ABOUT THE EDITORS

HERBERT H. HYMAN is Chairman of the Department of Sociology and Associate Director of the Bureau of Applied Social Research at Columbia University. He is the author of many books and articles, among them *Survey Design and Analysis* and *Political Socialization* (both published by The Free Press) and *The Psychology of Status*, which first elaborated the reference group concept. Professor Hyman is a past President of the American Association for Public Opinion Research.

ELEANOR SINGER (Ph.D., Columbia University) is Assistant Professor of Sociology at Columbia University. Before resuming graduate study, Professor Singer was for many years an editor of social science books.

Readings in
Reference Group Theory
and Research

Readings in
Reference Group Theory
and Research

Edited by
Herbert H. Hyman and
Eleanor Singer

The Free Press, NEW YORK

Collier-Macmillan Limited, LONDON

Collier-Macmillan Canada, Ltd., Toronto, Ontario

Library of Congress Catalog Card Number: 68-10366

FIRST PRINTING

For
Lisa, David, and Alex,
and
Emily and Lawrence

Preface

Fifteen years ago Muzafer Sherif warned that "reference group" was in danger of becoming a "magic term to explain anything and everything concerning group relations"—and, he might have added, many other social facts besides. Though the passage of time can serve only to increase the danger, there has appeared no collection of writings that might assist the reader in transforming magic into science.

This book aims to present such a collection. It represents, obviously, a drastic selection from among the many choices possible. The selection was guided by our desire to illuminate two central questions about reference group behavior *Why?*, which is the question of determinants; and *So what?*, which is the question of consequences. We have tried to sample the range of answers given to each of these questions. Our hope is that arraying them here will make it possible for the reader to relate them to one another and to identify the gaps that remain.

To further this aim, we have arranged the selections logically rather than chronologically. (The introduction, however, traces the historical development of the field; and the selections can of course be read in any order whatsoever). Part I is devoted to conceptual clarification; Part II, to the selection of reference groups; and Part III, to the consequences of such selection. Readings in Parts II and III are further divided according to their emphasis on the normative or comparison functions of reference groups. The general Introduction serves as a guide to the field as a whole; the introductions to the several parts concentrate on the readings included therein.

We wish to thank the authors and the publishers who have given us permission to reprint their work here. We also take this opportunity to thank Margaret Gannon, who prepared the authors' index and without whose help the manuscript would never have reached the printer. Above all, we would like to record our indebtedness to Helen Hyman, whose unfailing memory for anniversaries provided the instigation for this book.

New York City

H.H.H.
E.S.

CONTENTS

[ix]

Contents

Readings in
Reference Group Theory
and Research

Introduction

SOCIOLOGISTS, social psychologists, and cultural anthropologists have always operated on the fundamental principles that an individual's attitudes and conduct are shaped by the group in which he has membership and that self-appraisal and the correlative feelings and behavior flow from the individual's location in a particular group within a social hierarchy. "That men act in a social frame of reference yielded by the groups of which they are a part is a notion undoubtedly ancient . . ."[1] The evidence in support of such principles is, indeed, abundant, but, at times, faith in the principles becomes shaky in the face of contradictory examples: upper-class individuals with radical ideologies and revolutionary allegiances, those who feel deprived despite relatively advantaged positions, the products of an orthodox milieu who end up nonconformist. Ordinary language is rich in terms that describe such individuals who do not show the stamp of their group: the renegade Catholic, shabby gentility, the Tory worker.

Via the concept *reference group*, our confidence in the fundamental principles has been restored and theory and research on group influences has been invigorated. In the process of self-appraisal, from many possible groups available as a framework for social comparison, individuals make their own particular selection, thus reflecting the true complexities of their social location but not necessarily the arbitrary social position to which the scientist may have assigned them. In shaping their attitudes "men frequently orient themselves to groups other than their own . . .,"[2] thus reflecting the influences of the group to which they refer themselves, if not their membership group. If the groups to which individuals refer themselves, their reference groups, are empirically determined,

1. See Robert K. Merton and Alice Kitt Rossi, "Contributions to the Theory of Reference Group Behavior," p. 35 below.

2. *Ibid.*

[3]

knowledge and predictions of attitude, self-evaluation, and conduct will be enhanced; the cherished principles about group influences can be protected; and an understanding of the complex processes by which men relate themselves to groups can be enriched. Such is the hope of reference group theory and research, and the basis of its attractiveness to social scientists.

That hope dawned twenty-five years ago, when the concept was first given systematic treatment, but the hope has yet to be fully realized. Some, following Ebbinghaus, might say that reference group theory "has a long past, but only a short history" of empirical study—far too short for the consolidation of a field. Perhaps so, but it is certainly none too soon to present that history as it was written in the works of the period. Joining the pieces that have been separated or lost in time may form a structure to guide inquiry, may point to neglected but important problems, and call attention to fruitful but fugitive ideas from the past. These *Readings* may serve, therefore, to speed the progress and realize the hopes of *Reference Group Theory and Research.*

The structure that takes on form in these *Readings* is, naturally, incomplete. No matter how many fragments may be collected, some of the pieces essential to that structure do not yet exist. And the character of the partial structure, as well as the clarity of its form, depends on the way the pieces are arranged and joined. It is like the hidden figure in the puzzle that becomes visible only when the child joins in pencil a series of discrete points that were artfully arranged on a page. So, too, the pages of this book could have been arranged in many sequences to present to the eye of the reader different figures. Some art is involved, and some arbitrariness cannot be avoided in the final arrangement, if only because discrete articles may be complex and fit in several places. As the pencil serves to make the hidden figure visible, this general introduction and the later, shorter introductions outline the figure implicit in the pages and indicate some of the missing pieces needed to create a comprehensive structure.

The fact that men may shape their attitudes by reference to groups other than their own and their self-evaluations by the choice of unusual points of social comparison is perhaps the most distinctive contribution of reference group theory. To be sure, anomalous patterns of behavior may be understood without recourse to the concept. Some members of a group may depart from the modal pattern of behaviour simply because of their simultaneous membership in other groups. Some individuals in a particular status may have an incongruent self-image because they occupy other statuses as well and the status-set, rather than the discrete status, governs the process. But even here the concept of reference group makes a distinctive contribution to what otherwise would remain problematical. Which of the multiple memberships and multiple statuses is governant over the individual; what weights best represent their respective contributions?[3] The dilemma of the theorist facing these problems, but stripped

3. The need for the concept is suggested by the fact that the problematic aspects of multiple membership, although identified clearly and repeatedly long ago, have remained unresolved all these years. Forty years ago, in his lectures on *The Public and Its Problems,*

of the tool of reference group, is suggested in a discussion of probability and prediction by the philosopher of science Hans Reichenbach, and the utility of such a tool is emphasized by the odd fact that his methodological solution invokes a concept labeled *reference class.*

The probability of a certain attribute, e.g., death within the year, is predicted by locating an individual in a certain reference class, e.g., twenty-one years of age. ". . . [T]he probability of the prediction for the single case is greatly improved if the reference class is narrowed down. . . . It is advisable, instead of incorporating a person merely in the class of persons having his age, to narrow the reference class down by considering . . . other pertinent factors. The selection of a suitable reference class requires a great deal of technical knowledge. And there is no such thing as the best reference class; we can only proceed step by step to better reference classes."[4] In our field of inquiry, perhaps, the step-by-step classification or the arbitrary assignment to a reference class from among the many memberships and statuses can be obviated by empirically determining the group to which the individual refers himself.

HISTORY OF THE CONCEPT

The term was first used by Hyman, who elaborated the concept and explored some of its properties in an inquiry in 1942 into *The Psychology of Status.*[5] Seeking to understand the way individuals ranked themselves in terms of their choice of a social framework for comparison, he first explored by interview the

John Dewey remarked: ". . . an individual as a member of different groups may be divided within himself, and in a true sense have conflicting selves, or be a relatively disintegrated individual. A man may be one thing as a church member and another thing as a member of the business community. The difference may be carried as in water-tight compartments, or it may become such a division as to entail internal conflict." Yet while Dewey identified the problem so clearly, nowhere did he provide a principle for analyzing the way individuals resolve conflicts of multiple membership. (John Dewey, *The Public and Its Problems,* New York: Henry Holt and Company, Inc., 1927, p. 191.) Thirty years ago Floyd Allport reformulated the problem in the terms of the concept of *partial incorporation* of individuals into publics: "Now let us suppose . . . that an individual may belong simultaneously in two or more groupings because of different opinions or interests he possesses on different issues. In such a case if we try to state, or discover by a canvass, the opinion of a certain partially inclusive grouping . . . we might not know where a certain individual should be placed. Since he is in two groupings, he may have attitudes which tend to contradict each other on certain questions. One of these attitudes must be suppressed in favor of the other. If we place him arbitrarily in one of the publics we may be misjudging which attitude is dominant, thus producing a false result." In this vein, Allport ushered in the problem in the first article in the very first number of the *Public Opinion Quarterly* back in 1937, but it remained to be resolved. See F. H. Allport, "Toward a Science of Public Opinion," *Public Opinion Quarterly,* 1:9, 1937.

4. Hans Reichenbach, "Probability Methods in Social Science," in Daniel Lerner and Harold D. Lasswell (eds.), *The Policy Sciences: Recent Developments in Scope and Method,* Stanford, Calif.: Stanford University Press, 1951, p. 126.

5. Herbert H. Hyman, "The Psychology of Status," *Archives of Psychology,* No. 269, 1942. See pp. 147–165 below for excerpts from this study.

reference groups and reference individuals that subjects employed and some of the dynamics underlying such selection, and then determined the effects of particular reference groups on self-appraisal by experimental manipulations. At about the same time, Newcomb, searching to understand processes of attitude change, or lack of change, among individuals all of whom had prolonged membership in Bennington College, explored systematically by interview and repeated testing the various ways in which they related themselves to the Bennington community—in other words, chose it as a reference group.[6] These first systematic studies by social psychologists in *comparative* and *normative* reference group processes respectively (to use the distinction later developed by Kelley) stimulated no one but a few other social psychologists, notably, the Hartleys and Sherif, to continue research on reference groups. Sherif emphasized reference groups in his 1948 *Outline of Social Psychology*,[7] which included a summary by Newcomb of his Bennington study, rephrased in terms of the explicit concept *reference group*.

The concept had clarified for Newcomb various paradoxical findings. Similarly, Stouffer and his associates were led in their studies of *The American Soldier* to the concept of *relative deprivation*, a close cousin to the concept of comparative reference group, as they confronted the apparent contradictions between feelings of satisfaction or deprivation and the objective situation among groups of soldiers.[8] They then invoked the interpretive principle that the soldier's sense of deprivation was not dependent on an absolute level, but was relative to the perceived level in the groups with which he compared himself.

These ideas and concepts, however, had little prominence until 1950, when Merton and Rossi synthesized and presented in systematic form their "Contributions to the Theory of Reference Group Behavior."[9]

This historical sequence, despite its shortness, seems a faithful account of the early life of the concept. Certainly in the distant past, one can find precursors of the ideas implicit in reference group theory. Sumner's 1906 idea of in-groups and out-groups is a distant relation; Cooley's 1902 discussion of selective affinity to groups outside of one's immediate environment is an even earlier and closer relative: ". . . [t]he one who seems to be out of step with the procession is really keeping time to another music. As Thoreau said, he hears a different drummer. . . . Environment, in the sense of social influence actually at work, is far from the definite and obvious thing it is often assumed to be. . . . The group to which we give allegiance, and to whose standards we try to conform, is determined by our own selective affinity, choosing among all the personal influences accessible to us." His

6. Theodore M. Newcomb, *Personality and Social Change*, New York: Dryden Press, 1943; see pp. 374–386 below for a brief summary of this study.

7. Muzafer Sherif, *An Outline of Social Psychology*, New York: Harper & Row, 1948.

8. Samuel A. Stouffer et al., *The American Soldier: Adjustment during Army Life*, Vol. 1 Princeton: Princeton University Press, 1949.

9. Merton and Rossi, *op. cit.*

notion of imaginary conversation with an "interlocutor" anticipates the concept of *reference individual* and has inspired recent research that applies reference group concepts to mass communication. And his remark that "people differ much in the vividness of their imaginative sociability" is suggestive of later findings on individual differences in the use of multiple reference groups.[10] Earlier yet, in 1890, William James, in his account of the "social self," suggested that our *potential* social self was developed and inwardly strengthened by thoughts of remote groups and individuals who functioned as normative points of reference.[11] But these early glimmerings did not lead to the elaboration of the concept or its exploration by systematic research.

Since 1950 the concept has achieved, in Turner's phrase, "meteoric prominence" and has figured in so many writings that the more recent history defies brief review. The concept appears in Australia, Israel and India; in studies of farmers, scientists, drunkards, and newspapermen; it has been applied to problems of mental illness, formal organization, marketing and public relations, mass communication, acculturation, political behavior, consumer behavior, labor relations, and juvenile delinquency, as well as to opinion formation.[12] This sketchy sampling

10. C. H. Cooley, *Human Nature and the Social Order*, New York: Charles Scribner's Sons, 1902; reprinted by The Free Press, 1956, p. 301 and Chap. 3. In these passages, as Merton notes, Cooley clarifies the problem of nonconformity, one type of which he conceptualized most clearly, albeit implicitly, as conformity to the norms of a nonmembership group taken by the individual as a reference group. But the limitations and purely speculative character of these precursive writings is conveyed in Cooley's account of the kind of interlocutor likely to be chosen by different types of people. "The more simple, concrete, dramatic, their habit of mind is, the more their thinking is carried on in terms of actual conversation with a visible and audible interlocutor. Women, as a rule, probably do this more vividly than men, the unlettered more vividly than those trained to abstract thought, and the sort of people we call emotional more vividly than the impassive. Moreover, the interlocutor is a very mutable person, and is likely to resemble the last strong character we have been in contact with. I have noticed, for instance, that when I take up a book after a person of decided and interesting character has been talking with me I am likely to hear the words of the book in his voice. The same is true of opinions, of moral standards, and the like.... In short, the interlocutor, who is half of all thought and life, is drawn from the accessible environment." (p. 95.)

11. William James, *Principles of Psychology*, Vol. 1, New York: Henry Holt and Company, 1890, Chap. 10.

12. For some of these examples see F. E. Emery and F. M. Katz, "Social Theory and Minority Group Behavior," *Australian Journal of Psychology*, 3: 22–35, 1951; Ronald Taft, "Minority Group Behavior and Reference Group Theory," *Australian Journal of Psychology*, 4: 10–23, 1952; B. N. Varma, "Community Studies and the Concept of Caste," *Indian Journal of Social Research*, 6: 251–262, 1965; Everett M. Rogers and George M. Beal, *Reference Group Influence in the Adoption of Agricultural Technology*, Iowa Agricultural and Home Economics Experiment Station Project No. 1236, 1958; Everett M. Rogers, "Reference Group Influences on Student Drinking Behavior," *Quarterly Journal of Studies on Alcohol*, 19: 244–254, 1958; I. de Sola Pool and I. Shulman, "Newsmen's Fantasies, Audiences, and Newswritings," *Public Opinion Quarterly*, 23: 145–158, 1959; W. G. Bennis, N. Berkowitz, M. Affinito, and M. Malone, "Reference Groups and Loyalties in the Out-Patient Department," *Administrative Science Quarterly*, 2: 481–500, 1958; *Group Influence in Marketing and Public Relations*, Ann Arbor, Mich.: Foundation for Research on Human Behavior, 1956; J. S. Duesenberry, *Income,*

conveys the wild growth, but it should also be noted that despite the general flowering, some branches have not flourished. If we take as a comprehensive outline Merton's formulation: "Reference group theory aims to systematize the determinants and consequences of those processes of evaluation and self-appraisal in which the individual takes the values or standards of other individuals and groups as a . . . frame of reference," the deficiencies as well as the accomplishments will become apparent.[13] We shall also summarize developments in reference group measurement, since any field should be mapped along the two coordinates, theory and method.

CLARIFICATION OF CONCEPTS

Kelley's distinction between *comparative* and *normative* reference groups, corresponding to the two functions of reference groups as standards of comparison for self-appraisal or as the source of the individual's norms, attitudes, and values, is basic.[14] These two types of reference groups are sometimes regarded as separate but equal in importance for study, having only the common property that the individual's choice of a point of reference is the key to understanding either the process of self-appraisal or the formation of attitudes. The two types, however, may not always be empirically distinct. Contained within the structure of norms in a group may be the directive that one should not compare himself with his betters, or look down on his inferiors, or even be aware of their existence. Indeed, in Hyman's interviews, some subjects claimed that they did not employ any comparative reference group whatsoever, because of ideological distaste, and the comparative groups that other subjects employed were clearly shaped by their political attitudes. Given the possible interdependence of the two types of processes, it is all the more strange that although the study of the normative reference group has been cultivated, that of the comparative reference group has been neglected. The paths that Hyman, the Hartleys, Stouffer, and Merton took are now only byways, trodden by occasional investigators.[15]

The equally basic distinction between reference *individuals* and reference *groups* has been neglected despite the emphasis on the reference individual as a

Saving, and the Theory of Consumer Behavior, Cambridge: Harvard University Press, 1949; H. L. Wilensky, "The Moonlighter: A Product of Relative Deprivation," *Industrial Relations,* 3: 105–124, 1963; M. R. Haskell, "Toward a Reference Group Theory of Juvenile Delinquency," *Social Problems,* 8: 220–230, 1960–61. Other examples are scattered throughout this book.

13. Merton and Rossi, *op. cit.,* p. 35 below.

14. See Harold H. Kelley, "Two Functions of Reference Groups," pp. 77–83 below.

15. E. L. and R. Hartley, *Fundamentals of Social Psychology,* New York: Alfred A. Knopf, Inc., 1952, *passim;* Manford H. Kuhn and T. S. McPartland, "An Empirical Investigation of Self-Attitudes," *American Sociological Review,* 19: 68–76, 1954; Ralph Turner, "Reference Groups of Future-Oriented Men," *Social Forces,* 34: 130–136, 1955; James A. Davis, "A Formal Interpretation of the Theory of Relative Deprivation," *Sociometry,* 22: 280–296, 1959; in addition to the articles included in the appropriate sections of Parts II and III of this book.

point of social comparison in the early work and the obvious connection to such a prestigious concept as role-model. The parenthetical remark by Newcomb that a membership group may be a potent normative reference group "(particularly as symbolized by leaders ...)" strongly suggests the role of the reference individual as the carrier of the reference group's norms, but it appears to have been lost inside the parenthesis. It would be greatly to our advantage to reinstate the concept. Merton incorporated into his original formulation both concepts, and in his subsequent essay gave greater prominence to the "reference individual."[16] Sherif described that glorified variety of reference individual to which he gave the apt title, the "reference idol."

The reference group concept reminds us that individuals may orient themselves to groups other than their own, not merely to their membership groups, and thereby explains why the attitudes and behavior of individuals may deviate from what would be predicted on the basis of their group membership. Thus a theory of the group determination of attitude has been properly enlarged by the concept of reference group. Parallel to a theory of group influences on attitude, a recent fruitful development of theory and research has dealt with social influences of an interpersonal sort mediated through direct interaction and communication, and has become known to us under the headings of "opinion leadership," "the influential," and "personal influence." But this latter theory would take on enlarged significance by some stress on "reference individuals" as sources of influence. Just as reference group reminds us of the influence of nonmembership groups, the concept of reference individual would remind us that there are influentials, or opinion leaders, with whom we are not in direct social relations. We model ourselves not only on those who are near but on those who are far away. Certainly the emphasis in recent research on intimates as sources of influence is an understandable and wholesome reaction to the earlier emphasis on hierarchical and feudal types of influence from superiors, but perhaps the balance has swung too far. The point to be stressed is that the links in the interpersonal chain do not have to be forged exclusively via direct social relations.

For the study of normative reference groups, Newcomb's distinction between the *positive* and *negative* type reminds us that individuals may form their attitudes in opposition to the norms of a group as well as in accordance with them. The concept of negative reference groups helps us understand not only the affective tone and content of an individual's attitude, but also such *formal* features as the congruence and organization of his attitudes. Clearly there are some instances in social life where to oppose the norms of a particular group—for example, the Republican Party in the United States—is to be thrown into the arms of its opposite, the Democratic Party. But there are many other instances where social relations between groups are not patterned in terms of polar opposites. Thus to regard one's parents or community as a *negative* reference group may provide no other

16. Robert K. Merton, "Continuities in the Theory of Reference Groups and Social Structure," in Robert K. Merton, *Social Theory and Social Structure*, New York: The Free Press, 1957, pp. 281–368.

directive to the individual than to choose from among the norms of the myriad groups available. Individuals who form a constellation of attitudes under such conditions may well show the consequences in terms of diffuseness, lack of crystallization, inconsistency, and so on. But this remains a hypothesis to be tested when investigators pursue Newcomb's fruitful distinction.

The concept *referent power*, employed by French and Raven, suggests many fundamentals of normative reference group processes.[17] The power of a non-membership reference group inheres essentially in the fact that the individual by his sheer identification with the group willingly accepts what he perceives to be its norms. By contrast, membership groups often have the power, even when the individual does not take them as reference groups, to exact conformity in behavior through brutish means or rewards and to induce attitudes through prolonged doses of socialization. Certainly, when there is no bond of identification, their influence may be attenuated, and the concept of reference group reminds us that the psychological equipment of an individual can provide some escape from victimization by a membership group. Of course, when referent power is joined to real power, that is an unbeatable combination.

From these distinctions flows the hypothesis that the attitude *held* tends to reflect the reference group, whereas the attitude *expressed* tends to reflect the membership group.[18] It is only when the individual reveals his nonconformity that he is in danger of sanctions from his membership group. Thus the membership group and the reference group normally divide the realm, the former holding sway over the sphere of expression and the latter over the sphere of private thoughts. More refined hypotheses follow. As a membership group develops apparatus and institutions that threaten privacy, even the attitudes that are formed and then held in mind may come under its sway, since the truly private sphere shrinks. Conformity to the membership group then becomes more comprehensive. But when nonconformity is expressed, it, no doubt, requires that the person have some reference group or individual strongly in mind to steel his resolve. William James put it very well: "When for motives of honor and conscience I brave the condemnation of my own family, club, and 'set'. . . . I am always inwardly strengthened in my course and steeled against the loss of my actual social self by the thought of other and better *possible* social judges than those whose verdict goes against me now. The ideal social self which I thus seek in appealing to their decision may be very remote. . . . Yet still the emotion that beckons me on is indubitably the pursuit of an ideal social self, or a self that is at least *worthy* of approving recognition by the highest possible judging companion, if such companion there be. . . . All progress in the social self is the substitution of higher

17. John R. P. French, Jr., and Bertram Raven, "The Bases of Social Power," in Dorwin Cartwright (ed.), *Studies in Social Power*, Ann Arbor: University of Michigan Press, 1959, pp. 150–167.

18. M. Brewster Smith, Jerome Bruner, and Robert W. White, *Opinions and Personality*, New York: John Wiley and Sons, Inc., 1956; see Part III for other illustrations.

tribunals for lower."[19] On a miniature scale, the support of reference groups for nonconformity is revealed in the selection from the studies of the Encampment for Citizenship, where observations were made of youth as they moved back and forth between the larger society and a special community whose norms were in conflict. And on a more extended time scale, these processes are examined in Newcomb's follow-up study of Bennington graduates twenty-five years removed from its influence.

Merton's concept of *anticipatory socialization* is essential to this discussion.[20] Individuals may take as a reference group a nonmembership group to which they aspire to belong, and begin to socialize themselves to what they perceive to be its norms before they are ever exposed to its influence. The power of some reference groups thus inheres in the fact that they will ultimately be membership groups—at least such is the belief of the aspirant—and therefore can exact some conformity as the price of admission or of more comfortable passage into their ranks. Eulau advanced and then tested twice an ingenious hypothesis bearing upon this discussion. He reasoned that anticipatory socialization may be an effective means for learning *attitudes*, but not *conduct*, since the aspirant will have had little real opportunity to practice the skills required and to be taught the correct performance of the role.

Basic to reference group theory is the fact that individuals often have *multiple* reference groups. Certainly, there are some individuals who have limited capacity to use many reference groups, who lack rich "imaginative sociability." Others, however, in appraising the many facets of the self, employ various reference groups, each specialized as a point of comparison for one particular dimension.[21] In forming their total constellation of attitudes, several reference groups may be employed, each accorded a limited jurisdiction over some specialized attitude sphere. Studies of normative reference groups have found differences in the legitimacy that individuals accord to groups promulgating norms in various spheres.[22] There are also instances where multiple reference groups impinge simultaneously on the same sphere of comparison or the same realm of attitude, and then they may either reinforce the same outcome or produce conflicting consequences for the individual.[23]

19. James, *op. cit.*, pp. 315–316.

20. Merton and Rossi, *op. cit.*

21. Ralph H. Turner, "Reference Groups of Future-Oriented Men," *Social Forces*, 34: 130–136, 1955.

22. Angus Campbell, Philip E. Converse, Warren E. Miller, and Donald Stokes, *The American Voter*, New York: John Wiley and Sons, Inc., 1960.

23. In his delightful chapter on "The Consciousness of Self," William James anticipated these problems. As he put it, the person "has as many different social selves as there are distinct *groups* of persons about whose opinion he cares. He generally shows a different side of himself to each of these different groups. . . . From this there results what practically is a division of the man into several selves; and this may be a discordant splitting, as where one is afraid to let one set of his acquaintances know him as he is elsewhere; or it may be a perfectly

Over the life span of any person there will have been a multiplicity of reference groups, specialized less by sphere than by the life-segment to which they were keyed. Some are long departed, but since reference groups are represented by the symbolic processes of the individual, old reference groups may be carried over in memory. Recent groups may also be cast out of mind in the zealous adoption of a still newer reference group. The relations of multiple reference groups within a sequence suggest many fascinating problems that tie into the processes of social mobility.[24] Discussions of social mobility often assume that the past and future reference groups conflict, since the individual presumably wishes to break his ties to the old, inferior group. Litwak, however, presents an interesting reformulation, using the concept of the *stepping-stone reference orientation*. In a situation characterized by ordered change, "where integration into one group is considered to be a prerequisite for integration into a second group . . . it is possible for the individual to view both his current membership group and his future membership group as reference groups, without endangering his integration into his current group and without preventing his joining a different future group."[25] Each group is valued by the individual as a stepping stone to help him in his advance.

The concepts reviewed in no way exhaust the literature, but are those basic to any clarification of the field. Merton's 1957 essay describes many other conceptual refinements and the extended network of connections to other branches of theory.[26]

---

harmonious division of labor." Later, in a discussion of conflict of the selves, he states: "I am often confronted by the necessity of standing by one of my empirical selves and relinquishing the rest. Not that I would not, if I could, be both handsome and fat and well dressed, and a great athlete, and make a million a year, be a wit, a *bon-vivant*, and a lady-killer, as well as a philosopher; a philanthropist, statesman, warrior, and African explorer, as well as a 'tone-poet' and saint. But the thing is simply impossible. The millionaire's work would run counter to the saint's; the *bon-vivant* and the philanthropist would trip each other up; the philosopher and the lady-killer could not well keep house in the same tenement of clay. . . . So the seeker of his truest, strongest, deepest self must review the list carefully, and pick out the one on which to stake his salvation. All other selves thereupon become unreal, but the fortunes of this self are real. . . . This is as strong an example as there is of that selective industry of the mind. . . . Our thought, incessantly deciding, among many things of a kind, which ones for it shall be realities, here chooses one of many possible selves or characters, and forthwith reckons it no shame to fail in any of those not adopted expressly as its own." *Op. cit.*, p. 294, pp. 309–310. For recent studies of conflicting consequences of multiple reference groups, see E. L. Hartley, "Psychological Problems of Multiple Group Membership," in John H. Rohrer and Muzafer Sherif (eds.), *Social Psychology at the Crossroads*, New York: Harper & Row, 1951, pp. 371–386; Bernard C. Rosen, "Conflicting Group Membership: A Study of Parent-Peer Group Cross-Pressures," pp. 402–412 below.

24. Merton and Rossi, *op. cit.*

25. Eugene Litwak, "Reference Group Theory, Bureaucratic Career, and Neighborhood Primary Group Cohesion," *Sociometry*, 23: 72–73, 1960.

26. *Op. cit.* See also Turner, *op. cit.*; Tamotsu Shibutani, "Reference Groups as Perspectives," pp. 103–113 below; and Manford H. Kuhn, "The Reference Group Reconsidered," *Sociological Quarterly*, 5: 5–21, 1964.

RESEARCH AND THEORY ON THE SELECTION OF REFERENCE GROUPS

The concept *reference group* has always implied that one cannot make arbitrary assumptions about the groups to which an individual refers himself. Given the multiplicity of groups and the variability among individuals and situations, must we then, as a symposium put it in 1956, "determine which kinds of groups are likely to be referred to by which kinds of individuals under which kinds of circumstances in the process of making which decisions . . ."—over and over again?[27] There will always be a large amount of empiricism needed, and the development of simple instruments to measure a person's reference groups is of great importance. But, fortunately, research has already established certain regularities in the choices individuals make and some major factors governing selection.

Theorizing about the choice of reference groups and reference individuals is often based on simple assumptions about motivation. The individual chooses a normative reference group so that in fantasy, or ultimately in fact, he can feel himself part of a more favored group. Or, facing rapid social change, the individual latches onto a reference group. Thus anchored, he has a ready-made perspective to order the distressing complexities of the environment.[28] For social comparisons, he chooses a group so as to enhance his self-regard or protect his ego. Certainly in the search for reference groups, such fundamental strivings play an important part. The pleasure principle is at work, but so too is the reality principle.

Recall Stouffer's inference that the *more* advantaged soldiers felt deprived because they chose to compare themselves with others who were even better off. It seems plausible that the institutional arrangements gave such sharp definition and prominence to certain groups that the soldier's attention was drawn to them as points of comparison. Perhaps when reality is less highly structured, there is more freedom for the pleasure principle to guide the selection of reference groups.

Turner hypothesized that only those groups will be taken as points of comparison which are *relevant* to a particular aspect of self-appraisal—when a group's standing is *so* high or *so* low that it is not meaningful to the individual, it will not be used as a comparative reference group.[29] The similarity principle Festinger derived in his "theory of social comparison processes,"[30] that an individual chooses others who are close to his level of ability, is congruent with Turner's relevance principle, as is Merton's hypothesis, based on findings in *The American Soldier*, that "some similarity in status attributes between the individual and the reference group must be perceived or imagined, in order for the comparison to occur at all."[31] The Amba of East Africa dramatically illustrate that principle.

27. Foundation for Research on Human Behavior, *Group Influence in Marketing and Public Relations*, Ann Arbor, Michigan, 1956.

28. Shibutani, *op. cit.*; S. N. Eisenstadt, "Studies in Reference Group Behavior," pp. 413–429 below.

29. Turner, *op. cit.*

30. L. Festinger, "A Theory of Social Comparison Processes," pp. 123–146 below.

31. Merton and Rossi, *op. cit.*, p. 42 below.

They worked for Europeans for a much lower price than for employers from another tribe, and "are quite willing to explain this state of affairs. They say that a European is on a much higher social plane, and therefore comparisons are out of the question. Europeans are so wealthy that an increase in their wealth makes no difference in the . . . standing" of the Amba relative to Europeans.[32] Qualitative evidence in Hyman's interviews also suggested the operation of the similarity principle, or what he called "affinity" in the choice of reference groups, but he observed instances where contrast in status made a reference group salient and likely to be chosen.

The principle of relevance or similarity still leaves much room for the play of psychological factors. As Merton remarks, *perceived* similarity is what counts, and there are many dimensions of similarity, only some of which are noted by the individual.[33] And inside the range of similarity, in which direction will the individual turn then—toward relevant groups that are superior or inferior to him? Turner's college students seemed to compare themselves with higher reference groups, perhaps to their present discomfort, but because they were "future-oriented," desiring to surpass such groups in their future lives.

Patchen's study of industrial workers provides systematic evidence on the variables affecting the choice of a reference individual or reference group for economic comparisons and fundamentally clarifies the motivational assumptions of reference group theory. Men often choose reference groups which increase their *present* sense of relative deprivation, not only because formal institutional arrangements force such groups into attention, but, as Patchen demonstrates, when informal social influences make such groups salient.[34] Men may choose groups above them at the price of present dissatisfaction because they are laying a claim to a future when their status will be higher and their relative deprivation diminished.

Research on the selection of *normative* reference groups is meager. That individuals identify with advantaged groups and thereby gain gratification must be qualified in terms of the societal context. Such modes of selection may be

32. E. H. Winter, *Bwamba Economy*, Kampala, Uganda: East African Institute of Social Research, East African Studies, No. 5, 1955, p. 40.

33. The article by Strauss on the comparative reference groups selected by totally blind individuals provides a dramatic demonstration of the ambiguity in the notion of similarity, and is perhaps an extreme instance where dissimilars are chosen for comparison. See pp. 222–237 below.

34. What is suggested, by extension, is the role of *organized* social influences in making particular, comparative reference groups salient. By manipulation, one organized interest could heighten the sense of relative deprivation by emphasizing a relevant reference group receiving greater benefits; another organized interest could dampen the feeling of deprivation by urging for comparison a group receiving lesser rewards. The natural history of social conflicts no doubt provides many examples of the manipulation of the salience of comparative reference groups and the consequences that flow from such activities, all of which await the analysts sensitive enough to perceive the gains to be reaped for reference group theory. We are indebted to Charles R. Wright for the original suggestion of this strategic source of data.

characteristic of societies with high rates of upward mobility,[35] or where upward mobility is a strong value or is perceived, correctly or not, to be frequent. Comparative research is clearly required.

Experimental research demonstrates that situational factors may heighten the salience of a membership group and increase the likelihood of its being used as a reference group whose perceived norms then affect some specific sphere.[36] Whether such situational influences have enduring effects on the choice of normative reference groups remains unknown.

That normative reference groups are chosen in the spirit of identification perhaps also needs qualification. It may be true for many individuals seeking a source of norms, values, and attitudes, although the existence of *negative* reference groups obviously qualifies the proposition. Certainly the reference individual who is an idol or hero may be chosen with a sense of his distance and little feeling of identification. And what about the individual seeking a system of beliefs and *knowledge*? He may then choose his reference group in terms of its authority or expertness, and with the full awareness that he has no bond of identification. Systematic research on such determinants of choice does not exist, since the effects of reference groups on cognition have been neglected, to the detriment of an improved sociology of knowledge. Carlson, who demonstrated differences in the effectiveness with which rural Southern Negroes dealt with syphilitic infections, depending on their reference groups, and Beal and Rogers, who demonstrated that farmers who adopted better practices chose particular reference groups, illustrate the prospect for future research.[37]

Ruth Hartley's work represents a unique program of systematic research on psychological factors that influence the selection of a membership group as a normative reference group. Using a large college community, she measured the degree to which students adopted their new community as a reference group, and correlated such individual differences with other characteristics.[38] Taking on a

35. Merton and Rossi, *op. cit.*

36. See W. W. Charters and Theodore M. Newcomb, "Some Attitudinal Effects of Experimentally Increased Salience of a Membership Group," pp. 95–102 below; Harold H. Kelley, "Salience of Membership and Resistance to Change of Group-Anchored Attitudes," pp. 297–310 below; and L. Festinger, "The Role of Group-Belongingness in a Voting Situation," pp. 311–317 below.

37. Rogers and Beal, *op. cit.*; Robert O. Carlson, "The Influence of the Community and the Primary Group on the Reactions of Southern Negroes to Syphilis," Ph.D. dissertation, Columbia University, 1952; Morton Deutsch and Harold B. Gerard, "A Study of Normative and Informational Social Influences Upon Individual Judgment," *Journal of Abnormal and Social Psychology*, 51: 629–636, 1955; Theodore M. Newcomb, "The Influence of Attitude Climate Upon Some Determinants of Information," *Journal of Abnormal and Social Psychology*, 41: 291–302, 1946.

38. Ruth E. Hartley, "Personal Characteristics and Acceptance of Secondary Groups as Reference Groups," pp. 247–256 below; "Relationships between Perceived Values and Acceptance of a New Reference Group," *Journal of Social Psychology*, 51: 181–190, 1960; "Personal Needs and the Acceptance of a New Group as a Reference Group," *Journal of Social Psychology*, 51: 349–358, 1960; and "Norm Compatibility, Norm Preference, and the Acceptance of New Reference Groups," pp. 238–246 below.

new reference group is dependent on an acceptant personality pattern. A particular reference group is then likely to be chosen if it is seen as fulfilling personal needs, and if there is congruity between the individual's personal values and norms and the norms and values he perceives as characteristic of the group. Thus some of the apparent effect of reference groups on the values of individuals may be spurious, since their values were prior in time and determined the choice of the reference group.

Perception of the Norms and Standing of a Reference Group

For an individual to guide himself by a reference group requires some perception or cognition of its norms. Otherwise he may refer himself to the group all he wants, but no direction is indicated. Since reference groups may often be distant, nonmembership groups, perception of the true norms may be hazy and incorrect and not subject to any correction from the group. But even membership groups functioning as reference groups pose problems of perception, since the visibility of group norms is not always high and varies depending on one's position in the group.[39] Comparative reference group processes also require some perception or knowledge of the standing of others on the dimensions selected for comparison.

Deviation from the objective position of a group thus may be inspired by conformity to a false norm that the individual has taken to be the true norm of the reference group, and conformity to the objective norms may be the perverse fate of a deviant who thinks he is flouting the norms, but who has misperceived them. Attempts to understand the *motivation* of conformists and deviants must for sure distinguish among these varieties, and therefore measure the norms imputed to groups.

The environmental conditions and psychological processes that aid or obstruct perception vary greatly depending on the nature of the reference group or reference individual. Organized groups announce their views to members and to outsiders; diffusion is aided by the mass media and spread by word of mouth. But self-appointed communicators and the diffusion process may also distort the norms that finally reach the individual. More fundamental problems must be considered. Even organized groups do not announce all of their views all of the time. A norm may not yet have been promulgated; a fundamental value may remain implicit and taken for granted. On other issues, the norms may be confused, not shared throughout the organization, exceedingly complex in nature, or not distinctive from other groups. There are even occasional groups whose fundamental value is that the individual shall be autonomous in regulating his conduct, thereby creating difficulty for those individuals seeking cues. Such are the burdens on the perceiver, but what comes to his aid is *time*. He has abiding loyalties to

39. Merton and Rossi, *op. cit.*; K. Chowdhry and Theodore M. Newcomb, "The Relative Abilities of Leaders and Non-Leaders to Estimate Opinions of Their Own Groups," *Journal of Abnormal and Social Psychology*, 47: 51–57, 1952.

some reference groups or individuals, and what at first is dimly perceived finally takes on clarity.

Not all reference groups are organized entities. They may be vague collectivities, or sprawling social categories, or groups out of the dead past or not yet born. Some reference individuals may also be long departed. They are living structures only in the mind of the perceiver and do not communicate or transact behavior.[40] Here there is relatively free rein for autistic perception of norms.

With respect to conditions governing knowledge of norms, surveys of political behavior provide some relevant evidence. Members of a given social category have greater awareness than nonmembers that a voting norm characterizes the group. Among nonmembers, awareness of the norm of another group is greater for those whose environment contains many representatives of the group.[41] One may speculate that the choice of reference groups from the immediate environment, or from membership groups, or the choice of *reference individuals* rather than groups, may be motivated by the individual's need to simplify his perceptual tasks.

Consequences of Reference Group Selection

The recent popularity of reference group theory brings the danger, in Sherif's words, that the concept "is becoming a *magic* term to explain anything and everything concerning group relations."[42] The concept is often invoked and the influence of a particular reference group alleged without benefit of direct evidence. Operating under the protection of such reckless practices, the claims of reference group theory can easily be exaggerated and the consequences overstated. Under such a semiscientific regime, the true extent of the consequences can also be underestimated, since investigators may neglect to observe the influence of a particular reference group.

40. The selection of particular reference groups from out of the past or the present or future may be a consistent tendency reflecting the more general orientation towards time. A substantial literature establishes differences in the *time perspectives* of age groups and cultural groups. The codification of such old findings plus the systematic study of the problem would contribute not only to reference group theory but also, as Gouldner suggests, to fundamental social theory. He stresses the "need for a new concept analogous to that of the 'reference group,' but in which the actor's orientation to a time period, rather than to a group, is taken as problematic. A generalized concept such as this, which may be called the 'reference period,' would withhold commitment to the dubious assumption that all social action is equally anticipatory and future-oriented. It would seem sufficient to stress that men do have some time orientations which affect their behavior, and to submit the question of the degree of their past or future-orientation to empirical examination." Alvin W. Gouldner, "Some Observations on Systematic Theory, 1945–55," in Hans L. Zetterberg (ed.), *Sociology in the United States of America*, Paris: UNESCO, 1956, p. 37.

41. Angus Campbell, Gerald Gurin, and Warren E. Miller, *The Voter Decides*, Evanston, Ill.: Row, Peterson & Company, 1954; Herbert H. Hyman, "Reflections on Reference Groups," *Public Opinion Quarterly*, 24: 383–396, 1960.

42. See Muzafer Sherif, "The Concept of Reference Groups in Human Relations," p. 85 below.

Certainly in the long past, before the short history of the concept, the reference group must have been missed many times. And although investigators, in the current period, often assert the influence of a *normative* reference group whose presence has not been measured, this excess is counterbalanced by the state of neglect into which the concept of the *comparative* reference group has fallen. That notion only seems to come back to life when we study categories of people whose self-regard is so obviously vulnerable to social arrangements, or who respond in paradoxical ways to being elevated or degraded. Is it not significant that two out of three studies included on the consequences of selecting a particular comparative reference group deal with Negroes, who, despite improvements in their status, still remain deprived *relative* to what they deserve and others get?[43] Is it not a commentary on the general state of neglect of the comparative reference group that a dozen years after so prestigious a theorist as Festinger presented his theory of social comparison processes, there remains a "virtual absence of any experimental tests of its key assumptions"?[44]

If the varied consequences of reference group selection are to be accurately assessed, there must be a new scientific regime. Magical invocation of the concept must give way to empirical measurement, which will act to restrain arbitrary conclusions and lead cumulatively to knowledge. For this reason our general introduction concludes with a brief summary of research procedures. The present treatment is intended as suggestive of the consequences, and such details as can be established are reserved for the Introduction to Part III of the Readings.

As one ponders the consequences of selecting a particular comparative reference group, one sees once again the convergence of comparative and normative reference group processes. Self-appraisal rests on the framework of social comparison, and the choice of a comparative reference group maintains, enhances, or injures self-regard. Certainly this is enough of a consequence in itself to make the comparative reference group worthy of study. The concept of the self has always been central to social psychology. McDougall long ago described the central importance in social life of the self-regarding sentiment, and traced the ebb and flow of negative and positive self-feeling as the child grows and takes as his point of comparison various social circles through which he moves. His English illustration is old-fashioned, but the point is up-to-date. He remarks about the student: ". . . [a]fter a successful career in the schools and the playing fields, how changed again is his attitude towards his college society! The dons he regards with kindly tolerance, the freshmen with hardly disguised disdain; and very few remain capable of evoking his negative self-feeling—perhaps a 'blue,'

43. Other readings bearing on comparative reference processes simularly focus on socially disadvantaged groups. Two—one by Patchen, the other by Form and Geschwender—investigate job satisfaction among blue-collar workers; a third—by Strauss—examines comparison processes among the blind.

44. In this fashion, the editor introduces a recent number of a journal devoted to the theory. See B. Latane, "Studies in Social Comparison—Introduction," *Journal of Experimental Social Psychology*, 2:1, 1966, Supplement 1.

or a 'rugger-international,' or a don of worldwide reputation; for the rest—he has comprehended them, grasped their limits, labelled them, and dismissed them to the class that ministers to his positive self-feeling. And so he goes out into the world to repeat the process and to carry it as far as his capacities will enable him to do."[45]

But the process does not end there. From the deprived self, the fattened ego, flow corresponding attitudes and behavior. Thus although comparative and normative reference group processes may follow different courses, they arrive at the same end point: the comparative reference group working through the intervening variable of the self, and the normative more directly through the internalization of what is perceived as appropriate behavior. Both processes start with the same raw materials: society provides the rich assortment and complex arrangement of groups from which the choices may be made. Some are pressed upon the individual but he is creative and his symbolic equipment is highly developed and can present to the mind's eye a much larger assortment than is given in immediate experience. Thus he maintains some control over his own self-regard by his choice of comparative reference groups and guides his own fate accordingly. Similarly, by his choice of normative reference groups, he can escape from the confines of a narrow social world. Otherwise provincialism would be the law of life, conformity to the parochial the rule. We would all be like those "portions of the sovereign people" whom Lippmann describes in his *Public Opinion* as moving "as if on a leash, within a fixed radius of acquaintances, according to the law and gospel of their social set."[46]

MEASUREMENT PROCEDURES

The purpose of this brief discussion has already been suggested. The need is underscored by the fact that these Readings do not include any article specifically on methodology. To be sure, research and measurement procedures are implicated in many of the theoretical and substantive pieces presented, but it may be helpful to outline here some of these procedures.

A person's reference groups have been measured by such simple and yet predictive questions as those on subjective class identification.[47] When this self-location question is combined with a question on class awareness, prediction of attitudes is improved.[48] Other simple questions on the importance or the intimacy

45. William McDougall, *An Introduction to Social Psychology*, Boston: John W. Luce & Co., 1921, pp. 200–201. For recent treatments of the concept of the self in the context of reference group theory, see Muzafer Sherif, "The Self and Reference Groups: Meeting Ground of Individual and Group Approaches," *Annals New York Academy of Sciences*, 96(3): 1962, 797–813; John Sherwood, "Self-Identity and Referent Others," *Sociometry*, 28:66-81, 1965.

46. Walter Lippmann, *Public Opinion*, New York: Pelican Books, 1946, p. 37.

47. Richard Centers, *The Psychology of Social Classes*, Princeton: Princeton University Press, 1949.

48. Campbell et al., 1960, Chap. 14.

of a series of groups for the individual predict his attitudes.[49] Strength of attachment to one of a series of possible normative reference groups has been measured by a forced-choice instrument developed by Melikian and Diab.[50] Ruth Hartley's elaborate instrument to measure the acceptance of a normative reference group has high reliability and has been validated. The comparative reference groups that individuals normally employ have been studied by direct questions,[51] via the spontaneous group references that individuals make in the course of surveys on personal satisfaction,[52] and by applications of Kuhn's "Who Am I?" test, which elicits spontaneous definitions of the self and its incorporation into various social categories.[53]

Perception of the norms of a reference group is measured by having the subject estimate the opinion of various other groups or individuals or indicate his lack of awareness of any norm.[54] Centers reversed this procedure by presenting subjects with statements of beliefs or norms and asking them to impute the belief to some group.[55] Hyman, Wright, and Hopkins obtained perception of the norms by asking the respondent questions on the way he thought the conduct of an ideal member of the group differed from that of other people in the community.[56] Perception of the *differentiated* norms within a complex group has been examined in surveys of political behavior and by Hartley's battery on "perceived cohesiveness" of a reference group; the perceived clarity and perceived uniqueness of norms as well as the legitimacy an individual accords to a reference group exercising a norm in a particular sphere have all been measured by simple batteries of questions.[57] Experimental techniques to study the influence of reference groups on the behavior of a communicator have been developed by Zimmerman and Bauer,

49. Herbert Hyman, "Reflections on Reference Groups," *Public Opinion Quarterly*, 24, 383–396, 1960.

50. Levon H. Melikian and Lutfy N. Diab, "Group Affiliations of University Students in the Arab Middle East," *Journal of Social Psychology*, 49: 145–159, 1959.

51. Martin Patchen, "A Conceptual Framework and Some Empirical Data Regarding Comparisons of Social Rewards," pp. 166–184 below.

52. Eric Stern and Suzanne Keller, "Spontaneous Group References in France," pp. 199–206 below.

53. Harold A. Mulford and Winfield W. Salisbury II, "Self-Conceptions in a General Population," *Sociological Quarterly*, 5: 35–46, 1964.

54. Newcomb, 1943, *op. cit.*; Chowdhry and Newcomb, *op. cit.*; Norman Kaplan, "Reference Group Theory and Voting Behavior," Columbia University, 1955. See pp. 461–472 below for an excerpt from Kaplan's dissertation.

55. Richard Centers, "Social Class, Occupation, and Imputed Belief," *American Journal of Sociology*, 58: 543–555, 1953.

56. H. H. Hyman, C. R. Wright, and T. K. Hopkins, *Applications of Methods of Evaluation*, Berkeley: University of California Press, 1962.

57. For a summary, see Hyman, "Reflections . . . " *op. cit.*

and by Pool and Shulman.[58] Experiments to test the effects of manipulating such variables as the salience of reference group have also been designed.[59]

Current investigators have no excuse for neglecting existing measurement procedures. But they also have an obligation to refine these methods. In 1951 Newcomb remarked: ". . . [T]he concept of reference group is almost unique among the tools available to the social psychologist. . . . It is a variable intimately associated with that central problem of social psychology: the relating of self to society. The hand-to-hand advancement of reference group theory and of the research procedures which can make it possible would therefore seem to be one of social psychology's greatest needs."[60] After twenty-five years of history, the need is still not fully met. Hopefully, these Readings will stimulate progress toward that end.

58. For a summary, see Raymond A. Bauer, "The Communicator and the Audience," pp. 430–442 below.

59. Charters and Newcomb, *op. cit.*; Kelley, "Salience of Membership and Resistance to Change of Group-Anchored Attitudes"; Festinger, "The Role of Group-Belongingness in a Voting Situation."

60. Theodore M. Newcomb, Review of "Continuities in Social Research," *American Journal of Sociology*, 57: 90–92, 1951.

PART I

Conceptual Clarification and Elaboration

WITH one exception, the readings included in Part I are concerned primarily with making the concept *reference group* available to research, whereas those included in later sections report the results of such research. Thus, for example, among the problems for reference group theory raised by Merton and Rossi in the selection included in Part I is the relative potency of general status categories versus primary groups in shaping attitudes and behavior. This question is answered, at any rate for voting behavior, by Norman Kaplan in the selection included in Part III. Another problem area identified by Merton and Rossi is that of communication and perception of a group's norms if it is to serve as a point of reference. Converse and Campbell, in another selection included in Part III, investigate these problems of communication and perception of norms in some detail, again in relation to voting behavior; and Eulau's article extends the analysis by distinguishing between attitudinal norms, for which knowledge is sufficient, and behavioral norms, for which practice as well as knowledge may be required.

Still another problem identified by Merton and Rossi is that of the conditions under which unfavorable comparisons lead to a negative self-evaluation, and those under which they lead to a negative evaluation of institutional arrangements. The formulation of this problem is carried a step further in the selection by Runciman, who proposes that survey research ascertain not only whether, and in relation to whom, the respondent feels deprived; but also the extent to which he considers the *groups* with which he identifies to be deprived in relation to other groups. Presumably it is the latter kind of deprivation which is most conducive to a negative evaluation of social justice. Interestingly enough, Runciman found little evidence of this kind of perceived deprivation in an English survey carried out in 1962.[1] Systematic application of this procedure to cross-national studies could go a long way toward identifying empirically the conditions under which unfavorable comparisons lead to one or another outcome.[2]

Although Merton and Rossi formulate the distinctive concern of reference group theory as "those processes in which the individual takes the values or standards of other individuals and groups as a comparative frame of reference," their own analysis includes instances in which the central process involves *conformity to* the norms of some group, rather than *comparison with* some aspect of that group. Kelley has formalized this distinction by defining two functions of reference groups, which he calls the "normative" and the "comparison." His distinction has served as the framework for organizing the readings in this book, although it is recognized that both functions require the person to take some aspect of the group as normative for him. When a group is used as a standard of comparison for judging some aspect of the self, what distinguishes that judgment from a trivial psychophysical one is that it carries with it some implication of *ought* or *should*. Negative evaluation may lead to dissatisfaction with one's own status, or to dissatisfaction with institutional arrangements. When a group serves a normative rather than comparative function, failure to conform to the norm presumably leads to a negative *self*-evaluation only.

In their article, Merton and Rossi define the immediate task of reference group theory as investigating those problems centered around the individual's orientation to groups in which he is *not* a member. But, as the selections in this book testify, subsequent research has concerned itself as much, if not more, with the individual's relation to a variety of membership groups. In part, this emphasis reflects the relative lack of recent interest in the comparative functions of reference groups. Sherif, for example, characterizes reference groups as "those groups to which the individual relates himself as a part or to which he aspires to relate himself psychologically." The distinctive problems associated with reference group theory arise, as Sherif sees it, primarily in societies which are relatively differentiated, relatively unintegrated, relatively unstable—in short, in modern societies. "Modern man, especially in Western societies, is caught in the throes of vertical mobility, in the 'dilemmas and contradictions of statuses,' and painful predicament of marginality created by the demands and goals originating in diverse groups. He finds himself betwixt and between situations as he

1. *Relative Deprivation and Social Justice*, London: Routledge & Kegan Paul, Ltd., 1966. See pp. 207–221 below for an excerpt from this study.

2. An experimental attempt to create conditions of social injustice is reported by Martin Patchen in the selection included in Part III.

carries on the business of living in different roles in relation to diverse groups which not infrequently demand contradictory adjustment of his experience and behavior." Thus the problems identified by Sherif involve conformity to conflicting demands, rather than processes of comparison and evaluation.

Shibutani goes even further than Sherif, explicitly urging restriction of reference group theory to processes that do not involve comparison at all. He distinguishes three denotations of the term *reference group*: (1) that group which serves as the point of reference in making comparisons or contrasts; (2) the group in which the actor aspires to gain or maintain acceptance; (3) that group whose perspective constitutes the frame of reference of the actor. Shibutani proposes limiting the concept to the third usage, which is akin to Kelley's normative function but carries broader imperatives for defining the situation in which the actor finds himself. Like Sherif, Shibutani locates the distinctive concerns of reference group theory in modern mass societies. "The proposition that men think, feel, and see things from a standpoint peculiar to the group in which they participate is an old one, repeatedly emphasized by students of anthropology and of the sociology of knowledge. Why, then, the sudden concern with reference-group theory? . . . First of all, in modern societies special problems arise from the fact that men sometimes use the standards of groups in which they are *not* recognized members. . . . Second, in our mass society, characterized as it is by cultural pluralism, each person internalizes several perspectives and this occasionally gives rise to embarrassing dilemmas which call for systematic study." Certainly, conflicting group memberships are more common in mass society, but whether they are *peculiar* to that society is much less certain.[3]

The fifth selection in Part I, by Charters and Newcomb, might with equal appropriateness have been assigned to Part II. It is included here because it explicitly introduces the important concept of "negative" reference groups. Once this concept is identified, certain distinctive problems present themselves. An unknown portion of childhood and subsequent

---

3. In his discussion of "Psychological Problems of Multiple Group Membership," for example, Hartley remarks: "Lest we get the impression from the references to our contemporary, rapidly changing society that conflict of group memberships is historically a new problem, let me cite a few illustrations from an earlier day." He then describes the mutiny of the British fleet in 1797 as a case in point. See J. H. Rohrer and M. Sherif, *Social Psychology at the Crossroads*, New York: Harper & Row, 1951, p. 375. In analyzing the institution of caste, normally regarded as operating as a most potent membership group, Varma suggests that "Indians, even in the villages, show such orientation to other castes besides their own as well as other groups beside caste," and suggests the usefulness of conceptualizing caste as a reference group process. To be sure, he has in mind India in its present, transitional state, but this certainly suggests caution in thinking of reference groups and multiple group orientations as peculiar to mass society. Baidya Nath Varma, "Community Studies and The Concept of Caste," *Indian Journal of Social Research*, 6: 258, 1965.

socialization, for example, consists in the deliberate creation and manipulation of negative reference groups and reference individuals. "Don't be a cry-baby. . . . Only sissies cry. . . . Tattle-tale!" The usefulness of such injunctions for teaching appropriate behavior, and their effect in perpetuating negative stereotypes and stereotyped reactions, have yet to be systematically explored.[4]

In their study of Negro youth in Louisiana in the thirties, Davis and Dollard described a Creole girl, Jeanne, who said:

> "There are some nice dark people but most of them are low-down, mean, and rough." She disavows prejudice, of course, just as most white people do, but shows it nevertheless at every turn; the "nice" dark people are those of her own class. Her attitudes toward color and hair come from her mother, who instructed her girls "not to play with the little black ones." Jeanne makes the class point against them by saying that the little "dark ones" were always fighting and "didn't want to play right." Even now, she does not associate with dark people and said that in her "bunch" even the brown-skinned girls would not go with very dark people. She said in explanation, "I might walk in the street with them, but I feel funny. The light people criticize you. When I was little, I sometimes played with them at school, but when I'd meet 'em on the street, I'd turn my head from them and didn't speak." Jeanne is a "Y" girl, and the interviewer noticed that almost all the girls in this group were light; Jeanne said, "There are some dark girls, but they were in the club when it started, and

4. Long ago Miller and Dollard provided a framework of theory which might be used to systematize the normal developmental process by which children distinguish positive and negative reference groups or individuals and model their own behavior in ways similar or opposite to these respective points of social reference. In effect, the cardinal principle in their learning theory is that a reference group takes on negative qualities for the child when he is punished for engaging in imitation. Supplementary principles involve generalization from the original learning experience, and the plausible assumption that there are distinctive, recognizable cues which permit the learner to make the necessary discriminations between the several reference groups and individuals. For the formulation and experimental evidence, see N. E. Miller and J. Dollard, *Social Learning and Imitation*, New Haven: Yale University Press, 1941, especially pp. 165–168, 188–189. It is paradoxical, but the writings of Kurt Lewin provide another theoretical framework for analyzing the formation of negative reference groups. Although, as Gordon Allport states in his foreword to a collection of papers, a unifying theme in Lewin's thought was that "the group to which an individual *belongs* is the ground for his perceptions, his feelings, and his actions," Lewin must have intended the proposition to include behavior opposed to a membership group toward which the individual feels negative. In his classic essay of 1941, "Self-Hatred Among Jews," Lewin conceptualized the forces initiated by the larger society which make underprivileged minorities develop negative orientations toward their own group. " . . . [T]he more the reaching of the individual's goal is furthered or hindered by the group, the more likely it is that the balance of forces toward or away from the group will be positive or negative." For the essay and Allport's foreword, see Kurt Lewin, *Resolving Social Conflicts*, New York: Harper & Row, 1948.

they haven't taken in any more since." The "Y" authorities probably forced some dark girls in at the start, but once the girls got control of the club, they stopped that. Asked if she played with a certain girl who lives fairly near her, Jeanne said, "No, indeed, you don't have to go that far to find black people to go around with. I really don't have prejudice, but the kids we play with just happen to be mostly our color."[5]

It has long been recognized that certain transitions of status involve taking the former status as a negative reference point (as, for example, the children of immigrant parents often do), whereas other transitions do not (when, for example, one status is a recognized prerequisite for another). Merton and Rossi explore some possible consequences of such negative orientations (see pages 62–64), but the precise conditions under which they are likely to occur have not been investigated in any detail, nor have the social costs of such discontinuities been systematically assessed.[6]

Taken together, the readings included in Part I provide a setting for the research questions posed in later selections; and they identify a number of problems that have not been investigated at all, or have received relatively little attention, in subsequent research.

5. A. Davis and J. Dollard, *Children of Bondage*, Washington: American Council on Education, 1940, pp. 136–137.

6. For a recent analysis of the complex reference group processes arising in a "contact" situation, with particular emphasis on the costs to those individuals who fail to conform to the prevailing pattern, see G. D. Berreman, "Aleut Reference Group Alienation, Mobility, and Acculturation," *American Anthropologist*, 66: 231–250, 1964.

Contributions to the Theory of Reference Group Behavior

Robert K. Merton and Alice Kitt Rossi

$\mathbf{T}$HIS chapter proceeds on the assumption that there is two-way traffic between social theory and empirical research. Systematic empirical materials help advance social theory by imposing the task and by affording the opportunity for interpretation along lines often unpremeditated, and social theory, in turn, defines the scope and enlarges the predictive value of empirical findings by indicating the conditions under which they hold. The systematic data of *The American Soldier*,[1] in all their numerous variety, provide a useful occasion for examining the interplay of social theory and applied social research.

More particularly, we attempt to identify and to order the fairly numerous researches in *The American Soldier* which, by implication or by explicit statement, bear upon the theory of *reference group behavior*. (The empirical realities which this term denotes will presently be considered in some detail. It should be said here, however, that although the *term* "reference group" is not employed in these volumes, any more than it has yet found full acceptance in the vocabulary of sociology as distinct from social psychology, reference group *concepts* play an important part in the interpretative apparatus utilized by the Research Branch of the Information and Education Division of the War Department.) . . .

A common procedure for extracting and attempting to develop the theoretical

Reprinted in part from R. K. Merton, *Social Theory and Social Structure*, rev. ed., pp. 225–275, by permission of the authors and the publisher, The Free Press. Copyright 1949, 1957 by The Free Press.

1. The authors of the first of these volumes, "Adjustment during Army Life," are S. A. Stouffer, E. A. Suchman, L. C. DeVinney, S. A. Star, and R. M. Williams, Jr.; of the second, entitled "Combat and Its Aftermath," S. A. Stouffer, A. A. Lumsdaine, M. H. Lumsdaine, R. M. Williams, Jr., M. B. Smith, I. L. Janis, S. A. Star, and L. S. Cottrell, Jr. Both were published in 1949 by the Princeton University Press.

implications of *The American Soldier* is adopted throughout the analysis. This entails the intensive re-examination of *cases* of research reported in these volumes, with an eye to subsuming the findings under higher-level abstractions or generalizations. In the volumes themselves, the authors austerely (and, in our judgment, wisely) limit their analysis to the interpretation of the behavior of soldiers and to the organizational contexts in which that behavior occurred. But manifestly, the analytical concepts hold not merely for the behavior of soldiers. By provisionally generalizing these concepts, we may be in a position to explore the wider implications of the materials for social theory.

Our discussion thus grows out of an internal analysis of every research study in these volumes in which some reference group concept was used by the authors as an interpretative variable. The object of collating these cases is to determine the points at which they invite extensions of the theory of reference group behavior which can be followed up through further strategically focused research. Occasionally, the effort is made to suggest how these theoretical extensions might be incorporated into designs for empirical research which will thus build upon the findings of the Research Branch. In this way, there may be provision for continuity in the interplay between cumulative theory and new research.

The inductive re-examination of cases admits also the linking of these reference group conceptions with other conceptions prevalent in social psychology and sociology which have not ordinarily been connected with the theory of reference group behavior. In the degree that such connections are established, *The American Soldier* will have served a further function of empirical research: the provisional consolidation of presently scattered fragments of theory.

Along these lines, an effort will be made to indicate the coherence between reference group theory and conceptions of functional sociology. It appears that these deal with different facets of the same subject: the one centers on the processes through which men relate themselves to groups and refer their behavior to the values of these groups; the other centers on the consequences of the processes primarily for social structures, but also for the individuals and groups involved in these structures. It will be found that reference group theory and functional sociology address different questions to the same phenomena but that these questions have reciprocal relevance. . . .

The Concept of Relative Deprivation

Of the various concepts employed by the authors of *The American Soldier* to interpret their multiform materials, there is one which takes a major place. This is the concept of relative deprivation. Its central significance is in some measure evidenced by its being one of the two concepts expressly called to the attention of the reader in the chapter introducing the two volumes. As the authors themselves put it, after a brief allusion to the conception of varying profiles, "Other conceptual tools, notably a theory of *relative deprivation,* also are introduced to help in more generally ordering otherwise disparate empirical findings." (I, 52)

Although the concept of relative deprivation is periodically utilized for the interpretation of variations in attitudes among different categories of men, varying, for example, with respect to age, education and marital status, it nowhere finds formal definition in the pages of these volumes. Nevertheless, as we shall presently discover, the outlines of this conception gradually emerge from the various instances in which it is put to use. It is in the very first instance of such use, for example, that the authors refer to the nature of the theoretical utility of the conception and to its possible kinship to other, established concepts of sociological theory:

> The idea [of relative deprivation] is simple, almost obvious, but its utility comes in reconciling data, especially in later chapters, where its applicability is not at first too apparent. The idea would seem to have a kinship to and, in part, include such well-known sociological concepts as "social frame of reference," "patterns of expectation," or "definitions of the situation." (I, 125)

The following list represents, albeit in much abbreviated form, every research in which some version of the concept of relative deprivation (or a kindred concept, such as relative status) is explicitly drawn upon in *The American Soldier:*

> 1. *With reference to the drafted married man: "Comparing himself with his unmarried associates in the Army*, he could feel that induction demanded greater sacrifice from him than from them; and *comparing himself with his married civilian friends*, he could feel that he had been called on for sacrifices which they were escaping altogether." (I, 125)

> 2. The average high school graduate or college man was a clear-cut candidate for induction; marginal cases on occupational grounds probably occurred much more often in groups with less educational attainment. On the average, the non high school man who was inducted *could point to more acquaintances* conceivably no more entitled to deferment than himself, who nonetheless had been deferred on occupational grounds . . . when they *compared themselves with their civilian friends* they may have been more likely to feel that they were required to make sacrifices which *others like them* were excused from making. (I, 127)

> 3. The concept of *relative deprivation* is particularly helpful in evaluating the role of education in satisfaction with status or job, as well as in some aspects of approval or criticism of the Army. . . . With higher levels of aspiration than the less educated, *the better educated man had more to lose in his own eyes and in the eyes of his friends* by failure to achieve some sort of status in the Army. Hence, frustration was greater for him than for others if a goal he sought was not attained. . . . (I, 153)

> 4. . . . the concept of differential deprivation and reward . . . may help us understand some of the psychological processes relevant to this problem. In general, it is of course true that the overseas soldier, *relative to soldiers still at home*, suffered a greater break with home ties and with many of the amenities of life in the United States to which he was accustomed. But it was also true

that, *relative to the combat soldier*, the overseas soldier [in rear areas of an active theater] not in combat and not likely to get into combat suffered far less deprivation than the actual fighting man. (I, 172)

5. The concept of differential deprivation would lead us to look further for a reason why the actually more deprived group of soldiers seemed little more critical than the less deprived group ... the less *the differential between officers and men* in the enjoyment of scarce privileges—the extreme case being that of actual combat—the less likely was the enlisted man to be critical of the officers and the easier it was for him to accept the inevitability of deprivation. (I, 181)

6. ... as would be expected ... those soldiers who had advanced slowly *relative to other soldiers of equal longevity* in the Army were the most critical of the Army's promotion opportunities. *But relative rate of advancement can be based on different standards by different classes of the Army population.* For example, a grade school man who became a corporal after a year of service would have had a more rapid rate of promotion *compared with most of his friends at the same educational level* than would a college man who rose to the same grade in a year. Hence we would expect, at a given rank and a given longevity, that the better educated would be more likely than others to complain of the slowness of promotion. ... A similar phenomenon appeared to operate between different branches of the service. (I, 250)

7. From the studies of enlisted men reported previously in this chapter, it would be expected that attitudes of officers about promotion, like those of enlisted men, would reflect some relationship with level of expectation and with level of achievement *relative to that of one's acquaintances.* Thus we would expect a captain who had been in grade a long time *compared with other captains* to be less happy about the promotion situation than a lieutenant in grade a relatively short time. (I, 279)

8. ... it seems likely that both Northern and Southern Negroes may have been considerably influenced in their overall adjustment by other psychological compensations in being stationed in the South, which can be understood if we look at their situation as one of *relative status.*

Relative to most Negro civilians whom he saw in Southern towns, the Negro soldier had a position of comparative wealth and dignity. (I, 563)

9. Putting it simply, the psychological values of Army life to the Negro soldier in the South *relative to the Southern Negro civilian* greatly exceeded the psychological values of Army life to the Negro soldier in the North *relative to the Northern Negro civilian.* (I, 564)

These nine excerpts touch upon the core interpretative statements in which the notion of relative deprivation or affiliated concepts were expressly utilized to interpret otherwise anomalous or inconsistent findings.[2] To these explicit uses

2. It thus appears, as we shall have occasion to note in some detail, that the concept of relative deprivation grows out of what we have called "the serendipity pattern" of the impact of empirical research upon theory, namely, "the fairly common experience of observing an *unanticipated, anomalous and strategic datum* which becomes the occasion for developing a new theory or for extending an existing theory."

of the concept we shall later add several research cases not subjected by the authors to interpretation in terms of reference group concepts which nevertheless seem explicated by such concepts.

In all these cases, it should be noted, the concept of relative deprivation serves the same theoretical purpose: it is used as an interpretative intervening variable. The researches were designed to study the sentiments and attitudes of American soldiers—their attitudes toward induction, for example, or their appraisals of chances for promotion. These attitudes are typically taken as the *dependent variables*. The analysis of data finds that these attitudes differ among soldiers of varying status—for example, older or married men exhibited more resentment toward induction than younger or unmarried men; those enjoying the status of high school and college graduates were less likely to be optimistic about their prospects for promotion in the Army. These status attributes are in general taken provisionally as the *independent variables.* Once the relationships between independent and dependent variables are established, the problem is one of accounting for them: of inferring how it comes to be that the better educated are typically less optimistic about their chances for promotion or how it comes to be that the married man exhibits greater resentment over his induction into military service. At this point of interpretation, the concept of relative deprivation is introduced, so that the pattern of analysis becomes somewhat as follows: the married man (independent variable) more often questions the legitimacy of his induction (dependent variable), because he appraises the situation within the frame of reference (interpretative variable) yielded by comparing himself with other married men still in civilian life, who escaped the draft entirely, or with un- married men in the Army, whose induction did not call for comparable sacrifice. We may thus tag the major function of the concept of relative deprivation as that of a provisional after-the-fact interpretative concept which is intended to help explain the variation in attitudes expressed by soldiers of differing social status. And since after-the-fact interpretations have a distinctive place in the ongoing development of theory, we shall later want to consider this characteristic of the concept of relative deprivation at some length.

The collation of these key excerpts serves as something more than a thin summary of the original materials. Since the studies employing the concept of relative deprivation deal with diverse subject-matters, they are scattered through the pages of *The American Soldier* and thus are not likely to be examined in terms of their mutual theoretical linkages. The juxtaposition of excerpts admits of a virtually *simultaneous inspection* of the several interpretations and, in turn, per- mits us to detect the central categories which were evidently taken by the Research Branch as the *bases of comparison* presumably implicit in the observed attitudes and evaluations of soldiers. And once the categories of analysis employed by the Research Branch are detected, their logical connections can be worked out, thus leading to formulations which seem to have significance for the further develop- ment of reference group theory.

If we proceed inductively, we find that the frames of reference for the soldiers under observation by the Research Branch were provisionally assumed to be of three kinds. First of all are those cases in which the attitudes or judgments of the men were held to be influenced by comparison with the situation of others with whom they were in *actual association*, in sustained social relations, such as the "married civilian friends" of the soldier in excerpt 1, or the "acquaintances" of the non-high-school man in excerpt 2.

A second implied basis of comparison is with those men who are in some pertinent respect *of the same status* or in the *same social category*, as in the case of the captain who compares his lot "with other captains" in excerpt 7 without any implication that they are necessarily in direct social interaction.

And third, comparison is assumed with those who are in some pertinent respect of *different status* or in a *different social category*, as in the case of the non-combat soldier compared with combat men in excerpt 4, or the enlisted men compared with officers in excerpt 5 (again without social interaction between them being necessarily implied).

For the most part, as we learn from this inspection of cases, the groups or individuals presumably taken as bases for comparison by soldiers do not fall simply into one *or* another of these three types, but involve various combinations of them. Most commonly, presumed comparison is with *associates* of the same status, as the grade-school man compared with friends of the same educational level in excerpt 6, or with various unassociated "others" who are of a *status similar in some salient respect and dissimilar in other respects*, such as the Negro soldier who compares himself with the Negro civilian in excerpts 8 and 9.

If these attributes of the individuals or groups serving as presumed frames of reference are arranged in a matrix, then the conceptual structure of the notion of relative deprivation (and affiliated concepts) becomes more readily visible. The schematic arrangement enables us to locate, not only the frames of comparative reference most often utilized in the interpretation of data by the Research Branch, but additional possible frames of reference which found little place in their interpretation. It thus affords an occasion for systematically exploring the theoretical nature of relative deprivation as an interpretative tool and for indicating the points at which it possibly deepens and broadens the apposite theory of reference group behavior.

In substance, the groups or individuals taken as points of reference in the nine excerpts are explicitly characterized by these few attributes. The presence of sustained social relations between the individual and those taken as a basis for comparison indicates that they are to this degree, in a common *membership group* or *in-group*, and their absence, that they are in a *non-membership* or *out-group*. When it comes to comparative status, the implied classification is slightly more complex: the individuals comprising the base of comparison may be of the same status as the subject or different, and if different, the status may be higher, lower, or unranked. The array of reference points implied in the interpretations of the Research Branch thus appears as follows:

Attributes of Individuals, Social Categories and Groups
Taken as a Frame of Comparative Reference by Individuals*

IN SUSTAINED SOCIAL RELATIONS WITH INDIVIDUAL	SAME STATUS	DIFFERENT SOCIAL STATUS		
		Higher	Lower	Unranked
Yes—(membership- or in-group)	# 1 married friends # 2 non-high-school acquaintances # 6 friends at same educational level	# 5 officers	# 8, 9 Negro civilians in South	# 3 friends # 7 acquaint- ances
No—(non-member- ship or out-group)	# 4 soldiers in United States or in active combat # 6 soldiers of equal longevity # 7 other captains	# 5 officers	# 8, 9 Negro civilians in South	

* The numbers refer to the appropriate excerpts which are here being provisionally classified.

Examination of this matrix of variables implied by the notion of relative deprivation at once directs attention to several empirical and theoretical problems. These problems, as will presently become evident, not only bear specifically upon the concept of relative deprivation but more generally upon a theory of reference group behavior.

It will be noted from the preliminary survey of cases contained in the matrix that, at times, the authors of *The American Soldier* assume that individuals take as a base for self-reference the situation of people with whom they are in direct social interaction: primarily, the in-group of friends and associates. At others, the assumed frame of reference is yielded by social categories of people—combat soldiers, other captains, etc.—with whom the individual is not in sustained social relations. In order to highlight the connection of the concept of relative deprivation with reference group theory, these "others" with whom the individual does not interact are here designated as non-membership groups or out-groups.[3] Since both membership groups and non-membership groups, in-groups and out-groups,

3. We recognize that this sentence is replete with implicit problems which it would be premature to consider at this point. It involves, for example, the problem of criteria of "membership" in a group. Insofar as frequency of social interaction is one such criterion, we must recognize that the boundaries between groups are anything but sharply drawn. Rather, "members" of given groups are variously connected with other groups of which they are not *conventionally* regarded as members, though the sociologist might have ample basis for including them in these latter groups, by virtue of their frequent social interaction with its conventional membership. So, too, we are here momentarily by-passing the question of distinctions between social *groups* and social *categories*, the latter referring to established statuses between the occupants of which there may be little or no interaction. It will also be noticed by some that the formulation contained in *The American Soldier* extends the formulations by such theorists of social psychology as George H. Mead who confined himself to *membership groups* as significant frames of reference in his concept of the "generalized other" and in his account of the formation of self-attitudes. All this bears only passing mention at this point since it will be considered at a more appropriate place.

have in fact been taken as assumed social frames of reference in these interpretations, this at once leads to a general question of central importance to a developing theory of reference group behavior: *under which conditions are associates within one's own groups taken as a frame of reference for self-evaluation and attitude-formation, and under which conditions do out-groups or non-membership groups provide the significant frame of reference?*

Reference groups are, in principle, almost innumerable: any of the groups of which one is a member, and these are comparatively few, as well as groups of which one is not a member, and these are, of course, legion, can become points of reference for shaping one's attitudes, evaluations and behavior. And this gives rise to another set of problems requiring theoretical formulation and further empirical inquiry. For, as the matrix arrangement of cases drawn from *The American Soldier* plainly suggests, the individual may be oriented toward any one *or more* of the various kinds of groups and statuses—membership groups and non-membership groups, statuses like his own or if different, either higher, lower, or not socially ranked with respect to his own. This, then, locates a further problem: if *multiple* groups or statuses, with their possibly divergent or even contradictory norms and standards, are taken as a frame of reference by the individual, how are these discrepancies resolved?[4]

These initial questions may help establish the range of our inquiry. That men act in a social frame of reference yielded by the groups of which they are a part is a notion undoubtedly ancient and probably sound. Were this alone the concern of reference group theory, it would merely be a new term for an old focus in sociology, which has always been centered on the group determination of behavior. There is, however, the further fact that men frequently orient themselves to groups *other than their own* in shaping their behavior and evaluations, and it is the problems centered about this fact of orientation to non-membership groups that constitute the distinctive concern of reference group theory. Ultimately, of course, the theory must be generalized to the point where it can account for *both* membership- and non-membership-group orientations, but immediately its major task is to search out the processes through which individuals relate themselves to groups to which they do *not* belong.

In general, then, reference group theory aims to systematize the determinants and consequences of those processes of evaluation and self-appraisal in which the individual takes the values or standards of other individuals and groups as a comparative frame of reference.

From our brief preliminary examination, it appears that the researches in *The American Soldier* utilizing the concept of relative deprivation can act as a catalyst quickening theoretical clarification and the formulation of problems for further empirical study. . . .

4. Though this problem is reminiscent of the traditional but only slightly clarified problem of conflict between multiple group *affiliations* or multiple *roles*, it is by no means identical with it. For, as we have seen, frames of reference are yielded not only by one's *own* membership groups or one's own statuses, but by non-membership groups and other statuses, as well.

Toward this end, the essential facts and basic interpretation as these are set out by the Research Branch will be summarized for each case, and followed by a statement of its apparent implications for the advancement of reference group theory.

By way of preview, it may be said that these cases generate the formulation of a wide range of specific problems which will be taken up in detail and which are here roughly indicated by the following list of headings:

Membership-groups operating as reference groups;
Conflicting reference groups and mutually sustaining reference groups;
Uniformities of behavior derived from reference group theory;
Reference group theory and social mobility;
Functions of positive orientations to non-membership groups;
Social processes sustaining or curbing these orientations;
Psychological and social functions of institutions regulating passage from one membership group to another.

Membership Group as Reference Group

CASE # 1.

This research deals with soldiers' evaluations of promotion opportunities as these were elicited by the question, "Do you think a soldier with ability has a good chance for promotion?" A generalized finding, necessarily and too much abbreviated in this summary, holds that for each level of longevity, rank and education, "the *less* the promotion opportunity afforded by a branch or combination of branches, the *more favorable* the opinion tends to be toward promotion opportunity." (I, 256) Within the limits of the data in hand,[5] this paradoxical response of greater satisfaction with opportunities for mobility in the very branches characterized by less mobility finds clear demonstration. Thus, although the Air Corps has a conspicuously high rate of promotion, Air Corps men were definitely far more critical of chances for promotion than, say, men in the Military Police, where the objective chances for promotion "were about the worst in any branch of the Army." So, too, at any given rank and longevity, the better educated soldiers, despite their notably higher rates of promotion in general, were the more critical of opportunities for promotion.

This paradox is provisionally explained by the Research Branch as a result of evaluations occurring within the frame of reference provided by group rates of promotion. A generally high rate of mobility induces excessive hopes and expecta-

5. It is important that we introduce this caveat, for it is scarcely probable that this relationship between actual mobility rates and individual satisfaction with mobility chances holds throughout the entire range of variation. If promotion rates were reduced to practically zero in some of these groups, would one then find an even more "favorable opinion" of promotion chances? Presumably, the relationship is curvilinear, and this requires the sociologist to work out toward the conditions under which the observed linear relation fails to obtain.

tions among members of the group so that each is more likely to experience a sense of frustration in his present position and disaffection with the chances for promotion. As it is put by the authors, "Without reference to the theory that such opinions represent a relationship between their expectations and their achievements *relative to others in the same boat with them*, such a finding would be paradoxical indeed." (I, 251, italics supplied)

THEORETICAL IMPLICATIONS

First of all, it should be noted that it was an anomalous finding which apparently elicited the hypothesis that evaluations of promotion chances are a function of expectations and achievements "relative to others in the same boat with them." And, in turn, the raw uninterpreted finding appears anomalous only because it is inconsistent with the commonsense assumption that, in general, evaluations will correspond to the objective facts of the case. According to common sense, marked differences in objective rates of promotion would presumably be reflected in corresponding differences in assessments of chances for promotion. Had such correspondences been empirically found, there would seemingly have been little occasion for advancing this hypothesis of a group frame of reference. As it turns out, the data suggest that men define the situation differently. But it is not enough to mention these "definitions of the situation"; it is necessary to *account for* them. And the function of the concept of relative deprivation (as with other concepts of reference groups) is precisely that of helping to account for observed definitions of a situation.

In this case, it required *systematic* empirical data, such as those assembled in *The American Soldier*, to *detect* the anomalous pattern, not detectable through impressionistic observation. And this illustrates a basic role of systematic empirical research in reaching unanticipated, anomalous and strategic findings that exert pressure for initiating or extending theory. The data and the hypothesis advanced to account for them open up further theoretical and research problems, which can here receive bare mention rather than the full exposition they deserve.

The hypothesis makes certain important assumptions about *the* group taken as a point of reference by the soldiers and thus affecting their level of satisfaction with promotion opportunities. This assumption is stated, as we have seen, in the form that evaluations are "relative to others in the same boat." And the data are consistent with the view that four groups or social categories have presumably been taken as a context or frame of reference: men with similar longevity, similar educational status, similar rank, and in the same branch of the Service.

Now, this hypothesis, suitably generalized, raises all manner of further questions germane to reference group theory and requiring renewed inquiry and analysis. Which conditions predispose toward this pattern of selecting people of the same status or group as significant points of reference? The idiomatic phrase, "in the same boat," raises the same sociological problems as the idiomatic phrase, "keeping up with the Joneses." Who are the specific Joneses, in various social structures, with whom people try to keep up? their close associates? people in immediately higher social or income strata with whom they have contact? When are the Joneses people whom one never meets, but whom one hears about (through public media of communication, for example)? How does it happen that some select the Joneses to keep up with, others the Cabots, or the Cassidys, and finally that some don't try to keep up at all?

In other words, the hypothesis advanced in *The American Soldier* regarding individuals of similar status being taken as frames of reference for self-evaluations at once opens up an interrelated array of problems, amenable to research and constituting important further links in the development of reference group theory. When are one's membership-groups *not* taken as reference groups in arriving at evaluations? After all, many men were apparently aware of the differences between the table of organization of the Air Corps and their own branch. When would these mobility rates among men *not* in the same boat affect their own level of satisfaction? And these sociological problems, though they might have originated elsewhere, were in fact generated by the anomalous empirical findings developed and provisionally interpreted in this study.

That new systematic experience, such as that represented by the data and hypothesis of *The American Soldier*, does indeed generate the formulation of further theoretical questions is suggested by glancing briefly at the somewhat contrasting work of a notable theorist in social psychology, George H. Mead, who did not steep himself in *systematic* empirical materials. Mead was, of course, a forerunner and an important forerunner in the history of reference group theory, particularly with respect to his central conception, variously expressed in his basic writings, but adequately enough captured in the statement that "The individual experiences himself as such, not directly, but only indirectly, from the particular standpoints of other individual members *of the same group*, or from the generalized standpoint of the social group as a whole *to which he belongs*."[6]

In this formulation and in numerous others like it,[7] Mead in effect advances the hypothesis that it is the groups of which the individual *is a member* that yield the significant frame of reference for self-evaluations. And this he *illustrates* abundantly with anecdotal instances drawn from his varied personal experience and insightful reflection. But, possibly because he was not exposed to *systematic* empirical evidence, which might prove seemingly inconsistent with this formulation *at specific points*, he was not driven to ask whether, indeed, the group taken as a point of reference by the individual is invariably the group of which he is a member. The terms "another," "the other" and "others" turn up on literally hundreds of occasions in Mead's exposition of the thesis that the development of the social self entails response to the attitudes of "another" or of "others." But the varying status of "these others" presumably taken as frames of self-reference is glossed over, except for the repeated statement that they are members of "the"

6. George H. Mead, *Mind, Self and Society* (The University of Chicago Press, 1934), 138 (italics supplied).

7. For example, see *ibid.*, 151–156, 193–194.

group. Thus, Mead, and those of his followers who also eschew empirical research, had little occasion to move ahead to the question of conditions under which non-membership-groups may also constitute a significant frame of reference.

Not only does the research from *The American Soldier* point directly to that question, but it leads further to the problems raised by the facts of *multiple* group affiliations and *multiple* reference groups. It reminds us that theory and research must move on to consider the *dynamics of selection* of reference groups among the individual's several membership groups: when do individuals orient themselves to others in their occupational group, in their congeniality groups, or in their religious group? How can we characterize the *structure of the social situation* which leads to one rather than another of these several group affiliations being taken as the significant context?

Following out the hypothesis advanced in the text, we note as well the problem raised by the simultaneous operation of multiple reference groups. Further steps call for study of the *dynamic processes* involved in the theoretically supposed counter-tendencies induced by multiple reference groups. For example, what are the dynamics of evaluation, and not merely the final evaluation, of the mobility system among college graduates relatively new to the Military Police: on the hypothesis advanced in *The American Soldier*, they would be moved, through reference to the status of other college graduates, toward dissatisfaction, but as comparatively new replacements and as M.P.'s they would be moved toward relative satisfaction. How are these counter-tendencies ultimately resolved in the evaluation which comes to the notice of the observer?

Turning finally to the dependent variable in this study, we note that it consists in soldiers' evaluations of the *institutional system* of promotion in the Army, and not to *self-evaluations* of personal achievement within that system.[8] The men were in effect asked to appraise the system of promotion in terms of its effectiveness and legitimacy, as can be seen from the carefully worded question which elicited their judgments: "Do you think a soldier with ability has a good chance for promotion?"

This introduces a problem, deserving attention which it has not yet received: do the two types of evaluations, self-appraisals and appraisals of institutional arrangements, involve similar mechanisms of reference group behavior? At this point, it is clear that research is needed to discover the structure of those social situations which typically elicit self-evaluations or internalized judgments—for example, where comparison with the achievements of specified others leads to invidious self-depreciation, to a sense of personal inadequacy—and the structure of those situations which typically lead to evaluations of institutions or external-

8. True, as the text implies, the institutional evaluations probably reflect soldiers' assessments of their own position as compared with their legitimate expectations, but this is not at issue here. The reference group hypothesis attempts to account for variations in the nature of these expectations in terms of the social contexts provided by the distribution of statuses in significant in-groups.

ized judgments—for example, where comparison with others leads to a sense of institutional inadequacies, to the judgment that the social system militates against any close correspondence between individual merit and social reward.

Here, as with many of *The American Soldier* researches, the implications of procedure, analysis, and interpretation are of course not confined to further studies of behavior of soldiers. They bear upon some of the more strategic areas of study in the larger social system. For example, the sociological factors which lead men to consider their own, relatively low, social position as legitimate, as well as those which lead them to construe their position as a result of defective and possibly unjustified social arrangements clearly comprise a problem area of paramount theoretical and political importance. When are relatively slim life-chances taken by men as a normal and expectable state of affairs which they attribute to their own personal inadequacies and when are they regarded as the results of an arbitrary social system of mobility, in which rewards are not proportioned to ability?[9] The concepts of relative deprivation and of relative reward help transfer these much-discussed but little-analyzed patterns of behavior from the realm of impressionistic speculation to that of systematic research.

Multiple Reference Groups

Several researches in *The American Soldier* afford occasion for looking into theoretical problems arising from the conception that multiple reference groups provide contexts for evaluations by individuals. Two of these cases have been selected for attention here because they apparently exhibit different patterns of multiple comparison: in the first of these, multiple reference groups provide contexts which operate at cross-purposes; in the second, they provide contexts which are mutually sustaining.

CONFLICTING REFERENCE GROUPS. CASE # 2

During the latter part of 1943 and the early part of 1944, the Research Branch conducted a series of surveys from which they developed a picture of differences in attitudes (reflecting personal adjustment) of noncombat men overseas and of men stationed in the United States. Though consistent, the differences in attitudes were not large. Among noncoms still in the United States, for example, 41 per cent

9. Such questions have of course been raised on numerous previous occasions. But they have ordinarily been regarded as distinct and self-contained problems of interest in their own right and not as special problems subsumable under a theory of reference group behavior. For example, it has been suggested that conspicuously "successful" individuals who have risen rapidly in a social hierarchy and who are much in the public eye, function as models or reference-figures testifying to a mobility-system in which, apparently, careers are still open to talents. For some, these success-models are living testimony to the legitimacy of the institutional system and in this comparative context, the individual deflects criticism of the system onto himself. See Merton, Fiske and Curtis, *Mass Persuasion*, 152ff. But these observations remain impressionistic and anecdotal, since they do not provide *systematic* designs for inquiry into this behavior along the lines suggested by the researches of *The American Soldier*.

reported themselves as "usually in good spirits" in comparison with 32 per cent of those overseas; 76 per cent of the one held that the "Army is run pretty well or very well" compared with 63 per cent of the other. (I, 167, Chart IV) But since other surveys found that the major concern of the men overseas was to get back home (I, 187), the authors observe that considerably greater differences in attitudes expressing personal adjustment might well have been expected.

Three factors are tentatively adduced to account for the absence of greater differences, factors operating to curb the expectable[10] degree of dissatisfaction expressed by the noncombat soldier overseas. Of these, we attend only to the interpretative concept of "differential deprivation and reward"[11] which, it will be remembered from an earlier excerpt,

> may help us understand some of the psychological processes relevant to this problem. In general, it is of course true that the overseas soldier, *relative to soldiers still at home*, suffered a greater break with home ties and with many of the amenities of life in the United States to which he was accustomed. But it was also true that, *relative to the combat soldier*, the overseas soldier not in combat and not likely to enter into combat suffered far less deprivation than the actual fighting man. (I, 172)

THEORETICAL IMPLICATIONS

In effect, the authors suggest that two contexts of comparison, operating at cross-purposes, affected the evaluations of overseas noncombat troops. What, then, can be learned from this case about the grounds on which certain contexts rather than others become pertinent for such evaluations?

It should be noted at the outset that the status of those constituting the contexts of evaluation is, in some significant respect, *similar* to the status of the men making the evaluation. Thus, the soldiers still at home are similar in that they too are not in combat, and the combat soldiers are similar in that they too are overseas. Beyond this, other similarities and dissimilarities, pertinent to the situation, affect the resulting evaluations in contrasting ways. Thus, the overseas noncombat soldier is, by the standards of Army life, worse off than the soldier at home in that

10. Here we see again that the concept of relative deprivation (just as the notion of "definition of the situation" generally) is introduced to account for an apparently anomalous finding. In this case, the finding seemingly deviates, not from common sense expectation merely, but from other facts uncovered in the course of research. It would thus seem to illustrate the type of serendipity pattern in research in which "the observation is anomalous, surprising, either because it seems inconsistent with prevailing theory or with other established facts. In either case, the seeming inconsistency provokes curiosity; it stimulates the investigator to 'make sense of the datum.' "

11. The other two are, first, physical selection since men overseas had to meet more rigorous standards and second, "a sense of the significance of one's army job." In this latter connection, the authors remark: "While the difference between theaters . . . cannot prove or disprove hypotheses, the fact that, on the average, United States-overseas differences on attitudes toward Army jobs were negligible or reversed—as compared with United States-overseas differences in personal esprit or attitudes toward the Army—is a fact not to be overlooked." (I, 173)

he is comparatively deprived of amenities and cut off from social ties, and better off than the combat soldier in that he is not exposed to the same measure of deprivation and risk. It is as though he had said, "Bad off as we are, the others are worse off," a comparison not seldom adopted by those who would accommodate themselves to their position. His definition of his situation is then presumably the resultant of these counteracting patterns of comparison.

This suggests the general hypothesis that some similarity in status attributes between the individual and the reference group must be perceived or imagined, in order for the comparison to occur at all. Once this minimal similarity obtains,[12] other similarities and differences pertinent to the situation, will provide the context for shaping evaluations. Consequently, this focuses the attention of the theorist immediately upon the factors which produce a sense of pertinent similarity between statuses, since these will help determine which groups are called into play as comparative contexts. The underlying similarities of status among members of in-groups, singled out by Mead as *the* social context, thus appear as only one special, though obviously important, basis for the selection of reference groups. Out-groups may also involve *some* similarity of status.

By implication, the hypothesis of the Research Branch at this point provides a clue to the factors affecting the selection of reference groups. The hypothesis does not hold that the two categories of men—the combat men overseas and the noncombat men at home—constituted the *only* ones with which *any particular individual* among the overseas combat men compared himself. He may indeed have compared his lot with that of numerous and diverse others—a civilian friend in a cushy job back home, a cousin enjoying life as a war correspondent, an undrafted movie star whom he had read about in a magazine. But such comparisons by an individual, precisely because they involve personal frames of reference, might well be idiosyncratic. They would not provide contexts *common* to (many or most of) the individuals in the status of overseas noncombat men. To the degree that they are idiosyncratic, they would vary at random among the various categories of soldiers. Consequently, they would not aggregate into statistically significant differences of attitudes between *groups* or *social categories* of soldiers.

In other words, the statistics of *The American Soldier* on differential definitions of their situation among combat men,[13] overseas noncombat men and men

12. This minimum status similarity apparently presupposed by reference group behavior clearly requires systematic study. *Some* similarity in status can of course always be found, depending only on the breadth of the status category. One can compare oneself with others, if only in the most general social capacity of "human being." And more germane to the case in question, the overseas combat man could (and did) compare himself with the noncombat man back home by virtue of their similar status as soldiers, and with civilians by virtue of their similar status as young adult American males. The theoretical and research problem at this point is to determine how the structure of the social situation encourages certain status-similarities to become the basis for such comparisons, and leads other status-similarities to be ignored as "irrelevant."

13. *The American Soldier* does not supply data on the attitudes of combat men at this point in the text, although apposite data are found at other places in the volumes. (*e.g.*, I, 111)

still in the United States are taken to manifest the impact of *socially structured* reference groups more or less common to men in each category. It is not mere indolence or lack of insight which keeps the sociologist from seeking to track down all the comparative contexts which hold for any given individual; it is, rather, that many of these contexts are idiosyncratic, not shared by a large fraction of other individuals within the same group or social category. The comparative statistics in *The American Soldier* are plainly not intended to manifest and cannot manifest those numerous private contexts peculiar to individuals and hence varying at random to the social category. One does not look to these sociological data for idiosyncratic contexts of appraisal.

The reference groups here hypothesized, then, are not mere artifacts of the authors' arbitrary scheme of classification. Instead, they appear to be frames of reference held in common by a proportion of individuals within a social category sufficiently large to give rise to definitions of the situation characteristic of that category. And these frames of reference are common because they are patterned by the social structure. In the present case, for example, the degree of closeness to combat provides a socially organized and socially emphasized basis of comparison among the three categories of soldiers—overseas combat, overseas noncombat, and troops back home. It is, accordingly, categories such as these which provide the *common* comparative contexts for definition of the situation among these men. This is not to deny that other contexts may be of great consequence to particular individuals within each of these social categories. But these become relevant for the sociologist only if they are shared sufficiently to lead to group differences in evaluations.

In these pages, *The American Soldier* affords a clue, and possibly an important clue, for solving the sociological problem of finding the common residual which constitutes the reference groups distinctive for those in a social status category.

There is another problem implicit here about which little can be learned from this case: what are the patterns of response among members of a group or status category when they are subject to multiple reference groups operating at cross-purposes? In the present case, the net evaluation of their lot among overseas noncombat men apparently represented a compromise, intermediate between the evaluations of noncombat men at home and of men in actual combat. But it is not implied by the authors of *The American Soldier* that this is the only pattern of response under such circumstances. It is possible, for example, that when several membership groups exert diverse and conflicting pressures for self-appraisal, the individual tends to adopt other, non-membership groups as a frame of reference. In any event, there arises the large and imperfectly defined problem, previously alluded to, of searching out the processes of coming to terms with such conflicting pressures.[14] That the social scientists of the Research Branch were cognizant of

14. Thus, a study of political behavior found that individuals, under cross-pressure, were more likely to delay their final vote decision. And as the senior author goes on to say: "But such delay is not the only possible reaction. Other alternatives range all the way from individual neurotic reactions, such as an inability to make any decision at all, to intellectual solutions

this line of inquiry, emerging from their wartime studies, is suggested by the fact that the director, Stouffer, is now developing researches on the varying patterns of response to the simultaneous but conflicting demands of primary groups and of formal organizational authorities.[15]

MUTUALLY SUSTAINING REFERENCE GROUPS. CASE # 3

In its bare outlines, this study (I, 122–130) is concerned with the feelings of legitimacy ascribed by men to their induction into service. Patterns of response to the question, "At the time you came into the Army, did you think you should have been deferred?" showed that married men, over 20 years of age, who had not been graduated from high school were most likely to maintain that they should have been deferred. In this status category, 41 per cent, as compared, for example, with only 10 per cent of unmarried high school graduates under 20 years of age, claimed that they should not have been inducted at all. More generally, it is found that the statuses of age, marital condition and educational level are consistently related with willingness for military service.

Since the hypotheses advanced to account for these findings are essentially of the same type for each of the three status categories, we need concern ourselves here with only one of these for illustrative purposes. As we have seen in an excerpt from this case, the authors provisionally explain the greater reluctance for service of married men in terms of the standards of comparison yielded by reference to two other status categories. The key interpretative passage bears repetition at this point:

> *Comparing himself with his unmarried associates* in the Army, he could feel that induction demanded greater sacrifice from him than from them; and *comparing himself with his married civilian friends* he could feel that he had been called on for sacrifices which they were escaping altogether. Hence the married man, on the average, was more likely than others to come into the Army with reluctance and, possibly, a sense of injustice. (I, 125, italics supplied)

THEORETICAL IMPLICATIONS

However brief and tentative the interpretation, it helps us to locate and to formulate several further problems involved in developing a theory of reference group behavior.

First of all, it reinforces the supposition, hinted in the preceding case, that it is

which might lead to new social movements. Many of the baffling questions about the relationship between individual attitudes and social environment may be answered when these problems of cross-pressures and reactions to them are thoroughly and properly studied." Lazarsfeld, Berelson, and Gaudet, *The People's Choice* (New York: Columbia University Press, 1948, second edition), xxii.

15. Samuel Stouffer, "An analysis of conflicting social norms," *American Sociological Review*, 1949, 14, 707-717.

the institutional definitions of the social structure which may focus the attention of members of a group or occupants of a social status upon certain *common* reference groups. Nor does this refer only to the fact that soldiers will take the official institutional norms (the rules governing induction and exemption) as a *direct* basis for judging the legitimacy of their own induction into the service. These same rules, since they are defined in terms of such statuses as marital condition and age, also focus attention on certain groups or statuses with which individuals subject to service will compare themselves. This is, in effect, implied by the authors who, referring to the greater sacrifices entailed by induction of the married man, go on to say: "This was officially recognized by draft boards. . . . The very fact that draft boards were more liberal with married than with single men provided numerous examples to the drafted married man of *others in his shoes* who got relatively better breaks than he did." (I, 125, italics supplied) The institutional norms evoke comparisons with others similar in *particular* aspects of status—"others in his shoes"—thus encouraging *common* reference groups for these married soldiers. In addition to these common reference groups, as previously stated, there may well have been all manner of idiosyncratic reference groups, which, since they vary at random, would not have resulted in the statistically discernible reluctance for service which was comparatively marked among married men.

A second problem is highlighted by the hypothesis which uniformly assumes that the married soldier compares himself with like-statused individuals with whom he is or has been in *actual social relations: associates* in the Army or civilian *friends*. This, then, raises a question concerning reference group behavior when the frame of comparative reference is provided by *impersonal status categories* in general (other married men, noncoms, *etc.*) and by those representatives of these status categories with whom he is in *sustained social relations*. Which, for example, most affects the evaluations of the individual when these operate at cross-purposes (a problem clearly visible in the matrix of variables set out earlier in this paper)?

This question leads at once to the comparative significance of general status categories and intimate subgroups of which one is a member. Suppose, for example, that all or almost all of a married soldier's married associates have also been drafted, even though, *in general*, this status category has a smaller proportion of inductions than the category of the unmarried male. Which basis of comparison will, on the average, prove more effective? Will he compare himself with the other drafted benedicts in his clique or subgroup and consequently be the more ready to accept induction for himself, or will he compare himself with the larger status category of married men, who are in general more often deferred, and consequently feel aggrieved over his own induction? The question has, of course, more general bearing. For example, are workers' expectations regarding their personal prospects of future employment shaped more by the present employment of themselves and their associates on the job or by high rates of unemployment prevailing in the occupation at large?

This case from *The American Soldier* thus points to the need for cumulative research on *the relative effectiveness of frames of reference yielded by associates and by more general status categories*. It suggests the salient items of observation which must be incorporated in such projected studies, so that this problem, at least in its major outlines, can lend itself to research, here and now, not in some remote future. Such projected studies could readily include items of data on the norms or situation of close associates as well as data on knowledge about the norms or situation prevailing in the given status at large. Subsequent analysis would then be in terms of systematic comparison of individuals in the *same status* but with immediate *associates* who have distinctly opposed norms or who are in contrasting situations. Replicated studies including such materials would substantially advance our present understanding of the workings of reference group behavior.

Third, the theory assumes that individuals comparing their own lot with that of others have some *knowledge* of the situation in which these others find themselves. More concretely, it assumes that the individual *knows about* the comparative rates of induction among married and single men, or the degree of unemployment in their occupation at large.[16] Or, if the individual is taken to be positively oriented toward the norms of a non-membership group, the theory of course assumes that he has some knowledge of these norms. Thus, the theory of reference group behavior must include in its fuller psychological elaboration some treatment of the dynamics of perception (of individuals, groups and norms) and in its sociological elaboration, some treatment of channels of communication through which this knowledge is gained. Which processes make for accurate or distorted images of the situation of other individuals and groups (taken as a frame of reference)? Which forms of social organization maximize the probabilities of correct perception of other individuals and groups, and which make for distorted perception? Since *some* perceptual and cognitive elements are definitely *implied* even in a description of reference group behavior, it will be necessary for these elements to be explicitly incorporated into the theory.

A fourth problem emerging from this case concerns the empirical status of reference group concepts. In this study, as well as in others we consider here, the interpretative concept of relative deprivation was introduced *after* the field research was completed.[17] This being the case, there was no provision for the

16. It may of course turn out that, under certain conditions, individuals extrapolate their knowledge of the situation of associates in a given social category to that social category at large. Or, it may develop that the situation of one's associates is accorded greater weight by the individual than the contrasting situation which he knows to obtain in the social category at large. These are questions amenable to empirical research and salient for reference group theory.

17. Although the concept is after-the-fact of *data collection*, it was introduced early enough in the *analysis* to permit its use in suggesting types of tabulations which would otherwise not have been undertaken. From the interpretative standpoint, therefore, relative deprivation was not confined to use as an *ex post facto* conception.

collection of *independent systematic*[18] *evidence* on the operation of such social frameworks of individual judgments. That a significant proportion of married soldiers did indeed compare their lot with that of married civilian friends and un-married associates in the Army in arriving at their judgment remains, so far as the data in hand go, an assumption. These comparisons are inferred, rather than factually demonstrated, intervening variables. But they need not remain assump-tions. They not only happen to square with the facts in hand, but are of a kind which can be directly tested in future inquiries employing the concept of reference group.[19] These studies can be designed to incorporate systematic data on the groups which individuals actually do take as frames of reference for their behavior and can thus determine whether variations in attitude and behavior correspond to variations in reference group contexts.

This possibility of converting the intervening variable of reference groups from assumption into fact brings us to a fifth problem. Before plunging into re-search on the conditions under which individuals compare themselves with *specified* other individuals or groups, it is necessary to consider the psychological status of these comparisons. For when individuals *explicitly* and consciously adopt such frames of reference, sociological researches involving interviews with large numbers of people face no great procedural difficulties. Appropriate ques-tions can elicit the needed information on the groups, status categories or indi-viduals which are taken as a frame of reference. But there is, of course, no reason to assume that comparisons of self with others are uniformly conscious. Numerous experimental studies in social psychology have shown that individuals *unwittingly*

18. The emphasis on *systematic* data is essential, for *The American Soldier* has abundant indications that *in many cases* assumed reference groups were indeed taken as a context of comparison. For example, their text includes remarks by overseas soldiers which clearly indicate that the soldiers back home are sometimes taken as a point of reference in assessing their own situation: "I think I've had my share being overseas over two years. That's plenty for any man. . . . Let them USO boys get some of this chow once in a while, then they will know what it is to sleep in the mud with mosquitoes buzzing around them like a P-38." "We should have a chance to breathe a little fresh air for a while. But I guess you better keep them USO boys back there or there won't be any USO." "It is hard as hell to be here and read in every paper that comes from home where Pvt. Joe Dokes is home again on furlough after tough duty as a guard in Radio City." "We receive letters from soldiers who have not yet left the States and who are on their second furlough." (I, 188) These remarks also contain passing allusions to the source of information regarding the situation of the men back home: "read in every paper," "we receive letters," *etc.* But such telling anecdotal materials are properly enough not regarded as a basis for *systematic* analysis by the authors of *The American Soldier.*

19. A recent example of the possibility of now anticipating the need for data on reference group behavior is provided by the 1948 voting study in Elmira (since published as B. Berelson, P. F. Lazarsfeld and W. N. McPhee, *Voting*, University of Chicago Press, 1954). Under a grant from the Rockefeller Foundation for the study of panel techniques in social research, a conference at Swarthmore on reference group concepts was arranged, with an eye to having materials bearing on these concepts introduced into the Elmira voting study. *The American Soldier* provides numerous further conceptions which can be similarly incorporated in further research.

respond to different frames of reference introduced by the experimenter. To the extent that unwitting reference groups are involved in the ordinary routines of daily life, research techniques must be extended to detect their operation.

Appropriate research procedures must also be designed to discover which reference groups are spontaneously and explicitly brought into play, as distinguished from the study of responses to reference group contexts provided by the experimenter or suggested by the interviewer. Both interview and experimental studies have heretofore been largely centered on responses to reference group contexts supplied for the subjects. These studies can be further advanced by providing ordered arrays of comparative contexts, somewhat as follows:

> Compared with others on your work-team [or other membership-group], do
>   you feel you are getting a fair income for what you do?
> Compared with the men in the front office, do you . . . etc. . . . ?
> Compared with the president of the firm, do you . . . etc. . . . ?

Or similarly, information about the salaries of various individuals and groups could be given an experimental group and withheld from a matched group of workers to determine whether the subsequent self-appraisals and satisfactions of the experimental group are modified by possible reference groups supplied by the investigator.

But such tentative types of inquiry, in which the particular reference groups are provided, do not, of course, enter into the uncharted region of the *spontaneous selection of reference groups* in varying situations. Why will A, in one situation, compare himself with B, and in another, with C? Or, more concretely and illustratively: when do workers compare their lot with that of fellow-workers in close association, and when with others of markedly different status? which aspects of the social structure and which psychological processes limit the range of individuals and groups regarded as pertinent frames of reference? It is this type of problem—the processes shaping the selection of reference groups—that stands in most conspicuous need of research.[20]

Uniformities of Behavior Derived from Reference Group Theory

To this point, we have examined researches in which the concept of relative deprivation was explicitly utilized by Stouffer and his associates to interpret empirical findings. In doing so, we have attempted, first, to indicate how this concept can be incorporated in a more general, though still primitive, theory of

---

20. A notable beginning is found in the pioneering study by Herbert H. Hyman, *The Psychology of Status*, Archives of Psychology, No. 269, 1942. Hyman sought to have his subjects report the groups or individuals which they had taken for comparison with their own status. This kind of direct questioning can of course elicit only the conscious and remembered frames of comparison. But the advancement of reference group theory has suffered by the general failure to follow up Hyman's suggestive lead on spontaneously emerging frames of group reference.

reference group behavior and second, how these studies give rise to further empirical and theoretical problems that can become the object of new and cumulative research.

We want now to consider whether the theory of reference groups does indeed have wider applicability than the seemingly special concept of relative deprivation. Fortunately, the numerous researches of *The American Soldier* enable us to check this, at least to some degree. For some of these researches involve findings which are apparently not germane to the concept of relative deprivation—since they deal with self-images, but not with levels of satisfaction with one's lot—yet which can, we believe, be explicated by applying reference group conceptions to them. In the course of seeing whether this theory permits us to detect sociological uniformities underlying apparently disparate patterns of behavior, we shall also have occasion to add to the list of specific problems needing solution if reference group theory is to be advanced.

CASE # 4 (II, 242–72)

Combat groups were in general subject to high personnel turnover. It is true that some outfits were trained and entered into combat with few changes in personnel, but even in these instances, casualties required frequent replacements. The Research Branch seized upon the sociologically significant fact that inexperienced soldiers thus found themselves in two distinctly different social structures: some being for a time in homogeneous outfits comprised wholly of similarly green troops, and others, in divisions with combat veterans. And here the study took a decisive sociological turn. Unlike the ordinary polling studies in social psychology, which compare *aggregates of individuals of different status* (age, sex, class, *etc.*), they did not merely compare the attitudes of inexperienced and of veteran troops. This would have been only a comparison of aggregates of men in two distinct statuses, an important type of comparison but of severely limited value for sociology. Rather, they defined this as an occasion for studying the impact of *group contexts* upon the attitudes of types of individuals, a problem which is of course old, older than sociology itself, but which has less often been the object of systematic empirical research than of impressionistic discussion.

The Research Branch therefore centered upon the group contexts in which these troops found themselves: green troops in outfits comprised wholly by their own kind; equally inexperienced replacements in divisions otherwise composed of combat veterans; and the veterans themselves in these divisions.[21] Questions were put to these three groups of soldiers in several of what the Research Branch calls "attitude areas" (willingness for combat, confidence in their ability to take charge of a group in combat, appraisal of their physical condition, and so on). These surveys found apparently diverse *patterns of differences* in response among the

21. There is, of course, a fourth group context which might have entered strategically into the systematic comparison, namely, the divisions comprised wholly of combat veterans, except that the replacement practices of the Army did not make it possible for the Research Branch to include such all-veteran divisions in this study.

three groups. In the first "attitude area," for example, veterans expressed greater reluctance to get into combat than the troops in green outfits, with the replacements being intermediate to the two. Whereas 45 per cent of the green troops were "ready to get into an actual battle zone," this dropped to 28 per cent among the replacements and to only 15 per cent among the veterans. It is, of course, the contrast between the green troops and the replacements which is most significant, since these were alike in their *individual attribute* of lack of combat experience, but different with respect to the *kind of group* in which they found themselves. This same pattern, with the replacement *intermediate* to those of the veteran and green troops, occurred in responses to questions about attitudes towards noncoms.

But, the Research Branch reports, this is only one pattern of response. Quite another pattern was found with regard to the men's confidence in their ability "to take charge of a group of men" in combat. As some might expect on common-sense grounds, the veterans more often expressed confidence in their capacity to fulfill this role than did the green troops in green outfits. But it is of crucial significance that, unlike the first instance of willingness for combat, where the replacements were intermediate in their responses, in this case, they were consistently the least confident of the three groups.

Again, on yet another type of "attitude"—toward his own physical condition—the replacement was virtually indistinguishable from the other green troops, but far more likely than the veteran to consider himself "in good physical condition."

These three sets of data, then, seem to show three different patterns of response, in the first of which the replacement responds more like the veteran than the green troops; in the second, most remote from the veteran and also unlike other green troops; and in the third, quite like his counterpart in green outfits. And since these are diverse patterns, the Research Branch has advanced diverse interpretations. With regard to the replacements' approximation to the veterans' reluctance to go into combat, it is suggested that "to some extent the replacements took over the attitudes of the combat veterans around them, whose views on combat would have for them high prestige." (II, 250) With regard to capacity for leading a group in combat, where the replacements differ most from the veterans, it is suggested that "for the veterans, experience was their strong point, and also the point at which replacements in contact with them felt the greatest inferiority, standing as they did in the shadow of the veterans." (II, 251) And when the replacement is quite like his counterpart in green outfits, as with appraisals of physical conditions, this is tentatively explained by saying that these judgments probably reflect an actual (objective) difference in physical condition between veterans and others.

THEORETICAL IMPLICATIONS

It will be at once granted that this poses an intriguing challenge and problem for sociological theory. For the response-behavior of the replacements seems to exhibit almost random variation, a situation distasteful to the theorist whose task it is to perceive underlying uniformities amid such apparent disorder. It is reminiscent of the situation confronting Durkheim when he found an immense variety of suicide rates, differing among the sexes, rural-urban areas, military and civilian populations, religious groups, and so on. Rather than advance new and separate interpretations of each set of differentials, he attempted to derive these numerous variations from a limited set of propositions. So here, these various patterns of response of replacements set sociological theory the task of discerning the significant variables and conditions which bring about this seeming diversity of response-behavior.

As is well-known, the first step in the search for sociological order amid apparent disorder is to re-examine, in theoretical terms, the *concepts* in terms of which the data are reported. More often than not, it will be found that these concepts may profit by clarification and reformulation. That appears to be the case here. These several sets of data are all reported as *attitudes* falling into distinct "attitude-areas." The theorist might at once consider the possibility that basic conceptual differences in these data might be obscured by use of a singly crudely defined concept.[22] The single blanket concept of "attitude" may also fail to direct the analyst's attention to the appropriate body of theory for interpreting the data. And finally, by tacitly including significantly different elements in the data under this one undifferentiated concept, the empirical findings may exhibit anomalies, contradictions, and lack of uniformities which are only apparent, not real.

What does a conceptual reformulation of these data show ? The first variable, "willingness for combat," may indeed be usefully described as an "attitude" in the approximate sense of "a mental and neural *state of readiness,* organized through experience, exerting a directive or dynamic influence upon the individual's response to all objects and situations with which it is related."[23] But the second variable, "self-confidence in leadership capacities," as here indexed, appears not so much a preparatory set for behavior, as a *self-image and a self-appraisal.* Two consequences flow from this provisional reformulation of a single "attitude" concept into the two concepts of attitude and of self-appraisal. First, it is no longer assumed that the data bearing on these two variables need manifest the same comparative distributions: that now becomes a moot question and not a tacit presumption. And second, the reformulation in terms of self-appraisal leads us at once to the reference group theory of self-appraisals. Reformulation of the concept in which the dependent variables are stated thus provides a tentative link

22. In the introduction, Stouffer calls special attention to the looseness of the concept "attitude" as adopted in these studies: ". . . in the main work of the Research Branch and in most of the text of the present volumes there is no operational definition of attitudes—whence, concepts like 'attitudes,' 'tendencies,' and 'opinions' are used more or less loosely and even sometimes interchangeably. . . ." (I, 42) We are here engaged in exploring some of the empirical and theoretical consequences of the *respecification* of a concept. For a clear statement of this procedure, see W. J. Goode and P. K. Hatt, *Methods in Social Research* (New York: McGraw Hill, 1952), 48–53.

23. The particular definition cited is that by G. W. Allport, but various current conceptions of "attitude" have essentially this same core-denotation.

with theory of the past: we are not forced to improvise wholly new hypotheses, standing alone and unconnected with a general body of theory, but can, perhaps, derive these findings from an established set of hypotheses centered about the structure, functions, and dynamic mechanisms of self-appraisals in diverse group contexts. This is, moreover, the theory which incorporates the concept of relative deprivation, used elsewhere in these volumes, but not here.

With this new conceptual basis, we are prepared to re-examine the data of *The American Soldier* to see whether they do indeed exhibit the anomaly of three distinct patterns of response under the same conditions. If a general theory is to move out from these data and beyond the interpretations advanced in the text, then it should be able to incorporate these seemingly different patterns of response as expressions of an underlying regularity.

Stemming then from the theoretic background provided by James, Cooley and Mead, and by Hyman, Sherif and Newcomb, the hypothesis holds that, insofar as subordinate or prospective group members are motivated to affiliate themselves with a group, they will tend to assimilate the sentiments and conform with the values of the authoritative and prestigeful stratum in that group. The function of conformity is acceptance by the group, just as progressive acceptance by the group reinforces the tendency toward conformity. And the values of these "significant others" constitute the mirrors in which individuals see their self-image and reach self-appraisals. Applied to the specific case in hand, the significant others in the membership-group are similarly inexperienced men for the green soldier in a green outfit, whereas for the replacement, the significant others are experienced veterans, with their distinctive sets of values and sentiments.

In applying the general hypothesis, it must be anticipated that the replacements, as "outsiders" motivated to affiliate themselves with the prestigeful and authoritative stratum (the veterans), would more nearly conform to *all* of the veterans' values and sentiments here under inspection. We should be clear on this point. If its interpretative utility is to be properly assessed, the hypothesis must stand on its own feet, and not be modified or abandoned because the text of *The American Soldier* reports that the responses of replacements in these distinct "attitude areas" were in fact different. The present hypothesis gives us a set of instructions to the effect that we must re-examine these reportedly different patterns in order to determine whether they are actually different, or merely speciously so.

In a provisional way, and to the extent that the reported data allow us to say, it appears that the differences are only apparent. Underlying these manifest differences in the percentage distribution of replies to the given questions by veterans, replacements, and green troops, are regularities of response corresponding to those anticipated in the hypothesis.

Thus, first, with respect to willingness for combat, the sentiments of veterans held, in effect, that "combat is hell", and consequently, veterans most frequently expressed reluctance to enter into combat. The green troops, in contrast, who had more lately quitted civilian ranks, were more likely to have at the outset the values of the wartime civilian population, with all its "conventional stereotypes" of combat as affording occasions for dramatic heroism. This is in fact borne out by the text at another place and in another connection, where it is reported that "probably the strongest group code [among combat men] . . . was the taboo against any talk of a flagwaving variety. . . . The core of the attitude *among combat men* seemed to be that any talk that did not subordinate idealistic values and patriotism to the harsher realities of the combat situation was hypocritical, and a person who expressed such ideas a hypocrite."[24]

In this first instance, then, our hypothesis drawn from reference group theory would lead us to anticipate that the replacements, seeking affiliation with the authoritative and prestigeful stratum of veterans, will move from the civilian-like values toward the more tough-minded values of the veterans. And this, as we know, is indeed the case. For replacements, the assumed function of assimilating the values of the veterans is to find more ready acceptance by the higher-status group, in a setting where the subordinate group of replacements does not have independent claims to legitimate prestige.

But if the hypothesis is consistent with the first set of data on willingness for combat, can it also hold for the second set of data dealing with the so-called attitude of self-confidence regarding capacity for leadership, particularly since it was found that, in this instance, the replies of replacements were *remote* from those of the veterans, even more so than the replies of the green troops? Indeed, the text refers to this as a "different" or "divergent" pattern of response. To be sure, the manifest distribution of replies differs from the first. But, viewed in terms of reference group theory, it is, we believe, only another expression of the same underlying dynamic regularities of behavior in this group context.

This can be tested by applying the hypothesis. In the case of self-confidence, as we have seen, we deal with a self-appraisal rather than with an attitude in the sense of a preparatory set for action. The values and sentiments of the veteran stratum hold, in effect, that "actual combat experience is needed to prepare a private to take charge of a group of men in combat."[25] Now, if, as the hypothesis anticipates, replacements seek to assimilate *this* value and judge themselves accordingly, if they see themselves in the mirror provided by the values of the prestigeful veterans, they can only appraise themselves as, by and large, unprepared for spontaneous leadership in battle. On the hypothesis, the replacements

24. II, 150 (italics supplied). Essentially the same point of a contrast in values regarding combat between the civilian population and combat men is made at numerous places in the two volumes; *e.g.*, at II, 111–112, 151; I, 484. Notice should also be taken of Chart VIII in Chapter 3 of volume II, showing that veterans were far more likely than inexperienced troops to say that "this war is not worth fighting." And finally, it should be said that this contrast between the definitions of the combat situation by civilians and by combat men is drawn by Brewster Smith, who also conducted the analysis of replacement behavior now under review.

25. The statistical data of replies to the question, "Do you think you have been given enough training and experience so that you could do a good job of taking charge of a group of men on your own in combat," constitute one basis for the view that veterans hold this value. Discussions of the values of combat men, especially in II, Chapter 3, bear this out.

would, in short, behave just as they do, being most likely to say that they are *not* ready to take charge of men in combat (involving a lower self-estimate than that found among the green troops, *not* vis-à-vis the veterans). Thus, although their *distribution* of replies differs markedly from that of the veterans, leading the Research Branch to describe this as another pattern of response, the replacements are engaging in the same pattern of behavior in the two instances—when this is construed in terms of reference group theory. They are assimilating the values of the veterans, and thus presumably affiliating themselves with this authoritative and prestigeful stratum. In the first instance of "willingness for combat," this calls only for direct reaffirmation of the veterans' sentiments, leading the replacements' distribution of responses to resemble that of the veterans. In the second instance of self-confidence in leadership capacity, they also assimilate the veteran standards but since this is not merely an attitude but a self-appraisal, they apply these standards to themselves, find themselves comparatively wanting, and thus give distributions of responses to the self-appraisal questions differing from those of the veterans. Thus, a uniformity of social process apparently underlies the different patterns of manifest replies.

The same hypothesis can be tested anew on other items from these data on "attitudes" of veterans, replacements, and green troops; for example, those dealing with "attitudes toward physical condition." In this case, the green troops and replacements respond alike, with 57 per cent and 56 per cent respectively saying that they are in good physical condition, whereas only 35 per cent of the veterans make that claim. This is reported as a third pattern of response, again on the manifest empirical level of response-frequencies, leading the Research Branch to another interpretation of this apparently new pattern: the similarity of answers by replacements and green troops, it is suggested, "undoubtedly parallels similarity in the men's actual physical condition."[26]

Here, it is said, the responses represent, not an assimilation of veterans' attitudes, but more nearly a faithful reporting of objective differences in the physical condition of fatigued veterans—"beat-up Joes"—and of the fresh replacements and green troops.

But this only poses another problem for theory: Under which conditions do men respond by reporting the objective situation rather than a socially reflected image? Does this third, apparently different, pattern of response require a new hypothesis? It seems that, again, no additional *ad hoc* variables need be introduced although in the absence of the required data, this must of course remain for future research to examine. It appears that the veterans do not hold poor physical condition as a distinctive and positive social *value* (except, as the text indicates, as a possible rationalization for escaping further combat) in the same sense that they hold the belief that "combat is hell" or that "combat experience equips a private

---

26. II, 263. This refers to their "absolute" ratings in response to the question, "Do you think that you are in good physical condition?" Alternative questions which refer to "combat" conditions possibly introduce the factor of replacements' assimilated reluctance for combat; they tend to be intermediate to veterans and green troops in their responses to these.

to take charge of men in combat." Replacements seeking to affiliate themselves with the prestigeful and socially validated veterans will therefore not be served by asserting that they are in poor physical shape, that they, too, are in effect "beat-up Joes." If anything, this claim would only be the occasion for rejection of replacements by veterans, since it would represent, not a bid for affiliation with the group, but for equality of *status*. Moreover, the replacements' recognition of their comparatively good physical condition does not affirm a counter-value, which might also threaten their acceptance by the veterans. Within the same group context, then, there is no functional or motivational basis for replacements to reproduce the self-judgments of the veterans, and apparently objective differences in the physical condition of fatigued veterans and of fresh replacements and green troops find expression.

In so far as differences in these three patterns of manifest response can be theoretically derived from a functional theory of reference group behavior, this case illustrates one major service of theory for applied social research: the reconstruction through conceptual clarification of apparent irregularities in data leads to the provisional discovery of underlying functional and dynamic regularities. But, as we have suggested, the avenues between social theory and applied research carry two-way traffic: not only can theory reformulate some of the materials in *The American Soldier*, but on the basis of the same materials we can specify the types of further sociological indices and observations needed to achieve continuity and cumulation in the theory of value-assimilation, the group context of self-appraisals, and the objective assessment of situations. A brief list of such indices must stand in lieu of a detailed analysis of their potential for the advancement of this theory.

1. *Index of actual social relations:* There is plainly need for systematic data on the social relations actually obtaining between the prestigeful and authoritative stratum, and the newcomers to a group. Is there an empirically discoverable tendency for those in most frequent or most enduring affiliative contact to exhibit value-assimilation?

2. *Index of motivations of incoming group members:* The theory presupposes a concern among newcomers to affiliate themselves with the higher status group. For research purposes, it would of course be necessary to divide newcomers in terms of the presence, absence, or degree of such motivations. A derivative analytical procedure, moving in another direction, would consist in taking such affiliative motivations not as given, but as problematical, in turn requiring explanation.

3. *Index of social cohesion and of associated values:* Do the newcomers represent a scattered *aggregate* of individuals, or an organized subgroup? If the latter, do they have their own group values with distinctive claims to moral legitimacy? And in such instances, does continuous contact lead to more nearly reciprocal, rather than one-sided, assimilation?[27]

27. It will be noted that the materials in *The American Soldier* did not allow in general for study of the effects of replacements upon veterans, a problem manifestly involved in an

Inclusion of indices such as these, and systematic use of the panel-interview method, as well as direct observation, would encompass systematic study of the *processes* of value-assimilation as part of reference group behavior, and not only, as in the applied researches of *The American Soldier*, the study of certain net results of such processes. There could then be, for example, inquiry into the possibly circular and cumulative process[28] through which value-assimilation furthers social contact between the groups which in turn reinforces value-assimilation, greater social acceptability and increased contact. . . .

Reference Group Theory and Social Mobility

Other researches reported in *The American Soldier* which do not make explicit use of the concept of relative deprivation or kindred concepts can also be recast in terms of reference group theory. One of the more rigorous and seminal of these is the panel study of relationships between the conformity of enlisted men to official values of the Army and their subsequent promotion.

This study also illustrates the widely-known but seldom elucidated point that the same social research can be variously analyzed in at least three separate, though related, respects: its documented empirical findings, its methodology or logic of procedure, and its theoretical implications.

Since the methodology and the empirical findings of this study have been amply discussed—the one in the paper by Kendall and Lazarsfeld, the other in *The American Soldier* itself—we need not concern ourselves with them here. Instead, we limit our discussion to some of its theoretical implications.

These implications divide into three related kinds. First, the implications for reference group theory as the empirical findings are re-examined within the context of that theory. Second are the implications which enable us to connect reference group theory with hypotheses of functional sociology. And third, the implications which, once suitably generalized, enable us to see that this study bears, not only on the conformity-and-mobility patterns of American soldiers in World War II, but possibly also on more general and seemingly disparate patterns of behavior, such as group defection, renegadism, social climbing, and the like.

Tracing out these implications comprises a large order which can scarcely be entirely filled, not because of limitations of space but because of limitations of our own sociological knowledge. But even an approximation to achieving our purpose should help us recognize the theoretical linkages between presently separated types of social behavior.

extended setting of the problem. However, the Research Branch was clearly sensitive to the problem. At one point, for example, they were able to determine, roughly, if veterans' pride in their company was affected by a comparatively high proportion of replacements. (See II, 255–257).

28. For an example of the type of process analysis required to treat problems of this kind, see P. F. Lazarsfeld and R. K. Merton, "Friendship as social process: a substantive and methodological analysis," in M. Berger, T. Abel and C. H. Page (eds.) *Freedom and Control in Modern Society* (New York: D. Van Nostrand, 1954), 18–66.

We begin by following our now customary practice of briefly sketching out the chief findings of the study as these are set forth in *The American Soldier*.

CASE # 5 (I, 258–275)

This research was concerned, not with *rates* of promotion which were determined by changes in the table of organization, but with the *incidence* of promotion: which men were the more likely to be advanced? Since the decision of the commanding officer regarding promotions was by no means based upon objective tests of capacity or performance by enlisted men, there was much occasion for interpersonal relations and sentiments to play their part in affecting this decision. Accordingly, the Research Branch advanced the hypothesis that, "One factor which hardly would have failed to enter to some extent into the judgment of an officer in selecting a man for promotion was his conformity to the officially approved military mores." (I, 259) It is noted further, and we shall have occasion to return to this point in some detail, that "in making subjective judgments, the commanding officer necessarily laid himself wide open to charges of favoritism and particularly of succumbing to the wiles of those enlisted men most skilled at 'bucking'." (I, 264)

A panel study of three groups of enlisted men was designed to find out whether the men who expressed attitudes in accord with the established military mores subsequently received promotions in proportions significantly higher than the others. This was consistently found to be the case. For example, "of the privates who in September 1943 said they did not think the Army's control was too strict, 19 per cent had become Pfc's by January 1944, while only 12 per cent of the other privates had become Pfc's." (I, 261–2) So, too, when men in the three samples are arranged according to their scores on a "quasi-scale of attitudes of conformity," it was uniformly found in all three groups "that the men whose attitudes were most conformist were the ones most likely to be promoted subsequently." (I, 263)[29]

THEORETICAL IMPLICATIONS

In discussing this panel study, we want to bring into the open some of the connections between reference group theory and functional sociology which have remained implicit to this point,—an objective to which this study lends itself

29. As the authors themselves say and as Kendall and Lazarsfeld indicate in some detail, these data do not conclusively demonstrate that conformist attitudes, rather than other correlates of these attitudes, make for significantly higher likelihood of promotion. In principle, only a completely controlled experiment, obviously not feasible in the present instance, would demonstrate this beyond all reasonable doubt. But controlled experiment aside, this panel study, holding constant the factors of age and education which had been found to be related both to attitudes and promotion, goes a long way towards demonstrating a relationship between the incidence of conformist attitudes and subsequent advancement. In this respect, the study moves well beyond the point reached by the use of less rigorous data, indicating a static correlation between rank and conformist attitudes, inasmuch as it can show that those with conformist attitudes were more likely to be *subsequently* promoted. See I, 272–3.

particularly well, since the findings of the study can be readily reformulated in terms of both kinds of theory, and are then seen to bear upon a range of behavior wider than that considered in the study itself.

The value of such reformulation for social theory is perhaps best seen in connection with the independent variable of "conformity." It is clear, when one thinks about it, that the type of attitude described as conformist in this study is at the polar extreme from what is ordinarily called "social conformity." For in the vocabulary of sociology, social conformity usually denotes conformity to the norms and expectations current in the individual's *own* membership-group. But in this study, conformity refers, not to the norms of the immediate primary group constituted by enlisted men but to the quite different norms contained in the official military mores. Indeed, as data in *The American Soldier* make clear, the norms of the in-groups of associated enlisted men and the official norms of the Army and of the stratum of officers were often at odds.[30] In the language of reference group theory, therefore, attitudes of conformity to the official mores can be described as a positive orientation to the norms of a non-membership group that is taken as a frame of reference. Such conformity to norms of an out-group is thus equivalent to what is ordinarily called nonconformity, that is, nonconformity to the norms of the in-group.[31]

This preliminary reformulation leads directly to two interrelated questions which we have until now implied rather than considered explicitly: what are the consequences, functional and dysfunctional, of positive orientation to the values of a group other than one's own? And further, which social processes initiate, sustain or curb such orientations?

FUNCTIONS OF POSITIVE ORIENTATION TO
NON-MEMBERSHIP GROUPS: ANTICIPATORY SOCIALIZATION

In considering, however briefly, the possible consequences of this pattern of conformity to non-membership group norms, it is advisable to distinguish between the consequences for the individuals exhibiting this behavior, the sub-group in which they find themselves, and the social system comprising both of these.

30. Although the absolute percentages of men endorsing a given sentiment cannot of course be taken at face value since these percentages are affected by the sheer phrasing of the sentiment, it is nevertheless suggestive that data presented earlier in the volume (*e.g.*, I, 147ff.) find only a small minority of the samples of enlisted men in this study adhering to the officially approved attitudes. By and large, a significantly larger proportion of officers abide by these attitudes.

31. There is nothing fixed about the boundaries separating in-groups from out-groups, membership-groups from non-membership-groups. These change with the changing situation. Vis-à-vis civilians or an alien group, men in the Army may regard themselves and be regarded as members of an in-group; yet, in another context, enlisted men may regard themselves and be regarded as an in-group in distinction to the out-group of officers. Since these concepts are relative to the situation, rather than absolute, there is no paradox in referring to the officers as an out-group for enlisted men in one context, and as members of the more inclusive in-group, in another context.

For the individual who adopts the values of a group to which he aspires but does not belong, this orientation may serve the twin functions of aiding his rise into that group and of easing his adjustment after he has become part of it. That this first function was indeed served is the gist of the finding in *The American Soldier* that those privates who accepted the official values of the Army hierarchy were more likely than others to be promoted. The hypothesis regarding the second function still remains to be tested. But it would not, in principle, be difficult to discover empirically whether those men who, through a kind of *anticipatory socialization,* take on the values of the non-membership group to which they aspire, find readier acceptance by that group and make an easier adjustment to it. This would require the development of indices of group acceptance and adjustment, and a comparison, in terms of these indices, of those newcomers to a group who had previously oriented themselves to the group's values and those who had not. More concretely, in the present instance, it would have entailed a comparative study among the privates promoted to higher rank, of the subsequent group adjustment of those who had undergone the hypothesized preparation for status shifts and those who had previously held fast to the values of their in-group of enlisted men. Indices of later adjustment could be related to indices of prior value-orientation. This would constitute a systematic empirical test of a functional hypothesis.

It appears, further, that anticipatory socialization is functional for the individual only within a relatively open social structure providing for mobility. For only in such a structure would such attitudinal and behavior preparation for status shifts be followed by actual changes of status in a substantial proportion of cases. By the same token, the same pattern of anticipatory socialization would be dysfunctional for the individual in a relatively closed social structure, where he would not find acceptance by the group to which he aspires and would probably lose acceptance, because of his outgroup orientation, by the group to which he belongs. This latter type of case will be recognized as that of the marginal man, poised on the edge of several groups but fully accepted by none of them.

Thus, the often-studied case of the marginal man[32] and the case of the enlisted man who takes the official military mores as a positive frame of reference can be identified, in a functional theory of reference group behavior, as special cases of anticipatory socialization. The marginal man pattern represents the special case in a relatively closed social system, in which the members of one group take as a positive frame of reference the norms of a group from which they are excluded in principle. Within such a social structure, anticipatory socialization becomes dysfunctional for the individual who becomes the victim of aspirations he cannot achieve and hopes he cannot satisfy. But, as the panel study seems to

---

32. Qualitative descriptions of the behavior of marginal men, as summarized, for example, by E. V. Stonequist, *The Marginal Man* (New York, Scribner's, 1937), can be analytically recast as that special and restricted case of reference group behavior in which the individual seeks to abandon one membership group for another to which he is socially forbidden access.

indicate, precisely the same kind of reference group behavior within a relatively open social system is functional for the individual at least to the degree of helping him to achieve the status to which he aspires. The same reference group behavior in different social structures has different consequences.

To this point, then, we find that positive orientation toward the norms of a non-membership group is precipitated by a passage between membership-groups, either in fact or in fantasy, and that the functional or dysfunctional consequences evidently depend upon the relatively open or closed character of the social structure in which this occurs. And what would, at first glance, seem entirely unrelated and disparate forms of behavior—the behavior of such marginal men as the Cape Coloured or the Eurasian, and of enlisted men adopting the values of military strata other than their own—are seen, after appropriate conceptualization, as special cases of reference group behavior.

Although anticipatory socialization may be functional for the *individual* in an open social system, it is apparently dysfunctional for the solidarity of the *group* or *stratum* to which he belongs. For allegiance to the contrasting mores of another group means defection from the mores of the in-group. And accordingly, as we shall presently see, the in-group responds by putting all manner of social restraints upon such positive orientations to certain out-group norms.

From the standpoint of the larger social system, the Army as a whole, positive orientation toward the official mores would appear to be functional in supporting the legitimacy of the structure and in keeping the structure of authority intact. (This is presumably what is meant when the text of *The American Soldier* refers to these conformist attitudes as "favorable from the Army's point of view.") But manifestly, much research needs to be done before one can say that this is indeed the case. It is possible, for example, that the secondary effects of such orientations may be so deleterious to the solidarity of the primary groups of enlisted men that their morale sags. A concrete research question might help clarify the problem: Are outfits with relatively large minorities of men positively oriented to the official Army values more likely to exhibit signs of anomie and personal disorganization (*e.g.* non-battle casualties)? In such situations, does the personal "success" of conformists (promotion) only serve to depress the morale of the others by rewarding those who depart from the in-group mores?

In this panel study, as well as in several of the others we have reviewed here—for example, the study of soldiers' evaluations of the justification for their induction into the Army—reference group behavior is evidently related to the legitimacy ascribed to institutional arrangements. Thus, the older married soldier is less likely to think it "fair" that he was inducted; most enlisted men think it "unfair" that promotions are presumably based on "who you know, not what you know"; and so on. In part, this apparent emphasis on legitimacy is of course an artifact of the research: many of the questions put to soldiers had to do with their conception of the legitimate or illegitimate character of their situation or of prevailing institutional arrangements. But the researchers' own focus of interest was in turn the result of their having observed that soldiers were, to a significant degree, actually concerned with such issues of institutional legitimacy, as the spontaneous comments of enlisted men often indicate.[33]

This bears notice because imputations of legitimacy to social arrangements seem functionally related to reference group behavior. They apparently affect *the range of the inter-group or inter-individual comparisons* that will typically be made. If the structure of a rigid system of stratification, for example, is generally defined as legitimate, if the rights, perquisites and obligations of each stratum are generally held to be morally right, then the individuals within each stratum will be the less likely to take the situation of the other strata as a context for appraisal of their own lot. They will, presumably, tend to confine their comparisons to other members of their own or neighboring social stratum. If, however, the system of stratification is under wide dispute, then members of some strata are more likely to contrast their own situation with that of others, and shape their self-appraisals accordingly. This variation in the structure of systems and in the degree of legitimacy imputed to the rules of the game may help account for the often-noticed fact that the degree of dissatisfaction with their lot is often less among the people in severely depressed social strata in a relatively rigid social system, than among those strata who are apparently "better off" in a more mobile social system. At any rate, the *range of groups* taken as effective bases of comparison in different social systems may well turn out to be closely connected with the degree to which legitimacy is ascribed to the prevailing social structure.

Though much remains to be said, this is perhaps enough to suggest that the pattern of anticipatory socialization may have diverse consequences for the individuals manifesting it, the groups to which they belong, and the more inclusive social structure. And through such re-examination of this panel study on the personal rewards of conformity, it becomes possible to specify some additional types of problems involved in a more comprehensive functional analysis of such reference group behavior. For example:

1. Since only a fraction of the in-group orient themselves positively toward the values of a non-membership group, it is necessary to discover the social position and personality types of those most likely to do so. For instance, are isolates in the group particularly ready to take up these alien values?

33. For example, in response to the question, "If you could talk with the President of the United States, what are the three most important questions you would want to ask him about war and your part in it?", a substantial proportion of both Negro and white troops evidently raised questions regarding the legitimacy of current practices and arrangements in the Army. The Negro troops of course centered on unjust practices of race discrimination, but 31 per cent of the white troops also introduced "questions and criticisms of Army life." (I, 504 *et passim*.)

2. Much attention has been paid to the processes making for positive orientation to the norms of one's own group. But what are the processes making for such orientations to other groups or strata? Do relatively high rates of mobility serve to reinforce these latter orientations? (It will be remembered that *The American Soldier* provides data tangential to this point in the discussion of rates of promotion and assessment of promotion chances.) Suitably adapted, such data on actual rates of mobility, aspirations, and anticipatory socialization to the norms of a higher social stratum would extend a functional theory of conformist and deviant behavior.

3. What connections, if any, subsist between varying rates of mobility and acceptance of the legitimacy of the system of stratification by individuals diversely located in that system? Since it appears that systems with very low rates of mobility may achieve wide acceptance, what other interpretative variables need be included to account for the relationship between rates of mobility and imputations of legitimacy?

4. In civilian or military life, are the mobile individuals who are most ready to reaffirm the values of a power-holding or prestige-holding group the sooner accepted by that group? Does this operate effectively primarily as a latent function, in which the mobile individuals adopt these values because they experience them as superior, rather than deliberately adopting them only to gain acceptance? If such orientations are definitely motivated by the wish to belong, do they then become self-defeating, with the mobile individuals being characterized as strainers, strivers (or, in the Army, as brown-nosers bucking for promotion)?

SOCIAL PROCESSES SUSTAINING AND CURBING
POSITIVE ORIENTATIONS TO NON-MEMBERSHIP GROUPS

In the course of considering the functions of anticipatory socialization, we have made passing allusion to social processes which sustain or curb this pattern of behavior. Since it is precisely the data concerning such processes which are not easily caught up in the type of survey materials on attitudes primarily utilized in *The American Soldier*, and since these processes are central to any theory of reference group behavior, they merit further consideration.

As we have seen, what is anticipatory socialization from the stand-point of the individual is construed as defection and nonconformity by the group of which he is a member. To the degree that the individual identifies himself with another group, he alienates himself from his own group. Yet although the field of sociology has for generations been concerned with the determinants and consequences of group cohesion, it has given little *systematic* attention to the complementary subject of group alienation. When considered at all, it has been confined to such special cases as second-generation immigrants, conflict of loyalties between gang and family, *etc.* In large measure, the subject has been left to the literary observer, who could detect the drama inherent in the situation of the renegade, the traitor, the deserter. The value-laden connotations of these terms used to describe identification with groups other than one's own definitely suggest that these patterns of behavior have been typically regarded from the standpoint of the membership group. (Yet one group's renegade may be another group's convert.) Since the assumption that its members will be loyal is found in every group, else it would have no group character, no dependability of action, transfer of loyalty to another group (particularly a group operating in the same sphere of politics or economy), is regarded primarily in affective terms of sentiment rather than in detached terms of analysis. The renegade or traitor or climber—whatever the folk-phrase may be—more often becomes an object of vilification than an object of sociological study.

The framework of reference group theory, detached from the language of sentiment, enables the sociologist to identify and to locate renegadism, treason, the assimilation of immigrants, class mobility, social climbing, *etc.* as so many special forms of identification with what is at the time a non-membership group. In doing so, it affords the possibility of studying these, not as *wholly* particular and unconnected forms of behavior, but as different expressions of similar processes under significantly different conditions. The transfer of allegiance of upper class individuals from their own to a lower class—whether this be in the pre-revolutionary period of 18th century France or of 20th century Russia—belongs to the same family of sociological problems as the more familiar identification of lower class individuals with a higher class, a subject which has lately begun to absorb the attention of sociologists in a society where upward social mobility is an established value. Our cultural emphases notwithstanding, the phenomenon of topdogs adopting the values of the underdog is as much a reference group phenomenon lending itself to further inquiry as that of the underdogs seeking to become topdogs.

In such defections from the in-group, it may turn out, as has often been suggested, that it is the isolate, nominally in a group but only slightly incorporated in its network of social relations, who is most likely to become positively oriented toward non-membership groups. But, even if generally true, this is a static correlation and, therefore, only partly illuminating. What needs to be uncovered is the process through which this correlation comes to hold. Judging from some of the qualitative data in *The American Soldier* and from other studies of group defection, there is continued and cumulative interplay between a deterioration of *social relations* within the membership group and positive *attitudes* toward the norms of a non-membership group.

What the individual experiences as estrangement from a group of which he is a member tends to be experienced by his associates as repudiation of the group, and this ordinarily evokes a hostile response. As social relations between the individual and the rest of the group deteriorate, the norms of the group become less binding for him. For since he is progressively seceding from the group and being penalized by it, he is the less likely to experience rewards for adherence to the group's norms. Once initiated, this process seems to move toward a cumulative detachment from the group, in terms of attitudes and values as well as in terms of social relations. And to the degree that he orients himself toward out-group values, perhaps affirming them verbally and expressing them in action, he only widens the gap and reinforces the hostility between himself and his in-group associates. Through the interplay of dissociation and progressive alienation from the group values, he may become doubly motivated to orient himself toward the values of another group and to affiliate himself with it. There then remains the distinct question of the objective possibility of affiliating himself with his reference group. If the possibility is negligible or absent, then the alienated individual becomes socially rootless. But if the social system realistically allows for such change in group affiliations, then the individual estranged from the one group has all the more motivation to belong to the other.

This hypothetical account of dissociation and alienation, which of course only touches upon the processes which call for research in the field of reference group behavior, seems roughly in accord with qualitative data in *The American Soldier* on what was variously called brown-nosing, bucking for promotion, and sucking up. Excerpts from the diary of an enlisted man illustrate the interplay between dissociation and alienation: the outward-oriented man is too sedulous in abiding by the official mores—"But you're *supposed* to [work over there]. The lieutenant said you were supposed to."—this evokes group hostility expressed in epithets and ridicule—"Everybody is making sucking, kissing noises at K and S now"—followed by increasing dissociation within the group—"Ostracism was visible, but mild . . . few were friendly toward them . . . occasions arose where people avoided their company"—and more frequent association with men representing the non-membership reference group— "W, S and K sucked all afternoon; hung around lieutenants and asked bright questions." In this briefly summarized account, one sees the mechanisms of the in-group operating to curb positive orientation to the official mores[34] as well as the process through which this orientation develops among those who take these mores as their major frame of reference, considering their ties with the in-group as of only secondary importance.

Judging from implications of this panel research on conformity-and-mobility, then, there is room for study of the consequences of reference group behavior patterns as well as for study of their determinants. Moreover, the consequences pertinent for sociology are not merely those for the individuals engaging in this behavior, but for the groups of which they are a part. There develops also the possibility that the extent to which legitimacy is accorded the

---

34. An official War Department pamphlet given to new recruits attempted to give "bucking" a blessing: " 'Bucking' implies all the things a soldier can honestly do to gain attention and promotion. The Army encourages individuals to put extra effort into drill, extra 'spit and polish' into personal appearance. At times this may make things uncomfortable for others who prefer to take things easier, but it stimulates a spirit of competition and improvement which makes ours a better Army." I, 264.

structure of these groups and the status of their members may affect the range of groups or strata which they ordinarily take as a frame of reference in assessing their own situation. And finally, this panel research calls attention to the need for close study of those processes in group life which sustain or curb positive orientations to non-membership groups, thus perhaps leading to a linking of reference group theory and current theories of social organization.

Psychological and Social Functions

In our review of the foregoing case, an effort was made to distinguish between the consequences of positive orientation toward a non-membership group for the individual, the membership-group and the larger social system. If, as we assume, an established pattern of behavior typically has such diverse consequences, it can be usefully examined from both a psychological and sociological standpoint. On occasion, *The American Soldier* analyzes behavior only in terms of a psychological framework. In some of these instances, the same situation may be profitably re-examined in terms of its implications for a framework of functional sociology. This is not to say that the sociological orientation is necessarily "superior" to the psychological, or that it is necessarily at odds with it. But it *is* different. And by regarding these materials from a perspective differing from that in the text itself, we may, perhaps, bring out further implications of these applied researches for social theory.

CASE # 6 (II, 272-84)

Among the cases exhibiting a marked psychological orientation is the brief account of the experiences of men in replacement depots, those army stations through which they filtered from their training outfits to some depleted combat outfit in need of personnel. The author paints a vivid psychological portrait of the replacement depot: of the "apparently irreducible sources of psychological disturbance" characteristic of the depot, with its replacements handled in bulk and impersonally by permanent depot cadre, having only a casual status, and lacking the "support of social ties and the security of having an established niche in some organization." Probably, "the most salient psychological characteristic of depot life . . . was that the situation led to a state of anxious uncertainty without opportunity for resolving the tension." (II, 274) One consequence of the depot experience was to make the replacement "welcome many aspects of a permanent assignment." While this did not mean they welcomed combat itself, "even in this regard . . . the termination of anxious uncertainty was probably in some respects a psychological gain. The new combat man could say to himself, for better or for worse, 'This is it.' " (II, 176)

The Research Branch, then, was centrally concerned with the question: what were the effects of these experiences upon *the replacement*? But the same data involve another type of problem, this time from the standpoint of functional sociology: the problem, not of the effect of the depot upon the replacement, but upon his subsequent incorporation in a combat group.

Functional analysis of this situation would begin by conceptualizing the social role of the replacement depot, which falls into the category of an organization providing for *the movement of individuals from one group to another*. As typically follows upon a somewhat more generalized description of a situation, other situations nominally different on a common-sense level, are seen as belonging to the same general category. Materials presently scattered in the numerous pages of *The American Soldier* become cases in point of this pattern of transition from one group to another: for example, the replacement depot is, *in this respect*, essentially no different from the reassignment station as an intermediary between a combat outfit and a new domestic post. Furthermore, sociologists have long been interested in the standardized social patterns providing for passage from one group to another in various institutional areas, for example, the transition of the high school graduate to a first year at college.

The personal and social difficulties involved in such transfers are assumed to arise primarily from the dual process of breaking down old group affiliations (or of putting them into secondary place) and of building new group ties. That, in a sense, is comparable to the process of the recruit's initial absorption into his first army outfit, with all the attendant growing pains of group-formation. But in this special setting, the individual is immeasurably eased in his adjustment since it is not a problem peculiar to him. Every other member of the newly-forming group is experiencing a similar problem, whether he is a first-year college student or a raw army recruit.

Once he is a part of this group, however, transfer to another already established group is quite a different matter, as any child who is transferred from one school to another in mid-semester can report. In this case, his initial exposure to the new group is most apt to involve an intensification of old ties—his old friends, his former teachers, his old school are imbued with disproportionately great affect. This is much the same phenomenon as that of soldiers separated from their old combat outfits and settling into new domestic army stations. One study in *The American Soldier* reports that such returnees place tremendous importance on being permitted to "continue to wear the insignia of their old units" (II, 507-8),—just as the abruptly transferred school child may intensify his old group ties. Both reflect resistance to a sudden weaning from a former group affiliation. The school child, being a lone individual, presents no challenge to the unity of the new group,[35] and in time, he is usually

35. On this, see how C. S. Lewis, in the first part of his autobiography, mockingly describes the functional requirement for 'fagging' (hazing) in the English public schools or, at least, in the one school which he had the fortune to attend. "The interesting thing is that the public-school system had thus produced the very thing which it was advertised to prevent or cure. For you must understand (if you have not been dipped in that tradition yourself) that the whole thing was devised to 'knock the nonsense' out of the smaller boys and 'put them in their place.' 'If the junior boys weren't fagged,' as my brother once said, 'they would become insufferable.' . . . Obviously a certain grave danger was ever present to the minds of those who built up the Wyvernian hierarchy. It seemed to them self-evident that, if you left things to themselves, boys of nineteen who played rugger for the county and boxed for the school would

taken into the ranks. But should a sizable number of new youngsters confront the group with their emphasis on old school ties, we might well find a need emerging for an "educational depot," to forestall the dysfunctional consequences of these challenges to the unity of the group. This is precisely the problem of the army situation. Being built on fragile enough grounds, the unity of an army outfit might be seriously impaired by the introduction of a sizable number of replacements, if their former group attachment had not broken down prior to their admittance to the new outfit.

Thus from the perspective of the replacements' eventual ease of absorption into a combat group, new to them, as well as from the point of view of their potential effect upon the group they enter, there may well be a functional requirement for their *not* being transferred immediately from the training outfit to the outfit with which they will shortly serve in combat. One alternative is that which was in fact the practice utilized during the war years: filtering the newly trained soldier through replacement depots. This suggests the latent function possibly performed by the replacement depot: it may serve to loosen the soldier's previous army group ties, thus making him more amenable to ready absorption into his combat outfit. In much the same way that the sandhog adjusts to normal atmospheric pressure at the end of a day's work under water by going through de-compression chambers, so the soldier is *"de-grouped"* by passing through replacement depots. This would seem all the more important in view of the speed with which replacements were actually sent into combat upon joining a combat outfit. In one study, it was found that *half* the replacement infantrymen went into combat less than three days after joining their outfit.

In other words, the excessive psychological anxiety noted by the Research Branch as characteristic of depot life may also be regarded as a behavioral index of a state of temporary "grouplessness." But whichever is emphasized— the underlying sociological phenomenon of grouplessness or the external and visible psychological anxiety—the functional sociologist would seek to trace out its organizational consequences, *i.e.*, its impact on the absorption of the replacement into his most important army group, the unit with which he serves in combat.[36]

everywhere be knocked down and sat on by boys of thirteen. And that, you know, would be a very shocking spectacle. The most elaborate mechanism, therefore, had to be devised for protecting the strong against the weak, the close corporation of Old Hands against the parcel of newcomers who were strangers to one another and to everyone in the place, the poor, trembling lions against the furious and ravening sheep." C. S. Lewis, *Surprised by Joy: The Shape of My Early Life* (New York: Harcourt, Brace and Company, 1955), 104–106.

36. We have previously mentioned the similarity between the function of the replacement depot and that of the reassignment station through which the returnee soldier is transferred from his combat outfit to his domestic army post. An examination of the study of the returnee in *The American Soldier* (II—Chapter on problems of Rotation and Reconversion) suggests that the degrouping process of the returnee is of much longer duration, for the returnee has been removed from his most cohesive army group. Thus in a survey of returnees and non-

This anxiety accompanying the degrouping process may well be dysfunctional for the individual soldier at the time he is experiencing it, and for some soldiers, it may have had serious effects upon overall personal adjustment. Yet this same process of de-grouping may have functional consequences for other organizational units, particularly the combat outfit in which the de-grouped replacement is the more readily absorbed.[37] Empirical test of this hypothesis could be provided by an extension of the procedure adopted in the study of returnees (see the foregoing footnote). For each level of men's attachment to their previous outfit, it could be determined, first, whether the longer the period that men have spent in a replacement depot, the more effectively they have divested themselves of their previous group solidarity, and second, whether those men who had been thus "de-grouped" were the more effectively incorporated into their new combat outfit. To the extent that this was found to be the case, it would have bearing on the more general problem of factors and processes affecting the passage from old to new membership groups. And, in some measure, this would supplement the perceptive analysis of the replacement depot provided by *The American Soldier* . . . .

overseas men in which the soldiers were asked about their sense of belonging to their new outfit, the returnees were much more apt to say they did not feel they belonged to their outfits than the non-returnees, *even though in a large proportion of the cases the returnees had been with the outfit longer than the non-returnees.* In the Air Force, for example, 34 per cent of the returnees and 15 per cent of the non-returnees said they did not feel they "belonged" to their outfits. The difference between returnee and non-returnee in other branches of the Army decreases slightly from the difference of 17 per cent in the more cohesive air corps to 11 per cent in the quartermaster corps. (II, 507) The rapidity and ease of the de-grouping process and subsequent re-absorption into a new group would appear to depend on the intensity of the former group ties.

37. To note this possible function of anxiety is not thereby to *advocate* anxiety. In this instance, for example, one's values may lead one to conclude that organizational efficiency, through de-grouping with its attendant anxieties, exacts too high a price. This is scarcely the first time that such moral problems of social engineering have occurred.

Problems of Research on Relative Deprivation

W. G. Runciman

IN THIS note I shall discuss on the basis of a pilot survey now being analyzed[1] some of the issues raised by the concept of "relative deprivation" as a topic for survey research. In the first section, I shall deal with some of the theoretical considerations involved, and in the second with some of the problems of method.

I

The two related notions of relative deprivation and reference groups now command a very considerable literature, which I do not propose to review here.[2] The basic insight (or truism) which underlies both is that a person's attitudes, values and motives depend on (or are a function of) the frame of reference within which they are conceived. Although the term "reference group" has passed into current use, it is clear that it need not in fact be a group which is

Reprinted from *The European Journal of Sociology*, 2 : 315–323, 1961, by permission of the author and the publisher.

1. I am indebted to the Institute of Community Studies for support. I am also indebted for comments on earlier versions of this paper to Professors Herbert Hyman, T. H. Marshall, and Hanan C. Selvin.

2. The standard discussions remain Robert K. Merton and Alice K. Rossi, "Contributions to the Theory of Reference Group Behaviour," reprinted in Merton, *Social Theory and Social Structure* (New York: The Free Press, 1957), pp. 225–280; and Herbert H. Hyman, "The Relation of the Reference Group to Judgments of Status," reprinted in R. Bendix and S. M. Lipset, eds., *Class, Status and Power* (New York: The Free Press, 1953), pp. 263–270.

the crucial referent; as several writers have pointed out,[3] the referent may be anything from a single person to an abstract idea. Further, there is an important distinction between what have been labelled "comparative" and "normative" reference groups[4]; a group may be either a source of standards or an actual standard in itself, and it may or may not be an enforcer of these standards. This distinction, however, is irrelevant to the notion of relative deprivation, where the important question is simply what is the referent by which the level of a person's aspirations and standards is set. (This referent may, of course, be either positive or negative, both in the case of membership and of non-membership groups).[5] Relative deprivation may then be broadly defined by saying that a person is relatively deprived when (1) he does not have X, (2) he sees some other person or persons, which may include himself at some previous or imagined time, as having X (whether or not they do have X), and (3) he wants X (whether or not it is feasible that he should have X). "To be without Y" can, of course, be substituted where relevant for "to have X."

On the basis of this definition, we may say that the further the positive referent (or its equivalent) from a given person, the greater his relative deprivation. This, however, raises two further problems. First, there is no measure of social distance by which "greater" relative deprivation may be given a meaning; and second, a "greater" deprivation need not necessarily be more intensely felt than a lesser one. These difficulties can only be answered by reference to the particular person's own standards. The intensity even of the most measurable deprivations may not correlate at all with their magnitude; for instance, marginal differences of income within a family might be more deeply resented than greater external differences. Moreover, different people have very different pictures of the social structure of which they form a part, as has recently been shown for three European countries by Willener,[6] Popitz[7] and Elizabeth Bott.[8] It is only in terms of a person's own image of social distance that, for instance, a relative status deprivation may be seen as such. Of course, interpersonal comparisons are possible in certain cases, such as the percentage gap between desired and actual income; but a great many relative deprivations are impervious to such treatment and must logically remain so. I shall later be suggesting a

3. Merton, *op. cit.* pp. 302–304; S. N. Eisenstadt, "Studies in Reference Group Behaviour, I: Reference Norms and the Social Structure," *Human Relations*, VII (1954), p. 213; Tamotsu Shibutani, "Reference Groups as Perspectives," *AJS*, LX (1955), p. 565; Ralph H. Turner, "Role-taking, Role Standpoint and Reference Group Behaviour," *AJS*, LXI (1956), p. 329.

4. H. H. Kelley, "Two Functions of Reference Groups," in G. E. Swanson et al., eds., *Readings in Social Psychology* (New York, 1952), pp. 404–414.

5. Merton, *op. cit.* pp. 300—302; F. M. Martin, "Some Subjective Aspects of Social Stratification," in D. V. Glass, ed., *Social Mobility in Britain* (London, 1954), pp. 59–60.

6. A. Willener, *Images de la société et classes sociales* (Berne, 1957).

7. H. Popitz et al., *Das Gesellschaftsbild des Arbeiters* (Tübingen, 1961).

8. Elizabeth Bott, *Family and Social Network* (London, 1957), ch. vi: "Norms and Ideology: Concepts of Class."

fourfold typology of relative deprivation, but I do not thereby wish to imply that either relative deprivation or social distance can be measured by any kind of continuous monotonic scale.

There are two sorts of non-relative deprivation which must be distinguished both from relative deprivation and from each other. The first, for which the term "absolute deprivation" is sometimes used, is that which underlies the notion of "primary poverty"; that is to say, deprivation seen in terms of simple subsistence level.[9] This notion, however, is not really very satisfactory. In the first place, there are cases other than at subsistence level where we wish intuitively to speak of a person as absolutely deprived; an example would be deprivation of all social intercourse, although this is not necessary for survival. Secondly, even in terms of food and health there can be no purely objective criterion of deprivation; the standards both of the observer and of the person deprived may be equally likely to vary.[10] It would perhaps be less ambiguous to use "absolute deprivation" for any noticeable lack, whether felt or not (for instance, we might wish to speak of a Mexican village as absolutely deprived of sanitation even if its inhabitants refused the offer of it). On the other hand, "absolute deprivation" could instead be used for any felt need not dependent upon comparison with another person or group (for instance, hunger). The choice of terminology is, of course, arbitrary. But it is important to distinguish the two types of non-relative "deprivation"; first, objectively ascertained need, whether felt as such or not by the people concerned; and second, affective deprivation, whereby people are only deprived (even non-relatively) if they feel that they are.

In addition, there are two further sorts of attitude to be distinguished from relative deprivation, both of which have been found in answers to questions in the pilot survey mentioned above. First, there are people (particularly older people) whose satisfactions are closely bound up with those of their children, and who, although they may feel relatively deprived on behalf, as it were, of their children, should not be called relatively deprived themselves. Of course, some aspirations on behalf of children do reflect a relative deprivation felt by the parents; but these must be distinguished from cases where the parents share the relative deprivations (or satisfactions) of the children but are not themselves necessarily relatively deprived. The second and somewhat similar case is where a person feels disapproval of the existing social or economic structure without himself being relatively disadvantaged by it. It is quite possible for someone, whatever his picture of the social structure, to feel both that his own position within it is satisfactory and also that the relative positions of others are not what they should be. Once again, we may speak of relative deprivation as it were on behalf of others. But it would be incorrect in such a case to speak of the person as being relatively deprived himself.

9. R. Dahrendorf, *Class and Class Conflict in Industrial Society* (Stanford, 1959), p. 217.

10. P. E. P., "Poverty: Ten Years After Beveridge," *Planning*, No. 344 (1952), p. 36.

Within the category of what may be properly labelled relative deprivations, there are obviously a great number of different topics which may be covered. A man may feel himself relatively deprived of anything from his pre-war salary differential to his neighbour's pretty wife, and he may have a whole range of different referents for his different deprivations. Moreover, both the referents and the deprivations will be able to change over even quite a short period of time. It is thus evident that anything approaching a full analysis of a person's relative deprivations must take the investigator well beyond the scope of sociological analysis and into individual psychology. To map all of someone's relative deprivations would involve discovering the number of dimensions in which he felt himself deprived, and the extent or intensity of his deprivations in each. The correlation matrix of a person's whole set of deprivations might, of course, factor analyze into a very few dimensions, but this is unlikely in many cases to be so. However, the usefulness of the concept in survey research is not limited to such exhaustive and intricate analysis. We may still wish to ask such broader questions as whether a particular social or economic deprivation is relative or not, how far the members of a given social group impute to other groups a situation which affects their own aspirations, what sort of person or group (if any) is taken as referent on a given topic, and so on. In particular, there are two very general dimensions in which a person may be placed and which may be applicable in large-scale survey research on a total social structure. The first is a person's satisfaction with his position in what he sees as his group; the second is his satisfaction with the position of what he sees as his group in the total social structure.

It is at once evident that these two dimensions are not intended to cover the whole range of a particular person's relative deprivations. I do mean to suggest, however, that these are the two principal sociological dimensions of relative deprivation. If we consider the respondents to a national survey in their capacity as members of the total social structure, then (whatever the topic in question) it makes sense to ask in terms of their picture of their social location whether they are relatively deprived in either or both of these dimensions. This applies to questions about general political and social attitudes just as much as to questions about specific economic needs. Indeed, it is possible simply to ask whether there is any general topic about which a given person feels relatively deprived, and, if so, with reference to what group (or person or past situation, or whatever it may be). Curiously little work seems to have been done on relative deprivation at the level of total social structures (although I shall be referring to two particular examples in the next section). In Britain, for instance, although much has been written on the social, economic and political effects of the welfare state, there have been few if any studies of the needs and attitudes of different groups as related to the social circumstances and images of society by which they may be shaped. Professor Titmuss, in his essay on "Social Administration in a Changing Society," has forcibly pointed out how important it is from a purely practical point of view to understand the effect of recent social and economic changes on the relative attitudes and deprivations of different social groups and their consequent patterns of social needs.[11] Similarly, an understanding of people's relative deprivations as members of a group or class is likely to be crucial to the explanation of political behaviour; but little has so far been done beyond the topic of self-selected social status in relation to party preference.[12] There may, of course, be considerable difficulties (some of which I shall mention in the next section) in precisely assessing the influence of relative deprivation as an independent variable acting on social or political attitudes. Its theoretical importance, however, is surely unquestionable.

It would obviously be rash to hazard any ambitious theoretical generalizations on the basis of a small pilot survey. However, these few responses seem to show that it is fairly rare for people to take as a standard (and, in consequence, feel relatively deprived) what they see as the situation of a superior social stratum. If this is so, it may seem surprising in view of the degree of inequality, both of class and status, which still exists in contemporary England. But it could, on the other hand, be argued that it is precisely the awareness of these inequalities which reduces relative deprivation in reference to higher social strata; it may be that only where opportunity is believed to be equal do higher strata come to be taken as positive referents. This raises familiar general issues which I do not propose to embark on here. However, if it is true that it is in general membership groups by which people's social aspirations and standards are set, then the questions to what extent this holds good and under what conditions should be feasible topics for a national survey even if the material obtained is likely to be less explanatory than descriptive. In the next section, I shall consider some problems of method and discuss the proposed typology in more detail.

II

The typology can be best represented by the four-fold table on page 74.

I have labelled the four types simply by letter, for want of any satisfactory adjective to describe them, but some additional comment may make them clearer. Type A might be labelled "orthodox," being neither personally ambitious nor personally resentful of the existing social structure. If he is low in class- and status-situation we could label him "deferent" in Bagehot's sense (recently revived by R. T. McKenzie); if he is at the top, we could label him "boss." However, type A will also include the "altruist" or "prosperous radical" who, as mentioned in the previous section, would like to see the social structure

11. Richard M. Titmuss, *Essays on "The Welfare State"* (London, 1958), pp. 13–33; Cf. Henning Friis, "The Application of Sociology to Social Welfare, Planning and Administration" in *Transactions of the Fourth World Congress of Sociology* (London, 1959), II, pp. 66–67.

12. E.g. Mark Abrams and Richard Rose, *Must Labour Lose?* (Penguin Books, 1960), p. 18 (table 4).

altered without himself being relatively deprived. Type B, on the other hand, is likely to be the sort of "striver" described by Hollingshead and Redlich[13] as being less satisfied with his role and expecting more from the future than the stable person content with his situation as it is. Although not resentful of the existing social structure, he may still feel his personal resentment more intensely than type C, who although he compares the situation of his own group unfavourably with that of others is nevertheless satisfied with his position within it.

Satisfaction with position in own group

	+	−
Satisfaction with position of own group in social structure +	A	B
−	C	D

Type C will exemplify the sort of lateral solidarity described within the working class by Hoggart,[14] where an unambitious loyalty to class or occupational group is combined with the feeling that the class as a whole is relatively deprived. Finally, type D, whom we might describe as altogether disgruntled, will be the most relatively deprived of all, since he is not only resentful of the position of his group but also dissatisfied with his position within it.

There is one sort of person who needs separate comment, namely the person who must in some sense be regarded as altogether alienated from the social structure and who does not explicitly see himself as belonging to any group at all. Even in this case, however, I think that one does wish to speak of the person as being or not being relatively deprived. The complete recluse, no matter how cut off he may be from the rest of his society, must still be either satisfied or not with his situation. If his dissatisfactions do not depend in any way on comparison with others, we may fairly speak of him as not being relatively deprived; if, on the other hand, he has some picture of the way the

13. A. B. Hollingshead and F. Redlich, *Social Class and Mental Illness* (New York, 1958), p. 105. The authors also comment that "strivers" identify in significantly larger numbers with a higher class.

14. Richard Hoggart, *The Uses of Literacy* (London, 1957), esp. ch. III.

rest of society lives and if this picture affects his own felt dissatisfactions, then we do wish to talk about his relative deprivation. Thus even the person most alienated from his society can still in principle be categorized according to the typology. If his alienation is of the form of retreatism and apathy, this is likely to place him with type A. If, however, he is both conscious and resentful of the rest of society or his class as a "them" opposed to himself, he may belong more properly with type D. I do not mean to suggest that the "alienated" man is not importantly different from those who may fall more neatly into the categories. I do, however, mean to suggest that any member of a society can in principle be classified according to these two dimensions of relative deprivation.

Clearly, shifts from one type to another will be possible or indeed likely even over quite short periods of time, and if these could be ascertained they might well prove particularly interesting. Thus shifts from C to B might throw light on recent patterns of British voting behavior; or an oscillation between D and A might correlate with some independent measure of authoritarianism. To test such notions accurately, however, would require either panel data or purposively sampled trend data. But irrespective of changes, which could only be traced by an elaborate and expensive research design, it should be possible to obtain useful and interesting results from quite simple procedures of questioning and analysis. Out of previous work done on this topic, two particular studies suggest this: one by Hyman in the United States and one by Stern and Keller in France.

Hyman, in a well-known study of the value-systems of different classes,[15] shows by secondary analysis of public opinion data how different strata in American society modify their occupational goals in accordance with their social position and their corresponding view of the opportunities open to them. The second study, by Stern and Keller, is the analysis of the spontaneous group references given by a small national sample in France.[16] In this less well-known survey, which was carried out in the summer of 1951, the respondents were asked what they would consider a satisfactory standard of living for people like themselves. Despite the author's plea, the study has unfortunately not been replicated elsewhere, but its results are suggestive as far as they go. Stern and Keller found few references to out-groups and little evidence of status-striving or class resentment; and the study thus tentatively supports the hypothesis that in a society such as France, which is seen by its members as comparatively rigidly stratified, not many people feel explicitly relative deprivations although they may nevertheless be anxious to improve their absolute position.

15. Herbert Hyman, "The Value Systems of Different Classes: a Social Psychological Approach to the Analysis of Stratification," in R. Bendix and S. M. Lipset, eds., *Class, Status and Power* (Free Press, 1953), pp. 426–442.

16. Eric Stern and Suzanne Keller, "Spontaneous Group References in France," *Public Opinion Quarterly*, XVII (1953), pp. 208–217.

These two studies both show how a very straightforward type of question, easily applicable in large-scale survey research, may elucidate the pattern of relative deprivation in a total society. However, as was suggested in the previous section, an accurate assessment of relative deprivation as an independent variable is likely to be much more difficult. In particular, it is bound to be beyond the scope of survey research to establish which of a number of referents is the crucial one for the attitude concerned.[17] In a properly experimental situation, as in Hyman's original study [18] or the even earlier experiment by Chapman and Volkmann,[19] an attempt at direct assessment will of course be feasible; but in survey research, the different roles of relative deprivation as an independent and a dependent variable may be impossible to disentangle. Does a restricted frame of reference (and therefore a low level of relative deprivation) tend to reduce people's social and economic goals? Or is it because people's goals are restricted that their general feeling of relative deprivation is kept low? Presumably there is likely to be a reciprocal interaction, but survey data will not be adequate to elucidate the process in detail. There is also the risk of tautology if (to follow the example given) we take as an indicator of relative deprivation the stated goals of the people concerned; but this is obviously avoidable in practice. Thus, we may test, for instance, whether the giving of predominantly in-group references correlates with an independent measure of satisfaction, or whether identification with a higher class or status group correlates with a right-wing political preference. Such correlations will not be a substitute for the explanation of the psychological processes which must be assumed to underlie them; but they may still greatly enlarge our understanding of the national structure of social and political attitudes. . . .

Lastly, it is worth mentioning the implications of the proposed typology for comparative research. If by questions appropriate to different countries respondents in a national sample can be classified according to the proposed typology, then it becomes possible to compare the different national distributions of the four types. It might, for instance, turn out that the results could be arranged into an isotropic contingency table, or that the distributions as plotted in adjacent bar charts approximated to the shape of the normal (or some other) distribution. Even without such refinements, however, it seems worthwhile to suggest that relative deprivation provides an interesting and important theme for the cross-national comparison of social structures based on sample survey research.

17. This difficulty appears to have been encountered in a recent American attempt to relate reference group theory to voting behaviour. See Norman Kaplan, *Reference Group Theory and Voting Behaviour* (unpubd. Ph.D. Thesis, Columbia University, 1955), abstracted in *Dissertation Abstracts*, XV (1955), p. 1458.

18. See note 2, above.

19. Dwight W. Chapman and John Volkmann, "A Social Determinant of the Level of Aspiration," reprinted in E. E. Maccoby et al., eds., *Readings in Social Psychology* (New York, 1958), pp. 281–290.

Two Functions of
Reference Groups

Harold H. Kelley

$\mathbf{A}$ CONSIDERABLE number of every person's attitudes are related to or anchored in one or more social groups. The nature of this social anchorage of attitudes is by no means clear or simple. On the one hand, it is apparent that a person's attitudes are related to the attitudes commonly expressed within groups to which he belongs (his membership groups[1]). On the other hand, studies of prestige influence, opinion leadership, rejection of membership groups by underprivileged persons, and the influence of outgroups upon levels of aspiration, have indicated that attitudes are often related to nonmembership groups.

In recognition of this fact, the term *reference group*, first used by Hyman,[2] has come into use to denote *any* group to which a person relates his attitudes. Paralleling this usage has been the development of a general theory of reference groups, largely the work of Sherif,[3] Newcomb,[4] and Merton,[5] which is

Reprinted from Guy E. Swanson, T. M. Newcomb, and E. L. Hartley (eds.), *Readings in Social Psychology*, rev. ed., pp. 410–414, by permission of the author and the publishers, Holt, Rinehart & Winston, Inc. Copyright 1947, 1952 by Holt, Rinehart & Winston, Inc.

1. Here we follow T. M. Newcomb's definition of membership group as ". . . one in which a person is recognized by others as belonging . . . " *Social Psychology*, N.Y.: Dryden, 1950, p. 225.

2. H. H. Hyman, The Psychology of Status, *Arch. of Psychol.*, 1942, No. 269.

3. M. Sherif, *An Outline of Social Psychology*, N.Y.: Harper, 1948.

4. T. M. Newcomb, *op. cit.*

5. R. K. Merton and A. K. Rossi, "Contributions to the Theory of Reference Group Behavior," pp. 40–105 in R. K. Merton, and P. F. Lazarsfeld (eds.), *Studies in the Scope and Method of "The American Soldier,"* New York: The Free Press, 1950.

designed to take account of anchorage in both membership and nonmembership groups. Although this theory is still in the initial stages of development, because of the problems it formulates it promises to be of central importance to social psychology. In particular, it is important to those social scientists who desire to interpret the development of attitudes, to predict their expression under different social conditions, to understand the social basis of their stability or resistance to change, or to devise means of increasing or overcoming this resistance.

The purpose of the present paper is to clarify certain aspects of "reference-group theory" by drawing a distinction between two major functions which reference groups play in the determination of an individual's attitudes. This distinction is necessary because the term *reference group* has heretofore been applied to two rather different phenomena, each of which poses its own theoretical and research problems. However, the ultimate usefulness of the distinction should be, first, to indicate that a more complete theory of reference groups must integrate a variety of perceptual and motivational phenomena and, second, to outline the kinds of concepts and research problems that are necessary for an analysis of reference groups.

1. Current Usages of "Reference Group"

The concept "reference group" has been used to describe two kinds of relationships between a person and a group. *The first usage* has been to denote a group in which the individual is motivated to gain or maintain *acceptance*. To promote this acceptance, he holds his attitudes in conformity with what he perceives to be the consensus of opinion among the group members. Implicit here is the idea that the members of the reference group observe the person and evaluate him.

An example of this usage is found in Merton's reinterpretation of relevant material in the two volumes of *The American Soldier*, prepared by the Research Branch, Information and Education Division of the War Department.[6]

EXAMPLE I

Three soldier populations were interviewed about their willingness to go into combat. They were: (1) inexperienced soldiers in units composed wholly of their own kind, (2) inexperienced soldiers who were replacements in units otherwise composed of combat veterans, and (3) the veterans themselves in the latter units. Other data indicated that combat veterans generally felt that "combat is hell" and had a strong group code against any tendencies to glamorize it or express eagerness for combat. In this comparison, it was found that while 45% of the men in completely unseasoned units were "ready to get

6. S. A. Stouffer, *et al.*, *The American Soldier*, Vols. I and II of *Studies in Social Psychology in World War II.*, Princeton: Princeton University Press, 1949.

into an actual battle zone," only 15% of the veterans felt ready. The important fact for our purposes was that green replacements in combat units were intermediate between the two groups mentioned, with 28% expressing readiness. In this and other attitudinal areas, it appeared that the replacements had to some degree assimilated the attitudes of the veterans. Merton interprets this result in the following manner:

". . . [Our] hypothesis drawn from reference group theory would lead us to anticipate that the replacements, *seeking affiliation* with the authoritative and prestigeful stratum of veterans, will move from the civilian-like values toward the more tough-minded values of the veterans. . . . For replacements, the assumed function of *assimilating the values* of the veterans is to find more ready acceptance by the higher-status group, in a setting where the subordinate group of replacements does not have independent claims to legitimate prestige."[7]

Newcomb's use of "reference group" clearly falls into this category. Other persons are said to constitute a reference group for a person if his attitudes are influenced by a set of norms which he assumes he shares with them. The motivational aspects of this usage are emphasized in his distinction between positive and negative reference groups. A positive reference group is defined as one in which the person is motivated to be accepted and treated like a member. A negative reference group is one which the person is motivated to oppose or in which he does not want to be treated as a member. Sherif's usage is also of this variety. He emphasizes the individual's striving to maintain his standing in his reference groups and points out that the norms of the reference group become the person's attitudes.

The second usage of "reference group" has been to denote a group which the person uses as a reference point in making evaluations of himself or others. Examples are found in Hyman's paper on the "psychology of status."

EXAMPLE II

Defining status as the relative position of individuals, Hyman points out that the person's conception of his own position depends upon which other persons he considers. These other persons with whom a person compares himself in judging his status form a reference group for him. Hyman demonstrates that changes in judgments of one's own status can be brought about by changes in the reference group used. For instance, his subjects were first asked to indicate the proportion of all adults *in the U.S.* who are lower than they in economic status. This judgment was compared with that of the proportion of people *in their occupation* who are lower economically than they.

In this type of example, any evaluation of the person by members of the reference group is largely irrelevant. A group may become a reference group because *other persons* compare the individual with it. Hyman gives this example.

7. Merton and Rossi, *op. cit.*, p. 76. Italics supplied.

EXAMPLE III

". . . [If] a woman goes for a job as a model and her physical attractiveness is the desideratum, it may be irrelevant to the situation what her physical attractiveness is in relation to her friends, Hottentot women, etc. The relevant reference group is composed of the available women models."[8] In other words, the relevant reference group is the one with which she'll be compared by her prospective employers.

Whereas in the foregoing examples the reference group is a collection of persons to which the individual belongs, in one of Merton's examples that fits this general category this is not the case.

EXAMPLE IV

A survey of the morale attitudes of noncombat soldiers overseas revealed more expressed satisfaction with their lot than was expected. The interpretation of the authors of *The American Soldier*, in which Merton concurs, is that the noncombat soldiers overseas compared themselves with men in combat and consequently found their own circumstances to be relatively good. In this instance an outside, nonmembership group presumably served as a reference group.

In both Hyman's and Merton's examples the reference group is used in making self-evaluations. However, there would seem to be no reason why we should not also consider as reference groups those collections of persons who are used as reference points in judging others. In fact, it seems likely that the reference groups used in judging one's self would frequently be used in making judgments of others.

2. Two Functions of Reference Groups

From the foregoing it is apparent that the term "reference group" is used to describe two quite different kinds of groups. In the first case (Example I) the group is in a position to award recognition to the person or to withhold it. In the second (Examples II, III, and IV) the group is merely a standard or checkpoint which the person uses in making judgments. This dual usage of the term suggests that reference groups can play different functions in the determination of a person's attitudes.

The first of these is that of setting and enforcing standards for the person. Such standards are usually labelled *group norms* so we shall call this the *normative function* of reference groups. A group can assume this function of norm-setting and norm-enforcement whenever it is in a position to deliver rewards or punishments for conformity or nonconformity. A group functions as a normative reference group for a person to the extent that its evaluations of him are based upon the degree of his conformity to certain standards of

8. Hyman, *op. cit.*, p. 47.

behavior or attitude and to the extent that the delivery of rewards or punishments is conditional upon these evaluations. In Example I above, the veterans in combat units presumably defined certain attitudes as being "correct," evaluated how well each replacement accepted these standards, and accordingly rewarded him with acceptance or punished him by withholding any recognition or acceptance.

The second of these functions is that of *serving as* or *being* a standard or comparison point against which the person can evaluate himself and others. We shall refer to this as the *comparison function* of reference groups. A group functions as a comparison reference group for an individual to the extent that the behavior, attitudes, circumstances, or other characteristics of its members represent standards or comparison points which he uses in making judgments and evaluations. In Example II the particular comparison group which Hyman suggested to his subjects (e.g., all adults in the U.S., one's friends and acquaintances, or the persons in one's occupational group) was a comparison point for each person to use in judging his own status. In Example IV, the combat soldiers served as a comparison reference group for the overseas noncombat men in their evaluations of their own situation.

These two functions, the normative and comparison functions, will frequently be served by one and the same group. This will usually be the case with membership groups. In Example I the combat veterans' attitudes provided comparison points for the replacements' self-evaluations (the comparison function), while at the same time the veterans defined these attitudes as "proper" and awarded acceptance and approval on the basis of their adoption (the normative function). This example well illustrates the integrated character of these functions: The veterans' attitudes served as comparison points primarily *because* the veterans also functioned in the normative or sanction-applying role. Both functions are also frequently served by nonmembership groups in which membership is desired. For the undergraduate who hopes eventually to be tapped by a senior fraternity that group acts both as a standard (the behavior and attitudes of its members provide examples for the aspirant) and as the source of sanctions related to conformity to these standards (since it may invite membership or withhold it). On the other hand, normative and comparison functions need not be localized within a single group. A membership group may define an external group as the standard of behavior (the parents may insist that their child model his behavior after that of other children in the neighborhood) or it may subdivide its members in such a way that the same norms do not apply to all (pledges vs. full fraternity members).

3. Implications

The distinction between the two functions suggested above is important because it makes explicit the two main aspects of reference group theory: the motivational and the perceptual. A more complete theory of reference groups must consist of at least two parts, one having to do with groups as sources and enforcers of standards and the other having to do with groups as the standards themselves. These two parts of reference-group theory should prove to be merely special cases of more general theories about the *sources* and *nature* of standards which, in turn, should ultimately derive from fundamental theories of motivation and perception. The normative functions of reference groups may be expected to become part of a general theory of goal-setting and motivation which will also include other social determinants of standards (such as important individuals having the power to reward or punish), nonsocial factors in motivation, and the processes of self-motivation whereby social influences become internalized and operate through self-delivery of reward and punishment. The comparison functions of reference groups will be part of a general theory of perception and judgment such as is presently represented by the psychological theories of frames of reference. Comparison groups are, after all, only one of many kinds of comparison points within referential frameworks. Hyman found that individuals (as well as groups) are often the points against which a person compares himself in judging his status. Other standards would be inanimate objects or units of measurement (e.g., a child may use a table or a yardstick to judge his height) and impersonal descriptions of desired behavior (e.g., legal formulations of group norms).

Finally, a consideration of the normative and comparison functions of reference groups points to two major areas of research for students of reference-group behavior. In the study of *normative* reference groups such problems as the following will come under consideration: What is the motivational relationship between the person and each of his various reference groups? How much does he value his membership or, in the case of a nonmembership group, how much does he desire to become a member? What kind of motives are involved in his membership aspirations? What are the consequences of different kinds and degrees of motives? What factors permit a group member to resist the group pressures toward conformity without being rejected? With respect to what issues do norms develop within groups? What are the peculiar patterns of standards and norms associated with various special roles or offices within the group? What kind of sanctions are applied to produce conformity and what are the consequences of different kinds? How are these sanctions related to the degree of nonconformity? What factors in the person's relation to the group promote internalization of the group norms?

A study of *comparison* reference groups will involve different questions having largely to do with perceptual and judgmental processes. The following are some examples: What kind of stimulus does the comparison group present to the individual? Does it provide a highly structured and definite comparison point or is it an ambiguous stimulus capable of a variety of interpretations? What are the consequences of these different cases? In self-evaluations, what factors affect the size of the discrepancy the person perceives to exist between himself and the group norms? What are the effects of extremely high or low standards or comparison points? What is the nature of the scale along which comparisons are made?

Reference-group theory will be advanced by the answers to these and similar questions. Through the research and conceptual development necessary to yield these answers we may expect great advances in our understanding of the social basis of attitudes.

The Concept of Reference Groups in Human Relations

Muzafer Sherif

SOCIAL psychology, on the whole, has been approached historically in contrasting ways. One approach starts with one or a few sovereign principles, such as imitation, suggestion, instinct, libido, etc. On the other hand, there have been attempts to study empirically every social psychological topic, every specific case of attitude in its own right, as though the results concerning the topic at hand are insulated from other facts in that general area.

The approaches which utilize one or a few sovereign concepts tended to start and end with premature formalizations, resulting in rather "closed-system" schools of social psychology, in spite of claims at being systematic and comprehensive. In view of the diverse problems that have to be considered, it has become evident that especially in social psychology we cannot just sit down and write off all the major principles and concepts in one or a few stretches.

On the other hand, approaches which claim that facts speak for themselves uncontaminated with theorizing end up, or rather scatter around, in almost endless discrete results, in lists, inventories, or unrelated social psychological syllabuses. The main trend of "public opinion" polling and attitude studies of diverse kinds has, on the whole, been of the latter sort until very recently.

Fortunately we do not have to be bound by either of these alternatives. There has been growing concern with attaining concepts which stem from serious preoccupation with persistent problems in social psychology, which are organically related to actual research (experimental and otherwise) and which

Reprinted from M. Sherif and M. O. Wilson (eds.), *Group Relations at the Crossroads*, pp. 203–207, 219–231, by permission of the author and the publishers, Harper & Row, Publishers. Copyright 1953 by Harper & Brothers.

can be utilized for pulling together in a comprehensive way seemingly unrelated facts in a major problem area. The concept of reference groups seems to be such a concept.

Even though this concept has started to spread only during the last four or five years, it has already received varied interpretations and usages. There are incipient signs of its becoming a magic term to explain anything and everything concerning group relations. It may more than pay if we spend some time at this early stage in clarifying our understanding of the concept in terms of the experimental work of which it is an extension, and in terms of its application to problems in group relations.

The general problem is obviously that of individual-group relationship. During the past decades the impact of vital events brought the problem of individual–group relationships into sharp focus, and this trend continues to gain momentum. The major character of this trend, as contrasted with the individualistic emphasis, is the realization that group situations generate differential effects of significant consequence. Group interaction is seen as the major determinant in attitude formation and attitude change, and other phenomena of vital consequence to the individual. During the last decades both sociologists and psychologists, with various approaches, contributed to an ever fuller realization of this trend. In several chapters of this volume, we have instructive surveys of this general trend.

Then what is the use of cluttering the already confusing inventory of concepts relative to the individual–group relationship with another? The necessity of the concept of reference group as differentiated from the more general term, group, needs justification. For concepts are not mere constructs which people, even scientists, can posit at will. Nor does consensus of opinion among professionals in an area make the use of a concept valid. As we look historically, consensus of opinion has been abandoned a good many times because, I suspect, it did not do justice to the understanding of events dealt with.

Two sets of events in particular have forced some such specified group concept as reference group to the foreground. One is related to socio-economic conditions; the other set is on the psychological side.

In a stable, integrated and relatively less differentiated society, there would probably be little necessity for the use of reference group as a separate concept. Modern man, especially in Western societies, is caught in the throes of vertical mobility, in the "dilemmas and contradictions of statuses," and painful predicament of marginality created by the demands and goals originating in diverse groups. He finds himself betwixt and between situations as he carries on the business of living in different roles in relation to diverse groups which not infrequently demand contradictory adjustment of his experience and behavior. He is exposed through actual face-to-face contacts, through the mass media of communication, to pressures, demands, goals of diverse trends and ideologies. These are some of the many aspects of the setting in which he operates, through which he becomes indoctrinated, forms his identifications, faces a great variety of alternatives to choose from in line with his special needs, etc. If his psychological level of functioning were restricted largely to the impact of immediate stimulus situations and his behavior were regulated solely in terms of the immediate ups and downs of his biogenic motives and conditionings on that basis, he would probably not be troubled so much by the demands of overlapping and contradictory groups.

This leads to the second consideration, which relates to man's conceptual level of functioning. As he passes from one group situation to another from time to time, he reacts to the demands, pressures and appeals of new group situations in terms of the person he has come to consider himself to be and aspires to be. In other words, he reacts in terms of more or less consistent ties of belongingness in relation to his past and present identifications and his future goals for security of his identity, and also his status and prestige concerns. In short, this conceptual level of functioning makes possible regulation of experience and behavior in relation to values and norms that lie at times far beyond immediate group situations.

The conceptual level of functioning is, on the whole, taken too much for granted. We may be gaining a great deal if this conceptual level of functioning is deliberately brought into the discussion of motives and goals in relation to group situations. Of course, this idea is tied up with the notion of *levels* so cogently stressed by Schneirla, Lindesmith and Strauss, and others.[1]

It is apparent, then, that the groups to which the individual relates himself need not always be the groups in which he is actually moving. His identifications need not always be with groups in which he is registered, is seen to be, or announced to be a member. The concept of reference groups forces itself through such facts. The concept becomes almost indispensable in dealing with the relation of individuals to groups in highly differentiated and poorly integrated societies, in societies in the process of acculturation and high tempo of transition.

With the above considerations in mind, reference groups can be characterized simply as *those groups to which the individual relates himself as a part or to which he aspires to relate himself psychologically*. It is apparent that the characterization of reference groups just presented is a psychological one, that is, it is made from the standpoint of the individual in the individual–group relationship.

In many cases, of course, the individual's reference groups are at the same time his membership groups.[2] However, in cases where the individual's

1. T. C. Schneirla, "The 'Levels' Concept in the Study of Social Organization in Animals," in J. H. Rohrer and M. Sherif, eds., *Social Psychology at the Crossroads*, New York: Harper & Brothers, 1951; T. C. Schneirla, "Problems in the Biopsychology of Social Organization," *J. Abnorm. Soc. Psychol.*, 41: 385–402, 1946; and A. R. Lindesmith and A. L. Strauss, *Social Psychology*, New York: Dryden Press, 1949.

2. To make this point clear, our previous treatment of membership and reference groups is introduced under the title "Effects of Membership and Other Reference Groups." (M. Sherif, *An Outline of Social Psychology*, Harper & Row, 1948.)

membership groups are not his reference groups, it does not follow that the groups in which the individual actually interacts will not have an effect on him. On the contrary, this creates important psychological problems for him to which we shall have occasion to refer later when we deal with *marginality* as one instance of being caught between the positive attractions of one's reference group, which is not the membership group of the individual at the time, and demands and pressures of the membership group, which is not his reference group.

Numerous studies coming both from psychologists and from sociologists have shown that the major sources of the individual's weighty attitudes are the values or norms of the groups to which he relates himself, that is, of his reference groups. In fact, the values or norms of his reference groups constitute the major anchorages in relation to which his experience of self identity is organized. This conception enables us to pull together a host of discrete data in various areas. At this point, we shall mention just one illustration. Textbooks on adolescence used to give rather lengthy lists of adolescent interests and attitudes which included some items that appear as oddities. All such lists of adolescent attitudes and interests can be pulled together under a unified conceptual scheme if they are related to the adolescent's reference groups. These are, on the whole, cliques spontaneously formed under the motivational stresses to which the youngsters are exposed, especially in societies in a high tempo of transition.[3] Likewise, psychological problems of gang behavior, problems of marginality, problems of status regulation by individuals, etc., acquire conceptual unification when approached with some such concept as reference groups. . . .

Concept of Reference Groups Applied to Various Group Problems

It seems that this kind of conceptualization can handle a good many significant facts more easily. Many of these are scattered around although we know they are related. We tend to deal with each by itself under such headings as *consistency-inconsistency in social behavior, status problems and status equilibrium, marginality, attitude change, adolescent attitudes,* and so forth.

We have mentioned the relative consistency and continuity of the individual's identity. However, especially in modern complex societies, his behavior may appear highly contradictory and inconsistent in various situations. As an example, Jahoda takes the case of some union members who actively participated in the Detroit race riots of 1942 even though in their union they were taught and practiced nonsegregation. Now if these union members had been *nothing but* good and staunch union members, they would not have participated in the riots. But they were also members of families, neighborhood groups, churches,

3. K. Davis, "The Sociology of Parent-Youth Conflict," *Amer. Sociol. Rev.*, 5: 523–535, 1940.

ethnic groups and, as they have been reminded in so many ways from childhood on, a "White" group, which, they have learned, stands at definite distances from other groups. These groups were major reference groups long before these individuals became members of a union with an antidiscrimination policy. It is not surprising that in a situation in which they could either act as a "regular person" in terms of their major reference groups of neighborhood, color, etc., or as good union members, many of them—probably with no thought of doing otherwise—acted contrary to their union's practices.

To be sure, behavior of individuals may be inconsistent for a number of reasons, perhaps idiosyncratic ones related to continual thwarting of basic biogenic motives, or persistent conflict situations of a personal nature. However, a large proportion of instances of inconsistencies in *social* behavior can be understood in relation to conflicting norms of various reference groups which have been internalized and may be situationally aroused. Charters and Newcomb,[4] for example, showed that when Catholic subjects are situationally ego-involved as Catholics, their reactions to general statements are substantially different than their reactions to the same items when Catholic group reference is not activated.

When an individual has multiple reference groups, the norms of which conflict in various areas, he will sooner or later find himself in a situation where the norms of different reference groups point in different, even opposite directions. Consider the situation of the modern professional woman. At work, of course, the major reference group is her professional group; in social life, perhaps the ladies of the community; in her home, her family. It is not unusual for her to find herself in a situation where the norms of two or more of these reference groups are in conflict. Of course, she will probably react in terms of one or the other. She may even be aware of the source of her dilemma, feeling resentment toward one or the other of her reference groups responsible for the conflict in this area. It is doubtful, however, that this situation is clarified by speaking of a reference group as a negative reference group in one respect and positive in another respect. Probably at some time or other almost every group member is negatively inclined toward at least some norms of his group. If these terms were used, every group to which the individual relates himself could be both a positive and negative reference group. Lewis Killian of Florida State University has made an interesting analysis of the conflict of civilian and army norms in a military railway service.[5] Although the men he studied were all in the army and subject to all rules and customs of "military courtesy," the usual behavior among them, whether officers or enlisted men, was in terms of status in civilian railroad groups. In spite of "constant pressure from the general headquarters for compliance with traditional military practice," the

4. See T. M. Newcomb, *Social Psychology*, New York: Dryden Press, 1950.

5. "The Conflict of Civilian and Military Norms in a Military Railway Service," available from the author.

railroad group and its norms persisted as the major reference group, with resultant behavior quite inconsistent with the army situation.

In an analysis of the significance of multiple-group membership in disaster situations in four southwestern communities, Killian studied the reactions of individuals to situations where by necessity a choice in reference groups had to be made.[6] For example, frequent conflict was found between loyalty to family or friends and to occupational groups. An example of apparently inconsistent behavior in the eyes of those who watched was that of the state trooper who decided, after a tornado struck, that as a patrolman his job was to drive to the next town for help. To the friends and acquaintances who called for his help as he drove out of town, his action must have seemed inconsistent, even heartless. He stated that this was "one of the hardest things I ever had to do."

The behavior of telephone workers on strike in two disaster communities reveals the conflict between reference groups within the community and those outside of the community. "In both communities the striking workers were allowed to return to duty by union leaders, but were ordered to walk out again a few days later. In both cases the union officials considered the emergency to be over sooner than did the townspeople of the stricken communities. In one town the workers obeyed the union's orders only to find themselves subjected to harsh criticism by their fellow-townsmen. In the other community the workers resigned from the union rather than forsake their loyalty to their other membership group."

To the degree that the individual has interiorized the norms of his various reference groups, conflict or contradictions of these norms will be experienced as personal conflict. This relationship becomes more precise when the individual's status in his various reference groups is specified. Groups are necessarily hierarchical along some dimension or another. Status denotes the relative position of each member in these respects. Of course, to have a relative position the individual must in some degree relate himself or belong to the group. This relatedness implies experience of the hierarchy of the group and ego-involvement with it. Once a member, his aspirations for status and standards of attainment are determined in terms of this scale.

Now what happens when the individual's status in various reference groups differs? In delineating the concept of *status equilibration*, the sociologist, Benoit-Smullyan,[7] suggests that "there is a real tendency for the different types of status to reach a common level." For example, a millionaire who finds himself admired only for his money teams up with a college professor or public relations expert, or endows a research foundation, in the effort to attain prestige

---

6. Lewis Killian, "The Significance of Multiple-Group Membership in Disaster," *Amer. J. Sociol.*, 57: 309–314, 1952.

7. E. Benoit-Smullyan, "Status, Status Types, and Status Interrelations," *Amer. Sociol. Rev.*, 9: 151–161, 1944.

socially commensurate with his financial status. Or a lady newly arrived in a
financial sense may indulge in literature or the arts, or psychology, in order to
bring her social status in the community to the level of her financial status.
In the process of striving, she may be a little ashamed of her associates on the
wrong side of the tracks, and may try to minimize or even break off her relationship with them. As Hartley suggests, the individual may seek to adjust his
status by trying to raise the prestige of one of his reference groups to the level
of the higher group. Hartley's interesting study with Fenchel and Monderer[8]
on college students' status and status strivings in five significant reference groups
found the tendency to be expected from the notion of status equilibration.
Striving for status was significantly greater in reference groups in which status
was lower. "The results indicate a definite tendency for the status ratings to
approach a common high anchorage level within the individual's status
structure, as defined by his different reference groups." The explanation for
this, we should think, lies in the ego-involvement in these anchorages defined
by reference groups, and the personal uneasiness at being exposed to situations
of conflict and contradiction.

Personal conflict, uncertainty, or insecurity follows lack of stability of
anchorings in reference groups. These situations have been extensively studied
by sociologists—notably Park and Stonequist—as "marginality."[9]

The state of *marginality* gives a good opportunity to emphasize certain
points which we could touch upon only indirectly in the course of this discussion.
Since the topic is reference groups, the emphasis has been on instances in
which the groups are not face-to-face—or not within the perceptual range of
the individual. However, such emphasis should not imply that immediate
face-to-face group situations in which the membership group is *not* a reference
group do not have considerable effect on the individual. On the contrary, even
in cases in which a sharp cleavage exists between the group in which he is
registered or taken for granted and his reference group, he is bound to feel the
immediate pressures of the group situation he moves in. In such cases, he'll
be pushed in one direction by his actual membership group—pulled in the
opposite direction by his reference group.

In cases of marginality, however, the situation is ordinarily one of lack of
stability in reference group ties. The individual cannot relate himself in a
consistent way to either group. Both groups are reference groups for him,
however unstable his ties. The degree to which he is ego-involved with the
value scales of one or the other may vary.

The most common example of marginality is that of individuals belonging
to an ethnic group, religious group or color group in a minority position who
because of their inability to be accepted in larger society and their tendency to

8. G. H. Fenchel, J. H. Monderer, and E. L. Hartley, "Subjective Status and the
Equilibration Hypothesis," *J. Abnorm. Soc. Psychol.*, 46: 476–479, 1951.

9. E. V. Stonequist, *The Marginal Man*, New York: Charles Scribner's Sons, 1937.

reject standards or position of their own group, feel insecure in their reference group affiliations in a major way.

Among psychologists, Kurt Lewin[10] has written on these problems and Hartley[11] has done most interesting studies with children on the conflicting values of groups to which they relate themselves.

Marginality is not confined to members of minority groups. The *foreman* in industrial life is often in a similar position. Ordinarily, of course, the foreman rises out of the rank and file of workers. But as a foreman he is betwixt and between management and the workers. He can't consistently relate himself to management, partly because of his origins, his economic situation, and because he does not actually take part in making policy decisions but just carries out the directives of management. Roethlisberger pointed out[12] that management calls the foreman the "grass roots level of management" or "front-line personnel man." But the foreman calls himself a "go-betweener." He has to uphold management's standards and regulations and at the same time try to get workers to conform to them spontaneously. "Again and again he is put in a position of either getting the worker's cooperation and being 'disloyal' to management or of incurring the resentment and overt opposition of his subordinates."

The workers, in turn, think of the foreman as "the boss." Quoting an interview from a study by Whyte and Gardner one worker said: "You can't talk about this sort of thing with the boss. After all, he's part of management and you couldn't expect him to see things as we do. He's a good guy, as far as that goes, but he's a management man."[13]

The foreman thus is unable to take either management or the workers as his reference group in a consistent way. The result may be, in the words of one foreman: "You don't know where you stand. It's a hell of a situation because I get on edge and blow my top and say things that I really didn't mean to say."

In the studies of The American Soldier, Stouffer and associates apply a similar analysis to the conflicting situation of the noncommissioned officer. Here the "noncom finds himself in a conflict situation involving official responsibility to his officers on one hand and unofficial obligations to the other enlisted men on the other."[14]

10. Kurt Lewin, *Resolving Social Conflicts*, New York: Harper, 1948.

11. E. L. Hartley, M. Rosenbaum, and S. Schwartz, "Children's Use of Ethnic Frames of Reference: An Exploratory Study of Children's Conceptualizations of Multiple Ethnic Group Membership," *J. Psychol.*, 26: 367–386, 1948; "Children's Perception of Their Ethnic Group Membership; Note on Children's Role Perception," *J. Psychol.*, 26: 387–398; 399–405 1948.

12. F. J. Roethlisberger, "The Foreman: Master and Victim of Double Talk," *Harvard Bus. Rev.*, 23: 283–298, 1945.

13. W. F. Whyte, and B. Gardner, "Problems of the Foreman," *J. Appl. Anthrop.*, Spring, 1945.

14. S. A. Stouffer et al., *Studies in Social Psychology in World War II*, Princeton: Princeton University Press, 1949.

We have already mentioned attitude change in connection with the well-known Bennington study. It is sufficient to note here that attitude change of the greatest scope and degree is found when individuals shift or change reference groups, in contrast to effects of exposure to discrete stimuli or events.

In this connection, we will speak again of the adolescent period. Most of the changes in attitudes, interests, and conception of self are clarified when related to shifts in reference groups at this period. However, not quite the same thing happens with changes of reference groups in younger children or older adults. So it is necessary to refer briefly to antecedent conditions, some of which take place on a physiological level.

Of course, bodily and sexual maturation during adolescence in itself has dramatic effects. The changes in the adolescent's body, his desires, the way he sees himself, demand changes in relation to other persons in general and the opposite sex in particular. These changes are, of course, on a conceptual level. The adolescent must step from his "childish" relationship. He gets specific ideas and values of becoming a full-fledged man or woman in his society. And at this stage, he ardently desires to fulfill them.

On the other hand, parents, grownups, the social organization and its norms have very definite and, in complicated societies, often conflicting ideas or norms of how the transition from childhood to adulthood should be made.

In less differentiated societies, the young person settles down in his appropriate adult role shortly after puberty with a definite sexual role, with a definite work role and other roles. This may occur in a dramatic, even abrupt fashion, through "transition" ceremonies and rites, which often involve prescribed trials of various degrees of severity—as illustrated in the works of Van Gennep, Webster, Radin, and others.

But in more complex societies, e.g., America today, settling down is a delayed, prolonged process. During this period the fulfillment of the adolescent's desires and his dreams must be postponed in many instances. At the same time, although he is no longer a child, he is not consistently treated or accepted as an adult. Consequently, the youth and his parents and other grown-ups, whose job it is to help carry through these restrictions, are in conflict. As Kingsley Davis writes, this is especially true in countries where the values of adults and adolescents by virtue of a rapid rate of social change are miles apart, as in China or Turkey or many other countries today.[15]

In this state of instability and conflict, the adolescent tries to belong *some place* at any rate. In a setting where social mixing of various groups is not encouraged, these attempts to *become somebody* may be through daydreams and fantasy. But in most modern societies, on the whole, adolescents gravitate toward one another.

Thus arises a "peer culture" or "adolescent culture," as Blos, Zachry,

15. Davis, *op. cit.*

Harold Jones[16] and other writers on the subject have called it, which is peculiar to the adolescents, at least in some dimensions of their lives. Frequently it is peculiar to a particular group of youngsters.

Although adolescents of course *know* perfectly well what grownups want them to learn, they are in this state of affairs centered in their own group of adolescents. For the time being at least these become the dominant reference groups which regulate their attitudes and interests, their activities and aspirations to a considerable degree. In this setting, parents and adults may simply constitute annoyances in so many aspects of living important to them. One high school girl in California, peeved by her parents' interferences in her activities, remarked: "I am afraid my friends will think I have no control over my parents."

In more stable strata of society, adolescents may keep the major norms of the family reference group intact. Depending on the youngsters they associate with, many of these norms may not even bring up questions of great importance to them. For example, questions relating to political or social norms may be of very little importance to a group of upper-class adolescents.

It should be noted, of course, that this period of resistance to adults and preoccupation with age-mate reference groups, in some cases to the point of rebellion, is usually transitory.

Ordinarily, within an age range considered acceptable by society, the adolescent does "settle down," taking on economic and social roles in the adult society, including those of husband and wife. With these events, his reference group ordinarily becomes that adult group or groups in which he functions and moves, and the interests, attitudes and values of his youthful adolescent group appear even to him as silly youthful adventure.

Whenever individuals cannot consistently relate themselves to the scale of values of the groups within which they move and function, there is a tendency for these individuals to gravitate toward one another and to form *informal* reference groups, deriving their major self-identity, aspirations and values from those informal groups, at least for the time being.

Another excellent example of this tendency is found in "interstitial areas"— slum areas of large cities. The children and young people in such areas are very frequently in the position of being rejected by society at large, hence are unable to identify with society, and at the same time they reject the values of their families. These family values, which are often carry-overs of Old World norms, are unacceptable to children in constant contact with the established American setting. These interstitial areas and their conflicts and problems have been rather extensively studied by a number of sociologists.

Such interstitial areas may appear from the outside to be "disorganized,"

16. P. Blos, *The Adolescent Personality*, New York: Appleton-Century-Crofts, 1941; C. B. Zachry, *Emotion and Conduct in Adolescence*, New York: Appleton-Century-Crofts, 1940; and H. E. Jones, *Development in Adolescence*, New York: Appleton-Century-Crofts, 1943.

but as William Whyte pointed out, there is actually a high state of organization on an *informal* basis.

Such informal reference groups may become so all important that their standards may counteract chances to improve in status or to have contacts with the opposite sex. For example, Whyte[17] found that one group of young men broke off contact with a group of attractive girls when these contacts threatened to be a disruptive influence to the solidarity and integrity of the group.

Clifford Shaw's Jack-Roller[18] ran away from the opportunity to become a member of a well-to-do family, the father of which was the vice-president of a company and an influential man in the community. In this case, the boy's major identification was with a reference group which, in the eyes of society, was delinquent. But he had come from a slum area which the rest of society looked down upon, and he found no secure identification with his family group. When he became a member of a neighborhood gang as a young boy, he began to feel he was somebody in his own right—a person with a place in life. The informal groups of boys in which he functioned at various times in his development were the ones that gave him a sense of personal identity—they were his reference groups in everything that counted for him.

The knowledge of how he was supposed to behave and the opportunity to do so in a life of comparative ease were not enough for him. The norms of society were not the norms of his reference group and hence were not his norms.

This means that one has to analyze goals, standards and the like in relation to those of the individual's reference groups.

For example, ordinarily we think of a person who gives information to authorities as "repentant"—they have "seen the light" and are on their way to being reformed. But that is not the way these fellows view these events. In the Jack-Roller's words: "To squawk on a fellow-prisoner is an unpardonable sin and only the lowest characters will squawk. . . . *They are not fit to be associated with decent boys.*"

17. W. F. Whyte, *Street Corner Society*, Chicago: University of Chicago Press, 1943.

18. Clifford Shaw, *The Jack-Roller*, Chicago: University of Chicago Press, 1930.

Some Attitudinal Effects of Experimentally Increased Salience of a Membership Group

W. W. Charters, Jr., and Theodore M. Newcomb

A COMMONPLACE subscribed to by the man-in-the-street as well as by the social scientist is the proposition that many of the attitudes of an individual are greatly influenced by the norms of groups to which he belongs. Most individuals, however, are members of more than one group, and consequently may face a particular problem when these different groups prescribe opposing attitudes toward the same object. It seems reasonable to hypothesize that an individual's resolution of this problem will be a function of the relative potencies of his various group memberships. If the potency of one of the groups is extremely high in relation to the others, he may adopt the attitude prescribed by this particular group; if the potencies of the groups are of equal strength, he may either reach a compromise between the conflicting norms, or he may yield to the attitudinal position prescribed by the group the potency of which is highest at the moment.

We have attempted a simple test of the proposition that attitudinal response is a function of the relative strengths of momentary forces toward or away from membership in groups with conflicting norms. By increasing the potency of one of an individual's membership groups, we would expect to find that his expressed attitudes would resemble more closely the attitudes prescribed by the norms of that group. There are many ways by which the potency of group membership may be varied experimentally for an individual, but we shall limit ourselves to

Reprinted from Eleanor E. Maccoby, T. M. Newcomb, and E. L. Hartley (eds.), *Readings in Social Psychology*, 3d ed., pp. 276–281, by permission of the authors and the publishers, Holt, Rinehart & Winston, Inc. Copyright 1947, 1952, (c) 1958 by Holt, Rinehart & Winston, Inc.

the one H. H. Kelley has called "salience." Operationally, this means simply heightening the individual's awareness of his membership in the specified group by vivid reminders of this membership.

· *Experimental Procedure*

From a large class of introductory psychology students we selected those who we knew were also members of one of three strong religious organizations whose norms with respect to attitudes on religious matters differed from the norms associated with membership in the university community at large. We chose as subjects students who had indicated during college registration their religions as Roman Catholic, Jewish, or Protestant. Among the Protestants, we used as subjects only those students who indicated membership in a church we judged to be "evangelical"; these students were primarily Lutheran.

We randomly divided members of the Jewish and evangelical Protestant groups into control and experimental groups; Catholics were separated into one experimental and two control groups. Students assigned to experimental groups were instructed to meet in small rooms with the other members of their religious groups, while the control subjects (except for one of the Catholic control group subjects) received no instructions and reported along with other class members to the auditorium at which they ordinarily attended a psychology-class lecture.

The control selectees had no knowledge that they had been singled out among the other psychology students as participants in the experiment. Members of one of the Catholic control groups were assigned to a small room in a manner identical with that of the experimental subjects, but the experimental procedure of arousing awareness of their group membership was omitted. (We shall refer to this Catholic control group as the "alone" controls and to the Catholic control group that met in the lecture hall as the "auditorium" controls.)

In the experimental groups, the group leaders (each of whom was a member of the same religious group as the students in his group) attempted to establish an unambiguous awareness of common religious membership. The leaders explained that all in the room were Catholics (or Jews or Protestants) brought together to help construct a questionnaire on religious beliefs.

Following the statement of alleged purpose, in which considerable emphasis was put on the common group membership of all in the room, the leaders conducted uncontroversial discussions on the "basic assumptions which *underlie* the opinions of all Catholics (or Jews or Protestants)," carefully avoiding expressions of what loyal Catholics (or Jews or Protestants) *should* believe and expressions of opinions on specific issues. The leaders continued the discussions until they judged that the students were quite conscious of their common religious affiliations and then distributed a set of "preliminary questions" to which students were asked to respond with their *own personal opinions*. Judging from the frequency of "dissident" replies, there were few if any subjects who answered consistently as "good Catholics (or Jews or Protestants) are supposed to answer" instead of giving their own opinions. They were assured anonymity and told that only by responding with their own opinions would their contributions be of any value in constructing the final questionnaire. In order to keep their religious affiliations before them as they filled out the questionnaires, the leader asked them to check statements they believed to be especially important to their religious groups.

In the auditorium, the regular lecturer asked all the students (including the control subjects) to respond to a self-explanatory questionnaire. The lecturer explained that several different groups meeting elsewhere also were taking part in an experiment which had to do "with certain attitudes and values concerning which students differ." No intimation was given to the students of the religious bearing of the experiment prior to answering the questionnaire. The Catholic "alone" controls were instructed the same way as the auditorium group. In both experimental and control groups, leaders explained candidly and in detail the purpose of the experiment after all questionnaires had been returned.

We evaluated our success in equalizing control and experimental groups through random assignment by comparing the distributions of age, sex, and political preference. (Members of each group provided these data at the end of the questionnaire.) The proportions of subjects in the control and experimental groups with respect to these personal characteristics were sufficiently similar to indicate they were from the same population.[1]

The questionnaires, consisting of 72 Likert-type statements, were identical for all groups. There were nine statements eliciting opinions of a generally religious nature, twenty-three statements directed specifically to the three religious groups —seven each for Catholics and Protestants and nine for Jews, twenty-four items adapted from Thurstone and Chave's scale of attitudes toward the Church, seven items from Kirkpatrick's feminism scale, and nine other statements from Newcomb's political and economic progressivism scale considered to be irrelevant to the norms of any of the three religious groups. Feminist statements were included as part of a parallel investigation of the potency of sex-group membership, but the equivocal results will not be reported here. Irrelevant statements were included for two reasons, one, to ascertain, if control-experimental differences were found, whether they were due to the effects of the proper group norms, in which case reponses to statements irrelevant to the religious group norms would not show differences; and, two, to disguise the religious nature of the questionnaire in order not to arouse awareness of religious-group membership among the controls. Subjects were asked to respond to each statement by circling the appropriate letters from "strongly agree" to "strongly disagree," as in the following illustration:

Every person should have faith in some supernatural power to which he willingly subordinates himself.

SA   A   ?   D   SD

1. No Chi-square tests of control-experimental differences exceeded the .05 level of significance.

We expected all experimental group members to reply in greater agreement than persons in control groups to this general religious question in our illustration. (Illustrations of other types of statements are found in the appendix to this article.)

We undertook two kinds of analyses of the data. We evaluated the probability of control-experimental differences in distributions of responses to each item by means of the Chi-square test and then estimated the probability of finding consistent differences over a series of items by a formula for combined probabilities.[2] In addition, scores were assigned to each individual on the basis of his responses to a series of items, and differences in mean scores of control and of experimental subjects were evaluated by means of "t" tests. Items were weighted 1, 2, 3, 4, or 5, according to whether an individual's response was SA, A, ?, D, SD, respectively, so that a low store indicated conformity to the norms of the religious group. (About half the statements were reversed in such a way that disagreement indicated conformity, in which cases the scoring was correspondingly reversed.) Scores were computed similarly for the nonreligious items, and for the feminism and progressivism scales, on the basis of Kirkpatrick's and Newcomb's published methods, respectively.[3]

Catholic Results

Our initial hypothesis was clearly confirmed for the Catholic religious group. Catholic subjects in the experimental group for whom the potency of religious-group membership was deliberately increased more closely approximated the orthodox Catholic position than control subjects whose awareness of membership was not increased. Table 1 shows that for all three groups of relevant items the control-experimental differences in mean scores are significant at the .01 level or less. (The two Catholic control groups are combined for this demonstration.) Results for the Jewish and Protestant groups were ambiguous and will be discussed in the next section.

Significant differences between control and experimental subjects did not appear in attitudes toward matters irrelevant to the Catholic religion—attitudes toward political, feminist, Jewish, and Protestant matters. This fact supports the contention that the differences which *were* demonstrated resulted from the increased potency of the religious-group membership.

As we have suggested, the expression of an individual's attitudes is influenced by the norms associated with the various groups of which he is a

2. To discover if the combined probabilities of any series of tests are so great as to exceed chance, even though the individual probabilities do not reach significance, we have used the method described in E. F. Lindquist, *Statistical Analysis in Educational Research* (Boston: Houghton Mifflin Company, 1940), p. 46f.

3. See Clifford Kirkpatrick, "The Construction of a Belief-Pattern Scale for Measuring Attitudes toward Feminism," *J. Soc. Psychol.*, 1936, VII, 421–437, and T. M. Newcomb. *Personality and Social Change* (New York: Dryden Press, 1943).

Table I—Mean Scores of Catholic Subjects, Classified by Type of Item

Type of Item	Theoretical Orthodoxy	Experimental Group	Both Control Groups	University Norms (Residual Group)
Catholic	1.00	2.09*	2.36	2.73*
General religious	1.00	2.04*	2.41	2.77*
Church	1.00	1.50*	1.80	2.15*
Protestant	1.00	2.56	2.67	2.60
Jewish	1.00	2.36	2.38	2.23
Feminist	1.00	1.76	1.78	1.65
Political	1.00	1.95	2.07	2.17

* Difference between mean scores of control subjects and experimental or residual subjects is at or beyond the .01 level of significance.

member. We hypothesized that the attitudes of our Catholic students would be influenced, on the one hand, by their membership in the Catholic religious group and, on the other hand, by their membership in the university community. At this point, therefore, we must establish the polar positions of the university community and of the theoretically orthodox Catholic group.

We may take the mean scores of the group of 338 students who did not participate either as experimentals or controls, composed largely of non-"evangelical" Protestants and students with no religious affiliation, to represent roughly the dominant norms of the university community. These scores are reported in Table 1. In addition, we may consider the orthodox Catholic pole of the continuum with regard to the general religious, Catholic, and church items to be represented by consistently favorable responses (or unfavorable responses, in the case of reversed items), which would yield a theoretical mean score over all relevant items of 1.00.

The scores of both the combined Catholic control and the Catholic experimental groups fall between the extreme poles of the continuum, indicating that subjects in both groups are subject to other than Catholic or university community influences. Inasmuch as the mean scores of Catholic experimental subjects on items relevant to Catholic group norms are more nearly in accord with the orthodox Catholic pole than are the mean scores of the control subjects, we have evidence that their membership in the Catholic group had relatively greater potency for them than for control subjects. Controls, on the other hand, were less affected by the Catholic influence and more affected by the influence of the university community.

Thus far in our analysis we have treated the two Catholic control groups as one. How justified are we in assuming that the mere difference in conditions under which the groups met (in groups of 35 to 60 for the experimentals, but as part of a group of 500 for the controls) do not account for our findings? A comparison of the responses of Catholics in the "alone" and in the "auditorium" control situations assures us that the different conditions did not influence subjects' attitudes. (The condition under which the "alone" controls replied to the questionnaire was precisely the same as the condition under which the experimentals responded, except for the deliberate arousal of their awareness of religious membership.) No differences between "alone" and "auditorium" control subjects' responses were significant beyond the .05 level on the general religious and Catholic items.[4] We therefore have some justification for considering the "auditorium" group an adequate control in our consideration of Jewish and Protestant results.

Results for Jews and Protestants

The findings for Jews and evangelical Protestants do not confirm our initial hypothesis. On only one statement out of the eighteen general religious and specific statements for the Jews and on one out of the sixteen for the Protestants were their control-experimental differences significant beyond the .10 level. Although on fourteen of the eighteen statements differences between the Jewish controls were in the expected direction, the combined probabilities reveal that this distribution of probabilities would occur by chance about 50 times out of 100. Less than half the Protestant control-experimental differences were in the expected, "more religious" direction. Neither Jewish nor Protestant experimental subjects responded significantly more favorably than their controls with respect to attitudes toward the church.

We hestitate to reject our hypothesis on the basis of these results in view of the supporting evidence among the Catholic subjects. We shall therefore propose some reasonable explanations to account for the negative results for Jews and evangelical Protestants. We hasten to emphasize that *post factum* explanations cannot be accepted without further investigations designed explicitly to test them.

There is some indication that the norms associated with evangelical Protestantism had a less powerful influence upon the Protestant college population which we studied than the influence of Catholic norms on the Catholic students. Inspection of our data reveals that the attitudes of Protestant control subjects were quite similar to those of the residual group, but that attitudes of Catholic controls were considerably "more religious". If this is the case, then salience of religious membership would be less effective in inducing attitude change among Protestants than among Catholics. This cannot be a sufficient explanation, because Jewish controls also manifested attitudes quite dissimilar to attitudes among the residual group.

We do not overlook the possibility that some Jews and evangelical Protestants may react negatively to a recognition of their religious membership—

---

4. Chi-square analyses of responses to individual items of the church scale are not available, but analysis of the mean scores revealed no significant differences between "alone" and "auditorium" controls.

that is, their group may serve them as a negative reference group.[5] If this were the situation, these subjects would respond antithetically under the experimental condition while the remainder would respond according to our expectations. This would cancel differences which might otherwise appear. There is some evidence in our data to support this explanation, but because of the small number of subjects involved, we cannot evaluate its importance. If we compare the proportions of subjects in each control and experimental group who deviated from the modal response of their fellows on a relatively large number of items, we find that there are slightly more deviants among the experimentals. *Fewer* Catholic experimental subjects gave deviant responses as compared with Catholic controls. Table 2 shows these comparisons.

Table 2—Percentage of Subjects in Each Group with High Deviation Scores*

Religious Group	Control	Experi-mental
Catholic	24	8
Jewish	3	6
Protestant	9	16

* Figures entered in this table represent the proportion of subjects in the respective categories with high deviation scores. Total number of subjects in each category is:

Catholic "auditorium" control	58
Catholic experimental	46
Jewish control	92
Jewish experimental	58
Protestant control	45
Protestant experimental	33

There is, then, some equivocal evidence that the lack of confirmation of our initial hypothesis is due, in the case of evangelical Protestants, to the relatively small influence upon them of religious group norms; and in the case of both Protestants and Jews, to some persons who reacted negatively to awareness of their religious affiliation. These limiting conditions must be substantiated by further experimentation. The data from the Catholic groups strongly suggest that an individual's expression of attitudes is a function of the relative momentary potency of his relevant group memberships.

5. See Theodore M. Newcomb, *Social Psychology* (New York: Dryden Press, 1950), especially pp. 225–232.

Appendix: Sample Questionnaire Items[6]

GENERAL RELIGIOUS:

One of the things wrong with this country is that so many Americans have ceased to have any strong sense of right and wrong.

CATHOLIC:

All American children should receive at least part of their education in public (state-supported) schools.

Birth-control information should be provided to all married individuals who desire it.

JEWISH:

Our government should take a more active part in attempts to solve the problems of European DPs (displaced persons).

Under no conditions is there any justification for quotas limiting admission to schools and colleges on a racial or religious basis.

EVANGELICAL PROTESTANT:

If one is deeply convinced of one's values, one should do everything one can to demonstrate their supreme importance to others.

Religious experience of the kind which occurs at revivals is purely the result of crowd excitement.

6. Examples of feminist, political, and church items may be found in the published sources. See Kirkpatrick, *op. cit.*, Newcomb, *Personality and Social Change*, *op. cit.*, and L. L. Thurstone and C. J. Chave, *A Scale for Measuring Attitude toward the Church* (Chicago: University of Chicago Press, 1930).

Reference Groups as Perspectives

Tamotsu Shibutani

ALTHOUGH Hyman coined the term scarcely more than a decade ago, the concept of reference group has become one of the central analytic tools in social psychology, being used in the construction of hypotheses concerning a variety of social phenomena. The inconsistency in behavior as a person moves from one social context to another is accounted for in terms of a change in reference groups; the exploits of juvenile delinquents, especially in interstitial areas, are being explained by the expectations of peer-group gangs; modifications in social attitudes are found to be related to changes in associations. The concept has been particularly useful in accounting for the choices made among apparent alternatives, particularly where the selections seem to be contrary to the "best interests" of the actor. Status problems—aspirations of social climbers, conflicts in group loyalty, the dilemmas of marginal men—have also been analyzed in terms of reference groups, as have the differential sensitivity and reaction of various segments of an audience to mass communication. It is recognized that the same generic processes are involved in these phenomenally diverse events, and the increasing popularity of the concept attests to its utility in analysis.

As might be expected during the exploratory phases in any field of inquiry, however, there is some confusion involved in the use of this concept, arising largely from vagueness of signification. The available formal definitions are inconsistent, and sometimes formal definitions are contradicted in usage. The fact that social psychologists can understand one another in spite of these ambiguities, however, implies an intuitive recognition of some central meaning, and an explicit statement of this will enhance the utility of the concept as an analytic tool. The literature reveals that all discussions of reference groups involve some

Reprinted from *American Journal of Sociology*, 60 : 562–569, 1955, by permission of the author and the publisher, The University of Chicago Press. Copyright 1955 by the University of Chicago.

identifiable grouping to which an actor is related in some manner and the norms and values shared in that group, However, the relationship between these three terms is not always clear. Our initial task, then, is to examine the conceptions of reference group implicit in actual usage, irrespective of formal definitions.

One common usage of the concept is in the designation of that group which serves as the point of reference in making comparisons or contrasts, especially in forming judgments about one's self. In the original use of the concept Hyman spoke of reference groups as points of comparison in evaluating one's own status, and he found that the estimates varied according to the group with which the respondent compared himself. Merton and Kitt, in their reformulation of Stouffer's theory of relative deprivation, also use the concept in this manner; the judgments of rear-echelon soldiers overseas concerning their fate varied, depending upon whether they compared themselves to soldiers who were still at home or men in combat. They also propose concrete research operations in which respondents are to be asked to compare themselves with various groups. The study of aspiration levels by Chapman and Volkmann, frequently cited in discussions of reference-group theory, also involves variations in judgment arising from a comparison of one's own group with others.[1] In this mode of application, then, a reference group is a standard or check point which an actor uses in forming his estimate of the situation, particularly his own position within it. Logically, then, *any* group with which an actor is familiar may become a reference group.

A second referent of the concept is that group in which the actor aspires to gain or maintain acceptance: hence, a group whose claims are paramount in situations requiring choice. The reference group of the socially ambitious is said to consist of people of higher strata whose status symbols are imitated. Merton and Kitt interpret the expressions of willingness and felt readiness for combat on the part of inexperienced troops, as opposed to the humility of battle-hardened veterans, as the efforts of newcomers to identify themselves with veterans to whom they had mistakenly imputed certain values.[2] Thus, the concept is used to point to an association of human beings among whom one seeks to gain, maintain, or enhance his status; a reference group is that group in which one desires to participate.

In a third usage the concept signifies that group whose perspective constitutes the frame of reference of the actor. Thus, Sherif speaks of reference groups as groups whose norms are used as anchoring points in structuring the perceptual

1. H. H. Hyman, "The Psychology of Status," *Archives of Psychology*, XXXVIII (1942), 15; R. K. Merton and A. Kitt (Rossi), "Contributions to the Theory of Reference Group Behavior," in R. K. Merton and P. F. Lazarsfeld (eds.), *Studies in the Scope and Method of "The American Soldier"* (New York: Free Press, 1950), pp. 42–53, 69; D. W. Chapman and J. Volkmann, "A Social Determinant of the Level of Aspiration," *Journal of Abnormal and Social Psychology*, XXXIV (1939), 225–238.

2. *Op. cit.*, pp. 75–76.

field,[3] and Merton and Kitt speak of a "social frame of reference" for interpretations.[4] Through direct or vicarious participation in a group one comes to perceive the world from its standpoint. Yet this group need not be one in which he aspires for acceptance; a member of some minority group may despise it but still see the world largely through its eyes. When used in this manner, the concept of reference group points more to a psychological phenomenon than to an objectively existing group of men; it refers to an organization of the actor's experience. That is to say, it is a structuring of his perceptual field. In this usage a reference group becomes any collectivity, real or imagined, envied or despised, whose perspective is assumed by the actor.

Thus, an examination of current usage discloses three distinct referents for a single concept: (1) groups which serve as comparison points; (2) groups to which men aspire; and (3) groups whose perspectives are assumed by the actor. Although these terms may be related, treating together what should be clearly delineated as generically different can lead only to further confusion. It is the contention of this paper that the restriction of the concept of reference group to the third alternative—that group whose perspective constitutes the frame of reference of the actor—will increase its usefulness in research. Any group or object may be used for comparisons, and one need not assume the role of those with whom he compares his fate; hence, the first usage serves a quite different purpose and may be eliminated from further consideration. Under some circumstances, however, group loyalties and aspirations are related to perspectives assumed, and the character of this relationship calls for further exploration. Such a discussion necessitates a restatement of the familiar, but, in view of the difficulties in some of the work on reference groups, repetition may not be entirely out of order. In spite of the enthusiasm of some proponents there is actually nothing new in reference-group theory.

Culture and Personal Controls

Thomas pointed out many years ago that what a man does depends largely upon his definition of the situation. One may add that the manner in which one consistently defines a succession of situations depends upon his organized perspective. A perspective is an ordered view of one's world—what is taken for granted about the attributes of various objects, events, and human nature. It is an order of things remembered and expected as well as things actually perceived, an organized conception of what is plausible and what is possible; it constitutes the matrix through which one perceives his environment. The fact that men have such ordered perspectives enables them to conceive of their ever changing

3. M. Sherif, "The Concept of Reference Groups in Human Relations," in M. Sherif and M. O. Wilson (eds.), *Group Relations at the Crossroads* (New York: Harper & Row, 1953), pp. 203–231.

4. *Op. cit.*, pp. 49–50.

world as relatively stable, orderly, and predictable. As Riezler puts it, one's perspective is an outline scheme which, running ahead of experience, defines and guides it.

There is abundant experimental evidence to show that perception is selective; that the organization of perceptual experience depends in part upon what is anticipated and what is taken for granted. Judgments rest upon perspectives, and people with different outlooks define identical situations differently, responding selectively to the environment. Thus, a prostitute and a social worker walking through a slum area notice different things; a sociologist should perceive relationships that others fail to observe. Any change of perspectives—becoming a parent for the first time, learning that one will die in a few months, or suffering the failure of well-laid plans—leads one to notice things previously overlooked and to see the familiar world in a different light. As Goethe contended, history is continually rewritten, not so much because of the discovery of new documentary evidence, but because the changing perspectives of historians lead to new selections from the data.

Culture, as the concept is used by Redfield, refers to a perspective that is shared by those in a particular group; it consists of those "conventional understandings, manifest in act and artifact, that characterize societies."[5] Since these conventional understandings are the premises of action, those who share a common culture engage in common modes of action. Culture is not a static entity but a continuing process; norms are creatively reaffirmed from day to day in social interaction. Those taking part in collective transactions approach one another with set expectations, and the realization of what is anticipated successively confirms and reinforces their perspectives. In this way, people in each cultural group are continuously supporting one another's perspectives, each by responding to the others in expected ways. In this sense culture is a product of communication.

In his discussion of endopsychic social control Mead spoke of men "taking the role of the generalized other," meaning by that that each person approaches his world from the standpoint of the culture of his group. Each perceives, thinks, forms judgments, and controls himself according to the frame of reference of the group in which he is participating. Since he defines objects, other people, the world, and himself from the perspective that he shares with others, he can visualize his proposed line of action from this generalized standpoint, anticipate the reactions of others, inhibit undesirable impulses, and thus guide his conduct. The socialized person is a society in miniature; he sets the same standards of conduct for himself as he sets for others, and he judges himself in the same terms. He can define situations properly and meet his obligations, even in the absence of other people, because, as already noted, his perspective always takes into

5. R. Redfield, *The Folk Culture of Yucatan* (Chicago: University of Chicago Press, 1941), p. 132. For a more explicit presentation of a behavioristic theory of culture see *The Selected Writings of Edward Sapir in Language, Culture and Personality*, ed. D. G. Mandelbaum (Berkeley: University of California Press, 1949), pp. 104–109, 308–331, 544–559.

account the expectations of others. Thus, it is the ability to define situations from the same standpoint as others that makes personal controls possible.[6] When Mead spoke of assuming the role of the generalized other, he was not referring to people but to perspectives shared with others in a transaction.

The consistency in the behavior of a man in a wide variety of social contexts is to be accounted for, then, in terms of his organized perspective. Once one has incorporated a particular outlook from his group, it becomes his orientation toward the world, and he brings this frame of reference to bear on all new situations. Thus, immigrants and tourists often misinterpret the strange things they see, and a disciplined Communist would define each situation differently from the non-Communist. Although reference-group behavior is generally studied in situations where choices seem possible, the actor himself is often unaware that there are alternatives.

The proposition that men think, feel, and see things from a standpoint peculiar to the group in which they participate is an old one, repeatedly emphasized by students of anthropology and of the sociology of knowledge. Why, then, the sudden concern with reference-group theory during the past decade? The concept of reference group actually introduces a minor refinement in the long familiar theory, made necessary by the special characteristics of modern mass societies. First of all, in modern societies special problems arise from the fact that men sometimes use the standards of groups in which they are *not* recognized members, sometimes of groups in which they have never participated directly, and sometimes of groups that do not exist at all. Second, in our mass society, characterized as it is by cultural pluralism, each person internalizes several perspectives, and this occasionally gives rise to embarrassing dilemmas which call for systematic study. Finally, the development of reference-group theory has been facilitated by the increasing interest in social psychology and the subjective aspects of group life, a shift from a predominant concern with objective social structures to an interest in the experiences of the participants whose regularized activities make such structures discernible.

A reference group, then, is that group whose outlook is used by the actor as the frame of reference in the organization of his perceptual field. All kinds of groupings, with great variations in size, composition, and structure, may become reference groups. Of greatest importance for most people are those groups in which they participate directly—what have been called membership groups—especially those containing a number of persons with whom one stands in a primary relationship. But in some transactions one may assume the perspective attributed to some social category—a social class, an ethnic group, those in a given community, or those concerned with some special interest. On the other hand, reference groups may be imaginary, as in the case of artists who are

6. G. H. Mead, "The Genesis of the Self and Social Control," *International Journal of Ethics*, XXXV (1925), 251–277, and *Mind, Self and Society* (Chicago: University of Chicago Press, 1934), pp. 152–164. Cf. T. Parsons, "The Superego and the Theory of Social Systems," *Psychiatry*, XV (1952), 15–25.

"born ahead of their times," scientists who work for "humanity," or philan-thropists who give for "posterity." Such persons estimate their endeavors from a postulated perspective imputed to people who have not yet been born. There are others who live for a distant past, idealizing some period in history and longing for "the good old days," criticizing current events from a standpoint imputed to people long since dead. Reference groups, then, arise through the internalization of norms; they constitute the structure of expectations imputed to some audience for whom one organizes his conduct.

The Construction of Social Worlds

As Dewey emphasized, society exists in and through communication; com-mon perspectives—common cultures—emerge through participation in common communication channels. It is through social participation that perspectives shared in a group are internalized. Despite the frequent recitation of this proposi-tion, its full implications, especially for the analysis of mass societies, are not often appreciated. Variations in outlook arise through differential contact and association; the maintenance of social distance—through segregation, conflict, or simply the reading of different literature—leads to the formation of distinct cultures. Thus, people in different social classes develop different modes of life and outlook, not because of anything inherent in economic position, but because similarity of occupation and limitations set by income level dispose them to certain restricted communication channels. Those in different ethnic groups form their own distinctive cultures because their identifications incline them to interact intimately with each other and to maintain reserve before outsiders. Different intellectual traditions within social psychology—psychoanalysis, scale analysis, *Gestalt*, pragmatism—will remain separated as long as those in each tradition restrict their sympathetic attention to works of their own school and view others with contempt or hostility. Some social scientists are out of touch with the masses of the American people because they eschew the mass media, especially television, or expose themselves only condescendingly. Even the out-look that the *avant-garde* regards as "cosmopolitan" is culture bound, for it also is a product of participation in restricted communication channels—books, magazines, meetings, exhibits, and taverns which are out of bounds for most people in the middle classes. Social participation may even be vicarious, as it is in the case of a medievalist who acquires his perspective solely through books.

Even casual observation reveals the amazing variety of standards by which Americans live. The inconsistencies and contradictions which characterize modern mass societies are products of the multitude of communication channels and the ease of participation in them. Studying relatively isolated societies, anthropo-logists can speak meaningfully of "culture areas" in geographical terms; in such societies common cultures have a territorial base, for only those who live to-gether can interact. In modern industrial societies, however, because of the development of rapid transportation and the media of mass communication, people who are geographically dispersed can communicate effectively. Culture areas are coterminous with communication channels; since communication networks are no longer coterminous with territorial boundaries, culture areas overlap and have lost their territorial bases. Thus, next-door neighbors may be complete strangers; even in common parlance there is an intuitive recognition of the diversity of perspectives, and we speak meaningfully of people living in different social worlds—the academic world, the world of children, the world of fashion.

Modern mass societies, indeed, are made up of a bewildering variety of social worlds. Each is an organized outlook, built up by people in their interaction with one another; hence, each communication channel gives rise to a separate world. Probably the greatest sense of identification and solidarity is to be found in the various communal structures—the underworld, ethnic minorities, the social elite. Such communities are frequently spatially segregated, which isolates them further from the outer world, while the "grapevine" and foreign-language presses provide internal contacts. Another common type of social world consists of the associational structures—the world of medicine, of organized labor, of the theater, of café society. These are held together not only by various voluntary associations within each locality but also by periodicals like *Variety*, specialized journals, and feature sections in newspapers. Finally, there are the loosely connected universes of special interest—the world of sports, of the stamp collector, of the daytime serial—serviced by mass media programs and magazines like *Field and Stream*. Each of these worlds is a unity of order, a universe of regularized mutual response. Each is an area in which there is some structure which permits reasonable anticipation of the behavior of others, hence, an area in which one may act with a sense of security and confidence.[7] Each social world, then, is a culture area, the boundaries of which are set neither by territory nor by formal group membership but by the limits of effective communication.

Since there is a variety of communication channels, differing in stability and extent, social worlds differ in composition, size, and the territorial distribution of the participants. Some, like local cults, are small and concentrated; others, like the intellectual world, are vast and the participants dispersed. Worlds differ in the extent and clarity of their boundaries; each is confined by some kind of horizon, but this may be wide or narrow, clear or vague. The fact that social worlds are not coterminous with the universe of men is recognized; those in the underworld are well aware of the fact that outsiders do not share their values. Worlds differ in exclusiveness and in the extent to which they demand the loyalty of their participants. Most important of all, social worlds are not static entities; shared perspectives are continually being reconstituted.

7. Cf. K. Riezler, *Man: Mutable and Immutable* (Chicago: Henry Regnery Co., 1950), pp. 62–72; L. Landgrebe, "The World as a Phenomenological Problem," *Philosophy and Phenomenological Research*, I (1940), 38–58; and A. Schuetz, "The Stranger: An Essay in Social Psychology," *American Journal of Sociology*, XLIX (1944), 499–507.

Worlds come into existence with the establishment of communication channels; when life conditions change, social relationships may also change, and these worlds may disappear.

Every social world has some kind of communication system—often nothing more than differential association—in which there develops a special universe of discourse, sometimes an argot. Special meanings and symbols further accentuate differences and increase social distance from outsiders. In each world there are special norms of conduct, a set of values, a special prestige ladder, characteristic career lines, and a common outlook toward life—a Weltanschauung. In the case of elites there may even arise a code of honor which holds only for those who belong, while others are dismissed as beings somewhat less than human from whom bad manners may be expected. A social world, then, is an order conceived which serves as the stage on which each participant seeks to carve out his career and to maintain and enhance his status.

One of the characteristics of life in modern mass societies is simultaneous participation in a variety of social worlds. Because of the ease with which the individual may expose himself to a number of communication channels, he may lead a segmentalized life, participating successively in a number of unrelated activities. Futhermore, the particular combination of social worlds differs from person to person; this is what led Simmel to declare that each stands at that point at which a unique combination of social circles intersects. The geometric analogy is a happy one, for it enables us to conceive the numerous possibilities of combinations and the different degrees of participation in each circle. To understand what a man does, we must get at his unique perspective—what he takes for granted and how he defines the situation—but in mass societies we must learn in addition the social world in which he is participating in a given act.

Loyalty and Selective Responsiveness

In a mass society where each person internalizes numerous perspectives there are bound to be some incongruities and conflicts. The overlapping of group affiliation and participation, however, need not lead to difficulties and is usually unnoticed. The reference groups of most persons are mutually sustaining. Thus, the soldier who volunteers for hazardous duty on the battlefield may provoke anxiety in his family but is not acting contrary to their values; both his family and his comrades admire courage and disdain cowardice, Behavior may be inconsistent, as in the case of the proverbial office tyrant who is meek before his wife, but it is not noticed if the transactions occur in dissociated contexts. Most people live more or less compartmentalized lives, shifting from one social world to another as they participate in a succession of transactions. In each world their roles are different, their relations to other participants are different, and they reveal a different facet of their personalities. Men have become so accustomed to this mode of life that they manage to conceive of themselves as reasonably consistent human beings in spite of this segmentalization and are generally not aware of the fact that their acts do not fit into a coherent pattern.

People become acutely aware of the existence of different outlooks only when they are successively caught in situations in which conflicting demands are made upon them, all of which cannot possibly be satisfied. While men generally avoid making difficult decisions, these dilemmas and contradictions of status may force a choice between two social worlds. These conflicts are essentially alternative ways of defining the same situation, arising from several possible perspectives. In the words of William James, "As a man I pity you, but as an official I must show you no mercy; as a politician I regard him as an ally, but as a moralist I loathe him." In playing roles in different social worlds, one imputes different expectations to others whose differences cannot always be compromised. The problem is that of selecting the perspective for defining the situation. In Mead's terminology, which generalized other's role is to be taken? It is only in situations where alternative definitions are possible that problems of loyalty arise.

Generally such conflicts are ephemeral; in critical situations contradictions otherwise unnoticed are brought into the open, and painful choices are forced. In poorly integrated societies, however, some people find themselves continually beset with such conflicts. The Negro intellectual, children of mixed marriages or of immigrants, the foreman in a factory, the professional woman, the military chaplain—all live in the interstices of well-organized structures and are marginal men.[8] In most instances they manage to make their way through their compartmentalized lives, although personal maladjustments are apparently frequent. In extreme cases amnesia and dissociation of personality can occur.

Much of the interest in reference groups arises out of concern with situations in which a person is confronted with the necessity of choosing between two or more organized perspectives. The hypothesis has been advanced that the choice of reference groups—conformity to the norms of the group whose perspective is assumed—is a function of one's interpersonal relations; to what extent the culture of a group serves as the matrix for the organization of perceptual experience depends upon one's relationship and personal loyalty to others who share that outlook. Thus, when personal relations to others in the group deteriorate, as sometimes happens in a military unit after continued defeat, the norms become less binding, and the unit may disintegrate in panic. Similarly, with the transformation of personal relationships between parent and child in late adolescence, the desires and standards of the parents often become less obligatory.

It has been suggested further that choice of reference groups rests upon personal loyalty to significant others of that social world. "Significant others," for Sullivan, are those persons directly responsible for the internalization of

8. Cf. E. C. Hughes, "Dilemmas and Contradictions of Status," *American Journal of Sociology*, L (1945), 353–359, and E. V. Stonequist, *The Marginal Man* (New York: Charles Scribner's Sons, 1937).

norms. Socialization is a product of a gradual accumulation of experiences with certain people, particularly those with whom we stand in primary relations, and significant others are those who are actually involved in the cultivation of abilities, values, and outlook.[9] Crucial, apparently, is the character of one's emotional ties with them. Those who think the significant others have treated them with affection and consideration have a sense of personal obligation that is binding under all circumstances, and they will be loyal even at great personal sacrifice. Since primary relations are not necessarily satisfactory, however, the reactions may be negative. A person who is well aware of the expectations of significant others may go out of his way to reject them. This may account for the bifurcation of orientation in minority groups, where some remain loyal to the parental culture while others seek desperately to become assimilated in the larger world. Some who withdraw from the uncertainties of real life may establish loyalties to perspectives acquired through vicarious relationships with characters encountered in books.[10]

Perspectives are continually subjected to the test of reality. All perception is hypothetical. Because of what is taken for granted from each standpoint, each situation is approached with a set of expectations; if transactions actually take place as anticipated, the perspective itself is reinforced. It is thus the confirming responses of other people that provide support for perspectives.[11] But in mass societies the responses of others vary, and in the study of reference groups the problem is that of ascertaining *whose* confirming responses will sustain a given point of view.

The Study of Mass Societies

Because of the differentiated character of modern mass societies, the concept of reference group, or some suitable substitute, will always have a central place in any realistic conceptual scheme for its analysis. As is pointed out above, it will be most useful if it is used to designate that group whose perspective is assumed by the actor as the frame of reference for the organization of his perceptual experience. Organized perspectives arise in and become shared through participation in common communication channels, and the diversity of mass societies arises from the multiplicity of channels and the ease with which one may participate in them.

9. H. S. Sullivan, *Conceptions of Modern Psychiatry* (Washington, D.C.: W. A. White Psychiatric Foundation, 1947), pp. 18–22.

10. Cf. R. R. Grinker and J. P. Spiegel, *Men under Stress* (Philadelphia: Blakiston Co., 1945), pp. 122–126; and E. A. Shils and M. Janowitz, "Cohesion and Disintegration in the Wehrmacht in World War II," *Public Opinion Quarterly*, XII (1948), 280–315.

11. Cf. G. H. Mead, *The Philosophy of the Act* (Chicago: University of Chicago Press, 1938), pp. 107–173; and L. Postman, "Toward a General Theory of Cognition," in J. H. Rohrer and M. Sherif (eds.), *Social Psychology at the Crossroads* (New York: Harper & Row, 1951), pp. 242–272.

Mass societies are not only diversified and pluralistic but also continually changing. The successive modification of life-conditions compels changes in social relationships, and any adequate analysis requires a study of these transformational processes themselves. Here the concept of reference group can be of crucial importance. For example, all forms of social mobility, from sudden conversions to gradual assimilation, may be regarded essentially as displacements of reference groups, for they involve a loss of responsiveness to the demands of one social world and the adoption of the perspective of another. It may be hypothesized that the disaffection occurs first on the level of personal relations, followed by a weakening sense of obligation, a rejection of old claims, and the establishment of a new perspective. The conflicts that characterize all persons in marginal roles are of special interest in that they provide opportunities for cross-sectional analyses of the processes of social change.

In the analysis of the behavior of man in mass societies the crucial problem is that of ascertaining how a person defines the situation, which perspective he uses in arriving at such a definition, and who constitutes the audience whose responses provide the necessary confirmation and support for his position. This calls for focusing attention upon the expectations the actor imputes to others, the communication channels in which he participates, and his relations with those with whom he identifies himself. In the study of conflict, imagery provides a fertile source of data. At moments of indecision, when in doubt and confusion, who appears in imagery? In this manner the significant other can be identified.

An adequate analysis of modern mass societies requires the development of concepts and operations for the description of the manner in which each actor's orientation toward his world is successively reconstituted. Since perception is selective and perspectives differ, different items are noticed and a progressively diverse set of images arises, even among those exposed to the same media of mass communication. The concept of reference group summarizes differential associations and loyalties and thus facilitates the study of selective perception. It becomes, therefore, an indispensable tool for comprehending the diversity and dynamic character of the kind of society in which we live.

PART II

Selection and Acceptance of Reference Groups

THE readings in Part II all identify one or more factors leading to the selection or acceptance of a particular group or status category as a reference point for comparative or normative judgments.

The study by Hyman attempts to identify, by means of semistructured interviews, the groups and individuals spontaneously used by subjects in making comparative judgments of their status (rank) along a variety of specified dimensions (for example, intellectual, social, economic). Hyman found that both similarity and contrast served as principles for the selection of comparative reference groups and that realistic appraisal of one's rank was only one of several possible motives governing the direction of comparison. For example, he explicitly commented on the mechanisms of status enhancement and status depreciation, but noted also that the feeling accompanying comparison with groups having either superior or inferior status could not be inferred from the direction of comparison alone. All these points are taken up again in subsequent selections.

Festinger's "Theory of Social Comparison Processes" grew out of a considerable body of experimental work on opinion formation and influence processes in small groups. Festinger accounts for the often observed pressures toward uniformity of opinion in such groups by postulating (1) a universal need to evaluate the correctness of one's opinions; (2) reliance on comparison with other people if more "objective" means are not available; (3) the impossibility of making precise evaluations unless others hold opinions "close" to one's own. In the selection reprinted here, the theory is extended to include evaluation of one's abilities as well as opinions; and in subsequent work it has been extended to include, in addition, evaluation of the appropriateness of emotional responses.[1]

Festinger's theory is perhaps the most precisely worked out statement of comparative reference group processes for the special case when (1) the purpose of comparison is accurate appraisal of one's abilities or opinions and (2) other possible dimensions of comparison are experimentally held constant.[2] Both of these qualifications are important. Concerning the first, Hyman's study has indicated, and several later selections demonstrate in greater detail, that accurate appraisal is only one of several possible motives underlying comparison with others. Concerning the second, one would want to know which of several possible bases of relationship to others is selected as crucial by a given individual. In order to evaluate the correctness of his political opinions, for example, will he choose for comparison someone close in opinion but dissimilar in, say, occupational and educational status, or will he rather choose someone close in occupational and educational status but dissimilar in opinion? Questions such as these, which lie at the heart of comparative reference group theory, have not been posed by social comparison theory.[3]

Patchen's study of wage comparisons derives from the "relative deprivation" rather than the "social comparison" branch of reference group theory.[4] Patchen's major contribution is to test explicitly the

1. See, for example, Stanley S. Schachter, *The Psychology of Affiliation*, Stanford, Calif.: Stanford University Press, 1959; H. B. Gerard and J. M. Rabbie, "Fear and Social Comparison," *Journal of Abnormal and Social Psychology*, 62: 586–592, 1961; I. Sarnoff and P. G. Zimbardo, "Anxiety, Fear, and Social Affiliation," *Journal of Abnormal and Social Psychology*, 62: 356–363, 1961.

2. The experiments do not deliberately eliminate variation in other dimensions of status, but by selecting subjects who *are* similar in significant respects (usually, undergraduates), and by making the opinion or ability the only salient basis of comparison, they eliminate such variations for all practical purposes.

3. Jerome Singer makes this point in a recent review article entitled "Social Comparison—Progress and Issues," in Bibb Latane (ed.), "Studies in Social Comparison," special supplement to the *Journal of Experimental and Social Psychology*, 1966.

4. Since some of the key terms are common to both branches, it may be well to note here some of the different uses to which they have been put. *Evaluation*, in social comparison theory, is given several operational meanings. It is sometimes used to refer to the degree of confidence with which an opinion is held, or to the readiness with which it is abandoned under pressure. In relation to ability, it sometimes refers to a qualitative appraisal (good, fair, poor, etc.) but often to a subject's estimate of the score he made, or will make, on some test of performance. As used in connection with relative deprivation, *evaluation* invariably refers to a qualitative appraisal of some sort.

These differences in meaning follow from more fundamental differences. Social comparison theory is a "cognitive" theory, in the sense that its basic postulate is that

hypothesis that feelings of satisfaction or dissatisfaction with a particular comparison depend, not on the direction of that comparison but on the congruence or incongruence of other relevant factors. If, for example, a worker compares himself with someone earning more, who has also had more training and experience, the fact of greater earnings is congruent with these other factors and is likely to lead to relatively greater satisfaction than comparison with someone earning more, but with less training and less experience than the subject.[5] Indirectly, the article by Form and Geschwender also tends to support Patchen's hypothesis, since those workers who have experienced more occupational mobility relative to others like themselves—their brothers, fathers, and the sons of fathers with similar occupational backgrounds—also report greater satisfaction with their present jobs.

Patchen, however, also hypothesized that under certain circumstances individuals may be motivated to make "dissonant" rather than "consonant" comparisons. Such comparisons, and the consequent dissatisfaction, can act as a lever for change (of jobs, for example) or lead to demands for change (in pay, for example). One might speculate that willingness to make such comparisons is dependent in part on perceived opportunity to bring about the desired changes. Patchen does not test this subsidiary hypothesis, but he does show that men who accept little personal responsibility for their relatively disadvantaged position make more dissonant comparisons, and express more dissatisfaction with them, than men who accept a great deal of responsibility. Among the former, presumably no

---

there exists a universal drive to know, accurately, how correct, adequate, or appropriate one's opinions, abilities, or emotions are. Researchers working with the concept of relative deprivation, or with comparative reference processes generally, have not made this exclusive assumption. They have, on the one hand, examined the individual's motivations in making a particular comparison (cognitive accuracy may be one of these); and, on the other, they have examined variations in the structure of the situation that, quite apart from individual motives, may force a comparison of one kind rather than another.

The excerpt from Patchen's study which is reprinted here focuses on motivations for particular kinds of comparisons, and on their consequences, but the original study also gave attention to structural factors. See Martin Patchen, *The Choice of Wage Comparisons*, Englewood Cliffs, N.J.: Prentice-Hall, Inc., 1961.

5. In a different context, Homans has labeled the former condition as one of "distributive justice," and has hypothesized that "the more to a man's disadvantage the rule of distributive justice fails of realization, the more likely he is to display the emotional behavior we call anger." (George C. Homans, *Social Behavior: Its Elementary Forms*, New York: Harcourt, Brace & World, Inc., 1961, p. 75.) Both Patchen and Homans assume that if earnings are perceived as congruent with merit, discrepancies in earnings will be perceived as "just." Runciman, on the other hand, proposes that perceived congruence of earnings with need is an even more important condition for the existence of "social justice." (Cf. W. G. Runciman, *Relative Deprivation and Social Justice*, London: Routledge & Kegan Paul, Ltd., 1966, Chaps. 12 and 13.)

feelings of inferiority are attached to the comparison, and the dissatisfaction is directed outward; among the latter, inferiority feelings do come into play, and dissatisfaction is directed inward. Patchen has thus provided one answer to the question posed by Merton and Rossi: "When are relatively slim life-chances taken by men as a normal and expectable state of affairs which they attribute to their own personal inadequacies and when are they regarded as the results of an arbitrary social system of mobility . . . ?"[6]

The article by Stern and Keller, unfortunately one of the few studies of reference group processes in a society other than that of the United States, is of interest for methodological as well as substantive reasons. Like Hyman's study, but with a larger sample and traditional survey methods, it aims to identify what their respondents would consider a satisfactory standard of living. It has been shown (for example by Chapman and Volkmann[7] and by Hyman) that subjective status can be made to vary by experimentally varying the reference groups to be used by the subject. But it has also been shown that such subjective estimates of status are reliable (that is, remain constant over time) for only some of the reference groups specified by the experimenter. Hyman, for example, has shown that economic status is judged reliably only in relation to the occupational group, and social status in relation to the reference group of friends.[8] Presumably, reliable judgments are made in relation to those groups habitually and spontaneously used by the subject, and it is these which it is the task of reference group research to discover. In assessing the groups spontaneously mentioned by their French respondents, Stern and Keller conclude that close associates—particularly family and friends— constitute the major self-selected points of reference for comparative as well as normative judgments about living standards.

The selection by Runciman is part of a larger study[9] in which the author reports the results of a 1962 survey, of the adult population of England and Wales, which was specifically designed to assess relative deprivation with respect to both economic class position and social status or prestige. In addition to reporting the results of the survey, Runciman summarizes the historical changes presumed to underlie present attitudes and outlines a theory of "social justice," which is

6. The answer is only one step removed from the question, since the conditions under which men accept much or little responsibility for their fate obviously remain to be identified.

7. D. W. Chapman and J. Volkmann, "A Social Determinant of the Level of Aspiration," *Journal of Abnormal and Social Psychology*, 1939, 34: 225–238.

8. H. H. Hyman, "The Psychology of Status," *Archives of Psychology*, No. 269, 1942, p. 57.

9. Runciman, *op. cit.*

essentially a very general statement of the conditions under which people *ought* to feel relatively deprived.

The major finding emerging from his study is that, with respect to economic position,[10] there is much less relative deprivation in contemporary English society—whether on behalf of oneself, or of one's social group—than the facts of inequality might lead one to expect. This is true regardless of whether comparative references are spontaneously elicited or whether comparisons are suggested by the interviewer; whether the comparison is "other people who are earning more" or the size of income required "to maintain a proper standard of living for people like yourself"; whether the comparison is made in terms of earnings or ownership of consumer goods. In each case, the sense of relative deprivation is limited because comparative reference groups are restricted in scope, being chosen most often from those whose class situation approximates to that of the respondent. A corollary is that class-conscious, or, as Runciman puts it, "fraternalistic" comparisons, are at a minimum.

Although both Runciman and Stern and Keller suggest that a more mobile society, such as that of the United States, might yield a wider variety of comparative reference groups, the article by Form and Geschwender suggests that there, too, family and close associates constitute the most significant frame of reference for assessing occupational achievement. The conditions under which comparisons tend to be made more randomly, or even with those of widely discrepant status, have yet to be adequately specified both theoretically and empirically.

As we have seen, the implication of most of the articles in this section is that comparisons will tend to be made with persons or groups "close" to the respondent in some way. Generally, however, "closeness" includes both similarity and propinquity.[11] What happens when these two factors work in opposite directions? Helen Strauss's analysis of comparison processes among the blind is particularly interesting because it separates the two. The overwhelming majority of her blind respondents chose to compare themselves with persons who are dissimilar—that is, with the seeing. Surrounded by people who are not blind, they reflect this fact in their choice of reference groups. When their environment and socialization

10. With respect to *status*, Runciman argues, and presents some evidence to support his argument, that relative deprivation has increased among the less well placed at the same time that their actual advance toward equality has also increased. He suggests, however, that aspirations for higher status have increasingly taken the form of rising *out* of one's class, rather than *with* it.

11. For an investigation of the effects of both occupational similarity and residential propinquity on mate selection in Oslo, see Natalie Rogoff Ramsoy, "Assortative Mating and the Structure of Cities," *American Sociological Review*, 31: 773–786, 1966. Ramsoy finds that there is no relation between residential nearness and occupational similarity, and concludes that the two are independently related to choice of marriage partners.

emphasize isolation from the seeing, their reliance on other blind persons increases correspondingly.

Strauss's study thus suggests that under certain conditions, and not only among the blind, propinquity may be more important than similarity in structuring the choice of comparative reference groups, but we are obviously far from being able to specify what those conditions are. How many dissimilars in close propinquity (interaction?) are required to shift the direction of comparison? What other factors can substitute for propinquity? When, for example, does the Negro in the affluent society stop comparing his lot with that of other Negroes?[12]

Similarity and propinquity also enter into the choice or acceptance of *normative* reference groups. The first article by Ruth Hartley demonstrates that the more similar the values of a new membership group are perceived to be to those already held by the subject, the more readily will he accept that group as a normative reference group. Newcomb's twenty-five-year follow-up of a group of his Bennington subjects extends this formulation, indicating that one important factor in the *selection* of new reference individuals (or groups) is the perceived congruence of their values with the subject's own.[13] The selection by Festinger, Schachter, and Back, on the other hand, demonstrates that among persons who are similar, propinquity—or, in the authors' words, "functional distance"—is a powerful determinant in the formation of friendship groups, which subsequently function as potent normative reference groups.

In addition to similarity and propinquity, the selections included in this section identify several other factors pertinent to the choice or acceptance of normative reference groups. The second selection by Hartley, for example, points to the importance of a personality variable— a tendency toward "acceptance of the cultural *status quo*"—in determining

12. Concerning this point, see the Introduction to Part III.

13. That people are sometimes motivated to adopt as a point of reference a group whose values are quite dissimilar from their own has often been noted, but the determinants of this choice are less well known. Merton and Rossi provide an illustration of this phenomenon in Case # 5, which relates rates of promotion among enlisted men to their conformity to Army, and officer, norms (see pages 56–65 above). The classic instance is that of the "assimilation" of immigrants, or of their children. In either case, what seems to be required is a perception by the individual that the reward for adopting the divergent values will be greater than his cost in relinquishing familiar ones; this, in turn, presupposes some familiarity, and perhaps interaction, with the group(s) embodying the divergent values. But both the visibility of groups and their ability to confer rewards are socially patterned. As Merton has stated: "To the extent that status-conferral [one form of reward] represents a major basis for the selection of non-membership groups, the social structure, which assigns varying degrees of prestige and authority to groups and which determines the degree of accessibility to them, will tend to pattern this selection for those variously located in the society." (Robert K. Merton, "Continuities in the Theory of Reference Groups and Social Structure," *Social Theory and Social Structure*, rev. ed., New York: The Free Press, 1957, p. 305.)

the ease with which a new membership group of a certain kind is also accepted as a reference group. Merton's article on local and cosmopolitan influentials identifies two contrasting reference orientations among people perceived as influential by respondents in a small town on the Eastern seaboard. Though not explicitly concerned with the determinants of these orientations, Merton does identify two related factors: degree of "rootedness" in the community, and whether the influential person has achieved success in his career within the community or outside it. From these contrasting reference orientations flow a variety of predictable differences in group memberships, communications behavior, and styles of influence.

Merton's article has several larger implications worth stressing. It is one of the very few instances where the reference groups of *elite*, rather than rank-and-file, subjects have been studied. We may well think of a kind of social chain in which ordinary people take as normative reference individuals some elite persons, who in turn take their reference orientations from still others. Recall the old-fashioned phrasing of the phenomenon of the "influential" in the writing of E. A. Ross, who is part of the tradition of thought from which the concept of *reference group* grew. In 1908, he spoke of the "radiant points of conventionality" which guide us lesser lights. He went on to say: "Every editor, politician, banker, capitalist, railroad president, employer, clergyman, or judge has a following with whom his opinion has weight. He, in turn, is likely to have his authorities. The anatomy of collective opinion shows it to be organized from centers and subcenters, forming a kind of intellectual feudal system."[14]

Localism-cosmopolitanism as a dimension for ordering the selection of normative reference groups seems very relevant to current social problems. For example, as the people, and leaders, of Southern communities orient themselves to local reference groups and norms, integration is less likely to be spurred.[15] It would be valuable applied social research to determine and foster the conditions leading to the selection of cosmopolitan reference groups.

The two final articles in this section call attention to the fact that reference groups are multiple. A variable number may function as reference groups for any given individual, who in turn may use a given group as a frame of reference for one or many aspects of his behavior. Consequently, situational factors can give potency to the norms of a particular reference group that otherwise might have remained latent. Although, in the two experiments cited, the "aroused" reference groups were also membership

14. E. A. Ross, *Social Psychology*, New York: The Macmillan Company, 1908, p. 348.

15. See, for example, the study of a community in North Carolina by M. Tumin and R. Rotberg, "Leaders, the Led, and the Law: A Case Study in Social Change," *Public Opinion Quarterly*, 21 : 355–370, 1957.

groups, the same principle applies with equal validity to the norms of non-membership groups.

The articles by Kelley and by Festinger remind us again of the considerable importance of structural variables for reference group processes. Regardless of the absolute ordering of importance of an individual's reference groups, situational factors may make the norms of some group more salient than those of another, and therefore more likely to be acted upon. As with similarity and propinquity, one set of questions to which this formulation gives rise is how much absolute importance can be traded for how much situational salience, for which kinds of norms, people, and situations.

A Theory of
Social Comparison Processes

Leon Festinger

IN THIS paper we shall present a further development of a previously published theory concerning opinion influence processes in social groups. This further development has enabled us to extend the theory to deal with other areas, in addition to opinion formation, in which social comparison is important. Specifically, we shall develop below how the theory applies to the appraisal and evaluation of abilities as well as opinions.

Such theories and hypotheses in the area of social psychology are frequently viewed in terms of how "plausible" they seem. "Plausibility" usually means whether or not the theory or hypothesis fits one's intuition or one's common sense. In this meaning much of the theory which is to be presented here is not "plausible." The theory does, however, explain a considerable amount of data and leads to testable derivations. Three experiments, specifically designed to test predictions from this extension of the theory, have now been completed.[1] They all provide good corroboration. We will in the following pages develop the theory and present the relevant data.

Hypothesis I There exists, in the human organism, a drive to evaluate his opinions and his abilities.

Reprinted from *Human Relations*, 7 : 117–140, 1954, by permission of the author and the publisher.

The development of this theory was aided by a grant from the Behavioral Sciences Division of the Ford Foundation. It is part of the research program of the Laboratory for Research in Social Relations.

1. A. Dreyer, "Behavior in a Level of Aspiration Situation as Affected by Group Comparison," Ph.D. dissertation, University of Minnesota, 1953; L. Festinger, J. Torrey, and B. Willerman, "Self-Evaluation as a Function of Attraction to the Group," *Human Relations*, 7: 161–174, 1954; P. J. Hoffman, L. Festinger, and D. H. Lawrence, "Tendencies toward Comparability in Competitive Bargaining," *Human Relations*, 7: 141–159, 1954.

While opinions and abilities may, at first glance, seem to be quite different things, there is a close functional tie between them. They act together in the manner in which they affect behavior. A person's cognition (his opinions and beliefs) about the situation in which he exists and his appraisals of what he is capable of doing (his evaluation of his abilities) will together have bearing on his behavior. The holding of incorrect opinions and/or inaccurate appraisals of one's abilities can be punishing or even fatal in many situations.

It is necessary, before we proceed, to clarify the distinction between opinions and evaluations of abilities since at first glance it may seem that one's evaluation of one's own ability is an opinion about it. Abilities are of course manifested only through performance which is assumed to depend upon the particular ability. The clarity of the manifestation or performance can vary from instances where there is no clear ordering criterion of the ability to instances where the performance which reflects the ability can be clearly ordered. In the former case, the evaluation of the ability does function like other opinions which are not directly testable in "objective reality." For example, a person's evaluation of his ability to write poetry will depend to a large extent on the opinions which others have of his ability to write poetry. In cases where the criterion is unambiguous and can be clearly ordered, this furnishes an objective reality for the evaluation of one's ability so that it depends less on the opinions of other persons and depends more on actual comparison of one's performance with the performance of others. Thus, if a person evaluates his running ability, he will do so by comparing his time to run some distance with the times that other persons have taken.

In the following pages, when we talk about evaluating an ability, we shall mean specifically the evaluation of that ability in situations where the performance is unambiguous and is known. Most situations in real life will, of course, present situations which are a mixture of opinion and ability evaluation.

In a previous article[2] the author posited the existence of a drive to determine whether or not one's opinions were "correct." We are here stating that this same drive also produces behavior in people oriented toward obtaining an accurate appraisal of their abilities.

The behavioral implication of the existence of such a drive is that we would expect to observe behavior on the part of persons which enables them to ascertain whether or not their opinions are correct and also behavior which enables them accurately to evaluate their abilities. It is consequently necessary to answer the question as to how persons go about evaluating their opinions and their abilities.

Hypothesis II   To the extent that objective, non-social means are not available, people evaluate their opinions and abilities by comparison respectively with the opinions and abilities of others.

2. L. Festinger, "Informal Social Communication," *Psychological Review*, 57: 271–282, 1950.

In many instances, perhaps most, whether or not an opinion is correct cannot be immediately determined by reference to the physical world. Similarly it is frequently not possible to assess accurately one's ability by reference to the physical world. One could, of course, test the opinion that an object was fragile by hitting it with a hammer, but how is one to test the opinion that a certain political candidate is better than another, or that war is inevitable? Even when there is a possible immediate physical referent for an opinion, it is frequently not likely to be employed. The belief, for example, that tomatoes are poisonous to humans (which was widely held at one time) is unlikely to be tested. The situation is similar with respect to the evaluation of one's abilities. If the only use to which, say, jumping ability was put was to jump across a particular brook, it would be simple to obtain an accurate evaluation of one's ability in this respect. However, the unavailability of the opportunity for such clear testing and the vague and multipurpose use of various abilities generally make such a clear objective test not feasible or not useful. For example, how does one decide how intelligent one is? Also, one might find out how many seconds it takes a person to run a certain distance, but what does this mean with respect to his ability—is it adequate or not? For both opinions and abilities, to the extent that objective physical bases for evaluation are not available, subjective judgments of correct or incorrect opinion and subjectively accurate assessments of one's ability depend upon how one compares with other persons.

Corollary II A In the absence of both a physical and a social comparison, subjective evaluations of opinions and abilities are unstable.

There exists evidence from studies on "level of aspiration" which shows clearly the instability of evaluations of abilities in the absence of comparison with other persons.[3] The typical situation in an experiment designed to study "level of aspiration" is as follows: a person is given a task to perform which is serial in nature. This may be a series of trials of throwing darts at a target or a series of information tests or a series of puzzles or the like. After each trial the person is told what he scored (how many points he made or how many correct answers or how long it took) and is asked to state what score he expects to get or will try for on the next trial. These experiments have previously been interpreted in terms of goal directed behavior. If we examine the situation closely, however, it is apparent that the individual's stated 'level of aspiration" is actually a statement of what he considers a good performance to be. In other words, it

3. J. W. Gardner, "Level of Aspiration in Response to a Prearranged Sequence of Scores," *Journal of Experimental Psychology*, 25: 601–621, 1939; R. Gould, "An Experimental Analysis of 'Level of Aspiration,'" *Genetic Psychology Monographs*, 21: 1–116, 1939; F. Hoppe, "Erfolg und Misserfolg," *Psychologische Forschung*, 14: 1–62, 1930; K. Lewin, T. Dembo, L. Festinger, and P. S. Sears, "Level of Aspiration," in *Personality and the Behavior Disorders*, New York: Ronald Press Co., 1944, Vol. I, pp. 333–378; P. S. Sears, "Levels of Aspiration in Academically Successful and Unsuccessful Children," *Journal of Abnormal and Social Psychology*, 35: 498–536, 1940.

is his evaluation, at that time, of what score he should get, that is, his evaluation of his ability. The data show clearly that if the person scores as well as he said he expected to do, he feels he has done well (experiences success) and if he scores less than his "aspirations" he feels he has done poorly (experiences failure).[4]

Let us examine, then, the stability of these evaluations in a situation where the person performing the task has no opportunity for comparison with others. The data from these studies show that the "level of aspiration" fluctuates markedly as performance fluctuates. If the person makes a score better than his previous one, then what was formerly considered a good performance is no longer good and his "level of aspiration" goes up. If his performance drops, his "level of aspiration" drops. Even after a person has had a good deal of experience at a task, the evaluation of what is good performance continues to fluctuate.

Similar instability is found in the case of opinions. When, using the autokinetic effect, persons are asked to make judgments of how far the point of light moves, these judgments continue to fluctuate before there are any comparison persons.[5]

To the extent, then, that there are relevant data available, they tend to confirm *Corollary II A* concerning the instability of evaluations in the absence of comparisons.

Corollary II B   When an objective, non-social basis for the evaluation of one's ability or opinion is readily available persons will not evaluate their opinions or abilities by comparison with others.

Hochbaum[6] reports an experiment concerning the effect of knowledge of others' opinions on one's own opinion which corroborates *Corollary II B*. Half of the subjects in this experiment were persuaded by the experimenter that they were extremely good at being able to make correct judgments concerning things like the issue they were to discuss. The other half of the subjects were made to feel that they were extremely poor in making such judgments. They were then asked to write their opinions down and were handed back a slip of paper presumably reporting to them the opinions of each other person in the group. In this way the subjects were made to feel that most of the others in the group disagreed with them. Those subjects who were given an objective basis for feeling that their opinion was likely to be correct did not change their opinions very often in spite of the disagreement with others in the group. Those who had

---

4. E. R. Hilgard, E. M. Sait, and G. A. Magaret, "Level of Aspiration as Affected by Relative Standing in an Experimental Social Group," *Journal of Experimental Psychology*, 27: 411–421, 1940.

5. Although published material on the autokinetic effect does not present the data in this form, it is clearly shown in special analysis of data from an experiment by J. W. Brehm, "A Quantitative Approach to the Measurement of Social Influence," Honors thesis, Harvard University, 1952.

6. G. M. Hochbaum, "Certain Personality Aspects and Pressures to Uniformity in Social Groups," Ph.D. dissertation, University of Minnesota, 1953.

an objective basis for feeling their judgments were likely to be poor changed their opinion very frequently upon discovering that others disagreed with them.

Hypothesis III The tendency to compare oneself with some other specific person decreases as the difference between his opinion or ability and one's own increases.

A person does not tend to evaluate his opinions or his abilities by comparison with others who are too divergent from himself. If some other person's ability is too far from his own, either above or below, it is not possible to evaluate his own ability *accurately* by comparison with this other person. There is then a tendency not to make the comparison. Thus, a college student, for example, does not compare himself to inmates of an institution for the feeble minded to evaluate his own intelligence. Nor does a person who is just beginning to learn the game of chess compare himself to the recognized masters of the game.

The situation is identical with respect to the evaluation of opinions. One does not evaluate the correctness or incorrectness of an opinion by comparison with others whose opinions are extremely divergent from one's own. Thus, a person who believes that Negroes are the intellectual equals of whites does not evaluate his opinion by comparison with the opinion of a person who belongs to some very anti-Negro group. In other words, there is a self-imposed restriction in the range of opinion or ability with which a person compares himself.

Corollary III A Given a range of possible persons for comparison, someone close to one's own ability or opinion will be chosen for comparison.

There is some evidence relevant to this corollary from an experiment by Whittemore.[7] The purpose of the study was to examine the relation between performance and competition. Subjects were seated around a table and given tasks to work on. There was ample opportunity to observe how the others were progressing. After the experimental session, in introspective reports, the subjects stated that they had almost always spontaneously selected someone whose performance was close to their own to compete against.

Corollary III B If the only comparison available is a very divergent one, the person will not be able to make a subjectively precise evaluation of his opinion or ability.

There is evidence supporting this corollary with respect to abilities but no relevant evidence in connection with opinions has been found.

Hoppe[8] in his experiment on level of aspiration reports that when subjects made a score very far above or very far below their level of aspiration they did not experience success or failure respectively. In other words, this extremely

7. I. C. Whittemore, "The Influence of Competition on Performance," *Journal of Abnormal and Social Psychology*, 20: 17–33, 1925.

8. Hoppe, *op. cit.*

divergent score presented no grounds for self-evaluation. Dreyer[9] performed an experiment in which high school children were made to score either: very far above the reported average for boys like themselves; at the reported average; or very far below the reported average. After a series of trials they were asked, "How well do you feel you did on the test?" There were five possible categories of response. The top two were good or very good; the bottom two were poor or very poor. In the middle was a noncommittal response of fair. Both those who scored very far below and those who scored very far above the reported group average gave the response "fair" significantly more often than did those who scored at the reported group average. Also, on the average, the persons who had scored at the reported average felt they had done better than did those scoring far above the group. Again the data support the hypothesis.

We may then conclude that there is selectivity in comparison on abilities and opinions and that one major factor governing the selectivity is simply the discrepancy between the person's own opinion or ability and that of another person. Phenomenologically, the appearance of this process is different for opinions and for abilities but conceptually it is exactly the same process. In dealing with opinions one feels that those with whom one does not compare oneself are different kinds of people or members of different groups or people with different backgrounds. Frequently this allegation of difference, to support the non-comparability, is made together with some derogation. In the case of abilities, the phenomenal process is that of designation of status inferior or superior to those persons who are non-comparable to oneself. We will elaborate on this later.

Derivation A (*from I, II, III*) Subjective evaluations of opinions or of abilities are stable when comparison is available with others who are judged to be close to one's opinions or abilities.

Derivation B (*from I, II, III*) The availability of comparison with others whose opinions or abilities are somewhat different from one's own will produce tendencies to change one's evaluation of the opinion or ability in question.

There are also data to show the effect which knowledge of group opinions or group abilities has on the person's evaluations which were initially formed privately. If the evaluation of an opinion or an ability formed in the absence of the possibility of comparison with others is indeed unstable, as we have presumed, then we would expect that, given an opportunity to make a comparison with others, the opportunity would be taken and the comparison would have a considerable impact on the self evaluation. This is found to be true for both abilities and opinions. "Level of aspiration" experiments have been performed where, after a series of trials in which the person is unable to compare his performance with others, there occurs a series of trials in which the person has available to him the knowledge of how others *like himself* performed on

9. Dreyer, *op. cit.*

each trial.[10] When the "others like himself" have scores different from his own, his stated "level of aspiration" (his statement of what he considers is good performance) almost always moves close to the level of the performance of others. It is also found that under these conditions the level of aspiration changes less with fluctuations in performance, in other words, is more stable. When the reported performance of others is about equal to his own score, the stability of his evaluation of his ability is increased and, thus, his level of aspiration shows very little variability. Dreyer, in an experiment specifically designed to test part of this theory[11], showed clearly that the variance of the level of aspiration was smaller when the subject scored close to the group than when he scored far above or far below them. In short, comparison with the performance of others specifies what his ability should be and gives stability to the evaluation.

Festinger, Gerard, et al.[12] find a similar situation with respect to opinions. When a person is asked to form an opinion privately and then has made available to him the consensus of opinion in the group of which he is a member, those who discover that most others in the group disagree with them become relatively less confident that their opinion is correct and a goodly proportion change their opinion. Those who discover that most others in the group agree with them become highly confident in their opinion and it is extremely rare to find one of them changing his opinion. Again, comparison with others has tended to define what is a correct opinion and has given stability to the evaluation. This result is also obtained by Hochbaum.[13]

We may then conclude that *Derivations A* and *B* tend to be supported by the available data.

Derivation C (from I, IIIB) A person will be less attracted to situations where others are very divergent from him than to situations where others are close to him for both abilities and opinions.

This follows from a consideration of *Hypothesis I* and *Corollary IIIB*. If there is a drive toward evaluation of abilities and opinions, and if this evaluation is possible only with others who are close enough, then there should be some attraction to groups where others are relatively close with respect to opinions and/or abilities. There are data confirming this for both opinions and abilities.

---

10. H. H. Anderson and H. F. Brandt, "Study of Motivation Involving Self-Announced Goals of Fifth Grade Children and the Concept of Level of Aspiration," *Journal of Social Psychology*, 10: 209–232, 1939; D. W. Chapman and J. A. Volkmann, "A Social Determinant of the Level of Aspiration," *Journal of Abnormal and Social Psychology*, 34: 225–238, 1939; L. Festinger, "Wish, Expectation, and Group Standards as Factors Influencing Level of Aspiration," *Journal of Abnormal and Social Psychology*, 37: 184–200, 1942; Hilgard, Sait, and Magaret, *op. cit.*

11. Dreyer, *op. cit.*

12. L. Festinger, H. Gerard, et al., "The Influence Process in the Presence of Extreme Deviates," *Human Relations*, 5: 327–346, 1952.

13. Hochbaum, *op. cit.*

Festinger, Gerard et al.[14] report an experiment in which after each person had written down his opinion on an issue he was handed back a slip of paper presumably containing a tabulation of the opinions in the group. Some in each group were thus given the impression that most of the others in the group held opinions close to their own. The rest were given the impression that most others in the group held opinions quite different from their own. After the experiment they were each asked how well they liked the others in the group. In each of the eight different experimental conditions those who thought that the others held divergent opinions were less attracted to the group.[15]

The previously mentioned experiment by Dreyer[16] has as one of its main purposes the testing of this derivation in connection with abilities. He used a "level of aspiration" situation and falsified the scores he reported to the subjects so that some thought they were scoring very far above the group, some thought they were scoring very far below the group, while others thought they were scoring about at the same level as the average of others like them. After each trial they were asked whether they wanted to continue for another trial or whether they would prefer to stop. The reasoning was that if those scoring well above or well below the group average were not able to evaluate their ability accurately, the situation would be less attractive to them and they would stop sooner. On the average, those scoring very much above the group stop after the fifth trial, while those scoring below or at the average of the group stop after the ninth trial.[17] There is no difference between those scoring at and those scoring well below the average of the group. The derivation in the case of abilities seems confirmed for deviation from the group in one direction then but not in the other. This is probably due to the presence of another pressure which we shall discuss in detail later, namely, the value placed in our culture on being better and better with the result that the subjects scoring below the group wanted to, and felt that they might, improve and achieve comparability with the group average.

This result from the experiment by Dreyer[18] is also corroborated in the previously mentioned experiment by Hochbaum.[19] It will be recalled that half the subjects were made to feel that their ability in judging situations of the kind they were to discuss was extremely good and very superior to the abilities of the others in the group. The other half of the subjects were made to feel that their

14. Festinger, Gerard et al., *op. cit.*

15. This result is not reported in the article cited. It was obtained by analyzing the data for this particular purpose.

16. Dreyer, *op. cit.*

17. It is interesting to note that on this point, the usual theory of level of aspiration would lead to a quite different prediction, namely, that those scoring consistently below the group would stop earliest. Lewin, Dembo, Festinger, and Sears, *op. cit.*

18. Dreyer, *op. cit.*

19. Hochbaum, *op. cit.*

ability was poor and considerably worse than the ability of the others in the group. At the end of the experiment all the subjects were asked whether, if they returned for another session they would like to be in the same group or a different group. Of those who felt they were very much above the others in the group, only 38 per cent wanted to return to the same group. Of those who felt that they were considerably inferior to the others, 68 per cent wanted to return to the same group.

With the qualification concerning the asymmetry with regard to abilities the derivation may be regarded as confirmed. We will discuss the unidirectional drive upwards for abilities, which produces the asymmetry, in more detail later.

Derivation D (from I, II, III)   The existence of a discrepancy in a group with respect to opinions or abilities will lead to action on the part of members of that group to reduce the discrepancy.

We have stated in *Hypotheses I, II and III* and in the corollaries to these hypotheses that there is a drive to evaluate accurately one's opinions and abilities, that this evaluation is frequently only possible by comparison with others and that the comparison tends to be made with others who are close to oneself on the particular ability or opinion in question. This implies that the drive to evaluate one's ability or opinion will lead to behavior which will produce for the person a situation where those with whom he compares himself are reasonably close to him, in other words, there will be action to reduce discrepancies which exist between himself and others with whom he compares himself.

Before we can discuss the data relevant to this derivation it is necessary to point out two important differences between opinions and abilities which affect the behavioral manifestations of the action to reduce discrepancies. We will state these differences in the form of hypotheses.

Hypothesis IV   There is a unidirectional drive upward in the case of abilities which is largely absent in opinions.

With respect to abilities, different performances have intrinsically different values. In Western culture, at any rate, there is a value set on doing better and better which means that the higher the score on performance, the more desirable it is. Whether or not this is culturally determined, and hence culturally variable, is an important question but one with which we will not occupy ourselves here.[20]

With respect to most opinions, on the other hand, in the absence of comparison there is no inherent, intrinsic basis for preferring one opinion over another. If we thought of opinions on some specific issue as ranging along a continuum, then no opinion in and of itself has any greater value than any other opinion. The value comes from the subjective feeling that the opinion is correct and valid.

20. There is some evidence, for example, that among the Hopi Indians this preference for better performance is absent. S. E. Asch, "Personality Developments of Hopi Children," Unpublished manuscript referred to in Murphy, Murphy and Newcomb, *Experimental Social Psychology*, New York and London: Harper & Brothers, 1931, 1937 (rev. ed.).

Hypothesis V   There are non-social restraints which make it difficult or even impossible to change one's ability. These non-social restraints are largely absent for opinions.

If a person changes his mind about something, deserts one belief in favor of another, there is no further difficulty in the way of consummating the change. It is true that there are sometimes considerable difficulties in getting someone to change his mind concerning an opinion or belief. Such resistance may arise because of consistency with other opinions and beliefs, personality characteristics that make a person lean in one direction or another and the like. But the point to be stressed here is that once these resistances are overcome, there is no further restraint which would make it difficult for the change to become effective.

There are generally strong non-social restraints, however, against changing one's ability, or changing one's performance which reflects this ability. Even if a person is convinced that he should be able to run faster or should be more intelligent, and even if he is highly motivated to improve his ability in this respect, there are great difficulties in the way of consummating the change.

We may now examine the implications of *Derivation D*. Considering *Hypothesis IV* it is clear that the action to reduce the discrepancy which exists is, in the case of opinions, a relatively uncomplicated pressure towards uniformity. When and if uniformity of opinion is achieved there is a state of social quiescence. In the case of abilities, however, the action to reduce discrepancies interacts with the unidirectional push to do better and better. The resolution of these two pressures, which act simultaneously, is a state of affairs where all the members are relatively close together with respect to some specific ability, but not completely uniform. The pressures cease acting on a person if he is just slightly better than the others. It is obvious that not everyone in a group can be slightly better than everyone else. The implication is that, with respect to the evaluation of abilities, a state of social quiescence is never reached.

Competitive behavior, action to protect one's superiority, and even some kinds of behavior that might be called cooperative, are manifestations in the social process of these pressures which do not reach quiescence. We shall now elaborate this further in considering the specific nature of the social action arising from pressures toward uniformity. There are three major manifestations of pressure toward uniformity which we shall list below together with the relevant data.

Derivation D_1   When a discrepancy exists with respect to opinions or abilities there will be tendencies to change one's own position so as to move closer to others in the group.

Derivation D_2   When a discrepancy exists with respect to opinions or abilities there will be tendencies to change others in the group to bring them closer to oneself.

Considering *Hypothesis V* in relation to the above two subderivations we can see that a difference is implied between the resulting process for opinions and for abilities. Since opinions are relatively free to change, the process of changing the positions of members of a group relative to one another is expressed in action which is predominantly socially oriented. When differences of opinion exist, and pressures toward uniformity arise, these pressures are manifested in an influence process. Members attempt to influence one another, existing opinions become less stable and change occurs. This process of social influence, as we have mentioned before, ceases if and when uniformity of opinion exists in the group.

When pressures toward uniformity exist with respect to abilities, these pressures are manifested less in a social process and more in action against the environment which restrains movement. Thus, a person who runs more slowly than others with whom he compares himself, and for whom this ability is important, may spend considerable time practicing running. In a similar situation where the ability in question is intelligence, the person may study harder. But, needless to say, movement toward uniformity may or may not occur. Even if it occurs, it will take much, much longer than in the case of opinions.

This process would, of course, not be competitive if it were not for the simultaneous operation of the unidirectional push upward which is stated in *Hypothesis IV*. Because of this unidirectional push and the pressure toward uniformity, the individual is oriented toward some point on the ability continuum slightly better than his own performance or the performance of those with whom he is comparing himself. If uniformity concerning an ability were reached this would not lead to a cessation of competition as long as the unidirectional push upward is operating.

There are data which corroborate the two derivations with regard to both abilities and opinions. Back[21], Festinger and Thibaut,[22] Festinger, Gerard, et al.[23] and Gerard[24] have shown clearly that the presence of disagreement in a group concerning some opinion leads to attempts to influence others who disagree with them and also to tendencies to change own opinion to agree more with the others in the group. The effect of this process is to have the group move closer and closer to agreement. In groups where uniformity concerning some issue is reached the influence process on that issue ceases.

In the case of abilities the evidence is less direct for a number of reasons. First, there have been fewer studies conducted relevant to this point. Second, since the process resulting from pressure to reduce discrepancies concerning

21. K. Back, "The Exertion of Influence through Social Communication," *Journal of Abnormal and Social Psychology*, 46: 9–24, 1951.

22. L. Festinger and J. Thibaut, "Interpersonal Communications in Small Groups," *Journal of Abnormal and Social Psychology*, 46: 92–100, 1951.

23. Festinger, Gerard, et al., *op. cit.*

24. H. Gerard, "The Effect of Different Dimensions of Disagreement on the Communication Process in Small Groups," *Human Relations*, 6: 249–272, 1953.

abilities is not clearly shown in a social process, and since it is complicated by the drive to do better and better, it is harder to identify. Some evidence is available from the literature on level of aspiration.[25] It has been shown that in most situations, an individual's level of aspiration is placed slightly above his performance. When told the average performance of others like himself, the level of aspiration is generally set slightly above this reported group average. These results are what we would expect if the resolution of the simultaneous unidirectional drive upward and the pressure toward uniformity is indeed a drive to be slightly better than the others with whom one compares oneself. These data can then be viewed as an indication of the desire to change one's position relative to others.

An experiment by Hoffman, Festinger, and Lawrence[26] specifically designed to test parts of the present theory, shows this competitive process clearly. In a performance situation where one of three persons is scoring considerably above the other two, these two can and do act so as to prevent the high scorer from getting additional points, Thus, when the situation is arranged such that the performance of each person is controllable by the others in the group, action is taken to change the position of the members to reduce the discrepancies which exist.

Let us also examine what we would expect of the behavior of someone whose performance is considerably higher than the other members of the group and who has no other possible comparison group to turn to for his evaluation of this ability. Since the others are considerably poorer, they will not effectively serve as a comparison for his own evaluation. The pressure acting on him toward comparability can manifest itself in two ways. It is possible that under these conditions his performance will actually deteriorate slightly over a period of time. It is also possible that he will devote considerable time and effort to trying to improve the performance of the others in the group to a point where at least some of them are close to, but not equal to, him. This could take the form of helping them practice, coaching them, motivating them to improve and the like. Once comparability has been achieved, however, the process should change to the familiar competitive one.

There is some indirect corroboration of this from experimental evidence. Greenberg[27] reports a study in competition in which pairs of children, seated together at a table, were to construct things out of "stones" (blocks) which were initially all in one common pile. Grabbing blocks from the pile was one of the indications of competition while giving blocks to the others was taken as one indication of lack of competition. The author reports the case of two friends, E. K. and H. At a time when E.K.'s construction was clearly superior to that of

25. Lewin, Dembo, Festinger, and Sears, *op. cit.*

26. Hoffman, Festinger, and Lawrence, *op. cit.*

27. P. J. Greenberg, "Competition in Children: An Experimental Study," *American Journal of Psychology*, 44: 221–248, 1932.

H., H. asked for "stones" and was freely given such by E. K. Subsequently E. K. asked H. whether or not she wanted more "stones". At the end of the session, although privately the experimenter judged both constructions to be nearly equal, when the children were asked "whose is better?" E. K. said "mine" and H., after a moment, agreed.

From many such pairs the author summarizes as follows: "Sometimes when a child gave another a "stone", it was not at all an act of disinterested generosity, but a display of friendly competition and superior skill."

Derivation D_3 When a discrepancy exists with respect to opinions or abilities there will be tendencies to cease comparing oneself with those in the group who are very different from oneself.

Just as comparability can be achieved by changing the position of the members with respect to one another, so can it also be achieved by changing the composition of the comparison group. Thus, for example, if pressures toward uniformity exist in a group concerning some opinion on which there is a relatively wide discrepancy, there is a tendency to redefine the comparison group so as to exclude those members whose opinions are most divergent from one's own. In other words, one merely ceases to compare oneself with those persons.

Here again we would expect the behavioral manifestation of the tendency to stop comparing oneself with those who are very divergent to be different for opinions and for abilities. This difference arises because of the nature of the evaluation of opinions and abilities and because of the asymmetry introduced by the unidirectional push upward for abilities. We will consider these in order.

It will be recalled that opinions are evaluated in terms of whether or not subjectively they are correct while abilities are evaluated in terms of how good they seem. In other words, the existence of someone whose ability is very divergent from one's own, while it does not help to evaluate one's ability, does not make, in itself, for discomfort or unpleasantness. In the case of opinions, however, the existence of a discrepant opinion threatens one's own opinion since it implies the possibility that one's own opinion may not be correct. *Hypothesis VI*, which we will state below, leads us then to expect that the process of making others incomparable (ceasing to compare oneself with others) will be accompanied by hostility or derogation in the case of opinions but will not, generally, in the case of abilities.

Hypothesis VI The cessation of comparison with others is accompanied by hostility or derogation to the extent that continued comparison with those persons implies unpleasant consequences.

Thus, in the case of opinions we expect the process of making others incomparable to be associated with rejection from the group. In the case of abilities, this may or may not be the case. It would be plausible to expect that there would rarely be derogation in making those below oneself incomparable.

When making those above oneself incomparable, the presence of unidirectional push upward might lead to derogation in some instances.

The asymmetry introduced in the case of abilities is another difference we may expect to find. While in the case of opinions, deviation on either side of one's own opinion would lead to the same consequences, in the case of abilities there is a difference. The process of making others incomparable results in a "status stratification" where some are clearly inferior and others are clearly superior.

Corollary VI A   Cessation of comparison with others will be accompanied by hostility or derogation in the case of opinions. In the case of abilities this will not generally be true.

Festinger, Schachter, and Back[28] and Schachter[29] have shown that when there is a range of opinion in a group there is a tendency to reject those members of the group whose opinions are very divergent from one's own. This rejection tends to be accompanied by a relative cessation of communication to those who are rejected. This is undoubtedly another evidence of the cessation of comparison with those persons.

There are data relevant to this point in connection with abilities from the experiment by Hoffman, Festinger, and Lawrence.[30] In this experiment, one out of a group of three persons was made to score very much higher than the other two on a test of intelligence. When the nature of the situation allowed, the two low scoring subjects ceased to compete against the high scorer and began to compete against each other. When they did this they also rated the intelligence of the high scorer as considerably higher than their own, thus acknowledging his superiority. In those conditions where they continued to compete against the high scorer they did not rate his intelligence as higher than their own. In other words, when the situation allowed it they stopped comparing their scores with the score of someone considerably higher than themselves. This cessation of comparison was accompanied by an acknowledgment of the others' superiority. A number of sociometric questions showed no hostility toward or derogation of the high scorer.

Having discussed the manifestations of the "pressure toward uniformity" which arises from the drive to evaluate opinions and abilities, we will now raise the question as to the factors which determine the strength of these pressures.

Derivation E (from I, II and III)   Any factors which increase the strength of the drive to evaluate some particular ability or opinion will increase the "pressure toward uniformity" concerning that ability or opinion.

28. L. Festinger, S. Schachter and K. Back, *Social Pressures in Informal Groups*, New York: Harper & Row, 1950.

29. S. Schachter, "Deviation, Rejection, and Communication," *Journal of Abnormal and Social Psychology*, 46: 190–208, 1951.

30. Hoffman, Festinger, and Lawrence, *op. cit.*

Hypothesis VII Any factors which increase the importance of some particular group as a comparison group for some particular opinion or ability will increase the pressure toward uniformity concerning that ability or opinion within that group.

To make the above statements relevant to empirical data we must of course specify the factors involved. The corollaries stated below will specify some of these factors. We will then present the data relevant to these corollaries.

Corollary to Derivation E An increase in the importance of an ability or an opinion, or an increase in its relevance to immediate behavior, will increase the pressure toward reducing discrepancies concerning that opinion or ability.

If an opinion or ability is of no importance to a person there will be no drive to evaluate that ability or opinion. In general, the more important the opinion or ability is to the person, the more related to behavior, social behavior in particular, and the more immediate the behavior is, the greater will be the drive for evaluation. Thus, in an election year, influence processes concerning political opinions are much more current than in other years. Likewise, a person's drive to evaluate his intellectual ability will be stronger when he must decide between going to graduate school or taking a job.

The previously mentioned experiment by Hoffman, Festinger, and Lawrence[31] corroborates the Corollary to *Derivation E* with respect to abilities. It will be recalled that this experiment involved groups of three persons who took an "intelligence test." The situation was arranged so that one of the subjects (a paid participant) started out with a higher score than the other two. From then on the two subjects could completely control how many points the paid participant scored. The degree to which they prevented him from scoring points was taken as a measure of the extent to which they were competing against him and hence as an indication of the strength of the pressure toward uniformity acting on them. Half of the groups were told that this test which they were to take was an extremely valid test and hence a good measure of intelligence, an ability which these subjects considered important. The other half of the groups were told that it was a very poor test and the research was being done to demonstrate conclusively that the test was no good. For these subjects their performance was consequently not important. The results showed that the competition with the high scorer was significantly greater for the high importance than for the low importance condition.

Unfortunately there are no relevant data from experiments concerning opinions. The Corollary to *Derivation E* applies to opinions also, however, and is testable.

The data which we have presented refer to changing the position of members in the group. As the pressure toward uniformity increases there should also be observed an increase in the tendency to cease comparison with those who are

31. *Ibid.*

too different from oneself. Specifically, this would mean that the range within which appreciable comparison with others is made should contract as the pressure toward uniformity increases. This leads to an interesting prediction concerning abilities which can be tested. The more important an ability is to a person and, hence, the stronger the pressures toward uniformity concerning this ability, the stronger will be the competition about it and also the greater the readiness with which the individuals involved will recognize and acknowledge that someone else is clearly superior to them. And just as in influence processes, where, once rejection has taken place there tends to be a cessation of communication and influence attempts toward those who have been made incomparable,[32] so we may expect that once inferior or superior status has been conferred, there will be a cessation of competition with respect to those who have been thus rendered incomparable.

Thus, for example, let us imagine two individuals who are identical with respect to some particular ability but differ markedly in how important this ability is to them personally. The prediction from the above theory would say that the person for whom the ability is more important would be more competitive about it than the other; would be more ready to allocate "inferior status" to those considerably less good than he; and would be more ready to allocate "superior status" to those considerably better than he. In other words, he would be more competitive within a narrow range.

Corollary VII A   The stronger the attraction to the group the stronger will be the pressure toward uniformity concerning abilities and opinions within that group.

The more attractive a group is to a member, the more important that group will be as a comparison group for him. Thus the pressure to reduce discrepancies which operate on him when differences of ability or opinion exist will be stronger. We would expect these stronger pressures toward uniformity to show themselves in all three ways, increased tendency to change own position, increased effort to change the position of others and greater restriction of the range within which appreciable comparison is made.

There are a number of studies which corroborate *Corollary VII A* with regard to opinions. Back[33] showed that in groups to which the members were highly attracted there were more attempts to influence others than in groups to which the members were less attracted. This greater exertion of influence was accompanied by more change of opinion in the highly attractive groups. Festinger, Gerard, et al.[34] showed a tendency for members of highly attractive groups to change their opinions more frequently than members of less attractive groups upon discovering that most others in the group disagreed with them.

32. Festinger, Gerard, et al., *op. cit.*; Schachter, *op. cit.*

33. Back, *op. cit.*

34. Festinger, Gerard, et al., *op. cit.*

This change of opinion was before any influence had actually been exerted on them by other members of the group. They also found that there was more communication attempting to influence others in the high than in the low attractive groups.

Schachter[35] shows that this same factor, attraction to the group, also increased the tendency to cease comparison with those who differed too much. Members of his highly attractive groups rejected the deviate significantly more than did members of the less attractive groups.

Festinger, Torrey, and Willerman[36] report an experiment specifically designed to test *Corollary VII A* with respect to abilities. If, given a range of performance reflecting some ability, the comparison, and hence the competition, in highly attractive groups would be stronger than in less attractive groups, then this should be reflected in the feelings of having done well or poorly after taking the tests. If *Corollary VII A* is correct we would expect those scoring slightly below others to feel more inadequate in the high than in the low attractive groups. Similarly we would expect those scoring equal to or better than most others to feel more adequate in the high than in the low attractive groups. Groups of four persons were given a series of tests supposed to measure an ability that these persons considered important. One of the subjects was caused to score consistently slightly below the others. The other three were made to score equally well. Those members who were highly attracted to the group, and scored below the others, felt they had done worse than similar persons who were not attracted to the group. Those who were attracted to the group and had scored equal to the others felt that they had done better than did similar persons who were not attracted to the group. Thus the results of the experiment corroborate the corollary for abilities.

Corollary VII B The greater the relevance of the opinion or ability to the group, the stronger will be the pressure toward uniformity concerning that opinion or ability.

The conceptual definition of relevance of an opinion or an ability to a group is not completely clear. There are, however, some things one can state. Where the opinion or ability involved is necessary or important for the life of the *group* or for the attainment of the satisfactions that push the members into the group, the need for evaluation in that group will be strong. Groups will thus differ on what one may call their "realm of relevance." A group of men who meet every Friday night to play poker, and do only this together, will probably have a narrow "realm of relevance." The abilities and opinions for which this group serves as a comparison will be very restricted. The members of a college fraternity, on the other hand, where the group satisfies a wider variety of the members' needs, will have a wider "realm of relevance."

35. Schachter, *op. cit.*

36. Festinger, Torrey, and Willerman, *op. cit.*

In spite of the conceptual unclarity which is involved it is possible to create differences in relevance of an issue to a group which are clear and unambiguous. Thus Schachter[37] created high and low relevance conditions in the following manner. Groups which were to discuss an issue relevant to the group were recruited specifically for that purpose. Other groups were recruited ostensibly for very different kinds of things and on a pretext were asked to discuss the particular issue in question. They were promised this would never happen again in the life of the group thus making this issue of low relevance to that particular group. Schachter found, confirming *Corollary VII B*, that the tendency to reject deviates was stronger in the high relevance condition than in the low relevance condition.

No other evidence bearing on *Corollary VII B* has been located.

Thus far we have discussed only factors which, in affecting the pressure toward uniformity, affect all three manifestations of this pressure in the same direction. There are also factors which affect the manifestations of pressure toward uniformity differentially. We will discuss two such factors.

Hypothesis VIII   If persons who are very divergent from one's own opinion or ability are perceived as different from oneself on *attributes consistent with the divergence*, the tendency to narrow the range of comparability becomes stronger.

There is evidence supporting this hypothesis with respect to both abilities and opinions. In the previously mentioned experiment by Hoffman, Festinger, and Lawrence[38] half the groups were told that the three persons in the group had been selected to take the test together because, as far as could be determined, they were about equal in intelligence. The other groups were told that one of the three was very superior to the others. This was reported in a manner which made it impossible for either of the subjects to suppose that he himself was the superior one. In the "homogeneous" condition the subjects continued to compete against the paid participant who was scoring considerably above them. In the condition where they thought one of the others was clearly superior they competed considerably less with the paid participant and tended to compete with each other. In other words, when there was the perception of a difference consistent with the fact that the paid participant was scoring above them, they ceased comparison with him.

There is additional evidence on this point from level of aspiration experiments. Festinger[39] reports an experiment where, on an intellectual task, subjects (college students) were told they were scoring considerably above another group which they ordinarily considered inferior to themselves (high school students)

37. Schachter, *op. cit.*

38. Hoffman, Festinger, and Lawrence, *op. cit.*

39. L. Festinger, "Wish, Expectation, and Group Standards as Factors Influencing Level of Aspiration," *loc. cit.*

or were told they were scoring considerably below a group which they considered superior to themselves (graduate students). In these circumstances there is practically no effect on the level of aspiration. Thus, the knowledge of this other group's being divergent in a direction consistent with the label of the group had no effect on their evaluation. It is interesting to note in this same experiment that if the reported direction of difference is inconsistent with the level of the group this destroys the incomparability and the effect on the level of aspiration is very great.

The evidence concerning opinions relating to *Hypothesis VIII* comes from experiments reported by Gerard[40] and Festinger and Thibaut[41]. In both of these experiments discussions were carried on in a group of persons with a considerable range of opinion on the issue in question. In each experiment, half of the groups were given the impression that the group was homogeneous. All the members of the group had about equal interest in and knowledge about the issue. The other half of the groups were given the impression that they were heterogeneously composed. There was considerable variation among them in interest in and knowledge about the problem. In both experiments there was less communication directed toward those holding extremely divergent opinions in the heterogeneous than in the homogeneous condition. In other words, the perception of heterogeneity on matters related to the issue enabled the members of the groups to narrow the range within which they actively compared themselves with others.

It is interesting, at this point, to look at the data from these two experiments in relation to *Hypothesis III* which stated that the tendency to compare oneself with others decreased as the divergence in opinion or ability increased. In both the Gerard experiment and the Festinger and Thibaut experiment it was found that most communication was directed toward those whose opinions were most different from the others. Since we have just interpreted a reduction in communication to indicate a reduction in comparison with others, it is necessary to explain the over-all tendency to communicate most with those holding divergent opinions in the light of *Hypothesis III*.

From *Hypothesis III* we would expect comparison to be made mainly with those closest to oneself. This is indeed true. The support one gets for one's opinion is derived from those close to one's own. However, it will be recalled that, in the case of opinions, comparison with others who are divergent represents a threat to one's own opinion. It is for this reason that communication is directed mainly toward those most divergent but still within the limits where comparison is made. This communication represents attempts to influence them. Reduction in communication to these extreme opinions indicates that the existence of these extreme opinions is less of a threat to one's own opinion. In other words, one is comparing oneself less with them. In the case of abilities we would not expect to find any such

40. Gerard, *op. cit.*

41. Festinger and Thibaut, *op. cit.*

orientation toward very divergent persons. Comparison behavior in the case of abilities would follow very closely the simple relation stated in *Hypothesis III*.

Hypothesis IX When there is a range of opinion or ability in a group, the relative strength of the three manifestations of pressures toward uniformity will be different for those who are close to the mode of the group than for those who are distant from the mode. Specifically, those close to the mode of the group will have stronger tendencies to change the positions of others, relatively weaker tendencies to narrow the range of comparison and much weaker tendencies to change their own position compared to those who are distant from the mode of the group.

Some data are available to support this hypothesis, with reference to opinions, from experiments by Festinger, Gerard, et al.,[42] and by Hochbaum.[43] In both of these experiments some persons in each group were given the impression that the rest of the group disagreed with them while others were given the impression that most of the group agreed with them. In both experiments there was considerably more change of opinion among the "deviates" than among the conformers. In both experiments there were considerably more attempts to influence others made by the conformers than by the deviates. While there exist no adequate data relevant to the tendency to narrow the range of comparison, corroboration is suggested in the experiment by Festinger, Gerard, et al. In this experiment it was found that the deviates actually communicated less to those holding most divergent opinions than to those somewhat closer to their own position. The conformers showed the more familiar pattern of communicating most to those with extremely divergent opinions in the group.

The question may also be raised as to the determinants of the extent to which the group actually does move closer toward uniformity when pressures in this direction exist. In part, the degree of such movement toward uniformity will be dependent upon the strength of the pressures. In part they will be dependent upon other things. In the case of opinions it will be dependent upon the resistances to changing opinions, and upon the power of the group to successfully influence its members. The theory concerning the determinants of the power of the group to influence its members is set forth elsewhere.[44] We will not repeat it here since the power of the group to influence its members is relatively unimportant with regard to abilities. The social process itself, no matter how much power the group has, cannot achieve movement toward uniformity on abilities. The power of the group successfully to influence its members will be effective only insofar as changing members' values concerning a given ability and increasing motivations can be effective. With respect to values and motiva-

42. Festinger, Gerard, et al., *op. cit.*

43. Hochbaum, *op. cit.*

44. L. Festinger, "Informal Social Communication," *loc. cit.*

tions concerning the ability the situation is identical with the social process that goes on concerning opinions.

Implications for Group Formation and Societal Structure

The drive for self evaluation concerning one's opinions and abilities has implications not only for the behavior of persons in groups but also for the processes of formation of groups and changing membership of groups. To the extent that self evaluation can only be accomplished by means of comparison with other persons, the drive for self evaluation is a force acting on persons to belong to groups, to associate with others. And the subjective feelings of correctness in one's opinions and the subjective evaluation of adequacy of one's performance on important abilities are some of the satisfactions that persons attain in the course of these associations with other people. How strong the drives and satisfactions stemming from these sources are compared to the other needs which people satisfy in groups is impossible to say, but it seems clear that the drive for self evaluation is an important factor contributing to making the human being "gregarious."

People, then, tend to move into groups which, in their judgment, hold opinions which agree with their own and whose abilities are near their own. And they tend to move out of groups in which they are unable to satisfy their drive for self evaluation. Such movement in and out of groups is, of course, not a completely fluid affair. The attractiveness to a group may be strong enough for other reasons so that a person cannot move out of it. Or there may be restraints, for one or another reason, against leaving. In both of these circumstances, mobility from one group to another is hindered. We will elaborate in the next section on the effects of so hindering movement into and out of groups.

These selective tendencies to join some and leave other associations, together with the influence process and competitive activity which arise when there is discrepancy in a group, will guarantee that we will find relative similarity in opinions and abilities among persons who associate with one another (at least on those opinions and abilities which are relevant to that association). Among different groups, we may well expect to find relative dissimilarity. It may very well be that the segmentation into groups is what allows a society to maintain a variety of opinions within it and to accommodate persons with a wide range of abilities. A society or town which was not large enough or flexible enough to permit such segmentation might not be able to accommodate the same variety.

The segmentation into groups which are relatively alike with respect to abilities also gives rise to status in a society. And it seems clear that when such status distinctions are firmly maintained, it is not only members of the higher status who maintain them. It is also important to the members of the lower status to maintain them for it is in this way that they can relatively ignore the differences and compare themselves with their own group. Comparisons with members of a different status group, either higher or lower, may sometimes be made on a phantasy level, but very rarely in reality.

It is also important to consider whether or not the incomparability consequent upon group segmentation is a relatively complete affair. The conferring of status in the case of abilities or the allegation of "different kind of people" in the case of opinions may markedly lower the comparability but may not completely eliminate it. The latter is probably the more accurate statement. People are certainly aware, to some extent, of the opinions of those in incomparable groups. To the extent that perfect incomparability is not achieved, this has important bearing on differences in behavior to be expected from members of minority groups. Members of minority groups, if they are unable to achieve complete incomparability with other groups, should be somewhat less secure in their self evaluations. One might expect from this that within a minority group, the pressures toward uniformity would be correspondingly stronger than in a majority group. The minority group would seek stronger support within itself and be less well able to tolerate differences of opinion or ability which were relevant to that group.

In connection with opinion formation, there is experimental evidence that this is the case.[45] Subgroups which were in the minority within larger experimental groups showed evidence of stronger pressures toward uniformity within the subgroup than did the majority subgroups. In minority groups where particular abilities were relevant, we would, by the same line of reasoning, also expect stronger pressures toward uniformity and hence fiercer competition with respect to that ability than in majority groups.

We may recall that stronger pressure toward uniformity also implies the existence of stronger tendencies to regard as incomparable those who deviate markedly. Since others are made incomparable with respect to opinions by means of rejection from the group, this gives us a possible explanation of the persistent splitting into smaller and smaller factions which is frequently found to occur in minority groups which are under strong pressure from the majority segments of the population.

Consequences of Preventing Incomparability

There are predominantly two kinds of situations in which comparability is forced despite the usual tendencies not to compare oneself with those who deviate markedly. One such situation occurs when the attraction of the group is so strong, for other reasons, that the member continues to wish to remain in the group in spite of the fact that he differs markedly from the group on some opinion or ability. If, together with this state of affairs, he has no other comparison group for this opinion or ability, or if the opinion or ability is highly relevant to that group, then comparability is forced to a great extent. The

45. Gerard, *op. cit.*

psychological tendencies to make incomparable those who differ most will still be present but would not be as effective as they might otherwise be.

Under these circumstances where the attraction to the group remains high, the group has power to influence the member effectively and, in the case of opinion difference, we would expect an influence process to ensue which would be effective enough to eliminate the difference of opinion. In short, there would be movement toward uniformity. But what happens in the case of an ability? Here, while the group will probably succeed in motivating the member concerning this ability it is quite likely that the ability itself may not be changeable. We have then created a situation where a person's values and strivings are quite out of line with his performance and we would expect, if he is below others, deep experiences of failure and feelings of inadequacy with respect to this ability. This is certainly not an unusual condition to find.

The other major situation in which comparability is forced upon a person is one in which he is prevented from leaving the group. The theory concerning the effect of this situation on opinion formation is spelt out elsewhere. We will touch on the main points here in order to extend the theory to ability evaluation. In circumstances where a person is restrained from leaving a group either physically or psychologically, but otherwise his attraction to the group is zero or even negative, the group does not have the power to influence him effectively. Uniformity can, however, be forced, in a sense, if the group exerts threats or punishment for non-compliance. In the case of opinions, we may here expect to find overt compliance or overt conformity without any private acceptance on the part of the member. Thus a boy who is forced to play with some children whom he does not particularly like would, in such circumstances, where threat was employed, agree with the other children publicly while privately maintaining his disagreement.

Again, when we consider abilities, we find a difference which arises because abilities may be difficult if not impossible to change on short notice. Here the deviating member who is restrained from leaving the group may simply have to suffer punishment. If he deviates toward the higher end of the ability scale, he can again publicly conform without privately accepting the evaluations of the group. If he deviates toward the lower end of the ability scale this may be impossible. Provided he has other comparison groups for self evaluation on this ability he may remain personally and privately quite unaffected by this group situation. While publicly he may strive to perform better, privately his evaluations of his ability may remain unchanged.

Summary

If the foregoing theoretical development is correct, then social influence processes and some kinds of competitive behavior are both manifestations of the same socio-psychological process and can be viewed identically on a conceptual level. Both stem directly from the drive for self evaluation and the necessity for such evaluation being based on comparison with other persons. The differences between the processes with respect to opinions and abilities lie in the unidirectional push upward in the case of abilities, which is absent when considering opinions, and in the relative ease of changing one's opinion as compared to changing one's performance.

The theory is tentatively supported by a variety of data and is readily amenable to further empirical testing. One great advantage, assuming the correctness of the theory, is that one can work back and forth between opinions and ability evaluations. Some aspects of the theory may be more easily tested in one context, some in the other. Discoveries in the context of opinions should also hold true, when appropriately operationally defined, in the context of ability evaluation.

The Psychology of Status

Herbert H. Hyman

THE concept of status has been of interest to psychologists, since status may be thought to produce or correspond with certain predictable attitudes of the individual. Status also corresponds with aspects of behavior, by definition, since role and status are inseparable.[1] It affects one's social perspective because people in different positions in society will have different views of social change. Status is also an integral part of social organization, and any understanding of the relation of "culture and personality" demands analysis of status. . . .

Most determinations of status have in the past been made on the basis of some *objective* criterion such as income, or some institutional feature such as membership in a given occupational group or caste. In this study it is proposed to deal with an area of status which may be called "subjective status" which may be defined as a person's conception of his own position relative to other individuals. The term subjective is not associated in this study with the connotations unverifiable or unreliable. The reliability of measures of subjective status will be dealt with later. The word refers only to the dependence of the measure upon the subject's report. . . .

A research program in the field falls into two parts: *A*. A study of the nature of people's views of their own status. This study can be approached in part through the avenue of the psychology of judgment, since the individual can be asked to make a judgment of his own position relative to others. A judgmental approach has two important consequences. The results may extend the generality of principles of judgment to new materials of a "social" nature. More important, within this methodological framework, we already have at our

Reprinted in part from "The Psychology of Status," *Archives of Psychology*, No. 269 (1942), pp. 5–38, 80–86.

1. R. Linton, *The Study of Man*, New York: D. Appleton-Century Company, 1936.

disposal certain leads as to what are the variables that determine subjective status, by reference to the variables that determine the properties of judgments in general. *B.* A study of the relation of subjective status to social attitudes and other dependent variables. This aspect of the program will be limited to a study of radical attitudes. Of necessity the first area will be the major one dealt with, since we have to know the properties of subjective status before we can determine the functional relationships demanded by the second problem.

Since the entire study represents one of the first ventures into a new field, its chief value will be exploratory rather than definitive.

Two procedures were used in the investigation of the nature of subjective status: 1. *Controlled interview:* Since the area is relatively unknown, it was decided to do a series of intensive interviews on a heterogeneous population in an attempt to obtain suggestions as to the kind of experimental work to be done, and to obtain information about aspects of the problem not readily amenable to experimental study. 2. *Experimental studies:* On the basis of the interview materials, three experiments were devised which demonstrate more conclusively certain results suggested in the interviews. . . .*

Procedure

The interviews lasted approximately two hours per subject. They were relatively intense "clinical" examinations. The questions were not standardized in their presentation. It was thought that complete standardization would not permit sufficient modification of the questions to bring out the idiosyncrasies of the subjects, nor permit the investigator to extend the issue in question when necessary. Complete lack of standardization, however, would lead to chaotic results. Hence, the aims of the interview were categorized under seven headings and a number of possible wordings of each question were prepared. Leading questions were avoided, but the precise form of the question was modified wherever necessary to elicit an answer. The atmosphere of the interview was as informal as possible. Rapport and sincerity were achieved in the following ways: 1. The individuals were selected by recommendation and were therefore willing to cooperate. They were not, however, intimates of the experimenter and hence fewer personal barriers of shame or self-consciousness were imposed. 2. The interview was prefaced by the experimenter's statement to the effect that the data were confidential, and that, though they would be published in an academic article, no name would be attached.

The occupations that were represented include doctors, nurses, college teachers, students, clerks, salesmen, editors, housewives, waitresses, managers, engineers, and domestic workers. All of the subjects were drawn from an urban population.

The seven aims and categories of questions in the interview were as follows:

---

*None of these is included in the present selection. (*Editors' note.*)

1. THOUGHTS ABOUT STATUS

Subject was asked whether he had ever thought *his* standing was *higher* or *lower* than that of other individuals. Where the subject said *yes*, the examiner attempted to find out the frequency of such thoughts. Wherever the subject said *no*, he was asked why he did not think of his status. The reasons for lack of thought were determined for all such subjects wherever possible. While it might be assumed that all individuals in a competitive society would be concerned with status, our own society is not competitive in all respects and the reaction of different individuals to competitive situations is not uniform. Hence, it was necessary to discover empirically whether the subjects were actually concerned with their statuses.

2. DIMENSIONS OF STATUS

The subject was asked in what ways he had thought of his status. Here, the attempt was made to elicit all the dimensions of status that he habitually used or thought about. When the subject had ostensibly exhausted the dimensions, the investigator named others to find out their presence or absence.

3. FRAMES OF REFERENCE

a. Reference Groups

For each status reported, the subject was asked what group of people he compared himself with. Were they actual people he knew? Were they conceptual or "reified" people whom he did not know, but whose existence he postulated? Were they of higher or lower status than he?

b. Reference Individuals

He was asked for each status whether he compared himself, not with a group, but with a particular, crucial individual, and these individuals were identified.

4. GENESIS OF STATUS

For each dimension of status reported, he was asked when he had first thought about it (*e.g.*, at what age, at what school level, etc.), the precipitating factors, changes with time in the nature of thoughts about the dimension, affective accompaniments associated with his status, and behavioral consequences of an adjustment to his particular status.

5. CRITERIA FOR THE DEFINITION OF STATUS

For each dimension of status, the subject was asked *how* he decided what his standing was in terms of criteria used.

6. VALUES OF DIFFERENT STATUSES

The subject was asked to place the statuses reported in a rank order of values. The question was generally phrased thus: In which standing would you like to be most superior, next most superior, etc., or which status means the most to you, next, etc.

7. SATISFACTION WITH STATUS

The subject was asked which status he was satisfied with, which ones he would like to improve, which he was dissatisfied with, and whether striving for status had been important as a source of motivation to him. He was also asked to judge what would be the maximum and minimum yearly incomes that he would like to have in order to be contented.

Additional facts spontaneously reported and other data that appeared of interest were recorded. Personal data were secured about the individual's name, occupation, education, yearly income, source of income, marital status, parent's status and income, number of siblings, dependents, age, and religion. . . .

Results:

Thoughts of Status

While most of the subjects reported thinking about status, a number of them (6 out of 31) reported practically no thoughts. These data must be considered with two qualifications: 1. Lack of thoughts about status should be regarded probably as lack of concern with status rather than complete absence of the concept of status. 2. Lack of thought may represent verbalized opposition to the concept of status rather than actual absence of its use. . . .

. . . Case #30 presents a confused picture. She thinks about matters of status continually but resented E's questions on the subject. She became so emotional during the interview, that an intermission was necessary. She kept saying "that's a rotten word" (status). She says also that she does not go about making obvious status comparisons. There are several reasons for her point of view: 1. She says that she might feel terribly inferior if she made status comparisons. Hence the lack of comparison is partly a protection against insecurity. 2. She has a "radical" point of view; her feeling is that status differences may be a function of social dislocation rather than personal lacks. . . . Case #31, a member of the Communist Party, thinks of his status in a vicarious way. He thinks of it in terms of elevating the status of others in society, and thus vicariously raising his own. There is very little comparative phrasing of status in terms of *higher* and *lower* position. He reported that even where his status was high he never felt that he was better than any other person. The interpretation of this is partly due to S's conceptualization of the differences, not in terms of personal adequacy but as socially allocated differences. Related to such a view is Case #11 who considers differences in status but does not use them to flaunt her superiority. She understands that superior opportunity has made her superior rather than personal ability. She also values cooperation with others more highly than the enhancement of status differences between people.

It might be thought that all individuals in a competitive society, particularly those drawn from an urban competitive center such as New York, would think of and be striving for high status. Actually, people do not think of status in an indiscriminate fashion. For a variety of reasons, some people, as noted in the above cases, do not use any dimension of status. In two cases the lack of thought correlates with radical attitudes, but this is not characteristic of the four other subjects. As will be shown later, those who do strive for status are selective in using particular statuses rather than all possible statuses. Similarly, there is wide divergence in the amount of concern with status, answers varying from little or no thought to much or continuous thought. . . .

Reference Groups

The reference groups used are reported in Table 1 for each status with the relative frequencies of occurrence. Some individuals used several reference

Table I—The Habitual Reference Groups within Which Status Was Judged*

Status	Reference Groups		Frequency of Multiple Reference Groups
Social	Friends.	6	
	Work group	4	
	Those in same field	2	
	Similar background	4	
	Neighbors	2	5
	Same race	1	
	Family	1	
	People casually encountered	4	
	Economic classes	2	
Intellectual	Total population	4	
	Acquaintances	12	
	Similar background	4	
	Same occupation	4	
	Work group	4	
	People in contact with in business	1	11
	Same race	1	
	Writers S reads	1	
	People casually encountered	5	
	Definite classes	1	
Cultural	Acquaintances	2	
	Work group	2	
	Same occupation	6	
	Same race	1	
	Great artists	1	2
	People casually encountered	1	
	No reference group**	1	
	No group offered†	2	

Table I—(Continued)

Status	Reference Groups		Frequency of Multiple Reference Groups
Looks	Friends	6	
	Same occupation	2	
	Work group	2	
	Movie actresses	4	7
	People casually encountered	8	
	No reference group	1	
	No group offered	2	
General	Total population	1	
	Same occupation	1	
	People casually encountered	1	0
	No reference group	6	
	No group offered	2	
Economic	Total population	4	
	Friends	10	
	Work group	2	
	Same occupation	5	
	Similar background	1	8
	Employer	2	
	Family	2	
	People casually encountered	10	
	Classes	4	
	No reference group	1	
Prestige	Friends or acquaintances	3	
	Work group	2	
	Definite classes	1	
	Those of very high prestige ("best in field") .	2	1
	People casually encountered	3	
	No reference group	1	
	No group offered	1	

* Not all 31 subjects reported habitually using each dimension of status. The specific N's are as follows: social, 20; intellectual, 27; cultural, 15; looks, 18; general, 12; economic, 28; prestige, 12.
** No reference group means that the subject *said* he had no reference group.
† No group offered means that the subject did not volunteer a response or the examiner did not elicit one.

groups. For example, a subject might think about his economic status in relation to his friends and the total population. The frequency of such cases is reported in the table under "Frequency of Multiple Reference Groups."

The responses to the question of the reference groups used may be classified under a number of tendencies. Examples of these tendencies are given below.

VARIANTS IN STRUCTURING

A few individuals had singularly well structured reference groups which were common to the judgment of all statuses. This was the case with #28 and #21 who use their friends for the judgment of all statuses and #15, a nurse, who uses her occupational group. Hierarchical structuring *within* the reference group as a function of values is illustrated in #6, whose main dimension of status is intellectual. His spontaneously selected reference group is made up of those individuals who write the books he reads. The group is fairly large and amorphous; so the more salient group within it consists of those authors in the sciences and arts which he values most: mathematics, linguistics, anthropology, poetry, and philosophy. Similarly, #9 uses all academic people in the United States as a reference group for intellectual status. (S's aspiration is to do academic work.) This group is large and vague, and the more structured sub-group consists of social scientists. The subject reports that he has no desire to teach other subjects than the social sciences. A variant of hierarchical structuring is the case of #4 whose union was his major reference group. S was one of the leaders in the policy making nucleus within the group. He states that there was no need for comparison with union members below the nucleus. This is due to the fact that the group was organized so that the relations of leaders to ordinary members were formalized.

CLASS CONCEPTS

A few individuals have elaborate reference groups schematized in class terms. Such is the case with #7 who, for example, states that in the case of social status there are four classes, the ultra, above average, average, and low classes. He compares himself primarily with the above average class of which he is a member, but this class is not nationally represented, *i.e.*, he considers only the above average class in his community. Similarly, #31, a member of the Communist party, has two such reference groups for the judgment of intellectual status. These are respectively: 1. Proletarian intellectuals whom S considers as having higher intellectual status than he has because they have greater knowledge and are putting their knowledge to use. This group is composed of actual friends and acquaintances. 2. Bourgeois intellectuals, some of whom are former acquaintances and some are conceptual.[2] The members of this group are lower than S in intellectual status, since they are not putting their knowledge to productive use. Similarly, #23, a radical, states that there are three classes in society, the working, middle, and upper classes. These groups are not face-to-face groups, but portions of the total population. The subject regards himself as between the middle and working classes but identifies himself with the workers. His major reference group consists of the better paid members of the working class. Occasionally, he may compare himself with the middle class because of the fact that he can afford many things which they can. For intellectual status, he uses members of the middle class but only those individuals who are "educated" in the sense of having political sophistication. Class structuring of the reference

2. S does not know these people. He postulates their existence.

group is also seen in #17, who uses the total society as a reference group for economic status. She thinks of herself, however, as a white-collar worker and then places this class in the total structure to facilitate a determination of status.

MOTIVATIONAL PROCESSES, AUTISTIC AND REALISTIC, IN THE USE OF THE REFERENCE GROUP

There are certain instances where the use of particular reference groups is autistic, *i.e.*, directed by the subject's motives or desires, where the contradiction with reality is ignored. In other instances the use of the reference group is drive determined but does not stand in major contradiction with reality; the term "realistically motivated" is used in this context.

A case in point is #30, who realistically compares herself with groups who have what she desires. Her reference group for economic status consists of friends who live alone. S states that she is envious of such people. For the same dimension of status she compares herself with friends who have careers. S states that she desires a career. The same individual shows an autistic process in her choice of reference groups for social and intellectual status. In both instances she has two reference groups, one higher in the given status and the other lower. When she uses the higher groups, she says she does not feel that she is lower than they are or inferior to them. With the use of the lower reference groups S states that she feels she is superior in that status. The feeling of superiority exists despite her realization that she should not feel that way, since their lower status may be a function of social dislocation (see case 30 under "thoughts of status"). She rationalizes the mechanics of the upper reference group by saying that she does not feel inferior, since there is always something she can learn to equal them.

Another instance of autism is #29, who reports a reference group for social status the members of which include people like Sinclair Lewis and Heywood Broun. S would have liked to be in the company of such people, who represented his ideal—intellectually honest, free, and yet funny. For prestige status this same individual uses a reference group composed only of those individuals (men) who are the best in his occupation. The use of the reference groups is unrealistic since the subject can have no actual contact with them. The economic reference group is also representative of his economic aspirations. The group includes a few people who make a little more money than he, and S would like to be able to spend as much as they. He reports less irritation when he thinks of a wealthy reference group than when he thinks of the people who make just a little more money than he.

The case of #27 is an instance of the development of a reference group and the formation of a dimension of status as a result of "realistically motivated" considerations. This German refugee went to a school in Germany along with Nazi pupils. The Nazi children were privileged, but due to mistreatment, the Jewish children began to think that they could not do anything. Jews were not supposed to be good in athletics. S tried to do better in athletics just to show that she could do it. She compared herself with a reference group of Nazi girls, although in normal times (she says) she abhorred competition. Case #15 illustrates temporary changes in the reference group for motivational purposes. For economic status her customary reference group is made up of members of her occupation at her income level. She does, however, compare herself with people of higher and lower incomes when figuring expenditures and says—"if only I were rich" or thinks the converse to the effect that she makes more money than those of lower status and should be able to get along well. Case #24 chooses an autistic reference group when considering her character. She compares herself with girls from "home" who "went wayward." S says she had the same chance as they and did not "go wayward." S thereby feels that her character is superior to other girls. The reference group is apparently chosen with this purpose in mind.

INTRA-INDIVIDUAL COMPARISON

One person, #22, has no salient reference group for any dimension of status. She may use the casual reference group with whom she is in contact at the moment. S phrases her "status" in comparison with herself. She has her own idea of where she should be and asks herself if she is doing as well as she can. Satisfaction with status is a function of such comparison. . . .

REJECTION OF THE REFERENCE GROUP

One case, #3, rejects the concept of reference group although he does not reject reference individuals. To classify people as members of a given reference group cuts across the situation they are in. He does not look at another person without analyzing his total life situation. The approach is a functional one. An indication of rejection of a reference group for different reasons is seen in Case #4, who was a member of a W.P.A. work group. There was competition for high status within the group, but among certain individuals questions of superior status were set aside because these people were dependent on each other, trusted each other, and all had equality of status within the group.

SUMMARY

Certain interesting facts may be noted in the findings on reference group. The rare occurrence of the total population as a reference group and the great frequency of more intimate reference groups are characteristic of the process of judging status. Individuals operate for the most part in small groups within the total society, and the total population may have little relevance for them. Far more important are their friends, people they work with. . . . Examples have been cited to indicate such processes in connection with the reference group as structuring of the group, possible rejection of the group which would imply rejection of the concept of status, class structuring, autistic distortions, and absolute judgments and intra-individual comparisons of status in the absence of actual reference groups. Extreme reference groups may act via end anchoring[3] or other principles of judgment to enhance status differences. The operation of a given reference group may be affected by various motivational factors, and an extreme reference group may in the presence of these factors not enhance status differences. This is apparent in certain of the above instances where high status groups operate via identification, rationalization, or compensation by the use of an alternative reference group, so as not to cause depreciation in status.

Crucial Reference Individuals

Seventeen subjects reported the use of particular individuals as bases for status comparisons. Fourteen cases did not report such instances. In the great percentage of these latter cases, however, the subjects do make inter-individual comparisons of a casual sort, although their reference individuals are not crucial ones who are always kept in mind. Certain interesting trends may be noted in the use of reference individuals.

REJECTION OF REFERENCE INDIVIDUALS AS BASES FOR STATUS COMPARISONS

Case #23 says that there are no special individuals who should be used as measures for one's status. This is based on a sort of egalitarian view that all people are fundamentally alike and that therefore there are no particular people

---

3. When an individual is asked to make absolute judgments upon a group of stimuli, his judgments give evidence that he has formed a scale. This scale is anchored by the end stimuli, so that when the range of stimuli is changed the position of the scale shifts. The scale may be anchored at one end by a presented stimulus which redefines one end of the scale. Such an end anchor causes an extension of the scale toward the specified end, while the scale remains fixed at its other end by the former anchoring stimulus. Consequently, a judgment made formerly, now occupies a different position on the scale since the scale has been extended by the introduction of the new anchoring agent. With reference to the status scale, the reference group is analogous to anchoring by the end stimuli. For example, a person's economic status scale (if income is the criterion) may habitually be anchored by the incomes of a Negro share cropper and Henry Ford at the bottom and top ends respectively. When the reference group is changed, the range of values which anchor the status scale shifts. Consequently, a person's subjective status is a function of the reference group which operates through stimulus anchoring. An extreme reference group or reference individual may act in an analogous fashion to be an end-anchor. For example, a person whose top end of the economic scale is anchored by a $100,000 a year man has a given status. When the new end-anchor of Henry Ford is presented, the scale is extended and the subject has a lower status. Here the scale has been extended upwards, and a given stimulus, therefore, falls into a lower category than formerly. Hence as the scale moves up, the judgment moves down. This discussion has dealt with the material in the light of actual stimuli. Reference groups are not really presented stimuli. Volkmann, and Hunt and Volkmann however, have shown that values the individual selects and holds in mind operate in the same manner as presented stimuli to anchor the absolute scale. (See J. Volkmann, "The Anchoring of Psychological Scales," *Psychological Bulletin*, 33: 742, 1936; and W. A. Hunt and J. Volkmann, "The Anchoring of an Affective Scale," *American Journal of Psychology*, 49: 88–92, 1937.)

to be singled out as reference points. Case #11 has no salient reference individuals because she says she is not interested in people very much. Case #7 states that he does not believe in using particular reference individuals. He knows wealthy friends but he does not go around wishing he were like them. Perhaps the subject rejects an obvious reference individual to avoid depreciation in his status.

REFERENCE INDIVIDUALS AS ASPIRATION LEVELS

In talking of the genesis of intellectual status, Case #5, a psychologist, indicates two reference individuals acting as aspiration points. He says that he began to compare himself with Pavlov and Helmholtz and states that the greatest achievement or status that he could think of would have been to bring back one of Pavlov's dogs from Russia. Here is a graphic instance of the inability to understand the individual's view of his intellectual status without knowledge of this unusual reference point for the judgment of status. Another example of the same trend is Case #12, a secretary, who uses her boss, her boss's boss, and the top boss as well as certain people in the Blue Book for comparisons of prestige. She states that these people have more prestige than she, but that she never thinks of people lower in prestige. She is uncomfortable with these reference individuals. By using such individuals, this subject's judgment of her status should be lowered, but she apparently gets a sort of vicarious prestige from identifying with reference individuals of higher status. Likewise Case #29 compares his intellectual status with Steinmetz and Berzelius. He always compares himself unfavorably with these individuals. Yet he probably uses them as aspiration points. Case #6 uses as reference individuals the people for whom he has most admiration, such as Ruth Benedict and Franz Boas, who represent admired persons in his own profession. . . .

REFERENCE INDIVIDUALS CHOSEN BY VIRTUE OF AFFINITY OR CONTRAST WITH THE SUBJECT

The reference individuals in many cases are chosen by virtue of similarity to the subject, proximity to him in life situation, or as the result of objective facts which facilitate such comparison. The term *affinity* is used to cover such instances. Other reference individuals are chosen for comparisons of status by virtue of contrast with the subject's status. They are so different from him that they stand out as sources for comparison. The following cases illustrate these processes. An example is Case #15 who uses a good friend for comparison in social status. This reference individual does not get along as well with others as she herself does. In trying to find out the basis for this and to help her she has become conscious of comparisons of status. Case #28 illustrates a similar process. She used to compare her social status with a girl who went out socially quite often, whereas she did not. The subject felt unhappy and felt that there was something wrong with her. The comparisons continued because she knew the girl well. Whenever this subject saw her or called her on the telephone, she found out that she had a date. Thus objective proximity and contact facilitated the comparison.

Cases in which familiarity or similarity between the reference individual and the subject is operative are illustrated by #20 whose reference individual for all status dimensions is a person who belongs to the same church and whom she has known since they were children. They played together and today have about the same status. Case #21 possibly illustrates this process as well as a degree of autism. Her reference individual for attractiveness is Rita Hayworth since many friends have said that the two look alike.

Instances of "contrast" are seen in cases in which certain individuals are reference points because they contrast with the subject or because they stand out and are easy to use as reference individuals. Subject #9 reports that for cultural status the manager of the bookstore where he works acts as a reference individual. The man is very different from the subject. The manager is particularly distinctive in his own shop, since he has no knowledge of literature and the arts. This subject also states that Robert Lynd is a reference individual for intellectual status because he is so different from other academic people. Other examples reported are: strikingly beautiful or ugly women, people of great superiority, people of great personal attraction, brilliant classmates, disliked or admired people, very thrifty or extravagant people.

AUTISTIC TENDENCIES IN THE USE OF REFERENCE INDIVIDUALS

Case #27 uses her mother as a reference individual in considering character and intellectual status. S feels that she is of higher character and intellectual status than her mother, and consequently feels superior through the comparison. Case #28 uses one female friend as a reference individual for the judgment of economic status. S is much better off than her friend and feels *happy* by comparison. Yet she does not feel *superior* as a result of the comparison and there is little emotional involvement. The reason lies in the general finding reported before. Where the status of another person or the subject can be removed from personal focus and interpreted as someone else's fault or the fault of the social order, there is little inferiority feeling, as in this case. S states that her friend's low economic status is a consequence of dependency upon her parents. Consequently, it is not her friend's fault. The case suggests that such "social displacement" may not represent a rationalization to enhance the subject's status, since in this case it operates to rob the subject of any enhancement of status.

IMPOSITION OF THE DIMENSION BY THE REFERENCE INDIVIDUAL

In the preceding cases the subjects have had a dimension of status and have then considered certain reference groups in judging status within that dimension. In the following instances the presence of a given reference group operates to impose a dimension of status not formerly present. By way of analogy, when a person goes to a baseball game and sees the players he may start thinking about athletic status or his standing in relation to the players, or a person invited to

J. P. Morgan's home may begin thinking about his relative financial standing. This process is somewhat akin to a set imposed by the presence of another person which then specifies the aspect perceived or judged. Such processes are noted in the following: Case #3 reports that he never spontaneously considers income or economic status, but when he sees people who are earning much more or much less than their deserts he begins to think about economic status. S regards such people as representatives of a dislocated social order. They arouse annoyance and contempt in S if they try to appear superior by means of high incomes. Likewise, Case #18 states that she rarely thinks of economic status spontaneously. If she is confronted by some situation in which there is a person of much lower economic status, S thinks of the dimension and feels sorry for these people. She says that she feels no ego-enhancement in such situations. Similarly, if she is confronted by people exceedingly high in economic status, the dimension becomes salient. In such instances, however, the subject states that she is not personally involved. She may either feel amused and say to herself that she is happier than they or feel resentment toward the situation when she realizes that others are impoverished.

First Recollections of Status

. . . In the following discussion "genesis" of status refers to the recollection of the earliest concern with status. The results are of limited significance for the following reasons: 1. Only a limited number of subjects were able to state the approximate age for the appearance of given statuses. Most often the subject would say that he had thought of economic status, for example, when he was in public school or high school. Errors in the ability to recollect first thoughts of status are probably large. 2. Age has different meaning for different statuses. For certain statuses age is not significant since such dimensions may be precipitated by a variety of experiences. The age of genesis varies with the incidence of these experiences. For example, the incidence of economic status varies from six to twenty. Early genesis was associated with such factors as death of parents, necessity of working, and privation at an early age. Later genesis in adolescence was often associated with the need of money so as to be successful socially. Late genesis in adult life may be associated with the end of school, the independence of the subject, and the necessity of work. . . .

A number of hypotheses may be offered concerning the genesis of status.

1. Status dimensions are precipitated by given kinds of experiences or limited or emphasized by given stages of development.

2. Different status dimensions develop at different times, and concern with status is historically specific. No subject reported a general notion of status out of which particular statuses individuated. The tendency towards specificity is supported by the different ages at which particular statuses appear, and the different experiences which give rise to specific dimensions. Also, relatively few subjects reported a general status at all. . . .

3. Statuses operate with other variables to determine feelings of security. Low status may act as a potent source of insecurity feelings, and high status may serve various ego needs. When a given status no longer serves a function in the personality it may lose importance or vanish. Such dynamic tendencies may be offset by a number of factors. For example: a. Low status may not correspond with inferiority feelings if the subject interprets such status as a consequence of social dislocation rather than personal inadequacy. b. Low status may not serve to produce inferiority if the reference group has the same status and there is consequently little opportunity for invidious comparison. c. Low status may not be associated with much affect if the dimension of experience is not valued by the subject.

4. Striving for high status is directed in specific channels. One protocol, Case #3, will be presented to indicate many of these trends. His first experiences of intellectual status were in elementary school when he found out that he was a superior student. Yet he says that he did not get much pleasure from superior status for several reasons. 1. He did not like being thought superior since it meant being exposed to public scrutiny. Such exposure was painful to him and his extreme bashfulness outweighed any of the advantages of superior status. 2. He felt that this achievement was what he was competent to do and some pleasure was derived from having done a good job. (There is considerable ambivalence in this instance between the pleasure of achievement and the painful feeling of public exposure.) 3. He did not care much about intellectual status because he had the other children's values which emphasized athletic ability. Consequently, when he became a good athlete at about the age of twelve, he derived great pleasure. Athletic status became most important and he was apologetic about being a good student. His high status served the function of making him feel a more well-rounded person, whereas previously he had felt one-sided because of the attitude of his playmates towards him as an intellectual. The athletic dimension became less important with age. However, it is still present to some degree and he derives enjoyment from being a good ball player. It did lose potency because he developed security by other means and it was no longer needed.

Thoughts of economic status were precipitated by early experiences of being poor. His parents were in dire economic straits and, even at the pre-school level, low status was a potent factor in his insecurity. His extreme bashfulness and sensitiveness reinforced by social stigmatization made him feel worse. This economic area of insecurity narrowed because he noted that all the other people he knew were in the same economic position. He also says that with maturity and a body of knowledge within which to interpret his status, feelings of insecurity lessened. He realized that low economic status was not his fault but due to social dislocation. He put his childhood experience into this context, and this social perspective tended to throw thoughts of his economic status out of awareness and continually reinforced the dissociation of economic factors and feelings of security.

STATUS AS A MEANS TO AN END

Other examples of the "rise and fall" of a dimension of status in accordance with its functional value to the individual are seen in several women subjects. These data were reported only by women and reflect probably a sex difference in respect of the degree to which the status dimension of looks is emphasized in our culture for women rather than men. Subjects #12, #13, and #20 thought about the matter of their looks a good deal until they were married, at which time the dimension ceased to be important. Looks were conceived of as a means through which they might get married and once marriage was achieved the subjects no longer needed high status in respect of looks. In addition, marriage demonstrated the adequacy of their looks, hence worry about the dimension ceased. An analogous instance is Case #11 who says that at 18, she would have much preferred being told she was beautiful to being told she had a mind. Today, looks are unimportant to her. She says "My husband thinks I'm beautiful." Other instances in which looks were demonstrated by success with men are Cases #18, #24, and #17. Number seventeen says that at the age of 16 she thought she was the "world's ugliest duckling," but when she achieved social success with a beau, her estimation of her looks went up. Similar data of interest are found in Case #21 where there was no need for the dimension in her doings with men. She says that she did not worry about looks since the dates with the men she knew were not on the basis of looks. Then at the age of 19 she became concerned with looks since she conceived of looks as an instrumentality in dramatic success which is her goal.

Not all women used looks as such an instrumentality. Case #26 reports that she was always conscious of her looks and that after marriage, looks became even more important to her. Looks are not regarded as a device to get men since she says she wanted to be attractive even with girls. She likes to look well at all times, and looks imply rather an aesthetic dimension for her. Consequently, there was no change after marriage.

Examples of other statuses used as instrumentalities may be seen in Case #29 who is concerned with his prestige, which is a very important factor in his capacity as a consulting chemist. Case #18 indicates the loss of a status dimension when it no longer served a purpose. This subject was very conscious of her high social standing when she reached high school. When she found out she was not wanted within the group, she realized that people must like you for other reasons more important than social status. Then she was accepted in the group because of her abilities rather than her social status. These facts operated to vitiate the importance of this status.

INSTANCES OF CHANGES IN STATUS FOR MOTIVATIONAL REASONS

Case #10, an Italian refugee, said cultural status first assumed importance for him when he came to America. In Italy, culture had been important, but not as a tool with which to manifest superior status. There was little need to enhance his status while in Italy. In America, with the feeling of continual need to enhance his status, his cultural knowledge became used in a competitive way as an instrument of high status. Number five sought high intellectual status and his main intellectual aspirations up to this period were in the arts. He began to discover his inadequacy in this field, and was afraid to compete. Yet he wanted to assert his superiority. He sought another avenue for high intellectual status and chose a field in which he thought there were few people, i.e., Psychology. Here is an instance of changing a status dimension when it does not function adequately. Similarly #9 placed tremendous emphasis on intellectual status. He sought a way to assert his superiority, and high status in a number of dimensions was precluded for various reasons. Consequently, he found intellectual status the only dimension in which to assert his desire for high status. . . .

SIMILARITY OF STATUS IN THE REFERENCE GROUP

There are two consequences of similarity of status in the reference group. A. Thoughts of status may be associated with little inferiority because of the equality of status of the reference group. For example, Subject #20 stated that she began to work when she was twelve. She began to think about her economic status at this time and felt very bad that she was poor. She did not, however, feel inferior to others because all the people she associated with were equally poor. B. The lack of differences in status in the reference group may prevent the arousal of thoughts of status. This is indicated in the following cases: Subject #27 noted no differences in social status until she went to a party and saw how people in other social strata lived. Up to this time she had operated in one social milieu, and had gone to a private school, where the individuals all came from the same income group. Case #24 said that she had little knowledge of differences in economic status until she was about 19. She had gone to a clerical school and all the girls wore uniforms so that differences in the economic status of the girls mediated via differences in clothing were not noticed. . . .

Satisfaction with Status and Values

Various examples of the importance of values have been presented in different parts of the discussion of the interview material. Striving for status is generally directed in the channel of the valued status. Degree of dissatisfaction with a given status varies inversely with status, providing there is high valuation of the status dimension. Satisfaction with status is, consequently, also a function of the reference group, since the reference group is a variable in the judgment. Furthermore, status is a function of valuation of the reference group, as in the case of #18, who says that her status only concerns her within the context of a reference group of professional associates, and that her status outside of these groups makes no difference to her.

Satisfaction with status is also a function of aspiration for status. Mere position is not indicative of satisfaction. A person of low status may not feel inferior if he has no higher aspiration in that direction. This result may be indicated in the material on economic status. Besides reporting his income, each subject reported his aspirations for income. There were 24 cases for whom data on economic aspiration, income, and satisfaction were available. Eightteen were dissatisfied with their economic status, and 6 were satisfied. In the satisfied subjects the income range was from $900–$6100 a year, so that mere income does not specify satisfaction. Similarly, in the dissatisfied cases the income range was from $336–$4000 a year, so that mere income does not specify dissatisfaction with status.[4] Two contrasting cases may illustrate this point. One subject who earns $336 a year from Relief and domestic work says that if she had an income of $900 "I'd be joyous over it" and that with $500 a year, she could live happily. As a contrast, a person who earned $3676 a year, valued economic status first of six statuses, and reported an aspiration of $25,000.

Mean data were secured on these two groups and are presented, though they obscure the individual trend, and although six cases in the satisfied group are not an adequate sample. Aspiration for income was treated in terms of the difference between desired income and actual income expressed as a percent increment of the actual income.

The mean increment for the dissatisfied group was 836.7 per cent and for the satisfied group 290.4 per cent. This means that the dissatisfied people wanted on the average to increase their incomes to about eight times the present level and the satisfied to about three times the present level.[5] . . .

Social Implications

. . . The variables of status are mediated through an individual who acts selectively in his choice of reference group, who strives selectively for status, whose personal values affect the composition of status and the emotional concomitants of a given status, whose conceptualization of a reference group may be different from its actual character, who is not affected by all aspects of the culture nor by all references in the environment. Lynd states the case. "Understanding of institutions and social problems must be based upon analysis of what these institutions and problems *mean* to specific, differently situated people, how they look and feel to these different people, and how they are used."[6] . . .

. . . The writer interviewed one Negro subject whose reference group for a variety of statuses included white persons. Inconsistencies in the operation of

4. While there is a slight difference in the level of income for the two groups, the difference is probably not significant.

5. The magnitude of these increments is a function of the question which was worded as follows: "What is the *maximum* income that you would like to have in order to be satisfied?" The magnitude of the aspiration would have been less with different wording, but the contrasting result for both groups is probably not an artifact.

6. R. Lynd, *Knowledge for What?* Princeton: Princeton University Press, 1940.

our class structure are striking in the case of Negroes. Mobility is valued and emphasized in the culture and denied to them in practice. This pattern may not impinge in the same way on all Negroes. When the reference group for status is a high status white group and mobility is denied, we have an inconsistent pattern that is highly operative at the personal level as in the case of this subject. If the inconsistency, however, does not operate at the personal level and the reference group is intra-racial or intra-class, there may be fewer unfortunate consequences. Sutherland[7] discusses these problems: The extent to which minority status is effective depends on the accommodations to inferior status, and the hopes of many Negro youths are defined by the culture of the Negro world itself. The imposition of a white reference group is probably a function of interaction with whites, and such interaction varies with the Negro's life situation.

An interesting suggestion about race and status may be found in Brenman's work.[8] In the paragraph above the suggestion was made that status comparisons might be intra-racial and that less discontent would follow. Yet Brenman notes that in the absence of extreme economic differences among urban northern Negroes, which differences exist in the white group with a consequently differentiated social scale, the felt necessity to establish socially distinct lines has been met by subtler scales. She lists seven determinants of status within the group which differentiate subclasses. Thus it seems that given the values and motives of a surrounding culture which stress mobility and enhancement of status, status distinctions may find avenues for development. . . .

. . . The suggestion that stability and personal security are a function of fixity of status, intra-class goals, or intra-class reference groups has already been made. The theory derives some support from our data on the relation of aspiration and satisfaction. Where the discrepancy between aspirations and achievement was large, there was dissatisfaction. The use of an intra-class reference group may operate to lessen the difference between aspiration and achievement and also anchors the scale for judgment so as not to lower one's status markedly. Yet there is also contrary material on the problem: A. The American Dream has apparently operated to lessen the discontent of individuals. In this case there is a high reference group and dissatisfaction is not a consequence. B. There is the suggestion that if individuals of low status recognized their low status and their different possibilities, and lack of chance for betterment, there would be more discontent. This is contrary to the earlier relation between intra-class goals and satisfaction. C. Empirical interview data have been presented to indicate the wide use of reference groups and individuals of exceedingly high status who

7. R. L. Sutherland, *Color, Class, and Personality*, Washington, D.C.: American Council on Education, 1942.

8. M. Brenman, "The Relationship between Minority-Group Membership and Group Identification in a Group of Urban Middle-Class Negro Girls," *Journal of Social Psychology*, 11: 171–197, 1940.

vicariously *enhance* the subject's status. D. Lewin, Lippitt, and White[9] have suggested a positive correspondence between rigidity of group structure and aggression. How are these facts to be reconciled?

Several suggestion may be offered:

A. Reference groups, classes and castes operate through the medium of individuals and a reference group may be manipulated in different ways to give different results. Two contrasted processes might be involved in the use of reference groups. There may be identification with the status of a high reference group. There may be the judgmental situation in which a high reference group or individual operates by stimulus anchoring or end anchoring to define the absolute scale. In the case of identification with a high reference group, there may be vicarious satisfaction. Correspondingly, identification with a low group and recognition of low status may cause dissatisfaction. Where the reference group operates as an anchoring agent, a high reference group produces low status and discontent, and a low reference group produces higher status and greater satisfaction. Hence, the process by which the variables are manipulated may hold the key to the consequences.

B. If we assume that the process is one of judgment in which a reference group or individual anchors the scale for the judgment of status, an alternative hypothesis may be suggested. Rogers[10] has shown that the degree of change in the scale when an additional anchoring agent (in this case a reference group) is introduced is a rectilinear function of the remoteness of the anchor. Beyond a certain degree of remoteness, however, the function breaks. This would mean with respect to status and the reference group that the use of an inter-class reference group might operate to lower the judgment of a person of low status up to a certain point. If the status of the reference group were very remote from the person's status (e.g., if a share cropper used Henry Ford as a reference individual), there would be little additional loss in status.

C. The understanding of the phenomenon may not lie in the structure of class or caste societies per se, but in inconsistencies in their operation. A person who has a high status reference group in a society where there is actual mobility and a reasonable life chance of achieving higher status, may not manifest insecurity. Where there is in actuality no mobility and little realistic chance of achieving the higher status, there may be much insecurity. In this latter case it is necessary that the individual realize the impossibility of the aspiration. If mobility is unlikely and the individual, nevertheless, regards mobility as possible, as in the American Dream, the situation may not produce insecurity. . . .

9. K. Lewin, R. Lippitt, and R. K. White, "Patterns of Aggressive Behavior in Experimentally Created 'Social Climates'," *Journal of Social Psychology*, 10: 271–299, 1939.

10. S. Rogers, "The Anchoring of Absolute Judgments," *Archives of Psychology*, No. 261, 1941.

A Conceptual Framework and
Some Empirical Data Regarding
Comparisons of Social Rewards

Martin Patchen

A NUMBER of investigations, including the wartime researches reported in the *American Soldier* volumes, have made it clear that people's aspirations, satisfactions, and self-evaluations are determined not so much by their objective position as by their standing relative to specific persons with whom they compare.[1] These findings raise general questions about what determines how an individual will react to a given comparison—e.g., whether with satisfaction or with dissatisfaction. They also raise general questions about what determines the *choice* of specific comparisons from among a number of possible alternatives.

Reprinted from *Sociometry*, 24: 136–156, 1961, by permission of the author and the publisher, the American Sociological Association. The research reported here is part of a larger study conducted by the Organizational Behavior and Change Programs of the Survey Research Center. The study was under the general supervision of Dr. Floyd C. Mann, who played an important part in making the research possible. Most of the data and ideas presented here are part of a doctoral dissertation submitted to the University of Michigan in August 1959.

1. D. W. Chapman and J. Volkmann, "A Social Determinant of the Level of Aspiration," *Journal of Abnormal and Social Psychology*, 34: 225–238, 1939; H. H. Hyman, "The Psychology of Status," *Archives of Psychology*, 38, 15, 1942; A. McIntosh, "Differential Effect of the Status of the Competing Group on Levels of Aspiration," *American Journal of Psychology*, 55: 546–554, 1942; M. Patchen, "The Effect of Reference Group Standards on Job Satisfactions," *Human Relations*, 11: 303–314, 1958; and S. A. Stouffer et al., *The American Soldier* 2 vols., Princeton, N.J.: Princeton University Press, 1949–50.

Festinger[2] and Davis[3] have presented formal theoretical analyses of the comparison process. Davis states that he has not attempted to derive the formal relations between his theory and that of Festinger, though he suggests that his theory treats comparisons "where perceptions and evaluations are unambiguous" while Festinger's theory treats comparisons "where perceptions and evaluations are ambiguous."[4]

The present paper points out what appear to be serious weaknesses in Davis's formulation of comparison phenomena. A conceptual approach to the comparison process will be outlined which is intended to be more general than either the Davis or Festinger formulation. This conceptual approach will treat comparisons in terms closely related to the theory of dissonance proposed by Festinger.[5] Our consideration of what determines the choice of comparisons will, in turn, suggest some implications for dissonance theory. Data relevant to these theoretical ideas, from a study of wage comparisons made by workers in an oil refinery, will be presented.

Some Theoretical Ideas

THE SUBJECTIVE MEANING OF GIVEN COMPARISONS

Davis divides comparisons into those made with members of an "in-group" (same marital status, same education, etc.) and those made with members of an "out-group".[6] The meaning of comparisons to those in an in-group is clear. For example, as Davis points out, those who are deprived with respect to some social reward, and who compare to someone in the same in-group who is not deprived, will experience feelings of relative deprivation and, presumably, dissatisfaction. However, the meaning of comparisons with those in an out-group is not as clear. Those who are deprived and who compare to an out-group person will, Davis says, experience an "attitude" of "relative subordination." Those who are not deprived and compare to an out-group person who is deprived, will experience an "attitude" of "relative superiority".[7] But how will the comparer *react* to his position of, say, relative subordination compared to the out-group person? Will he be satisfied? Will he maintain a feeling of high self-esteem? Or will he be dissatisfied, angry, or ashamed?

We obviously cannot answer these questions until we know what the "out-group" is, what characteristics it has, and what relevance these characteristics

2. L. Festinger, "A Theory of Social Comparison Processes," *Human Relations*, 7: 117–140, 1954.

3. J. A. Davis, "A Formal Interpretation of the Theory of Relative Deprivation," *Sociometry*, 22: 280–296, 1959.

4. *Ibid.*, p. 282.

5. L. Festinger, *A Theory of Cognitive Dissonance*, Evanston, Ill.: Row, Peterson & Company, 1957.

6. Davis, *op. cit.*, pp. 283ff.

7. *Ibid.*, p. 283.

are seen by the comparers as having for deprivation with regard to some social reward. Without knowing these things, we cannot predict the subjective meaning of the comparisons made with this "out-group."

This point is of very general significance. It applies not only to comparisons to true out-groups—in the sense of persons who are widely and generally different from the comparer. It applies also to the large number of comparisons to persons who are similar to the comparer in some ways but different in others. Take the case of wage comparisons. A man may compare to someone who has generally equal education, but the comparison person may have three years of college instead of four, or a year of post-graduate work, or have gone to an Ivy League College instead of a state university, or majored in a different subject. Or, given complete identity of education, the comparison person may differ in any one of a number of other characteristics—age, family background, seniority, etc.—which are relevant to the wage comparison. Indeed, when we consider specific comparisons, the lines between in-groups and out-groups blur. The question of how the individual will react to various comparisons where the comparison person differs from himself in ways *other* than on the dimension being judged becomes, therefore, very important.

Festinger shows an awareness of the importance of the relative position of comparer and comparison person on a *variety* of dimensions when he states the hypothesis, "If persons who are very divergent from one's own opinion or ability are perceived as different from oneself on *attributes consistent with the divergence,* the tendency to narrow the range of comparability becomes stronger."[8] But, rather than considering additional attributes only in their possible role of limiting the range of comparisons, we may consider comparison on such secondary attributes as a fundamental part of the comparison process.

It is possible to think of any given social comparison as not one, but two or more, simultaneous comparisons. On the one hand individuals compare themselves on a primary dimension being judged (e.g., earnings). But comparisons on this primary dimension cannot be made in a cognitive vacuum. Such comparisons become meaningful to the individual only when he also compares himself to others on secondary dimensions which are believed to be bases of standing on the primary dimension (e.g., skill, seniority, education— where pay is the primary dimension) or which are otherwise relevant to standing on the primary dimension (e.g., for pay, how interesting various jobs are).

Continuing in our use of the example of wage comparisons,[9] the individual, in effect, makes a cognitive relation of the following sort:

8. Festinger, "Social Comparison, ... *op. cit.,*" p. 133.

9. The present discussion is phrased in terms of wage comparisons in order to give substantive flavor to abstract ideas and because the research to be described has been concerned with wage comparisons. However, the general conception is thought to hold true for other types of social comparisons as well, especially those of other social rewards—e.g., prestige, popularity, rank, affection, and material goods.

$$\frac{\text{my earnings}}{\text{his (their) earnings}} \quad \text{compared to} \quad \frac{\text{my position on dimensions related to earnings}}{\text{his (their) position on dimensions related to earnings}}$$

We may define a *perceived consonant comparison* as one in which the comparer perceives one side of this relation (i.e., the ratio of one's own earnings to another's earnings) as congruent with, or appropriate to, the other side of the relation (i.e., the ratio of one's own position on related dimensions to another's position on related dimensions). Similarly, a *perceived dissonant comparison* is defined as one in which the comparer perceives the ratio on one side of the relation as incongruent with, or inappropriate to, the ratio on the other side of the relation.[10]

It is also possible to distinguish among comparisons according to the degree of *objective* dissonance present. Some comparisons—e.g., to men of the same education and age as the comparer who are earning more than he—provide more objective bases for the comparer to perceive dissonance in than do other comparisons—e.g., to older men with more schooling who are earning more than he. We define *objectively consonant comparisons* as those in which the ratio of the comparer's position on dimensions relevant to pay to another's position on these relevant dimensions is culturally considered congruent with, or appropriate to, the ratio of their earnings. *Objectively dissonant comparisons* are, similarly, defined as those in which the ratio of the two persons' positions on dimensions relevant to pay is culturally considered incongruent with, or inappropriate to, the ratio of their earnings.[11]

From the preceding general description of the comparison process, it is apparent that the following kinds of pay comparisons (as shown in Figure 1) are likely to be perceived as *dissonant in favor of the comparison person:*

1. Comparison to someone earning *more*—who is generally *similar* to the comparer on attributes related to earnings (cell F).
2. Comparison to someone earning *more*—who is generally *inferior* to the comparer on attributes related to pay (cell I).
3. Comparison to someone earning the *same*—who is generally *inferior* on attributes related to pay (cell H).

10. This definition appears closely similar to Festinger's definition of dissonance, although the present formulation was conceived without intentional linkage to Festinger's work. Festinger states, "Two cognitive elements are in a dissonant relation if, considering these two alone, the obverse of one follows from the other" (*Cognitive Dissonance*, pp. 260–261).

11. It is sometimes useful to separate presently consonant comparisons into those which will remain consonant over time and those which are *potentially* dissonant. This subject is discussed in detail in M. Patchen, "The Choice of Wage Comparisons," Ph.D. dissertation, University of Michigan, 1959.

The following types of comparisons (again shown in Figure 1) are likely to be perceived as *dissonant in favor of the comparer:*

1. Comparisons to those earning *less*—who are generally *superior* to the comparer on attributes related to earnings (cell A).
2. Comparisons to those earning *less*—who are generally *similar* to the comparer on attributes related to earnings (cell D).
3. Comparisons to those earning the *same*—who are generally *superior* to the comparer on attributes related to earnings (cell B).

Cell E of Figure 1 shows the type of comparison which is most likely to be perceived as consonant—i.e., comparisons to those who earn the *same* as oneself and who are also closely *similar* on attributes relevant to earnings. It would be

Figure I—Types of Wage Comparisons

Over-all Position of Comparison Person on Attributes Relevant to Earnings	COMPARISON PERSON		
	Earns Less	Earns Same	Earns More
Superior	Dissonant—in favor of comparer A	Dissonant—in favor of comparer B	1. Consonant 2. Dissonant—in favor of comparison person 3. Dissonant—in favor of comparer C
Similar	Dissonant—in favor of comparer D	Consonant E	Dissonant—in favor of comparison person F
Inferior	1. Consonant 2. Dissonant—in favor of comparison person 3. Dissonant—in favor of comparer G	Dissonant—in favor of comparison person H	Dissonant—in favor of comparison person I

expected that perfect consonance in comparisons—either as objectively determined by the observer or as perceived by the comparer—is rare. However, it is probable that many comparisons which are close to perfect consonance may—for all practical purposes—be treated as consonant.

Perhaps the most interesting cells in Figure 1 are cells C and G. Cell C, for example, shows the possible types of comparisons which may occur when the comparison person earns more than the comparer and is also generally superior to the comparer on attributes relevant to earnings. Such comparisons may be consonant, dissonant in favor of the comparison person, or dissonant in favor of the comparer. Which it is depends on *how much more* the comparison person earns in relation to *how much superior* he is considered.

Some concrete comparisons which fit in cell C, drawn from interviews with oil workers, should make this point clearer.

Comparison type C1 (consonant) is illustrated by the remarks of a plant protection worker who compared his earnings to that of a certified accountant who earns more than himself. The comparer said he was "satisfied" with the way their earnings compared, explaining, "He has more education; he is a college graduate; he should be earning more."

Comparison type C2 (dissonant in favor of comparison person) is illustrated by the case of an assistant mechanic who chose "the fellow I work with"— a full mechanic—with whom to compare his earnings. The assistant said he was "not too satisfied" with the way their earnings compared, explaining, "We do the same work and there's three pay rates difference; I didn't have my papers when he did; he's quite a bit older than I am. He had 'em for a quite few years." While this man is willing to acknowledge the other to be superior to him in some ways, he evidently doesn't think the amount of difference justifies three rates of difference in pay.

Comparison type C3 (dissonant in favor of comparer) is illustrated by the case of a welder who chooses for comparison his brother-in-law who is a chemist and who earns more than he. The welder checks the most extreme category of satisfaction with the comparison ("very satisfied") and comments, "Well, he has gone to the University for five years and the difference in our wages is very small." In a similar case, a production worker who compared to a teacher who earned more than he, commented, "Considering the difference in our educations, I figure I'm doing better than he is."

These cases illustrate vividly why it is necessary to go beyond a mere identification of the reference groups or persons who are pertinent to given individuals. Such an approach tends to assume that once the comparison persons are identified, it is immediately obvious whether the comparison is favorable to the comparer (e.g., by whether he earns more or less). The present analysis indicates that identifying relevant comparison persons is only one part of the job of understanding the comparisons involved.

If the picture of the comparison process outlined above is adequate, then we should be able to predict individuals' satisfaction with specific wage comparisons when we have sufficient objective information about how the comparer and comparison person stand on dimensions culturally considered relevant to pay, as well as about the difference in their earnings.

Hypothesis I Satisfaction with wage comparisons will be a function not of objective difference in earnings, in itself, but of the objective dissonance of the comparison as a whole.

We would expect also, if our picture of the comparison process is meaningful, that individuals will consciously base their feelings of satisfaction or dissatisfaction with wage comparisons not on the actual money difference, nor on their need for money, nor on why they would like to have the money, but on the appropriateness of the wage difference in view of other relevant differences between themselves and the comparison persons.

We may state this expectation more formally, as follows:

Hypothesis II   Men who are satisfied with specific wage comparisons will explain their satisfaction in terms of a consonance between relative wage standing and relative standing on attributes related to pay; men who are dissatisfied with specific wage comparisons will explain their dissatisfaction in terms of a dissonance between relative wage standing and standing on attributes relevant to pay.

THE CHOICE OF COMPARISONS

What determines which specific comparisons, from among many possible alternatives, will be chosen? Davis's crucial assumption, in this regard, is that "Within the population comparisons are random".[12] Though he admits that this assumption may appear dubious, he sees "no reason to introduce a more complicated one." The rest of Davis's further theoretical derivations rest on this fundamental assumption.

It seems likely that some of the variance in the choice of comparisons can be accounted for on the basis of Davis's assumption of randomness. However, the present theoretical approach to comparisons would emphasize also that some individuals have stronger *motivation* than do others to choose dissonant rather than consonant comparisons.

One determinant of the individual's motivation to choose dissonant or consonant comparisons was expected to be whether or not he accepts *personal responsibility* for his present position. If the individual sees himself as responsible for his present job position, a dissonant wage comparison will make him feel ashamed. Compared to the other person, he is a failure. For men who accept personal responsibility for their fate, there should, therefore, be strong pressures to avoid such dissonant comparisons.

This picture of motivations which impel the individual to choose consonant comparisons has parallels to Festinger's discussion of the forces which determine the choice of comparisons. Festinger sees the motivational push behind comparisons as the drive to evaluate oneself (one's opinions or abilities). However, the individual wants this evaluation to be favorable, to show him as being as good as or a little better than others like himself. Festinger states:

> The action to reduce the discrepancy which exists is, in the case of opinions, a relatively uncomplicated pressure towards uniformity. When and if uniformity of opinion is achieved there is a state of social quiescence. In the case of abilities,

12. Davis, *op. cit.*, p. 282.

however, the action to reduce discrepancies interacts with the unidirectional push to do better and better. The resolution of these two pressures, which act simultaneously, is a state of affairs where all the members are relatively close together with respect to some specific ability, but not completely uniform. The pressures cease acting on a person if he is just slightly better than the others.[13]

In the terminology used in this paper, the individual is described as motivated to choose comparisons which are at least consonant.

However, according to the present theory, the comparer may, in some cases, be motivated to make comparisons which are dissonant in favor of the other person. For the man who rejects personal responsibility—who blames his boss, the union, society, etc.—for the existence of the dissonance, dissonant comparisons will usually evoke righteous indignation, instead of feelings of shame. Such a comparer can also use dissonant comparisons to justify protests over his present status and to legitimate (to himself as well as to others) a claim that he deserves a higher status.

For the case of wage comparisons, the following hypothesis concerning personal responsibility is advanced:

Hypothesis III Men who see the responsibility for their occupational and wage position as not being their own will be more likely than others to choose dissonant wage comparisons.

If Hypothesis III is correct, we would expect as a corollary that "non-responsible" men will, more often than "responsible" men, be dissatisfied with wage comparisons.

It may be noted that the question of the acceptance or non-acceptance of personal responsibility, which is so relevant to wage comparisons, probably has little relevance for the types of comparisons—opinions and abilities—discussed by Festinger. In most instances the individual would be hard put to blame his opinions or his abilities on someone else. But comparisons such as those concerning prestige, material goods and affection relate to things which are determined to some extent by other people. If we imagine a continuum which shows the relevance of personal responsibility to comparisons, then the types of comparisons which Festinger discusses would cover only one part of the continuum.

Another difference between Festinger's theory of comparison processes and the present theoretical approach may be noted. Festinger stresses the importance to the comparer of narrowing the range of comparisons to those like himself. Where the comparer's main motivation is evaluation of the self *per se* (as perhaps in comparisons of some opinions and abilities), such pressures to narrow the range of comparisons may be very strong. It may also be that, where it is difficult to compare some attribute with accuracy (e.g., again, in the case of some opinions and abilities), then a narrowing of the range of comparisons will be

13. Festinger, "Social Comparison,.*op. cit.*" p. 125.

encouraged. However, in the case of other comparisons, such as wage comparisons, we would not expect such pressures to narrow the range of comparability to be strong. For if the comparer is actually motivated to create dissonance, such dissonance can sometimes best be established in comparisons to those who are unlike the comparer on the attribute being judged. For example, the most common and direct way to make a dissonant wage comparison is to compare to someone whose earnings are *much higher* than one's own, but who is, nevertheless, similar to oneself in some relevant ways.

Finally, the present theoretical approach has some interesting implications for the general theory of dissonance which Festinger has proposed.[14] Festinger postulates that when dissonance occurs, forces to reduce this dissonance will arise. Festinger also discusses factors which create resistance to the reduction of dissonance. However, he seems to hold that, whatever the resistance to its reduction, the dissonance itself is anxiety producing. The present conception of dissonance with regard to comparisons of social rewards assumes, however, that under certain conditions even great dissonance may produce little anxiety and that the dissonance itself may serve the purpose of the comparer.

Research Setting and Operations

Having outlined a conceptual framework for understanding comparisons and having stated three hypotheses, we turn now to the presentation of some empirical data which bear on these ideas.

THE SITE

The research reported here was conducted at an oil refinery located in a small Canadian city of approximately 40,000 population. Several other oil and chemical plants are located in this area. There are about 1500 non-supervisory employees working at the refinery. All employees, except a few office workers, are male and only men were interviewed. Almost all of the men are married and the great majority have children.

The largest group (34 per cent) work at traditional trades—such as pipefitter, mason, machinist—in the task of maintaining refinery equipment. Another large group of men (31 per cent) control and regulate the actual production of oil, jobs which require the watching and adjusting of control dials, as well as related tasks. Smaller groups of men work at assembly-line jobs, mainly at packaging and manufacturing oil drums (15 per cent), at the testing laboratory (6 per cent), at common labor and janitorial work (8 per cent), and at other miscellaneous jobs, such as driving trucks (6 per cent).

SAMPLE

A one-third sample of male non-supervisory employees was interviewed. This sample was stratified by occupational groups and by pay level. Excluding

14. Festinger, *Cognitive Dissonance, op. cit.*

those who could not be reached for interviewing, the number of men included in the final sample was 489, or 90.5 per cent of the original sample drawn.

MEASURES

During the interview, the respondent was told: "Now I'd like to ask you a few questions about how your earnings compare with the wages of other people you know about. Who would be someone either here at 'Atlas' or outside the refinery whose yearly earnings are *different* from yours?"[15] After one comparison person was named and identified as to kind of work, the respondent was asked: "Who would be someone else whose yearly earnings are different from yours?" For each of the two comparison persons, the following information is available:

Direction of Comparison

The respondent was asked: "Is he earning more or less than you are right now?"

Occupational Level of Comparison Person

Responses concerning the type of work done by the comparison persons, as described by the respondent, were coded into these ten occupational categories: (a) Professionals; (b) Proprietors and Managers; (c) Clerical or Sales; (d) Blue-collar, foreman; (e) Blue-collar, skilled and semi-skilled, non-supervisory; (f) Blue-collar, unskilled; (g) Blue-collar, unspecified; (h) Farm Owners and Farm Workers; (i) Unemployed; (j) Other.

It seems reasonable to assume that those who are on a different occupational level from our respondents will differ from the respondents in a number of ways which are culturally considered relevant to pay. These differences include educational level, social class, style of life, and the kinds of skills involved in work. Comparison persons who are professional men are most likely to be superior to our blue-collar respondents in all of these ways. Men in white-collar occupations (clerical and sales) and men who are proprietors or managers of businesses are also likely to have backgrounds different from those of our respondents, though not so much superior as that of professional persons.

Respondent's Satisfaction with the Way Earnings Now Compare

After a respondent had indicated whether he or the comparison person was earning more, he was asked, "Which of these statements best shows how you feel about the way your earnings now compare to his earnings?" He was then handed a card which listed five alternatives, ranging from "very satisfied" to "not at all satisfied."

15. This rather indirect way of obtaining wage comparisons was adopted after more direct questions caused resentment and defensiveness among some respondents during exploratory interviews. Since time pressure permitted only two comparisons to be obtained and probed, comparisons only to those with *different* earnings were asked for. This restriction was intended to maximize the chances for dissonant comparisons to be chosen.

Reasons for Satisfaction or Dissatisfaction with Comparison

After the respondent indicated his degree of satisfaction with the way earnings compare, he was asked, "Could you tell me why you feel this way?" The great majority of responses to this question were in terms of comparison on dimensions other than pay. These responses were coded in terms of the type of dimension compared on and the placement the respondent gave himself in relation to the comparison person on this non-pay dimension.

Other data available on each respondent include:

Absolute Pay Rate

These were available from company records.

Relative Pay Position

Respondents reported their age, education, length of service at the refinery, and the occupations of their brothers and brothers-in-law. On each of these criteria, every respondent was coded as below the median, at the median, or above the median on pay for men like himself. For example, the distribution on pay for men in each age category was calculated so that every man in the category was assigned a score showing his relative position on pay for men of his age. In the same manner, each man was given a score showing his pay position relative to men of his educational category, relative to men of his seniority category, and relative to men of his family. In addition to the scores showing each man's relative pay position on each of these four dimensions, an overall index of relative pay position was constructed by adding each man's score (corresponding to below, at, or above the median) on all four dimensions.

Perception of Personal Responsibility for Wage Position

This is indicated by answers to two questions asked in the interview. (a) "For men who grew up when you did, how much would you say a man's chances for getting ahead in life depended on himself and how much on things beyond his control?" (Five alternatives were given on a printed card, ranging from "Almost entirely on the man himself" to "Not at all on the man himself.") (b) "Thinking about Atlas, how much would you say advancement usually depends on how well a man can do a job and how much on other things?" (Five alternatives were given on a printed card, ranging from "Almost entirely on how well a man can do a job" to "Not at all on how well a man can do a job.") These questions were intended to tap two separate, though related, components of personal responsibility in the life history of the individual. When numbers from one to five are assigned to alternative answers to each of these questions, there is a moderate positive correlation between acceptance of responsibility as measured by one question and as measured by the other ($r = + .29$). Moreover, each question, taken separately, was found to have a similar relation to the direction of comparisons chosen and to satisfaction with such comparisons. An index of acceptance of personal responsibility was constructed simply by adding each respondent's scores on the two questions.

CONSONANCE AND DISSONANCE

With the present data we can distinguish well only a limited number of concrete types of consonance and dissonance from among the many possible types shown in Figure 1. Comparisons to those earning the same as the comparer (cells B, E, and H of Figure 1) are not available, since we asked men to choose persons whose earnings are different from their own.

The data available also make it difficult to classify various comparisons to those earning less than the comparer (cells A, D, and G) as more or less dissonant. This is because comparison persons who earn less than our respondents are almost all on the same general occupational level (blue-collar, non-supervisory) and it is not possible to tell whether these comparison persons are objectively superior, similar, or inferior on attributes relevant to earnings.

However, when we examine comparisons to those who earn *more* than the comparer, it is possible to make some rough distinctions between those comparisons which are objectively consonant and those which are objectively dissonant in favor of the comparison person. Comparisons to those who earn more but are on a higher occupational level fall in cell C and may, in general, be considered as more objectively consonant than comparisons to those on the same occupational level who earn more (cell F).[16] This is because higher earnings for persons on a higher occupational level (with accompanying higher social status, higher education, etc.) are, in general, culturally defined as appropriate, while differences in earnings for men on the same occupational level are not as often culturally defined as appropriate.

Results

OBJECTIVE DISSONANCE AND SATISFACTION

Our first hypothesis is that satisfaction with earnings will be a function not of the difference in earnings, as such, but of the difference in earnings in relation to the objective status differences between comparer and comparison person—i.e., of the objective dissonance of the comparison. A specific prediction based on this hypothesis was that men who choose "upward" wage comparison persons on the same occupational level as themselves (Cell F of Figure 1) will more often be dissatisfied with such comparisons than will men who choose upward comparison persons of a higher occupational level (Cell C of Figure 1). This prediction ignores the absolute amount of difference in earnings among men on

---

16. The number of comparisons to persons who earn more but who are on a lower occupational level is too small to be included in the analysis.

various occupational levels. However, since the gap in earnings is likely to be larger between occupational levels than within them, this factor should work against our hypothesis, rather than for it.

Table 1 presents the data on satisfaction with upward comparisons,[17] separately for different occupational levels of the person with whom comparison is made. Those who choose comparison persons who earn more but who are on a higher occupational level are more satisfied with the comparisons than are men who choose comparison persons who earn more but are on their own occupational level. This difference is most marked when we compare satisfaction

Table I—Satisfaction with Wage Comparisons to Those Earning More, in Relation to Occupational Level of Comparison Person[a]

Occupational Level of Upward Comparison Person	Mean Satisfaction with Comparison[b]	Number of Comparers[c]
Professional	2.23	66
Clerical or sales	2.33	24
Proprietor of own business; manager	2.42	64
Blue-collar: foreman	2.59	76
Blue-collar: skilled or semi-skilled	2.63	252
All other (including farm and no mention)	2.43	37
Total	2.52	519

[a] Low scores indicate greater satisfaction with comparisons.
[b] Solid line joining two mean scores indicates that the difference is significant at the .01 level (1-tailed t test). Broken line joining two mean scores indicates that the difference is significant at the .10 level (1-tailed t test).
[c] For each comparer, a maximum of one comparison in a single row is included in the table, to avoid giving any comparer greater weight than any other. Where a comparer chose two upward comparison persons of the same occupational level, the first comparison was taken.

with comparison persons who are professionals to satisfaction with comparison persons who are blue-collar non-supervisory personnel like our respondents (difference between means significant at beyond .01 level; one-tailed *t* test). However, men are also more satisfied with comparisons to "clerical-sales" or "proprietory-managerial" persons who earn more than themselves than they are with comparisons to blue-collar workers who earn more than they do (difference between means significant at .10 level in both cases). These data consistently support Hypothesis I.

17. The greater the satisfaction a man expressed with the specific comparisons he chose, the more content he was with his wages. A questionnaire item asked respondents, in a context other than that of comparisons, "How well do you feel you've done up to now as far as earnings go?" At one extreme, among those who said they were "very satisfied" with both wage comparisons chosen, 90.2 per cent said they felt they had, in general, done "very well" or "quite well" with respect to their earnings. At the other extreme, among men who said they were "not too satisfied" or "not at all satisfied" with both specific wage comparisons, only 16.0 per cent said they had, in general, done "very well" or "quite well."

PERCEIVED CONSONANCE AND DISSONANCE

We have predicted not only that *objective* dissonance will lead to feelings of dissatisfaction with comparisons, but that feelings of satisfaction or dissatisfaction will be *subjectively* based on perceptions of consonance or dissonance (Hypothesis II). Table 2 shows the reasons given by respondents for feelings of satisfaction or dissatisfaction with comparisons to those who earn more than themselves.

Table 2—Reasons Given by Respondents for Feeling Satisfied or Dissatisfied with Specific Comparisons to Persons Who Earn More[a] *(Read Table Vertically)*

	DEGREE OF SATISFACTION WITH COMPARISON		
Reasons Given for Feeling of Satisfaction or Dissatisfaction	*Satisfied per cent*	*Neither Satisfied nor Dissatisfied per cent*	*Dissatisfied per cent*
Respondent has compensating advantages	44.6	19.5	0.0
Financial	16.1	5.4	0.0
Non-financial	28.5	14.1	0.0
Comparison person is superior	55.8	34.8	17.8
In what his job requires (education, skill, etc.)	44.6	22.8	13.7
In seniority, experience, age	6.8	8.7	1.4
In personal qualities	4.4	3.3	2.7
Comparison person's job is different—unspecified	8.0	16.3	2.7
Respondent is equal or superior	1.2	9.8	75.4
In what his job requires (education, skill, etc.)	0.8	8.7	64.4
In seniority, experience, age	0.4	1.1	11.0
Respondent is not interested in comparing earnings	5.6	18.5	0.0
Respondent earns enough for his needs	2.8	4.4	0.0
Respondent wants more money, higher living standard	0.0	0.0	8.2
Other, or vague	3.6	10.9	16.4
Number of comparers	(249)	(92)	(73)

[a] The percentages in each column add up to more than 100, since a maximum of two reasons was coded for each respondent. The reasons given by each man for his feelings about a maximum of one comparison are included in any single column.

REASONS FOR FEELING SATISFIED

Of those who said they are satisfied with comparisons to men who earn more, over half (56 per cent) mentioned ways in which comparison persons are superior to themselves, thus justifying the difference in wages. More education, more seniority, being older, having more skills, having more responsibility, and having worked harder for advancement are among the superior attributes of the comparison person named.

A large proportion (about 45 per cent) of those who expressed satisfaction with upward comparisons explained their feelings by pointing to compensating advantages which they enjoy. Such items as having a better benefit program at

Atlas, working more steadily, liking their own work better, and having a cleaner job are typical of the compensating advantages mentioned.

About 8 per cent of those satisfied emphasized the difference in jobs per se, without specifying which man deserves more pay. These men mentioned the fact of working for different companies, different departments, or different industries, implying that these essential differences explain the difference in wages. About 6 per cent of those satisfied said they were not interested in comparing wages; about 1 per cent mentioned ways in which they are equal or superior to the men who earn more; and about 4 per cent gave other reasons.

These data show that an overwhelming majority of men explain their satisfaction with upward comparisons in terms of differences between themselves and the comparison person on dimensions related directly or indirectly to pay. These differences are usually either some superiority of the comparison person or some compensating advantage enjoyed by the respondent. In either case, what these men seem to be saying, in effect, is: "I am satisfied to be earning less, because there is some other difference between us which makes the wage difference okay." Or, in our theoretical terms, "I am satisfied because the difference in wages is consonant with other differences between us."

It is noteworthy that so few respondents (about 3 per cent) answered merely in terms of the wage difference—saying they earned enough for their needs—without relating the wage difference to some other relevant differences between the individuals.

REASONS FOR DISSATISFACTION

Among those who are dissatisfied with earning less than comparison persons, a large majority (about 75 per cent) justify their feeling in terms of their own equality or superiority in ways directly relevant to pay. Mention of one's own high level of education, skill, responsibility, seniority, and experience and/or the comparison person's low standing in these respects are typical of the kinds of reasons included in this category.

Again, very few men explained their dissatisfaction merely in terms of the money difference or in the closely related terms of their wish for more material things. Only 8 per cent mentioned these reasons and, among these men, many gave additional answers in terms of the relative standing of comparer and comparison person on attributes other than earnings.

About 18 per cent of those dissatisfied also mention some *superiority* of the comparison person—most often in an attempt to give both sides of the issue. Three per cent mention the differences in occupation, industry, etc.

There are also a relatively large number of answers (about 16 per cent) by dissatisfied men which do not fit in the categories mentioned. Detailed examination of these uncategorized answers reveals that many are vague and non-specific, sometimes a mere restatement of dissatisfaction.

The data for dissatisfied men thus also support Hypothesis II. The great majority of men explain their feeling of dissatisfaction in terms of dissonance between differences in pay and differences on attributes related to pay.

In general, Table 2 provides striking empirical confirmation of a basic tenet of the conceptual scheme presented—that comparisons on some primary dimension (e.g., pay) are almost always made in the context of simultaneous comparisons on other culturally relevant dimensions.

REASONS FOR FEELING "NEUTRAL" ABOUT COMPARISON

The reasons given by those who say they are "neither satisfied nor dissatisfied" with upward comparisons indicate that their "neutrality" of feeling is based on cross-pressures exerted by perceptions of consonance and perceptions of dissonance. About one-third of these men mention some way in which the *comparison person* is superior, but about 10 per cent mention some way in which they themselves are equal or superior.

The most striking difference shown by this group is the relatively large proportion (about 19 per cent) who say they are not interested in comparing earnings. There appears to be a tendency in this group to avoid thinking about comparisons and to shut off their feelings about comparisons ("neither satisfied nor dissatisfied") when they are forced to compare.

RESPONSIBILITY AND DISSONANCE

Our third hypothesis is that men who accept personal responsibility for their occupational fate will be more likely than others to choose consonant comparisons. One specific expectation derived from this hypothesis was that, among men who choose comparison persons who earn more than themselves, those who accept personal responsibility will be more likely than others to choose persons on a higher occupational level (Cell C).

In general, the data tend to support this prediction. But the differences among those who accept varying degrees of responsibility are small and statistically non-significant. However, when we consider separately those men who differ in their position on the Relative Pay Index, a more complete picture emerges. Men who stand medium or high on the Relative Pay Index tend to choose a high proportion of consonant comparisons regardless of whether or not they accept responsibility for their present position. But among men whose pay is low compared to others like themselves (low on Relative Pay Index), acceptance or rejection of personal responsibility for this poor position makes a difference in the choice of consonant comparisons. Table 3 shows this result. Especially noteworthy in this table is the fact that, among those who are relatively low on pay and accept responsibility, 19.2 per cent choose upward comparison persons who are professionals (consonant comparisons) while among those who stand relatively low but reject responsibility, only 4.8 per cent choose professionals (p of difference < .01; one-tailed test). And while those who accept great personal responsibilty choose only 40.4 per cent of upward comparisons on their own occupational level, those who accept little personal responsibility

Table 3—Occupational Level of "Upward" Comparison Persons Chosen by Men in Low Relative Pay Position, in Relation to Whether Comparer Accepts Personal Responsibility for His Position[a, b]

Occupational Level of Upward Comparison Person	RESPONSIBILITY ACCEPTED BY COMPARER		
	Little per cent	Moderate per cent	Great per cent
Professional	4.8	8.8	19.2
Clerical-sales	1.6	2.9	0.0
Manager-proprietor	16.1	4.4	11.5
Blue-collar, foreman	9.7	16.2	13.5
Blue-collar, skilled, semi-skilled	67.7	57.4	40.4
Other[c]	0.0	10.3	15.4
Total	100.0	100.0	100.0
N of Comparers	62	68	52

[a] For each respondent, only the first upward comparison chosen is included in this table.

[b] Solid line joining two percentages indicates difference is significant at the .01 level (1-tailed tests except "Other" category, where 2-tailed test was used, since difference was not specifically predicted). Dashed line indicates difference is significant at .05 level (1-tailed test).

[c] Includes primarily comparison persons in farm occupations and in occupations which could not be sufficiently identified. Also included in "Other" are unskilled or unemployed.

choose 67.7 per cent upward comparisons on their own occupational level (p of difference <.01; two-tailed test).

These data, while presenting some evidence that "non-responsible" men more often choose dissonant comparisons, undoubtedly underestimate the percentage of consonant comparisons chosen by all groups, since only one specific type of consonance is distinguished. It seems probable that the differences between the comparisons chosen by the "responsible" and "non-responsible" groups would be greater if our measures of consonance and dissonance were more refined.

The data concerning the choice of consonant and dissonant comparisons are exactly paralleled by the results concerning satisfaction with comparisons. Table 4 shows that the combination of low relative pay position and rejection of personal responsibility brings a sharp decrease in satisfaction with upward comparisons. Among those whose relative pay position is low, men who reject personal responsibility are significantly more likely than those who accept moderate or great responsibility to be dissatisfied with comparisons ($p < .01$ for each difference; one-tailed t tests). Similarly, among those who reject responsibility, men who stand relatively low on pay are significantly more likely than those whose position is medium or high to be dissatisfied ($p < .01$ for each difference; one-tailed t tests). In other words, the same persons who were most likely to choose objectively dissonant comparisons were also most likely to be subjectively dissatisfied with comparisons. This parallel, while not surprising, gives a reassuring consistency to the data.

Table 4—Mean Scores of Present Satisfaction[a] with Upward Comparisons, in Relation to Comparer's Relative Pay Position and Acceptance of Responsibility[b, c] (Number of Comparers in Parentheses)

	ACCEPTANCE OF RESPONSIBILITY			
Relative Pay Position	Little	Moderate	Great	Total
Low	3.02 (64)	2.60 (68)	2.38 (52)	2.68 (184)
Medium	2.43 (41)	2.20 (27)	2.21 (17)	2.31 (85)
High	2.28 (44)	2.12 (33)	2.22 (37)	2.21 (114)
Total	2.64 (149)	2.39 (128)	2.30 (106)	2.46 (383)

a Lower score indicates greater satisfaction.
b Three men who did not answer both questions comprising the acceptance of responsibility index are not included in this table.
c Solid line joining two mean scores indicates that the difference is significant at the .01 level or beyond (1-tailed t test). Dashed line joining two mean scores indicates significant difference at the .05 level or beyond (1-tailed t test).

These results concerning the effect of feelings about personal responsibility on the choice of and satisfaction with comparisons generally support Hypothesis III. However, the data qualify and broaden the hypothesis. They indicate that the *combination* of an unfavorable position with regard to some social reward *and* rejection of personal responsibility for one's fate with regard to this reward will lead to the choice of dissonant comparisons. These data are also consistent with our assumption that an important motivation behind the choice of dissonant comparisons is the wish to protest one's present status and to help legitimate a claim for higher status. Men whose present objective wage position is low but who reject responsibility for this low position would be especially likely to have these motives.

The general conclusion that comparisons are often motivated is supported by other data from the present study concerning the effect of mobility chances on the choice of comparisons. These data, presented elsewhere,[18] show that men whose upward mobility chances are relatively poor and uncertain are more likely to choose dissonant comparisons than are men whose upward mobility chances are assured. Again, however, the factor of personal responsibility is important, since men with uncertain mobility chances were most likely to choose dissonant comparisons when they reject responsibility for their occupational position.

Summary

This paper has presented a conceptual framework for categorizing comparisons in terms of consonance and dissonance. A number of specific empirical types of consonant and dissonant wage comparisons were indicated. One advantage of this conceptual approach over previous formulations, it was argued, is to enable us better to predict the affective reaction (satisfaction-dissatisfaction) to specific kinds of comparisons.

It was hypothesized that individuals' satisfaction with wage comparisons will be a function of the objective and perceived dissonance of the comparisons, as defined, rather than of the difference in earnings alone. Data relevant to these predictions from a study of wage comparisons among workers at an oil refinery were presented. These data generally support the hypothesis that satisfaction with wage comparisons is based on the consonance or dissonance of the total comparison rather than on the wage difference alone.

Concerning the choice of comparisons, it was postulated that such choices are not, as Davis has assumed, wholly random, but are often motivated. One possible motive is the wish to protest one's present status and to claim a higher status. It was hypothesized that those who reject personal responsibility for their job position will be more likely to have such a motive and would be more likely, therefore, to choose dissonant wage comparisons. The data support this prediction for men whose wage position, relative to those like themselves, is low. These data also give support to the general proposition that the individual may tolerate and even seek dissonance in his situation if he rejects personal responsibility for the dissonance.

18. Patchen, "The Choice of Wage Comparisons," *op. cit.*

Social Reference Basis of Job Satisfaction: The Case of Manual Workers

William H. Form and James A. Geschwender

Introduction

THE purpose of this study is to demonstrate the utility of a social explanation for personal appraisals of life situations. The life situation here selected is job satisfaction, but the model of explanation may be applied to any area of life. Several probably fallacious assumptions underlie traditional studies of job satisfaction.[1] They are that all workers have a clear perception of a hierarchical occupational structure; that they all have a desire for upward occupational mobility, and that their degree of job satisfaction is a function of success in this

Reprinted from *American Sociological Review*, 27: 228–237, 1962, by permission of the authors and the publisher, the American Sociological Association. The data reported in this study are part of a larger study conducted earlier by J. Allan Beegle, William H. Form and Sigmund Nosow, under a grant made by the Rockefeller Foundation to Michigan State University to conduct regional studies. The authors are deeply indebted to the above named for the use of the data and to the Foundation for financial support of the original project.

1. See for example R. Hoppoch, *Job Satisfaction*, New York: Harper Brothers, 1935; D. E. Super, "Occupational Level and Job Satisfaction," *Journal of Applied Psychology*, 23 (October, 1939), pp. 547–564; and R. P. Bullock, *Social Factors Related to Job Satisfaction*, Columbus: Bureau of Business Research, Ohio State University, 1952. Nancy C. Morse, *Satisfaction in the White Collar Job*, Ann Arbor: Survey Research Center Institute for Social Research, University of Michigan, 1953, is a case of a work that departs from the traditional job satisfaction studies in that it treats satisfaction as being a function of the relationship between rewards desired and those received. In this sense it is similar to the present study. It differs from the present study to the extent that Morse deals with satisfaction with aspects of the job rather than with total job satisfaction. In addition, Morse does not investigate non-job related causes of level of reward desired.

graded occupational structure.[2] Such assumptions ignore the stratification realities of urban society, the different experiences and aspirations of sub-groups in such a society, and the operations of different forces on various segments of the society. In line with these considerations this study proposes that personal evaluations of life situations are relative to the precise social locations which people occupy in society and the specific groups to which they commit their identities.[3]

In accord with this theoretical position we may propose that sub-groups in a society respond differently to the occupational structure,[4] that their evaluations of their occupational status is a response to their social and mobility experiences, and that changes in their objective positions condition their job evaluations. The evidence on each of these points is sparse but supportive of the theoretical position assumed here. Thus Hatt has shown that the occupational structure is not a simple hierarchy but a series of interrelated situses.[5] Knowledge about the complexities of the structure is differentially distributed in the society.[6] Although there is general consensus about the rank of well-known occupations, lower status persons are less knowledgeable of the entire structure and tend to evaluate jobs in simple economic terms.[7] In short, it appears that different segments of the population respond differently to concrete situations in the occupational world.

Centers, Jones, Knupfer, and others have indicated that manual workers do not share the strong belief in the realities of opportunities for upward mobility characteristic of white collar workers.[8] Davis further indicates that under-

2. There is, however, wide recognition that aging tends to be a structural feature associated with increased job satisfaction.

3. This is harmonious with the general position of Alex Inkeles, "Industrial Man: The Relation of Status to Experience, Perception and Value," *American Journal of Sociology*, 66 (July, 1960), pp. 1–31; Herbert H. Hyman, "The Psychology of Status," *Archives of Psychology*, No. 269, 1942, and Robert K. Merton and Alice K. Rossi, "Contributions to the Theory of Reference Group Behavior," in R. K. Merton, *Social Theory and Social Structure*, New York: The Free Press, 1957, pp. 225–280.

4. Indeed, there may not be a single hierarchical structure as Paul Hatt has suggested in "Occupation and Social Stratification," *American Journal of Sociology*, 55 (May, 1950), pp. 533–543.

5. *Ibid.*

6. See the survey of this research examined by Arthur F. Davies, "The Prestige of Occupations," *British Journal of Sociology*, 3 (June, 1952), pp. 134–147.

7. See Delbert C. Miller and William H. Form, *Industrial Sociology*, New York: Harper Brothers, 1951, Part III, "The Social Adjustment of the Worker."

8. Richard Centers, *The Psychology of Social Classes*, Princeton: Princeton University Press, 1949; Alfred W. Jones, *Life, Liberty and Property*, Philadelphia: J. B. Lippincott Co., 1941; Genevieve Knupfer, "Portrait of the Underdog," *Public Opinion Quarterly*, 11 (Spring, 1947), pp. 103–114; R. S. Lynd and H. M. Lynd, *Middletown in Transition*, New York: Harcourt, Brace and Company, 1937.

privileged workers lack motivation for social climbing and thus tend to derive their satisfactions from their present situations rather than from expected mobility.[9] This situation makes it unlikely that they would use the middle status groups as reference points in the evaluation of their life situations and their jobs. Rather, they would tend to use their work associates and relevant family members as social references since they have similar origins.

Rogoff and Lipset and Bendix have demonstrated that changes in the occupational structure are as much responsible for social or occupational mobility as other factors.[10] Their evidence further suggests that changes in social position force changes in aspirations rather than the reverse process. Thus changes in opportunites and life situations foster changes in evaluations of life situations, aspirations, and ideologies, not the other way around.[11] Such a position makes it possible to account for a seemingly contradictory phenomenon —that upward mobility, though not internalized as a realistic goal, nonetheless does operate to provide persons greater satisfactions when they experience it, but dissatisfaction does not automatically result when mobility is not experienced. There is some evidence that workers are quickly desocialized from the aspirational complex learned in school, for aspirations are related to reality soon after full-time entry into the world of work.[12]

Research Design

The research task then is to demonstrate that for manual workers in an industrial community, job evaluations are not so much a function of their aspirations or of that of their parents, but a response to the occupational position which their parents and brothers occupy. If these relevant others occupy positions above the subject, he should feel less satisfied with his job situation, or if they are at the same or lower level, he should feel relatively more satisfied.[13] These expectations were formalized into the following hypotheses.

1. There will be no association between job satisfaction of the subject and his occupational level relative to his parents' occupational aspirations for him.

9. Allison Davis, "The Motivation of the Underprivileged Worker," in William Foote Whyte, editor, *Industry and Society*, New York: McGraw-Hill Book Co., Inc., 1946.

10. Natalie Rogoff, *Recent Trends in Occupational Mobility*, New York : The Free Press, 1953; Seymour M. Lipset, and Reinhard Bendix, *Social Mobility in Industrial Society*, Berkeley, University of California Press, 1959.

11. *Ibid.*, especially p. 61.

12. Miller and Form, *op. cit.*

13. As Merton states, "Some similarity in status attributes between the individual and the reference group must be perceived or imagined, in order for the comparison to occur at all." Merton, *op. cit.*, p. 242.

2. There will be a positive association between job satisfaction and occupational level of the subject relative to that of his father.
3. There will be a positive association between job satisfaction and occupational level of the subject relative to that of his brothers.
4. There will be a positive association between job satisfaction and generational occupational mobility of the subject relative to that of all those of similar origin, i.e., those whose father's occupation was similar to that of the subject's father (generational occupational mobility score, GOMS).[14]

Data for this study are taken from 545 interviews with manual workers in Lansing, Michigan taken in 1950–51. Lansing is primarily an industrial community of about 90,000 persons. Its main industries are automobile and metal fabrication. It is also the state capital and service center for a population of 250,000. The industrial work force is comprised mostly of native born persons who came from small cities and rural areas of Michigan and nearby states. The sample for this study was every tenth male name appearing in *Polk's Directory* 1950. Any person who was not a manual worker was rejected.[15] Eleven cases were retained of "sales, clerical and related occupations" because it was felt that their occupations were in fact manual. The final sample contained 11.4 per cent unskilled workers, 59.8 per cent semi-skilled, 26.8 per cent skilled and 2.0 per cent "manual clerical."

These people were then interviewed and data were obtained with respect to their occupation, income, education, age, job tenure, marital status, number of children, father's occupation, occupations and ages of all brothers in the labor force, parents' occupational aspirations for the respondent, job satisfaction, and other related data.

Job satisfaction was measured by the question, "How do you like your job?" Five possible response categories were used: very good; pretty good; average; not so good; and not at all, which were scored 5, 4, 3, 2, and 1 respectively.[16] The mean score was 3.84.

14. As defined by Melvin M. Tumin and Arnold S. Feldman, "Theory and Measurement of Occupational Mobility," *American Sociological Review*, 22 (June, 1957), pp. 283–284.

15. For the extended description, see Sigmund Nosow, "Labor Distribution and the Normative System," *Social Forces*, 35 (October, 1956), p. 28.

16. This measure of job satisfaction was constructed after the method of attitude scaling pioneered by Rensis Likert and followed by countless others including Allan Edwards. See, for example, Rensis Likert, *A Technique for the Measurement of Attitudes*, Archives of Psychology, No. 140, 1932; Gardner Murphy and Rensis Likert, *Public Opinion and the Individual*, New York: Harper and Brothers, 1937; and Allan Edwards, *Attitude Measurement*, New York: Appleton Century-Crofts, Inc., 1957. Edwards clearly considers satisfaction as an attitude which can be so measured. In the cited study (p. 2) Edwards states: "When you ask someone about his attitude towards something, say his job, what is it that you are interested in finding out? If you are primarily interested in how he *feels* about his job and, in particular, whether he *likes* or *dislikes* his job, then you are using the concept of attitude in much the

Prestige levels of occupation were assigned values as follows: professionals and semi-professionals, 7; owners, managers, officials and self employed, 6; clerical, office, and sales, 5; skilled workers, foremen and direct supervisors, 4; farm owners, managers, tenants (farmers unspecified), 3; semi-skilled workers and apprentices, 2; service workers, unskilled laborers, and farm laborers, 1.

Findings

Hypothesis I: There will be no association between job satisfaction and occupational achievement relative to parents' occupational aspirations for the respondent.

Data presented in Table 1 indicate that almost four fifths of the respondents reported that their parents had no occupational aspirations for them.[17] Since 37 per cent had parents who were farmers they possibly had little knowledge of the urban labor market to project job aspirations for their children. However,

Table I—Mean Job Satisfaction Scores for Respondents Grouped According to Their Occupational Achievement Relative to Their Parents' Occupational Aspirations for Them

Occupational Achievement Relative to Parents' Occupational Aspirations for Respondents	Mean Job Satisfaction Score	Number of Cases
No parental aspirations	3.83	296
Occupational level lower than parental aspirations	3.88	66
Occupational level same as parental aspirations	4.50	8
Occupational level higher than parental aspirations	4.00	3
Total	3.85	373
Total with expressed parental aspirations	3.95	77

same way that it will be used in this book." In the same study (p. 151) Edwards provides us with support for this manner of assigning weights to the five response categories: "In the development of the method of scale construction . . . Likert found that scores based on relatively simple assignment of integral weights correlated .99 with the more complicated normal deviate system of weights. He therefore used the simpler system. We shall do likewise." This method was also used by Nancy C. Morse, *op. cit.* We realize that this method of assigning values does not give us a zero neutral point. This is not a major problem as we are not concerned with giving *absolute* scores for degree of job satisfaction or dissatisfaction but are rather concerned with comparing mean scores of groups in terms of *relative* amounts of job satisfaction. Edwards supports this usage as well as the correlation of this scale value with other scales or measures of interest without need for reference to the zero point on a favorable-unfavorable continuum. (Edwards, *op. cit.*, p. 157ff.) The responses to the question were distributed 164, very good; 193, pretty good; 131, average; 44, not so good; 10, not at all; and 3, no response.

17. The question used to gather this data was: "Did your parents want you to get into any particular line of work? Yes——No——. *If yes*, what was it?——."

even urban dwellers had few aspirations for their children. It may be that in both cases a low belief in occupational mobility made the whole question irrelevant for both parents and children.[18] This interpretation is consistent with the findings of Davis and others.[19]

The number of respondents who did report any parental aspirations is too small to permit meaningful statistical analysis. However, it is worth noting that all who did had higher job satisfaction scores than those who did not report parental aspirations. This is even true for those who reported occupational achievements lower than parental aspirations. Those who achieved an occupational level equal to, or higher than that to which their parents aspired for them exhibited higher mean job satisfaction scores. There are too few cases in the group that exceeded their parents' aspirations to have confidence in the trend observed.

Hypothesis II: There will be a positive association between job satisfaction and occupational level relative to that of one's father.

Data in Table 2 indicate that upwardly mobile sons (those who achieved

Table 2—Job Satisfaction and Occupational Level of Sons Relative to That of Fathers

Sons' Occupational Level Relative to Fathers' Occupation	Mean Job Satisfaction Score of Sons	Number of Cases
1. Sons' occupation lower than fathers' occupation	3.39	122
2. Sons' occupation the same as fathers' occupation	4.01	101
3. Sons' occupation higher than fathers' occupation	4.03	77
Total	3.76	300

$t_{13} = 4.57, P < .0005$, df, 197.

an occupational level higher than their fathers) exhibited a significantly higher mean job satisfaction score than did sons who were downwardly mobile. The mean job satisfaction score of the stationary or immobile sons, i.e., those whose occupational level is similar to that of their father, is significantly higher than that of the downwardly mobile sons, but is only slightly below that of the upwardly mobile sons. This may indicate that the degree of job satisfaction exhibited by a working class male will be seriously impaired if he fails to achieve

18. Sons of farmers were excluded from this analysis because they are in a different situs. The t-test was used after Helen M. Walker and Joseph Lev, *Statistical Inference*, New York: Henry Holt and Co., 1953, p. 154. Significance level for this study was arbitrarily set at the .05 level.

19. Davis, *op. cit.*, and William A. Faunce, "Occupational Involvement and the Selective Testing of Self Esteem," unpublished manuscript, 1959.

an occupational level comparable to that of his father, but achieving a higher level will not significantly add to his satisfaction. The middle class worker with a strong belief in upward mobility may experience greater frustration from lack of it because he lives in a world where greater mobility does in fact occur.[20]

Hypothesis III: There will be a positive association between job satisfaction and occupational level relative to that of one's brothers.

The following analysis is limited to workers having only one working brother in order to avoid the complicating effects which subsequent brothers might have. Data in Table 3 indicate that workers who achieve a higher occupational level than that of their brother exhibit a significantly higher mean job satisfaction score than those whose occupational level is equal to that of their brother. In turn, the mean job satisfaction score of those whose occupational

Table 3—Job Satisfaction and Occupational Level Relative to Occupational Level of Brother*

Occupational Level Relative to That of Brother	Mean Job Satisfaction Score	Number of Cases
1. Occupational level lower than that of brother	3.67	42
2. Occupational level same as that of brother	3.88	42
3. Occupational level higher than that of brother	4.33	18
Total	3.87	102

$t_{12} = .88$, $P < .10$, df, 82; $t_{23} = 2.05$, $P < .025$, df, 58; $t_{13} = 7.59$, $P < .0005$, df, 58.

* In order to avoid the complicating effect that second and third brothers might have, we include in this table only those individuals who had one and only one brother.

level is equal to that of their brother is higher (but not statistically significant [p of t = >. 10]) than that of those whose occupational level is lower than that of their brother. The observed trend, the sizes of the differences, and the fact that two of the three differences are statistically significant lead to the conclusion that the occupational level of the worker relative to his brother is important to the degree of his job satisfaction.

It is important to note that the mean job satisfaction score of all respondents whose brother was in farming was 3.85 and the score of all those whose brother was in a non-farm occupation deemed to be non-comparable to that of the respondent was 3.90. Both of these scores approximate the mean job satisfaction score, 3.88, of those respondents whose occupational level was equal to that of their brother. The closeness of these scores is quite consistent with reference group theory. If individuals whom one would normally use as social references in evaluating one's occupational position are in an occupational situs that is not

20. See Centers, *op. cit.*, Rogoff, *op. cit.*, Lipset and Bendix, *op. cit.*

comparable to one's own, then no comparisons can be made that would result in feelings of relative gratification or deprivation. This is precisely analogous to the situation in which one is in the same occupation as the social reference. No invidious comparisons can be made in either case and one would expect the mean job satisfaction scores to be similar.

*Table 4—Job Satisfaction and Vertical Occupational Mobility as Measured by the Revised Generational Occupational Mobility Score**

G OMS z Score	Job Satisfaction	Number of Cases
8.39	3.50	2
8.59	4.13	8
8.64	3.79	29
8.67	2.67	3
8.74	4.14	7
8.78	3.43	7
8.87	3.67	3
9.08	3.89	9
9.19	3.47	15
9.22	3.91	11
9.24	3.00	11
9.32	3.81	57
9.33	3.44	45
9.38	3.62	34
9.39	3.68	124
9.48	4.50	4
10.33	4.20	5
10.41	3.67	9
10.43	4.31	36
10.46	4.40	5
10.52	4.43	7
10.67	4.50	12
10.70	4.50	4
10.78	4.14	21
10.88	5.00	1
10.89	4.27	41
10.98	5.00	1
11.15	4.00	1
11.32	4.50	2
11.51	4.67	3
11.65	4.33	3

$r = .251$, $P < .0005$, df, 538.

* Computations are made from individual scores. Data are grouped for clarity of presentation.

This relationship was further analyzed controlling for the relative ages of the respondent and his working brother with no predictable alterations occurring.[21] This suggests that the occupational niche is found early in work life and that job satisfaction reaches a stable level quickly for manual workers.

21. Workers having two brothers were then analyzed by comparing occupational level to that of two brothers simultaneously and no regular ordering of mean job satisfaction scores resulted. However, this later finding must be considered of limited utility as all cell frequencies were exceedingly small.

Hypothesis IV: There will be a positive association between job satisfaction and generational occupational mobility score.

Testing this hypothesis necessitated using an index of the subject's mobility relative to the mobility of all sons of fathers occupationally similar to the subject's father. Such a scale, called the "generational occupational mobility score" (GOMS), was constructed by Tumin and Feldman,[22] and revised by Geschwender.[23] The scoring used for prestige levels of the occupations presented above in the discussion of the research design was modified after Tumin and Feldman.[24]

The data presented in Table 4 show a highly significant, if only moderate, relationship between job satisfaction and GOMS z scores. This suggests that manual workers do use those of similar origin as social references in evaluating their occupational achievements. When they have achieved relatively greater amounts of upward mobility they exhibit higher job satisfaction scores. In order to gain more insight into this relationship the sample was analyzed by both occupation of destination (present occupation) and occupation of origin (father's occupation).

The breakdown by occupation of destination presented in Table 5 reveals a moderate negative (not statistically significant) association between job satisfaction and amount of occupational mobility for the small category of sales, clerical, and related occupations and small positive or negligible relationships for all other categories. These results are of interest for reference group theory and the original assumption that manual workers do not believe strongly in the existence of opportunities for upward mobility. In appraising these results cognizance must be taken of the fact that the comparisons are being made among workers who are on the same occupational level. Since the amounts of satisfaction received are about equal for all concerned and the range is small, few invidious comparisons can be made. The deviating pattern for clerical workers who have the highest mobility but low satisfaction lends indirect support to the assumption that belief in opportunities for upward mobility is an intervening variable. . . .

The breakdown of the sample into groups by occupation of origin (father's occupation) as shown in Table 6 yielded a positive association between job satisfaction and occupational mobility for all occupational categories. This association was statistically significant for all categories except "semi-skilled." These results lend support to the original interpretation that working class males tend to use the peers with which they began life as social references in evaluating their occupational achievement.

22. *Op. cit.*

23. James A. Geschwender, "Theory and Measurement of Occupational Mobility: A Reexamination," *American Sociological Review*, 26 (June, 1961), pp. 451–452.

24. In the computation of GOMS z scores, brothers in the armed forces, still in school, disabled, or retired were excluded.

Table 5—Job Satisfaction and Vertical Occupational Mobility as Measured by the Revised Occupational Mobility Score, by Occupation of Destination

Occupation of Destination	GOMS z Score	Job Satisfaction	Number of Cases
Sales, clerical and related occupations	10.88	5.00	1
	10.98	5.00	1
	11.15	4.00	1
	11.32	4.50	2
	11.51	4.67	3
	11.65	4.33	3

r = −.292, P >.05, df, 9.

Skilled workers and foremen	10.33	4.20	5
	10.41	3.67	9
	10.43	4.31	36
	10.46	4.40	5
	10.52	4.43	7
	10.67	4.50	12
	10.70	4.50	4
	10.78	4.14	21
	10.89	4.27	41

r = + .024, P > .05, df, 138.

Semi-skilled	9.08	3.89	9
	9.19	3.47	15
	9.22	3.91	11
	9.24	3.00	11
	9.32	3.81	57
	9.33	3.44	45
	9.38	3.62	34
	9.39	3.68	124
	9.48	4.50	4

r = + .036, P > .05, df, 308.

Unskilled	8.39	3.67	2
	8.78	3.43	7
	8.59	4.13	8
	8.64	3.79	29
	8.67	2.67	3
	8.74	4.14	7
	8.87	3.67	3

r = − .042, P > .05, df, 57.

Table 6—Job Satisfaction and Occupational Mobility as Measured by the Revised Generational Occupational Mobility Score, by Father's Occupation

Father's Occupation	GOMS z Score	Job Satisfaction	Number of Cases
Professional, self-employed, sales, clerical, and related occupations	8.39	3.50	2
	8.67	2.67	3
	9.08	3.89	9
	9.19	3.47	15
	9.22	3.91	11
	10.33	4.20	5
	10.41	3.67	9
	10.46	4.40	5
	10.88	5.00	1
	11.15	4.00	1

$r = .404$, $P < .005$, df, 59.

Skilled and supervisory	8.78	3.43	7
	9.24	3.00	11
	9.33	3.44	45
	10.43	4.31	36
	10.52	4.43	7
	10.98	5.00	1

$r = .476$, $P < .0005$, df, 105.

Farmer	8.64	3.79	29
	9.39	3.68	124
	10.89	4.27	41
	11.65	4.33	3

$r = .212$, $.01 < P < .025$, df, 195.

Semi-skilled	8.59	4.13	8
	9.32	3.81	57
	10.78	4.14	21
	11.51	4.67	3

$r = .153$, $P > .05$, df, 87.

Unskilled and service	8.74	4.14	7
	8.87	3.67	3
	9.38	3.62	34
	9.48	4.50	4
	10.67	4.50	12
	10.70	4.50	4
	11.32	4.50	2

$r = .293$, $.005 < P < .01$, df, 64.

In our discussion, thus far, we have viewed job satisfaction as resulting from mobility relative to one significant social reference at a time. Actually, people use many social references simultaneously. Thus, it would appear that an analysis of the subject's mobility relative to the three above used social references simultaneously would provide even more striking evidence for the suggested interpretation. Table 7 compares the mean job satisfaction scores of

Table 7—Job Satisfaction and Occupational Mobility Relative to Three Significant Social References

Occupational Mobility Relative to Three Social References	Mean Job Satisfaction Score	Number of Cases
Overachievement on GOMS z scores, occupational level higher than that of father and brother	4.33	9
Underachievement on GOMS z scores, occupational level lower than that of father and brother	3.40	15

$t = 2.02$, $P < .05$, df, 22.
Mean of total sample of 545 = 3.84.

those workers who are upwardly mobile relative to their peers of origin, their father, and their brother with those workers who are downwardly mobile relative to all three references. The difference between the two mean job satisfaction scores is relatively large. This fact, combined with the observation that the mean job satisfaction score for the entire sample falls about midway between the two mean scores, strongly suggests that manual workers use all three social references simultaneously in arriving at a level of job satisfaction. . . .

The relationship between job satisfaction and hourly wages presented in Table 8 warrants special consideration. It may be noted that with hourly wage rates above $1.50 increased income is associated generally with increased satisfaction. However, all wage categories below $1.50 have job satisfaction scores

Table 8—Job Satisfaction and Hourly Wages

Hourly Wage	Mean Job Satisfaction Score	Number of Cases
Under $1.00	3.92	13
1.00– 1.24	4.00	16
1.25– 1.49	3.63	40
1.50– 1.74	3.42	184
1.75– 1.99	3.54	101
2.00– 2.24	3.69	32
2.25– 2.49	4.33	30
2.50– 2.74	4.80	20
2.75– 2.99	4.96	29
3.00– up	4.98	53

$r = .440$, $P < .01$, df, 518.

higher than those between $1.50 and $2.00. When the three lowest categories were analyzed separately, it was discovered that southern born, rural born, and foreign born workers were proportionately over-represented as compared to the total sample (.203 to .125 for southern born; .435 to .400 for rural born; and .101 to .089 for foreign born). Negroes were over-represented .101 to .076; workers under thirty and over sixty were over-represented .290 to .217 and .212 to .153 respectively, and those with six years of schooling or less were over-represented .221 to .118.

These finding are consistent with reference group theory, for the relatively well satisfied low wage earners are comprised of groups who are probably not using native born urban industrial workers as their social references. The southern born, rural born, foreign born, and Negroes might all tend to use standards prevailing in their families and sub-communities in evaluating their present jobs.[25] For each of these groups the standards used would tend to be lower than for native workers in a northern industrial city who have better job opportunities.[26] Workers with little education probably compare their jobs with those who have a similarly low level of education, thus not coming off badly in the comparison. Younger lower class workers who see school attendance as income depriving find satisfaction in jobs which provide substantial income. Older workers might represent a low opportunity group which has become adult socialized to their present positions. Although these interpretations are *post hoc* they still appear to lend support to the reference group position postulated here.

Conclusion

The findings of this study tend to show that reference group theory does provide a meaningful framework for the analysis of the relationship between job satisfaction and inter-generational occupational mobility among male manual workers. Three different referential measures of occupational achievement were used and all were found to be significantly related to degree of job satisfaction. One non-structural aspirational measure was used and it was not significantly associated with job satisfaction. Improvement in the amount and precision of data on peers and kin (education, income, residence, amount of contact with the subject) would no doubt improve statistical confidence in the general trends.

This study did not provide direct evidence of the role of ideology as an intervening variable on the relationship between position in the social structure and the subjective evaluation of life circumstances. Enough indirect evidence

25. These findings have been corroborated in a separate study of social integration among unionized automobile workers in the same community. See William H. Form and H. Kirk Dansereau, "Union Member Orientations and Patterns of Social Integration," *Industrial and Labor Relations Review*, 11 (October, 1957), pp. 3–12.

26. That this does indeed occur in this community has been clearly demonstrated in the research of Sigmund Nosow, *op. cit.*

was provided to propose the hypothesis that the relationship between occupational mobility and job satisfaction is mediated by the belief in opportunities or lack of opportunities for workers to rise in the occupational hierarchy. It also appears clear that the position taken on the ideology of opportunity does not arise randomly, but is rather a response to certain changing structural features of the social economy.[27] This fact almost by itself tends to account not only for the differences in mobility found in studies done during periods of economic depression and prosperity, but also for findings on life satisfactions and dissatisfactions.

Studies have shown that during any period, prosperous or not, the most difficult occupational barrier to pierce is the manual-white-collar division.[28] Thus it is the *normal* condition for most manual workers not to expect great upward mobility and for them not to internalize strongly the ideology of opportunity. Lacking the ideology of opportunity they tend to use their peer groups and the male members of their family of orientation as social references in evaluating their occupational positions. The greater the amount of mobility a worker has experienced relative to these social references, the more job satisfaction he will feel. This relationship will continue to hold as long as the worker has not come into sufficient contact with the middle class ideology of opportunity or as long as he has not had sufficient life experiences to accept it partially. When a working class male has become imbued with this ideology he tends to shift his social references to the incumbents of positions above him, and tends to exhibit relatively more job dissatisfaction. The more mobility he experiences, the more he will believe in the existence of opportunities and in his own ability to rise. When mobility is blocked he will become increasingly dissatisfied with his present position. Thus, it appears that limited occupational mobility is a self-defeating process for the manual worker who is imbued with the middle class ideology of opportunity and who is faced with the relatively rigid barrier which exists between the manual and white collar occupational strata.

27. See Lipset and Bendix, *op. cit.*, p. 61, and William Kornhauser, *The Politics of Mass Society*, New York: The Free Press, 1959, pp. 142–158, 213–222.

28. Among others, see Rogoff, *op. cit.*, Lynd, *op. cit.*, Lipset and Bendix, *op. cit.*, Miller and Form, *op. cit.*

Spontaneous Group References
in France

Eric Stern and Suzanne Keller

AMERICAN social scientists have become increasingly concerned with the problem of the concept of the self as this is influenced and determined by groups in the social environment. Reference group theory has developed as one systematic attempt to deal with this problem. A distinction has been made between orientation toward "membership groups" (groups with which one is in continuous and sustained contact) and "non-membership groups" (groups representative of social strata outside of one's immediate social environment). The term "reference groups" has been applied to those "non-membership groups" which serve as referents for people's aspirations and values.

In a recent paper, Merton and Kitt stated a list of prerequisites for the development of reference group theory. Among other items, they suggested that an effort be made ". . . to discover which reference groups are spontaneously and explicitly brought into play, as distinguished from the study of responses to reference group contexts provided by the experimenter or suggested by the interviewer."[1] In the summer of 1951, material was made available to the authors which contributed some of the requisite data. In addition, the material had been gathered in a cultural context different from that in which most of the recent studies have taken place, and which might thus provide useful comparative material. The following paper describes what was found, and attempts to relate these findings to present thinking on this problem.

Reprinted from *Public Opinion Quarterly*, 17: 208–217, 1953, by permission of the authors and the publisher.

1. Robert K. Merton and Alice S. Kitt, (Rossi) "Contribution to the Theory of Reference Group Behavior" in *Continuities in Social Research*, R. K. Merton and P. F. Lazarsfeld, eds., New York: The Free Press, 1950, p. 69.

Methodology

In the summer of 1951, approximately two hundred unstructured interviews were carried out in a pilot study aimed at the construction of a formal
questionnaire on the standard of living in France.[2] Interviewers called on 200
people selected to represent an approximate cross section of the French population according to geographic location, city size, age, sex, occupation, and
economic level. The interviewer opened with the following remarks:

> We are making a study of the standard of living of the French people,
> but we realize that when one speaks of the standard of living, everyone under-
> stands something different by that expression. I would therefore like to ask
> you what would be, for you, a satisfactory standard of living?

No further question was asked until the respondent had said all he could
possibly say, but repeated encouragements were used, such as, "Is there anything else?" Only after no further responses could be elicited were a few specific
questions posed, among them: "How much would you have to earn to live the
way you have described?" and "How much do you earn at present?"

After the material had been used for its original purpose, it became evident
that these interviews offered an opportunity to find out what social groups are
spontaneously mentioned when people talk about their living conditions and
their aspirations. Analysis of these spontaneous responses might usefully be
considered from the point of view of reference group theory in a non-American
cultural setting.

The 198 interviews, ranging in length from three to twelve or more typed
pages, were carefully scrutinized for every explicit group reference they contained. Each reference noted was then coded as either a "we" reference, referring
to a membership group, or a "they" reference, referring to a non-membership
group. A statement was classified as a "we" statement if the person making the
statement either explicitly said "we . . . the workers," or "we . . . the young . . .,"
etc., or if the group he mentioned was one with which he had some explicit
connection. Background data were available for each respondent, such as age,
sex, education, economic level, occupation, marital status, and size of family.
The statements made were then checked back against the objective data available.
A statement was classified as a "they" statement if the group mentioned was
different from those which the respondent had any contact with. For example,
a teacher who referred to the shopkeepers would be coded as having made a
"they" statement. A further breakdown judged the context of the reference as
"favorable," "unfavorable," or "factual." The judgments of the authors constituted the criterion determining the classifications. All the information was

2. The material was obtained by Dr. Eric Stern, Foreign Opinion and Market Research,
New York.

put on separate cards for each respondent, making possible a variety of cross-references for the questions of interest to us.

The Findings

One hundred eighty-three of 198 respondents made a total of 663 group references, an average of 3.6 per person. The least talkative people who expressed themselves only in the most general terms—there were fifteen—did not mention any groups. As Table 1 shows, 69 per cent of the 663 references were "we" statements, and 31 per cent were "they" statements. It is the 207 "they" statements which would seem most important in light of existing hypotheses concerning reference groups.

SOCIAL CLASS MENTIONS

Social class was mentioned by 84 (46 per cent) of the 183 people who mentioned any group. The references were made nearly as often in a context of self-identification as in a context of "other identification."

Table 1—Frequency and Nature of Group References

Category	"We" References	"They" References	Total
(1) Social Class (such items as "the workers," "the capitalists")	72	85	157
(2) Family ("my wife," "my children")	152	—	152
(3) Occupation ("the teachers," "in our profession")	70	12	82
(4) Sex ("a man should . . . ," "a woman should . . .")	41	19	60
	41	19	60
(5) General ("the people," "everyone")	33	26	59
(6) Age groups ("the old," "the young," "at our age")	24	20	44
(7) Social life ("our friends," "my colleagues")	37	—	37
(8) National groups ("the French," "the Americans")	17	15	32
(9) Special groups or Institutions ("the State," "the Government")	5	24	29
(10) Rural-Urban ("the city people," "we country women")	5	6	11
	n = 456	207	663

While the references to one's own class tended to be largely favorable, it may seem surprising that no small proportion of the respondents made favorable references to social classes other than their own. Here it is important to note the social class background of the respondents making these references. It was the upper class respondents who tended to make favorable (usually sympathetic) references to "the working class," "the poor," "those less fortunate than we."

Lower class respondents, who did make social class references, tended to make "favorable" statements about their own class and "unfavorable" statements about upper class people.

Table 2—Favorability of Class References

	"We" References (72)	"They" References (85)
Favorable	83%	35%
Unfavorable	7	53
Factual	10	12

Although our sample of people tended to be aware of social class differences, they did not at the same time exhibit any great degree of class *resentment* or class consciousness.

FAMILY

References to one's family were made nearly as often as references to social class. Since they were all membership-group references, they cannot contribute much to the specific problem we are dealing with here. One important thing to note, however, is that family references, more than any other, contained the most articulated statements involving a patterning of one's behavior, wishes, and values after those of others.

OCCUPATIONAL GROUP MENTIONS

Apart from references to the family, occupational references were found to be the second most frequent ones made, and they seemed important in terms of people's self identifications, since 70 of the 82 occupational references were favorable "we" statements. The most common unfavorable "they" reference was to the trades people (*les commercants*), generally blaming them for the high cost of food.

The two most common reasons for mentioning occupations at all were: (1) demands for better salaries, and (2) discussion of the nature of the work and the personal demands it made. In all these references there was a tendency to broaden the specific occupation which a person exercised so as to include one's self in a large general social category rather than a small specific group. It seemed that people gained in self importance when they associated themselves with a large social aggregate, and also, that the statement of their personal desires and demands gained in scope by being made the desires and demands of the largest group with whom the respondent felt he could associate.

AGE GROUP MENTIONS

One fourth of the respondents mentioned age, and the references were evenly divided between "we" and "they" mentions. The age of the respondent seemed to be related to the kind of statement he would make about age. Those over fifty years old and those between thirty and forty years old made age references most frequently, but the nature of the references differed sharply between these two groups. The younger group mentioned age in a membership-group context, such as "we . . . the young," or "when one is in his thirties like I am. . . ." Those over fifty were concerned with (1) the social, economic and emotional problems connected with aging, and (2) the young people. It was this group who made the largest proportion of favorable "they" references, either looking at young people with nostalgia, or sympathizing with the young for the difficulties they face in these turbulent times.

SOCIAL LIFE

Friends or colleagues were mentioned as being important to them by 24 per cent of the respondents. It was in these mentions that social status awareness appeared to any considerable degree. People did want to impress their friends with a certain style of life, but this did not mean that they were trying to keep "up with the Joneses." Rather, if the "Joneses" were important at all, it was as members of the immediate social circle. These comments generally centered around wishes for one's own home, but the stress was on being able to share with one's friends: "being able to invite people, to entertain them properly," "to serve good food," etc. Social status was accepted as given, and the problem of how to improve it or of how to move up in the world hardly seemed to exist for the majority of the respondents.

FURTHER FINDINGS

There were several other group mentions which will be cited only briefly since they indicate little of value for reference group theory. The only national groups mentioned were the "Americans" and "the French." The former was mentioned mostly by upper class respondents, always in a context of resentment of the greater and more widespread availability of comforts in America. The latter tended to receive uniformly favorable comments, usually concerned with some national characteristic which was cited with good humor, such as "the French like their good food," or "we French just are like that." The only institution mentioned was the Government, always referred to in an unfavorable context. This points to a suggestive practical split in attitudes toward France. The French tend to credit everything that is found satisfactory to "the French" people, whereas everything that is found wanting is blamed on the Government. This mechanism operates as a technique for preserving an integrated self-image for the Frenchman, while at the same time allowing him to be highly critical and expressing disfavor with the externalized "collective whole." By making the Government a kind of "out-group," he can criticize the collective whole without at the same time feeling guilty about its failures and imperfections. This split in attitudes toward the government and toward the people varies from national group to national group, and may serve as a useful focus for comparative cultural studies.

The French seem not to be significantly aware of rural-urban differences; only eleven out of 663 references were so directed, and all of these were made by rural people. There is no doubt that by use of a structured questionnaire, questions about rural-urban differences would elicit a response from every respondent, but the low rank of this type of mention among spontaneous references would indicate that its importance is a relatively minor one. This difference between spontaneous reactions and reactions obtained by a pointed questionnaire is an example of one of the major values of studies of this kind.

It might be worthwhile to note that there was not a single reference to religious groups or to the Church, and no mention of local communities. This might be characteristic of France or a function of the form of our inquiry. The meaning could not be ascertained.

INCOME SATISFACTION AND GROUP REFERENCES

At the end of the interview, each respondent was asked two questions concerning his actual and his desired income: "How much would you need to earn to live the way you have just described?" and "How much do you actually earn at present?" Of 198 respondents, 138 answered both questions with sufficient precision to be tabulated; the results are shown in Table 3.

Table 3—Income Levels and Aspirations

Income level	No. of cases	Desired income (per cent of actual)
1 (lowest)	8	340%
2	30	220
3	33	190
4	16	144
5	18	159
6	18	178
7 (highest)	15	122

As we go up the income scale, the actual and the desired income tend to become more nearly equal. Thirteen people (mostly on income levels 6 and 7) were completely satisfied with their present incomes and said so. There also tends to be a steady decrease in the proportion demanded over and above what is presently earned as we go from the lowest income level upward. The data are admittedly inadequate, but one interesting suggestion emerges from them. Checking back on the number of group references made by income level, we find that the greatest number occurred in the middle income groups. At the lower levels (1 and 2) the major concern seemed to be the availability of basic material necessities, and at the upper income levels the concern was one for greater and more diverse comforts. For the middle income groups, however, one concern seemed to be with groups outside of the membership-group context.

Meaning of the Study

One finding which deserves further testing was the evidence of little class friction or class "resentment" in this French sample. People did note differences in behavior and values among the members of the different social classes, but this awareness did not lead to their making collective judgments about their own class or the other social classes which they mentioned. There were few aggressive statements made by the poor respondents about those better off than they, and there were hardly any statements which might be interpreted in terms of "status strivings." People mentioned concrete things that they would like to acquire; they expressed disappointment that they could not do everything they would like to do, but they did not seem to be concerned with their social status at present, or refer with envy to those groups which are socially favored.

A recent paper raises the question:

> ... do ... self-appraisals and appraisals of institutional arrangements involve similar mechanisms of reference group behavior? At this point, it is clear that research is needed to discover the structure of those social situations which typically elicit self-evaluations or internalized judgments ... and the structure of those situations which typically lead to evaluations of institutions or externalized judgments, for example, where comparison with others leads to a sense of institutional inadequacies, to the judgments that the social system militates against any close correspondence between individual merit and social reward.[3]

Some findings in the present study relate to this question. Closer examination of the nature of the "social class" references showed that it was the upper class people who tended to make social class references in a context of evaluating institutional arrangements; that is, they referred to those less fortunate than they in terms of "the system" which makes for the inequitable distribution of social privileges and life chances. It was the lower class people who made their social class references in a context of personal evaluations, such as, "well, when one works hard, or is good, or has the ability, etc.," one can rise in the world. We might expect the reverse to have been the case; namely that lower class people would be concerned with "the system," with the arrangement of social institutions which limit the improvement of their status positions, and that upper class people would explain their own superior social positions and the failure of others to achieve them in terms of personal abilities, drives, energies, and talents. That this was not the case suggests the following hypothesis: In a society which no longer allows for a large amount of upward social mobility, lower class people tend to evaluate those of higher status in terms of superior personal qualities, whereas upper class people tend to see the classes below them as a result of institutional arrangements. In a society where there is a great

---

3. Merton and Kitt, *op. cit.*, p. 58.

deal of upward social mobility, the reverse may be the case; namely, those now on top appraise those beneath them in personal terms, and those on the bottom of the social scale appraise other classes and groups in terms of institutional arrangements.

Looking at the contents of the "we" references, the point which stands out most clearly is that their aim is to arrive at the *harmonious continuance of social units*. Group mentions tended to express a desire to keep relationships functioning smoothly. It may well be that this is the central function of referring to the behavior and values of others in a membership group setting. It has usually been assumed in studies of the influence of social status and social class on certain kinds of behavior that awareness of the material possessions of others evokes jealousy and envy, and results in striving to reach that status which would provide these material comforts. The present material seems rather to point to the desire to have harmonious social relations with people close to one. This is not easily possible if there are widespread discrepancies in material comforts at the disposal of the different members of the group. The desire to be alike, to have what others have (provided that there is some social interaction), to minimize differences where socially valued things are involved, may be functional to the continuance of the membership group as a harmonious, intimate group.

Another point closely linked with patterns of social mobility concerns the presence of resentment or envy directed towards an "in-group" as contrasted with that directed towards an "out-group." In a society where there is little social mobility, one's horizon of possibilities is relatively limited, thus confining comparison between one's self and others to members of one's family, occupation, and social circle. In a society of greater social mobility, the self-other comparison is allowed freer range and takes in more groups, as well as groups outside of one's membership or "in-group" environment.

The material of this survey presents very few indications that French values, behavior, and ideas are formed and influenced through the values of "out-groups." The wishes and desires which were expressed in our data were stated in a context of wanting those things which would procure the possibility of harmony within the membership group. One of the characteristics of French society is the relative immobility of social groups. Similar investigations undertaken in other social systems may yield different results. Our findings should be tested in a society where there is less traditionalism than is the case in France, and where upward social mobility is more prevalent. If we were to take a society such as the United States in which basic needs are more widely satisfied, presumably the pattern of reference group behavior would be quite different. . . .

Reference Groups and Inequalities of Class

W. G. Runciman

W<small>E</small> are now in a position to turn to the 1962 survey with several specific questions in mind. Without the survey, generalizations about the relative deprivation felt by different groups could only be drawn from very indirect inference. With it, generalization is still a matter of inference, but it can be rather more solidly based. . . .

The sample . . . was a stratified random sample taken from electoral registers. 2,000 names were drawn at random from two wards within each of 50 constituencies in England and Wales, and 1,415 respondents interviewed. The questionnaire had been previously tested on a quota sample of 100 respondents in four different areas. Respondents in the main survey were classified as manual or non-manual on the basis of occupation; wives were classified according to their husband's occupation, and retired or unemployed people on the basis of their last occupation. The criteria of classification were based on the standard procedure used by Research Services Ltd., who carried out the interviewing, coding and preliminary cross-tabulations. . . .

Incomes

A sequence of three questions was put to the respondents for the purpose of finding out their comparative reference groups on the topic of income: first, "Do you think there are any other sorts of people doing noticeably better at the

Reprinted in part from W. G. Runciman, *Relative Deprivation and Social Justice*, pp. 151, 192–217, by permission of the author and the publishers, Routledge & Kegan Paul, Ltd. Copyright 1966 by W. G. Runciman. In this selection, Runciman discusses some of the major findings from a 1962 survey of the adult population of England and Wales.

moment than you and your family?"; second (if the person had answered yes), "What sort of people do you think are doing noticeably better?"; and third, "What do you feel about this, I mean, do you approve or disapprove of this?" This sequence was chosen in order to tie the answers to people's own immediate situations and to exclude the sort of extravagant or fantastic replies which could not be interpreted as a genuine reference group. It might be thought that even with this wording, so many obvious answers would occur in people's minds that the question would produce long lists of the notoriously rich. Everyone knows, after all, that film stars and industrial tycoons are very much better off than themselves. But in fact, the replies offer ample confirmation that comparative reference groups are limited in scope. On the evidence of this question, relative deprivation is low in both magnitude and frequency even among those who are close to the bottom of the hierarchy of economic class. Over a quarter of the total sample said that there were no other sorts of people that they could think of as doing noticeably better than themselves and their families. The proportion rises, as one would expect, with income. But even in the bottom third of incomes, it is 18 per cent (with an additional 19 per cent of "Don't Knows"); and in the manual stratum as a whole it is 27 per cent (with an additional 14 per cent of "Don't Knows") as against 25 per cent of the non-manual (with 14 per cent of "Don't Knows"). These figures are by themselves a demonstration of a considerable discrepancy between inequality and relative deprivation. . . .

The figures are shown in full in Table 1.

Table 1—"Do you think there are any other sorts of people doing noticeably better at the moment than you and your family?"; by Income within Occupational Stratum

| | NON-MANUAL | | | MANUAL | | |
	High per cent	Medium per cent	Low per cent	High per cent	Medium per cent	Low per cent
Yes	59	66	62	51	56	63
No	31	25	21	39	32	17
Don't know	10	9	17	10	12	20
Total	100%	100%	100%	100%	100%	100%
	(N = 160)	(N = 107)	(N = 75)	(N = 99)	(N = 278)	(N = 368)

At the bottom level of incomes, there is virtually no difference between the two strata. It is still remarkable that so many of the poor should be unable (or unwilling—in either event, their reticence is remarkable) to think of others who are doing better. But the difference between the two strata emerges only at the middle and upper levels of income. At the upper level, the difference is striking if only because the manual respondents who have reached it are nonetheless very much less rich than the non-manual who are shown in the same category.*

*Because the criterion is an income of over £15 per week. It should be noted that only 1087 of 1415 respondents could be coded on income. (*Editors' note.*)

This comparison accordingly supports the argument that for manual workers to reach the top level of incomes will make them satisfied in terms of their traditional comparisons rather than heightening the frequency of relative deprivation among them. In the same way, the greater readiness with which non-manual respondents at the middle level of incomes named others as doing better than themselves suggests that even a modest affluence among manual workers and their wives tends to be seen in terms of traditional working-class comparisons and therefore to lead to a lower frequency of relative deprivation than among non-manual workers at the same level of income. But to interpret these figures more fully, it is necessary to discover who the "other sorts of people" were who were cited by those who did think of at least some others as doing noticeably better than themselves. Among those who did express a sense of relative deprivation, what was the magnitude of it?

The question used was an open-ended one, and the coding therefore calls for some comment. The replies of particular interest to the argument were those which were explicitly tied to people in either the manual or the non-manual stratum. If my earlier argument is correct, then manual respondents should have in mind other manual workers more often than non-manual, even though the incomes which are higher than their own occur more often, and are more likely to be very much higher, among the non-manual stratum. This expectation is

**Table 2—"What sort of people do you think are doing noticeably better?";
by Occupational Stratum**

	Non-Manual per cent	Manual per cent
Higher earnings (including less dependents, more earners in household, opportunities for overtime, more prosperous industries, etc.)	31	39
Non-manual job or class	33	19
Manual job or class	22	25
Friends, neighbors, town or country dwellers	2	2
Specific age group	3	2
Welfare beneficiaries (including paying less tax, retirement pension, family allowances, etc.)	3	2
Educated (including professionally qualified) people	2	4
Everybody else	3	4
Other	4	6
Don't know	4	4
Total	107	107
	(N = 304)	(N = 517)

borne out by the answers given. But the answers most often given by the sample as a whole were references which were not explicitly tied to one stratum or the other. The category shown in Table 2 as "Higher earnings, etc." is the general category used for responses of this kind. It covers a diversity of replies, ranging from people with less dependents to people in more prosperous industries to people with unspecified "better jobs." They all, however, have in common that the point of the comparison made did not derive from the fact that the reference group was on one side or the other of the manual/non-manual line. Almost all of them imply a comparison close to the actual situation of the respondent. None could be termed in any sense "class-conscious," and most of them suggest or, sometimes, directly state a comparison based on a particular feature of the respondent's personal situation.

A few direct quotations may bring out both the flavour and the range of the replies coded under this heading. "People with no children," said a woman with four of them. "Where there is a man working in the family," said an unmarried woman. "People who get extra money by letting off part of the house," said an 82-year-old widow. "Army officers retiring since I did," said a retired army officer. "People that have good health and are able to be in full time work," said a retired draper. "People on night work," said a 63-year-old brazier in the engineering industry, "I have now had to do day work—I'm getting old." "People farming in a bigger way who can get subsidies," said a smallholder, "I don't have enough acreage to be entitled to any." "University research people who went into research instead of teaching," said a schoolteacher's wife.

These replies all relate directly to the immediate position of the respondent, and though they may apply only within one or the other stratum this is not the point of the comparison as stated. The answers coded under this heading do, however, shade over into references to occupations where a less personal comparison is implied but where it is unclear whether the respondent has members of the manual or the non-manual stratum in mind. It might have been legitimate to code some of these as either manual or non-manual—for example, a gardener's wife who referred to "factory people" probably had works, not staff, in mind—but where the reference seemed to be to people in other industries rather than in manual or non-manual jobs as such, they were assigned to "higher earnings, etc." This category therefore includes, for example, a grocer's wife who said "people working in government offices and factories—they get far more money and better hours," or a joiner who said "people in the motor-car industry like mechanics, manufacturers etc.," or a bus-driver who said "people in key jobs in factories down the road." Some of the replies coded into the other categories could also be interpreted as referring only to the manual or the non-manual stratum: for example, a retired shipping clerk who cited those who had paid in to their firms for a retirement pension presumably had fellow clerical workers, not dockers or seamen in mind. He was, however, coded under the heading of "welfare beneficiaries" on the grounds that this represented his choice of reference group better than the occupational stratum to which those whom he had in mind in fact belonged. In the same way "other farmers," when said by a poultry farmer's wife, was coded with "higher earnings etc."; but if a factory worker had said simply "farmers," his reply would have been coded under "non-manual."

The distinction is not always easy to draw, and the percentages for the "higher earnings etc." category in Table 2 must therefore be regarded as less strict than those shown for questions answered by "yes" or "no." All the answers to this question were, however, individually examined, and the distribution shown in Table 2 is certainly accurate enough to support the argument which follows. Double codings were permitted, but were rarely used. One or two of the more sophisticated respondents gave what amounted to a list of others doing better: a schoolteacher in a secondary modern school cited "People on expense accounts, professionals with their own practice, shopkeepers, personnel engaged on important industrial work with wives working, newspapermen, publishers, airline pilots." A solicitor in his early forties listed "More senior people in professions, professional footballers, judges, television and radio stars, cabinet ministers." But replies like these were exceptional. Almost all the answers given were short, and most of them suggested limited comparisons which could be directly related to the respondent's personal situation. The full distribution of replies under the codings used is shown above.

The most interesting figures are those for the frequency of references to the non-manual stratum. Not only is such a reference considerably likelier among non-manual than among manual respondents, but the manual respondents are less likely to refer to the non-manual stratum than to their own. If it is true that reference groups tend to be closely circumscribed at all levels of society except under some abnormal stimulus, then this is just what one should expect. But it affords a striking demonstration of the way in which the narrow scope of comparison produces a discrepancy between relative deprivation and inequality. Given the actual distribution of wealth, the answer to the question which would most obviously and naturally accord with the facts of inequality would be a reference by both manual and non-manual workers to those in business or the professions. Although a few manual workers are earning more than some non-manual, the incomes of very many members of the non-manual stratum are far above those of even the most prosperous manual workers. But when asked a question directly tied to inequalities of class, few members of the manual stratum drew a comparison from the other side of the manual/non-manual line. Even if some of those listed under "higher earnings etc." could have been coded as referring by implication to members of the non-manual stratum, less than a quarter of manual respondents, at most, could be described as choosing a specifically non-manual reference group; and this quarter is a quarter of those who were able to name any sort of people as doing noticeably better than themselves—that is, a quarter of only 56 per cent of the manual stratum.

When self-rated "class" is introduced into the analysis, it makes no difference. A difference is, however, made by income. The likelihood of a reference to the non-manual stratum by manual respondents rises markedly with income; at the bottom level, it is roughly half what it is at the top. This at the same time confirms that reference groups tend to be chosen from close to people's own situation and offers further evidence for the width of the discrepancy between relative deprivation and inequality among the poor. Accordingly, those at the bottom level of incomes are more likely to see some other group as doing better than themselves; but if they do, this comparative reference group is seldom drawn from the non-manual stratum. Those at the top level, by contrast, are more likely to cite members of the non-manual stratum if they cite anybody; but they are the least likely to cite anybody at all.

When those who did see some other sort of people as doing better were asked whether they approved or disapproved of this, there was a slight but interesting difference between manual and non-manual respondents. The proportion coded as "indifferent" or "don't know" was almost identical in each stratum. But the non-manual respondents were not only more likely to see some other group as doing better, but more likely, if they did so, to disapprove: 28 per cent of the non-manual respondents expressed disapproval as against 23 per cent of manual. The difference is not a very large one, but it is interesting that there should be a difference in this direction at all. It, too, is unaffected by self-rating. An egalitarian sense of grievance among manual workers and their wives seems to be inhibited not only by circumscribed reference groups but by the lack of intensity with which a relative deprivation of class, if any, is felt. A possible explanation of this might be that middle-class people are more likely to feel that their particular situation is worsening, and this in turn predisposes them to disapproval of others. But although those who thought that they and their families were "worse off than a year ago" were indeed found to be likelier to disapprove of others, the frequency of disapproval remained higher among non-manual than manual respondents. Irrespective of whether or not they feel that their own position is worsening, middle-class people are more likely to feel the prosperity of others as a grievance.

The frequency of disapproval has, however, little meaning by itself until it is related to the categories of people for whom it is felt. If the comparisons made

Table 3—Manual or Non-Manual references; by Disapproval or Approval/Indifference within Occupational Stratum

	NON-MANUAL		MANUAL	
	Approve or Indifferent	Disapprove	Approve or Indifferent	Disapprove
Non-manual reference	36%	24%	21%	15%
Manual reference	16%	37%	24%	32%
	(N = 205)	(N = 85)	(N = 378)	(N = 117)

by the two strata are as I have suggested, references to manual workers will be commoner among manual than non-manual respondents but disapproving references to manual workers will be commoner among non-manual than manual respondents. This expectation is borne out by the figures shown in Table 3. When incomes are introduced into the analysis, manual respondents at the top level of incomes are more likely to express disapproval than those at the middle or bottom. Since this group is at the same time the likeliest to refer to non-manual workers, it might appear that among the most prosperous manual workers and their wives there is, after all, a good deal of disapproval extending across the manual/non-manual line. But in fact, a further breakdown shows that those who expressed disapproval and those who made a reference to non-manual workers are not to any significant extent the same people. Even at the top of the manual stratum, disapproval does not extend across the manual/non-manual line to the extent that it does among non-manual respondents who are thinking of manual workers. The kinds of references made to either manual or non-manual workers by members of the two strata are shown above. Perhaps the most remarkable feature of the table is that the disapproving references by manual workers to non-manual are the smallest single category of all.

The spontaneous comparisons which people make, however, may not show at all the same pattern as the answers which they give when specific comparisons are put to them. The comparative reference groups spontaneously given have shown first, that there is a wide discrepancy between relative deprivation and inequality; second, that those at the top of the manual stratum are least likely of all to think of any other sorts of people as doing better; and third, that disapproval, and particularly disapproval of manual workers seen as doing better, is more frequent in the non-manual stratum than the manual. But what happens when people are directly asked whether they think that manual workers are doing better than white-collar and whether they think that manual workers ought to be doing as well as they are?

Certain differences between manual and non-manual respondents are readily predictable—the manual respondents will surely be less likely to think that manual workers are doing better, and more likely to think that they ought to be doing at least as well as they are. It can also be safely predicted that age will make a difference to these attitudes—older manual workers and their wives will be less likely than younger ones to think that manual workers ought to be doing as well as they are. Both these expectations are confirmed by the survey; the actual figures are only interesting in that over half the manual respondents agreed that "manual workers are doing much better nowadays than white-collar workers." This finding provides abundant confirmation of the way in which comparison has helped to diminish the relative deprivation felt by manual workers. But what is less predictable is the influence of income and of self-rating.

The two questions used were as follows: first, "Some people say that manual workers are doing much better nowadays than white-collar workers. Do you think this is so or not?"; and second, "Do you think that manual workers ought to be doing as well as they are doing compared with white-collar workers?" . . .

Almost two-thirds of manual workers and their wives describing themselves as "middle-class" agreed that manual workers are doing much better than white-collar, and this proportion is exactly the same among those of the non-manual stratum who described themselves as "working-class." Of manual respondents describing themselves as "working-class," however, under half agreed that manual workers are doing much better. The difference holds good at all three levels of income, and particularly at the top. Of manual workers and their wives at the top level of incomes, 78 per cent of those describing themselves as "middle-class" agreed that manual workers are doing much better. The figure for those at the same income level who described themselves as "working-class" is 48 per cent.

It is clear from this that relative deprivation of class of what I have called a fraternalistic kind can be strongly affected by the choice of normative reference group. But there is an important qualification to be made. Self-rating has almost no effect when manual workers and their wives are asked whether manual workers *ought* to be doing as well as they are by comparison with white-collar workers. . . . [A] middle-class self-rating does not mean that manual workers and their wives will agree with the non-manual stratum about whether manual workers ought or ought not to be doing as well as they are. They may be less likely than those describing themselves as "working-class" to express a relative deprivation on behalf of manual workers as a whole by comparison with white-collar. But they are hardly more likely to agree that manual workers ought not to be doing as well as they are; indeed, because of the higher proportion of Don't Knows among those who describe themselves as "working-class," those who describe themselves as "middle-class" are the more likely of the two to say positively that manual workers ought to be doing as well as they are. Table 4

Table 4—(1) Agreement that Manual Workers are Doing "Much Better Now-adays" than White-Collar Workers, and (2) Assertion that They Ought Not to be Doing as Well as they Are; by Self-Rated "Class" within Occupational Stratum

	NON-MANUAL		MANUAL	
	Self-Rated Middle	Self-Rated Working	Self-Rated Middle	Self-Rated Working
(1) Yes, doing better	72%	64%	64%	45%
(2) Should not be doing as well as they are	41%	25%	15%	12%
	(N = 365)	(N = 124)	(N = 303)	(N = 610)

thus shows both how much and how little the choice of reference group can affect the attitudes of manual workers and their wives to the relative position of manual and white-collar workers in the system of inequalities of class. . . .

Those at the middle level of income who describe themselves as "working-class" are, however, of particular interest. This category of manual respondents shows less agreement that manual workers are doing much better than white-collar than does any other category once income and self-rating are held constant, including those who are poorer than they are but also describe themselves as "working-class." The difference is not overwhelming, and is partly explained by the old age pensioners who are at the bottom level of incomes. But it suggests a tentative conclusion which other tabulations seem also to bear out. Manual workers and their wives who have reached the top level of incomes are likely not to feel relatively deprived because in terms of the comparisons natural to them they have done well. Those at a slightly lower level of incomes, however, will be more likely to feel a relative deprivation in terms of what other manual workers have achieved; and if they think of themselves as "working-class," they will be particularly likely to feel that manual workers in general are not doing all that well. They are, in a sense, the true "fraternalists" of the manual stratum, for they are not only the likeliest to think that manual workers are not doing much better than white-collar; they are also the likeliest of those who describe themselves as "working-class" to agree that manual workers ought to be doing as well as they are. . . .

There is a further way in which relative deprivations of income may be elucidated, apart from either asking for spontaneous comparisons or testing reactions to a particular comparison which is suggested. Without being conscious of any particular comparison with another group, people may still feel relatively deprived by reference to what their own situation was or, perhaps, ought to be. This is bound to have a relation of some kind to what others are seen as getting; no one has an attitude about personal incomes in a vacuum. But if people are asked what they think is the proper standard of living for "people like themselves," then this will furnish another and perhaps different conclusion about the relative deprivations of the different strata. It would obviously be foolish to ask "How much more do you want?," for this does take the question out of any defined social context and into the realm of fantasy. But the gap between what people say they have and what they say they think would be proper for "people like themselves" may be a better measure of the frequency and magnitude of relative deprivation than a question about others seen as doing better. The question used was worded as follows: "What income do you think is necessary for you (your husband) in order to maintain a proper standard of living for people like yourself?"

It is often assumed by writers on the distribution of income or wealth that everyone always thinks that they ought to be given a little more than they have at the moment. "In the American Dream," says Merton, "there is no final stopping point. The measure of 'monetary sucess' is conveniently indefinite and relative. At each income level, as H. F. Clark found, Americans want just about 25 per cent more (but of course this 'just a bit more' continues to operate once it is obtained)."[1] As it is put by Michael Young in his fantasy on *The Rise of the Meritocracy*, "An early sociologist, a Professor Hobhouse, once stated a profound truth. *Question:* What is the ideal income? *Answer:* 10 per

---

1. Robert K. Merton, "Social Structure and Anomie," in *Social Theory and Social Structure*, rev. ed., New York: The Free Press, 1957, p. 136.

cent more than you've got."[2] The notion that people's wants can expand indefinitely is not only to be found in both Marx and Freud; it is a good deal older even than Aristotle, who quotes from Solon to just this effect.[3] But in practice, there is a fair proportion of people who will give a desired income little or no higher than their actual income, and, as we shall see, an even higher proportion who will say that they are satisfied with what they are getting. The present situation is not, any more than the question about incomes themselves, as reliable a guide as the table by itself might suggest. But when the answers to it are compared with incomes as stated, it is immediately apparent that people do not always think they ought to have a constant percentage more than they do.

The members of the sample for whom the calculation could be made fell fairly neatly into four categories. 303 people said that they thought a proper income would be less than, as much as, or only up to 10 per cent more than their stated earnings (and half of these gave a figure equal to their stated earnings); 329 people gave a figure 15 per cent to 44 per cent more; 281 people a figure 45 per cent to 99 per cent more; and 151 gave a figure twice as high or more. For the rest of the sample, unfortunately, the calculations could not be made, usually because the respondent's income was not known. But there are enough respondents in the first category, and the spread of the answers is sufficiently wide, for it to be clear that it would be a mistake to assume that people think they ought "properly" to have more in any fixed ratio to what they say they do have. The answers may, of course, be taken as evidence for how far people understate their earnings; it may be naive to suppose that anyone will say that he ought to be getting less than he is. But the discrepancy is hardly less interesting if it arises partly because people are ashamed to say things in an interview which they fear will make them seem greedy; and it is certainly no less revelant to a comparison of the feelings of relative deprivation which the members of the two strata are willing to voice.

If the argument so far advanced is correct, then the most satisfied group in either stratum—in the sense of this comparison—should be the manual workers and their wives who are in the top third of the overall income distribution. These people are likely to have retained working class standards of income, and since they have done as well as anyone by these standards (but not so spectacularly well as to demolish them altogether) they will more often be content with their incomes than non-manual workers who may be earning a great deal more. We should therefore expect that a comparison between the manual and non-manual respondents at the top level of income will show that the manual workers are more likely to consider their earnings adequate for "people like themselves," even though the actual earnings of the non-manual workers are considerably higher.

This expectation is confirmed by the responses. Out of the six categories

2. Michael Young, *The Rise of the Meritocracy* 1870–2033 (London, 1958), p. 127.

3. *Politics*, 1256b, 33–34.

which result from a breakdown by occupation and income, the manual respondents in the top third of incomes are those most likely to give as a "proper" income a sum more or less equal to what they later say that they (or their husbands) are actually getting. In both strata, the high earners are very much likelier to do so than either the medium or the low earners; but the manual respondents at the top level are still more likely to do so than are the non-manual. The percentages are shown in Table 5.

Table 5—Proportion of Respondents Giving as a "Proper" Income (or Husband's Income) a Sum Less than, Equal to, or Under 10 per cent more than Stated Income; by Income within Occupational Stratum

| | Non-Manual | | | Manual | |
High	Medium	Low	High	Medium	Low
43%	15%	12%	56%	26%	22%
(N = 160)	(N = 107)	(N = 75)	(N = 99)	(N = 278)	(N = 368)

A corresponding relationship holds for the percentage in each category giving as a "proper" income double or more than double their (or their husband's) stated income. Only 2 per cent of the high manual earners did so as against 4 per cent of the non-manual, and more of the medium and low non-manuals also did so than of the medium and low manuals. But even if these figures are representative, they are likely to be misleading, since a much smaller absolute increase will be a percentage increase of 100 per cent for those whose actual incomes are low. In any case, the numbers involved are very small. It is better to observe simply that within each third of the overall income distribution, manual respondents are considerably more likely than non-manual to give a "proper" income more or less equivalent to what they say that they earn. This is, perhaps, a very obvious illustration of what the difference of standards and expectations between the two strata would lead one to expect. But it is noticeable that the manual respondents in the bottom third of the income distribution are likelier not only than their non-manual equivalents but even than non-manual respondents in the middle third of the distribution to say that they ought to be receiving little or no more than they are. The replies to this question, therefore, confirm the impression given by the answers about "other sorts of people" doing better: measured either by cross-class comparisons or by reference to the "proper" situation of the chosen membership reference group, the frequency of relative deprivation of income is lower at all three income levels among manual workers and their wives.

There is one final test, however, which needs to be applied before generalizing too freely. The three questions discussed all support the argument that the comparisons most natural to the different income groups within each stratum are such as to make prosperous manual workers least likely of all to feel relatively deprived. But a person may not think of others as doing better, or have any feelings about manual/white-collar differentials, or think a higher income necessary for a "proper" standard of living for someone like himself, but still feel dissatisfied with his present earnings. Indeed, a further cross-tabulation shows that roughly a third of the manual respondents who see others as doing better and disapprove of this are still quite willing to express themselves satisfied with their own (or their husband's) income. A question worded in terms of satisfaction with income may not reveal at all the same differences between the two strata as a question where the propriety of particular standards has been deliberately introduced. With this in mind, respondents were also asked the question: "Would you say you were satisfied with your (your husband's) present position as far as income is concerned?"

A comparison of the two strata on this different question does indeed reveal a different pattern from the answers to the question about other people. More non-manual than manual respondents said they were aware of others as doing better. But when asked a question in terms of satisfaction, fewer manual than non-manual respondents were prepared to express themselves satisfied with their (or their husband's) incomes. In both strata, the proportion is almost suspiciously high—57 per cent of non-manual respondents and 55 per cent of manual expressed themselves satisfied. Married women were particularly likely to express satisfaction, and this may well reflect a marital loyalty which inhibited them from expressing any dissatisfaction with their husband's income to an interviewer. But as before, it is the differences that are interesting, and the comparison with the result of the question about other people suggests that a further analysis is necessary. A slight difference is made by self-assigned "class," in that manual workers and their wives who describe themselves as "working-class" are less likely by 5 per cent to express themselves satisfied. But the important difference is made by income. When income is introduced as an independent variable, it turns out that the greater frequency of satisfaction in the non-manual stratum is due entirely to the greater frequency of dissatisfaction among the large number of manual workers and their wives who are at the bottom level of incomes. . . .

At the middle level, and even more at the top level, manual respondents are more likely to express satisfaction, so that the prosperous manual workers and their wives do turn out once again to be the least aggrieved of all. But at the bottom level of incomes, the manual more often express dissatisfaction than the non-manual. The proportion satisfied is still remarkably high—of those who gave their or their husband's income as £10 a week or less, 47 per cent of the manual and 56 per cent of the non-manual nonetheless pronounced themselves satisfied. But the difference at the top level confirms the argument that here the traditional framework of working-class comparisons will produce a high frequency of satisfaction among manual workers and their wives. At the bottom level of incomes, by contrast, manual workers and their wives are just as ready to see others as doing better than themselves (even if these others are not drawn from the non-manual stratum), and they are readier still to express themselves dissatisfied with their incomes. The difference between them and the non-manuals is that the non-manuals are considerably likelier, as shown in Table 5, to say that the "proper" standard of income for people like themselves is higher than what they are getting. When satisfaction, rather than propriety, is at issue, the distribution of replies at each level of incomes within the two strata is as shown in Table 6.

Table 6—Satisfaction with Own or Husband's Present Income; by Stated Income within Occupational Stratum

	Non-Manual High per cent	Non-Manual Medium per cent	Non-Manual Low per cent	Manual High per cent	Manual Medium per cent	Manual Low per cent
Yes	63	50	56	72	57	47
No	37	50	41	27	41	51
Don't know	0	0	3	1	2	2
Total	100	100	100	100	100	100
	(N = 160)	(N = 107)	(N = 75)	(N = 99)	(N = 278)	(N = 368)

Those who expressed themselves dissatisfied with their present incomes were then asked the further question: "Is that because the job you are doing (he is doing) is worth more pay, because you need more money, or for some other reason?." Of the total in either stratum who had expressed themselves dissatisfied, 17 per cent, of whom the great majority were at the bottom level of incomes, specifically mentioned retirement and dependence on pensions as their reason. Among the remainder, the non-manual were likelier by 6 per cent than the manual to give worth as their reason and less likely by 5 per cent to give need. This is not a large difference. But it is symptomatic of the difference in norms and outlook between the two strata, and it suggests what might be a part of the reason why the answers of the non-manual respondents more often implied not only an awareness but a disapproval of others.

The questions asked about income, therefore, confirm the expectations suggested by the earlier discussion. Not merely are comparative reference groups among manual workers and their wives so far restricted as to result in a marked discrepancy between relative deprivation and actual inequality; their retention of working-class standards of comparison means that manual workers and their wives are consistently less likely to feel relatively deprived than are non-manual workers and their wives who are earning the same (or at the top level probably a great deal more). Only among the poorest does this conclusion need to be qualified at all; and even here, it can only be said that manual workers and their wives are less often avowedly satisfied, not that they more often feel relatively deprived. . . .

Consumer Goods

In order to find out about attitudes not merely to incomes but to the possession of particular goods, two lists of items were drawn up. The first covered seven obvious and tangible consumer goods: television, telephone, car, refrigerator, washing machine, record player and central heating. The second covered a range of items which it was thought might be more naturally regarded as a prerogative of non-manual households: a house owned (or being bought on mortgage), a fur coat ("for your wife"), foreign holiday travel, a spare bedroom for visitors, first class travel on trains and a private education for children. Respondents were asked first, if they had these items, second, whether they wanted them, third (on the first list only), whether they expected to get those they wanted "in the next two or three years," and fourth, "Do you think other people are managing to afford (any items not possessed but wanted)?" Those who answered yes to the last question were then asked the open-ended question, "What sort of people are you thinking of?" . . .

The way in which comparative reference groups are limited is already suggested by the answers given when those who said they wanted one or more of the items listed were asked whether they thought that "other people" were managing to afford them. For example, 9 per cent of the non-manual and 16 per cent of the manual respondents who said they wanted foreign holiday travel, replied "no," 18 per cent of the non-manuals and 30 per cent of the manuals who said that they wanted a telephone, replied "no," and 53 per cent of the non-manuals and 61 per cent of the manuals who said that they wanted central heating, replied "no." On the face of it, it is at least as remarkable that there should be anyone answering "no" to these questions as that there should be anyone saying that nobody else is doing better than themselves. . . .

The distribution of answers among the manual and non-manual respondents who both wanted one or more items on the first list and said that they thought that "other people" were managing to afford them is shown in Table 7.

Table 7—"What sort of people are you thinking of?" (As Managing to Afford Items not Possessed but Wanted from First List of Goods); by Occupational Stratum

	Non-Manual per cent	Manual per cent
"Status-seekers," "big spenders," etc.	6	8
"More money," "higher incomes," etc.	10	16
More earners, less dependents, etc.	13	16
Non-manual job or class	20	16
Manual job or class	20	27
Friends, neighbours, etc.	8	7
Everybody, most people, etc.	8	6
"Ordinary" people	2	1
"People like self"	4	2
Beneficiaries of welfare	2	2
Age groups	4	3
Other	10	8
Unspecified, Don't know	5	3
Total	112	115
	(N = 263)	(N = 522)

The remarkable feature of this table is the distribution of references explicitly made to the manual or non-manual stratum. The figures shown should be qualified to the extent that a wide variety of specific comparisons are included in them: the distinction within the manual stratum between skilled and unskilled is, as we have already seen, salient in the minds of many people on either side of it, and it is this comparison which underlies many of the references made by manual respondents to other workers in manual jobs. This is obviously a very different comparison from either that made by a farm labourer between himself and workers in factories or by a clerical worker between himself and manual workers in general. In addition to this, some of the answers coded under these two headings were very general ones, including the phrases "middle class" or "working class" which, as has already been shown, may have a variety of meanings to different people. But these qualifications do not invalidate the conclusion to which the figures point. Manual workers and their wives who want one or more of the items listed are not only less likely than non-manual respondents to take a comparative reference group from the non-manual stratum; they are themselves much less likely to take a comparative reference group from the non-manual than from the manual stratum. . . .

There is no way of ascertaining in detail from the survey just what influences underlie this restriction of comparisons. If the normal response to economic inequality is to make comparisons only to those closest to oneself rather than to those by contrast with whom one is most unequally placed, then these results need, perhaps, no explanation whatever. But since it is clear that this is not universally true, the question remains to what extent and for what reasons reference groups are so restricted. A glance over the social history of Britain since 1918 reveals some, at least, of the reasons why on matters of economic class—but not status—there has not been a cumulative spiral of aspiration and prosperity since the collapse of the militant radicalism which followed the First World War. But the principal interest of the 1962 survey lies not in demonstrating what influences are at work—this must rest on the historical evidence for the period before the survey was taken—but in revealing to what extent the reference groups of the less well placed are limited in scope, unspecifically defined, and mildly expressed. Several different forms of question were used to elucidate the reference group comparisons made, and each served only to reinforce the same impression. Both the magnitude and frequency of relative deprivation among manual workers and their wives are very much lower than would accord with the facts of economic inequality. The lack of "class-consciousness" which is sometimes attributed to the British working class is in this sense, at least, amply confirmed.

Reference Group and Social Comparison Processes Among the Totally Blind

Helen May Strauss

HOW the totally blind locate themselves in the social world may seem to be a peculiar problem bearing on the behavior of only a tiny segment of the general population. Their situation is certainly most unusual; but it also provides a rare opportunity for the exploration of reference group processes and for a critical test of social comparison theory.

The totally blind are unequivocally set apart from the general population by a clearly defined physical handicap which affects their lives in many and important ways. The very rarity of the handicap—in the United States perhaps one person in 2,500 is totally blind—sharpens the contrast. But in addition they are circumscribed by many well-established arrangements provided or imposed by society. The special status of blindness is emphasized by the laws of the states and Federal government which provide public assistance for the visually handicapped, and by the educational system which until recently provided for their needs through special schools, often residential in character, in which the blind were taught in physical isolation from the sighted population.[1]

Prepared especially for this volume. This is a summary of some of the findings from the author's *A Study of Reference Group and Social Comparison Processes Among the Blind* (unpublished Ph.D. dissertation, Columbia University, 1966). It is printed by special permission of the author, and is part of a larger research program in which totally blind individuals are being studied to illuminate fundamental social psychological problems. The program is directed by Herbert Hyman under grants from the National Science Foundation.

1. In our total sample of adults, approximately half received all of their precollege education in schools for the blind. Although the other half were educated among sighted people in conventional schools, they may often have attended special classes or other special

Many less formal social patterns accentuate the situation. Special attitudes toward the blind have been reported throughout history, in sacred and secular writings, and there is abundant evidence of the special treatment accorded to them by many societies. Thus, the blind traditionally have been taught their proper place in man's, or God's, scheme, by virtue of normative influences at every stage of life.

And it is not easy for them to learn differently. Many of the characteristics which would permit the blind to differentiate themselves from one another are not visible to them, and they have an overriding ground of similarity to each other. They must certainly feel some common fate and some sense of isolation from the sighted world, denied by their handicap from sharing many forms of normal experience and from a major mode of social stimulation and communication. And that same handicap would also deny them the visual evidence to appraise their own performance objectively and to invalidate the social definition of reality which the sighted world has taught to them. The choice of a comparative reference group seems simple—almost overdetermined—in accordance with a theory of social comparison such as Festinger's, which postulates similarity as the basic principle governing the selection of a reference group, and which stresses the need for social comparison processes when objective, non-social means for self-appraisal are not available.[2] By this logic a totally blind person ought to choose the blind rather than the sighted as a comparative reference group. In the process, he would protect his self-regard from any damage that might occur in comparing his standing with competitors who have the unfair advantage of being sighted.

Weighty as the argument may appear, there are, nevertheless, grounds for an alternative view. Reference group theory in a permissive, perhaps indulgent, way has sought for empirical evidence on the variety of choices of comparison points in the course of many field studies, in contrast with the few laboratory tests of social comparison theory. And the evidence thereby accumulated does suggest that factors other than similarity may contribute to the selection of reference groups. For example, individuals sometimes choose dissimilars in the spirit of identification, and particular reference groups may become salient as a result of specialized social influences.[3] That the blind may also have some

---

facilities. Within our sample, in the stratum of those who were born blind or blinded in early childhood, over three-quarters were educated in separate schools for the blind. Among those who became totally blind after the age of fifteen, over three-quarters were educated in conventional schools, since they may have suffered no handicap or only a partial handicap during their school years.

2. See Leon Festinger, "A Theory of Social Comparison Processes," *Human Relations*, 7: 117–140, 1954, especially Hypothesis III and Corollary III A, and Hypothesis II and Corollary II B.

3. See, for example, H. H. Hyman, "The Psychology of Status," *Archives of Psychology*, No. 269, 1942; and Martin Patchen, "A Conceptual Framework and Some Empirical Data Regarding Comparisons of Social Rewards," *Sociometry*, 24: 136–156, 1961.

freedom of choice of reference groups was suggested by empirical observations in the course of the preliminary phases of our own research. The blind of today appear to be exposed to two sets of conflicting social pressures. On one side are those reformers who urge integration into the sighted world and who are pressing the blind to take part in its competition to the limit of their capacities. At the other pole, representing the traditional view, are those who view the blind as a group so handicapped as to be completely dependent. In the spirit of reform, the current view endorses schooling in integrated settings with the sighted. Thus, despite the severe handicap under which all totally blind individuals must labor, and which creates the objective grounds of similarity, it was suggested to us that there would be large individual differences in the internalization of the two ideologies and corresponding differences in reference group selection.

The individual differences in the conceptions of the self and its capabilities would depend on the experiences and immediate social influences impinging on the life of the particular blind person. Whatever the sources may be, they are evidenced in the striking fact that about a third of our totally blind respondents report that they do *not* conceive of themselves as blind! With such a self-conception, a blind person might find more links of similarity, albeit psychologically forged, with those who are sighted than with others who are blind as a basis for such social comparisons.

These are some of the mysterious and wondrous workings of the self. But, even among those who define themselves as blind, it is not difficult to discern a psychological principle which might make comparisons with the sighted not threatening to the self-regard of a blind person. Certainly, it is bitter to know that one's performance or position is inferior to some group's, but if this is not one's fault and is consonant with the limitations imposed by the handicap, it may not reflect on the self.[4]

Thus there are good grounds, both theoretical and empirical, for entertaining the hypothesis that the sighted as well as the blind are likely points toward which the totally blind can orient their social comparisons.

There is still another possibility. Social comparison behavior may be inhibited altogether among the blind, despite Festinger's postulation of a drive to evaluate the self which leads to social comparison under conditions where objective evidence on performance is not available. By avoiding all comparisons, anyone could protect himself from the sense of inferiority which might follow on an unfortunate choice of a superior reference group. Among the blind this pattern would appear especially likely for still another reason. The function of comparative reference group behavior is to appraise the self, which normally

4. See Patchen, *op. cit.* On the basis of long observational studies and psychoanalytic treatment of the blind, Dorothy Burlinghame suggests that "they suffer greatly when they compare themselves with the seeing; they are resentful and angry, and merely control their anger because they realize how much they need the seeing." "The Development of the Blind," *The Psychoanalytic Study of the Child*, 16: 131, 1961.

follows from knowledge of the relative position of an individual and his reference group. But if the blind were barred by their handicap from knowledge, not only of their absolute level of performance, but also of their position or performance relative to others, social comparison behavior could serve no function for them. Unless modalities other than vision yielded the information essential to the determination of their standing, evaluation by social comparison would be avoided, since when it is employed, uncertainty or inaccuracy would result. Following this line of thought, one would predict a general diminution in social comparison behavior, or a subtle pressure toward use of the sighted as a point of comparison. Using similars, other blind, for comparison would provide no simple cues to the determination of one's relative position. In using the sighted, a blind person could accept as authoritative knowledge the common view that the sighted are superior and have the basis for making a judgment.

An empirical study among the totally blind therefore seemed an especially fruitful way to test a theory of social comparison processes, and to enrich our knowledge of reference group behavior. The central questions to be answered were: Do the totally blind engage in social comparisons? Are they more likely to use the sighted or the blind consistently as their reference groups, or do their choices and the frequency of social comparisons vary with the dimension on which they are appraising themselves?

The Sample and the Method

There are severe difficulties in designing an unbiased sample of the universe of totally blind adults in the United States, and almost insuperable obstacles to completing such a design. A sample of totally blind, noninstitutionalized adults living in five cities spread over the country was obtained by the strictest, most scientific procedures possible, and various tests established that it approximates an unbiased sample of that universe.[5] For this inquiry, 197 totally blind, white adults, ranging in age from 18 to 70 were employed. They were drawn from two strata defined by the age at which they became totally blind. The "late" group became totally blind after the age of 15, and all the "early" group became totally blind before the age of 8.[6] The early blind have had the opportunity to

5. See the forthcoming monograph on the findings of the larger research program for a detailed description of the sample design and the tests of its quality. It should be noted that only 197 out of the larger sample of about 400 blind adults were used in this particular inquiry, but all the subjects who satisfied one essential requirement were included in the subsample.

6. The early-blinded group of 85 includes a subgroup of 44 congenitally totally blind individuals. The remaining 41 became blind before age 8, 21 of them before age 5. Great effort was devoted to finding as many *congenitally* totally blind respondents as possible. Because their entire lives have been lived without benefit of any vision, their responses do, of course, promise most toward the understanding of problems of social perception. Unfortunately for us, though happily for the human race, they are the rarest category of the blind. It was only by virtue of an exhaustive effort in five widely separated cities that 85 early-blinded individuals were found who agreed to cooperate in the study.

establish their identity as blind over a very long period and during their most formative years. Over half of them have had all their lives in which to establish such an identity, since they were born totally blind. The late blinded have all had the benefit of some or complete vision during their childhood, but many have also had long years in which to assume a new identity as blind, since about 40 per cent of them have been totally blind for over ten years.

For each early-blind and for every other late-blind subject, a sighted close relative was sought to serve as an informant on the socialization and current life patterns of the blind person. Sampling the relatives was an economy measure, but was not applied to the early blind because of the special interest we had in their behavior. Reference to Table 1 shows that the desired number

Table I—Composition of the Samples

	Blind	Sighted Relatives
Early-blinded	85	61
Late-blinded	112	55
Total	197	116

was obtained for the late blind, but that the sample fell short for the early blind.[7]

The data on which our findings are based were collected in the course of long interviews, in which specially trained interviewers, mainly recruited from the regular staff of the National Opinion Research Center and working under continuing supervision, administered a standardized questionnaire. The blind respondent was always interviewed first to eliminate any influence that the sighted relative might otherwise have exercised if he had known the questions to be asked. The interview with the relative was conducted as soon afterwards as could be arranged in order to minimize opportunity for discussion and contamination of his answers. The questionnaire and procedures were developed on the basis of two pretests, and interviewers' ratings of each interview plus a general report filed at the end of their total assignment provided additional evidence on the quality of the data.

A battery of three questions, administered in the order shown, and located

---

7. To prevent biased selection of relatives by the interviewer, a priority system was established for drawing relatives in a certain order, corresponding to their estimated knowledge-ability of the blind respondent, and their utility as a control group of sighted relatives who would be matched with the blind in social characteristics. Thus the influence of blindness on social attitudes, a prime focus for the larger research program, could be assessed. For the design of the sample of relatives, and tests of the unbiased character of the losses, see the forthcoming monograph. It should be noted that in about 15 per cent of the cases, no relative was available, and the informant was a party in the household or close by who filled the role of being in close contact and knowledgeable about the blind person.

about one-quarter of the way through the schedule, provided evidence on the comparative reference groups the blind select for three dimensions of self-appraisal.[8] While the interviewers reported deficiencies on some of the other questions, in no case did they express any doubt about the honesty of the respondents' answers to this battery, or report any difficulty or reluctance in answering them.

1. In judging your own personal appearance, are you likely to think of yourself in comparison with (men, women) of your own age who are blind, or who are sighted?

2. Supposing someone asked you if you were a quick learner—in thinking of your answer, would you be more likely to compare yourself with people of your own age who are blind, or people of your own age who are sighted?

3. When you think about your character, and whether you are a good person, do you usually think of yourself in comparison with other blind people or with people who can see?

The answers to these questions were recorded in precoded categories, but the interviewers were also instructed to record any spontaneous comments. Inspection of the comments indicated in every case a thoughtful reaction and suggests that the issue of social comparison is frequently affect-laden for the blind. A man of fifty-seven, blind for twenty-seven years, remarked in answer to the question on personal appearance: "They say I look good and they tell me I don't look my age, but I don't know." A blind woman says: "I *want* to look as good as a sighted person." The question on the reference group used for appraising learning ability drew more defensive comments from some respondents. In the few instances where the question on the comparison group for appraising character elicited comments, the respondent remarked that blindness had nothing to do with character.

The comments also provided informal validation of the assumption underlying the design of the battery. The three questions differ in the degree to which they implicate blindness as a relevant factor in reference group processes. The similarity the blind share with each other, but not with the sighted, varies with the dimension specified, and the perceived inadequacy of the blind and the corresponding feelings also varied. Learning ability was more likely to be viewed as the difficult area of competition and to arouse fear; personal appearance also occasioned uneasiness, but character none.

8. None of the previous questions nor the introduction would have heightened the tendency to engage in social comparisons. However, discussion of blindness in the earlier questions would no doubt have made the handicap salient for the respondent, and the findings to be presented on the choice of the sighted as a reference group are, in light of this, even more compelling.

The question on personal appearance might be regarded by some as an experimental vehicle to test Festinger's proposition that "if an . . . ability is of no importance to a person there will be no drive to evaluate that ability. . . . "[9] That personal appearance is, in fact, of importance to the blind is suggested not only by their comments, but also by a special battery of questions on which our respondents scored high in their endorsement of conventional visual-aesthetic values, by a literature which reveals the blind desiring the visually beautiful, and by the emphasis in their traditional schooling on neatness, clean-liness, and the creation of artistic products that appeal essentially to the visual modality. The question, therefore, tests another aspect of social comparison theory. When an ability is of importance and objective means for self-appraisal are, by definition, not possible, will comparison processes nevertheless be inhibited because the social comparison cannot serve its function in the absence of the perceptual cues needed to locate the self relative to others?

The contrast in the psychological contents of the three questions should make uniformities observed in social comparison processes quite a compelling finding. But while the questions differ in content, they are identical in technical form. The order in which the blind and sighted reference groups were mentioned is identical and the three questions were asked consecutively rather than being widely separated in the questionnaire. The possibility of a response set certainly may be entertained, but it should be stressed that the findings from twelve other questions scattered through the interview and worded in many different forms support the aggregate findings to be presented. Response set seems, in this light, to be a negligible factor. In any event, it cannot account for the findings of subgroup differences in comparison processes, since response set, in whatever minor degree it may operate, is a constant for all groups.

All three questions pressed the respondent to choose either the blind or the sighted as a comparative reference group, and did not present to him such alternative possibilities as "both blind and sighted," or "never compare myself." Moreover, the interviewers were instructed not to suggest such alternatives and to try to force the choice presented. However, answer boxes were provided to record such answers when they were volunteered spontaneously. Although the procedure cannot bias the findings on the relative frequency of choosing blind versus sighted reference groups, or obscure the differences between dimensions or subgroups, it does deflate reports of noncomparison. The estimates to be presented of such behavior are therefore conservative.

The reference group and social comparison processes revealed by these questions were examined in relation to many independent variables. Only selected findings will be presented for a number of the major variables which were measured by a variety of questions, and found to be relatively reliable on the basis of the interviewers' reports and other evidence.

9. *Ibid.*, p. 130.

The Findings

ABSENCE OF SOCIAL COMPARISONS

On each of the dimensions of self-appraisal, about one-fifth of the blind report that they do not compare themselves with anyone. Recalling the fact that such a response had to be volunteered, this is a startlingly large proportion. Given three invitations to choose a comparative reference group, it is, indeed, striking that 13 per cent of the blind consistently reported that they never compared themselves at all with respect to their personal appearance, learning ability, or character. The data are presented in Table 2, from which it can be

Table 2—Responses of Totally Blind to Three Social Comparison Questions

Dimension	Per Cent Making No Comparison
Personal appearance	26
Learning	17
Character	20
	$N = 197$

seen that social comparison behavior is least likely to occur in the sphere of personal appearance, the very realm in which objective means for self-appraisal would be minimal, and most likely to occur with respect to learning ability, where objective, nonsocial cues for self-appraisal are most available to the blind.

The absence of social comparisons was found, by many analyses, to be most characteristic of those blind who suffered the greatest social isolation, past or present. It was more frequent among the early blind, those who had been blind longer, and those who had been educated in residential schools for the blind, so that their contact with the world of the sighted was restricted from early life. In their current adult lives, the noncomparing respondents were less likely to belong to clubs or organizations. A larger proportion were regarded by their family and friends as "blind" and many more considered themselves "blind" than did those who reported using a comparative reference group.

In summary, every social or psychological or demographic characteristic (for example, age) that was examined showed a correlation between withdrawal from social comparison and factors that would isolate the individual from social relations. Yet, it would be a mistake to see these individuals as completely withdrawn from society. In their social participation our sample exhibits conventional and normal behavior, very similar to that of their sighted relatives. They go to church as often; they show even greater interest in news of the day. Considering the physical barriers in the way of a totally blind person casting a vote, it is dramatic that 57 per cent of the total sample reported voting in the last presidential election! But among individuals with high rates of such participation, the specialized life experiences mentioned above do make an independent contribution in dampening social comparison processes. The exact nature of the constellation that inhibits such processes is thus somewhat elusive, but certainly the fact that our blind respondents involve themselves in larger social concerns means that the isolation variable should not be construed in an extreme and generalized fashion.

How the noncomparing blind individuals actually evaluate themselves, when they apparently do not employ social comparison processes, remains a question for further research. In his early study, Hyman described nonhandicapped individuals who also did not engage in comparative reference group behavior, and who used personal, idiosyncratic methods for self-evaluation. The phenomenon which appears so prevalent among our blind subjects is clearly not unique to them, although blindness seems to increase its frequency. The empirical evidence of its association with influences isolating one from social relations suggests an avenue for exploration.

THE DIRECTION OF SOCIAL COMPARISON

We now examine the comparative reference groups chosen by those blind who do engage in social comparisons. The basic pattern can be conveyed simply by averaging the percent who choose the sighted on the three different dimensions. The fact that, on the average, 63 per cent choose the sighted qualifies strongly the principle of similarity. Only four of our totally blind respondents consistently chose the blind as a reference group for all three dimensions of comparison. Table 3 presents the more detailed findings for each dimension, separately for early- and late-blinded respondents.

Table 3—Direction of Comparisons for Each of Three Dimensions Among Comparing Respondents

DIMENSION	EARLY-BLINDED CHOOSING:			Percentages of	LATE-BLINDED CHOOSING:			
	Blind	Both Blind and Sighted	Sighted	Total Number	Blind	Both Blind and Sighted	Sighted	Total Number
Learning	16	32	52	66*	15	18	67	96*
Personal appearance	13	20	67	55	4	13	83	87
Character	3	47	50	66	6	24	70	92

* Adding the "noncomparers" to the totals of 66 and 96, respectively, makes up the grand totals of 85 early-blinded and 112 late-blinded respondents.

On each of the dimensions, the selection of an exclusively blind reference group is the least frequent pattern, and the finding is about equal in magnitude for both early- and late-blinded respondents. But certain interesting patterns may be observed. For learning ability, where the ability of the blind to compete with the sighted is most handicapped, the blind are more frequently employed as an exclusive reference group. On the dimension of character, where the handicap of blindness is least relevant to performance, the respondents are least likely to exhibit any exclusivity in their choices and to volunteer that they choose both blind *and* sighted for their reference groups. On personal appearance, a dimension where there is certainly a ground for dissimilarity, the strength of desire is perhaps suggested by the largest percentage of choices of the sighted as the reference group. On all three dimensions, the early blind are less likely to choose the sighted as their exclusive reference group, but this does not mean that they turn completely in the opposite direction. Rather, they tend to choose from among both the blind and sighted for a reference group.

DETERMINANTS OF THE CHOICE OF REFERENCE GROUP

In the analysis of factors accounting for the choice of reference group, we shall limit ourselves to the dimension of learning ability. The distribution of choices is most varied and thus provides greatest opportunity for studying individual differences. And it is this dimension of performance which brings into sharpest relief the handicap of blindness. To simplify the analysis, and presentation, the choice of the sighted exclusively will be contrasted with the choice either of the blind reference group or "both blind and sighted" as a reference group. The latter combination of choices into one grosser reference group provides the most comprehensive measure of those who will orient their reference group behavior, in some degree, toward the blind. Very few of our totally blind respondents will allow themselves (or admit to) an exclusive orientation toward other blind.

All the tests bear upon a general hypothesis: When psychological or social forces act upon the individual to increase his conception of blindness as a restricting or limiting condition, the tendency to compare himself with other blind persons will be increased. Clearly the coalition of all the forces is such as to make the sighted the preeminent reference group for the blind, as evidenced in the earlier findings. Consequently, when only one of these forces is abstracted from the total complex, its counter-influence cannot be expected to be of great magnitude.

The forces whose influence on reference group selection has been examined fall into three sectors: those that relate to the definition of the self and its capabilities; those that derive from the immediate family environment; those that derive from the wider environment through which the individual has passed or within which he is now contained. All the tests are presented separately for the early- and late-blinded respondents. Since many of these variables are correlated with the onset of blindness, this insures that the tests are not confounded by that overriding determinant of reference group selection, and incidentally shows the independent influence of onset of blindness apart from any of the specific factors examined. Listed below are the eleven questions used to provide indicators of the forces in the three sectors which direct reference group selection toward the blind or the sighted.

Self-Concept

1. (a) The self-image: considers self blind or not.
   (b) The reflected self-image: believes that family and friends consider him blind or not.
2. Likes or does not like his blindness to be known by others.
3. Thinks things through and acts on his own decisions or not.
4. Believes most important things to teach a blind child are skills which increase self-reliance and behavior which diminishes stigma rather than traits of resignation, acceptance of handicap and the specialized skills traditionally taught the blind.

Environmental Influences

5. Attended residential blind school or not.
6. Achieved only a low level of formal education or a higher level of formal education.
7. Membership only in organizations exclusively for the blind, or membership in organizations which include sighted people.

Family Influences as Reported in the Interview with the Sighted Relative

8. Family members think of him as blind or not.
9. Family member believes most important things to teach a blind child are skills which increase self-reliance and diminish stigma or not.
10. Family member thinks blind respondent should be watched more closely in the friends he makes than a sighted person, or not.
11. Family member thinks a blind child should be disciplined more strictly, more leniently, or the same as a sighted child.

The findings are presented in Table 4. Considering first the way in which the conception of the self and its capabilities influences the choice of a comparative reference group, the findings are quite dramatic among the early-blinded. All of these individuals have been totally blind, either from birth or early childhood, and yet their own definition of the self as handicapped or not has a very considerable influence on their choice of the blind or sighted as a framework for social comparison. But there are objective limits within which the self-conception can operate, as witnessed by the contrast in the reference group behavior of the late-blinded. Given a self-conception of the same character and capability, the early-blinded are more likely to choose the blind as their reference group than are the late-blinded. And an early-blinded person who endows his self with greater capabilities than does a late-blinded person shows no consistently greater tendency to select a sighted reference group. Among the late-blinded, the self-conception has a much smaller influence on the choice of reference group, their choices going overwhelmingly toward the sighted reference group, and one of the tests going contrary to expectation.

One other finding in this sector is dramatic. What we have called the reflected self-image, the blind person's perception of how his family regard him, is much less influential in determining his choice of a comparative reference group than his own self-conception. Certainly, one might expect such primary group influences—perhaps one might label them influence from a *normative* reference group—to have a stronger effect. We shall postpone discussion of the finding until the data on direct family influences are summarized.

Table 4—Determinants of the Direction of Social Comparison for Appraisal of Learning Ability

	Early-Blinded		Late-Blinded	
	PERCENTAGES SELECTING THE BLIND AS THEIR REFERENCE GROUP WHEN HYPOTHESIZED INFLUENCE IS TOWARD			
	Blind	Sighted	Blind	Sighted
Self-Concept				
1. a. Considers self blind or not (self-image)	65 (42)*	34 (24)*	39 (62)*	25 (35)*
b. Believes family and friends consider him blind or not (reflected self-image)	50 (24)	44 (36)	32 (38)	28 (39)
2. Likes his blindness known by others or not	53 (36)	50 (28)	38 (42)	26 (35)
3. Thinks things through and acts on own decisions or not	88 (9)	44 (57)	36 (11)	35 (83)
4. Believes blind child should be taught reliance, etc., or not	64 (17)	45 (49)	31 (51)	37 (41)
Environmental Influences				
5. Attendance at residential school	53 (56)	30 (10)	43 (21)	31 (76)
6. Low or high level of education	60 (20)	48 (33)	40 (44)	26 (23)
7. Membership in blind or sighted organizations	63 (19)	40 (26)	40 (30)	34 (26)
Family Influences				
8. Family and friends think of him as blind or not	37 (24)	40 (25)	29 (24)	45 (23)
9. Teach a blind child reliance or not	40 (10)	42 (36)	44 (25)	24 (20)
10. The friends the blind respondent makes should be more carefully watched or not	29 (7)	42 (43)	45 (11)	33 (37)
11. Blind child should be disciplined more strictly, leniently or the same as a sighted child	40 (10)	41 (39)	63 (11)	31 (35)

* Numbers in parentheses are the totals in each subgroup.

Larger environmental influences are presented in the second section of the table. Whether or not the blind individual had attended a special school for the blind was selected as a decisive developmental influence relating closely to his feelings of identification throughout life. We found, in fact, that those who had attended such schools were consistently more apt to withdraw from social comparison, a response-pattern which we took to indicate isolation from the sighted world. Inspection of the possible connection between this strong influence and the social comparison behavior of those subjects who do not withdraw from comparisons reveals that the same expectations are fulfilled. Those who have had special school training show a greater tendency to name "the blind" in making their comparison choice. The percentages are 53 per cent for the early-blind who had residential school training contrasted with 30 per cent for those who did not, and for the late-blind, 43 per cent for those who had special training as against 31 per cent for those who did not.

In contrast with *type* of education, level of formal education achieved provides a test of a rather complex constellation of experiences. In part, the level achieved reflects the actual equality the blind have demonstrated in their competition in the larger world. An early-blinded individual who has gone on to higher education, by definition among the sighted, has shown his motivation and capability; and the findings among the early-blinded who have been "low achievers" is just what one would predict. For the late-blinded, the findings have been presented in the table, but, of course, cannot be interpreted in the same fashion. For many of them, their education was completed before the onset of their blindness and thus does not reflect their predispositions as blind persons. The experience or general orientation toward achievement has, however, left its mark.

The high achievers among the early-blinded are less likely to choose the blind as their reference group, but the absolute magnitude is high: 48 per cent of such individuals still compare themselves with the blind. Reality must have intruded. Speed of learning ability is a dimension to which the blind are sensitive, and higher education would expose them unrelentingly to their limitation and sensitize them even more. The "retreat" to the objectively similar reference group is marked under this situation. The pressures and the motivation implied in the recruitment into higher education, which might direct reference group choices toward the sighted world, are apparently overridden by the consequences of the experience. In pressing toward such achievement, the blind individual has presented himself to the glaring exposure of his limitations. Understandably, he may grasp the comfort to be extracted from the fact that, in comparison with other *blind* individuals, his performance represents a very high level of accomplishment.

Voluntary association membership describes the contemporary environment of the blind person, rather than the past environment through which he traveled. In part his association with other blind individuals exclusively versus his association with the sighted represents self-selection and thus taps the respondent's motivation, but it also is indicative of the type of stimulation to which he is being exposed. In any case the influence is as expected, and is considerable for the early-blinded.

With respect to family influences, as revealed in an interview with a sighted informant in the family, the first variable examined in the table is the relative's direct report of the way he and the family define the blind person. This is in contrast with the blind person's *perception* of his family's definition of him, presented in the earlier part of the table under the label, the "reflected self-image." The family definition of the respondent is observed to have no effect among the early-blinded and an effect in a direction *opposite* to expectation among the late-blinded. To some extent, this perverse finding might be interpreted as indicative simply of the slippage or attenuation that arises from the blind person's misperceiving the way his family actually defines his character and capability. But, recall that the reflected self-image, based on his own perception, also had only a modest influence on the choice of reference group, whereas his own self-conception had a marked influence on his choice of reference group. More detailed analyses of the data, based both on the particular question and on various patterns which can be derived from the three questions on self-image, reflected self-image, and family image, clarify the findings, but cannot be presented here.[10] In part, it should be realized that the informant may not always be an accurate spokesman for the entire family, and that sometimes he did report that different family members saw their blind relative in differing ways. But the essential meaning of the finding is that the blind individual often is not controlled by his family's conceptions, and guides his reference group behavior by his own self-definition, the sources of which remain to be determined.

In the other tests of influences stemming from the family, the findings are negligible for the early-blinded, but substantial for the late-blinded. It should be stressed that the informant is reporting on *contemporary* features within the milieu, and these would have impinged on the late-blinded closer in time to the onset of their handicap. By contrast, the early-blinded made their adaptation long ago, and the informant's reports are therefore much less revealing about the circumstances that may have been critical at the time the reference group processes unfolded.

From the array of data in the total table, the dramatic fact that stands out is how rarely the totally blind choose their similars as a reference group, even in the presence of specific influences in that direction. And this is so despite the fact that the choice of "both the blind and the sighted" is combined with the exclusive choice of the blind, enlarging the magnitude of those who apparently select a blind reference group. But perhaps the finding would be different if we combined several of these variables, thereby testing the influence of a more powerful force on reference group selection.

CUMULATIVE EFFECTS OF SEVERAL FORCES ON REFERENCE GROUP SELECTION

Three variables have been selected for this analysis: The two aspects of the self-concept elicited by the questions, "Do you consider yourself blind or not?" and "How do you personally feel about having other people know about your trouble with seeing?" and one environmental factor, schooling in a residential training school for the blind. The effect of these three variables on reference

10. See Strauss, *op. cit.*

group selection is examined only for the group of early-blinded subjects, who are more likely to orient their behavior to other blind individuals. The findings are presented in Table 5.

Table 5—Percentage of Early-Blinded Choosing "The Blind" for Social Comparison of Learning Ability as Three Pressures toward This Choice Are Cumulated

None of three factors is present	0 (3)
One factor is present	30 (10)
Two factors are present	48 (29)
Three factors are present	58 (24)

It should be stressed that there are practically no early-blinded respondents who exhibit none of these characteristics, and only a small minority who exhibit only one of the three characteristics whose force is being examined. The statistical foundation for examining the problem in these cells is indeed precarious. Nevertheless, there is an orderly progression among the early-blinded in the choice of the blind as a reference group as the forces are cumulated. But even when the influence of three such forces has been compounded, about half of the early-blinded still orient their reference group behavior toward the sighted world. The cumulative effect of a set of strong forces is still insufficient to make most of the totally blind turn away from the reference group of the sighted world.

Conclusion

Social comparison and reference group processes have been examined in a group of totally blind adults, and the relationship of such processes to the self-concept, to primary group and larger environmental influences, has been demonstrated. Currently, few totally blind American adults will choose the blind as their comparative reference group for appraising themselves on several important dimensions. Societal pressures and their own self-regard militate against such a choice. Where that choice is made, however, the relationship to antecedent factors in the life history may be clearly traced.

The concept of similarity in social comparison theory needs considerable qualification and specification in the light of our studies of the blind. Our study points to an inherent vagueness and obscurity in the concept. The blind may interpret the concept in their own subtle way. Despite their fundamental similarity to each other, they often do not choose each other for social comparison. They may reject the obvious and objective ground of similarity with each other to protect their self-regard, which might be damaged by their accepting membership in a group that is labeled inferior. They may find a more comforting identity among those with whom they share some other bond of similarity, spontaneously felt or made salient to them. The dynamics of the self are perhaps the key to understanding the way the mind manipulates the manifold aspects of similarity, which in turn guides reference group processes and feeds back upon the self-regard.

Generally, the need to protect self-regard is assumed to motivate comparisons with similars rather than those who are markedly superior. The patterns noted among the blind suggest that self-regard may be protected by the avoidance of social comparison behavior altogether. But the comfort bought in this fashion might be at the price of having no way of appraising one's own abilities on a dimension where objective bases for self-appraisal are lacking. Festinger stresses the importance of a need to know. To be sure, the blind confront a most unusual dilemma with respect to such a need. Comparison processes which normally function to establish one's rank may not be able to render this function when the cognitive cues essential to completing the actual comparison are lacking. In their strange dilemma, the blind may highlight features of the general process which could improve the theory. The sighted person entering into some social comparison process may also find it difficult to obtain clear and simple cues as to his location relative to some other group, and thus might also refrain from social comparison or turn his eyes toward another reference group whose position is clearer. The perception of the standing of a reference group is certainly a neglected aspect of the theory, and one that has been taken for granted.

As far as learning ability is concerned, the reference group behavior of the blind also suggests that self-regard need not always be damaged by comparison with a superior reference group. The blind seem almost reckless in exposing themselves to such damage. And perhaps this ought to tell us that such comparisons are not necessarily so punishing to the ego. When the inferiority cannot be laid at the door of the self, it may hurt less. There is a built-in protection for the blind. They may know they are inferior in some respects, but they also know that it is not their fault. They are highly rewarded when they compete successfully, and perhaps even when they try, regardless of their success or failure. Certainly, there are strong motives for the blind to choose dissimilars and superiors. But, here again, the blind may not be alone. Among the sighted there may be similar balances of motivational forces which complicate the calculation of which choice of reference group leads to greatest gain or pleasure.

In a group apparently so homogeneous as the totally blind—even in more homogeneous subgroups among them—a variety of self-conceptions and social comparison processes is prominent. There are more things at work than we have realized, and reference group theory must deepen and widen its explorations. In these explorations, the blind have shown themselves to be a most strategic group for inquiry.

Norm Compatibility, Norm Preference, and the Acceptance of New Reference Groups

Ruth E. Hartley

A. Problem

IT is an inevitable aspect of life in most societies that man should change his reference groups. Changes in status defined by a wide variety of factors (e.g., age, economics, vocational functioning, marital role, etc.) are inescapably accompanied by shifts in reference groups. Understanding the dynamics of such shifts should contribute much to our total understanding of man in his social milieu, and eventually, to our ability to master that social milieu for the benefit of the individual more effectively.

Of the available studies focussing on the functioning of reference groups, most are concerned with the *effect* of such groups, very few with the *process* by which a new group comes to fill the role of a reference group for an individual. The study reported in this paper is one of a series of pilot investigations focussing on the factors associated with the dynamics of acquiring new reference groups. The results of several of these investigations have been reported elsewhere.[1] Here we shall report an investigation of the relationship of the perceived

Reprinted from *Journal of Social Psychology*, 52: 87–95, 1960, by permission of the author and the publisher, The Journal Press. The data reported here were collected as part of an exploratory program of studies focussing on the personal and social components associated with the acceptance of new groups as reference groups, conducted under Contract Nonr-1597 (01) with the Group Psychology Branch Office of Naval Research. We wish to acknowledge with thanks the participation of John Kunz in the capacity of research assistant in this phase of the project.

1. R. E. Hartley, "Acceptance of New Reference Groups," Technical Report 3, ONR Project NR 171–033, Contract Nonr-1597(01) (mimeo.), New York: The City College, 1956; "Affirmative Personality Trends and the Response to New Groups," Technical Report 9,

congruity between the *mores* of an individual's established groups and those of a new membership group to the acceptance of the new group as a reference group.

In most discussions of the functioning of reference groups, the assumption is made that the individual accepts as guides for his own behavior the standards and norms characteristic of his reference groups. This assumption has been supported by a variety of studies, especially those concerned with attitude formation and attitude change.[2] Only a few investigators, however, have concerned themselves with the part played by the norms and standards of a given group in making it acceptable as a reference group. Yet we know from common usage that this role is an important one. We speak of "our kind of people" or feeling "out of place" or "at home" in a new group to indicate a perceived congruence (or lack of it) with previously established standards of behavior.

Fragmentary findings from a number of research studies suggest that this area is an important one for systematic investigation. Newcomb, for example, reported a perceived gap in values and standards between established groups and a new group as inhibiting the acceptance of the new group for some college-age subjects.[3] Becker and Carper[4] found that compatibility of standards and norms with personal inclinations influences identification with vocational groups, and Eisenstadt has found this factor important in the successful assimilation of immigrants to their new national group.[5]

Most of the findings mentioned above were by-products of studies with

ONR Project NR 171–033, Contract Nonr-1597(01) (mimeo.), New York: The City College, 1958; "Personal Characteristics and Acceptance of Secondary Groups as Reference Groups," *J. Individ. Psychol.*, 13: 45–55, 1957; "Personal Needs and the Acceptance of a New Group as a Reference Group," Technical Report 6, ONR Project NR 171–033, Contract Nonr-1597(01) (mimeo.), New York: The City College, 1958; "Relationships between Perceived Value Systems and Acceptance of New Reference Groups," Technical Report 8, ONR Project NR 171–033, Contract Nonr-1597(01) (mimeo.), New York: The City College, 1958; "Selected Variables Associated with Acceptance of a New Secondary Group as a Reference Group," Technical Report 5, ONR Project NR 171–033, Contract Nonr-1597(01) (mimeo.), New York: The City College, 1957.

2. T. M. Newcomb, "Attitude Development as a Function of Reference Groups: the Bennington Study," in M. Sherif, *Outline of Social Psychology*, New York: Harper, 1948; B. C. Rosen, "The Reference Group Approach to the Parental Factor in Attitude and Behavior Formation," *Soc. For.*, 34: 137–144, 1955; A. E. Siegel, and S. Siegel, "Reference Groups, Membership Groups, and Attitude Change," *J. Abn. & Soc. Psychol.*, 55: 360–364, 1957.

3. Newcomb, *op. cit.*

4. H. S. Becker and J. W. Carper, "The Development of Identification with an Occupation," *American Journal of Sociology*, 61: 289–298, 1956; and "The Elements of Identification with an Occupation," *American Sociological Review*, 21: 341–348, 1956.

5. S. N. Eisenstadt, "Studies in Reference Group Behavior," *Human Relations*, 7: 191–216, 1954.

other objectives. Systematic investigations of the operation of norm congruity as related to reference group acquisition are still lacking. To help fill this gap, the present investigator proposed the following hypotheses for testing: (*a*) In general, the greater the perceived difference in norms between an individual's established groups and a new nominal membership group, the less readily the individual is likely to accept the new group as a reference group. (*b*) The degree of acceptance of a new group will be positively related to the degree of preference for the norms of that group, without regard to existing relationships between the norms of the new group and established groups.

A number of assumptions are implied in the above hypotheses. These may be stated briefly as follows:

Most adults or adolescents have an established hierarchy of reference groups. Accepting a new group can be expected to be accompanied by a re-evaluation of those previously established, and to place the latter in temporary competition for the individual's loyalty. The process by which a new group becomes a reference group could therefore be expected to subject the individual to competing pulls and the decision of the issue would depend on the balance of forces acting on him.

Individuals, however, do not necessarily join new groups because they are seeking like-minded companions. Their overt objectives may be entirely pragmatic, ulterior, and removed from any consideration of compatibility. The new group may be considered a tool for the achievement of an ultimate objective removed from the immediate membership, or nominal membership may be forced on the individual. The transformation of the new group from one of nominal membership to one serving a reference function, however, may depend to a critical extent on its compatibility with aspects of the individual's previous experience and his personal preferences. The pattern of accepted norms of behavior is assumed to be one of the crucial elements in that experience. Hence the congruity among the norms of established and new groups appears logically to be an important catalytic element involved in the transformation process.

B. Method

1. SUBJECTS, THE NEW GROUP, AND THE ESTABLISHED GROUPS

Subjects were 146 unselected male freshmen students enrolled in the College of Liberal Arts and Sciences of a municipal, tuition-free college in an urban setting. Since their membership in the college community was of recent occurrence, the College seemed an appropriate unit to use as the new group; off-campus associations were assumed to comprise the subject's established groups. Most of the subjects commuted daily from their homes to the college and continued to maintain some contact with their home neighborhoods. This fact was assumed to heighten the subjects' awareness of differences in norms where such differences existed, and to make these subjects a peculiarly appropriate population for testing the hypotheses presented.

2. MEASURES OF NORM-CONGRUITY AND PREFERENCES

For the purposes of this study "norms" were defined as "ways of behaving." A list of 15 items, which were judged to be substantively meaningful for our population, was drawn up on the basis of intensive interviews with a selected sample of students conducted during the exploratory phase of the general project. These items were presented to the subjects, together with a set of instructions for responses to be made on answer sheets designed for machine scoring, as follows:

> Below is a list of kinds of behavior which may vary between one group and another. We would like to know if there is a difference between students at _____ and your off-campus friends and associates with respect to these items. If there is a difference we also would like to know which way of behaving you prefer. Please note both parts of the instructions below.
>
> I. For each item please mark the answer sheet in the space that represents what you think, according to the following scale:
>
> A = there is no difference or a very slight difference between the two groups in this respect.
> B = there is a moderate difference between the two groups in this respect.
> C = there is a large difference between the two groups in this respect.
>
> II. For every item which you answer B or C on the answer sheet, also fill in D or E on the answer sheet, whichever is appropriate according to the description below:
>
> D = I personally prefer the attitude of my off-campus friends and associates in this respect.
> E = I personally prefer the attitude of students at _____ in this respect.
>
> 1. How one behaves toward friends of the same sex.
> 2. How one behaves toward friends of the opposite sex.
> 3. One's attitude toward people older than one's self—parents, teachers, employers, etc.
> 4. The importance of dress and grooming.
> 5. Attitude toward one's studies.
> 6. The kind of language one uses.
> 7. The importance of having high ambitions or goals.
> 8. Showing that one is keeping up with the latest fads and fashions.
> 9. The degree of interest one shows in sports.
> 10. The attitude one has toward religion.
> 11. The kinds of things one talks about.
> 12. Preferences in types of music.
> 13. Where one goes on dates.
> 14. Where one hangs out during any spare time.
> 15. The interest one shows in political affairs.

Acceptance of the college as a reference group was measured by a questionnaire especially designed for this purpose, composed of 58 multiple-choice items and having corrected reliability coefficient of .82 (Spearman-Brown formula). The items covered six aspects of reference-group feeling and behavior: personal involvement, valence of the group, influence of the group, public identification, interaction with the group, and evaluation of the group. The following are sample items for the first five aspects: "If you were to learn from the newspapers that_____had been attacked by a Congressman or Senator, how would you feel about it?" "Would you like to spend more time at the _____ if you could?" "If you were looking for people who might serve as models to pattern yourself by, among which of the following groups do you think you would most probably find such models?" "When you are introduced to a new group, and the person introducing you says, 'He (she) goes to_____,' how do you honestly feel?" "How active are you in the groups (formal and informal) with which you are connected here?" This questionnaire had been validated in a previous investigation by two methods: (a) reference to actual sub-group participation of subjects scoring at the upper and lower extremes of the response range, and (b) interview follow-ups of "high" and "low" acceptors. It had also been demonstrated to be reasonably immune to the operation of response set.[6] This questionnaire had demonstrated its usefulness in several other studies of this series.[7]

3. PROCEDURES OF ADMINISTRATION, SCORING, AND STATISTICAL ANALYSIS

Both questionnaires described above were administered to several sections of the Freshman Orientation course during two regular sessions of the Orientation program. An interval of a week occurred between administering the acceptance questionnaire and the norms items. The latter were imbedded in a much longer questionnaire form containing items designed to give information about personal values, personal needs, and generalized satisfaction-dissatisfaction. All questionnaires were administered after students had been members of the college community somewhat less than three months. The time for gathering the data was chosen on the assumption that a period of contact of about $2\frac{1}{2}$ months gave the subjects sufficient time to familiarize themselves with the College but was short enough so that the difference between those who accepted the group readily and those who were reluctant to do so would be most evident. Experience had shown that such differences tended to become less marked with the passage of time; in addition, waiting until the second semester to gather data could result in the loss of a significant number of subjects from the lower end of the range of acceptance scores.

6. Ruth E. Hartley, "Acceptance of New Reference Groups" and "Personal Characteristics and Acceptance of Secondary Groups as Reference Groups."

7. Ruth E. Hartley, "Personal Characteristics . . ."; "Personal Needs and the Acceptance of a New Group as a Reference Group"; and "Selected Variables. . . ."

The norms items were scored in two different ways. A *gross difference score* was derived by assigning a value of 0 to the *A*, 1 to the *B*, and 2 to the *C* choices and totalling these responses; the larger the score, the greater the perceived difference between the new and the subjects' established groups. A *gross preference score* was worked out by assigning a value of 0 to *D* responses, and of 1 to *E* responses, totalling the items, and dividing the total by the sum of the *D*'s and *E*'s marked: this score represented the ratio of college-oriented preferences to all preferences possible.

Product-moment correlations between each of the norms scores and the acceptance score, as well as correlations among the norms scores, were used to test the hypotheses. Correlations between the norms scores and other measures administered at the same time (mentioned above) gave evidence concerning the presumptive validity of the former and added to our understanding of their functioning.

C. Results and Discussion

In Table 1 we present the product-moment correlations between each of the scores derived from the norms questionnaire and the scores achieved on the acceptance measure.

Table I—Product-Moment Correlations Between Norms Scores and Acceptance of the New Group
(N = 146)

Score	r	p
Gross difference	−.26	<.01
Gross preference	.17	<.05

Both correlations are significant, though low, and occur in the expected directions. We interpret these results to indicate substantiation of our hypotheses.

The correlation between the two norms scores was .17 ($p<.05$).

An estimate of the presumptive validity and the meaning of a specific measure may sometimes be derived from the pattern of its intercorrelations with other measures. The significant correlations between our norms scores and other measures administered to the same subjects are therefore presented in Table 2. All correlations shown in Table 2 are significant above the level of $p = .01$.

The three significant correlations shown by the difference scores are all negative and are all associated with measures of satisfaction. Specifically, these correlations indicate that the tendency to report large differences in norms between established groups and the new group is associated with a tendency to report relatively little satisfaction of personal needs, either in the new group (*C*-need satisfaction) or in the previously established groups (*OC*- need satisfaction), and to be relatively dissatisfied with one's general cultural setting. These data suggest that those of our subjects who perceived large differences in norms between their old and new groups tended to be among the chronically dissatisfied.

Table 2—Significant Correlations Between Norms Scores and Additional Measures

Scores correlated	r
1. Difference and C-need satisfaction[a]	— .22
2. Difference and OC-need satisfaction[b]	— .26
3. Difference and generalized satisfaction-dissatisfaction[c]	— .27
4. Preference and OC-need satisfaction[b]	— .33
5. Preference and C-OC need satisfaction "balance" score[d]	.33
6. Preference and S-OC value congruity[e]	.22

[a] A measure of the extent to which the College community satisfies subject's personal needs.

[b] A measure of the extent to which subject's personal needs are satisfied by his off-campus groups and associates.

[c] A measure of generalized satisfaction-dissatisfaction with the culture.

[d] A measure of the relative extent to which the College community fills subject's personal needs when compared with the subject's off-campus groups and associates.

[e] A measure of the congruity between the subject's personal values and the perceived values of his off-campus groups and associates. This was derived so that a large S-OC score indicated large differences or a relative lack of congruity in perceived values.

The logical consistency of the patterns of significant correlations shown between the preferences scores and other measures in Table 2 gives further evidence that preference for the norms of a new group is likely to be associated with perceived incompatibility with established groups. For example, the negative correlation ($r = -.33$) with *OC*-need satisfaction scores indicates that a tendency to prefer the College norms is accompanied by a relatively low level of satisfaction of personal needs by off-campus groups. The positive correlation with the *C-OC* need satisfaction "balance" scores ($r = .33$) supplies the corollary that the College community is perceived to contribute relatively more to the satisfaction of personal needs than are off-campus groups, by subjects who prefer the norms of the College. Finally, we find that preference for College norms is associated with a relatively large difference between the individual's values and those he perceives as characterizing his off-campus groups and associates.

We have one additional bit of evidence bearing on the dynamics of the norms scores to consider. Three of the additional measures administered to our subjects made use of five-point response scales going from "extremely well satisfied" to "not satisfied at all." From these we derived a "positive response tendency" score for each subject by adding up the numbers of times he chose the "extremely well satisfied" response. (We shall refer to this as the p.r.t. score hereafter.) Since the "extremely well satisfied" response also could enter into each subject's specific score for each of the measures which were combined for its derivation, the p.r.t. score cannot be regarded as an entirely independent measure, and may well be tainted by the subject's actual attitudes toward the substance of the items to which he was responding. Despite this fact, in consideration of current preoccupation with the possibility of the operation of "response tendencies" to the detriment of clarity in the meaning of data, a sensitivity indicated by the number of recent publications concerned with this topic,[8] we believe it would be relevant to the purpose of this paper to note the relationships between the p.r.t. scores and others with which we are here concerned. Table 3 presents the correlations between the p.r.t. scores and the norms scores.

Table 3—Correlations Between P.R.T. Scores and Norms Measures
(N = 146)

Measure	r	p
1. Gross difference in norms	− .23	< .01
2. Gross preference for college norms	− .09	*

* Not significant.

We interpret these data to indicate the lack of operation of a positive response tendency in relation to the norms measures. If any general tendency is operating, it is in a negative rather than a positive direction.

D. Summary

This paper reports an investigation of the relationship between perceptions of norm-congruity, norm-preference, and the acceptance of a new group as a reference group. Subjects were 146 male freshman college students, who reported (a) the amount of difference they perceived in normative behavior in 15 selected areas between their established groups and the College, considered here as the new group, and (b) which norms they preferred. Two scores were derived from these materials: a gross preference score and a gross difference score. Correlations with a measure of acceptance of the College indicated that perception of relatively large differences in norms between established groups

8. B. M. Bass, "Development and Evaluation of a Scale for Measuring Social Acquiescence," *Journal of Abnormal and Social Psychology*, 53: 296–299, 1956; E. P. Hollander and R. E. Krug, "On Response Set Determination," Pittsburgh, Carnegie Institute of Technology, Department of Psychology (hectographed manuscript); D. N. Jackson and S. J. Messick, "A Note on 'Ethnocentrism' and Acquiescent Response Sets," *Journal of Abnormal and Social Psychology*, 54: 132–134, 1957.

and the new group was associated with relatively less acceptance of the new group as a reference group. Preference for the norms of the new group, however, was positively associated with acceptance of it as a reference group. Intercorrelations between the norms scores and several measures of need-satisfaction and value-congruity indicated that preference for the norms of the new group was associated with a relative lack of need-satisfaction by other groups and a perceived lack of congruity between the individual's values and those of other groups.

Personal Characteristics and Acceptance of Secondary Groups as Reference Groups

Ruth E. Hartley

THE relationship between man and the groups in which he moves interested Adler, as it interests present-day social psychologists. The importance of understanding the dynamics of this relationship was directly expressed by him in the following passage:

> In order to understand what goes on in an individual, it is necessary to consider his attitude toward his fellow men. The relationships of people to one another in part exist naturally and as such are subject to change. In part they take the form of institutionalized relationships which arise from the natural ones. These institutionalized relationships can be observed especially in the political life of nations, in the formation of states, and in community affairs. Human psychological life can not be understood without the simultaneous consideration of these coherences.[1]

Reprinted from *Journal of Individual Psychology*, 13: 45–55, 1957, by permission of the author and the publisher. The data reported in this paper were collected as part of a research project being administered under Contract Nonr-1597(01) with the Group Psychology Branch Office of Naval Research. This paper constitutes Technical Report No. 4 under that contract. Permission is granted for reproduction in whole or in part for any purpose of the United States Government.

We wish to acknowledge with thanks the participation of Joshua Fishman and John Kunz in various phases of this study.

1. H. L. Ansbacher and Rowena R. Ansbacher, eds., *The Individual Psychology of Alfred Adler*, New York: Basic Books, Inc., 1956, pp. 127–128.

When Adler tied the concepts of identification and empathy[2] to the concept of social interest, he came close to describing the essence of reference-group feelings as they are commonly understood today. "To see with the eyes of another, to hear with the ears of another, to feel with the heart of another,"[3] for example, may be a bit poetic for current scientific taste, but it is an essentially valid description of what we call "personal involvement," *a sine qua non* of the reference group concept. When applied to cultures and communities, as Adler applies them, these phrases essentially express, in figurative language, the acceptance of group standards, *mores*, and goals. . . .

However indicated, the acceptance of any group as a reference group is basically a state of feeling: a feeling of *being* an integral part of a larger unit, if group membership has been consummated; a feeling of *wanting* to be part of it, if actual membership has not been achieved. . . .

From a theoretical point of view, the bridge between individual dynamics and social behavior remains a tantalizing enigma. Elaborated speculation is not lacking in this area, but solid, empirical data is almost invisible.[4] Though much work is being carried out with primary or small groups, this statement is especially true concerning the positive aspects of the individual's relations with his *secondary* groups. While the characteristics of the *groups* evoking positive responses have received a good deal of attention, the characteristics of the *individuals* responding positively to large and impersonal groups have largely been neglected, probably on the assumption that individuals respond to groups in terms of the realistic functioning of the latter. The present investigator, however, has found some evidence, in an earlier study, that seems to point to the operation of a generalized acceptance tendency, more clearly expressive of the member than of the group to which he was responding.[5] In the study to which we are referring, this tendency was shown specifically in relation to the self, to a new membership group, and to the subject's peers in the new group. These findings suggested the value of further exploration of the relationship of personal dynamics to acceptance of new groups as reference groups—specifically, large, impersonal, and formally organized groups with all phases of which the individual member can have only limited contact.

The data reported below were collected as part of a program of exploratory studies dealing with the identification of factors associated with variation in the acceptance, by new members, of a secondary group as a reference group.

The personal characteristics selected for investigation in the study with

2. *Ibid.*, pp. 135–137.

3. *Ibid.*, p. 135.

4. See H. Guetzkow, "Multiple Loyalties: Theoretical Approach to a Problem in International Organization," Publication No. 4 of the Center for Research on World Political Institutions, Princeton University, 1955.

5. Ruth E. Hartley, "The Acceptance of New Reference Groups," Technical Report 2, Distributed under Contract Nonr-1597(01), Washington, D.C.: Group Psychology Branch of the Office of Naval Research, 1956.

which we shall deal here were *ease in interpersonal contacts* and several dynamics which seemed to be related to performance on the F scale:[6] *sense of victimization, authoritarian submission, cynicism,* and *lack of self-confidence.* This terminology is taken from Webster, et al.[7]

The "group" used as the focus for acceptance was a large publicly supported educational institution in an Eastern urban setting. To many of its students this institution appeared to be a last resource for a college degree, which they used *faut de mieux.* This sense of having no choice, of being arbitrarily involved with the group (the college as a whole) through the coercion of circumstances, suggests that attitudes developed in relation to it could be expected to be similar, in many respects, to attitudes developed toward other groups or collectives of which one might become a part without any real alternative: communities, nations, business organizations, the armed forces, etc.

It was hypothesized that "acceptance" of the college as a reference group would be (a) *positively* related to *ease in interpersonal contacts* and *authoritarian submission;* and (b) *negatively* related to *sense of victimization, cynicism,* and *lack of self-confidence.*

The first hypothesis was based on two assumptions: (1) that relatively greater ease in interpersonal contacts would make contacts with some members of a new group relatively more pleasant and that this feeling would be globally projected to the group as a whole; and (2) that individuals who accept and identify with authority would be most likely to accept and identify with almost any group functioning in a culturally prescribed manner, and particularly with one exhibiting a hierarchical authoritarian structure which is endowed with some degree of power relative to the individual.

The second hypothesis rests on several considerations: (1) the assumption that an individual who shows a generalized sense of victimization to a relatively high degree will associate that feeling with every group with which he comes into contact and will therefore be unable to identify with any group; (2) impressions derived from a series of interviews conducted during a preliminary phase of the project that students who tended toward cynical attitudes tended also to insulate themselves from attachments to groups; and (3) the assumption that lack of self-confidence would normally be accompanied by apprehension of rejection by a new group, which would in turn interfere with the individual's ability to accept and identify with a new group early in his experience with it.

Procedure

Subjects; The subjects were 73 unselected male freshmen in the College of Liberal Arts and Sciences who had been on the campus for about three months. They comprised the entire male contingent of five sections of the Freshman Orientation course, a non-credit course required of all entering students.

6. T. W. Adorno et al., *The Authoritarian Personality*, New York: Harper, 1950.

7. H. Webster, N. Sanford, and M. Freedman, "A New Instrument for Studying Authoritarianism in Personality," *Journal of Psychology*, 40: 73–84, 1955.

Instruments: (1) Acceptance of the college as a reference group was measured by a questionnaire especially designed for this purpose, composed of 58 multiple-choice items and having a corrected reliability coefficient of .82 (Spearman-Brown formula). The items covered six aspects of reference-group feeling and behavior: personal involvement, valence of the group, influence of the group, public identification, interaction with the group, and evaluation of the group. The following are sample items for the first five aspects. "If you were to learn from the newspapers that ———— had been attacked by a Congressman or Senator, how would you feel about it?" "Would you like to spend more time at the ———— if you could?" "If you were looking for people who might serve as models to pattern yourself by, among which of the following groups do you think you would most probably find such models?" "When you are introduced to a new group, and the person introducing you says, 'He (she) goes to ————,' how do you honestly feel?" "How active are you in the groups (formal and informal) with which you are connected here?" This questionnaire had been validated in a previous investigation by two methods: (*a*) reference to actual sub-group participation of subjects scoring at the upper and lower extremes of the response range, and (*b*) interview follow-ups of "high" and "low" acceptors.

(2) *Ease in interpersonal relations* was measured by a group of 15 true-false items, developed for this study, which had an odd-even reliability coefficient of .74 (corrected by the Spearman-Brown formula.) Some sample questions from this instrument are: "Do you feel that you are accepted and liked by *most* people that know you?" "Do you tend to wind up on the fringe of things after an evening at some social affair?" "Do you find that you really do not know many new people in your classes, even after meeting with them for several months?"

(3) Four different groups of true-false items originally tested by Webster *et al.* were used in slightly amended form to measure *sense of victimization, authoritarian submission, cynicism,* and *lack of self-confidence* respectively. These four dynamics were selected on the basis of a priori judgment concerning their relevance to our population from a questionnaire of 123 items, representing 13 different personality dynamics and reported to have a reliability coefficient of .88 and a correlation of .74 with the F scale. Time limitations prevented us from including all 13 dynamics. According to their report, Webster, *et al.* grouped the items on a theoretical rather than a statistical basis. Used discretely with our sample, these item-groupings had respective reliability coefficients (corrected by the Spearman-Brown formula) as follows: sense of victimization (9 items) .50; authoritarian submission (13 items) .60; cynicism (15 items) .61; lack of self-confidence (10 items) .58.

(4) One additional measure, called *"stereotypes" of group members,* was used as a follow-up on the findings of the earlier study referred to above.[8] This measure consisted of a list of 137 selected adjectives, which subjects indicated as being applicable or not applicable to "most students at (*their own*) College." The scoring of this list was so derived that it yielded a "pleasantness-unpleasantness" estimate of peers in the group.[9]

8. Ruth E. Hartley, "The Acceptance of New Reference Groups," *op. cit.*

9. For details on derivation and scoring of the "stereotype" list see *ibid.*, pp. 16–17.

Collecting the Data; The questionnaires were administered to relatively small groups of subjects (10 to 20) during two regular meetings of the Freshman Orientation program of the College, with the Acceptance Questionnaire being given first. The item-groupings dealing with personality dynamics were interspersed among a number of other questionnaire segments dealing with different aspects of groups and group-related attitudes and activities. Absentees were followed up for individual testing to rule out the possible operation of a relevant selective factor in our sample of subjects.

Results and Discussion

The various measures of personality tendency correlated with scores on the Acceptance Questionnaire as shown in Table I. These correlations offer confirmation of our first hypothesis. The second hypothesis was not confirmed since the correlations are not significant; yet it should be noted that they are all negative thus tending in the expected direction.

The pattern of the correlations is especially interesting in the light of the recent accumulation of studies[10] calling into question the meaningfulness of

Table I—Correlations Between Scores on the Acceptance Questionnaire and the Various Measures of Personality Tendency

(a) Ease in interpersonal contacts	.28 ($p < .02$)*
(b) Authoritarian submission	.46 ($p < .001$)
(c) Sense of victimization	− .05**
(d) Cynicism	− .12**
(e) Lack of self-confidence	− .14**
(f) "Stereotype" list (judgments of peers)	.30 ($p < .01$)

* For 73 subjects, correlations between .23 and .26 (inclusive), are significant at about a p level of .05; those between .27 and .29 are significant at about the .02 level; and those of .30 and above are significant at the .01 level and below.
** Not significant.

responses to the F scale. Although four of our item-groupings (*b, c, d,* and *e*) were drawn from a "personality" test correlating highly with the F scale, and these four were all scored in the same direction, only one of these groupings showed a positive correlation with the Acceptance Questionnaire. This indicates that negative as well as positive responses were used liberally. We conclude that in these data there is little evidence of a single pervasive response set to acquiesce which would influence reactions to all items.[11]

10. B. M. Bass, "Development and Evaluation of a Scale for Measuring Social Acquiescence," *Journal of Abnormal and Social Psychology*, 53: 296–299, 1956; L. J. Chapman and D. T. Campbell, "Response Set in F Scale," *Journal of Abnormal and Social Psychology*, 54: 129–132, 1957; D. N. Jackson and S. J. Messick, "A Note on 'Ethnocentrism' and Acquiescent Response Sets," *Journal of Abnormal and Social Psychology*, 54: 132–134, 1957; D. N. Jackson, S. J. Messick, and C. M. Solley, "How 'Rigid' is the 'Authoritarian'?" *Journal of Abnormal and Social Psychology*, 54: 137–140, 1957.

11. Webster et al. also report evidence that "a general tendency to agree" was *not* characteristic of the sample of 441 subjects responding to the 667 items from which the scale of 123 items was selected. *Op. cit.*, p. 76.

The fact that *authoritarian submission* shows a much closer association with acceptance of the college than does *ease in interpersonal contacts* may have important implications for our understanding of the relationship between an individual's attitude toward his face-to-face groups and his attitudes toward his secondary groups. It is often assumed, for example, that large-group identifications are mediated through primary-group experiences, and that the quality of these, in turn, depends largely on the social effectiveness of the individual. We believe our findings raise some questions concerning the validity of the assumption of this sequence.

Table 2—Intercorrelations Among Variables Significantly Related to "Acceptance"

	1	2	3
1. Authoritarian submission	—	.26	.16
2. Ease in interpersonal contacts		—	.01
3. Judgments of peers			—

The pattern of intercorrelations among the variables that related significantly to acceptance, and the level of various combinations of variables used in multiple correlations with acceptance scores lend some support to the foregoing suggestion. Tables 2 and 3 present these data.

Table 3—Multiple Correlations Between "Acceptance" (y) and Different Combinations of Variables

Ry authoritarian submission, ease in interpersonal contacts	.48
Ry authoritarian submission, judgments of peers	.52
Ry ease in interpersonal contacts, judgments of peers	.41
Ry authoritarian submission, ease in interpersonal contacts, and judgments of peers	.54

Although *ease in interspersonal contacts* correlates almost equally, and significantly (at the .05 level of confidence), with *authoritarian submission* and "acceptance," it adds little when combined with the former in accounting for variance in the latter. This suggests that the variable measured by the *authoritarian submission* items was also involved somehow in the judgments the subjects made of their own social ease.

This suggestion is substantiated by the partial correlations presented in Table 4.

We may note in Table 4 that partialling out *ease in interpersonal contacts* from the correlation between *authoritarian submission* and "acceptance" has little effect on the latter. When, however, *authoritarian submission* is partialled out of the correlation between *ease of interpersonal contacts* and "acceptance," the correlation is reduced below its former level of significance. The relationship between *judgments of peers* and "acceptance", on the other hand, is changed very little by eliminating the effect of either of the other two variables.

Table 4—Partial Correlations Between "Acceptance" (y) and Selected Variables

Ry authoritarian submission ease in interpersonal contacts	.42
Ry ease in interpersonal contacts authoritarian submission	.19
Ry authoritarian submission judgment of peers	.44
Ry ease in interpersonal contacts judgments of peers	.29
Ry judgments of peers authoritarian submission	.26
Ry judgments of peers ease in interpersonal contacts	.31

The question of why *authoritarian submission* and *ease in interpersonal contacts* should be tied together in this way is not easily answered. If we assume that "social interest," as used by Adler, is closely related to "acceptance of the group" as we are using the term, this tie might be interpreted as an indication of the validity of Adler's statement that "social interest" and "normal adjustment" are closely related. On the other hand, it is equally possible that the explanation lies in the same rationale that underlies the connection between *authoritarian submission* and acceptance of the college as a reference group.

Inspection of the items used to measure *authoritarian submission*, reproduced below, reveals that the first five deal with attitude toward parents, the next four express feelings about the state, and the last four indicate a respect for those occupying a position of power and importance.

It would be difficult to deny that respect for parents, the state, and established power are culturally approved sentiments. It seems logical to assume that

SCORING**	ITEMS*
T	One of my aims in life is to accomplish something that would make my parents proud of me.
T	Parents are much too easy on their children nowadays.
T	Children should associate more with children and less with their elders.
T	It is a pretty callous person who does not feel love and gratitude toward his parents.
F	At times I have very much wanted to leave home.
T	Disobedience to the government is never justified.
T	Army life is a good influence on most young men.
T	It is the duty of a citizen to support his country right or wrong.
T	Only a fool would try to change our American way of life.
T	It's a good thing to know people in the right places so you can get traffic tags, and such things, taken care of.
T	I would dislike being a member of a leaderless group.
T	When I take a new job, I like to be tipped off on who should be gotten next to.
T	I like to know some important people because it makes me feel important.

* As selected from Webster et al., *op. cit.*, p. 78.
** "T" and "F" as shown here are the responses that were scored as indicating the presence of this variable.

a high score on these items indicates a tendency to "go along with" the *status quo*, to accept it. Those who accept some aspects of the culture are likely to accept others, including the culturally defined and accepted groups in which they find themselves. The decision to join the group in question may, in fact, simply be a reflection of the individual's acceptance of the cultural evaluation of that class of groups (colleges, in this case). Once a nominal member, the tendency to accept the *status quo* is enough to account for the rest.

So, too, we might explain the relationship between *ease in interpersonal contacts* and *authoritarian submission*. None will deny that social ease is a culturally valued quality. Those who accept the culture generally may be expected to perceive themselves in culturally acceptable terms and so report. Accepting social ease as a good thing, they see themselves as partaking of it, and indicate this in their responses. (Since all our data are based on self-report, we have no way of checking on the validity of subjects' perceptions.) There is, of course, the alternative possibility that those who accept the tenets of the culture *do* move in it with greater ease than those who question or rebel. Accepting the culture, they have no reason to doubt themselves. The "feeling of belonging-ness" Adler[12] posits as characteristic of social interest would be theirs almost inevitably.

The literature of psychological research suggests that we find no difficulty with the concept of hostile or aggressive personality tendencies. Why not, then, the "acceptant" personality? Such a one would accept himself, his peers, a way of life, and any socially indicated group. Guetzkow's "habit of loyalty"[13] would be characteristic of him. He would, in general, tend to make a good member of any group acceptable to the larger culture of which he partakes.

The data reported above hold special interest because of the nature of the institution in which they were collected. The college is regarded in the community as "liberal" in relation to the social and political inclinations of its students, who pride themselves on individualism and disdain conformity. The accepted classroom attitude is one of challenge and scepticism. The *mores* of the peer group seem to have nothing in common substantively with the items in the *authoritarian submission* questionnaire; yet our subjects can apparently accept both. The dynamic of accepting rather than the substance of what is accepted seems to be involved here.[14] These considerations suggest that the precise nature of the functioning of any given group may be of less importance

12. Ansbacher and Ansbacher, *op. cit.*, p. 138.

13. Guetzkow, *op. cit.*, p. 42.

14. This tendency is reminiscent of Bass's "social acquiescence," and descriptions of the "conformist personality" by several other workers. Although it is referred to as "Babbittry" by Bass and has been connected with high degrees of ethnic prejudice in previous studies (e.g., Adorno et al., *op. cit.*; and E. L. Hartley and Ruth E. Hartley, "Tolerance and Personality Traits," in E. L. Hartley, *Problems in Prejudice*, New York: King's Crown Press, 1946), we believe these qualities are simply characteristic of the culture it reflects rather than intrinsic aspects of the tendency itself.

in motivating loyalty than is commonly asserted. The decisive dynamics may rest, rather, with quite global and generalized qualities which reside in the individual who occupies membership status.

It seems worth noting that our subjects' *judgment of their peers* (in terms of characteristics denoting degrees of pleasantness) seems to have little relation to either *authoritarian submission* or *ease in interpersonal contacts* though it does account for some of the variance in acceptance of the college. (The latter situation may be in part an artifact of the two tests, since the Acceptance Questionnaire also contains some items asking for judgments about peers, though not the same kinds of judgments called for by the "stereotype" list. It is logical to assume that those who find their fellow group members relatively high in characteristics rated as "pleasant" will also find them compatible in other ways.) This lack of correlation between *authoritarian submission* and *judgments of peers* may indicate the operation of a reality factor in addition to a global attitudinal factor in relation to acceptance of the group, or it may indicate the existence of two independent "acceptance" factors, one being person-oriented and the other culture- or institution-oriented. Both contribute to the prediction of acceptance of a new group having the characteristics we have described.

Summary and Conclusions

Adler's descriptions of *social interest* seem to relate it in several ways to the concept of *reference group* as used in contemporary social psychology. This concept offers an explanatory principle for many aspects of social behavior which in the past have been treated discretely and classified under a variety of rubrics. Despite the importance of understanding the psychological dynamics of reference-group membership, empirical research literature is conspicuously lacking in data in this area, particularly in relation to the personal qualities of the individual and his ability to identify with secondary (i.e. large, impersonal) groups. In previous studies the present investigator has found suggestive indications of the functioning of a generalized personality variable which seems relevant to this concern, and the present investigation is an attempt (1) to collect further evidence of such functioning, and (2) to begin to specify the nature of the variable (or variables).

About three months after admission, 73 male freshmen students in a large municipal college in the East responded to questionnaires designed to measure respectively their "acceptance" of the school as a reference group, their *ease in interpersonal contacts*, their *judgments of their peers*, and four different personality dynamics, referred to as *sense of victimization, authoritarian submission, cynicism,* and *lack of self-confidence*.

The hypotheses were advanced that "acceptance" of the college as a reference group would be (a) *positively* related to *ease in interpersonal contacts* and to *authoritarian submission* shown; and (b) *negatively* related to *sense of victimization, cynicism,* and *lack of self-confidence*.

Correlational analyses of the data supported the first hypothesis. With regard to the second hypothesis, the obtained correlations were not statistically significant; yet it should be noted that they were all negative thus tending in the expected direction.

When the significant results are considered in relation to substantive aspects of the measures by which they were achieved, they seem to justify the following conclusions: The tendency toward *authoritarian submission* is involved with the process of accepting a new secondary group (of a specific kind) as a reference group. Because the measure for *authoritarian submission* actually seems to be measuring acceptance of the cultural *status quo*, the response tendency elicited by it can be expected to operate generally in relation to culturally prescribed aspects of the individual's experience, hence toward the secondary groups that are a normal part of his culture. There is evidence for "acceptant" response tendencies oriented toward *persons* which may operate differently from those oriented toward *institutions*. While both *person-oriented* and *institution-oriented* response tendencies contribute to the individual's acceptance of a newly acquired secondary group as a reference group, the latter seem to be involved to a much greater extent.

Persistence and Regression of Changed Attitudes: Long-Range Studies

Theodore M. Newcomb

I

ONE-HALF score and seven years ago, here in Philadelphia, I read a paper before this society. It was properly, which is to say polysyllabically, titled— something about autistic hostility—and its manuscript pages numbered just 28. Doubtless I would long since have forgotten about it had I not discovered, several years later, that another man had stolen my central idea, some five-score years before I was born. The name of the thief was William Blake, and a striking feature of *his* paper was that its total number of *words* was just 28. Let me quote them:

> I was angry with my friend:
> I told my wrath, my wrath did end.
> I was angry with my foe:
> I told it not, my wrath did grow.

Though I'm not sure that Blake would accept the phrasing, our common theme had to do with the change and persistence of attitudes. What I, at least, was trying to say was that one's attitudes toward another person are not likely to change if one so manipulates one's environment that one cannot add to or correct one's information about that person. Today I shall pursue a similar theme, though in a somewhat different direction.

Originally delivered as the 1962 Kurt Lewin Memorial Award Address, this article is reprinted from *Journal of Social Issues*, Vol. 19, No. 4, pp. 3–13, by permission of the author and the publisher, the Society for the Psychological Study of Social Issues.

One's attitude toward something is not only a resultant of one's previous traffic with one's environment but also a determinant of selective response to present and future environments. Viewed in the latter way, existing attitudes may determine one's selection among alternative environmental settings, and these in turn may serve to preserve or undermine the very attitudes that had been initially responsible for one's selection among the alternatives. Insofar as attitudes are self-preserving, such tendencies to select a supportive environment would, if empirically supported, provide an important explanation of their persistence. In its most general form, the hypothesis would run somewhat as follows: Existing attitudes are most likely to persist, other things equal, when one's environment provides most rewards for their behavioral expression. But this platitudinous proposition ("things persist when conditions are favorable to their persistence") is not very interesting, and is probably not even testable. A more interesting and more testable form of the proposition would take account of both change and persistence, both of attitudes and of environmental supportiveness. In particular, it would say something about a changed selection of environments following attitude change, about the ways in which the recently formed attitude is or is not reinforced by the new environment, and about the persistence of the attitude in both supportive and hostile environments. Such a proposition, in its simplest form, would run somewhat as follows: A recently changed attitude is likely to persist insofar as it leads to the selection of subsequent environments that provide reinforcements for the behavioral expression of the changed attitude.

Among the many possible forms of environmental reinforcements of behavioral expressions of attitudes, I shall consider a single class: behavior on the part of other people that one perceives as supportive of one's own attitudes. With few exceptions, such support comes from persons or groups toward whom one is positively attracted, according to the principles of what is perhaps most frequently known as balance theory.[1] I am, in short, about to defend the limited proposition that a recently changed attitude is most likely to persist if one of its behavioral expressions is the selection of a social environment which one finds supportive of the changed attitude. This proposition differs from the one about austic hostility primarily in that persistence of a recently acquired attitude depends upon continuing rather than cutting off sources of information about the attitude-object.

II

There are various ways in which such a proposition might be tested in the laboratory. But insofar as one is interested, as I have been, in long-range effects,

1. Cf. F. Heider, *The Psychology of Interpersonal Relations*, New York: John Wiley & Sons, Inc., 1958; and R. Brown, "Models of Attitude Change," in R. Brown, E. Galanter, E. H. Hess, and G. Mandler, *New Directions in Psychology*, New York: Holt, Rinehart & Winston, Inc., 1962.

one will make use of "natural" settings. I shall therefore cite a few findings from two of my own studies, mentioning only briefly the less immediately relevant one,[2] which involved the daily observation of two populations of 17 male students, all initial strangers to one another who lived intimately together for four-month periods. The only attitudes of these subjects that showed much change, from first to last, were their attractions toward each other—attitudes which had not even existed, of course, before their initial encounters in this research setting. Expressions of interpersonal attraction during the first week or two were highly unstable, but after about the fifth week they showed only slow and slight changes.

Under the conditions of this research, imposed environments (in the form of arbitrarily assigned rooms, roommates, and floors) had no consistent effects beyond the first week or two in interpersonal preferences. That is, one could predict little or nothing about interpersonal attraction from the fact of being roommates or floormates. Self-selected interpersonal environment, however, was closely associated with interpersonal attraction. At all times later than the first week or two, pairs of subjects who were reported by others to belong to the same voluntary subgroups were almost invariably pairs whose members chose each other at very high levels of attraction. If this seems to be a commonplace observation (as indeed it is), let me remind you of my reason for reporting it; interpersonal environments are not only consequences of existing attraction but also sources of future attraction. It is an everyday phenomenon that, having developed differential attitudes toward one's several acquaintances, one manipulates one's interpersonal environment, insofar as one can, to correspond with one's interpersonal preferences. And insofar as one is successful, chances are that the preferences will be further reinforced. My data, showing stability both of preferences and of voluntarily associating subgroups following the first month or so, indicate that exactly this was occurring. The fact that it is an everyday occurrence enhances rather than negates the importance of the principle involved, namely, that a recently acquired attitude will persist insofar as it results in the selection of an environment that is supportive of that attitude.

III

I now turn to a totally different set of data, or rather to two sets of data from the same subjects, obtained over an interval of more than 20 years. The earlier responses were obtained between 1935 and 1939 at Bennington College;[3] the later ones, obtained in 1960 and 1961, were from almost all of the subjects who had been studied for three or more consecutive years during the 1930's. To

2. T. M. Newcomb, *The Acquaintance Process*, New York: Holt, Rinehart & Winston, Inc., 1961.

3. T. M. Newcomb, *Personality and Social Change*, New York: Holt, Rinehart & Winston, Inc., 1943.

be specific, out of 141 former students in this category who in 1960 were alive, resident in continental United States, and not hopelessly invalided, 130 (scattered in 28 states) were interviewed, and 9 of the remaining 11 completed more or less parallel questionnaires. The interview dealt primarily with their present attitudes toward a wide range of public-affairs issues, with attitudes of their husbands and other contemporary associates, and with their histories and careers since leaving the College.

Before telling you some of the follow-up findings, I ought to report a few of the original ones. During each of four consecutive years (1935–36 through 1938–39), juniors and seniors were on the average markedly less conservative than freshmen in attitude toward many public issues of the day. Studies of the same individuals over three-and four-year intervals showed the same trend, which was not attributable to selective withdrawal from the College. Comparisons with other colleges showed almost no intercollege differences in freshmen attitudes, but much less conservatism at Bennington than at the other institutions on the part of seniors. Individual studies showed that at Bennington nonconservatism was rather closely associated with being respected by other students, with participation in college activities, and with personal involvement in the College as an institution. The relatively few malcontents were, with surprisingly few exceptions, those who held conservative attitudes toward public issues.

Given these initial findings, one of my concerns in planning the follow-up study was the following: Under what conditions would individuals who had become less conservative during their college years remain relatively non-conservative 20-odd years later, and under what conditions would they "regress" to relatively conservative positions? (As to the problem of comparing attitudes toward one set of issues in the 1930's with those toward quite different issues in the 1960's, I shall for present purposes note only that at both times we used indices of relative, not absolute standing: each subject is compared with the same set of peers.)

By way of noting the general pattern of persistence vs. regression on the part of the total population, I shall first compare one early with one later datum. In the 1940 presidential election, 51 per cent of our interview sample who reported a preference for either major candidate chose the Democrat, F. D. Roosevelt, and 49 per cent the Republican, W. Willkie. Twenty years later, the comparable figures were 60 per cent for J. F. Kennedy and 40 per cent for R. M. Nixon. No single election, of course, provides a very good test of what might be termed "general conservatism concerning public affairs," but at any rate this particular comparison does not suggest any conspicuous regression toward freshman conservatism. This conclusion is also supported by the following finding: In six consecutive presidential elections (1940 through 1960), an outright majority of our interviewees (51 per cent) reported that they had preferred the Republican candidate either once or never, whereas only 27 per cent of them had preferred that candidate as many as five times out of the six times.

The problem of regressive effects can also be approached by comparing relative conservatism on the part of the same individuals over the interval of 20-odd years. In terms of party or candidate preference in 1960, the degree of individual stability is startling. As shown in Table 1, individuals who were in the

Table I—Presidential Preferences in 1960, According to Quartiles of PEP Scores on Leaving College in the Late 1930s

PEP Quartile	Nixon Preferred	Kennedy Preferred	Total
1 (least conservative)	3	30	33
2	8	25	33
3	18	13	31
4 (most conservative)	22	11	33
Total	51	79	130

least conservative quartile of the total population, on graduating, preferred Kennedy by frequencies of 30 to 3, and those in the next quartile by 25 to 8; 83 per cent of this half of the population preferred Kennedy 20 years later, while 37 per cent of the initially more conservative half preferred Kennedy after 20 years. Political party preferences, and also an index of general political conservatism, showed about the same relationship to political conservatism more than two decades earlier. These data provide no support for a prediction of general regression—either toward previous conservatism or in the statistical sense of regression toward the mean.

Other evidence concerning the general nonconservatism in this population in the early 1960's includes the following:

77% of them considered themselves "liberal" or "somewhat liberal," as com- pared with 17% who were "conservative" or "somewhat conservative";
76% "approved" or "strongly approved" of "Medicare" for the aged under Social Security;
61% "approved" or "strongly approved" of admitting Red China into the United Nations.

These and other data suggest that the population as a whole is now far less conservative than is to be expected in view of its demographic characteristics. Its socio-economic level may be judged from these facts: (1) 77 per cent of the 117 respondents who were or had been married were judged by the interviewer to be at least "fairly well-to-do," with annual incomes of not less than $20,000; and (2) of 113 mothers in the population, 65 per cent had sent at least one of their children to a private school. In religious backgrounds, about three-quarters of them were Protestants (more than half of whom were Episcopalian), and less than 10 per cent were either Catholic or Jewish. According to information assembled for me by the Survey Research Center of the University of Michigan,[4]

4. By my colleague Philip Converse, to whom I am most grateful.

the proportion of Protestant women college graduates at the income level of this population who in 1960 expressed a preference for Kennedy over Nixon was less than 25—as compared with 60 per cent of this alumnae population.

I shall now revert to my earlier theme: If this population is now less conservative than one might expect, to what extent is this explainable in terms of its members' selection of post-college environments that were supportive of non-conservative attitudes? It proves to be very difficult to categorize total environments from this point of view, and so for the present I shall limit myself to a single aspect of post-college environments: husbands. I am making no assumptions here except that (1) husbands were indeed a part of their wives' environments; (2) wives had had something to do with selecting this part of their environments; and (3) husbands, as environmental objects, were capable of being either supportive or nonsupportive of their wives' attitudes.

Nearly 80 per cent of our respondents both had a husband and were able to report on his attitudes toward most of the issues with which we were concerned, during all or most of the past 20 years; one reason for placing a good deal of confidence in their report is that they seem highly discriminating, as indicated by such responses as these: "I don't think I know how he'd feel on that particular issue," or "Now on *that* one he doesn't agree with me at all." Here are some summaries concerning all husbands whose wives were willing to attribute attitudes toward them (nearly all wives on most issues):

> 54% of the husbands in 1960 favored Kennedy over Nixon;
> 64% of them either "approved" or "strongly approved" of "Medicare" for the aged under Social Security;
> 57% of them either "approved" or "strongly approved" of admitting Red China into the United Nations.

And so it is almost as true of husbands as of wives that they are less conservative than is to be expected in view of their demographic characteristics: husbands' and wives' demographic characteristics are taken to be identical except for a very few couples differing in religious background, and their present attitudes are highly similar (90 per cent of 1960 presidential preferences by pairs of spouses, for example, being reported as the same in 1960). It would hardly seem to be a matter of sheer chance that a set of men who are less conservative than is to be expected are married to a set of women of whom just the same thing is true. It seems necessary, therefore, to assume that attitudes toward public affairs had something to do with husbands' and wives' reciprocal selection of one another, or with post-marital influence upon one another, or with both. Here is one statistical support for this assumption: the correlation between wives' scores on an instrument labeled Political and Economic Progressivism, as of their graduating from college in the late 1930's, with the number of Republican candidates that their subsequent husbands voted for between 1940 and 1960 was .32; this does not account for much of the variance, but its p value is $> .0005$.

Another interesting finding has to do with the number of women in our interview sample whose husbands had attended Ivy League colleges; one would expect this proportion to be high, since so many of the women's fathers and brothers had attended these colleges. The actual frequency turned out to be just 50 per cent. These Ivy League husbands' voting preferences in 1960, however, turned out to be much more like their wives' preferences than like their class-mates' preferences: 52 per cent of husbands whose wives were able to state a preference were for Kennedy—which is to say that they did not differ at all in voting preferences from all non-Ivy League husbands. This total set of facts can best be interpreted as follows: Our Bennington graduates of the late 1930's found their husbands in the kinds of places where their families expected them to be found, but they selected somewhat atypical members of these "proper" populations of eligibles; they tended not to have conservative attitudes that were then typical of these populations.

One evidence of this atypical selection is to be seen in the occupational distribution of these women's husbands. Only 38 per cent of all husbands are classifiable as "in management or business," the remaining 62 per cent represent-ing for the most part a wide range of professions (especially college teaching, entertainment, and the arts) and public employment (especially in government). Husbands in these two general categories (management and business vs. all others) differed sharply in their voting preferences in 1960; of the 113 husbands whose wives attributed preferences to them, 26 per cent of those in management and business preferred Kennedy, and 68 per cent of all other husbands preferred Kennedy. In sum, these women's husbands had typically come from "the right" places but a majority of them did not have "the right" attitudes or occupational interests.

If, therefore, I were to select a single factor that contributed most to these women's maintenance of nonconservative attitudes between the late 1930's and early 1960's, I think it would be the fact of selecting husbands of generally nonconservative stripe who helped to maintain for them an environment that was supportive of their existing attributes.

IV

Now I shall turn from the total population of interviewees to some com-parisons of subpopulations. The most crucial of these, from the point of view of my proposition about supportive environments, are to be found within the population of nonconservatives on leaving college in the late 1930's: What seems to be the differences between those who do and those who do not remain nonconservative in the early 1960's? Such comparisons will have to be im-pressionistic, since numbers of cases are small.

Among 22 individuals previously labeled as clearly nonconservative in their third or fourth year of attendance at the College, just half belong in the same category now. Only three of them are clearly conservative today, the remaining eight being classified as intermediate. Here are these wives' descriptions of their husbands' political positions over the years:

  3 presently conservative wives: 3 Republican husbands (100%)
  7 presently intermediate wives: 3 Republican husbands (42%)
  8 presently nonconservative wives: 2 Republican husbands (25%)

Of the three presently conservative women, none mentions having engaged in activities related to political or other public issues; of the eight who are intermediate, six mention some activity of this kind, but they identify their activity only in such general terms as "liberal" or "Democratic Party"; of the 11 still nonconservative women, eight mention such activities, more than half of them specifying such "causes" or organizations as labor unions, civil liberties, the ADA, or the NAACP.

Each interviewee was also asked about the general orientation of "most of your friends" toward political and other public affairs. More than half (12) of the 22 women originally labeled as clearly nonconservative described their environment of friends as "liberal," in spite of the fact that most of them lived in the suburbs or other geographical areas not generally renowned for liberalism. Interestingly enough, those who are now relatively conservative answered this question in just about the same way as did those who are still relatively nonconservative. The 16 women originally labeled as clearly conservative, on leaving college, answered this question somewhat differently; more than half of them (9) described their environment of friends as predominantly "conservative," but answers differed with the present attitudes of the respondents. That is, those who are now, in fact, relatively conservative with near-unanimity describe their friends as conservative, whereas those who are now relatively non-conservative consider a substantial proportion or even most of their friends to be "liberal." Thus only those who were quite conservative in the late 1930's and who still remain so see themselves surrounded by friends who are primarily conservative.

In sum, nearly all of the still nonconservative women mention either husbands or public activities (most commonly both) that have served to support and maintain previously nonconservative attitudes, while none of the three formerly nonconservative but presently conservative women mentions either husband or public activities which have served to maintain earlier attitudes.

What about attitude persistence on the part of those who, after three or four years in college, were still relatively conservative? Sixteen of those who were then labeled conservative were interviewed in the early 1960's, ten of them being categorized as still conservative and three as now nonconservative. Only one of the nonchangers reported having a husband who was a Democrat, and in this lone case he turned out to have voted for Nixon in 1960. Two of the three changers, on the other hand, report husbands who were Democrats and Kennedy voters in 1960. Only two of the persistent conservatives mentioned public activities presumably supportive of their attitudes (in behalf of the Republican

Party, in both cases); eight of the ten described most of their friends either as conservative or as Republicans. The conditions that favor the persistence of conservatism over the 20-odd years are thus about the same as those that favor the persistence of nonconservatism: supportive environments in the form of husbands, local friends, and (for the nonconservatives but not the conservatives) in the form of associates in activities related to public issues.

There is a special sub-population of students who, as of graduating in the late 1930's, were candidates for regression; that is, they became much less conservative during their college years. Of these, about one-third (9 of 28) were among the most conservative half of the same population in the early 1960's, and may be regarded as regressors, in some degree at least. Eight of these potential regressors were, for various reasons, unable to report on husbands' preferences. Among the remaining 19 respondents, five were actual regressors, four of whom reported their husbands to be Republicans or "conservative Republicans." Among 14 actual non-regressors reporting, ten described their husbands as Democrats or "liberal Democrats," two referred to them as "Republicans who have been voting Democratic," and only two call their husbands Republicans. These are highly significant differences: the actual regressors can pretty well be differentiated from the nonregressors merely by knowing their husbands' present attitudes. By this procedure only 3 of 19, or 16 per cent of all predictions would not have been correct.

This total set of data suggests that either regression and persistence of attitudes as of leaving college are, over the years, influenced by husbands' attitudes, or early post-college attitudes had something to do with the selection of husbands, or both. In either case, both regression and persistence are facilitated by the supportiveness of husbands.

V

If there is any very general principle that helps to account for this whole range of phenomena (both my 1946 and my 1963 versions), I believe that it is to be found in an extended version of "balance theory," as originally outlined by Heider.[5] Heider's formulations are formulated in individual and phenomenological terms; a balanced state is a strictly intrapersonal, psychological state. But it is also possible to conceptualize an objective, multi-person state of balance, referring to the actual relationships among different persons' attitudes, regardless of the persons' awareness of each other. Such a concept is psychologically useful not only because it describes an actual, existing situation—an environment of which each person is himself a part, as suggested by Asch[6]—but also because it describes a relationship which, given reasonably full and accurate communication, comes to be accurately perceived. My own recent work on the

5. F. Heider, "Attitudes and Cognitive Organization," *J. Psychol.*, 21: 107–112, 1946; and Heider, *The Psychology of Interpersonal Relations.*

6. S. E. Asch, *Social Psychology*, Englewood Cliffs, N.J.: Prentice-Hall, Inc., 1952.

acquaintance process has been interesting to me primarily because it inquires into the processes by which and the conditions under which *intra*personal states of balance come to correspond with *inter*personal ones. As outlined by Heider, and subsequently by many others,[7] the processes by which imbalanced states serve as goads toward the attainment of balanced ones include both internal, psychological changes and external modifications of the environment. Thus, one may achieve a balanced state with the important figures in one's social environment—whether by selecting those figures, by modifying one's own attitudes, or by influencing others' attitudes—and at the same time continue to perceive that environment accurately.

According to such an extended, *inter*personal concept of balance, an imbalanced state under conditions of continued interaction is likely to be an unstable one, simply because when it is discovered it arouses *intra*personal imbalance on the part of one or more of the interactors, and this state arouses forces toward change. Given marked attitude change on the part of one but not the other member of a dyad actually in balance with respect to that attitude, imbalance results. This was what typically happened to students at Bennington College vis-a-vis their parents, in the 1930's. A common way in which they attempted to reduce imbalance was by avoidance—not necessarily of parents but of the divisive issues as related to parents. As Heider might say, unit formation between issue and parents was broken up, and psychological imbalance thus reduced. Such a "solution" resembles autistic hostility in that it involves a marked restriction of communication.

But this solution, as many of my subjects testified, was not a particularly comfortable one. Hence, it would hardly be surprising if many of them, during early post-college years, were in search of environments that would provide less uncomfortable solutions—or, better yet, more positively rewarding ones. An ideal one, of course, would be a husband who was rewarding as a supporter of one's own attitudes as well as in other ways.

And so, vis-a-vis parents and fellow-students at first, and later vis-a-vis husbands (or perhaps working associates), forces toward balance were at work. Specifically, support from important people concerning important issues came to be the rule, and its absence the exception. Support sometimes came about by changing one's own attitudes toward those of needed supporters, or, more commonly, by selecting supporters for existing attitudes. The latter stratagem represented not merely an automatic tendency for attitudes to perpetuate themselves. More significantly, I believe, it represents an adaptation to a world that includes *both* persons and issues. Such a dual adaptation can be made, of course, by sacrificing one's stand on the issues (regression). But if the dual adaptation is to be made without this sacrifice, then an interpersonal world must be selected (or created) that is supportive—in which case we can say that the attitude has been expressed by finding a supportive environment.

7. Cf. Brown et al., *op. cit.*

According to my two themes (of 1946 and 1963) an existing attitude may be maintained by creating environments in which *either* new information can be avoided *or* in which other persons support one's own information. In either case, the fate of an attitude is mediated by the social environment in which the individual attempts to maintain or to restore balance regarding that same attitude. Insofar as that environment excludes disturbing information or provides reinforcing information, the attitude persists. And insofar as the selection or the acceptance of that environment is a consequence of holding the attitude, we have a steady-state, self-maintaining system. . . .

The Spatial Ecology of Group Formation

Leon Festinger, Stanley S. Schachter, and Kurt Back

Human ecology has dealt mainly with the study of the distribution of persons, institutions, or any social phenomena in space. Among the concerns of the human ecologist have been studies of the spatial distribution and patterning of such things as delinquency, truancy, crime, vice, suicide, mental disorders, divorce, desertion, poverty, morality, etc. Almost without exception these studies have followed a common pattern—a relatively large area, such as a metropolitan region, is subdivided into a number of zones or enumeration districts in each of which the rate of occurrence of a particular social phenomenon is computed. Little attention has been devoted to the possible effects of the spatial arrangement of smaller areas such as neighborhoods, nor has attention been focused on the relations between ecological factors and the formation of friendship and face-to-face groups.

Stouffer[1] in a study of mobility says, "Whether one is seeking to explain 'why' persons go to a particular place to get jobs, 'why' they go to trade at a particular store, 'why' they go to a particular neighborhood to commit a crime, or 'why' they marry the particular spouse they choose, the factor of spatial distance is of obvious significance."

Direct research on the ecological determinants of friendship and group

Reprinted in part from Leon Festinger, Stanley S. Schachter, and Kurt Back, *Social Pressures in Informal Groups*, pp. 33–46, by permission of the authors and the publisher, Stanford University Press. Copyright 1950 by Leon Festinger, Stanley S. Schachter, and Kurt Back.

1. S. A. Stouffer, "Intervening Opportunities: A Theory Relating Mobility and Distance," *American Sociological Review*, Vol. 5, pp. 845–867, 1940.

formation has, however, been minimal. A few studies[2,3] have examined the relationship between distance and marriage selection. Such studies show that there is an inverse relationship between the distance separating potential marriage partners and the number of marriages. Thus, in New Haven, 76 per cent of the marriages in 1940 were between persons living within twenty blocks of each other and 35 per cent between persons living within five blocks of each other.[3]

While such findings may not seem surprising, it is less obvious that differences in distance as small as twenty or thirty feet would play a major part in determining friendships. Within the Westgate and Westgate West housing projects,* however, even these small differences in distance are effective in determining patterns of friendship. This chapter outlines the relationships between the physical environment and the sociometric structure of these two communities.

The Ecological Basis of Friendship

In communities such as Westgate and Westgate West, where people moving into the area have few or no previous contacts in the community, friendships are likely to develop on the basis of the brief and passive contacts made going to and from home or walking about the neighborhood. These brief meetings, if they are frequent enough, may develop into nodding acquaintanceships, then into speaking relationships, and eventually, if psychological factors are right, into friendships. Such casual or involuntary meetings we will call passive contacts.

Passive contacts are determined by the required paths followed in entering or leaving one's home for any purpose. For example, in going from one's door to the stairway one must pass certain apartments; in walking to the butcher shop one must go by certain houses. These specific required paths are determined by the physical structure of the area.

In relating physical structure to the formation of friendships, it is necessary to distinguish between two ecological factors, (1) physical distance, and (2)

2. R. H. Abrams, "Residential Propinquity as a Factor in Marriage Selection," *American Sociological Review*, Vol. 8, pp. 288–294, 1943.

3. R. Kennedy, "Premarital Residential Propinquity," *American Journal of Sociology*, Vol. 48, pp. 580–584, 1943.

*These were post-World War II housing projects for married veteran students at the Massachusetts Institute of Technology. Westgate consisted of 100 single-family units arranged in nine courts, six of them containing 13 houses each and the others a smaller number of units. Westgate West consisted of 17 Navy barracks divided into ten apartments per building. Students were assigned to the two projects in the order in which their name appeared on a waiting list. The residents of the projects were similar with respect to age, educational background, interests, aspirations, and, of course, their status as either married veteran students or their wives. (*Editors' note.*)

positional relationships and features of design which we may call functional distance.

Physical distance is measured distance and is one of the major determinants of whether or not passive contacts will occur. Obviously there is a high negative relationship between the physical distance separating the homes of two people and the probability that these people will make passive contact. The smaller the physical distance the greater the number of required paths neighbors are likely to share and the greater the probability of passive contacts. For example, in hanging clothes out to dry, or putting out the garbage, or simply sitting on the porch one is much more likely to meet next-door neighbors than people living four or five houses away.

2. Factors such as the design of a building or the positional relationships among a group of houses are also important determinants of which people will become friends. It is these functional factors of design and position which determine the specific pattern of required paths in an area and consequently determine which people will meet. For example, if there is a stairway at each end of a floor, there is a good chance that people living at opposite ends of the floor will never or rarely meet. Functional distance is measured by the number of passive contacts that position and design encourage.

Both physical distance and functional distance, therefore will affect the pattern and number of passive contacts. Obviously, they cannot be considered as independent variables, for we can expect a high relationship between the two. In particular cases, however, the distinction becomes clear. For example, two back-to-back houses which are thirty feet apart and have neither back doors nor back yards would be considered functionally farther apart than two back-to-back houses, also thirty feet apart, which do have back doors and yards. Thus we can have varying functional distances while physical distance remains constant.

THE EFFECT OF PHYSICAL DISTANCE ON THE FORMATION OF FRIENDSHIPS

Figure 1 is a schematized representation of the front of a Westgate West building. The porch area provides the only means of entering or leaving the building and is, therefore, the only place within the building in which passive

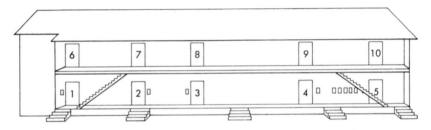

Figure 1. Schematic Diagram of a Westgate West Building

contacts can occur. Each of the doorways is the entrance to a different apartment and the numbers on the doorways will be used to designate each apartment position. Each floor consists of five directly adjoining apartments and the two floors are connected by stairways at each end of the porch. With two exceptions the doorways of all adjoining apartments are separated by almost 19 feet. Apartments 3 and 4 and apartments 8 and 9 are separated by 32 feet. The maximum separation on any one floor is the 88 feet between the end apartments.

In order to simplify the presentation of data we have adopted a unit of approximate physical distance to describe the difference between any two apartments in a building. Each unit is the equivalent of the physical distance separating any two neighboring doorways. Thus, in Figure 1, apartments 1 and 2 are one unit of approximate physical distance apart; apartments 1 and 3 are two units apart; apartments 1 and 5 and apartments 6 and 10 are four units apart, and so on. In specifying the distance between apartments on different floors, the letter S is employed as a symbol for the stairways between the first and second floors. Thus, apartments 9 and 1 are separated by two units of physical distance and a stairway and this distance is designated as 2S; apartments 2 and 7 are separated by 1 unit and a stairway and are 1S units apart, and so on. Despite the fact that the stairway on the right-hand side of the building ends midway between apartments 9 and 10, the units are calculated as if this stairway ended right in front of the door of apartment number 9. This procedure has been adopted for simplicity's sake and makes little difference in our results. Where there are two possible routes connecting any apartment on one floor to any apartment on the other floor, the units are always computed for the shorter route.

Table I—The Relationship Between Sociometric Choice and Physical Distance on One Floor of a Westgate West Building

(1)	(2)	(3)	(4)
Units of approximate physical distance	Total number of choices given	Total number of possible choices	Choices given (2) / Possible choices (3)
1	112	8 × 34	.412
2	46	6 × 34	.225
3	22	4 × 34	.162
4	7	2 × 34	.103

In order to study the effect of these physical design features on the formation of friendships we may relate such things as physical distance to sociometric choices. These sociometric data were gathered on all residents of Westgate and 166 of the 170 Westgate West residents by asking, "What three people in Westgate or Westgate West do you see most of socially?"

Table 1 presents the data for Westgate West on choices given to people living in the same building and on the same floor as the person who chooses them. The data for all seventeen Westgate West buildings are grouped since all of these buildings are exactly the same.

In column (1) of Table 1 are listed all the approximate physical distances which can separate any two persons living on the same floor. Column (2) presents the total number of choices given to persons living at each distance away from the people who are choosing. These figures, however, are inadequate in this form because there are great differences in the total number of potential choices between people separated by the various distances. There are, for example, many more 1 unit choices than 4 unit choices possible. These figures in column (2) must, consequently, be corrected on the basis of the total number of such possible choices.

Column (3) presents the correction factors for each distance of separation between apartments. The figures in this column represent the total number of choices that could exist in the entire Westgate West project at each separation distance. Thus, at three units distance, there are four possible choices within any one floor; apartments 4 to 1, 5 to 2, 1 to 4, and 2 to 5 on the first floor or, symmetrically, apartments 9 to 6, 10 to 7, 6 to 9, and 7 to 10 on the second floor. Since there are seventeen buildings, each with two floors, the number of possible choices at each distance is multiplied by thirty-four. Column (4) presents the corrected sociometric choices at each distance. These figures are arrived at by dividing the figures in column (2) by those in column (3). They state specifically the percentage of possible choices at each distance that were actually made. Thus, 41.2 per cent of the 272 possible one unit choices were actually made; 22.5 per cent of the 204 possible two unit choices were made.

The data in Table 1 show unequivocally that within the floor of a Westgate West building there is a high relationship between friendships and physical distance. The greatest percentage of possible choices are made to next-door neighbors. These percentages decrease constantly with distance to a minimum of 10.3 per cent of all choices that could be exchanged between people four units apart, that is, between those who live at opposite ends of the same floor. It must be remembered that these distances are actually small. Neighboring apartments are about 22 feet apart and apartments at opposite ends of the same floor are only 88 feet apart. Yet these small differences in distance seem to be major determinants of whether or not friendships will form.

These choices given to people living on the same floor represent a very sizeable proportion of the total number of choices given. Forty-four per cent of the 246 choices made were given to people living on the same floor as the chooser.

We find a similar relationship of sociometric choice to physical distance in choices given to people living in the same building but on a different floor. Table 2 presents data for between-floor choices. The meaning of each of the columns is the same as in Table 1. The letter S in column (1) is the symbol for stairway.

The data in Table 2 show a high relationship between choices exchanged among people living on different floors of the same barracks and the distance between these people. Again, those people having the smallest physical separation give each other the highest proportion of the total number of possible choices. Thus, 20.6 per cent of the 68 possible choices are made at S units, the shortest possible distance between apartments on different floors. These percentages decrease constantly with increasing distance to a low point of 5.9 per cent of possible choices between apartments with a separation of 3S or 4S units of approximate physical distance.

Table 2—The Relationship of Sociometric Choices Between Floors of a Westgate West Building to Physical Distance

(1)	(2)	(3)	(4)
Units of approximate physical distance	Total number of choices given	Total number of possible choices	Choices given (2) / Possible choices (3)
S	14	2 × 34	.206
1S	39	6 × 34	.191
2S	20	8 × 34	.074
3S	14	7 × 34	.059
4S	4	2 × 34	.059

Whereas 44 per cent of the total number of sociometric choices in Westgate West were made to others on their own floor, only 21 per cent of the total choices were made between floors. . . .

Data on the effects of physical distance on friendship formation are more difficult to obtain for Westgate. Within any one court there are houses next to one another and houses facing one another. Some of the back-to-back houses have back doors while others do not, and so on. Even if one wishes to ignore the possible effects of different functional relationships throughout this community, it would be almost impossible to compute the relationship of physical distance per se to friendship formation because of the extreme difficulty of determining the necessary correction factors for the number of possible choices at various distances.

However, for part of each side of a large Westgate U-shaped court it is possible partially to isolate the effect of physical distance. . . .

Analysis of the sociometric choices exchanged among the people living in each row of houses [two rows of five houses each per court] follows the same pattern as the analysis of choices among apartments on the same floor of a Westgate West building. Distance between houses is again handled in terms of units of approximate physical distance. . . . Choices are again categorized according to the units of distance separating the house of the person chosen from that of the person choosing. The data for all twelve rows [two rows in each of the six courts having the same number of houses] are pooled and are presented in Table 3. Again, there is the same marked relationship between sociometric choice and physical distance. The greatest proportion of possible choices is made to next-door neighbors. This proportion decreases with increasing distance to the low point of no choices at all to people living four units away. . . .

Table 3—The Relationship of Sociometric Choices Among the Houses in a Row in Westgate Courts to Physical Distance

(1)	(2)	(3)	(4)
Units of approximate physical distance	Total number of choices given	Total number of possible choices	Choices given (2) / Possible choices (3)
1	26	8 × 12	.271
2	6	6 × 12	.083
3	2	4 × 12	.042
4	0	2 × 12	.000

In summary, data for two differently designed housing projects show a strong relationship between sociometric choice and physical distance. In both projects the greatest number of choices were made to people living closest to the person choosing and the choices decreased continuously as distance from the home of the chooser increased. The actual measured distances involved were quite small, in no case being larger than 180 feet. Yet the effect of even these small distances is so marked that in a Westgate row no choices at all were made between houses with the maximum separation of four units or 180 feet.

THE EFFECT OF PHYSICAL DISTANCE ON CHOICES OUTSIDE OF OWN COURT

OR BUILDING

The data presented so far have explored the relationships between sociometric choices and physical distances within a court or building. This same relationship holds for choices outside of the court or building. The greater the physical separation between any two points in these communities, the fewer the friendships. Table 4 presents the data for choices given by Westgaters to people

Table 4—Sociometric Choices Given by Westgaters to People Living Anywhere in the Two Projects

(1)	(2)	(3)	(4)
Location of person chosen	Total number of choices	Total number of possibilities	Choices given (2) / Possible choices (3)
Own court	143	1076	.133
Adjacent court	51	2016	.025
Other courts	47	6794	.007
Westgate West	17	17,000	.001

living anywhere in the two projects. Column (1) lists the places of residence of
the people chosen. "Own court" refers to a choice made within the court of the
chooser; "adjacent court" refers to choices given to people living in immediately
neighboring courts. "Other courts" refers to any choice within Westgate which
does not fall into the first two categories. "Westgate West" includes all choices
given by Westgaters to people in Westgate West. In the order given, these
categories approximate a continuum of physical distance. In general, though not
in all cases, "own court" choices are physically closer than "adjacent court"
choices and so on.

Table 4 makes it obvious that the relationship between physical distance
and sociometric choice holds for out-of-court choices as well as in-court choices.
Column (4) again shows that the percentage of possible choices made decreases
with increasing distance.

Table 5—Sociometric Choices Given by Westgate West People to People Living Anywhere in the Two Projects

(1)	(2)	(3)	(4)
Location of person chosen	Total number of choices made	Total number of possibilities	Choices given (2) / Possible choices (3)
Own buildings	278	1530	.182
Own quadrangle	49	4000	.012
Other buildings	66	23,200	.003
Westgate	33	17,000	.002

The data for Westgate West present a similar picture. Table 5 shows that
for Westgate West, too, there is an inverse relationship between the percentage
of possible choices actually made and physical distance.

THE EFFECT OF FUNCTIONAL DISTANCE ON THE FORMATION OF FRIENDSHIPS

In describing the six large Westgate courts we mentioned that, with the
exception of the end houses at the tips of the U, all of the houses constituting
a court face into the courtyard area. All but two of these end houses face out
onto the street which runs through the project. . . .

Because of these differences in position we can expect marked functional
differences between these end houses and the rest of the houses in the court.
It is possible to come and go from the end houses facing the street without ever
passing the homes of court neighbors. One can work in the garden or sit out on
the porch and only rarely meet court neighbors. None of these things are true
for the houses facing into the court. Therefore, we can expect that the people
living in the end houses facing the street will have far fewer passive contacts
with their court neighbors than will people living in houses facing into the court.

If the hypothesis be true that in this community the formation of friendships depends upon the extent of passive contacts, the people living in these end houses will receive fewer sociometric choices from their court neighbors than will the people living in houses facing into the court. . . .

. . . The people living in these end houses do receive fewer choices than the people living in any other house position. The mean number of choices received by people living in end houses facing the street is 0.60 and by people living in inner court houses is 1.56. This difference is consistent throughout. In each of the six courts the inner court residents receive a larger mean number of choices than the residents in end houses facing the street.[4]. . .

The Ecological Basis for Formation of Groups

The data presented have been stated largely in terms of specific friendships between people living in particular house positions. We have shown that, in these two communities, friendships will be determined in large part by physical and functional distance. In terms of these ecological considerations we can further expect that a large proportion of all sociometric choices will be exchanged among people living within the same court or building. We know that in a Westgate court the houses are close to one another and with a few exceptions face into the same area. In general, the people living in each court are both physically and functionally closer to one another than to anyone else living in Westgate. This is obviously also true for the people living in each Westgate West building. The data corroborate the expectation. Of the 426 choices made by Westgate West people, 278 or 65.3 per cent were given to people living in the same building as the choosers. Similarly for Westgate, 143 or 55.5 per cent of the 258 choices made were given to people living in the same court as the choosers. Further, 85.5 per cent of all people in Westgate West chose at least one person living in the same building and 80 per cent of Westgaters chose at least one person in their court. If the end houses facing the street, which positionally at least are not members of the court, are excluded from this count, the figure for Westgate rises to 87.4 per cent. Thus, a large share of all friendships in both of these communities was among people living in the same court or building.

If one accepts the definition of a group as a number of interacting and sociometrically connected people, it follows that these ecological factors determine not only specific friendships but the composition of groups within these communities as well. Each court and building is populated by people who have most of their friends in the same living unit. Thus the people in each court or building will work together, play together, and, in general, see more of each other than of any other individuals living in the projects.

4. Significant at the 3 per cent level of confidence.

Summary

The hypothesis has been advanced that friendships and group membership will be determined in these communities by passive contacts between neighbors. The pattern and number of such contacts among particular people will depend upon physical and functional distance. Data have been presented which reveal a striking relationship between these ecological factors and sociometric choice.

Obviously, there are other methods of making friends. The men of the project undoubtedly meet one another in class and school activities. People probably meet at parties, and so on. However, the relationships between ecological and sociometric structures is so very marked that there can be little doubt that in these communities passive contacts are a major determinant of friendship and group formation. . . .

It should be remembered that Westgate and Westgate West represent homogeneous communities. Whether these ecological factors would be as effective in more heterogeneous communities is, of course, a question for further empirical study. It seems likely that in such communities ecological factors will play some part, though a less important one, in determining sociometric structure.

Patterns of Influence: Local and Cosmopolitan Influentials

Robert K. Merton

THIS is an exploratory study focused upon the place of mass communications in patterns of interpersonal influence. Based primarily upon interviews with eighty-six men and women drawn from diverse social and economic strata in "Rovere," a town of 11,000 on the Eastern seaboard, it is essentially a case study rather than a statistical analysis[1] of influence patterns. The initial substantive aim of this pilot study was fourfold: (1) to identify types of people regarded as variously influential by their fellows; (2) to relate patterns of communications behavior to their roles as influential persons; (3) to gain clues to the chief avenues through which they came to acquire influence; and (4) to set out hypotheses for more systematic study of the workings of interpersonal influence in the local community.

The body of this report is devoted to an analysis of basically different types of influential persons: types which we shall call the "local" and the "cosmopolitan." But before turning to these substantive materials, there may be some interest in glancing briefly at two procedural and methodological detours encountered on the way. The first detour was taken when an applied research in sociology, originally devoted to a delimited practical problem, gave rise to theoretic constructs which unexpectedly emerged in the process of investigation. Although the pilot study was in the beginning undertaken to learn the functions

1. Although figures summarizing our case-study materials are cited from time to time, these are merely heuristic, not demonstrative, in character. They serve only to indicate the sources of interpretative hypotheses which await detailed, systematic inquiry.

served by a national newsmagazine for various types of readers—a problem in the sociology of mass communications—it was soon reoriented as a result of initial impressions and findings. For it appeared that the magazine was utilized in markedly different ways by people who exercised varying degrees of inter-personal influence in their community. In rapidly retracing our steps over the second detour, we shall meet the obstacle which required us to devise alternative schemes for analyzing the same qualitative data. The plain fact is that our initial analysis was quite unproductive. With the emergence of the concepts of local and cosmopolitan *influentials*, however, the "same" qualitative data led to productive results which have since lent themselves to elaboration. After this brief procedural review of these two phases of our qualitative analysis, we shall be better prepared to assess the substantive account of local and cosmopolitan influentials. . . .

Two Phases of Qualitative Analysis of Influentials

. . . In prolonged interviews, informants were led to mention people to whom they turned for help or advice regarding various types of personal decisions (decisions ranging from choice of a job or educational plans for self and children to selections of books, plays or furniture). Informants were invited, further, to indicate those persons who, so far as they knew, were generally sought out for advice in these several spheres. Such tentative identifications of individuals exercising interpersonal influence were of course linked with reasons advanced by informants for singling out these individuals rather than others.

In the course of these interviews, our eighty-six informants came to mention a total of 379 people who, in one respect or another, were said to have exerted influence upon them in a concrete situation involving decisions. Some people turned up repeatedly in this canvass. (There were 1043 "mentions" referring to 379 persons, some of whom were referred to on thirty or more occasions.) Of the 379, fifty-seven, or 15 per cent, were mentioned four or more times and this was provisionally taken as our working criterion of "influentiality." As we shall presently see, this wholly tentative and arbitrary criterion enabled us to identify cases in which we could examine the operation of interpersonal influence. Thirty of these influential people were subsequently interviewed with regard to their own evaluation and image of their influence, evaluations of the influence exercised by others upon them, situations in which they exerted influence, their communications behavior, and the like. All this comprised the data for analysis. . . .

In what we now know to be the relatively sterile first phase of our analysis, we not only distinguished the influentials from the rank-and-file, but went on to distinguish influentials according to their dynamic position in the local *influence-structure*. Thus distinctions were drawn between the currently in-fluential (occupying a supposedly stable position), the potentially influential (the rising star—still upward mobile), the waning influential (passed the zenith—now downward mobile), and the dormant influential (possessing the *objective* attributes of the influential but not exploiting these for the exercise of influence). The non-influentials were in turn divided into the rank-and-file (with a limited range of social contacts in which they are typically the recipients rather than the dispensers of advice) and the isolates (largely shut off from social contacts).

This classification proved to be logically impeccable, empirically applicable, and virtually sterile. To be sure, our data could readily be arranged in these categories. But this resulted in few clear-cut uniformities of communications behavior or of other patterns of behavior. In short, the distinctions were valid but relatively fruitless for our purposes. . . . The sterility of this phase of our analysis *motivated the search* for new working concepts, but it was a series of observations incidentally turned up in the course of this analysis which directed attention to the *actual concepts* with which we came to operate.

Above all else, one strategic *fact* shaped the second phase of the analysis. The interviews with influentials had been centered on their relations with*in* the town. Yet, in response to the same set of queries, some influentials spoke wholly in terms of the local situation in Rovere, whereas others managed to incorporate frequent references to matters far beyond the reaches of Rovere. A question concerning the impact of the war upon the Rovere economy would elicit in the one instance a response dealing exclusively with problems within the town and in the other, to remarks about the national economy or international trade. It was this characteristic patterning of response within a peculiarly local or a more extended frame of reference—a patterning which could, perhaps, have been anticipated but which was not—that led to the conception of two major types of influentials: the "local" and the "cosmopolitan."

Whereas the first classification had dealt with phases in the cycle of personal influence, the second was in terms of influentials' *orientation*[2] toward local and larger social structures. The one centered on position within the influence-structure; the other on the grounds for influence and the ways in which this influence was exercised.

With the emergence of the concepts of local and cosmopolitan influentials, a number of new uniformities at once came to light. The "same" materials took on quite new implications as they were re-examined and re-analyzed in terms of these concepts. Facts which found no pertinent place in the first analysis became not only relevant but critical in the second. Thus the varying types of career-patterns of influentials—whether these developed largely within Rovere or were furthered in Rovere after having been initiated elsewhere—came to be an integral part of the second analysis whereas they had been "interesting" but unincorporated data in the first. Such seemingly diverse matters as geo-

---

2. A word of explanation is needed for this concept of "orientation." The social orientation differs from the social role. Role refers to the manner in which the rights and duties inherent in a social position are put into practice; orientation, as here conceived, refers to the theme underlying the complex of social roles performed by an individual. It is the (tacit or explicit) theme which finds expression in each of the complex of social roles in which the individual is implicated.

graphic mobility, participation in networks of personal relations and in voluntary organizations, the translation of influence-potentials into influence-operations, patterns of communications behavior—all these were found to be expressions of these major orientations toward the local community: orientations ranging from virtually exclusive concern with the local area to central concern with the great world outside. . . .

Types of Influentials: The Local and the Cosmopolitan

The terms "local" and "cosmopolitan"[3] do not refer, of course, to the regions in which interpersonal influence is exercised. Both types of influentials are effective almost exclusively within the local community. Rovere has few residents who command a following outside that community.[4]

The chief criterion for distinguishing the two is found in their *orientation* toward Rovere. The localite largely confines his interests to this community. Rovere is essentially his world. Devoting little thought or energy to the Great Society, he is preoccupied with local problems, to the virtual exclusion of the national and international scene. He is, strictly speaking, parochial.

Contrariwise with the cosmopolitan type. He has some interest in Rovere and must of course maintain a minimum of relations within the community since he, too, exerts influence there. But he is also oriented significantly to the world outside Rovere, and regards himself as an integral part of that world. He resides in Rovere but lives in the Great Society. If the local type is parochial, the cosmopolitan is ecumenical.

Of the thirty influentials interviewed at length, fourteen were independently

3. Upon identification of the two types of influentials, these terms were adopted from Carle C. Zimmerman, who uses them as translations of Toennies' well-known distinction between *Gemeinschaft* (localistic) and *Gesellschaft* (cosmopolitan). The sociologically informed reader will recognize essentially the same distinction, though with different terminologies, in the writings of Simmel, Cooley, Weber, Durkheim, among many others. Although these terms have commonly been used to refer to types of social organization and of social relationships, they are here applied to empirical materials on types of influential persons. Cf. Ferdinand Toennies, *Fundamental Concepts of Sociology* (New York, 1940), a translation by C. P. Loomis of his classic book, *Gemeinschaft und Gesellschaft*, and more importantly, a later article bearing the same title. See also Carle C. Zimmerman, *The Changing Community* (New York and London: Harper & Brothers, 1938), especially 80ff. For a compact summary of similar concepts in the sociological literature, see Leopold von Wiese and Howard Becker, *Systematic Sociology* (New York: John Wiley & Sons, Inc., 1932), especially 223–226n.

4. The concept of influentials has been taken up in a study of the influence-structure of a suburb which houses men of national reputation and influence. As the authors say, "It is hardly surprising then that the personal characteristics of these 'influentials' differ from those of the lower-ranking cosmopolitan influential in Rovere." Kenneth P. Adler and Davis Bobrow, "Interest and influence in foreign affairs," *Public Opinion Quarterly*, 1956, 20, 89–101. See also Floyd Hunter, *Power Structure: A Study of Decision-Makers* (Chapel Hill: University of North Carolina Press, 1953).

assessed by three analysts[5] as "cosmopolitan" on the basis of case-materials exhibiting their orientation toward the Rovere community, and sixteen, as "local."

These orientations found characteristic expression in a variety of contexts. For example, influentials were launched upon a statement of their outlook by the quasi-projective question: "Do you worry much about the news?" (This was the autumn of 1943, when "the news" was, for most, equivalent to news about the war.) The responses, typically quite lengthy, readily lent themselves to classification in terms of the chief foci of interest of the influentials. One set of comments was focused on problems of a national and international order. They expressed concern with the difficulties which would attend the emergence of a stable post-war world; they talked at length about the problems of building an international organization to secure the peace; and the like. The second set of comments referred to the war news almost wholly in terms of what it implied for interviewees personally or for their associates in Rovere. They seized upon a question about "the news" as an occasion for reviewing the immediate flow of problems which the war had introduced into the town.

Classifying influentials into these two categories, we find that twelve of the fourteen[6] cosmopolitans typically replied within the framework of international and national problems, whereas only four of the sixteen locals spoke in this vein. Each type of influential singled out distinctively different elements from the flow of events. A vaguely formulated question enabled each to project his basic orientations in his replies.

All other differences between the local and cosmopolitan influentials seem to stem from their difference in basic orientation.[7] The group-profiles indicate the tendency of local influentials to be devoted to localism: they are more likely to have lived in Rovere for a long period, are profoundly interested in meeting many townspeople, do not wish to move from the town, are more likely to be interested in local politics, etc. Such items, which suggest great disparity between

5. This complete coincidence of assessments is scarcely to be expected in a larger sample. But the cosmopolitan and local syndromes were so clearly defined for this handful of cases, that there was little doubt concerning the "diagnoses." A full-fledged investigation would evolve more formal criteria, along the lines implied in the following discussion, and would, accordingly, evolve an intermediate type which approaches neither the local nor the cosmopolitan pole.

6. It should be repeated that the figures cited at this point, as throughout the study, should not be taken as representative of a parent population. They are cited only to illustrate the heuristic purpose they served in suggesting clues to the operation of diverse patterns of interpersonal influence. As is so often the fact with quantitative summaries of case-studies, these figures do not confirm interpretations, but merely suggest interpretations. The tentative interpretations in turn provide a point of departure for designing quantitative studies based upon adequate samples.

7. Nothing is said here of the objective *determinants* of these differences in orientation. To asertain these determinants is an additional and distinctly important task, not essayed in the present study.

the two types of influentials, are our main concern in the following sections. There we will find that the difference in basic orientation is bound up with a variety of other differences: (1) in the structures of social relations in which each type is implicated; (2) in the roads they have traveled to their present positions in the influence-structure; (3) in the utilization of their present status for the exercise of interpersonal influence; and (4) in their communications behavior.

Structures of Social Relations

ROOTS IN THE COMMUNITY

Local and cosmopolitan influentials differ rather markedly in their attachment to Rovere. The local influentials are great local patriots and the thought of leaving Rovere seems seldom to come to mind. As one of them gropingly expressed it:

> Rovere is the greatest town in the world. It has something that is nowhere else in the world, though I can't quite say what it is.

When asked directly if they had "ever thought of leaving Rovere," thirteen of the sixteen local influentials replied emphatically that they would never consider it, and the other three expressed a strong preference to remain, although they believed they would leave under certain conditions. None felt that they would be equally satisfied with life in any other community. Not so with the cosmopolitans. Only three of these claim to be wedded to Rovere for life. Four express willingness to live elsewhere, and the remaining seven would be willing to leave under certain conditions. Cosmopolitans' responses such as these do not turn up at all among the locals:

> I've been on the verge of leaving for other jobs several times.

> I am only waiting for my son to take over my practice, before I go out to California.

These basic differences in attitude toward Rovere are linked with the different runs of experience of local and cosmopolitan influentials. The cosmopolitans have been more mobile. The locals were typically born in Rovere or in its immediate vicinity. Whereas 14 of the 16 locals have lived in Rovere for over twenty-five years, this is true for fewer than half of the cosmopolitans. The cosmopolitans are typically recent arrivals who have lived in a succession of communities in different parts of the country.

Nor does this appear to be a result of differences in the age-composition of the local and cosmopolitan groups. True, the cosmopolitans are more likely to be younger than the local influentials. But for those over forty-five, the cosmopolitans seem to be comparative newcomers and the locals Rovere-born-and-bred.

From the case-materials, we can infer the bases of the marked attachment to Rovere characteristic of the local influentials. In the process of making their mark, these influentials have become thoroughly *adapted to the community* and dubious of the possibility of doing as well elsewhere. From the vantage point of his seventy years, a local judge reports his sense of full incorporation in the community:

> I wouldn't think of leaving Rovere. The people here are very good, very responsive. They like me and I'm grateful to God for the feeling that the people in Rovere trust me and look up to me as their guide and leader.

Thus, the strong sense of identification with Rovere among local influentials is linked with their typically local origins and career patterns in this community. Economically and sentimentally, they are deeply rooted in Rovere.

So far as attachment to Rovere is concerned, the cosmopolitans differ from the locals in virtually every respect. Not only are they relative newcomers; they do not feel themselves rooted in the town. Having characteristically lived elsewhere, they feel that Rovere, "a pleasant enough town," is only one of many. They are also aware, through actual experience, that they can advance their careers in other communitites. They do not, consequently, look upon Rovere as comprising the outermost limits of a secure and satisfactory existence. Their wider range of experience has modified their orientation toward their present community.

SOCIABILITY: NETWORKS OF PERSONAL RELATIONS

In the course of the interview, influentials were given an occasion to voice their attitudes toward "knowing many people" in the community. Attitudes differed sharply between the two types. Thirteen of the sixteen local influentials in contrast to four of the fourteen cosmopolitans expressed marked interest in establishing frequent contacts with many people.

This difference becomes more instructive when examined in qualitative terms. The local influential is typically concerned with knowing *as many* people as possible. He is a quantitativist in the sphere of social contacts. Numbers count. In the words of an influential police officer (who thus echoes the sentiments of another "local," the Mayor):

> I have lots of friends in Rovere, if I do say so myself. I like to know every-body. If I stand on a corner, I can speak to 500 people in two hours. Knowing people helps when a promotion comes up, for instance. Everybody mentions you for the job. Influential people who know you talk to other people. Jack Flye [the Mayor] said to me one day, "Bill," he said, "you have more friends in town than I do. I wish I had all the friends you have that you don't even know of." It made me feel good. . . .

This typical attitude fits into what we know of the local type of influential. What is more, it suggests that the career-function of personal contacts and personal relations is recognized by local influentials themselves. Nor is this concern with personal contact merely a consequence of the occupations of local influentials. Businessmen, professionals, and local government officials among them all join in the same paeans on the desirability of many and varied contacts. A bank president recapitulates the same story in terms of his experience and outlook:

> I have always been glad to meet people. . . . It really started when I became a teller. The teller is the most important position in a bank as far as meeting people goes. As teller, you must meet everyone. You learn to know everybody by his first name. You don't have the same opportunity again to meet people. Right now we have a teller who is very capable but two or three people have come to me complaining about him. He is unfriendly with them. I told him, you've got to have a kind word for everyone. It's a personal and a business matter.

This keynote brings out the decisive interest of local influentials in all manner of personal contacts which enable them to establish themselves when they need political, business, or other support. Influentials in this group act on the explicit assumption that they can be locally prominent and influential by lining up enough people who know them and are hence willing to help them as well as be helped by them.

The cosmopolitan influentials, on the other hand, have notably little interest in meeting *as many* people as possible.[8] They are more selective in their choice of friends and acquaintances. They typically stress the importance of confining themselves to friends with whom "they can really talk," with whom they can "exchange ideas." If the local influentials are quantitativists, the cosmopolitans are qualitativists in this regard. It is not *how many* people they know but the *kind of people* they know that counts.[9]

The contrast with the prevailing attitudes of local influentials is brought out in these remarks by cosmopolitan influentials:

> I don't care to know people unless there is something to the person.

> I am not interested in quantity. I like to know about other people; it broadens your own education. I enjoy meeting people with knowledge and standing. Masses of humanity I don't go into. I like to meet people of equal mentality, learning and experience.

8. This was interestingly confirmed in the following fashion. Our informants were confronted with a random list of names of Rovere residents and were asked to identify each. Local influentials recognized more names than any other group of informants, and cosmopolitans, in turn, knew more persons than the non-influential informants.

9. In this pilot study, we have confined ourselves to the expression of attitudes toward personal contacts and relations. A detailed inquiry would examine the quantum and quality of *actual* personal relations characteristic of the local and cosmopolitan influentials.

Just as with the local influentials, so here the basic attitude cuts across occupational and educational lines. Professional men among the cosmopolitans, for example, do not emphasize the importance of a wide and extensive acquaintanceship, if one is to build up a practice. In contrast to a "local" attorney who speaks of the "advantage to me to know as many people as possible," a "cosmopolitan" attorney waxes poetic and exclusive all in one, saying:

> I have never gone out and sought people. I have no pleasure in just going around and calling. As Polonius advised Laertes,
>
> > "Those friends thou hast, and their adoption tried,
> > Grapple them to thy soul with hoops of steel,
> > But do not dull the palm with entertainment
> > Of each new-hatch'd unfledged comrade. . . ."

In a later section of this study, we shall see that these diverse orientations of locals and cosmopolitans toward personal relations can be interpreted as a function of their distinctive modes of achieving influence. At the moment, it is sufficient to note that locals seek to enter into manifold networks of personal relations, whereas the cosmopolitans, *on the same status level*, explicitly limit the range of these relations.

PARTICIPATION IN VOLUNTARY ORGANIZATIONS

In considering the sociability of locals and cosmopolitans, we examined their attidues toward informal, personal relationships. But what of their roles in the more formal agencies for social contact: the voluntary organizations?

As might be anticipated, both types of influentials are affiliated with more organizations than rank-and-file members of the population. Cosmopolitan influentials belong to an average of eight organizations per individual, and the local influentials, to an average of six. This suggests the possibility that cosmopolitans make greater use of organizational channels to influence than of personal contacts, whereas locals, on the whole, operate contrariwise.

But as with sociability, so with organizations: the more instructive facts are qualitative rather than quantitative. It is not so much that the cosmopolitans belong to *more* organizations than the locals. Should a rigorous inquiry bear out this impression, it would still not locate the strategic organizational differences between the two. It is, rather, that they belong to different types of organizations. And once again, these differences reinforce what we have learned about the two kinds of influentials.

The local influentials evidently crowd into those organizations which are largely designed for "making contacts," for establishing personal ties. Thus, they are found largely in the secret societies (Masons), fraternal organizations (Elks), and local service clubs—the Rotary, Lions, and the Kiwanis, the most powerful organization of this type in Rovere. Their participation appears to be less a matter of furthering the nominal objectives of these organizations than of using them as *contact centers*. In the forthright words of one local influential, a businessman:

> I get to know people through the service clubs; Kiwanis, Rotary, Lions. I now belong only to the Kiwanis. Kiwanis is different from any other service club. You have to be asked to join. They pick you out first, check you first. Quite a few influential people are there and I get to meet them at lunch every week.

The cosmopolitans, on the other hand, tend to belong to those organizations in which they can exercise their special skills and knowledge. They are found in professional societies and in hobby groups. At the time of the inquiry, in 1943, they were more often involved in Civilian Defense organizations where again they were presumably more concerned with furthering the objectives of the organization than with establishing personal ties.

Much the same contrast appears in the array of public offices held by the two types of influentials. Seven of each type hold some public office, although the locals have an average somewhat under one office. The primary difference is the *type* of office held. The locals tend to hold political posts—street commissioner, mayor, township boards, etc.—ordinarily obtained through political and personal relationships. The cosmopolitans, on the other hand, more often appear in public positions which involve not merely political operations but the utilization of special skills and knowledge (*e.g.*, Board of Health, Housing Committee, Board of Education).

From all this we can set out the hypothesis that participation in voluntary associations[10] has somewhat different functions for cosmopolitan and local influentials. Cosmopolitans are concerned with associations primarily because of the activities of these organizations. They are means for extending or exhibiting their skills and knowledge. Locals are primarily interested in associations not for their activities, but because these provide a means for extending personal relationships. The basic orientations of local and cosmopolitan influentials are thus diversely expressed in organizational behavior as in other respects.

Avenues to Interpersonal Influence

The foregoing differences in attachment to Rovere, sociability, and organizational behavior help direct us to the different avenues to influence traveled by the locals and the cosmopolitans. And in mapping these avenues we shall fill in the background needed to interpret the differences in communications behavior characteristic of the two types of influentials.

10. For types and functions of participation in such organizations, see Bernard Barber, "Participation and mass apathy in associations," in Alvin W. Gouldner (ed.), *Studies in Leadership* (New York: Harper & Brothers, 1950), 477–504.

The locals have largely grown up in and with the town. For the most part, they have gone to school there, leaving only temporarily for their college and professional studies. They held their first jobs in Rovere and earned their first dollars from Rovere people. When they came to work out their career-pattern, Rovere was obviously the place in which to do so. It was the only town with which they were thoroughly familiar, in which they knew the ins and outs of politics, business, and social life. It was the only community which they knew and, equally important, which knew them. Here they had developed numerous personal relationships.

And this leads to the decisive attribute of the local influentials' path to success: far more than with the cosmopolitans, *their influence rests on an elaborate network of personal relationships*. In a formula which at once simplifies and highlights the essential fact, we can say: *the influence of local influentials rests not so much on what they know but on whom they know*.

Thus, the concern of the local influential with personal relations is in part the product and in part the instrument of his particular type of influence. The "local boy who makes good," it seems, is likely to make it through good personal relations. Since he is involved in personal relations long before he has entered seriously upon his career, it is the path of less resistance for him to continue to rely upon these relations as far as possible in his later career.

With the cosmopolitan influential, all this changes. Typically a newcomer to the community, he does not and cannot utilize personal ties as his chief claim to attention. He usually comes into the town fully equipped with the prestige and skills associated with his business or profession and his "worldly" experience. He begins his climb in the prestige-structure at a relatively high level. It is the prestige of his previous achievements and previously acquired skills which make him eligible for a place in the local influence-structure. Personal relations are much more the product than the instrumentality of his influence.

These differences in the location of career-patterns have some interesting consequences for the problems confronting the two types of influentials. First of all, there is some evidence, though far from conclusive, that the rise of the locals to influentiality is slow compared with that of the cosmopolitans. Dr. A, a minister, cosmopolitan, and reader of newsmagazines, remarked upon the ease with which he had made his mark locally:

> The advantage of being a minister is that *you don't have to* prove yourself. You are immediately accepted and received in all homes, including the best ones. [Italics inserted.]

However sanguine this observation may be, it reflects the essential point that the newcomer who has "arrived" in the outside world, sooner takes his place among those with some measure of influence in the local community. In contrast, the local influentials *do* "have to prove" themselves. Thus, the local bank president who required some forty years to rise from his job as messenger boy, speaks feelingly of the slow, long road on which "I worked my way up."

The age-composition of the local and cosmopolitan influentials is also a straw in the wind with regard to the rate of rise to influence. All but two of the sixteen locals are over forty-five years of age, whereas fewer than two-thirds of the cosmopolitans are in this older age group.

Not only may the rate of ascent to influence be slower for the local than for the cosmopolitan, but the ascent involves some special difficulties deriving from the local's personal relations. It appears that these relations may hinder as well as help the local boy to "make good." He must overcome the obstacle of being intimately known to the community when he was "just a kid." He must somehow enable others to recognize his consistent change in status. Most importantly, people to whom he was once subordinate must be brought to the point of now recognizing him as, in some sense, superordinate. Recognition of this problem is not new. Kipling follows Matthew 13 in observing that "prophets have honour all over the Earth, except in the village where they were born." The problem of ascent in the influence-structure for the home-town individual may be precisely located in sociological terms: change of status within a group, particularly if it is fairly rapid, calls for the revamping of attitudes toward the mobile individual and the remaking of relations with him. The pre-existent structure of personal relations for a time thus restrains the ascent of the local influential. Only when he has broken through these established conceptions of him, will others accept the reversal of roles entailed in the rise of the local man to influence. A Rovere attorney, numbered among the local influentials, describes the pattern concisely:

> When I first opened up, people knew me so well in town that they treated me as if I still were a kid. It was hard to overcome. But after I took interest in various public and civic affairs, and became chairman of the Democratic organization and ran for the State legislature—knowing full well I wouldn't be elected—they started to take me seriously.

The cosmopolitan does not face the necessity for breaking down local preconceptions of himself before it is possible to have his status as an influential "taken seriously." As we have seen, his credentials are found in the prestige and authority of his attainments elsewhere. He thus manifests less interest in a wide range of personal contacts for two reasons. First, his influence stems from prestige rather than from reciprocities with others in the community. Secondly, the problem of disengaging himself from obsolete images of him as "a boy" does not exist for him, and consequently does not focus his attention upon personal relations as it does for the local influential.

The separate roads to influence traveled by the locals and cosmopolitans thus help account for their diverging orientations toward the local community, with all that these orientations entail.

Social Status in Action: Interpersonal Influence

At this point, it may occur to the reader that the distinction between the local and cosmopolitan influentials is merely a reflection of differences in education or occupation. This does not appear to be the case.

It is true that the cosmopolitans among our interviewees have received more formal education than the locals. All but one of the cosmopolitans as compared with half of the locals are at least graduates of high school. It is also true that half of the locals are in "big business," as gauged by Rovere standards, whereas only two of the fourteen cosmopolitans fall in this group; and further-more, that half of the cosmopolitan influentials are professional people as compared with fewer than a third of the locals.

But these differences in occupational or educational status do not appear to determine the diverse types of influentials. When we compare the behavior and orientations of professionals among the locals and cosmopolitans, their characteristic differences persist, even though they have the same types of occupation and have received the same type of education. Educational and occupational differences may *contribute* to the differences between the two types of influentials but they are not the *source* of these differences. Even as a professional, the local influential is more of a businessman and politician in his behavior and outlook than is the cosmopolitan. He utilizes personal relationships as an avenue to influence conspicuously more than does his cosmopolitan counterpart. In short, *it is the pattern of utilizing social status and not the formal contours of the status itself which is decisive.*[11]

While occupational status may be a major support for the cosmopolitan's rise to influence, it is merely an adjunct for the local. Whereas all five of the local professionals actively pursue local politics, the cosmopolitan professionals practically ignore organized political activity in Rovere. (Their offices tend to be honorary appointments.) Far from occupation serving to explain the differences between them, it appears that the same occupation has a different role in inter-personal influence according to whether it is pursued by a local or a cosmopoli-tan. This bears out our earlier impression that "objective attributes" (education, occupation, etc.) do not suffice as indices of people exercising interpersonal influence.

The influential businessman, who among our small number of interviewees is found almost exclusively among the locals, typically utilizes his personal relations to enhance his influence. It is altogether likely that a larger sample would include businessmen who are cosmopolitan influentials and whose

11. The importance of actively seeking influence is evident from an analysis of "the upward mobile type," set forth in the monograph upon which this report is based. See also Granville Hicks, *Small Town* (New York: The Macmillan Co., 1946), 154, who describes a man who is evidently a local influential in these terms: "He is a typical politician, a born manipulator, a man who worships influence, *works hard to acquire it*, and does his best to convince other people that he has it." (Italics supplied.)

behavior differs significantly in this respect. Thus, Mr. H., regarded as exerting great influence in Rovere, illustrates the cosmopolitan big-business type. He arrived in Rovere as a top executive in a local manufacturing plant. He has established few personal ties. But he is sought out for advice precisely because he has "been around" and has the aura of a man familiar with the outside world of affairs. His influence rests upon an imputed expertness rather than upon sympathetic understanding of others.

This adds another dimension to the distinction between the two types of influential. It appears that the cosmopolitan influential has a following because *he knows;* the local influential, because *he understands.* The one is sought out for his specialized skills and experience; the other, for his intimate appreciation of intangible but affectively significant details. The two patterns are reflected in prevalent conceptions of the difference between "the extremely competent but impersonal medical specialist" and the "old family doctor." Or again, it is not unlike the difference between the "impersonal social welfare worker" and the "friendly precinct captain," which we have considered in Chapter I. It is not merely that the local political captain provides food-baskets and jobs, legal and extra-legal advice, that he sets to rights minor scrapes with the law, helps the bright poor boy to a political scholarship in a local college, looks after the bereaved—that he helps in a whole series of crises when a fellow needs a friend, and, above all, a friend who "knows the score" and can do something about it. It is not merely that he provides aid which gives him interpersonal influence. It is *the manner in which the aid is provided.* After all, specialized agencies do exist for dispensing this assistance. Welfare agencies, settlement houses, legal aid clinics, hospital clinics, public relief departments—these and many other organizations are available. But in contrast to the professional techniques of the welfare worker which often represent in the mind of the recipient the cold, bureaucratic dispensation of limited aid following upon detailed investigation are the unprofessional techniques of the precinct captain who asks no questions, extracts no compliance with legal rules of eligibility and does not "snoop" into private affairs. The precinct captain is a prototype of the "local" influential.

Interpersonal influence stemming from specialized expertness typically involves some social distance between the advice-giver and the advice-seeker, whereas influence stemming from sympathetic understanding typically entails close personal relations. The first is the pattern of the cosmopolitan influential; the second, of the local influential. Thus, the operation of these patterns of influence gives a clue to the distinctive orientations of the two types of influentials.

There is reason to believe that further inquiry will find differing proportions of local and cosmopolitan influentials in different types of community structures. At least this implication can be provisionally drawn from the ongoing studies of technological and social change in a Pennsylvania city during the past fifty years being conducted by Dorothy S. Thomas, Thomas C. Cochran and their colleagues.[12] Their detailed historical and sociological analysis yields the finding that the city comprised two distinct types of population: "fairly permanent residents, many of whom had been born there, and a migrating group that continually came and went." On the basis of crude statistics of turnover of population in other American cities, the investigators conclude further that this condition is fairly widespread. It may well be that the first, more nearly permanent group includes the local type of influential and the second, relatively transient group, the cosmopolitan. Diverse types of communities presumably have differing proportions of the two kinds of population and of the two kinds of influentials.

Other recent studies have found more directly that the proportions and social situations of the two types of influentials vary as the social structure of the community varies. Eisenstadt reports, for example, that a traditional Yemenite community almost entirely lacks the cosmopolitan type, whereas both cosmopolitans and locals play their distinctive roles in several other communities under observation.[13] On the basis of Stouffer's study of civil liberties, David Riesman suggests ways in which the roles of local and cosmopolitan influentials may differ in different social structures. Cosmopolitans who take on positions of formal leadership in the community, he suggests, may be obliged to become middlemen of tolerance, as they are caught between the upper millstone of the tolerant élite and the nether one of the intolerant majority, and thus become shaped into being less tolerant than their former associates and more so than their constituency. As a result of differing structural context, also, cosmopolitans among the community leaders, themselves more "tolerant" of civil liberties than others, may be in more vulnerable situations in the South than in the East and West. For Stouffer has found that among all but the college-educated, Southerners are far less tolerant of civil liberties than Northerners of like education; "This means," Riesman points out, "that the college graduate in the South is, in these respects, quite sharply cut off from the rest of the community, including even those with some college attendance, for although education is everywhere associated with tolerance, the gradations are much less steep in the North.

12. As reported by Thomas C. Cochran, "History and the social sciences," in *Relazioni del X Congresso Internazionale di Scienze Storiche* (Rome, 4–11 September 1955), I, 481–504, at 487–488 on the basis of Sidney Goldstein, *Patterns of Internal Migration in Norristown, Pennsylvania, 1900–1950*, 2 volumes (Ph.D. thesis, multigraphed), University of Pennsylvania, 1953.

13. S. N. Eisenstadt, "Communication systems and social structure: an exploratory comparative study," *Public Opinion Quarterly*, 1955, 19, 154–167. A study of a small Southern town reports that the two types of influentials cannot be distinguished there; the present suggestion holds that, with the accumulation of research, it is no longer enough to report the presence or absence of the types of influentials. Rather, it is sociologically pertinent to search out the attributes of the social structure which make for varying proportions of these identifiable types of influentials. See A. Alexander Fanelli, "A typology of community leadership based on influence and interaction within the leader subsystem," *Social Forces*, 1956, 34, 332–338.

Moreover, much the same is true in the South for metropolitan communities against smaller cities, though in this dimension there are substantial differences in the East as well."[14]

From this evidence which is only now being accumulated, it would seem that the emergence of the two types of influentials depends upon characteristic forms of environing social structure with their distinctive functional requirements.

Against this background of analysis it is now possible to consider more fully the utilization of mass communications by the two types of influentials.

The Communications Behavior of Influentials

It appears that communications behavior is part and parcel of the routines of life and basic orientations characteristic of the two types of influentials. Their selections of magazines, newspapers, and radio programs at once reflect and reinforce the basic orientations. Although the *motives* of their selection of materials from the vast flow of mass communications may vary widely, the psychological and social *functions* fulfilled by the selection are fairly limited. Since the local and cosmopolitan make distinctly different demands of their social environment, they utilize mass communications for distinctly different results.

PATTERNS AND FUNCTIONS OF MAGAZINE READING

Cosmopolitan influentials apparently read more magazines—subscribing to four or five—than the locals, with their subscriptions to two or three. This is to be anticipated from what we know of their respective routines of life and orientations. The cosmopolitans, with their extra-local interests, devote themselves more fully to the kind of vicarious experience set forth in journals, whereas the locals are more immediately concerned with direct interpersonal relations. The one tends to read about the great world outside, the other, to act in the little world inside. Their reading practices reflect their ways of life.

It is the variations in the *types* of magazines read by the locals and cosmopolitans, however, which more directly indicate the functions of these reading patterns. The influential reader of the newsmagazine, for example, is prevalently of the cosmopolitan rather than the local type. This is entirely expectable, in the light of the functions fulfilled by a magazine such as *Time*.

The newsmagazine provides news and views on a broad front. Promising to give its version of the news behind the news, it deals with current developments in national and international politics, industry and business, education, science, the arts. These constitute the very spheres in which the influence of the

14. Samuel A. Stouffer, *Communism, Conformity, and Civil Liberties* (New York: Doubleday & Company 1955) provides the findings under review by David Riesman in his article, "Orbits of tolerance, interviewers, and elites," *Public Opinion Quarterly*, 1956, 20, 49–73.

cosmopolitans is to be found; for, as we have seen, they are considered the expert arbiters of "good taste," or "culture," and of trends in the Great Society. By the same token, the national newsmagazine had little to say to the local influentials. It does not, after all, devote much space to Rovere and its environs. The reading of *Time* will contribute neither to the locals' understanding of Rovere life nor to their influence in the town. It is an entirely dispensable luxury.

For the cosmopolitan, however, the newsmagazine serves several functions. It provides a transmission-belt for the diffusion of "culture" from the outside world to the "cultural leaders" of Rovere. (This is particularly true for the women among the cosmopolitans.) Among the little coteries and clubs of like-minded cosmopolitans, it provides the stuff of conversation. It enables the cultural élite of Rovere's middle class to remain well in advance of those who seek them out for advice in matters of taste or for opinions concerning the trend of international developments. *Time* not only builds a bridge across the gulf between the cosmopolitan influential and the influenced; it helps maintain the gulf separating the knower from the uninformed. It thus supplies diverse gratifications for the cosmopolitans of Rovere. It enables them to retain a kind of contact with the world outside and reduces their sense of cultural isolation. It gives some a sense of "self-improvement," as they "keep up with things." It enables them to buttress their own position in the community, by enabling them to flourish their credentials of knowledgeability when the occasion demands.

But since these are not the grounds of influence for the local influentials, since their social roles do not entail judgments about "culture" and the world at large, journals such as *Time* are superfluous.

Gratifications derived from mass communications, therefore, are not merely psychological in nature; they are also a product of the distinctive *social roles* of those who make use of these communications. It is not that the newsmagazine is *one man's meat* and *another man's poison*. It is, rather, that the newsmagazine is meat for one *social type* and poison for another *social type*. The analysis of the functions of mass communications requires prior analysis of the social roles which determine the uses to which these communications can and will be put. Had the social contexts of interpersonal influence not been explored, we could not have anticipated the selection of *Time* by one type of influential and its rejection by another.

Much the same can be said of the further magazine-reading of Rovere influentials. It so happens that for our handful of cases, the reading of *Time* most clearly differentiates the locals and the cosmopolitans. But the same patterns of selection operate with other magazines. *Atlantic Monthly, Harper's, National Geographic*—the so-called "class" magazines which devote much of their content to foreign and national affairs and to the arts are read by twice as many cosmopolitans as locals. For virtually all other magazines, there seems to be no difference between the two. *Reader's Digest* and *Life* appear with equal frequency. A large-scale study could readily check the impression that *upon the same educational level*, local and cosmopolitan influentials have different patterns of magazine reading and that these can be explained in terms of the magazines satisfying distinctly different functions for the two groups.

PATTERNS AND FUNCTIONS OF NEWSPAPER READING

Reading national newsmagazines is an act above and beyond the call of dutiful newspaper reading. It implies an interest in being "in on things," in "developing responsible opinions," in having a "distinctive point of view." Interestingly enough, it appears that the patterns of newspaper reading also reflect the different orientations of the local and the cosmopolitan influential.

Locals read more newspapers, but this is wholly accounted for by their greater proclivity for Rovere and other local newspapers (in a nearby city). The picture is quite different for metropolitan newspapers. Every one of the cosmopolitans reads the *New York Times* or the *New York Herald Tribune*, or both, while the locals less often turn to these papers with their wide and analytical coverage of world news. The contrast extends to details. Almost half of the locals read New York tabloids, with their capsule treatments of world affairs and their emphasis on "human interest" news—murder, divorce, and daring crimes appear to be major foci of contemporary human interest—but only one cosmopolitan includes a tabloid in his newspaper diet. However these statistical distributions might turn out in a detailed study, the consistency of these exploratory facts suggests that the basic orientations of influentials are also expressed in their patterns of newspaper reading.

PATTERNS AND FUNCTIONS OF LISTENING TO RADIO NEWS COMMENTATORS

There is some evidence that the predilection of cosmopolitans for an impersonal, analytical understanding of world events is reflected in their routines of listening to radio news commentators. On the basis of an earlier study by the Bureau of Applied Social Research, commentators were classified according to the degree to which they "analyzed" rather than "reported" news, particularly world news. The cosmopolitans prefer the more analytical commentators (Swing, Hughes) while the locals are more interested in those who forego analysis and are virtually newscasters (Thomas, Goddard, etc.).

Even in the realm of "extra-local news," the locals manage to import a localistic criterion. They distinctly prefer those commentators who typically convert news and public issues into *personalized* anecdotes. Gabriel Heatter with his infusions of sentiment into political and economic affairs is a favorite of the locals but not of the cosmopolitans. So, too, with Walter Winchell, who reports the Broadway version of intimate gossip across the backfence and personalizes national and international issues. The local influentials seek out the personal ingredients in the impersonal array of world news.

Communications behavior thus appears to reflect the basic orientations of local and cosmopolitan influentials. Further inquiry should provide a sound statistical check and make more rigorous tests of these impressions. Do locals and influentials who read "the *same*" magazines, for example, actually select the same contents in these magazines? Or do the locals characteristically focus upon the "personalized and localistic" components in the editorial material, whereas the cosmopolitans seek out the more impersonal and "informative" components? To what uses do these different types of readers put the materials which they have read? In other words, how do the contents of mass communications enter into the flow of interpersonal influence?[15] Studies in the sociology of mass communications must supplement analyses in terms of personal attributes of readers and listeners with analyses of their social roles and their implication in networks of interpersonal relations. . . .

15. This is precisely the focus in the study of influence patterns by Elihu Katz and P. F. Lazarsfeld, *Personal Influence* (New York: The Free Press, 1955).

Salience of Membership and Resistance to Change of Group-Anchored Attitudes

Harold H. Kelley

A BASIC finding in social psychology is that the attitudes a person holds depend in part upon his social contacts and particularly upon the groups in which he holds membership. At the same time, it is apparent that the typical individual, at least in our own culture, simultaneously belongs to a number of different organizations and is associated with a variety of groups. While these different sources of attitude anchorage sometimes mutually reinforce one another or affect non-overlapping areas of attitudes, they often exert contradictory influences upon the person. This phenomenon, termed *"cross-pressures,"* has been investigated primarily with respect to political issues.[1]

An important problem created by the existence of cross-pressures is whether, as an individual moves from one situation to another, there are concurrent variations in the extent to which his various social affiliations operate to support his attitudes and to determine the opinions he holds. We might expect that at any given moment conformity to a specific group's norms will depend upon the degree to which cues associated with that group successfully compete with other cues in the individual's environment, capture his attention, and arouse his conformity motives. The phenomenon singled out for consideration in the present research has to do with situational variations in

Reprinted from *Human Relations*, 3: 275–289, 1955, by permission of the author and the publisher.

1. M. Kriesberg, "Cross-Pressures and Attitudes," *Public Opinion Quarterly*, 13: 5–16, 1949; and P. F. Lazarsfeld, B. Berelson, and Hazel Gaudet, *The People's Choice*, 2d ed., New York: Columbia University Press, 1948.

whether or not symbols or "reminders" of a specific group are present for its members and the effects of this variation upon their resistance to communications contrary to the group's norms.

The degree to which, in a given situation, a specific group is present and prominent in a person's awareness is termed the *salience* of that group. In some instances high salience corresponds to presence in the center of the person's attention, but it is not the intention here to restrict the notion to instances where there is a fully conscious or reportable awareness of the group. Possible differences in the salience of the various aspects of the group or its norms will be disregarded and reference will be made only to general salience of the group, on the tentative assumption that salience of any aspect of the group heightens the tendency to conform to its norms at that particular time.

Several theoretical discussions are pertinent to this problem. In an outline of the psychological consequences of minority group membership, Lewin noted that sometimes a person's belonging to one group is dominant and sometimes his belonging to another. At any given time, the dominant group largely determines the person's feelings and actions. Lewin considered the particular group that dominates in a given situation to be related to the characteristics of that situation.[2] Elsewhere, he took account of the effects of motivational factors upon the relative dominance of different sets of behavioral and attitudinal determinants. In this regard, he postulated that an increase in the intensity of the need related to a certain goal increases the relative potency (read "salience") of the situation containing that goal.[3] Thus, it would seem reasonable to expect persons who are strongly motivated to achieve or maintain membership in a given group to relate controversial questions to its norms, whether or not the group or its symbols are immediately present.

Other related discussions are those which attempt to account for inconsistency in attitudes and behavior.[4] It is common knowledge that expressed opinions vary from situation to situation and often exhibit apparent self-contradictions. Undoubtedly, some of these variations are due to conformity to the social pressures of the moment and represent a more or less conscious, opportunistic attempt to avoid criticism and obtain approval. However, it is also possible that the apparent disregard for the norms of a group, which at other times and places plays an active part in the determination of attitudes and behavior, reflects its temporary absence as a psychological force.

Recently, Eugene and Ruth Hartley have discussed the problem of "evoking

2. K. Lewin, "Psycho-Sociological Problems of a Minority Group," *Character and Personality*, 3:175–187, 1935.

3. K. Lewin, "The Conceptual Representation and the Measurement of Psychological Forces," *Contributions to Psychological Theory*, 1:34–35, no. 4, 1938.

4. For example, cf. I. Chein, M. Deutsch, H. Hyman, and Marie Jahoda (eds.), "Consistency and Inconsistency in Intergroup Relations," *Journal of Social Issues*, Vol. 5, no. 3, 1949.

specific reference groups."[5] They describe several relevant findings, for example, the "interviewer effects" found in public opinion polling, which can be interpreted in terms of variations in the group roles that respondents assume when confronted by different social situations.

An investigation by Charters and Newcomb[6] was specifically directed at the problem of the effects of the immediate social situation upon opinions expressed on an attitude questionnaire. They administered the questionnaire to three comparable groups of Roman Catholics under the following conditions:

1. In a large class with many other students.
2. In a small group by themselves, but with no mention of their church membership or of the reason for their being together.
3. In a small group by themselves where, before answering the questionnaire, they were told that they had been called together as Catholics in order to obtain their help in constructing a questionnaire on religious beliefs and were asked to discuss the "basic assumptions" underlying the opinions of all Catholics.

In the last variation, the common religious affiliations of all subjects in the room was repeatedly emphasized. In all three variations, the subjects anonymously answered a questionnaire that contained, among other items, a number of critical ones related to Catholic norms but so worded that they could also be answered by the subjects in their roles as members of other groups. The results showed that subjects in the third variation answered these critical items more in the manner prescribed for Catholics than did subjects in the other two variations.

There is some ambiguity as to whether this result is, as the authors suggest, due simply to "heightening the individual's awareness of his membership in the specified group by vivid reminders of this membership" (p. 415). First is the possibility that the initial discussion of "basic assumptions" in the third variation gave the Catholics new information about their church's values, which enabled them to conform more closely than did their prior, less clear conceptions of the norms. Charters and Newcomb attempted to minimize this by asking their discussion leaders to avoid discussing what Catholics *should* believe or the opinions they would give on specific issues. Another possibility is that the subjects were motivated to answer as "good" Catholics. For example, being aware that all persons in the room were Catholics, the subjects may have foreseen the possibility that the data would be examined to determine how uniformly Catholics adhere to their church's norms and the subjects may have

5. E. L. Hartley and Ruth E. Hartley, *Fundamentals of Social Psychology*, New York: Alfred A. Knopf, Inc., 1952, pp. 478–481.

6. W. W. Charters, Jr., and T. M. Newcomb, "Some Attitudinal Effects of Experimentally Increased Salience of a Membership Group," in G. E. Swanson, T. M. Newcomb, and E. L. Hartley, eds., *Readings in Social Psychology*, rev. ed., New York: Henry Holt, Inc., 1952, pp. 415–420.

wanted to have their religious group make a good showing in this respect. Again, the investigators attempted to eliminate this factor by instructing the subjects to give their own personal opinions. Charters and Newcomb conclude from their findings that "an individual's expression of attitudes is a function of the relative momentary potency of his relevant group memberships" (p. 420).

If, as this suggests, situational cues affect the opinions a person expresses, they may also affect his resistance to counternorm communications. It would seem reasonable to assume that the salience of a group determines its availability as a possible source of resistance to change, the strength of the resistance being determined by other factors, such as how highly membership is valued. The purpose of the present experiment was to test the following hypothesis: When group-anchored attitudes are exposed to counter-pressures, their resistance to change at the particular time will be greater with high salience of the relevant group than with low. In addition, the procedure was designed so as to determine whether the phenomenon described by Charters and Newcomb would appear under more rigorous conditions than theirs, where subjects are mixed together in terms of their religious affiliation and are not told that this factor is involved in the investigation.

A further purpose of this study was to obtain some initial evidence on the relative permanency of attitudinal changes accomplished under conditions of high and low salience. If it proves to be true that a communication will produce more immediate change when opposing group norms are at a low level of salience than when they are highly salient, this might suggest that where group anchorage is important a communicator would be wise to approach his audience when the pertinent group is in the background and they are preoccupied with other loyalties and interests. However, the problem immediately arises as to the fate, with the passage of time, of changes produced under these conditions. When the group becomes salient in subsequent situations, we might expect the resistance to the communication to be restored and to produce a reversion to the old attitudes. This would reduce the difference in final attitudes between persons initially with low salience and those initially with high. There are still other lines of reasoning that lead one to expect changes produced under conditions fostering low salience to be maintained *less well* than those produced under conditions fostering high salience (cf. Discussion).

Procedure

Attitudes of members of the Roman Catholic Church were studied within high school and college age groups. This particular group membership was chosen in order to provide the possibility of comparing the results with those of Charters and Newcomb. The experiment was conducted during regular class sessions when members of all religious faiths were present and when, because of the presence of cues related to competing loyalties and interests, the salience of any particular religious affiliation could be expected to be relatively low.

The students were first given short readings, some of them receiving material intended to heighten the salience of Catholic membership and others receiving unrelated "neutral" material. They then answered an opinion questionnaire containing items that were related to Catholic norms but were carefully selected so as to involve other roles and memberships and to heighten the salience of Catholic membership as little as possible. In addition, two out of every three of the subjects received, as part of the questionnaire, a communication intended to modify their opinion responses. This was done by including for each item in their questionnaire, information purporting to give the opinion of the typical student at the same level in school. The "typical opinions" were indicated at positions fairly divergent from those most acceptable to Catholics and thus constituted a counternorm communication for them.

Through appropriate combinations of these materials, two main experimental conditions were created:

1. Communication, high salience.
2. Communication, low salience.

In addition, an experimental condition with no communication and high salience was used in order to check upon the effectiveness of the communication. A random procedure was used for assigning subjects to each experimental variation, so the subjects within the three samples can be assumed to be comparable initially, within the limits of sampling error. The basic data consist of a comparison of the attitudes expressed by members of various religious groups under these conditions, the questionnaire providing an immediate after-test of the experimental treatments.

Three days after the initial testing, most of the subjects were given a delayed after-test. The same questionnaire was readministered, but this time under the "no communication, high salience" condition for all subjects. The data from this delayed after-test provide the means for studying the loss of the initial opinion shifts as time passes and church membership becomes salient for all Catholic subjects.

The specific characteristics of the subjects and details of the procedure are as follows:

1. SUBJECTS

Two hundred and seven third-year students in a public high school and 247 second- and third-year students in a metropolitan university. The experimental procedure was carried out during regular class sessions (high-school English classes and introductory college courses in psychology and sociology) where students of various religious faiths were present. In order to avoid one extraneous possibility of salience arousal, the question of religious affiliation was not raised at any time during the experiment.

For the high-school Ss, identification of religious affiliation (whether "Catholic," "Jewish," or "other") was made on the basis of family names.

The judgments as to inclusion in the first two categories were made by two judges independently and with very high agreement. Only those names on which both judges agreed were included among the "Catholics." (These consisted mainly of Italian and Irish names and, in a few instances, Polish. Demographic studies of the community in which the high school is located show that over 95 per cent of persons from these national backgrounds are Catholics.) The classification "Jewish" was established to provide a category that could be assumed to contain virtually no Catholics. The results from the "Jewish" and "other" classifications proved to be so similar that they were combined to provide a single category of "non-Catholics." Religious affiliation of the college Ss was determined by a direct question asked at the conclusion of the experiment.

2. INTRODUCTORY INSTRUCTIONS

After being introduced by the class instructor, the experimenter gave instructions, the essence of which is as follows: "We've been making a study of the opinions of students in this area. With you, we'd like to try a somewhat different procedure from the usual. Before giving us your opinions on these questions, we want you to take your minds off the things you're thinking about now—your class work, things going on here at school, and your friends. To help you do this we want you to read some short articles. These have nothing to do with the questions we're going to ask but are simply articles about well-known men or organizations we thought you might find interesting. While you're reading these, relax and take your minds off the things you're thinking about now. Then we'll ask your opinions on various matters."

Booklets containing three articles and the questionnaire were distributed and the Ss were asked to give their birthday, sex, and (in the case of the high-school students) name. They were then instructed to begin with the first article and to read rapidly for a short time without turning to the questions.

3. READING-MATERIAL

The three articles dealt with either famous men or world organizations. (Classes receiving the "famous men" series at the first session received the "world organizations" series at the delayed after-test, and vice versa.) Only enough time was allowed for reading the first of the three articles, the content of which was varied in order to produce the high and low salience conditions. The other two articles were similar in content to the low salience reading. In the "famous men" series, the "high salience" article dealt with the life of Pope Pius XII and his role as international leader of the Catholic Church; the corresponding "low salience" reading summarized the life of (then) General Dwight D. Eisenhower. In the "world organizations" series, the "high salience" article described the world-wide missionary work of the Catholic Church; the "low salience" article described the work of UNESCO. (The "famous men" and "world organizations" series produced similar patterns of results and hence no distinction is made between them in the presentation of the data.)

All articles were selected from current books and magazines and were edited to ensure student interest. The "high salience" articles were carefully selected so as to contain no references to the issues raised in the opinion questionnaire. They constituted very favorable pictures of the Catholic Church, its activities, and leader, as drawn by outside observers. They were intended to make a Catholic feel proud of his church and, at the same time, bring his church membership into the forefront of his awareness.

4. OPINION QUESTIONNAIRE

After most Ss had finished reading the first article, the entire class was stopped and asked to complete the opinion questionnaire. The instructions included strong assurances that their answers would be treated confidentially.

The questionnaire consisted of 18 critical items, with six irrelevant "filler" items distributed among them. The critical items dealt with four broad topics, examples of which follow:

a. *Censorship* of books, movies, plays, etc.: "Censorship of books and movies is *not* good in our country; a truly free people must be allowed to choose their own reading and entertainment."

b. *Parental control* over children: "Parents should give their children complete freedom when it comes to deciding about matters like political and religious beliefs."

c. Traditionalism in *religious practices:* "Religion should move away from the traditional doctrines and practices and adapt itself to modern life."

d. *Loyalty* to nation versus loyalty to other organizations: "A person's loyalty to his country is far more important than his loyalty to any institution or organization of which he is a member."

Subjects responded to these items by indicating on a rating scale the extent of their agreement or disagreement with each. From the eighteen critical items, a total score was computed for each S, with a *high score representing a high degree of conformity to what the investigator prejudged to be the Catholic norms on these questions.*

5. COMMUNICATION

The communication delivered to certain of the Ss consisted of special check marks placed along the rating scales provided for responding to the questionnaire items. On the 18 critical items, these marks were placed in the half of the scale opposite the end thought to represent Catholic norms. These marks were placed in a standard pattern, which was the same for all subjects receiving the "communication."

Before the Ss started answering the questionnaire, the experimenter explained these marks as follows: "As I said before, we've already given these questions to a number of students in this area. We thought this might be more interesting for you if you could see how other students have answered these questions. So we've placed red check marks in your booklets to show where, *on the average*, other students have answered the questions. I'm sorry we didn't have time enough to put these check marks in all the booklets so some of you may not have them. Those of you who do have them need not pay any attention to them if you don't want to. Just give your own opinions about these matters."

For Ss given the communication, the initial opinion measurement constitutes a test given *immediately after* the communication since the S presumably responds to each item after reading it and noticing the location of the check mark. The effectiveness of this type of communication has previously been demonstrated. Kulp, for example, studied the effect of opinion responses attributed to various kinds of people (e.g. educators, lay citizens) and found that even unlabelled responses produce some effect.[7]

6. THE THREE EXPERIMENTAL CONDITIONS

The various reading-materials and the two versions of the questionnaire (with and without the special check marks) were combined into test booklets to produce three different experimental conditions:

  a. No communication, high salience.
  b. Communication, high salience,
  c. Communication, low salience.

The three types of test booklets were intermixed and distributed at random within each classroom. In the remainder of this paper, subjects will be identified in terms of the experimental booklet that they happened to receive during this first session.

7. DELAYED AFTER-TEST

For all high-school Ss and half of the college Ss, the above procedure was repeated in its major details three days later. However, at this time all Ss received the "no communication, high salience" set of materials, the purpose being to determine the relative retention under high salience conditions of opinion changes produced initially under different degrees of salience. The readministration of the procedure was explained to the subjects as an investigation of the variability of responses to the questionnaire. They were requested to try to answer the questions as if they had never seen them before and not to try to remember how they had answered them earlier.

---

7. D. H. Kulp, "II. Prestige, As Measured by Single-Experience Changes and Their Permanency," *Journal of Educational Research*, 27: 663–672, 1934.

Results

1. EFFECTS OF SALIENCE ON RESISTANCE TO CHANGE

The results for the high-school students are presented in Figure 1, where high scores represent close conformity to what were prejudged to be Catholic norms. The validity of this prejudgment is apparent from the fact that for the "no communication, high salience" variation the Catholic subjects showed significantly higher scores than the non-Catholic subjects (p. < .01). Thus, it seems clear that the questionnaire measures attitudinal dimensions on which Catholics differ from non-Catholics.

Figure I—The Effects on Attitude Scores of Variations in Salience of Catholic Membership for High-School Students

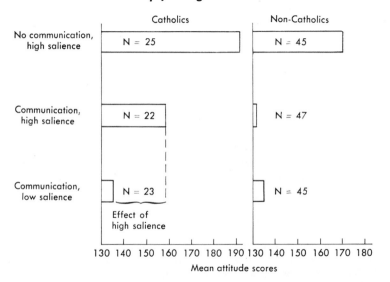

It is also evident in Figure 1 that the communication was effective in producing changes in attitude responses. The communication presented a more extreme position on the issues raised in the questionnaire than that taken by non-Catholics, so it operated to shift their responses as well as those of the Catholics. The difference between the "no communication, high salience" variation and the two communication samples is significant at beyond the one-per-cent level of confidence for both religious classifications.

The expectation of greater resistance to change for the Catholic subjects with high salience of their church than with low salience is borne out by the data in Figure 1. Of the Catholics receiving the communication, those for whom the church was highly salient showed higher attitude scores than those for whom it was not (p < .05 using a one-tailed test). Subjects of other religious affiliations who received the communication expressed much the same attitudes, whether receiving the salience-arousing materials or not, which is to be expected because the salience of the Catholic Church is not relevant to their attitude anchorage.

Table 1 presents the results for the college students. The evidence for the

Table I—The Effects on Attitude Scores of Variations in Salience of Catholic Membership for College Students

Experimental Condition	CATHOLICS		NON-CATHOLICS	
	N	Mean Score	N	Mean Score
No communication, high salience	36	178	42	147
Communication, high salience	32	157	53	123
Communication, low salience	39	162	45	127

relevance of the questionnaire and the effectiveness of the communication is similar to that obtained from the high-school students. In the "no communication, high salience" condition, Catholics score significantly higher than non-Catholics (p < .01). Subjects receiving the communication score lower than those without it, both for the Catholics (p < .01) and non-Catholics (p < .01).

With regard to salience and resistance to change, the results from the college students do not support the hypothesized relationship. Among Catholics receiving the communication, there is little difference between the scores of those in the "high salience" condition and those in the "low salience" one. So it appears that the experimental variation intended to produce differences in salience of Catholic membership failed to produce any difference in the Catholics' resistance to the communication.[8]

8. A correlational analysis was made of the college students' data, in which a tentative measurement of salience was substituted for the experimental manipulation. This measure of the degree to which their church membership was salient for Catholic college students in the testing-situation was based on answers to the instructions: "Write down the first things that come into your mind. Ready? Name two groups or organizations to which you belong." Catholic subjects who named a church group were considered as having their membership at a high level of salience and were compared with those mentioning other than church groups. The former subjects showed somewhat higher scores both within the samples receiving only the questionnaire (p = .06) and within the samples receiving the communication with the questionnaire (p = .28). These trends were especially marked (p = .06 and p < .05, respectively) for a part-score based only on the questionnaire items dealing with the topic of censorship. (Incidentally, it may be noted that this particular part-score appeared to be more sensitive than the other part-scores to the variations in salience produced experimentally for the high-school students.) In brief, this correlational analysis of the data for the college students yields some evidence, although somewhat tenuous, in support of the hypothesis that group members express more conforming attitudes when their membership is salient than when it is not, both when they are merely asked for their opinions and when they are exposed to a counternorm communication.

The trends described above remained even when age and a measure of valuation of membership (reported frequency of attendance at religious services) were taken into account. Both these variables were found to affect resistance to the counternorm communication. The

2. RETENTION OF CHANGES PRODUCED UNDER HIGH AND LOW SALIENCE

Because of the apparent failure of the experimental manipulation of salience with the Catholic college students, only the results from the Catholic high-school students will be considered from the point of view of the effect of salience upon the retention of opinion change. For subjects who were initially in the "no communication, high salience" condition there was virtually no change from the immediate to the delayed after-test. Since the two tests were given under identical conditions, the absence of any sizable change indicates that extraneous factors such as practice or intervening events did not systematically affect the results.

For the Catholic high-school students initially receiving the communication, a comparison of the high and low salience samples is shown in Figure 2. (The

Figure 2—Retention over Three-Day Interval of Opinion Changes Produced under Conditions of High and Low Salience

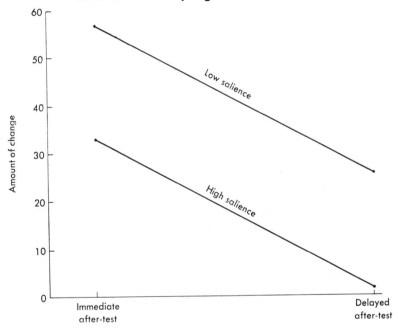

older Catholics were less influenced than the younger ones ($p < .01$) and the high-valuation members were less influenced than the low-valuation members ($p < .06$, using a one-tailed test). The latter finding is consistent with the finding by Kelley and Volkart ("The Resistance to Change of Group-Anchored Attitudes," *American Sociological Review*, 17: 453–465, 1952) that members' resistance to a counternorm communication is a direct function of how highly they value their membership in the group. Also consistent with that study was the finding that, although high- and low-valuation members apparently differed in their ability to withstand a counter-communication, they tended to express quite similar opinions in the absence of a communication of this type.

data for each sample are presented in terms of how much it differs from the "no communication" group, which serves as a control group.) It can be seen that both samples made large shifts on the delayed after-test in the direction of greater conformity to Catholic norms. The magnitude of this shift over the three-day interval was virtually identical for those given the communication initially under low salience and those exposed under high. In addition, it is apparent that the highs had returned to the level of the control (no communication) sample while the low salience sample still showed a sizable effect of the original communication. (For the difference between the high and low salience samples at the time of the delayed after-test, p = .06.) Thus the results bear out the common observation that the greater the initial change, the greater the opinion change shown on subsequent occasions. There is no evidence that changes induced under conditions of low salience tend to be lost completely or retained to any lesser degree than those produced under high salience.

Discussion

The experimental procedures intended to produce variation in salience of church membership were apparently successful with the high-school students. Although the correlational analysis of the college students' data (cf. footnote 8) suggests that their conformity may be related to salience of church membership, the attempt to vary salience experimentally for this population appears to have been quite ineffective. Several factors might account for this result. One possibility is that the Catholics sampled in a metropolitan college include large numbers who have drifted away from their church and feel little attachment to it. Consequently, heightening the salience of church membership would have little or no effect on their expressed opinions or resistance to counternorm communications. Another possibility is that college students are more sophisticated about how various controversial issues relate to the norms of their church, so that the questions on the opinion scale may have heightened the salience for all samples and thus eliminated the differences created by the reading materials.[9] As compared with a sample of high-school students, a sample of college-age Catholics would probably include more persons in both of these categories— those who have lost their earlier attachment to the church and those who have gained in awareness of the various implications of the church's norms. If these factors operated in the present case to attenuate the effects of the experimental

---

9. A related possibility is that students in college classes, and particularly those taking psychology, are especially aware that experiments often have hidden purposes. Consequently, they become interested in trying to figure out the purpose of any experimental procedure they are asked to follow. Even though they do not deduce the true purpose, their incorrect hypotheses may seriously modify their responses to the instructions. There is no reason to expect the effects of these "hunches" to cancel out one another and, hence, merely to contribute to the random error. It seems more likely that the various hypotheses will have enough in common to introduce systematic variance into the results.

salience-arousing cues, the phenomenon obtained with the high-school students may appear only for persons of high valuation of membership and relatively low sophistication about relevant opinion issues.

In general, we might expect a number of factors to determine the effects produced by situational variations in cues related to a given group. Whether or not such cues elicit increased conformity will depend upon whether or not the individual values his membership enough to find satisfaction in being like the other members and maintaining their approval. A problem for future research is whether the person who places very high value upon membership will be much affected by situational cues: he is more likely to furnish his own cues and to relate controversial questions to the group's norms whether or not it or its symbols are externally present. The specific kind of conformity behavior elicited by "reminders" of membership will be a function of the person's knowledge and beliefs about the kind of behavior that is expected and approved. In short, the effects of situational cues undoubtedly depend upon the various predispositional factors (e.g. valuation of membership, social rank, knowledge of norms) that have been found to affect the degree of conformity to group norms.

Assuming that a person is predisposed to conform to group norms and resist counter-communications when that membership is highly salient, there remains the question of the appropriate conditions for observing the effects of increases in salience. It is necessary, of course, that the group membership should exist initially at a low level of salience. This is accomplished, as in the present study, by finding a situation in which competing memberships or interests are aroused and active. Then, if variations in salience are to be detected in the person's expressed opinions, the questions used to elicit these opinions probably must tap areas of conflict between the influence of the group under study and the competing influences. Unless the measured opinions reflect an area of controversy or cross-pressures, there is no particular reason to expect opinions expressed with high salience of group membership to differ from those expressed with low. The existence of crosspressures is ensured in the procedure of the present study by the use of a counternorm communication. In the absence of such counter-pressures, whether or not there are variations in opinion associated with variations in salience may provide a means of determining the attitudinal areas in which a given group is in conflict with other attitude determinants. In this connection, it may be noted that in the present investigation the censorship items were most affected by variations in salience of Catholic membership. This suggests that, of the topics used in the questionnaire, the issue of censorship represents the most definite area of conflict between Catholic norms and other influences operating in the milieu of our subjects.

Of particular interest for further investigation is the problem of determining the conditions that affect the persistence of opinion changes produced under high and low salience. The above results indicate that in the specific circumstances of the present experiment, the greater immediate change made possible by low salience also appears at a later time. In other circumstances, particularly when group members encounter pro-norm opinions and become sharply aware of their earlier nonconformity, a complete loss of the initial change might be expected.

Several other theories would suggest not merely that the greater change produced under low salience will be completely lost, but that the end result will be a kind of boomerang effect, with the low salience condition giving rise to less persistent change than the high salience condition. One such possibility is that subsequent situations of high salience may produce guilt and anxiety among those persons initially low, if they become aware of having been caught off guard and seduced into deviating markedly from the group norms. One way of alleviating this guilt and of warding off possible social punishment for the nonconformity is to conform more closely to the group norms than ever before. As a result, those persons initially low in salience (and hence most influenced initially by the counternorm communication) would finally be more in conformity with the norms (and less in agreement with the communication) than those initially high.

A second mechanism would have almost the same end effect. If during the communication situation, the resistance stemming from the group can be aroused and dealt with, then the likelihood is increased that the change will endure through later situations in which the group happens to be salient. The problem becomes one of providing the person with a method either for resolving the conflict between the appeals of the communication and the counter-pressures of the group or for becoming adapted to it. This may involve revaluation of the group, redefining the issue, resigning oneself to a special role or position in the group, and so on. It may also be useful to prepare the individual for the social criticism that his new views will eventually evoke. The assumption here is simply that when a person changes an attitude in full awareness of the norm that has supported the old position, the reorganization produced will tend to have a better chance of enduring than one produced in the absence of the norm. Accordingly changes produced under high salience would endure more than those produced under low. This and other hypotheses related to the persistence of changes brought about under various conditions of salience require further experimental analysis.

Experiments in Group Belongingness

Leon Festinger

... I SHOULD like now to give a more detailed description of the procedure and results of an experiment[1] which I conducted to determine some of the conditions under which the behavior and attitudes of people toward other people are determined by the group membership labels of the people concerned. More specifically, the study dealt with a systematic investigation of the effect which knowledge of religious affiliation had in determining one's behavior toward other people.

I shall not try to report all there is to tell about the procedure and techniques used in conducting this experimental study. I shall only attempt to review the more salient features of the design as a necessary prelude to considering the results which we found.

The major theme was to gather a group of people in our laboratory who would function as a meeting of a club to elect officers for the club. It was further desired, for the purposes of the experiment, to have the membership of the "club" evenly divided as to Jewish and Catholic religious affiliation.

From the point of view of control over the factors which influence the situation and consequent ability to interpret our results unequivocally, there were a number of major problems which had to be solved.

How could we equate or control the previous history of interactions among the individuals concerned? In any existing group or real-life situation this history, through the attitudes which have developed in consequence of it, has an important bearing on behavior. For the purpose of not allowing this factor to obscure

Reprinted from James Miller, *Experiments in Social Process*, pp. 36–45, by permission of the author and the publishers, McGraw-Hill Book Company. Copyright 1950 by McGraw-Hill Book Company, Inc.

1. L. Festinger, "The Role of Group Belongingness in a Voting Situation," *Human Relations*, 1947, 154–180.

the variable which we wanted to observe in operation, we set up our group meetings so that the people involved were complete strangers to one another at the beginning. No one knew anyone else or anything about them—at least no more about them than he could surmise from looking at them.

This, however, only partly solves our problem. There are still, as everyone knows, marked differences among people. There are people we like at first sight, and there are people we do not like at first sight. With this powerful factor operating we would have a very difficult time singling out the effect which knowledge of religious affiliation had on behavior. Two solutions to this problem were devised, both of which were used.

One solution was to have exactly the same people, in exactly the same group, elect a club officer both before and after they knew the religious affiliation of the others. Accordingly, for half of the group meeting everyone referred to everyone else by means of an assigned number and no one knew the name or religion of anyone else in the group. Halfway through the meeting, on a pretext, it became necessary for everyone's name and religion to be written on a blackboard along side of their assigned number. The meeting then proceeded to further elections.

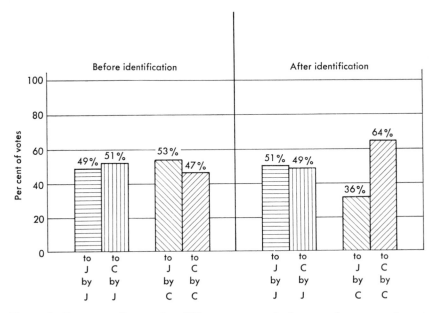

Figure I. Per cent of votes for different groups in face-to-face experiment

We were thus able to observe, for the same people, in the same group, in the same voting situation, what effect this knowledge of name and religion had on their voting preference.

Not completely satisfied with this control, however, we also decided to insert an even more rigorous one. Each group was composed of ten girls. They were told that each of the girls came from a different college in the Boston area. (This, incidentally, is quite plausible since there are more than enough such colleges to go around.) Actually, six of the girls at each meeting did come each from a different college. The other four girls, however, were paid participants. These same four paid participants were members of each group and were coached as to how to behave. When the time came for identification by name and by religion, two of these four said they were Jewish and the other two said they were Catholic. However, which two said they were Jewish and which two said they were Catholic changed from group to group. We were thus able to compare how many votes the same people received when identified as Jewish and when identified as Catholic.

We have thus succeeded in setting up a situation which it would be impossible to find in everyday life. The sum of these controls and safeguards enabled us, with a high degree of confidence, to single out changes in behavior due only to knowledge of religious affiliation.

Figure 1 shows the per cent of votes given to Jews and to Catholics before and after they were identified by name and religion. In this, and the subsequent figures, the first vertical bar shows the per cent of votes given to Jews by Jews; the second bar shows the per cent of votes given to Catholics by Jews; the third and fourth bars show the per cent of votes given to Jews and Catholics respectively by Catholics.

It is clear from the figure that before anyone was identified as to religion both the Jewish and the Catholic girls in the groups split their votes equally between Jews and Catholics. All the percentages hover about 50 per cent. We may come to the conclusion, which we certainly would have anticipated beforehand, that among a group as homogeneous as college girls, there is not enough difference among members of different religious groups to outweigh the wide variety of personality factors which make for being chosen an officer of a club.

The effect of knowing the name and religion of the other people introduces a considerable change in behavior. While the Jewish girls still split their votes about evenly between Jews and Catholics, the Catholic girls now give 64 per cent of their votes to Catholics and only 36 per cent to Jews.

Let us examine whether or not this holds up for our more rigorous comparison of votes given to the four paid participants when they identified themselves as Jewish and when they identified themselves as Catholic. The second figure shows these data.

We may see, by examining the figure, that the data are virtually identical with the data shown in the previous figure. Before the individuals are identified, both Jews and Catholics split their votes quite evenly between those who later on will be identified as Jewish and those who later will be identified as Catholics. All the percentages are very close to 50 per cent. After the identification is made, the pattern again changes markedly. The Jews still split their votes evenly between those paid participants who identify themselves as Jewish and those who identify themselves as Catholic. The Catholics, on the other hand, give 67 per cent of their votes to those paid participants who identify themselves as Catholics and only 33 per cent to those who identify themselves as Jewish.

It is well to mention once more at this point that the paid participants who identify themselves as Jewish are the same ones who identify themselves as Catholic. Each of the paid participants was identified as Jewish in half the groups and as Catholic in the other half.

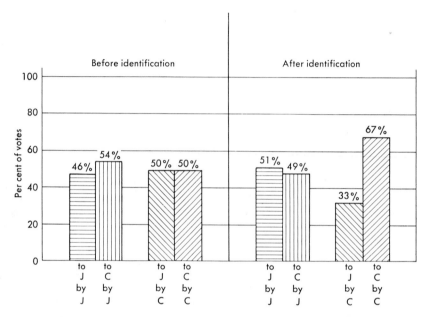

Figure 2. Per cent of votes for paid participants when identified as J or C

To check even further on these results a number of groups were conducted as control groups. The procedure was identical except for the fact that identification of the members of the group was omitted. Throughout the meeting these groups continued to refer to each other by number and did not know the name or religion of the other members. No changes occurred in these groups and the percentages of votes for Jews and for Catholics continued to stay close to 50 per cent.

We may unequivocally come to the conclusion that in this situation where the effect of personality factors and individual differences was adequately controlled, the knowledge of religious affiliation markedly affected for whom Catholics voted, but did not affect for whom Jews voted.

One of the first questions we asked ourselves concerned the nature of the effect of the identification on the Jewish members of the groups. It is possible that they were quite unaffected by the identification. On the other hand, it is possible that the identification may have aroused two sets of conflicting forces, the net result of which was to leave the distribution of votes to Jews and Catholics unchanged.

In an attempt to answer this question, another type of group was set up. In this group 10 girls, half of them Jewish and the other half Catholic (including the four paid participants), sat up on a platform at the front of a large room. About 50 girls sat in the room facing the front platform. The large group of 50 girls did the voting and could vote for any of the 10 girls on the platform. The 10 on the platform did not vote. Halfway through the meeting the 10 girls on the platform were identified by name and religion, as in the previous experiment, *but the girls who were doing the voting were never identified.*

The results for this large group are presented in Figure 3. The results prior

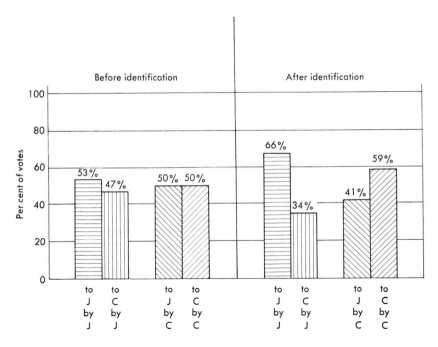

Figure 3. Per cent of votes for different groups in "large-group" experiment

to the identification are identical with the results for the small face-to-face groups. The results after the identification, however, present a rather different picture. Here *both* the Jewish and Catholic members of the group have altered their distribution of votes. The Jewish girls give 66 per cent of their votes to Jews and the Catholics give 59 per cent of their votes to Catholics. In short, in the large group the Jewish members of the group are no longer unaffected by the knowledge of name and religion. Indeed they are affected at least as much as the Catholic members of the group.

There must be some real differences between the small-group and the large-group situations to have produced this difference in behavior. Let us recapitulate and interpret these differences.

First, in the small groups the people doing the voting were at the same time the recipients of votes. In the large group the people doing the voting were *not* receiving the votes. It would then seem that in the small-group situation the group members would be concerned with both their reactions to other people and other people's reactions to them. In the large-group situation, however, the voting members of the group would only be concerned with their own reactions to the ten people who were receiving votes.

Second, in the small-group situation all the members were identified by name and religion halfway through the meeting. In the large-group situation only those who were the recipients of votes were identified. The voting members of the group were never themselves identified. In the large-group situation, then, the voting member of the group, whose behavior we are here examining, remained personally anonymous throughout the meeting, while in the small-group situation there was no anonymity for anyone.

It should be emphasized here that this anonymity applies to whether or not anyone knows who the person is and does not apply to knowing how anyone votes. All the ballots in all the experimental situations were secret ballots. All the ballots were, as far as the group members knew, unidentifiable as to who did the voting. They were, of course, identifiable to the experimenter.

How can we understand and explain the results which have been obtained? In the situation where the individual is anonymous and does not have to be concerned with the impression she makes on others, but only with the impression others make on her, we find that both Jews and Catholics react to knowledge of religious affiliation by voting more for members of their own group. We must then maintain that for both Jews and Catholics there are forces operating in the direction of favoring members of their own group. It must also be maintained that this force, for both Jews and Catholics, is strong enough at least partially to overcome personal preference for individuals. The reaction to the same individual in the same situation depends on whether or not a religious label is worn and which label it is.

But in the small face-to-face groups the Jewish girls do not show any effect of this identification. We must maintain, then, that in this situation a sufficiently strong counterforce was brought into operation. It is plausible that this counterforce should stem from the factors in the small-group situation which are different from the large-group situation, namely, that the individual doing the voting is not anonymous, and the nature of the situation pushes her to consider the impression she is making on others in the group. It would seem, then, that when the Catholic girl is identified before others as Catholic in a situation where the others are considering whether or not to vote for her, she is still able to express her preference for other Catholics. When the Jewish girl, however, is identified before others as Jewish under these same circumstances, she cannot express her own preferences for members of her own group—perhaps because she fears or feels rejection by the members of the other group.

What are the larger implications of this experiment and the larger implications of experiments such as this that might be done in the future?

Here we have a technique, a means of studying systematically the various facets of phenomena like intergroup conflict, prejudice, and the strength of the influence of group membership. We have already cast some light on the function of secrecy and anonymity in determining people's overt reactions toward others who can be labeled. We have begun to cast some light on the reactions of the members of minority groups to such labeling of themselves, and its effect on their behavior in mixed groups. We have begun to see very specifically what the relative strengths of various factors are in allowing or retarding the overt expression of prejudice.

One small experiment is of course only a bare beginning. Other experiments on these factors can and undoubtedly will follow. The ramifications of the problem are many and the answers such experiments can supply are important. The whole problem of what function group belongingness plays for us and what its effects are, must be the focus of attack by means of such systematic study.

PART III

Consequences of Reference Group Selection

Part III is concerned mainly with the consequences of normative and comparative reference orientations. Many of the readings in the preceding section have, of course, already touched on this aspect of reference group behavior. Festinger, for example, hypothesizes that comparison with others close in opinion or ability will lead to precision and stability of evaluation. If there is divergence of opinion in a group, "pressures toward uniformity" will arise, which may in turn lead to rejection of the deviant. Hyman notes that comparisons with others may permit realistic appraisal of one's own status, but may also result in status enhancement or depreciation. Patchen's major hypothesis is that consonant comparisons will result in feelings of satisfaction, whereas dissonant comparisons may lead to satisfaction or dissatisfaction, depending on the direction of dissonance. Form and Geschwender hypothesize that upward mobility relative to significant others will lead to feelings of satisfaction, regardless of the absolute rank the person achieves in "the" occupational ladder.

As for normative reference orientations, Newcomb's twenty-five-year follow-up study demonstrates that stability of attitudes is a consequence of support by significant reference individuals; Merton adduces a variety of behavioral consequences from contrasting reference orientations; Kelley shows that increasing the salience of a reference group increases resistance to a counternorm communication; and Festinger demonstrates, under controlled laboratory conditions, the phenomenon of loyalty to

[319]

the "in-group" when that group membership is made salient. Careful reading of the selections in Parts I and II will disclose still other consequences, either demonstrated or hypothesized to follow from taking some individual, group, or status category as an object of comparative or normative reference.

In Part III the selections that illustrate the consequences of comparative reference processes all focus on their *negative* implications, although, as we have seen, this need not be the most probable consequence of comparison. In the first selection Patchen attempts to produce, experimentally, two possible consequences of relative deprivation: dissatisfaction with one's job, and dissatisfaction with the norms governing the distribution of jobs. He succeeds in creating the first but not the second. It would be interesting to see whether a repetition of this experiment, omitting the explanation to subjects of how jobs were assigned, would result in more of the latter kind of dissatisfaction.

The selection by Pettigrew uses the concept of relative deprivation as a heuristic device to explain the dramatic rise in Negro discontent during a period of equally dramatic gains in Negro civil rights and standards of living. In essence, Pettigrew points to a shift in Negro reference groups, locating a number of structural factors conducive to this shift;[1] and, in addition, identifies a change in the relative position of one of the groups serving as a potential comparative reference group for American Negroes.

Although Parker and Kleiner happen also to be working with a population of urban Negroes, the theory of mental illness they propose is not limited to this group. In effect, the authors argue that discrepancy between aspirations and achievement is one form of stress conducive to mental illness.[2] In the chapter excerpted here, they demonstrate that the

---

1. Structural sources for the relative satisfaction and dissatisfaction of Negro soldiers stationed in the South and in the North are noted by Merton and Rossi (see p. 31 above). And, in studies done in four medium-sized cities in different regions of the country, in the early fifties, surveys established "consistently that Negroes were more likely to classify themselves as members of the upper class than were majority group members or other minorities." For example, in Elmira, 21 per cent of the Negro sample located themselves in the upper class compared with 3 per cent of the sample of native American white gentiles. The paradox is interpreted in terms of the fact that, at that period of time, Negroes were likely to choose, as a comparative reference group, the predominantly working-class Negro community rather than the total population. See Robin M. Williams, Jr., *Strangers Next Door, Ethnic Relations in American Communities*, Englewood Cliffs, N.J., Prentice-Hall, 1964, p. 251.

2. That mental illness is only one possible outcome of such stress is apparent from the not inconsiderable literature devoted to this topic. To cite only the more prominent: Merton's analysis of "anomie" as a social structural factor in deviance turns on the discrepancy between culturally patterned aspirations and structurally constrained achievements. His paper also suggests conditions that may predispose to one or another kind of deviance, mental illness being one possible outcome. Festinger's theory of cognitive dissonance would have discrepancy between aspirations and achievement

mentally ill groups, compared with community control groups, did, in fact, report a greater discrepancy between their own way of life and that of close friends, in a direction predominantly unfavorable to themselves. Other analyses of reference group behavior in this same chapter also tend to support the authors' contention that the comparison processes of the mentally ill reflect or support a greater perceived discrepancy between aspirations and achievement. Whether this discrepancy is consequence or cause of their illness is, however, less easily answered on the basis of the research design.

The first selection dealing with the consequences of *normative* orientations to reference groups is Newcomb's summary of his classic study of attitude change in a college community. The study demonstrates that, over time, those who take the college as a positive reference group become more liberal in their political attitudes, in accordance with the prevailing norms of the college community. In this brief summary, Newcomb calls attention to identification with the group, awareness of its norms, and supporting or conflicting identifications with other groups as mediating the processes of attitude change.[3] It should be noted, however, that some of Newcomb's subjects conformed to the norms of the college community

---

as a special case and predict a variety of attempts to reduce such dissonance, with some kind of deviant behavior as the outcome only under certain conditions. The hypothesis that prejudice toward minority groups is a consequence of downward mobility can also be conceptualized in terms of discrepancy between aspirations and achievement, and the concept of "status incongruity" is susceptible of a similar interpretation. (See Robert K. Merton, "Social Structure and Anomie" and "Continuities in the Theory of Social Structure and Anomie," in *Social Theory and Social Structure*, New York: Free Press, 1957, pp. 131–194; Leon Festinger, *A Theory of Cognitive Dissonance*, Bloomington, Ill.: Row, Peterson & Company, 1957; Bruno Bettelheim and Morris Janowitz, *The Dynamics of Prejudice*, New York: Harper & Brothers, 1950; Joseph Greenblum and Leonard I. Pearlin, "Vertical Mobility and Prejudice: A Socio-Psychological Analysis," in R. Bendix and S. M. Lipset, *Class, Status, and Power*, New York: The Free Press, 1953, pp. 480–491; Gerhard Lenski, "Status Crystallization: A Non-vertical Dimension of Social Status," *American Sociological Review*, 19: 405–413, 1954.) Despite the apparent fruitfulness of the discrepancy concept, questions have been raised about the interpretation of measures derived from it. For a methodological critique of such measures as used in psychological research, see Lee J. Cronbach, "Proposals Leading to Analytic Treatment of Social Perception Scores," in Renato Tagiuri and Luigi Petrullo (eds.), *Person Perception and Interpersonal Behavior*, Stanford, Calif.: Stanford University Press, 1958; and for a recent critique of sociological applications, see Hubert M. Blalock, "The Identification Problem and Theory Building: The Case of Status Inconsistency," *American Sociological Review*, 31: 52–61, 1966.

3. Pearlin reports similar findings in a study of white women students at a southern residential college with a relatively liberal climate of opinion. Depending on the way the conflict between home and parental identifications and identification with the college was resolved, students showed dramatic differences on a social distance scale toward Negroes. See Leonard I. Pearlin, "Shifting Group Attachments and Attitudes toward Negroes," *Social Forces*, 33: 47–50, 1954.

without apparent identification. Conformity was a price they knowingly and willingly paid in return for acceptance in or approval by a significant membership group. Still others adopted liberal attitudes primarily in a spirit of *negative* orientation toward their parents, who happened to embody and express conservative values.

Like Newcomb's study, the monograph by Hyman, Wright, and Hopkins finds reference group processes contributing in important ways to attitude change. In the excerpt reprinted here, they indicate that the *original* reference group need not be involved in the *maintenance* of such changes. When attitudes are to be expressed in action, however, the support of this group, or its representatives, does appear to make a difference.

In one of the most elegant field experiments devised in this area, Siegel and Siegel demonstrate that both reference groups and membership groups—whether or not these are taken as reference groups—are capable of bringing about attitude change. Rosen approaches a similar problem in a somewhat different way: If the individual belongs to two membership groups whose norms conflict, which of the two is he more likely to conform to? Not unexpectedly, Rosen finds that the group which is the more potent reference group also commands the greater conformity. This is exactly analogous to the Siegels' finding that those girls who were assigned to a non-Row house and, at the end of a year, chose to remain in it had lower authoritarianism scores than those who were assigned to a non-Row house but at the end of the year drew again for a Row residence. The only difference is that the Siegels are investigating the consequences of membership in one group; Rosen, in two.

Instead of examining the consequences of a particular reference orientation for some segment of behavior, Eisenstadt attempts to discern the consequences of reference orientations *in general*, for the individual and for society. He begins by identifying two general types of reference norms. The first translates the abstract values of a group into more specific role prescriptions. The second facilitates resolution of conflict between two or more roles. From the point of view of society, both types of norms function as mechanisms of social control. For the individual, they reduce conflict and anxiety and give meaning to various role performances by relating them to some value or valued group membership.

One of the problems with which Eisenstadt concerns himself is that of the communication of various types of reference norms. In that section of the Rileys' article on mass communication which is reprinted here, the authors focus on the *recipient* of such communications.[4] They remind us that this recipient is not an isolated individual, and that his perception of

4. In the remainder of the article, they discuss the communicator in relation to *his* reference groups, and the communicator-recipient relationship as part of a larger social structure.

a message, and his response to it, may be better understood in terms of his relationship to a variety of primary and secondary reference groups and their values.

Bauer's concern also is with communication, but his emphasis is, rather, on the effect that an actual or potential reference group has on the *communicator*. His formulation is intended to cover all types of communication, whether to a mass audience or to a small group of friends. The particular significance of the several related studies he reports lies in their implications for the process by which reference groups come to influence attitudes and beliefs. Briefly, the research supports the following propositions: (1) that the characteristics of the audience to which information is to be communicated influence "the way in which the communicator organizes new information and thereby what he himself may remember and/or believe at a later time"; and (2) "secondary audiences or reference groups, usually internalized and often imagined, are important targets of communication and may, at times, play a decisive role in the flow of communication." From these two propositions it follows that real or imagined communication with salient reference groups can significantly influence the individual's cognitive structuring of reality, in accordance with the attitudes and beliefs he attributes to these groups.

Although the last four papers in this section all deal specifically with the effects of reference groups on political behavior, the propositions they advance are not limited to that domain. D. Campbell's proposal to test the influence of public opinion polls in changing voting behavior derives from substantial experimental work demonstrating that groups tend toward consensus, and that "the communication of the opinions of members affects such consensus." Campbell proposes to specify this recurrent finding by investigating the effectiveness of various *kinds* of reported opinion (national, state, local) in changing the voter's own opinion on various kinds of political issues. In effect, he reformulates the "bandwagon" effect as the influence of the voting norm of an assumed reference group. Applications to other than political problems can readily be devised.

The chapter of Kaplan's dissertation which is reprinted here addresses itself to the question: How do individuals come to act in accordance with the norms of status categories to which they belong, in those situations where no organized group exists to transmit these norms? His answer is that they are transmitted by the small, face-to-face groups with which the person is in frequent interaction; when these groups do not communicate the appropriate norms, the individual is not likely to act in accordance with them, either.

Converse and A. Campbell concern themselves rather with other conditions that facilitate behavior in accordance with the norms of reference groups. In addition to identification with the group, they point to the following factors as crucial: strength and clarity of the standards emitted; their successful transmission to the membership; and the beliefs of members concerning the appropriateness of political behavior by the particular group.

Eulau, finally, distinguishes between norms that are purely attitudinal in their implications and those that require performance of some sort, hypothesizing that persons who take a non-membership group as a reference group will be more adept at conforming to the former than to the latter. Specifically, he predicts that *self*-identification, in terms of social class, will be more effective in shaping political values, whereas *objective* class situation will be more reliably related to *participation* in politics. In this as in the other readings concluding this section, the fact that Eulau is dealing with political behavior should not obscure the more general import of his results.[5]

5. An experiment by Maccoby and Wilson suggests not only another application, but also a possible modification of Eulau's principle. When the behavior of the non-membership group is portrayed realistically and in detail by the mass media, conformity to performance norms will be enhanced. See Eleanor E. Maccoby and William Wilson, "Identification and Observational Learning from Films," *Journal of Abnormal and Social Psychology*, 55 : 76–87, 1957.

The Effect of Reference Group
Standards on Job Satisfactions

Martin Patchen

SINCE the publication of *The American Soldier*,[1] investigators have been alert
to the effects of reference group standards on individual attitudes and satisfactions. There has been, however, surprisingly little verification of the original
"relative deprivation" hypothesis that an individual's satisfaction will depend
mainly on what his lot is relative to those with whom he compares himself. This
hypothesis was put forward as a convincing *ex post facto* explanation of survey
findings. Experimental testing under a variety of conditions is still needed.
Further knowledge is needed, moreover, about just what kind of satisfaction
will be affected by deprivation relative to one's fellows.

We may distinguish conceptually two types of satisfaction which may be
affected by the influence of a reference group: (a) Satisfaction derived by an
individual from the use of those rewards which are available to him. (b) Satisfaction with the norms governing how these rewards are distributed.

Both from a theoretical and from a practical point of view, this distinction
appears important. The first kind of satisfaction is immediately significant
mainly in determining the degree of individual happiness under the existing
social organization. The second may determine whether *change* will occur in
social organization—from the choosing of a new leader to violent revolution.
Moreover, these two kinds of satisfaction may relate differently to productivity.
In the long run, personal unhappiness may lead to dissatisfaction with present
norms. But whether one type of dissatisfaction or the other is widespread at
any given time can have important consequences for group life.

Reprinted from *Human Relations*, 11:303–314, 1958, by permission of the author and the
publisher.

1. S. A. Stouffer et al., *The American Soldier: Adjustment During Army Life*, 2 vols.,
Princeton, N.J.: Princeton University Press, 1949–50.

The relative deprivation concept was used by the *Soldier* investigators most often when discussing satisfaction with how the Army was run—with the promotion system, special privileges for officers, etc. In other words, satisfactions with the norms which governed available rewards were usually studied. But does relative deprivation also affect the enjoyment of what rewards one has, in addition to bringing more complaints about the distribution of rewards?

Similar conceptualizations by several investigators of what determines satisfaction would lead us to answer yes. Klass[2] found support for the hypothesis that intrinsic job satisfaction is a function of the ratio of the fulfillment of job expectations to initial job expectations. Morse[3] and Spector[4] have presented evidence to support similar hypotheses—essentially that the individual's satisfaction is determined by the ratio of what he gets to what he wants to get. These investigators have not been concerned with the social sources of such wants. It would seem, however, that in many instances a particular reference group (or several reference groups) would be crucial in determining what the individual's expectations are and thus what his wants are. The relative deprivation concept may be seen therefore as a particular case, with more sociological significance, of the general formulation regarding direct job gratifications advanced by these writers.

In line with this theoretical expectation, the first hypothesis of the present study was: Persons being advantaged relative to their fellows will derive more enjoyment from performance of their jobs than will those doing the same job but being disadvantaged relative to their fellows.

The second hypothesis concerns the second type of satisfaction we have distinguished and is derived more directly from the context of *The American Soldier* researches. It is: Persons being advantaged relative to their fellows will be more satisfied with the rules of job assignment and performance than those doing the same job but being disadvantaged relative to their fellows.

In short, the present research was intended to provide an experimental test of the relative deprivation hypothesis and to see whether relative deprivation would affect differentially the two types of satisfaction distinguished.

General Design

The essential design of the experiment used to test the hypothesis consisted of comparing the satisfactions of three groups of subjects, all of whom did the same job, B, a task of medium attraction to them. In one condition (the Advantaged Class), classmates were doing job A, a job of low desirability, at the

2. B. Klass, "The Role of Expectations in Determining Intrinsic Job Satisfactions," Unpublished Ph.D. dissertation, Boston University, 1952.

3. Nancy C. Morse, *Satisfactions in the White-Collar Job*, Ann Arbor: Institute for Social Research, 1953.

4. A. J. Spector, "Expectations, Outcomes, and Satisfactions," Unpublished Ph.D. dissertation, Boston University, 1953.

same time. Thus those doing job B were better off than their fellows. In a second condition (the Deprivation Class), classmates were doing job C, a highly desirable job. In this case, those doing job B were worse off than their fellows. In the third condition (the Non-Comparison Class) everyone did job B so that these subjects had no one with whom to compare themselves. These persons were a control group.

Procedure

SETTING OF STUDY

The study was conducted with four classes of seventh and eighth grade junior high school pupils, totaling sixty boys and sixty-four girls. The average age of the seventh graders was about 13 years and that of the eighth graders about 14 years.

The experiment was performed during one of the social studies periods of each of the classes, in the regular classroom. The experimenter and the social studies teacher were the only adults present.

PRE-EXPERIMENTAL LIKING FOR JOBS

Twenty days before the experimental sessions, a questionnaire was given to each of the four classes. Students were told that they would be asked to do a simple job during several class periods in connection with a study on "perception." Each student was presented with a list of 18 simple tasks and asked to "show how well you think you would like doing each of them" by marking each of the choices on a seven-point scale ranging from "like very much" to "dislike very much."

According to responses to this questionnaire: alphabetizing 100 names was a very unpopular job, copying a list of numbers was a job which the youngsters neither strongly liked nor strongly disliked, and modeling clay was a task highly attractive to the subjects.

ASSIGNMENT TO EXPERIMENTAL GROUPS

Each of the 16 subjects who was assigned to copying numbers in the Advantaged Class had indicated a greater liking for copying numbers than for alphabetizing cards. All 17 assigned to be copyers in the Deprivation Class had shown a greater liking for modeling clay than for copying.

These Deprived and Advantaged experimental groups—i.e. those assigned to copying in the two-job classes—were generally matched on the following criteria.

1. *Liking for job*

All had picked one of the middle three choices on the seven-point "job-liking" scale. The subjects in the Non-Comparison Classes who also picked one of these three "moderate" choices (*N* equals 37) represent the control group of the experimental design.

A numerical value was assigned to each of the possible scale choices and a mean initial "job-liking" score was computed for each experimental and control group. There were no significant differences among the mean scores of the different groups.

2. *Amount of deprivation*

The distance between each response and the next on the seven-point scale of liking for the job was counted as one unit. On the average those assigned to copy numbers in the Advantaged Group said they liked that job 2.7 units better than they liked alphabetizing cards. Those who copied numbers in the Deprived Group on the average liked their job 2.1 units less than the job their classmates were doing—that of modeling clay. Thus the potential feeling of deprivation in one group was roughly equated to the potential feeling of advantage in the other.

3. *Intelligence*

There were no systematic differences in the intelligence of the groups as measured by scores on the Pintner General Abilities Test. Almost all the subjects had taken this test less than six months before the experiment.

4. *Sex distribution*

In both two-job classes the proportion of males to females was about the same in the experimental group (those copying numbers) as in the rest of the class. Thus, the probability of the copyers' comparing themselves to persons doing the other job was increased. (The number of males and females among those copying in the Advantaged Group and in the Control Groups was about the same. But in the Deprived Group 12 out of 17 were females.)

5. *Sociometric choices*

The success of the experiment demanded that those copying in the two-job classes should compare themselves to classmates doing another job. It seemed wise, therefore, to make sure that one at least of each copyer's friends was outside his own job group. For this purpose, each pupil was asked by the social science teacher—with no reference to the coming experiment—to name the four persons with whom he would most like to work on a class project. Only one person assigned to copying (in the Advantaged Group) chose solely persons who were assigned to his own experimental work group.

THE EXPERIMENTAL SESSION

The subjects were not told in advance the date of the experimental session. The study periods and lunch periods of each class were arranged in such a way that those classes meeting later in the day could not mix prior to the session with those classes which had already taken part in an experimental session.

EXPLANATION OF STUDY

A standard fictitious explanation of some length about the purpose of the experiment was given to each class. The students were told, in part:

In general we're studying what psychologists call perception—which boils down pretty much to what people notice about objects. . . . First, we're trying to discover whether there are differences in the things that people of various age groups notice about objects. Dr. Fairfield (fictitious study director) believes that because of differences in perception, people of different age groups will perform differently in doing various tasks. . . .

The first "test run" of the study is being done with this group. This will be the first of three sessions for you people.

EXPLANATION OF JOB CHOICE

Every class was then told: "The study director decided that all of the jobs which are listed on the form you filled out last time are of equal value for our research purposes. So we just chose (one) of them at random. . . ."

DESCRIPTION OF JOBS

The jobs to be done were then described—before job assignments were made—in such a way as to strengthen the predisposition of Advantaged Group copiers to feel better off, and of the Deprivation Group copiers to feel worse off than their classmates.

EXPLANATION OF ASSIGNMENT

In the two-job classes, subjects were told that, although the researchers had hoped to assign people to the two tasks according to how well the subjects liked them, it turned out that just about everyone preferred one job to another. "So the directors of the study decided to just assign to the more popular job those people whose questionnaires we tabulated first—the ones which happened to be on top of the pile."

The officially announced methods of job choice and of job assignment were intended to be fairly ambiguous in their fairness so as neither to conform strongly nor to violate strongly the subjects' values. In this way, it was hoped that relative deprivation would have a maximum chance to influence satisfaction with the rules of the session.

WORK PERIOD

In every class and for every job, the subjects were given 20 minutes to do their tasks. They were told to work at a normal pace, but were not told at the start how long they would continue to work. The subjects were asked not to talk, so that exchange of opinions or feelings about the job or other aspects of the session was kept at a minimum—verbally at least.

RULES SATISFACTION

After the jobs had been done, the students were asked to fill out a first questionnaire. They were told, in part: "Since we're going to study perception with many other groups of this kind, we want to find out if we've arranged these sessions so that they'll go smoothly. We'd like to get your feelings about how the present session was arranged. . . ."

The subjects were asked to check one of a number of possible answers to questions about: the type of job chosen, the method of job assignment, whether enough attention was paid to making the session pleasant for them, the way in which they were told to do their jobs, and the amount of time allotted for the work. (Two other questions—about the adequacy of lighting and of amount of room—were added to help disguise the real purpose of the questionnaire.) This "Rules Satisfaction" questionnaire was ostensibly anonymous; however, every form was marked so that the respondent could be identified. A "Rules Satisfaction Index" was constructed on the basis of answers to these five questions.

EXPRESSION OF ENJOYMENT

After the Rules Satisfaction questionnaires were filled out, the subjects were informed that there would be "some changes in the procedure for the next two (fictitious) sessions, on the basis of your answers on the questionnaires you just filled out. . . . One change which we're going to make anyway is to have everyone do the same job the next time . . . we'd like to know also, when choosing one job for everyone to do the next session, how you feel *now* about the job which you did during this session. . . . "

The subjects were then asked to fill out a second questionnaire which included questions on: how well subjects would like to do the same job next time, enjoyment in doing the job this session, interest of the task, feeling of accomplishment, and how well other people "like yourself" would enjoy doing the same job. On the basis of answers to these five questions, a "Job Enjoyment index" was constructed.

DEPRIVATION IN THE TWO-JOB CLASSES

The Rules Satisfaction questionnaire included questions about which job the subject preferred and how strong this preference was. Deprivation scores were assigned, ranging from nine for those who preferred the other job very strongly to one for those who preferred their own job very strongly.

OTHER MEASURES

In addition to the measures already mentioned, other data on subjects obtained were: (a) A slightly modified form of the Authoritarian Submission Sub-Scale of the F-Scale. This scale was administered to all subjects at the same pre-experimental session where liking for various jobs was expressed. (b) Independent ratings by two male teachers of each subject's submissiveness to authority. Submissiveness, judged on a five-point scale, was defined as "willingness to accept the direction of teachers, principal and others in authority without question and without resentment." The correlation between the ratings of the two teachers (on 135 subjects in all four classes) was + .55. In no case did one instructor rate on the high side of the scale a subject whom the other teacher rated on the low side. The submissiveness score for each subject is a simple average of the ratings of both teachers. (c) The amount and quality of work done by each of the subjects who copied numbers (the experimental and control groups) was tabulated.

Results

EXPERIMENTAL GROUPS

1. *Job enjoyment*

Our first hypothesis led us to expect that subjects in the Advantaged Group would enjoy doing the job most, that those in the Deprived Group would enjoy their work least, and that those in the Control Groups would be intermediate in enjoyment. The mean job enjoyment scores for the different groups are shown in Table 1.

Table I—Job Enjoyment Index Scores* for Experimental and Control Groups

Group	Mean	S.D.	N
Advantaged	3.36	1.12	16
Deprived	3.65	.73	17
Control	3.24	1.01	37
Total	3.37	.99	70

* Highest satisfaction = 1; lowest = 5.

The Deprived Group showed, in line with our prediction, a substantially lower job enjoyment than the other groups. The difference between the mean job enjoyment scores of the Deprived Group and of the Control Group is shown by a *t*-test to be significant at the .10 level, a little short of the usual standard of statistical significance. However, in addition to the correctness of our prediction, the comments of several members of the Deprived Group give us confidence that the lower enjoyment of this group is the result of the operation of our independent variable, rather than that of chance. Four out of the 17 subjects answered the open-ended question, "Why did you feel this way about the job?" in terms of their deprivation relative to classmates modeling clay.

The lower job enjoyment of the Deprived Group is even more convincing in view of the fact that this group had the highest proportion of females, 12 out of 17. As will be noted again later, females generally reported greater enjoyment of their job than did males.

Table 1 shows also that the Advantaged Group did not, as predicted, score highest on job enjoyment. Its mean score is a little lower than, but not significantly different from, that of the Control Group.

There is some evidence relevant to why the Advantaged Group did not show greater job enjoyment. All those in this group had before the experimental session indicated a decidedly greater liking for their job, copying numbers, than for that of their classmates, alphabetizing names. But in answer to the post-experimental question, "Would you have rather done the other job instead of the one assigned to you?" only four of the 16 checked, "No, I prefer the one I did"; nine said they had no preference; while five said they would rather have done the other. Evidently copying numbers turned out to be a more tedious task than the subjects (and the experimenter) had bargained for. This tediousness of the copying task thus reduced whatever feeling of advantage had existed in the Advantaged Group, while it undoubtedly reinforced the feeling of deprivation in the Deprived Group.

The limited effectiveness of the relative deprivation variable in the Advantaged Group is in sharp contrast to its effectiveness in the Deprived Group. Fourteen of the 17 in the Deprived Group said, "I would rather have done the other (job)." The comments on the questionnaire of two of three subjects who checked, "I didn't have any preference at all," indicated that they also really preferred the other job.

2. *Rules satisfaction*

Our second hypothesis led us to predict that subjects in the Deprived Group would complain most about how the experimental session was arranged, that the Advantaged Group would complain least, and that the Control Group would be intermediate in its satisfaction with the rules.

These predictions regarding rules satisfaction were not supported (see Table 2).

The Deprived Group complained slightly more than the Control Group, but this difference was far short of statistical significance. The Advantaged Group, in a reversal of our prediction, complained most. The difference between the mean rules satisfaction of the Advantaged Group and that of the Control Group was significant in a *t*-test at the .05 level.

Table 2—Rules Satisfaction Index Scores* for Experimental and Control Groups

Group	Mean	S.D.	N
Advantaged	2.80	1.14	16
Deprived	2.33	.91	17
Control	2.23	.79	37
Total	2.39	.94	70

* Highest satisfaction = 1; lowest = 5.

These data for the experimental and control groups provide some evidence that relative deprivation affected job enjoyment (at least for the Deprived Group) but not rules satisfaction. So far the data have concerned only subjects who did the job of medium desirability—copying numbers. We will consider next whether the same relations hold for all those subjects (copiers and non-copiers) in the two-job classes who expressed a preference either for their own job or for the other job. There were 45 such cases.

The correlation between deprivation scores and job enjoyment scores for these subjects is + .73. Feeling deprived relative to classmates and less enjoyment in doing the job went together. Even when this relation is controlled for differences both in rules satisfaction and in submissiveness, the partial coefficient is + .66. The simple correlation between deprivation scores and rules satisfaction scores is + .46. That is, greater deprivation is moderately associated with lower satisfaction. Holding submissiveness ratings constant does not much affect this relation. However, when we control for job enjoyment as well as for submissiveness, the partial correlation between deprivation and rules satisfaction drops to + .18. Although we predicted its direction, a *t*-test shows that this partial coefficient is not significantly different from zero.

The correlation between rules satisfaction scores and job enjoyment scores was + .47. That is, as one kind of satisfaction increased, the other increased also. But when this relation is controlled for amount of deprivation, the partial coefficient between rules satisfaction and job enjoyment drops to + .23.

The high correlation between relative deprivation and job enjoyment, while the relation between deprivation and rules satisfaction is not significant, is in agreement with results in the Deprived experimental group. Thus, the correlational analysis confirms the positive relation between relative deprivation and job enjoyment (although it can offer no additional evidence on the causal direction of the relation). Moreover, the correlational findings provide additional evidence of the lack of relationship between deprivation and satisfaction with the rules.

SUBMISSIVENESS

One variable which was highly related to rules satisfaction is submissiveness to authority, as measured by teacher ratings. The effect of submissiveness to authority on complaints about the rules of the experimental session is shown for the experimental and control groups in Table 3.

In each of the four groups, those rated low on submissiveness had a lower rules satisfaction score (i.e. complained more) than those rated as more submissive. The difference between the scores of all "high submissives" and all "low submissives" is significant in a *t*-test at close to the .05 level.

The correlation between submissiveness ratings and rules satisfaction for all subjects who expressed a job preference (*N* equals 45 copiers and non-copiers) was − .51. That is, as submissiveness increased, amount of expressed dissatis-

Table 3—Mean Rules Satisfaction Index Scores* for Subjects High and Low on Submissiveness

	SUBMISSIVE RATING**		
Group	Low	High	Total
Advantaged	3.63	2.42	2.80
	5	11	16
Deprived	2.70	2.22	2.33
	4	13	17
Control-A	2.25	2.06	2.15
N	10	11	21
Control-B	2.56	2.13	2.34
N	8	8	16
Total	2.66	2.21	2.39
N	27	43	70
S.D.	1.22	.64	.94

* Highest satisfaction = 1; lowest = 5.
** Low submissiveness scores: 2–5; high scores: 6–10.

faction with the rules went down. The partial coefficient for this relation, with deprivation and job enjoyment held constant, is $-$ .47. Submissiveness ratings, which were not consistently related to job enjoyment in the experimental and control groups, are also not significantly correlated with job enjoyment for this group of all those who had definite job preferences.

SEX

The attribute which was most strongly related to rules satisfaction was sex. Table 4 shows that females expressed significantly greater satisfaction than males with the way the session was arranged. Males complained more than females in every group except one of the two control groups, where there was no difference

Table 4—Mean Rules Satisfaction Index Scores* for Males and for Females

Group	Male	Female	Total
Advantaged	3.42	2.00	2.80
N	9	7	16
Deprived	2.92	2.08	2.33
N	5	12	17
Control-A	2.15	2.15	2.15
N	11	10	21
Control-B	2.68	2.08	2.34
N	7	9	16
Total	2.74	2.09	2.39
N	32	38	70
S.D.	1.20	.45	.94

* Highest satisfaction = 1; lowest = 5.

between the sexes. The difference between the sexes for all groups is significant in a *t*-test at beyond the .01 level. (As already noted, females also express significantly greater enjoyment in doing the job.)

We have seen that both submissiveness ratings and sex are, when studied alone, related to satisfaction with the rules of the session. Moreover, the relation between each of these factors and rules satisfaction holds up when the other factor is controlled.

PRODUCTIVITY

In addition to comparison of satisfactions among the experimental and control groups, these groups were compared on the amount and quality of work done. The mean output of both the Advantaged and the Deprived Groups, as measured by number of sets of numbers copied, was lower than the output of either of the control groups. The difference between the output of the Advantaged Group and that of the combined control groups is significant in a *t*-test at beyond the .05 level. The difference in output between the Deprived Group and the combined control group does not reach statistical significance.

There were no great differences among the experimental and control groups in the quality of their work—as measured by the number of errors per set of numbers copied.

Within each of the groups, both quantity and quality of work were systematically related to only one attribute—sex. Females did markedly more work than males in the Advantaged Group, showing that the significantly lower output of the Advantaged Group was due primarily to the males. Females also did more work in each of the two control groups, but had slightly less output in the Deprived Groups. For all the groups combined, the output of the females was significantly higher in a *t*-test at beyond the .01 level.

Moreover, in every group, females did better quality work than males. For all groups combined, the difference between the sexes on quality of work is highly significant in a *t*-test at beyond the .001 level.

Negative results with respect to output are: (a) There was no consistent relation between job enjoyment scores and output. (b) The combination of extremely high or low rules satisfaction with extremely high or low job enjoyment did not have any consistent effect on volume of work. (c) Output was not related to teacher ratings of submissiveness. (d) Scores on the Authoritarian Submission Sub-Scale of the F-Scale were, likewise, not related to output. (Nor were F-scores related to either type of job satisfaction.)

Conclusions

We have found that those people who were deprived relative to their fellows derived less enjoyment from doing their jobs than did people who had no one with whom to compare themselves. This finding is in line with the proposition that the effect of relative deprivation on satisfaction is a special case of the general determination of satisfaction by what a person gets in relation to what he wants to get.

We found, however, that deprived persons did not differ from the control group in their satisfaction with the norms governing what gratifications they were allowed to have. This finding does not agree with the general findings reported in *The American Soldier*—that men deprived relative to their reference groups were more dissatisfied with Army rules. It appears from the present data that although deprivation relative to one's fellows will result in lessened personal enjoyment, it does not *necessarily* lead to discontent with existing rules governing the group.

Taking this next step of questioning the existing norms would appear to require some perception that one is being treated unfairly—i.e. that certain accepted values are being violated. *The American Soldier* researches concerned Army practices (e.g. promotion policy, special privileges of officers) about which the men could and did have definite values. But in the present experiment, as noted above, the method of job choice, job assignment, and job performance were made purposely ambiguous in their fairness so that the independent effect of relative deprivation would be maximized. It seems likely that, although the members of the Deprived Group were disappointed in drawing the poorer job, they could see no clear injustices in the rules of the session.

Dissatisfaction with norms is interpreted, then, as resulting from a violation of the values of the individual. Such violations of values may or may not accompany deprivation relative to others. This interpretation appears consistent with our finding that both submissiveness and being female were related to less complaining about the rules. Females in our culture tend to have values which favor the acceptance of direction rather than independent determination of their own activities. Submissive persons often have similar values which make them reluctant to question authority. It may be objected that both females and submissives may have been as dissatisfied as others, but that their particular personality make-up kept them from expressing this discontent. That such a difference in expressiveness had some effect seems probable. However, this explanation seems inadequate completely to explain sex and submissiveness differences on answers to an ostensibly *anonymous* questionnaire. Furthermore, the fact that the highly submissive persons were willing to express as much dissatisfaction concerning *job enjoyment* as did others supports the view that the values of the individual are important in determining how satisfied he will be with the *norms* governing his activities.

Contrary to our hypothesis, the Advantaged Group showed least satisfaction with the rules. We have seen that after the experiment most of the members of this group reported *not* preferring their own job to the other, although they had preferred their own job *before* the experiment. According to the relative deprivation hypothesis, then, it was not surprising that this group was not more satisfied, since they did not really feel better off than their fellows. However, the relative deprivation framework alone does not explain why this group actually complained *most*.

A plausible interpretation of this result, consistent with the theoretical ideas above, revolves about the fact that subjects in the Advantaged Group were assigned a job which turned out to be more tedious and disagreeable than the pre-experimental description of the job had led them to believe. They had indicated indifference when asked vaguely about "copying a list of numbers." The experimenter later described copying numbers as the preferable job. But when they received the work materials, they found they had to copy numerous columns of long numbers for 20 minutes.

In this context, subjects could well have felt that they had been misled in what to expect by the experimenter and that their standards of fair treatment had been violated. The Deprived Group, on the other hand, was aware from the beginning of the experimental session that there was a chance that they might get a very tedious job. Also, the method of assignment to jobs described (picking names from the top of a randomly ordered pile) was impersonal and reasonably fair. Thus, although these persons were disappointed in the job they got (as shown in their job enjoyment scores) they evidently saw little reason to complain about the rules which governed their assignment and activity. Once again, then, we may conclude that the crucial factor determining satisfaction with the rules is not merely how one stands relative to others, but also how legitimate (according to certain values) one considers the rules which placed him in that position.

In general, then, our data suggest that there is no simple relation between standing relative to a reference group, on the one hand, and satisfaction with the norms, on the other.

Moreover, although our data have indicated a close relation between relative deprivation and intrinsic job enjoyment, broadly defined, we should not always expect to find a strong relation of this sort. If, as we have proposed, the position of a particular reference group is only one determinant of wants, the possibility is present that other wants may occur, based on conflicting reference group standards, or independent of any particular reference group.

The data also offer some evidence that intrinsic job satisfaction varies relatively independently of satisfaction with norms. It is proposed that this empirical independence is based on an important theoretical difference.

An individual's wants may have at least two different components. One is what rewards he can *realistically hope* to get. The second is what he feels he is *entitled* to get. The enjoyment of available rewards appears to be a function of what the individual gets in relation to what he *realistically hoped* to get. Satisfaction with the operation of norms would depend on what he gets relative to what he felt *entitled to get*.

A reference group, as Kelley[5] points out, may serve to provide an objective

5. H. H. Kelley, "Two Functions of Reference Groups," in G. E. Swanson et al., eds., *Readings in Social Psychology*, rev. ed., New York: Henry Holt and Company, Inc., 1952.

criterion for hopes or it may serve to provide a value standard about what are legitimate expectations. It does not *necessarily* have to serve both functions in any given situation. Where a reference group provides an objective standard for hopes, its main effect will be in determining the enjoyment of what rewards become available. Where the reference group provides a *value norm* about what it is legitimate to expect, its main influence will be as a determinant of whether the operation of the norms will be accepted. Further knowledge is needed about the conditions under which a reference group will provide an objective standard and when it will provide a normative standard. Also, we need to know more about when these two kinds of standards will go together and when they will not.

Since job enjoyment and satisfaction with norms are influenced so heavily by such reference group standards, this kind of knowledge should lead to a better understanding of variations in the two types of satisfaction discussed and of the relation between them.

Actual Gains and Psychological Losses

Thomas Pettigrew

T HE late Samuel Stouffer, one of America's greatest sociologists, always became incensed when a layman blithely reacted to a finding of behavioral science with, "Who didn't know that?" He countered with a simple true-false test of ten items, the "obvious, common sense" answers to which had all been demonstrated to be incorrect by rigorous social research. Most of those who take Stouffer's test miss every item. The moral is clear: many behavioral science findings appear obvious only after the fact.

Stouffer's favorite illustration involved the relative morale of the Air Corps and the Military Police in World War II. Promotions were rapid and widespread in the Air Corps, but slow and piecemeal in the Military Police. Conventional wisdom predicts that the Air Corpsmen should have been more satisfied with their chances for promotion, for the "obvious" reason that they were in absolute terms moving ahead faster in their careers. But, as a matter of empirical fact, Stouffer found in his famous studies of *The American Soldier* that the Air Corpsmen were considerably more frustrated over promotions than the Military Police.[1] What was not so obvious was that the fliers' wide-open system of promotions led them to assume exceedingly high aspirations; most of them expected such swift elevation that even the generous promotions of their service left them *relatively* dissatisfied. By contrast, morale was reasonably high among the Military Police. The MP's did not expect rapid promotions and learned to

Reprinted from Thomas Pettigrew, *A Profile of the Negro American*, pp. 178–192, by permission of the author and the publisher, D. Van Nostrand Company. Copyright, 1964 by D. Van Nostrand Company, Inc.

1. S. A. Stouffer et al., *The American Soldier*, Vol. 1, Princeton, N.J.: Princeton University Press, 1949.

be content with what few advances they did achieve. It was not the absolute level of attainment that made for poor morale so much as relative deprivation— the discrepancy between what one anticipates and what one attains. . . .

Likewise, conventional wisdom dictates that Negro Americans should be more content today than any previous point in America's history. After all, have Negro gains not been faster in recent decades than any period since Emancipation? Why, then, are many Negroes so unusually restive, so openly angry, so impatient for further gains? Relative, not absolute, deprivation once again provides a social-psychological explanation. The great majority of Negroes in past years dared not cherish high aspirations. While never satisfied with their lot, they, like the Military Police, expected very little of life, and they had to be content with what crumbs they did receive. But Negro Americans in recent years hunger for much more than crumbs. Like the Air Corpsmen they have tasted significant progress and can fully appreciate what further progress could mean. Indeed, Negro aspirations have risen far more swiftly than Negro advances. Thus, while better off in absolute terms than ever before, Negroes today are relatively more deprived than they were before the last twenty-five years of racial progress.

This important social-psychological principle underlies the Negro American protest of the 1960's. To trace its operation, this chapter summarizes the actual gains of recent years, lists the simultaneous psychological losses of these same years, [and] offers a psychological interpretation of the protest movement itself. . . .

Actual Gains

The past quarter-century has witnessed the most rapid actual gains in Negro American history. Consider this sampling of recent advances culled from a variety of statistical sources:

The Negro's transition from rural Southerner to urbanite, North and South, continues apace. Today's Negro Americans are more urban than white Americans; 72 per cent of all non-whites in 1960 resided in urban areas, three times the non-white urban percentage in 1900. The Negro has migrated particularly to the very largest of American cities. Thus, in 1960 over half of all non-whites in the nation lived in metropolitan centers with at least a half-million people. Mark the Negro's growth in America's five largest cities. Between 1940 and 1960, the non-white percentages in New York and Philadelphia more than doubled and in Chicago, Los Angeles, and Detroit nearly tripled.

Behind these data lie literally millions of individual stories of migration, of picking up stakes in rural areas and moving into strange and bustling cities. The period from 1950 to 1960 alone witnessed the mass movement of more than a half-million Negro Southerners to the Northeast, another half-million to the Midwest, and a third of a million more to the West. Consequently, Negro migration has not only involved a moving from farm to city, but also a moving out of the South into other parts of the country. Clearly, race relations are no longer the problem and domain of a single region; with almost as many Negroes residing outside the South as in it, racial matters are definitely a national concern.

These enormous demographic alterations contribute to Negro progress in several ways. To begin with, this massive migration has lifted the bulk of the Negro population out of those areas most resistant to racial change and into the cities where racial change is least resisted. Within the South, the old rural Black Belt—named for its rich black soil—has traditionally had counties where Negroes outnumbered whites. A symbol and center of racial discrimination, this area is now breaking up. Today only one Southern county in eight has more Negroes than whites, while Negro populations in Southern cities have been growing at rates only slightly less than those of Northern cities. Between 1950 and 1960, the absolute number of Negroes residing in Miami almost tripled; in Dallas and Oklahoma City, more than doubled; and in Houston and Little Rock, almost doubled.

Moreover, this massive movement leads directly to a more sophisticated people capable of effective protest, a people more cognizant of what discrimination over the years has denied them. It also produces large concentrations of Negroes, facilitating communication and organization that simply could not be achieved in scattered rural districts. Finally, migration enables Negroes to benefit from the substantially higher urban standards of living. This factor greatly influences Negro progress in a wide range of domains: health, employment, business, income, housing, politics, and education.

. . . [L]ife expectancy at birth for Negroes from 1900 to 1960 has increased twice as rapidly as that of whites. Much of this advance reflects the better medical care available in large metropolitan areas, and most of the advance has occurred in recent years. In relation to the nation as a whole, age-adjusted, non-white total mortality rates improved from 1950 to 1960 virtually as much as they had in the previous half century.[2]

Likewise, gains have been registered in upgraded employment. The first few years of the Kennedy Administration witnessed a substantial growth in middle- and high-level federal employment of Negroes.[3] Although the positions involved are still relatively few, the number of Negroes in responsible government service jobs (GS 5 through 18) shot up 20 per cent from July, 1961, through June, 1962, while the number of whites in comparable jobs increased only 6 per cent. Responsible postal employment (PFS 5 through 18) revealed a similar trend. Lower level federal positions (GS and PFS 1 through 4) showed more modest Negro gains. While federal employment comprises only a small fraction of the nation's jobs, this swift improvement in occupational upgrading demonstrates what well-directed, crash programs can accomplish.

2. M. S. Goldstein, "Longevity and Health Status of the Negro American," *Journal of Negro Education, 1963 Yearbook*, 32 (4): 337–348.

3. J. Hope, II and E. Shelton, "The Negro in the Federal Government," *Journal of Negro Education, 1963 Yearbook*, 32 (4) : 367–374.

Employment opportunities have gradually expanded in recent years for Negro youth in the professional and clerical categories as well as the more traditional service fields; and non-white males have made gains somewhat faster than white males during the 1950's in both the professional and operative job classifications.[4] . . . Only a small portion of this professional and clerical progress, however, can be attributed to the development of Negro-controlled business itself, though some aspects of Negro business have prospered. The assets of Negro savings and loan associations, for instance, have multiplied over 32 times since 1947, a rate roughly three times that of all savings and loan associations combined.[5] Similarly, commercial banks owned and operated by Negroes increased their assets from 5 million dollars in 1940 to about 53 million by 1960, a growth rate over five times faster than that of all commercial banks. And the 51 Negro-controlled life insurance companies have doubled their assets since 1951 to a present total of at least 320 million dollars.[6]

These trends in turn generate income gains. From 1950 to 1960, the median annual income for individual non-whites fourteen years of age and older climbed 54 per cent and for non-white families 73 per cent.[7] The Negro middle class swelled; the percentage of non-white families earning $6000 or more in 1961, 20 per cent, was over five times larger than in 1945. The resulting purchasing power of Negroes has evolved into a potent factor even in the South. Thus, in 1961 it was estimated that the Negro participation in the total retail sales of ten standard metropolitan areas of the South amounted to 19 per cent, representing sales of almost two billion dollars. "This is not only suggestive of the impact of aggregate and concentrated purchasing power in the Negro market," remarks economist Vivian Henderson, "but it is also indicative of the kind of economic potential to which southern race relations must adjust."[8]

Increments in income are soon translated into better housing. The 1950's marked a doubling of the percentage of non-whites residing in census-defined "standard" housing.[9] And many Negroes became able for the first time to afford their housing without taking in boarders and extended family members;

4. W. G. Daniel, "The Relative Employment and Income of American Negroes," *Journal of Negro Education, 1963 Yearbook*, 32(4) : 349–357.

5. According to the *New York Times* (August 26, 1963, p. 37), savings and loan associations in general have expanded eleven times since 1945.

6. H. B. Young, "The Negro's Participation in American Business," *Journal of Negro Education, 1963 Yearbook*, 32(4) : 390–401.

7. N. D. Glenn, "Some Changes in the Relative Status of American Non-Whites, 1940 to 1960," *Phylon*, 24 : 109–122, 1963; V. W. Henderson, *The Economic Status of Negroes: In the Nation and in the South*, Atlanta, Ga.: Southern Regional Council, 1963.

8. Henderson, *op cit.*, p. 11.

9. Marian P. Yankauer and M. B. Sunderhauf, "Housing: Equal Opportunity to Choose Where One Shall Live," *Journal of Negro Education, 1963 Yearbook*, 32(4) : 402–414.

consequently, significantly fewer Negro households in 1960 included lodgers and three-generation families than in 1950.[10]

Important changes have occurred in political, as well as purchasing, power. Over a million more Negroes voted in 1962 than in 1950, and the power of this increased access to the ballot revealed itself in a wide range of elections. The first Negro elected to the Georgia legislature for generations won office in 1962, as did Negroes elected to statewide posts in Connecticut and Massachusetts. And it was no coincidence that the 1960 presidential campaign was the first in history where both major political parties vied intensively with one another as to which could write the stronger civil rights plank in its platform. Demographic shifts have established powerful concentrations of Negroes in most of the key electoral states: New York, Pennsylvania, Ohio, Michigan, Illinois, and California. In addition, Negro voters more than made the difference for Mr. Kennedy in 1960 in three crucial Southern states—North Carolina, South Carolina, and Texas.

Educational gains have also been evident. The percentage increments from 1940 to 1960 of Negro youth of all ages attending school are dramatic; and indices of educational quality, such as expenditures per pupil, number of pupils per teacher, and the academic preparation of teachers, have all risen in Southern schools for Negroes.[11] Educational attainments for the Negro adult population have climbed markedly in recent decades.[12] From 1940 to 1960, the percentage of Negroes who had attended college more than doubled[13]; from 1950 to 1960, the percentage of Negroes who had completed high school rose from 14 to 22 per cent, a faster rate than that of whites; and from 1950 to 1960, the median school years completed by all adult Negroes increased over a grade, 6.9 to 8.2 years.[14] Particularly indicative is the advance made by the twenty-five-to-twenty-nine-year-old age group. Negroes in this key age category in 1940 had received a median of only 7 years of training, while similar Negroes in 1960 recorded a median of 11 years.[15]

These recent advances have had a profound psychological effect upon Negro Americans. Despair and hopelessness have declined, new and proud aspirations have taken hold, and a determined optimism about the future has

10. G. F. Edwards, "Marriage and Family Life among Negroes," *Journal of Negro Education, 1963 Yearbook*, 32(4) : 451–464.

11. Eunice Newton and E. H. West, "The Progress of the Negro in Elementary and Secondary Education," *Journal of Negro Education, 1963 Yearbook*, 32(4) : 465–484.

12. Educational data cited throughout this chapter use the census definition for adults as all persons twenty-five years of age and older.

13. H. H. Doddy, "The Progress of the Negro in Higher Education, 1950–1960," *Journal of Negro Education, 1963 Yearbook*, 32(4) : 485–492.

14. Metropolitan Life Insurance Company, "Nationwide Rise in Educational Level," *Statistical Bulletin*, 44 : 3–5, August 1963.

15. Newton and West, *op. cit.*

developed. These trends became noteworthy by the early 1950's. A representative 1954 national public opinion poll asked: "On the whole, do you think life will be better for you or worse, in the next few years than it is now?"[16] . . . Of those with an opinion, 64 per cent of the Negro respondents felt life would soon be better. This figure compared with only 53 per cent of a white control sample equivalent to the Negro sample in region of residence, sex, age, education and occupation. . . . [T]his heightened Negro optimism, relative to comparable whites, was especially marked among the most deprived segments of the Negro population. Thus, the greatest relative optimism was evidenced by Negroes who were laborers, or had only a grammar school education, or resided in the South.

The public school desegregation ruling of the Supreme Court, of course, made 1954 a vintage year for rising Negro aspirations. But recent poll data suggest that, if anything, this high level of optimism has risen further. A 1959 national survey found that Negro Americans felt they had personally lost ground during the previous five years; but their hopes for the next five years revealed a relative increment roughly twice that of white Americans.[17] The 1963 *Newsweek* opinion survey of Negro Americans also uncovered revealing results: 73 per cent felt that the racial attitudes of whites would improve during the next five years; 63 per cent thought whites would accept racial change without violence; 85 per cent desired to own a private home; and 30 per cent believed they were qualified for elevation to professional or other white-collar employment.[18]

This same poll finds that much of this renewed hope for the future centers upon education. Although one in five families interviewed had a child who had dropped out of school before completing high school, 97 per cent wanted its children to finish high school. Ever since Abolitionist schoolmarms implanted faith in learning in Negroes after the Civil War, they have traditionally valued education as a means of achieving full acceptance in American society; and several additional studies point to the intensity of this faith at the present time. One investigation conducted in the middle 1950's in the Northeast noted that a sample of Negro mothers strongly valued achievement in terms of a future orientation that usually accompanies high educational aspirations.[19] Indeed, 83 per cent of these mothers intended for their sons to go to college.

Studies of the children themselves further confirm this emphasis upon education as a means for upward social mobility. One research project of the early 1950's tested and interviewed Negro and white children of matched

16. These results were derived from a reanalysis by the author of data from Samuel Stouffer's large polling study, *Communism, Conformity, and Civil Liberties*. These data were kindly furnished by the Roper Public Opinion Research Center, Williamstown, Massachusetts.

17. W. P. Janicki, "Cross-National Study of Satisfaction," unpublished paper.

18. *Newsweek* editors, "The Negro in America," *Newsweek*, 62 : 15–34, July 29, 1963.

19. B. C. Rosen, "Race, Ethnicity, and the Achievement Syndrome," *American Sociological Review*, 24 : 47–60, 1959.

intelligence from a desegregated elementary school.[20] The Negro youngsters expressed higher levels of aspiration and more ambitious hopes for the future than the white youngsters. And a recent investigation of Negro high school students throughout the South reveals that they, too, harbor a great desire for further education.[21]

Some observers interpret such heightened educational aspirations as "unrealistic" and indicative that Negroes learn early to separate their hopes from the stark reality that generally confronts them. But another study done in the late 1950's of high school seniors in Kentucky discovered that most of the Negro children who had reached this level had surprisingly well-conceived plans for the future.[22] Negro seniors in this sample were not only more optimistic than the white seniors, but they shrewdly appraised their position in American society, their better chances for white-collar jobs in the North, and their need to end discriminatory barriers.

Psychological Losses

Slowly, imperceptibly, the frame of reference for many Negro Americans has shifted during the past few decades. While formerly most Negroes judged how well off they were by their own previous conditions, the rising expectations of the present are increasingly framed in terms of the wider society. Negro protest today is moving away from an exclusive emphasis upon desegregation and equal opportunity toward a broader demand for a "fair share" and advantages directly comparable to those of whites. This shift merits special attention, for the actual gains just reviewed were all relative to previous Negro conditions. But such advances are not enough to meet the hopes of a people beginning to contrast their still-lowly position with the rich abundance surrounding them. The hard truth is that the Negro's recent progress does not begin to close the gap between the two races. Consider once again each of the realms in which changes have occurred.

Despite the large-scale migration since 1915, substantial segments of the Negro population remain in the most hostile and deprived areas of the nation. Mere mention of county names—such as Greene and Monroe in Alabama, Lee and Terrell in Georgia, Carroll and Tate in Mississippi, McCormick and Williamsburg in South Carolina, Fayette and Haywood in Tennessee, and Prince Edward in Virginia—serves to remind us that several millions of Negroes still reside in rural areas of the South which are resisting racial change by almost

20. G. F. Boyd, "The Levels of Aspiration of White and Negro Children in a Non-Segregated Elementary School," *Journal of Social Psychology*, 36:191–196, 1952.

21. M. Sherif and Carolyn Sherif, *Reference Groups: Explorations in Conformity and Deviance of Adolescents*, New York: Harper & Row, 1964.

22. A. J. Lott and Bernice E. Lott, *Negro and White Youth: A Psychological Study in a Border-State Community*. New York: Holt, Rinehart and Winston, Inc., 1963.

every means possible. The high promise of change is barely beginning in these Black Belt countries.

There is also another aspect to the recent improvements in Negro American health. . . . Life expectancy at birth still lags behind that of white Americans, though the discrepancy has shrunk to six to eight years.[23] And relative to white rates, non-white mortality rates for diabetes mellitus and cirrhosis of the liver actually increased between 1950 and 1960; this increase, however, may well reflect better reporting and diagnosis rather than actual retrogression.[24] The remaining racial disparities in health are principally due to conditions which can be drastically reduced with both improved medical care and a higher standard of living: tuberculosis, syphilis, childhood diseases, perinatal and maternal complications, etc.

Employment presents a similar picture. In spite of rapid upgrading in the past few years, Negroes employed by the federal government are still concentrated in the lower, blue-collar brackets and sparse in the upper, white-collar brackets; in most unionized industries, basic racial employment patterns remain unaltered; Negro youth suffer from almost twice the unemployment rate of white youth; and Negro adults in general are still vastly underemployed, downgraded, and underpaid relative to comparably-educated segments of the white community. The slow rise of Negro occupational trends during the 1950's is forcefully shown by projecting these trends into the future.[25] At the creeping 1950 to 1960 rate of change . . . , non-whites in the United States would not attain equal proportional representation among clerical workers until 1992, among skilled workers until 2005, among professionals until 2017, among sales workers until 2114, and among business managers and proprietors until 2730! Obviously, such a pace is ridiculously slow for a people whose expectations for the immediate future are among the most optimistic in the nation; hence, the significant slogan of the 1963 March on Washington—"Jobs and Freedom Now."

The projected eight centuries necessary to close the racial gap among business managers and proprietors illustrate once more the exclusion of Negroes from executive roles in the general society and the minuscule size of Negro business. Even in the savings and loan field, a strong Negro business area, the assets of Negro-controlled institutions constitute only approximately three-tenths of one per cent of total assets;[26] and in the insurance field, the strongest Negro business area, the assets of all Negro-controlled companies constitute only a fraction of any one of the very largest companies. Although minor

23. Metropolitan Life Insurance Company, "Progress in Longevity since 1850," *Statistical Bulletin,* 44:1–3, July 1963.

24. Goldstein, *op. cit.*

25. Glenn, *op. cit.*

26. The total assets of Negro savings and loan associations are approximately 300 million dollars (Young, *op. cit.*), while total assets of all associations passed the $100 billion mark during 1963 (*New York Times*, August 26, 1963, p. 37).

allowance must be made for a few publishing and insurance companies and financial institutions, the dour generalization of Franklin Frazier continues to hold true: " . . . 'Negro business,' which has no significance in the American economy, . . . [is] a social myth. . . . "[27]

Changes in Negro income relative to white income provide the most disappointing trend of the 1950's. The ratio of non-white to white median-family-income in 1959 (51.7 per cent) was virtually the same as in 1949 (51.1 per cent).[28] Korean War prosperity elevated the ratio to its highest point (56.8 per cent) in 1952, but since then white income gains have been markedly larger than those of non-whites. The racial discrepancy is especially great in the South, where in 1960 the median non-white family received $2687 less than the median white family; in no region, however, did the dollar difference narrow to less than $1500.[29] This means that, although the absolute level of Negro family income rose throughout the 1950's, white family income rose proportionately faster.

This sharp racial differential in family income persists in spite of a larger average number of Negro family members working and larger families to support. Differential tax payments balance this inequity slightly; but Negroes typically obtain less for their consumer dollar. This is especially true in housing. While some housing gains occurred in the 1950's, the quality of Negro housing remains vastly inferior relative to that of whites. For example, in Chicago in 1960, Negroes paid as much for housing as whites, despite their lower incomes. Median rents for both groups were $88, yet Negroes received much poorer accommodations. This situation exists because of essentially two separate housing markets; and the residential segregation that creates these dual markets "has increased steadily over past decades until it has reached universally high levels in cities throughout the United States, despite significant advances in the socio-economic status of Negroes."[30]

Even the accelerated political advances of Negro Americans leave much undone. Negroes still vote far less often than whites. Particularly in those Southern areas where racial change is most desperately needed, Negroes are least often found on the electoral rolls.[31] Indeed, there is a massive denial of the

27. E. F. Frazier, *Black Bourgeoisie*, New York: Collier Paperbacks (Macmillan), 1962, p. 193.

28. Glenn, *op. cit.*

29. Henderson, *op. cit.* One of the results of this relative lack of income improvement is that Negro family disorganization actually worsened during the 1950's. From 1950 to 1960, the percentage of nonwhite, husband-wife families slipped from 78 to 74, while the percentage of nonwhite families headed by a female increased from 18 to 21 (Edwards, *op. cit.*).

30. K. E. Taeuber and Alma F. Taeuber, "Is the Negro an Immigrant Group?" *Integrated Education*, 1: 25–28, 1963.

31. A recent ecological investigation of all the Southern counties with at least one per cent Negroes demonstrates that Negro voting is proportionately greatest in those counties with high white and Negro incomes, fairly large percentages of Negro white-collar workers, and relatively few Negroes. See D. R. Matthews and J. W. Prothro, "Political Factors and Negro Voter Registration in the South," *American Political Science Review*, 57: 355–367, 1963.

franchise in most of Alabama and Mississippi and large parts of Louisiana, Georgia, and South Carolina.[32] The proposed voting title of the 1964 Civil Rights Act provides limited help, but does not offer a definitive solution.

Finally, Negro education has yet to approach that generally available to whites. It remains in general "less available, less accessible, and especially less adequate."[33] In 1960, Negro college attendance was proportionately only about half that of whites; the percentage of adult Negroes who had completed college was considerably less than half that of whites; and the percentage who had completed high school was precisely half that of whites. These gaps are especially serious, for as we have seen, Negro hopes for the future are so centered upon education that training of poor quality at this stage could well undercut the determined thrust toward group uplift.

Thus, in each interrelated realm—health, employment, business, income, housing, voting, and education—the absolute gains of the 1950's pale when contrasted with current white standards. Numerous spokesmen for the status quo have boasted of the present status of the Negro in glowing international comparisons. Negroes in the United States today, goes one boast, have a consumer buying power comparable to that of similarly-populated Canada. And a larger percentage of Negroes, goes another, attends college than residents of the British Isles. But such glittering statements must not blind us to the fact of greatest psychological importance. Negro American standards have their psychological meaning relative to the standards of other Americans, not of Canadians or the British. The Negro American judges his living standards, his opportunities, indeed, even judges himself, in the only cultural terms he knows—those of the United States and its "people of plenty." Dr. Martin Luther King, Jr. made the point bluntly in his Washington March address: "The Negro lives on a lonely island of poverty in the midst of a vast ocean of material prosperity . . . and find himself an exile in his own land."

The resulting relative deprivation is the fundamental basis of mass Negro American dissatisfaction today. But it is not the only factor. Special frustrations are created by the appearance of proud new African nations upon the world scene. Emerging Africa has a dual psychological effect upon Negro Americans. On the one hand, it generates racial pride and lifts self-esteem—especially among the darkest members of the group. . . . On the other hand, it lends a desperate urgency to protest at home. Heretofore, Negro Americans have been the most sophisticated and respected black group in the Western world— regardless of their lowly position by American standards. But now many Africans can claim complete freedom, while Negro Americans still seek theirs. In this sense, then, independent African nations add to the Negro's keen sense of relative deprivation.

32. H. F. Gosnell and R. E. Martin, "The Negro as Voter and Office Holder," *Journal of Negro Education, 1963 Yearbook*, 32(4) : 415–425.

33. Newton and West, *op. cit.*

A similar phenomenon occurs regionally within the United States. Negro Northerners have typically prided themselves on being the products of the big-city North, on being superior to their Southern "country cousins." Yet Negro Southerners today lead the struggle for racial justice; many of them have willingly faced fire hoses, dogs, jail, and police brutality in order to demand and assert their rights; and one of them, Dr. King, has become the symbol of the protest movement throughout the country. A few Negro leaders in the South even hint wryly that the day may come when Negro Northerners will have to migrate southward to obtain true equality. And when Negroes in the North contrast their slow progress against de facto segregation in housing, schools, and employment with the dramatic desegregation of public facilities in many parts of the South, they must wonder if such wry hints do not possess some basis in truth.

Thus, the present-day Negro's feeling of being left behind springs from three sources. It derives partly from relating his situation to emerging Africa. For the Negro Northerner, it also stems from comparing his gains with those of his on-rushing Southern relatives. But its primary source is from contrasting his still meager lot with the abundance of other Americans.

Reference Group Behavior and Mental Disorder

Seymour Parker and Robert J. Kleiner

Introduction

THE central problem of this study developed from an attempt to replicate the early studies of Malzberg and Lee[1] on migration and mental disorder among Negroes. These investigators found that Negro migrants (predominantly from the South) to New York State during the period 1929–1939 had a significantly higher rate of mental disorder, as gauged by first admissions to public and private hospitals in the state, than those who were born in New York.

In view of Malzberg's and Lee's conclusive findings, we were surprised that the rate of first admissions of Negroes to the Pennsylvania public mental hospitals during the period 1951–1956 was significantly higher for natives than for migrants to the state, even when age and sex differences in the two populations were taken into account.[2] Explanations advanced by previous studies to account for the relationship between migration and mental illness might lead one intuitively to expect a higher first admission rate for migrants (e.g., the difficulties involved in adjusting to unfamiliar surroundings; the greater propensity of maladjusted individuals to move into a new environment, etc.). However, the statistically significant findings of our study raised questions about the plausibility of such a rationale. Our perplexity and interest increased on noting that in the Philadelphia Negro community the rate of juvenile delinquency

Reprinted in part from Seymour Parker and Robert J. Kleiner, *Mental Illness in the Urban Negro Community*, pp. 1–28, 137–165, by permission of the authors and the publishers, The Free Press. Copyright 1966 by The Free Press, a division of The Macmillan Company.

1. B. Malzberg and E. S. Lee, *Migration and Mental Disease: A Study of First Admissions to Hospitals for Mental Disease, New York, 1939–1941*, New York: Social Science Research Council, 1956.

2. R. J. Kleiner and S. Parker, "Migration and Mental Illness: A New Look," *American Sociological Review*, 24: 687–690, 1959.

was higher among adolescents native to Philadelphia than among those born in the South.[3] Also, "broken homes," as measured by the rate of divorces, separations, and desertions, were more numerous among natives than migrants.[4]

Although these studies reported the statistical distributions of the phenomena under consideration, they offered little rationale for understanding them. The theoretical problems posed by such findings excited our curiosity about possible explanations for the higher rates of deviant behavior (i.e., mental disorder, juvenile delinquency, and broken homes) of the Negro native to Pennsylvania. We determined that status position, often linked to such indices of deviancy, could not explain these results; in fact, using education as an index of status position, the native Negro rated considerably higher than the migrant. Were the reasons for similarity in direction of these rates of deviant behavior unrelated, or etiologically linked? Would it be possible to subsume them under a single theoretical formulation?

At about this time, Robert Kleiner and his associates completed an analysis of census data pertaining to the Negro community of Philadelphia. They found that, controlling for occupational level, the native group had significantly higher educational attainments than the migrant. Level of education was assumed to be roughly correlated with level of aspiration in significant areas of life.[5] The suggestion that the discrepancy between achievement and aspiration might be higher among native Negroes than among migrants provided the necessary conceptual wedge. We reasoned that the Negro who spent his formative years of socialization in the semi-caste system of the South would be prone to gear his aspirations to a relatively low level at an early age in order to accommodate to his social situation.[6] That such adjustments are common for the southern Negro has been amply documented in the writings of Allison Davis, John Dollard, and others. However, the Negro raised in the North would be more likely to partake for a longer period in an ethos that (ideally) sanctioned high success goals for everyone. Only at a later stage in life would he realize that the available means for achieving his relatively high aspirations were severely limited because he was a Negro, and because he probably occupied a low rung on the socioeconomic-educational ladder. Keeping in mind that the occupational achievements of both groups were similar, we assumed that the Negro raised in the North would be likely to experience a relatively larger discrepancy between his aspirations and achievements than the migrant Negro. We further assumed that the effect of this larger discrepancy would be psychologically stressful, and/or

3. L. Savitz, *Delinquency and Migration*, Philadelphia: Commission on Human Relations, 1960.

4. W. M. Kephart and T. P. Monahan, "Desertion and Divorce in Philadelphia," *American Sociological Review*, 17: 719–727, 1952.

5. J. Tuckman and R. J. Kleiner, "Discrepancy between Aspiration and Achievement as a Predictor of Schizophrenia," *Behavioral Science*, 7: 443–447, 1962.

6. A. J. Prange and M. M. Vitols, "Cultural Aspects of the Relatively Low Incidence of Depression in Southern Negroes," *International Journal of Social Psychiatry*, 8: 104–112, 1962.

that the pressure to lower one's aspirations would be accompanied by a serious loss of self-esteem and a propensity toward mental disorder.

For these reasons, we decided to focus our study on the psychopathogenic effects of goal-striving behavior. Migration and other sociological variables became subsidiary to this interest; the overall research design of the study would incorporate these variables in order to test the predictive power of our theoretical formulation of goal-striving stress. While other investigators[7] in this area inferred discrepancies from educational and occupational data, the present study elicited information on aspirations by means of direct interviews.

Although the relationship between goal-striving experience and mental disorder will be examined in a Negro population, it is not *specifically* a Negro problem. . . . The psychic burden of this striving is heavy for Americans in general, but particularly so for the Negro who battles for equality and status position in a social system that is *relatively* closed to him. Kardiner and Ovesey,[8] in their psychiatric study of Negroes, and Max Lerner,[9] in his analysis of American civilization, observed that a considerable proportion of the Negro's self-hatred and frustration stemmed from his acceptance of white goals, which for him were largely unattainable. This idea was expressed cogently by Frazier,[10] and further confirmed in a recent study by Parker and Kleiner.[11] We found that the Negro's status position varied with negative attitudes toward the Negro community. Although our selection of Negro subjects in order to study goal-striving behavior and orientation was partly an historical accident, in certain respects it was a fortunate choice. The additional social barriers to advancement encountered by the Negro make his goal-striving experience extremely painful; the investigation of these experiences may show a particularly clear relationship to mental disorder. In addition, because of the different prevailing ideologies and norms in the North and the South, a Negro sample allows us to study the psychic effects of varying levels and intensities of goal striving among individuals socialized in the two environments. . . .

Sociological and Social-Psychological Origins

Merton's views on goal-striving and reference group behavior[12] are relevant to this problem and add an important sociological dimension to the conceptual

7. E.g., Tuckman and Kleiner, *op. cit.*

8. A. Kardiner and L. Ovesey, *The Mark of Oppression: A Psychosocial Study of the American Negro*, New York: W. W. Norton and Company, Inc., 1951.

9. M. Lerner, *America as a Civilization: Life and Thought in the United States Today*, New York: Simon and Schuster, Inc., 1957.

10. E. F. Frazier, *Black Bourgeoisie*, New York: The Free Press, 1957.

11. S. Parker and R. J. Kleiner, "Status Position, Mobility, and Ethnic Identification of the Negro," *Journal of Social Issues*, 20: 85–102, 1964.

12. R. K. Merton, *Social Theory and Social Structure*, revised edition, New York: The Free Press, 1957, pp. 131–160, 161–194, 225–280, 281–386.

framework of the present study. In discussing the social and cultural precondi-
tions of deviant behavior, Merton noted that the American ethos "extols common success goals for the population at large." There is a strong emphasis on
high achievement goals and a widespread belief that hard work insures success.
Hyman[13] found that most people chose reference groups with achievements
above their own. In the past, such beliefs were both realistic and functional for
the individual. America has permitted upward social mobility, apparently to a
greater degree than other societies; the continually striving individual has had
a fairly good chance (i.e., high probability) of reaching his aspirations. Unfortunately, the striving Negro has been an exception to this "American dream."[14]
Like his fellow Americans, the Negro internalizes the common success values
and assumes (for varying periods of his life) that his chances of achieving his
aspirations are good. He, too, is led to believe in the ethos of the open social
system which permits a high rate of social mobility. Given the objective fact of
the limited opportunity structure for the Negro,[15] this estimate of reality is not
feasible and frequently leads to frustration.[16] It is not simply that he fails to
achieve specific valued goals, but rather that he considers himself a failure and
experiences concomitant and severe loss of self-esteem because he has internalized
the values of success orientation. In his discussion of reference group theory,
Merton[17] introduced the concept of "anticipatory socialization" by which he
explained some of the sources of deviant behavior and personal maladjustment.
According to this concept, the individual's role expectations and behavioral
norms are geared to the anticipation that he will achieve the standards of his
reference group. In a sense, he becomes partially socialized to a situation in
which he *expects* to be involved. The specific values and behavioral norms involved in this anticipatory socialization are embodied in his reference group,
which provides him with role models. Where the potential for social mobility
is high, these anticipations will be functional and psychologically adjustive, in
that they will facilitate the transition to new roles associated with higher status
positions. But if social mobility is restricted, as it is for most Negroes, the consequences of anticipatory socialization may be seriously dysfunctional. The individual in this situation becomes psychologically marginal to his peers and to
those at the level he aspires to reach. Thus, the consequences of high goal striving

13. H. H. Hyman, "The Psychology of Status," *Archives of Psychology*, Number 269, 1942.

14. Frazier, *op. cit.*, pp. 153–212.

15. E. Haveman and P. S. West, *They Went to College*, New York: Harcourt, Brace and
World, Inc., 1952, p. 96; S. M. Lipset and R. Bendix, *Social Mobility in Industrial Society*,
Berkeley and Los Angeles: University of California Press, 1963, p. 106.

16. Kardiner and Ovesey, *op. cit.*, p. 316; P. C. Glick and H. P. Miller, "Educational
Level and Potential Income," *American Sociological Review*, 21: 307–312, 1956; R. Dreger
and K. S. Miller, "Comparative Studies of Negroes and Whites in the United States," *Psychological Bulletin*, 57: 361–402, 1960.

17. Merton, *op. cit.*, pp. 225–280, 281–386.

differ depending on the nature of the social structure and the reference group behavior of the individual. ... ⌐

While goal-striving stress may itself increase susceptibility to mental disorder (for the reasons already discussed), its effects are probably conditioned by the manner in which the individual perceives and interprets his failure to reach important goals. The individual can perceive high goal-striving stress either as a prelude to success or failure. The consequences of these different perceptions for mental health may be very different. His interpretation of goal-striving stress will also differ, depending on whether he perceives his reference group situation as threatening to his concept of self and to his interpersonal relations. We assume that the individual's reference group behavior determines to a great extent how he interprets his goal-striving experience.[18] In some cases the actual position achieved by a reference group which one aspires to enter supplies the criteria for evaluation. In other instances the values of the current reference group (or individual) determine whether feelings of success or failure are associated with a specific achievement level. Reference group behavior is also significant for this study insofar as it provides an arena for the operation of individual psychological defenses against the potentially stressful consequences of goal-striving experiences. As conceived here, the reference group functions primarily to supply evaluative criteria for one's behavior. Festinger and his associates[19] noted that frequently "there is no objective, non-social basis for evaluating one's abilities. To the extent that such objective bases are lacking the individual again evaluates his abilities by comparing [them] with the abilities of others in groups of which he is a member." Research on reference groups indicates that their importance in determining feelings of success or failure increases (1) if the individual is a member of the group; (2) if it is attractive to him; and, (3) if the evaluative criteria it supplies are relevant or important to him. The individual will evaluate himself as a failure if, in an area relevant to his self-esteem, he perceives his performance as falling below that of a significant reference group (i.e., negative discrepancy), and he will regard himself as adequate or superior if he perceives that his performance is equal to or above it.[20]

18. K. Lewin, "Psychology of Success and Failure," *Occupations*, 14: 926–930, 1936; R. S. Lazarus and R. W. Baker, "Personality and Psychological Stress: A Theoretical and Methodological Framework," *Psychological Newsletter*, 8: 21–32, 1956; R. Simpson, "Parental Influence, Anticipatory Socialization, and Social Mobility," *American Sociological Review*, 27: 517–522, 1962; A. Zander and R. Quinn, "The Social Environment and Mental Health: A Review of Past Research at the Institute for Social Research," *Journal of Social Issues*, 18: 48–66, 1962; A. Zander and H. Medow, "Individual and Group Levels of Aspiration," *Human Relations*, 16: 89–105, 1963; C. N. Alexander and E. Q. Campbell, "Peer Influences on Adolescent Educational Aspirations and Attainments," *American Sociological Review*, 29: 568–575, 1964.

19. L. Festinger, J. Torrey, and B. Willerman, "Self-Evaluation as a Function of Attraction to the Group," *Human Relations*, 7: 161–174, 1954.

20. G. Rasmussen and A. Zander, "Group Membership and Self-Evaluation," *Human Relations*, 7: 239–251, 1954; Simpson, *op. cit.*; Zander and Quinn, *op. cit.*; Zander and Medow, *op. cit.*; Alexander and Campbell, *op. cit.*

We further hypothesize that the individual who experiences such feelings of failure will be more prone to mental illness. . . .

The use of the concepts of goal-striving stress and distance from reference group as interacting elements raises some questions about their meaning and whether, in fact, they reflect similar phenomena. Is not one's own level of aspiration (used to measure goal-striving stress) already determined by the performance level of his relevant reference groups? If this is true, then considering the stress levels arising from these respective sources is tantamount to adding the same phenomenon twice. Careful consideration of these concepts, however, suggests that they overlap to some degree but are not congruent. One's level of aspiration can be regarded as the historical, but still active, precipitate of *all* his significant reference group experiences, past and present, and the degree to which he has met with success and failure in the past. Although one's personal level of aspiration *includes* norms emanating from actual reference groups in his environment, these groups do not exclusively determine such norms.[21] Norms provided by one's existing reference group contain evaluative elements, or standards by which current performance and achievement are evaluated. . . .

Methods and Procedures

. . . The basic research design involved the comparison of two populations, both drawn from the Philadelphia Negro community: a representative sample of the community population, and a representative sample of individuals diagnosed as mentally ill. In order to determine with a high degree of confidence any significant differences between these two populations on any of the variables under consideration, the samples had to be large enough to permit comparisons when such factors as age, sex, achievement level, etc., were controlled, or held constant.

The sophisticated reader might question the implication that individuals in the community sample were necessarily "healthy" from a psychiatric viewpoint. Everyday observation, confirmed by Srole et al.[22] and Langner and Michael,[23] indicates that such an assumption is untenable. Clearly, a certain proportion of individuals in any community population will be afflicted with emotional symptoms of varying severity. Therefore, we included in our mentally ill sample all those from the community sample who reported being treated by a physician for "nervous or mental trouble" at the time of, or during the year preceding, the interview ($N = 99$). This procedure removed from the community

21. Simpson, *op. cit.*; Zander and Quinn, *op. cit.*; Zander and Medow, *op. cit.*; Alexander and Campbell, *op. cit.*

22. L. Srole, T. S. Langner, S. T. Michael, M. K. Opler, and T. A. C. Rennie, *Mental Health in the Metropolis: The Midtown Manhattan Study*, Vol. 1, New York: McGraw-Hill Book Company, 1962.

23. T. S. Langner and S. T. Michael, *Life Stress and Mental Health: The Midtown Manhattan Study*, Vol. 2, New York: The Free Press, 1963.

sample only current or recently treated cases; undoubtedly individuals remained who were not then in treatment but who probably required psychiatric care. Fifty-six (3.7 per cent) of the 1489 cases remaining in the community sample reported some contact with psychiatric facilities prior to the year preceding the study. We made two assumptions about our samples: (1) that the ill sample contained a significantly larger number of psychiatrically ill individuals than the community sample; and (2) that those who were psychiatrically ill in the treated sample were significantly more impaired than the untreated disturbed individuals in the community sample. These assumptions permitted us to test hypotheses concerning the relationship between particular variables and mental disorder. The questionnaire instrument administered to the community and ill samples also included a checklist of symptoms indicating the possible existence of psychopathology. This list facilitated a separation in the community sample of the relatively well and relatively ill and provided a method for confirming the hypotheses made about subgroups in the community population. . . .

Major Hypotheses and Findings

 . . . It is assumed here that one's perception of his goal-striving experiences and the psychological impact of this perception will be partly determined by the standards by which he evaluates his performance. Further, that these standards and norms of comparison are derived from the significant groups (or individuals) he desires to emulate. . . .

In this study, the reference group concept designates the group (or individual) which serves as a reference point or means of evaluating oneself. This was the major emphasis placed on the concept in Hyman's pioneering study.[24] It seems that the use of a reference group as an anchor point enabling the individual to make judgments concerning his own achievements and self-image is most relevant to his sense of self-esteem and ultimately to his state of mental health. Given two persons of identical objectively defined status, the individual who evaluates himself by the standards of a relatively higher status reference group may be less satisfied with his own status and thus more prone to various manifestations of maladjustment and psychopathology.

This chain of reasoning has appeared frequently in the research literature.[25] It is often assumed that people choose reference groups or reference individuals occupying a status relatively close to their own. Hyman[26] attributed this tendency to 'proximity to him [the individual] in life situations, or as the result of

24. Hyman, *op. cit.*

25. Hyman, *op. cit.*; Merton, *op. cit.*, 225–280; J. K. Myers and B. H. Roberts, *Family and Class Dynamics in Mental Illness*, New York: John Wiley and Sons, Inc., 1959, p. 142ff.; Zander and Quinn, *op. cit.*

26. Hyman, *op. cit.*

objective facts which facilitate such comparisons." Festinger, et al.[27] regarded similar or proximal status choices as a result of "the pressure toward uniformity which may exist in a group." In the context of this study we assume that, because of their objectively circumscribed range of social interaction with others of similar status, and because of the need to maintain feelings of competence, most people do tend to select reference points at, or close to, their own positions.

When an individual is below his reference group on a scale of status positions, we say he is characterized by a "negative discrepancy." If his own position is above that of his reference group, he is said to have a "positive discrepancy." Up to this point the discussion suggests that if we compare people of equal status, those with relatively high reference groups (i.e., negative discrepancies) will be more prone to self-devaluation and mental illness. The hypotheses presented in this chapter incorporate this idea of a direct relationship between degree of negative discrepancy from reference group and severity of mental illness (i.e., the more negatively discrepant, the greater the severity of illness.)

Hypothesis II. The degree of negative discrepancy from a reference group will vary directly with the severity of mental illness.

Hypothesis IIa. Within the mentally ill population, negative discrepancy from a reference group will be higher for the psychotics than for the neurotics.

Hypothesis IIb. Within the community population, negative discrepancy from a reference group will be larger for a high symptom group than for a low symptom group.

We have specified no formal predictions about positive discrepancies from reference group. Such predictions would involve the very problematic issue of using reference groups for psychologically defensive purposes, or alternatively, as a means to enable the individual to cope with his felt anxieties. In agreement with Festinger and Hyman, we assume that pressures toward uniformity are such that most people select a reference group close to their own status position. It has also been noted in the literature, however, that individuals experiencing threats to their interpersonal relations are likely to choose reference groups considerably above *and* below their own position—there can be wishfully high and low choices.

Hyman[28] distinguished between "realistic" and "autistic" reference group choices. As the term implies, an autistic choice is determined by felt pressures to minimize threats, and, to varying degrees, it ignores elements of the realistic situation. Realistic choices, on the other hand, do not "stand in major contradiction with reality." Hyman cited examples of people who, in order to be reassured of their own superiority, evaluated themselves by comparisons with

27. L. Festinger, K. Back, S. Schachter, H. H. Kelley, and J. Thibaut, *Theory and Experiment in Social Communication*, Ann Arbor, Michigan: Research Center for Dynamics, Institute for Social Research, University of Michigan, 1950, p. 4.

28. Hyman, *op. cit.*

individuals who were considered inferior. Other individuals used reference points considerably above their own positions in order to reassure themselves that they could and would reach higher levels. Similar examples demonstrating both defensive types of reference group choices were reported by Frenkel-Brunswik.[29] Based on carefully conducted clinical interviews she concluded:

> It would appear that we do not always see ourselves as we are but instead perceive the environment in terms of our own needs. Self-perception and perception of the environment actually merge in the service of these needs. Thus, the perceptual distortions of ourselves and the environment fulfil an important function in our psychological household.

A bimodal defensive pattern of reference group behavior in psychiatric patients was further evidenced in a large scale study conducted in New Haven.[30]

Although the hypotheses stated above constitute our only formal predictions, in view of these kinds of findings in the literature, we anticipate greater negative discrepancies from reference groups, and, to a lesser extent larger positive discrepancies, for the patients than for the community subjects.

In this chapter we shall principally be concerned with Hypotheses II, IIa, and IIb. . . .

In order to operationalize our measures of discrepancy from reference group and test the relevant hypotheses, certain assumptions and choices between alternative procedures were made. First, it was necessary that the respondent choose the criteria sufficiently salient *for him* to be used as the basis by which he compared himself to his reference group. Obviously, there were different criteria serving such functions. Second, we felt that the choice of reference group should be limited to those with which the respondent had face-to-face relations, rather than groups more psychologically remote. Previous research had indicated that such face-to-face groups were likely to provide more potent bases for self-judgments. Finally, within the range of face-to-face reference groups, we felt it was important to select a given reference point for all respondents that would maximize the comparability of responses. Hyman's study[31] indicated that one's friends and acquaintances constituted the most common reference group to which he compared his own achievements. Therefore, we decided to make our self-anchored striving scale measure a basis for deriving data on the degree of discrepancy from reference group.

The self-anchored striving scale has already been described: each respondent was presented with a diagrammatic representation of a flight of ten steps, the bottom one labelled the "worst possible way of life" and the top, the "best

29. E. Frenkel-Brunswik, "Personality Theory and Perception," in R. Blake and G. V. Ramsey (eds.), *Perception, an Approach to Personality*, New York: The Ronald Press Company, 1951, pp. 356–419.

30. Myers and Roberts, *op. cit.*, p. 147.

31. Hyman, *op. cit.*

possible way of life." After specifying the content of these two anchor points, the respondent selected the step that represented his own current position. . . . At a later point in the questionnaire he was asked to choose the step-position of his "close friends" and to specify "the things you had in mind when you compared the position of your close friends to yourself." . . . By determining the size and the direction of the difference between the respondent's own step-position on the striving scale and that of his "close friends," we were provided with a measure of his discrepancy from his reference group.

Brief mention should be made of the criteria specified by community and ill respondents by which they compared themselves to their close friends. The first and second criteria given in response to this question were tabulated separately in each population. Since correlations between first and second choices are extremely high (.94 and .92 respectively, $P = < .01$) for both populations, this discussion will be limited only to first choices. The distributions of responses for the two populations correlate significantly (.84, $P = < .01$; see Table 1). There are apparently no significant differences in the choices of criteria by which the two populations compare themselves to their respective reference groups. By far the most common criterion of comparison between self and friends used by patients and community respondents is "Economic factors." (Over 50 per cent of each population use this criterion.) The large percentage of responses falling into this category is consistent with reports from other relevant research.[32] The only response category for which there is a sizable percentage difference between the two samples is "Morality" (see Table 1).

The average discrepancy between one's own perceived position and that of his "close friends" for both populations and subgroups within these populations is a negative one—that is, the step chosen for self is usually lower than

Table I—Criteria for Comparing Self With Close Friends*

	COMMUNITY	ILL
	per cent	
Health	3	5
Economic factors		
(financial and occupational)	54	53
Relations with friends	4	3
Family relations	9	10
Morality ("good life")	14	6
Personality characteristics	10	12
Education and training	3	7
Miscellaneous	3	4
Total N	1446	1390

* The rank order correlation between repsonse distributions of the community and ill population is .84 ($P = \lhd .01$).

32. *Ibid.*

that chosen for reference group. This finding is consistent with other research.[33] As predicted in Hypothesis II, the mentally ill place themselves further below their reference group than do those in the community ($P = < .001$; see Table 2).

Table 2—Mean Negative Reference Group Discrepancy by Illness Status, Sex, and Age

(1)		(2)	Mean (1)	Mean (2)	N1	N2	P (By "t" test)
Total ill	vs	total comm.	1.63	.44	1390	1446	< .001
Ill males	vs	comm. males	1.67	.40	565	585	< .001
Ill females	vs	comm. females	1.60	.46	825	861	< .001
Ill young	vs	comm. young	1.63	.48	983	772	< .001
Ill old	vs	comm. old	1.62	.39	407	671	< .001
Psychotics	vs	neurotics	1.81	1.10	1036	354	< .001
High symp.	vs	low symp.	.95	.38	165	1281	< .001
Psychotics	vs	low symp.	1.81	.38	1036	1281	< .001
Neurotics	vs	low symp.	1.10	.38	354	1281	< .001

It should be remembered that respondents were free to use any criteria of comparison, and to place themselves and their reference group at any position on the ten-step scale. The mean discrepancy for the patients is significantly larger than the corresponding discrepancy for the community subjects.

These significant differences between the two populations persist when sex and age controls are applied. Not only is the average negative discrepancy consistently considerably larger for the mentally ill, but the variance of the mentally ill sample (9.49) is also significantly greater than that of the community sample (3.06). This tendency among the patients to manifest more dispersion on the discrepancy continuum is related to the previous discussion about the use of reference group comparisons as a psychological coping mechanism. The relative propensity for extreme discrepancies at both ends of the continuum will be explored more fully in subsequent analyses of the data.

The data in Table 2 confirm all three hypotheses involving reference group discrepancy. In support of Hypothesis II, there is a direct relationship between negative reference group discrepancy and severity of illness. The psychotics are significantly ($P = < .001$) more negatively discrepant than the neurotics (Hypothesis IIa). The high symptom group is characterized by a significantly ($P = < .001$) larger mean negative discrepancy than the·low symptom group (Hypothesis IIb).

At this point we should restate the assumption that the low symptom group, the high symptom group, the neurotics, and the psychotics constitute a continuum of increasing severity of mental illness. This sequence will be implied whenever subsequent reference is made to these four mental health groupings.

The mean negative discrepancy increases along our mental health continuum, as expected, and all comparisons of adjacent groupings are significant except for the high symptom-neurotics comparison. In Chapter 3, we reported

33. *Ibid.*

little difference between these two mental health groupings on goal-striving stress scores. In the present context, not only does the mean reference group discrepancy become increasingly negative with severity of mental illness, but the variances around the respective means for mental health groupings also increase with illness (2.79, 4.93, 7.02, and 10.24, respectively)—there is a greater spread of discrepancies above and below the mean position of the group as severity of illness increases. This general pattern of variability was also manifested in the goal-striving stress scores of the mental health groupings. . . .

Although the findings just reported strongly confirm our major hypotheses about the relationship between mental illness and reference group behavior, they also raise questions necessitating further investigation. The mean negative discrepancy from reference group becomes progressively larger with an increase in severity of illness, but this indicates little about the distributions of actual discrepancies within these groupings. Similar means may result from very dissimilar distributions. This problem relates to the possible defensive function of reference group behavior—that is, its function as a means of coping with threats to the self. We have speculated that such defenses may be characterized by a tendency to choose reference groups above and below one's own perceived position.

Table 3 presents the distributions of negative, positive, and zero reference

Table 3—Distribution of Reference Group Discrepancies, by Illness Status in Percentages

	TOTAL						CONTROL GROUP 1-3		4-6		7-10	
	III	Comm.	Low Symp.	High Symp.	Neur.	Psych.	III	Comm.	III	Comm.	III	Comm.
Relationship to Reference group												
Above	17	18	18	19	21	17	4	5	16	13	30	21
At	25	47	49	37	30	23	11	29	23	36	37	55
Below	57	35	33	44	50	61	85	66	61	50	33	24
Total N	1390	1446	1281	165	354	1036	330	79	536	473	461	838

group discrepancies within various population subgroups, with and without striving scale achievement controls. Twenty-two per cent more ill than community respondents place themselves below their reference group. There are almost no differences between the two populations in the proportions who place themselves above their reference group. Consequently, many more community than ill respondents place themselves at the same position as their reference group. This pattern of differences is also found in each of the sex and age subgroups and is significant in each instance ($P = < .001$). Apparently, the "defensive" response of placing oneself above his reference group does not occur. . . .

Some of the reference group discrepancy differences between the ill and community samples may be a function of the positions selected and the limitations imposed by the use of the ten-step scale. For example, although the patients tend to select lower positions on the scale than the community respondents, their potential discrepancy from reference group may be greater merely because there are more positions above them on the scale at which to place their reference group. An individual who places himself at step 9 can only be one step below his reference group, whereas an individual who selects step 3 as his position has a much larger potential negative discrepancy. This scale problem can be eliminated by controlling, or holding constant, the respondent's perceived position on the ten-step scale. As a further refinement of the reference group discrepancy analyses, we compared only those individuals who placed themselves at approximately the same position on the striving scale. This procedure was intended to determine whether the ill-community differences were maintained when striving scale achievement controls were used. In order to facilitate control group comparisons, we divided our populations into three achievement control categories: respondents who placed themselves at positions 1 through 3, 4 through 6, and 7 through 10. Table 3 presents the results of the total ill-community sample comparisons. We shall discuss in text the relevant trends for the four mental health groupings within these control groups.

Within each of the three control categories, more ill than community respondents place themselves below their reference group. Therefore, the differences already observed between the ill and community samples are not merely artifacts of respondents' selected striving-scale positions. In every control group, the percentage of individuals at the same position as their reference group is smaller among the patients than among the community respondents. However, differences among the three control groups *do* emerge when we consider respondents with positive discrepancies. Community and ill subjects in the lowest control category (self-step 1 through 3), show a negligible difference in positive discrepancy, but more patients than community individuals are characterized by a positive discrepancy in the next control category (self-step 4 through 6). This preference for a position above that of the reference group is significant only in the highest control group (self-step 7 through 10; $P = <.01$). The mentally ill in the two highest control groups are more likely to choose reference groups above *and* below their own position, but this tendency is particularly apparent and statistically significant in control group 7 though 10 (see Table 3). These findings suggest the occurrence of a larger proportion of defensively high and low reference group choices among the mentally ill in the high achievement groups. This is not meant to imply, however, that the majority of negative reference group discrepancies among the patients are of a psychologically defensive nature. . . .

Reference Group Behavior Determined by Subjective Social Status Position

A second measure was used in addition to the self-anchored striving scale to investigate the general relationship between reference group behavior and mental illness: the individual's subjective status position. Subjective status refers to one's evaluation of his own social status position compared to that of some relevant reference group. Perception of one's own position depends upon the status attributed to the others with whom he compares himself. As an example, individuals in a middle income range will perceive their own income level as low if compared to a Rockefeller, and as high if compared to that of a Southern sharecropper.

On the basis of this assumption we asked each respondent, "What things do you think of when you decide what social class a person belongs to?" . . . The respondent either selected factors from a precoded list of various criteria of social class, or else specified additional unlisted criteria. He was then asked: "Taking into account the things you just told me, which of these choices best describes where you are?" . . . The precoded alternatives were "Much above average," "Somewhat above average," "Average," "Somewhat below average," and "Much below average." We reasoned that most people probably compare themselves on overall status position to others who occupy a fairly similar position on the status continuum, and therefore regard themselves as "Average." In a group of individuals occupying the same objectively defined status position, those regarding themselves as "Below average" are comparing themselves with a higher status reference group, and those placing themselves "Above average" are comparing themselves with a status group lower than their own. This reasoning provided us with a procedure for determining the relative discrepancy from reference group and its direction. In order to simplify the presentation of these analyses, we combined the five subjective status categories into three: "Average," "Below average," and "Above average." The findings reported below were also obtained when all five subjective status categories were considered, however.

Table 4 presents data on the subjective status item for the total community

Table 4—Distribution of Subjective Social Status, by Illness Status in Percentages

	TOTAL						MULTI-STATUS 1		MULTI-STATUS 2		MULTI-STATUS 3		MULTI-STATUS 4	
	Ill	Comm.	Low Symp.	High Symp.	Neur.	Psych.	Ill	Comm.	Ill	Comm.	Ill	Comm.	Ill	Comm.
Much or somewhat above average	18	15	15	14	16	19	11	9	14	12	19	12	33	26
Average	43	63	63	63	48	42	40	54	45	65	46	69	40	62
Much or somewhat below average	39	22	22	23	36	40	50	36	42	22	35	19	28	12
Total N	1394	1457	1285	172	353	1041	332	340	349	348	430	379	273	373

Summary of significant chi-square analyses
Total Ill vs. Total Comm., $P = < .001$
Psychotics vs. High symptom, $P = < .001$
Psychotics vs. Low symptoms, $P = < .001$
Neurotics vs. High symptoms, $P = < .005$
Neurotics vs. Low symptoms, $P = < .001$

Multi-status: Ill vs. Comm., $P = < .01$
Multi-status: Ill vs. Comm., $P = < .001$
Multi-status: Ill vs. Comm., $P = < .001$
Multi-status: Ill vs. Comm., $P = < .001$

and ill samples, for the mental health continuum, and for each of four objectively determined multi-status positions* within each sample. Hypothesis II, which predicts that the degree of negative discrepancy from a reference group will be higher in the ill than in the general community population, is confirmed. The proportion of those regarding themselves as "Below average" (i.e., negative discrepancy from reference group) is significantly greater ($P = < .001$) for the patients than the community subjects. More of the community respondents regard their status position as "Average," but slightly more ill than community subjects consider their status "Above average." These same trends are evident in each of the four objective multi-status control groups and are significant in each case. These differences between the ill and the community populations also hold for each of the different sex and age subgroups and again are significant in every instance.

A more detailed examination of these four multi-status control groups reveals some additional findings. In each status control group more than half the responses of community respondents indicate "Average" subjective status. Among the mentally ill, all the corresponding percentages for the "Average" response are less than 50. As objective multi-status position increases from level 1 to 4, the proportion of those considering themselves "Below average" decreases among community and ill respondents, but it remains consistently higher among the mentally ill. Both mental illness and objective multi-status position appear to be influential in determining subjective social status position. It is important to note that as objective multi-status level goes from 1 to 4, "Above average" response choices tend to increase more rapidly among ill than among community respondents. The percentage difference between the ill and community populations on this response increases from 1 to 7 per cent. Thus, although respondents' objective and subjective social status positions rise simultaneously as expected, the ill are increasingly more likely to consider themselves "Above average." This suggests that as objective status increases, the mentally ill become relatively more prone to compare themselves with a reference group at a position below their own. The same tendency emerges in the analyses of the self-anchored striving scale: in the highest striving scale achievement control group, more patients than community individuals chose reference groups below their own position. This type of reference group choice may serve to (defensively) inflate self-esteem, but even in the mentally ill population such defenses are exaggerations, rather than complete distortions, of reality.

Earlier it was predicted that the psychotics would place themselves further below their reference group than the neurotics (Hypothesis 2a), and similarly, that the high symptom group would be more negatively discrepant than the low symptom group (Hypothesis IIb). Although the data on the subjective status item go in the predicted direction, neither hypothesis is supported by significant findings. When the four mental health groupings subsumed under the two

*Social class, or "multi-status position," refers to a composite index of education, income, and occupation.

hypotheses are considered on an illness continuum, the percentages of "Below average" responses increase progressively from the low symptom group to the psychotics (see Table 4). This sequential increase is statistically significant ($P = < .001$).

In addition, the percentages for both ill diagnostic groupings are significantly higher than either of the community sample groupings. There are no significant differences among the four mental health groupings on the "Above average" choice of subjective status position, nor is the direction of these responses consistent. Although there is no difference between the high and low symptom groups in the proportion of "Average" responses (i.e., no discrepancy from reference group), this percentage decreases progressively from the high symptom group, to the neurotics, to the psychotics. This tendency supports the idea that positive states of mental health are associated with little or no discrepancy from reference group. . . .

Reference Group Behavior Determined by Blue/White-Collar Occupational Choices

Our questionnaire instrument presented every subject with three pairs of occupations, each having a specified salary attached. The respondent was asked to select his own job preference from each pair. . . . Each paired choice consisted of one white- and one blue-collar occupation. The salary associated with the latter choice was always somewhat higher than for its white-collar counterpart. We assumed that when two individuals at the same objective socio-economic multi-status position were presented with these alternative choices, the one selecting the white-collar occupation with its lower salary did so because his reference norms were associated with a higher status nonmanual "middle-class" orientation (people, values, style of life, etc.). Since such occupations are considered to be higher and more prestigious on the social status continuum in our society, we felt that an analysis of these occupational choices constituted one index of the relative height of the reference groups selected by our subjects.

In order to insure additional validity for this assumption, we associated the white-collar occupations with particularly low weekly salaries ($60 to $80 range). Under such conditions, only those with a strong middle-class orientation would probably select the nonmanual job alternative. Two qualifications should be noted:

(1) Since some of the choices listed (e.g., bricklayer) are considered to be male occupations, we present only the responses given by males in our sample population.

(2) All those at multi-status positions 1 and 2 already have blue-collar occupations of differing degrees of skill. Position 3 contains individuals with both blue- and white-collar occupations, while level 4 includes only respondents in white-collar positions. Therefore, our assumption that the white-collar choice reflects a higher reference point applies mainly to subjects at the two lowest

multi-status levels. This assumption should be less applicable at status level 3, and not at all applicable at level 4.

The blue/white-collar occupations and their attached salaries are listed in Table 5. Consistent with Hypothesis II, we predict that significantly more

Table 5—Blue-Collar White-Collar Occupational Choice as an Indicator of Reference Group (Males) in Percentages

	MULTI-STATUS 1		MULTI-STATUS 2		MULTI-STATUS 3		MULTI-STATUS 4	
	Ill	Comm.	Ill	Comm.	Ill	Comm.	Ill	Comm.
Choice 1								
Blue-Collar: Bricklayer—$120	47	68	37	58	37	42	31	30
White-Collar: Teacher—$90	53	32	63	42	63	58	69	70
Total N	110	104	126	128	197	165	140	193
Choice 2								
Blue-Collar: Machine-								
Operator—$100	54	71	42	69	42	56	46	52
White-Collar: Gov't. Clerk—								
$80	46	29	58	31	58	44	54	48
Total N	110	104	126	128	197	165	140	193
Choice 3								
Blue-Collar: Factory								
Worker—$80	66	77	39	79	60	68	63	53
White-Collar: Sales Person								
(department store)—$60	34	23	61	21	40	32	37	47
Total N	110	104	126	127	197	163	140	187

Summary of significant chi-square analyses
Choice 1: Multi-status-1, Ill vs. Comm., $P = < .005$ Choice 2: Multi-status-2, Ill vs. Comm., $P = < .001$
Choice 1: Multi-status-2, Ill vs. Comm., $P = < .005$ Choice 2: Multi-status-3, Ill vs. Comm., $P = < .001$
Choice 2: Multi-status-1, Ill vs. Comm., $P = < .01$ Choice 3: Multi-status-2, Ill vs. Comm., $P = < .001$

patients at each multi-status level will choose the white-collar occupations, despite the lower weekly salaries. With regard to the first pair of choices, more patients at multi-status levels 1, 2, and 3 select the white-collar position, although it offers a salary below that of the blue-collar job. At levels 1 and 2, there is a 21 per cent difference between the ill and community respondents in number of white-collar choices ($P = < .005$). At level 3, the mentally ill are also more prone to choose the white-collar position, but the difference between the two populations is not significant. At the highest multi-status position there is virtually no difference between the two populations in occupational choices. As mentioned previously, since many level 3, and all level 4 individuals already occupy white-collar positions, the choice of this alternative (with its associated lower remuneration) does not tap any existing desire for upward social mobility.

With respect to the second paired set of jobs, at every multi-status position except the highest, significantly ($P = < .01$) more ill choose the white-collar job, despite its wage penalty of $20 and a fairly low absolute weekly salary

($80). Even at level 4, the percentage of white-collar choices is higher among the ill (although not significantly). As expected, the largest difference between the two populations in these choices occurs at levels 1 and 2 (17 and 27 per cent, respectively) and then decreases progressively at levels 3 and 4 (14 and 6 per cent, respectively).

The difference in salary between the third set of paired blue/white-collar positions is also $20, but the absolute weekly salary of the white-collar job is only $60. In addition, the status of a department store sales person is not as high as for the other white-collar alternatives. A relatively unattractive white-collar position was intentionally selected in order to see whether the expected pattern would continue to emerge. More mentally ill than community respondents at the first three status levels again choose the white-collar occupation (see Table 5). The differences between the ill and community populations are significant only at multi-status positions 1 and 2 ($P = < .05$). This trend is reversed at level 4, where the community respondents are more prone to choose the white-collar occupation. . . .

In summary, ten of the twelve comparisons indicate that the patients are more prone than the community respondents to choose the low-salary white-collar occupations. Seven of these ten analyses are statistically significant (by sign test, $P = < .01$). This ill-community difference is pronounced at the lowest multi-status position, becomes even more apparent at level 2, and then decreases considerably at level 3. At the highest multi-status position, differences between the ill and community respondents are inconsistent in magnitude and direction. The results for the two highest levels are not unexpected, but the relative increase in the difference between the two populations in white-collar choices from status level 1 to level 2 is puzzling. The possibility of white-collar occupational achievement may be so remote to a Negro at level 1 that it does not evoke strong achievement striving. At level 2 such a possibility is not as distant, and striving for white-collar jobs is more salient. It is at this position that differences between the community and ill populations become most pronounced.

In this connection it is also interesting that within the community, the percentage of respondents selecting the white-collar alternative increases directly with multi-status position: the higher the level, the higher the proportion of white-collar choices. Only one of twelve relevant comparisons shows the opposite trend. In the mentally ill population this percentage increases sharply from level 1 to level 2, and at the two higher levels becomes erratic and inconsistent. One interpretation of these findings suggests that the reference group choices of community respondents are determined to a considerable extent by the objective reality of their achievement.

Findings reported earlier in this chapter clearly indicate that community respondents tend to place themselves at the position of their reference group more frequently than the patients (who deviate in both directions, but are predominantly below their reference group). The data relevant to the community respondents conform to what would be expected on the basis of Festinger's "social comparison theory."[34] Festinger and his co-workers found that individuals in group situations tended to modify their opinions and aspirations so that they conformed to those of the other group members. Although the situation we are considering does not involve common membership in a formal group, most individuals will probably tend to adjust their opinions, attitudes, and aspirations to those of individuals with whom they commonly interact. This may account for the tendency of most community respondents to place themselves at, or close to, their reference group level. On the other hand, the mentally ill seem much less constrained by their objective status position and the pressures generated by their status peers. Their selections of goals may conform more to Hyman's designation of "autistic" choices.

Responses given by females to the three sets of paired occupational choices were also analyzed. Among females there are fewer white-collar choices, and no significant difference between the community and ill populations. The ability of the blue/white-collar questions to discriminate in the male population, and its failure to do so among females, suggests that males are more inclined to prove their adequacy and maintain their self-esteem in the vocational area. It is not surprising, then, that the occupational reference group should be higher for males than for females, and that it should constitute a more sensitive correlation of mental health among males.

Racial Identification of the Negro as an Indicator of Reference Group

The two questionnaire items analyzed in this section involve the degree to which respondents use other Negroes as a reference group. Almost every clinical study of psychopathology among Negroes indicates that the Negro who is not identified with other members of his group, or who aspires to "be white," is relatively more prone to manifest various forms of mental ill health. Sometimes this phenomenon is referred to as "self-hate" or "color denial." Its importance for mental health is extensively documented. Because this phenomenon cannot be conceptualized in terms of a quantitative scale, we shall use these data to explore the manifestation of this behavior in our various population subgroups rather than for the rigorous testing of our hypotheses.

One of the questions to be analyzed in this connection deals with the issue of "passing"—that is, a Negro's attempt to deny his racial membership and to "pass" as white. We felt that a Negro's attitude toward this issue was a good index of the strength of his identification with other Negroes, or the degree to which he used other Negroes as a reference group. It was assumed that if a Negro subject either condoned or showed no concern over the passing issue

34. L. Festinger, "A Theory of Social Comparison Processes," *Human Relations*, 7: 117–140, 1954.

(i.e., had no affective reaction to it), he did not use other Negroes as a salient reference group. The individual who strongly condemned such behavior was assumed to be more prone to use other Negroes as a reference group. We asked each respondent for his reactions to a hypothetical friend who said that he wanted to pass "because of the advantages that it would give him." . . . The responses to this open-ended question were subsequently categorized as follows:

(1) Condones passing (feels that it is a good decision, would like to do it himself, etc.).
(2) Not involved in the issue (does not care, or feels unconcerned about the matter).
(3) Ambivalent about the decision to pass (expresses both positive and negative affect toward the decision or toward the hypothetical friend).
(4) Condemns passing ("He is a traitor to his race"; "He is letting the rest of us down"; "I would have no use for him," etc.).

For purposes of analysis categories (1) and (2) were combined, with the assumption that individuals expressing either type of reaction were minimally inclined to use other Negroes as a reference group. We expected the mentally ill to show a greater inclination than the community individuals to condone or to feel uninvolved in the passing decision. At this point it is difficult to predict or speculate about the meaning of response categories (3) and (4); we shall merely examine the data and suggest possible interpretations.

Table 6 presents the percentage distributions of responses to passing. The

Table 6—Reaction to Hypothetical Friend's Desire to Pass, in Percentages

| | TOTAL | | | | | |
	Ill	Comm.	Low Symp.	High Symp.	Neur.	Psych.
Condones passing or not involved in issue	48	39	41	35	43	49
Ambivalent	21	34	36	31	24	21
Condemns	30	22	22	29	32	29
Other	+	4	1	5	1	1
Total N	1405	1479	1257	172	357	1048

Summary of significant chi-square analyses
Total ill vs. Total comm., $P = < .001$ Neurotics vs. High symptom, $P = < .02$
Psychotics vs. High symptom, $P = < .001$ Neurotics vs. Low symptom, $P = < .001$
Psychotics vs. Low symptom, $P = < .001$ High symptom vs. Low symptom, $P = <.001$

difference between the total ill and community sample is statistically significant ($P = < .001$). More ill than community respondents either condone or feel uninvolved in this issue, suggesting, as predicted, that the mentally ill are less inclined to use other Negroes as a salient reference group. It should be re-emphasized that this interpretation rests on the assumption of a positive correlation between group identification and its use as a reference group: the more strongly one identifies himself with a particular group, the more likely he is to use its norms and values in evaluating himself and events in his environment. Whatever its significance for understanding reference group behavior, the combination of response categories (1) and (2) is the modal one for individuals in both samples.

More patients than community subjects condemn the decision to pass (see Table 6). To be consistent with the interpretation offered in the above paragraph, we must maintain that, in this context, the patients are *more* prone than the community respondents to use Negroes as a salient reference group. It appears that the total ill population is characterized by the occurrence of both extreme responses, while the community population contains many more respondents who feel ambivalent about the passing decision. Community respondents apparently tend to consider both Negroes and whites as reference groups, while the patients are more absolute in choosing one or the other. . . .

These reactions to the passing question support some of the findings reported in clinical studies of mental illness among Negroes,[35] indicating that patients frequently use their Negro identity "as a defense against facing other problems . . . projecting all their difficulties onto the racial prejudice of the therapist or others . . . or denying the fact that being a Negro has any effect at all on their lives."[36] Therapists have often observed that Negro patients commonly accept many of the white negative stereotypes about Negroes, with a consequent rejection of self and other Negroes. This insight helps us to understand the rather high percentage of mentally ill in the present study who either condone passing or say that the issue does not concern them.

Assuming that the foregoing reasoning is valid, we expect an increase in both of these extreme reactions and a decrease in "Ambivalent" responses as severity of illness increases. As we move along the mental health continuum from the low symptom group to the psychotics, the proportion of extreme responses (i.e., "Condones," or "Not involved" responses, combined with "Condemns" responses) increase as predicted: 63, 64, 75, and 78 per cent, respectively. At the same time, the "Ambivalent" responses decrease progressively from 36 to 21 per cent through the four mental health groupings (see Table 6).

It is interesting that so many individuals in all mental health groupings select one of the extreme responses to passing, and also that the highest proportions of responses in all groupings fall into the "Condones–Not involved" category. Our data indicate that the community population is relatively inclined to use Negroes *and* whites as reference groups, whereas the patients apparently select one group or the other. The mentally ill may be less able to sustain the

35. W. A. Adams, "The Negro Patient in Psychiatric Treatment," *American Journal of Orthopsychiatry*, 20: 305–310, 1950; Kardiner and Ovesey, *op. cit.*; V. Bernard, "Psychoanalysis and Members of Minority Groups," *American Psychoanalytic Journal*, 1: 256–267, 1953.

36. M. Shane, "Some Subcultural Considerations in the Psychotherapy of a Negro Patient," *Psychiatric Quarterly*, 34: 1–19, 1960.

ambivalence and conflict implicit in the community responses and thus tend to give the more extreme responses. Although ambivalence in identification patterns has often been associated with psychopathology in the clinical literature, ambivalence in the present instance may very well be realistic and adaptive for the Negro. It is the polarization of racial identification or reference group behavior that is psychopathogenic. Our data show that the psychiatrically healthy Negro is an individual with conflicts about his racial identification. It is the mentally ill person who tends to remove this constant conflict from conscious awareness.

The problem concerning the use of other Negroes as a reference group warrants further investigation, both because the issue has been so frequently related to Negro mental health, and because our interpretation of the "passing" question is somewhat speculative. Each respondent was asked whether being a Negro "has prevented you from getting the things you wanted?" . . . The four precoded response choices were "Yes, very much"; "Yes, to some degree"; "Yes, slightly"; and "No." We assumed that a Negro who did not use other Negroes as a reference group would be more inclined to answer "No" to this question—that is, since he did not use Negro norms and values to evaluate the social barriers to which he was exposed, he would deny that being a Negro was a barrier to his goal achievements. Implicit in this reasoning is the assumption that Negroes in our society have actually been handicapped considerably by their skin color, and that the Negro who completely denies this is also denying his own racial membership.

Table 7 presents the responses to this barrier question. Relatively few

Table 7—"Being a Negro" as a Perceived Barrier to Achievement in Percentages

| | TOTAL | | | | | |
	III	Comm.	Low Symp.	High Symp.	Neur.	Psych.
Very much	11	8	8	7	11	11
Slightly or to some degree	32	57	58	52	40	29
Not at all	57	35	34	41	49	59
Total N	1416	1473	1299	174	358	1058

Summary of significant chi-square analyses

Total III vs. Total comm., $P = < .001$
Psychotics vs. Neurotics, $P = < .005$
Psychotics vs. High symptom, $P = < .001$

Psychotics vs. Low symptom, $P = < .001$
Neurotic vs. Low symptom, $P = < .001$

community and mentally ill respondents feel that being a Negro has been "Very much" of a barrier to their achievement, while a very high percentage of both samples say that it has not constituted any barrier. In this connection it should be noted that the modal response of the community and ill subjects to the "passing" question indicated either condonation or lack of concern about such behavior. The findings on both of these questionnaire items suggest a surprising lack of strong racial identification in these populations.[37] Significantly more mentally ill than community subjects ($P = < .001$) report that their racial membership has not been any barrier to achievement (see Table 7). This significant difference between the two samples is maintained for each of the sex and age control groups. If our assumptions about the meaning of this question are valid, we can conclude that considerably fewer ill than community respondents use Negroes as a salient reference group. Table 7 also shows that 57 per cent of the community respondents, compared to only 32 per cent of the patients, feel that being a Negro has constituted "Somewhat" of a barrier. Although more patients than community individuals see their racial membership as "Very much" of a barrier, the percentage difference between the two populations on this response is very small. As in the question on passing, the mentally ill are somewhat more inclined in this instance to select one or both of the extreme responses. . . .

A consideration of the relationship between "No barriers" responses and the four mental health groupings reveals a direct increase in the expected direction. The number of subjects giving this response increases from the low symptom group to the psychotics (see Table 7). This progressive increase in denial suggests that, as illness becomes more severe, individuals are less inclined to use other Negroes as a reference group. . . .

Summary

The findings presented in this chapter offer striking support for the three hypotheses concerning reference group behavior. In spite of some deviations from the predictions, the data indicate that the mentally ill place themselves further below their reference group than do those in the community sample. Consistent with data on goal striving presented in previous chapters, findings on reference group behavior confirm that mental disorder is linked to relatively high social mobility strivings. Not only do the mentally ill experience high levels of stress associated with goal striving, but they also tend to compare themselves with reference groups considerably above them on various status criteria. Such a configuration might result in feelings of relative deprivation, personal failure, and loss of self-esteem. . . . At this point we shall recapitulate some of the major findings on reference group behavior.

The major measure used to investigate this phenomenon was the discrepancy between the individual's perception of his own position and that which he attributed to his "close friends." The criteria involved in these evaluations were determined by the individual himself when he made these judgments. There is a high rank order correlation between the criterion choices of community and mentally ill respondents. Although the mean discrepancies in both populations are negative, the patients are significantly further below their

37. The data underlying this conclusion were gathered in 1960 and may not reflect the effects of current developments in the Negro civil rights movement.

reference group than the community subjects. This difference holds for comparisons using sex and age controls. Furthermore, when the position perceived for the self is controlled, the mentally ill continue to show significantly larger negative discrepancies than the community respondents at every control level. At the highest control level the mentally ill place themselves above their reference group more frequently than do community subjects.

There is a direct relationship between severity of illness and degree of negative discrepancy from reference group, thus confirming our predictions. We find significantly higher negative discrepancies among the psychotics than the neurotics, and among the high symptom group than the low symptom group.

Attitude Development as a Function of Reference Groups: The Bennington Study

Theodore M. Newcomb

MEMBERSHIP in established groups usually involves the taking on of whole patterns of interrelated behavior and attitudes. This was one of the hypotheses pursued in the study which is reported here in part. The group selected for study consisted of the entire student body at Bennington College—more than 600 individuals—between the years 1935 and 1939. One of the problems to be investigated was that of the manner in which the patterning of behavior and attitudes varied with different degrees of assimilation into the community.

Not all of the attitudes and behaviors that are likely to be taken on by new members, as they become absorbed into a community, can be investigated in a single study. A single, though rather inclusive, area of adaptation to the college community was therefore selected for special study, namely, *attitudes toward public affairs*. There were two reasons for this selection: (1) methods of attitude measurement were readily available; and (2) there was an unusually high degree of concern, in this community at this time, over a rather wide range of public issues. This latter fact resulted partly from the fact that the college opened its doors during the darkest days of the depression of the 1930's, and its formative period occurred in the period of social change characterized by the phrase "the New Deal." This was also the period of gathering war clouds in Europe. Underlying both of these circumstances, however, was the conviction on the part of the faculty that one of the foremost duties of the college was to acquaint its some-what oversheltered students with the nature of their contemporary social world.

In a membership group in which certain attitudes are approved (i.e., held by majorities, and conspicuously so by leaders), individuals acquire the approved attitudes to the extent that the membership group (particularly as symbolized by leaders and dominant subgroups) serves as a positive point of reference. The findings of the Bennington study seem to be better understood in terms of this thesis than any other. The distinction between membership group and reference group is a crucial one, in fact, although the original report did not make explicit use of it.

The above statement does not imply that no reference groups other than the membership group are involved in attitude formation; as we shall see, this is distinctly not the case. Neither does it imply that the use of the membership group as reference group necessarily results in adoption of the approved attitudes. It may also result in their rejection; hence the word *positive* in the initial statement. It is precisely these variations in degree and manner of relationship between reference group and membership group which must be known in order to explain individual variations in attitude formation, as reported in this study.

The essential facts about the Bennington membership group are as follows: (1) It was small enough (about 250 women students) so that data could be obtained from every member. (2) It was in most respects self-sufficient; college facilities provided not only the necessities of living and studying, but also a cooperative store, post office and Western Union office, beauty parlor, gasoline station, and a wide range of recreational opportunities. The average student visited the four-mile-distant village once a week and spent one week end a month away from the college. (3) It was self-conscious and enthusiastic, in large part because it was new (the study was begun during the first year in which there was a senior class) and because of the novelty and attractiveness of the college's educational plan. (4) It was unusually active and concerned about public issues, largely because the faculty felt that its educational duties included the familiarizing of an oversheltered student body with the implications of a depression-torn America and a war-threatened world. (5) It was relatively homogeneous in respect to home background; tuition was very high, and the large majority of students came from urban, economically privileged families whose social attitudes were conservative.

Most individuals in this total membership group went through rather marked changes in attitudes toward public issues, as noted below. In most cases the total membership group served as the reference group for the changing attitudes. But some individuals changed little or not at all in attitudes during the four years of the study; attitude persistence was in some of these cases a function of the membership group as reference group and in some cases it was not. Among those who did change, moreover, the total membership group sometimes served as reference group but sometimes it did not. An oversimple theory of "assimilation into the community" thus leaves out of account some of those whose attitudes did and some of those whose attitudes did not change; they remain unexplained exceptions. A theory which traces the impact of other reference groups as well as the effect of the membership group seems to account for all cases without exception.

The general trend of attitude change for the total group is from freshman conservatism to senior nonconservatism (as the term was commonly applied to the issues toward which attitudes were measured). During the 1936 presidential election, for example, 62 per cent of the freshmen and only 14 per cent of the juniors and seniors "voted" for the Republican candidate, 29 per cent of freshmen and 54 per cent of juniors and seniors for Roosevelt, and 9 per cent of freshmen as compared with 30 per cent of juniors and seniors for the Socialist or Communist candidates. Attitudes toward nine specific issues were measured during the four years of the study, and seniors were less conservative in all of them than freshmen; six of the nine differences are statistically reliable. These differences are best shown by a Likert-type scale labeled Political and Economic Progressivism (PEP) which dealt with such issues as unemployment, public relief, and the rights of organized labor, which were made prominent by the New Deal. Its odd-even reliability was about .9, and it was given once or more during each of the four years of the study to virtually all students. The critical ratios of the differences between freshmen and juniors-seniors in four successive years ranged between 3.9 and 6.5; the difference between the average freshman and senior scores of 44 individuals (the entire class that graduated in 1939) gives a critical ratio of 4.3.

As might be anticipated in such a community, *individual prestige was associated with nonconservatism.* Frequency of choice as one of five students "most worthy to represent the College" at an intercollegiate gathering was used as a measure of prestige. Nominations were submitted in sealed envelopes by 99 per cent of all students in two successive years, with almost identical results. The nonconservatism of those with high prestige is not merely the result of the fact that juniors and seniors are characterized by both high prestige and nonconservatism; in each class those who have most prestige are least conservative. For example, ten freshmen receiving 2 to 4 choices had an average PEP score of 64.6 as compared with 72.8 for freshmen not chosen at all (high scores are conservative); eight sophomores chosen 12 or more times had an average score of 63.6 as compared with 71.3 for those not chosen; the mean PEP score of five juniors and seniors chosen 40 or more times was 50.4 and of the fifteen chosen 12 to 39 times, 57.6, as compared with 69.0 for those not chosen. In each class, those intermediate in prestige are also intermediate in average PEP score.

Such were the attitudinal characteristics of the total membership group, expressed in terms of average scores. Some individuals, however, showed these characteristics in heightened form and others failed to show them at all. An examination of the various reference groups in relation to which attitude change did or did not occur, and of the ways in which they were brought to bear, will account for a large part of such attitude variance.

Information concerning reference groups was obtained both directly, from the subjects themselves, and indirectly, from other students and from teachers. Chief among the indirect procedures was the obtaining of indexes of "community citizenship" by a guess-who technique. Each of twenty-four students, carefully selected to represent every cross section and grouping of importance within the community, named three individuals from each of three classes who were reputedly most extreme in each of twenty-eight characteristics related to community citizenship. The relationship between reputation for community identification and nonconservatism is a close one, in spite of the fact that no reference was made to the latter characteristic when the judges made their ratings. A reputation index was computed, based upon the frequency with which individuals were named in five items dealing with identification with the community, minus the number of times they were named in five other items dealing with negative community attitude. Examples of the former items are: "absorbed in college community affairs," and "influenced by community expectations regarding codes, standards, etc."; examples of the latter are: "indifferent to activities of student committees," and "resistant to community expectations regarding codes, standards, etc." The mean senior PEP score of fifteen individuals whose index was $+15$ or more was 54.4; of sixty-three whose index was $+4$ to -4, 65.3; and of ten whose index was -15 or less, 68.2.

To have the reputation of identifying oneself with the community is not the same thing, however, as to identify the community as a reference group for a specific purpose—e.g., in this case, as a point of reference for attitudes toward public issues. In short, the reputation index is informative as to degree and direction of tendency to use the total membership group as a *general* reference group, but not necessarily as a group to which social attitudes are referred. For this purpose information was obtained directly from students.

Informal investigation had shown that whereas most students were aware of the marked freshman-to-senior trend away from conservatism, a few (particularly among the conservatives) had little or no awareness of it. Obviously, those not aware of the dominant community trend could not be using the community as a reference group for an attitude. (It does not follow, of course, that all those who are aware of it are necessarily using the community as reference group.) A simple measure of awareness was therefore devised. Subjects were asked to respond in two ways to a number of attitude statements taken from the PEP scale: first, to indicate agreement or disagreement (for example, with the statement: "The budget should be balanced before the government spends any money on social security"); and second, to estimate what percentage of freshmen, juniors and seniors, and faculty would agree with the statement. From these responses was computed an index of divergence (of own attitude) from the estimated majority of juniors and seniors. Thus a positive index on the part of a senior indicates the degree to which her own responses are more conservative than those of her classmates, and a negative index the degree to which they are less conservative. Those seniors whose divergence index more or less faithfully reflects the true difference between own and class attitude may (or may not) be using the class as an attitude reference group; those whose divergence indexes represent an exaggerated or minimized version of the true relationship between own and class attitude are clearly not using the class as an attitude reference group, or if so, only in a fictitious sense. (For present purposes the junior-senior group may be taken as representative of the entire student body, since it is the group which "sets the tone" of the total membership group.)

These data were supplemented by direct information obtained in interviews with seniors in three consecutive classes, just prior to graduation. Questions were asked about resemblance between own attitudes and those of class majorities and leaders, about parents' attitudes and own resemblance to them, about any alleged "social pressure to become liberal," about probable reaction if the dominant college influence had been conservative instead of liberal, etc. Abundant information was also available from the college personnel office and from the college psychiatrist. It was not possible to combine all of these sources of information into intensive studies of each individual, but complete data were assembled for (roughly) the most conservative and least conservative sixths of three consecutive graduating classes. The twenty-four nonconservative and nineteen conservative seniors thus selected for intensive study were classified according to their indexes of conservative divergence and of community reputation. Thus eight sets of seniors were identified, all individuals within each set having in common similar attitude scores, similar reputations for community identification, and similar degrees of awareness (based upon divergence index) of own attitude position relative to classmates. The following descriptions of these eight sets of seniors will show that there was a characteristic pattern of relationship between membership group and reference group within each of the sets.

1. *Conservatives, reputedly negativistic, aware of their own relative conservatism.* Four of the five are considered stubborn or resistant by teachers (all five, by student judges). Three have prestige scores of 0, scores of the other two being about average for their class. Four of the five are considered by teachers or psychiatrist, or by both, to be overdependent upon one or both parents. All of the four who were interviewed described *their major hopes,* on entering college, *in terms of social rather than academic prestige;* all four felt that they had been defeated in this aim. The following verbatim quotations are illustrative:

> E2: Probably the feeling that (my instructors) didn't accept me led me to reject their opinions. (She estimates classmates as being only moderately less conservative than herself, but faculty as much less so.)

> G32: I wouldn't care to be intimate with those so-called "liberal" student leaders. (*She claims to be satisfied with a small group of friends.* She is chosen as friend, in a sociometric questionnaire responded to by all students, only twice, and reciprocates both choices; both are conservative students.)

> F22: I wanted to disagree with all the noisy liberals, but I was afraid and I couldn't. *So I built up a wall inside me against what they said. I found I couldn't*

compete, so I decided to stick to my father's ideas. For at least two years I've been insulated against all college influences. (She is chosen but once as a friend, and does not reciprocate that choice.)

Q10: (who rather early concluded that she had no chance of social success in college) It hurt me at first, but now I don't give a damn. *The things I really care about are mostly outside the college.* I think radicalism symbolizes the college for me more than anything else. (Needless to say, she has no use for radicals.)

For these four individuals (and probably for the fifth also) the community serves as reference group in a *negative* sense, and the home-and-family group in a positive sense. Thus their conservatism is dually reinforced.

2. *Conservatives, reputedly negativistic, unaware of their own relative conservatism.* All five are described by teachers, as well as by guess-who judges, to be stubborn or resistant. Four have prestige scores of 0, and the fifth a less than average score. Each reciprocated just one friendship choice. Four are considered insecure in social relationships, and all five are regarded as extremely dependent upon parents. In interviews four describe with considerable intensity, and the fifth with more moderation, precollege experiences of rebuff, ostracism, or isolation, and all described their hopes, on entering college, in terms of making friends or avoiding rebuff rather than in terms of seeking prestige. All five felt that their (rather modest) aims had met with good success. Each of the five denies building up any resistance to the acceptance of liberal opinions (but two add that they would have resented any such pressure, if felt). Three believe that only small, special groups in the college have such opinions, while the other two describe themselves as just going their own way, *paying no attention to anything but their own little circles and their college work.* Typical quotations follow:

Q47: I'm a perfect middle-of-the-roader, neither enthusiast nor critic. I'd accept anything if they just let me alone. . . . I've made all the friends I want. (Only one of her friendship choices is reciprocated.)

Q19: *In high school I was always thought of as my parents' daughter.* I never felt really accepted for myself. . . . I wanted to make my own way here, socially, but independence from my family has never asserted itself in other ways. (According to guess-who ratings, she is highly resistant to faculty authority.)

L12: What I most wanted was to get over being a scared bunny. . . . I always resent doing the respectable thing just because it's the thing to do, but I didn't realize I was so different, politically, from my classmates. At least I agree with the few people I ever talk to about such matters. (Sociometric responses place her in a small, conservative group.)

Q81: I hated practically all my school life before coming here. I had the perfect inferiority complex, and I pulled out of school social life—out of fear. I didn't intend to repeat that mistake here. . . . I've just begun to be successful in winning friendships, and I've been blissfully happy here. (She is described by teachers as "pathologically belligerent"; she receives more than the average number of friendship choices, but reciprocates only one of them.)

For these five individuals, who are negativistic in the sense of being near-isolates rather than rebels, the community does not serve as reference group for public attitudes. To some extent, their small friendship groups serve in this capacity, but in the main they still refer such areas of their lives to the home-and-family group. They are too absorbed in their own pursuits to use the total membership group as a reference group for most other purposes, too.

3. *Conservatives, not reputedly negativistic, aware of their own relative conservatism.* Three of the five are described by teachers as "cooperative" and "eager," and none as stubborn or resistant. Four are above average in prestige. Four are considered by teachers or by guess-who raters, or both, to retain very close parental ties. All four who were interviewed had more or less definite ambitions for leadership on coming to college, and all felt that they had been relatively successful—though, in the words of one of them, none ever attained the "really top-notch positions." All four are aware of conflict between parents and college community in respect to public attitudes, and all quite consciously decided to "string along" with parents, feeling self-confident of holding their own in college in spite of being atypical in this respect. Sample quotations follow:

> Q73: *I'm all my mother has in the world. It's considered intellectually superior here to be liberal or radical. This puts me on the defensive,* as I refuse to consider my mother beneath me intellectually, as so many other students do. Apart from this, I have loved every aspect of college life. (A popular girl, many of whose friends are among the nonconservative college leaders.)

> Q78: *I've come to realize how much my mother's happiness depends on me, and the best way I can help her is to do things with her at home as often as I can.* This has resulted in my not getting the feel of the college in certain ways, and I know my general conservatism is one of those ways. But it has not been important enough to me to make me feel particularly left out. If you're genuine and inoffensive about your opinions, no one really minds here if you remain conservative. (Another popular girl, whose friends were found among many groups.)

> F32: *Family against faculty has been my struggle here.* As soon as I felt really secure here I decided not to let the college atmosphere affect me too much. Every time I've tried to rebel against my family I've found out how terribly wrong I am, and so I've naturally kept to my parents' attitudes. (While not particularly popular, she shows no bitterness and considerable satisfaction over her college experience.)

> Q35: I've been aware of a protective shell against radical ideas. When I found several of my best friends getting that way, I either had to go along or just shut out that area entirely. I couldn't respect myself if I had changed my opinions just for that reason, and so I almost deliberately lost interest—really, *it was out of fear of losing my friends.* (A very popular girl, with no trace of bitterness, who is not considered too dependent upon parents.)

For these five the total membership group does not serve as reference group in respect to public attitudes, but does so serve for most other purposes. At some stage in their college careers the conflict between college community and home and family as reference group for public attitudes was resolved in favor of the latter.

4. *Conservatives, not reputedly negativistic, not aware of their own relative conservatism.* All four are consistently described by teachers as conscientious and cooperative; three are considered overdocile and uncritical of authority. All are characterized by feelings of inferiority. All are low in prestige, two receiving scores of 0; all are low in friendship choices, but reciprocate most of these few choices. Two are described as in conflict about parental authority, and two as dependent and contented. All four recall considerable anxiety as to whether they would fit into the college community; all feel that they have succeeded better than they had expected. Sample statements from interviews follow:

D22: I'd like to think like the college leaders, but I'm not bold enough and I don't know enough. So the college trend means little to me; I didn't even realize how much more conservative I am than the others. *I guess my family influence has been strong enough to counterbalance the college influence.* (This girl was given to severe emotional upsets, and according to personnel records, felt "alone and helpless except when with her parents.")

M12: It isn't that I've been resisting any pressure to become liberal. The influences here didn't matter enough to resist, I guess. *All that's really important that has happened to me occurred outside of college,* and so I never became very susceptible to college influences. (*Following her engagement to be married, in her second year, she had "practically retired" from community life.*)

Q68: If I'd had more time here I'd probably have caught on to the liberal drift here. But I've been horribly busy making money and trying to keep my college work up. *Politics and that sort of thing I've always associated with home instead of with the college.* (A "town girl" of working-class parentage.)

Q70: Most juniors and seniors, if they really *get excited about their work, forget about such community enthusiasms as sending telegrams to Congressmen.* It was so important to me to be accepted, I mean intellectually, *that I naturally came to identify myself in every way with the group which gave me this sort of intellectual satisfaction.* (One of a small group of science majors, nearly all conservative, who professed no interests other than science and who were highly self-sufficient socially.)

For none of the four was the total membership group a reference group for public attitudes. Unlike the nonnegativistic conservatives who are aware of their relative conservatism, they refer to the total membership group for few if any other purposes. Like the negativistic conservatives who are unaware of their relative conservatism, their reference groups for public attitudes are almost exclusively those related to home and family.

5. *Nonconservatives, reputedly community-identified, aware of their relative nonconservatism.* Each of the seven is considered highly independent by teachers, particularly in intellectual activities; all but one are referred to as meticulous, perfectionist, or overconscientious. Four are very high in prestige, two high, and one average; all are "good group members," and all but one a "leader." None is considered overdependent upon parents. All have come to an understanding with parents concerning their "liberal" views; five have "agreed to differ," and the other two describe one or both parents as "very liberal." All take their public attitudes seriously, in most cases expressing the feeling that they have bled and died to achieve them. Interview excerpts follow:

B72: *I bend in the direction of community expectation*—almost more than I want to. I constantly have to check myself to be sure it's real self-conviction and not just social respect. (An outstanding and deeply respected leader.)

M42: My family has always been liberal, but the influences here made me go further, and for a while I was pretty far left. Now I'm pretty much in agreement with my family again, but it's my own and it means a lot. It wouldn't be easy for me to have friends who are very conservative. (Her friendship choices are exclusively given to nonconservatives.)

E72: I had been allowed so much independence by my parents that I needed desperately to identify myself with an institution with which I could conform conscientiously. Bennington was perfect. I drank up everything the college had to offer, including social attitudes, though not uncritically. I've become active in radical groups and constructively critical of them. (Both during and after college she worked with C.I.O. unions.)

H32: I accepted liberal attitudes here because *I had always secretly felt that my family was narrow and intolerant, and because such attitudes had prestige value.* It was all part of my generally expanding personality—*I had never really been part of anything before.* I don't accept things without examining things, however, and I was sure I meant it before I changed. (One of those who has "agreed to differ" with parents.)

Q43: It didn't take me long to see that liberal attitudes had prestige value. But all the time I felt inwardly superior to persons who want public acclaim. Once I had arrived at a feeling of personal security, I could see that it wasn't important—it wasn't enough. *So many people have no security at all. I became liberal at first because of its prestige value.* I remain so because the problems around which my liberalism centers are important. What I want now is to be effective in solving the problems. (Another conspicuous leader, active in and out of college in liberal movements.)

The total membership clearly serves as reference group for these individuals' changing attitudes, but by no means as the only one. For those whose parents are conservative, parents represent a negative reference group, from whom emancipation was gained via liberal attitudes. And for several of them the college community served as a bridge to outside liberal groups as points of reference.

6. *Nonconservatives, reputedly community-identified, not aware of their own relative nonconservatism.* The word *enthusiastic* appears constantly in the records of each of these six. All are considered eager, ambitious, hard-working, and anxious to please. Four are very high in prestige, the other two about average. None is considered overdependent upon parents, and only two are known to have suffered any particular conflict in achieving emancipation. Each one came to college with ambitions for leadership, and each professes extreme satisfaction with her college experience. Sample quotations follow:

> Qx: Every influence I felt tended to push me in the liberal direction: my under-dog complex, *my need to be independent of my parents, and my anxiousness to be a leader here.*

> Q61: I met a whole body of new information here; I took a deep breath and plunged. When I talked about it at home my family began to treat me as if I had an adult mind. *Then too, my new opinions gave me the reputation here of being open-minded and capable of change.* I think I could have got really radical but I found it wasn't the way to get prestige here. (She judges most of her classmates to be as nonconservative as herself.)

> Q72: I take everything hard, and so of course I reacted hard to all the attitudes I found here. I'm 100-per cent enthusiastic about Bennington, and that includes liberalism (but not radicalism, though I used to think so). Now I know that you can't be an *extremist if you're really devoted to an institution,* whether it's a labor union or a college. (A conspicuous leader who, like most of the others in this set of six, *judges classmates to be only slightly more conservative than herself.*)

> Q63: *I came to college to get away from my family,* who never had any respect for my mind. Becoming a radical meant thinking for myself and, figuratively, thumbing my nose at my family. *It also meant intellectual identification with the faculty and students that I most wanted to be like.* (She has always felt oppressed by parental respectability and sibling achievements.)

> Q57: It's very simple. *I was so anxious to be accepted that I accepted the political complexion of the community here.* I just couldn't stand out against the crowd unless I had many friends and strong support. (Not a leader, but many close friends among leaders and nonconservatives.)

For these six, like the preceding seven, the membership group serves as reference group for public affairs. They differ from the preceding seven chiefly in that they are less sure of themselves and are careful "not to go too far." Hence they tend to repudiate "radicalism," and to judge classmates as only slightly less conservative than themselves.

7. *Nonconservatives, not reputedly community-identified, aware of own relative nonconservatism.* Each of the six is described as highly independent and critical-minded. Four are consistently reported as intellectually outstanding, and the other two occasionally so. All describe their ambitions on coming to college in intellectual rather than in social terms. Four of the five who were interviewed

stated that in a conservative college they would be "even more radical than here." Two are slightly above average in prestige, two below average, and two have 0 scores. Three have gone through rather severe battles in the process of casting off what they regard as parental shackles; none is considered overdependent upon parents. Sample interview excerpts follow:

Q7: *All my life I've resented the protection of governesses and parents.* What I most wanted here was the intellectual approval of teachers and the more advanced students. Then I found you can't be reactionary and be intellectually respectable. (Her traits of independence became more marked as she achieved academic distinction.)

Q21: I simply got filled with new ideas here, and the only possible formulation of all of them was to adopt a radical approach. *I can't see my own position in the world in any other terms. The easy superficiality with which so many prestige-hounds here get "liberal" only forced me to think it out more intensely.* (A highly gifted girl, considered rather aloof.)

C32: *I started rebelling against my pretty stuffy family before I came to college.* I felt apart from freshmen here, because I was older. Then I caught on to faculty attempts to undermine prejudice. I took sides with the faculty immediately, against the immature freshmen. I crusaded about it. *It provided just what I needed by way of family rebellion,* and bolstered up my self-confidence, too. (A very bright girl, regarded as sharp tongued and a bit haughty.)

J24: *I'm easily influenced by people whom I respect,* and the people who rescued me when I was down and out, intellectually, gave me a radical intellectual approach; they included both teachers and advanced students. *I'm not rebelling against anything.* I'm just doing what I had to do to stand on my own feet intellectually. (Her academic work was poor as a freshman, but gradually became outstanding.)

For these six students it is not the total membership group, but dominant subgroups (faculty, advanced students) which at first served as positive reference groups, and for many of them the home group served as a negative point of reference. Later, they developed extracollege reference groups (left-wing writers, etc.). In a secondary sense, however, the total membership group served as a negative point of reference—i.e., they regarded their nonconservatism as a mark of personal superiority.

8. *Nonconservatives, not reputedly community-identified, not aware of own relative nonconservatism.* Each of the five is considered hard-working, eager, and enthusiastic but (especially during the first year or two) unsure of herself and too dependent upon instructors. They are "good citizens", but in a distinctly retiring way. Two are above average in prestige, and the other three much below average. None of the five is considered overdependent upon parents; two are known to have experienced a good deal of conflict in emancipating themselves. All regard themselves as "pretty average persons," with strong desire

to conform; they describe their ambitions in terms of social acceptance instead of social or intellectual prestige. Sample excerpts follow:

> E22: *Social security is the focus of it all with me.* I became steadily less conservative as long as I was *needing to gain in personal security, both with students and with faculty.* I developed some resentment against a few extreme radicals who don't really represent the college viewpoint, and that's why I changed my attitudes so far and no further. (A girl with a small personal following, otherwise not especially popular.)

> D52: *Of course there's social pressure here to give up your conservatism.* I'm glad of it, because for me this became the *vehicle for achieving independence from my family.* So changing my attitudes has gone hand in hand with two *very important things: establishing my own independence and at the same time becoming a part of the college organism.* (She attributes the fact that her social attitudes changed, while those of her younger sister, also at the college, did not, to the fact that she had greater need both of family independence and of group support.)

> Q6: I was ripe for developing liberal or even radical opinions because so many of my friends at home were doing the same thing. So it was really wonderful that I could agree with all the people I respected here and at the same time move in the direction that my home friends were going. (A girl characterized by considerable personal instability at first, but showing marked improvement.)

> Qy: I think my change of opinions has given me *intellectual and social self-respect at the same time.* I used to be too timid for words, and I never had an idea of my own. As I gradually became more successful in my work and made more friends, I came to feel that it didn't matter so much whether I agreed with my parents. It's all part of the feeling that I really belong here. (Much other evidence confirms this; she was lonely and pathetic at first, but really belonged later.)

These five provide the example *par excellence* of individuals who came to identify themselves with "the community" and whose attitudes change *pari passu* with the growing sense of identity. Home-and-family groups served as supplementary points of reference, either positive or negative. To varying degrees, subgroups within the community served as focal points of reference. But, because of *their need to be accepted, it was primarily the membership group as such which served as reference group for these five.*

Summary

In this community, as presumably in most others, all individuals belong to the total membership group, but such membership is not necessarily a point of reference for every form of social adaptation, e.g., for acquiring attitudes toward public issues. *Such attitudes, however, are not acquired in a social vacuum. Their acquisition is a function of relating oneself to some group or groups, positively or negatively.* In many cases (perhaps in all) the referring of social attitudes to one group negatively leads to referring them to another group positively, or vice versa, so that the attitudes are dually reinforced.

An individual is, of course, "typical" in respect to attitudes if the total membership group serves as a positive point of reference for that purpose, but "typicality" may also result from the use of other reference groups. It does not follow from the fact that an individual is "atypical" that the membership group does not serve for reference purposes; it may serve as negative reference group. Even if the membership group does not serve as reference group at all (as in the case of conservatives in this community who are unaware of the general fresh-man-to-senior trend), it cannot be concluded that attitude development is not a function of belonging to the total membership group. The unawareness of such individuals is itself a resultant adaptation of particular individuals to a particular membership group. The fact that such individuals continue to refer attitudes toward public issues primarily to home-and-family groups is, in part at least, a result of the kind of community in which they have membership.

In short, the Bennington findings seem to support the thesis that, in a community characterized by certain approved attitudes, the individual's attitude development is a function of the way in which he relates himself both to the total membership group and to one or more reference groups.

Reference Groups and the Maintenance of Changes in Attitudes and Behavior

Herbert H. Hyman, Charles R. Wright, and Terence K. Hopkins

This selection is drawn from a much larger study of attitude changes which occurred during the summer training programs of the Encampment for Citizenship. Over many years, approximately a hundred youth from diverse social backgrounds and different ethnic and racial groups have been brought together for six weeks on a residential school campus, where they are exposed to an educational program and communal experiences designed to prepare them for responsible citizenship, to educate them in the meaning of democracy, and to train them in techniques of democratic action. At the end of the 1955 session, it was found that the group had changed in many of the ways intended by the program, and considerable evidence was presented that these immediate changes were related to the emergence of the Encampment as a positive reference group and a clear awareness of its norms. Six weeks after return to their home communities, a follow-up study demonstrated that the immediate changes had persisted. In this excerpt, the authors examine the extent to which such changes were maintained four years after the campers had been back in their own communities, and inquire into the factors that tended to sustain or counteract the changes that had occurred. (Editors' note.)

THE ability of ex-campers to sustain their liberal attitudes, formed or reinforced during the Encampment, even under adverse post-Encampment circumstances, has been demonstrated. Does this mean that such attitudes, once formed,

[387]

are relatively autonomous? Or are they stable, perhaps, only because ex-campers continue to reinforce each other through frequent social contacts or communication, or by some other reference-group process? Either hypothesis is plausible. We know from the results of the six-week follow-up study of campers in their home communities in 1955 that many of them continued to preserve their Encampment norms even in the absence of various forms of contact with others in their Encampment group or use of them as a salient reference group. But such autonomy of attitudes may survive for only a short time. It is reasonable to hypothesize that over a long period there would be a greater loss of Encampment views on the part of ex-campers separated from interaction with others in their class. Therefore, in this section, data are presented on the extent to which ex-campers retain their liberal attitudes between 1955 and 1959 with and without further contacts with the Encampment staff and alumni, with and without the use of the campers as a salient, continuous reference group.

Consider first the stability of opinions under various conditions of isolation from Encampment staff and alumni. Several measures of contact with the Encampment, both in the past year and in earlier years, were obtained from the ex-campers: the frequency with which they had met socially with others from the 1955 group, spoken with them on the telephone, corresponded, worked together on a project, held reunions with alumni from other years, and received visits from staff members or literature from the Encampment. Each of the measures of contact or isolation was used independently to separate ex-campers who might have had post-Encampment support for their opinions from those who had not. Then comparisons were made between the views held by each group in 1955 and 1959.

No systematic difference in the stability of opinions appears between such contrasted groups, regardless of the specific index of social support or isolation used. To illustrate, ex-campers who had never attended reunions with Encampment alumni are just as stable in their favorable attitudes toward civil liberties as those who attended; nor have the isolates become more anomic, less tolerant, or more alienated from the Encampment norms than the others. (They do, however, show less stability on civil rights than the reunion group.) Ex-campers who were not visited by members of the Encampment staff do not regress in their opinions any more than those who were visited. Even in instances where *potential* support from other ex-campers seems limited (because the respondent thinks there are at best only a few ex-campers in his community), there is as much stability in post-Encampment views as when potential support is available. Finally, even failure to have social contacts of various sorts with fellow members of the 1955 group does not make such ex-campers any less firm in their opinions than others.

Following the lead obtained during the six-week post-Encampment study, a distinction was made between subsequent contacts of the face-to-face variety and others. Presumably face-to-face contacts are more powerful sources of control over the individual and therefore would provide stronger support for norms he originally shared with the group. Indirect contacts, such as correspondence, should be less effective, but better than no contact at all. Yet, six weeks after the Encampment, it may be recalled, even those ex-campers who had no face-to-face contact with their group were able to sustain the Encampment opinions and attitudes, although they seemed less likely to try to apply its principles toward the solution of some concrete problem in their new environment.

But perhaps six weeks is too short a time to detect such influences. Perhaps the ex-camper is able to sustain his liberal views for a short time even though isolated from face-to-face interaction with the old group, but weakens in the long run without such support. Evidence from the four-year follow-up shows otherwise. Those with no face-to-face contacts with other 1955 campers in the past year are no less firm than those with contacts, over the long run, in their attitudes toward civil liberties, civil rights, and tolerance, and have become only slightly less permissive of radio privileges for a Communist in peacetime. There is a slight decrease in the perception of society as anomic on the part of ex-campers who have interacted, while the others increase slightly, suggesting that face-to-face interaction may increase the ex-campers' feelings that one's opinions and behavior matter to others.

Of course, many of the ex-campers who did not have face-to-face contact with their cohort in the preceding year did have such contacts in other years, which might have sustained their opinions. Further analysis here is impossible, however, because there are too few ex-campers who had no face-to-face contact whatsoever with someone from the group sometime between 1955 and 1959.

What about action? On the six-week follow-up, it may be recalled, there was evidence that ideology was stable even without social supports, but action, in the form of trying to apply Encampment principles, was affected both by potential and actual interaction with ex-campers. Sentiments, it was argued, are private things that may operate autonomously because they need not be expressed in situations where they engender conflict. Action, on the other hand, is overt, may well engender conflict, and therefore is less likely to occur if the ex-camper does not perceive the possibility of support from others.

During the longer run of four years, the relationship held between social support and action, but not in all instances. To illustrate, attempts at applying Encampment ideas are reported by 16 per cent more of the ex-campers visited by the staff than by those not visited; 12 per cent more of the ex-campers who had some form of contact with the 1955 campers in the past year; and by 9 per cent more of the persons who attended reunions. On the other hand, neither potential interaction nor face-to-face contacts per se played the part they had in the six-week follow-up. Those ex-campers who had the potential for interaction (because they thought there were many ex-campers in their community), and even those who had *face-to-face* interaction with others from the 1955 group in the past year, were no more likely to have tried to apply Encampment ideas than those who had no potential for direct interaction or no face-to-face contact to support them. Forty-one per cent of the ex-campers living in communities with several other ex-campers report trying to act on Encampment ideals, in comparison with 48 per cent of the others; 37 per cent of the persons with face-to-face interaction acted on Encampment ideals, in comparison with 43 per cent without such contacts.

Returning to the issue of stability of opinions during four years, one might argue that contacts, face to face or otherwise, are not so important in the maintenance of opinions as is the retention of the Encampment as a reference group in the minds of the ex-campers. Evidence of the degree to which the Encampment serves as a salient, current reference group is available from a variety of indirect indices, such as how frequently ex-campers stop and think about the former campers and staff members, whether they count several members of the 1955 group as really close friends today, and whether they consider persons from other Encampments as current friends.

Is stability of opinions dependent upon the *saliency* of the Encampment as a reference group? Apparently not. Persons who do not have the Encampment constantly in mind still are as stable in their views between 1955 and 1959 as the others for whom the 1955 cohort is a frequent object of thought and reference. To illustrate, those who only occasionally stop to think about the staff and campers are only a little less constant in their views about civil rights and tolerance than those who think about the Encampment frequently, and equally stable on civil liberties. Those who count none of the 1955 group as really close friends today still retain their post-Encampment positions on civil liberties, civil rights, and tolerance as well as, and sometimes better than, persons who have several such friends.

Again, while ideology seems autonomous, action is affected by reference groups. Fully 21 per cent more of the ex-campers who think frequently about the Encampment report trying to apply its ideas in some specific situation. And instances of applying Encampment principles occur among a slightly higher percentage of ex-campers who have an Encampment alumnus as a current friend than among people lacking such friendships.

Of course, it may be possible that any one of these measures of reference group is misleading if taken alone. Perhaps the presence of any one factor— either close friends or frequent remembrances—is sufficient to support the 1955 views, so that both must be missing before the ex-camper loses his liberal views. To a limited extent this hypothesis can be tested, although the number of cases for comparison is fewer than would be desired. Let us contrast the stability of opinions held by 20 ex-campers who frequently think about the Encampment and who also count at least one 1955 alumnus as a close friend today with the opinions of 26 ex-campers who neither think about the Encampment very often nor have any close friends from their group. The results are presented in Table 1.

Again the evidence is clear: there is no appreciably greater general loss of liberal views on the part of ex-campers who are without benefit of the reference group. Even without a constant reference group ex-campers still retain their

Table I—Stability and Change in Opinions as Related to Post-Encampment Reference-Group Support

Opinions	Ex-campers who frequently think about Encampment and who have a close friend from 1955 cohort (N = 20)	Ex-campers who think about Encampment only occasionally and who have no close friends from 1955 cohort (N = 26)	Findings
Civil liberties			
Median score, end of Encampment, 1955	2.4	1.3	No differential change
Median score, 1959	2.7	1.2	
Civil rights			
Per cent scoring no prejudice, end of Encampment, 1955	65	88	No differential change
Per cent showing no prejudice, 1959	70	88	
Tolerance			
Per cent "more tolerant," end of Encampment, 1955	75	100	No differential change
Per cent "more tolerant," 1959	65	85	
Communist on radio in peacetime			
Per cent permissive, end of Encampment, 1955	70	92	Differential change
Per cent permissive, 1959	65	69	
Anomie			
Median score, end of Encampment, 1955	2.4	2.0	No differential change
Median score, 1959	2.4	2.2	
Conduct			
Per cent applying Encampment ideas	50	30	Difference

liberal attitudes toward civil liberties and civil rights, and become no more anomic and hardly less tolerant than those who keep the reference group. But those with reference-group support are more likely to have tried to translate the Encampment ideas into conduct than those lacking support—50 per cent versus 30 per cent.

Despite occasional exceptions, the general pattern of the findings is now clear. The opinions and attitudes expressed by the campers at the close of the 1955 Encampment were, on the whole, equally well maintained by ex-campers with or without subsequent contacts with the Encampment or use of the 1955 campers as a reference group, Action, on the other hand, is somewhat more likely to be dependent upon such contacts and supports. This pattern was observed in the studies of both short-term and long-term stability.

The relative independence of opinion from subsequent reference-group support during the four years after the Encampment may seem paradoxical in view of the important role that the group played in the dynamics of opinion formation during the Encampment summer itself. As noted in Chapter V,* communal living and the incorporation of the campers into the group experience seemed to play a greater part than the formal didactic program itself in shaping

*Of the original study. (*Editors' note.*)

opinions and attitudes during the summer. These two findings form an interesting contrast worthy of additional thought, for they provide the basis for several hypotheses concerning the connection between reference groups and individual opinions. They suggest, for example, that the connection may depend upon the functional relations among the individual, his opinions, and the reference groups, as well as upon the larger situational context which determines visibility of opinions.

To elaborate, reference groups seemed especially important in producing change in opinions or attitudes during the summer. Perhaps such opinions change because they serve the function of relating the individual to the new group that surrounds him at the time, a group in which the individual's attitudes and opinions are made highly visible and a group into which he would like to be accepted.

Under the conditions of life at the Encampment it was rather difficult for sentiments and opinions to remain private. There was, in effect, a relatively thin line between private and public realms during the summer. Both formal and informal pressures worked to change opinions from private to publicly expressed phenomena. Formally, for example, the Encampment encouraged the tapping of private sentiments and the verbalization of opinions through such institutionalized parts of the program as small discussion groups (in which each camper was drawn into a conversation about civil liberties, civil rights, tolerance or, whatever other subject had just been treated by a lecturer), workshops, personal biographies and group reports delivered before other campers, and so on. Informally, the general atmosphere, the close living, the evening "bull sessions," and other elements combined to make talking easy and hiding one's views difficult. Expression of opinion then became a necessary condition for acceptance into the group; and verbalization of an opinion is in itself a form of conduct.

The process of change of individual opinions toward the group norm is facilitated by the atmosphere, which makes expression of opinions almost mandatory, plus the close community living, which increases the mutual dependence of members of the group. The extent to which the individual is involved in group activities affects his exposure to the group's norms and his susceptibility to change during the summer.

Once the new opinions are formed and expressed, however, they become part of the individual's personal viewpoint which can be maintained in subsequent life with as much tenacity as his other private opinions. They can function on their own, without group support, even in a hostile environment, as they are once again private matters. Thus in the ordinary, day-to-day experiences of life at home, in the community, or on the campus, the individual can protect his Encampment norms either by keeping them private, as there is no institutional pressure to make them public, or by selecting new friends and environments that support the liberal views. In either event he is no longer dependent upon the original group of campers who played so important a role in developing or reshaping his pre-Encampment ideas. One might conjecture, however, that the actual or potential psychological support of the original group would again take on significance if the individual were forced to make his opinions known before a hostile larger society, just as group supports increase the probability of playing the visible role of active alumnus who tries to apply Encampment ideas in the larger community.

Findings such as those summarized here, then, suggest new hypotheses for future research which promise to increase our knowledge about the distinctive functions of reference groups for opinion formation, or maintenance and change, as well as the conditions under which reference groups are likely to affect opinions and behavior. The testing of such new hypotheses requires new research beyond the current project.

Reference Groups, Membership Groups, and Attitude Change

Alberta Engvall Siegel and Sidney Siegel

I N social psychological theory, it has long been recognized that an individual's *membership groups* have an important influence on the values and attitudes he holds. More recently, attention has also been given to the influence of his *reference groups:* the groups in which he aspires to attain or maintain membership. In a given area, membership groups and reference groups may or may not be identical. They are identical when the person aspires to *maintain* membership in the group of which he is a part; they are disparate when the group in which the individual aspires to *attain* membership is one in which he is not a member. It has been widely asserted that both membership and reference groups affect the attitudes held by the individual.[1]

The present study is an examination of the attitude changes which occur over time when reference groups and membership groups are identical and when they are disparate. The study takes advantage of a field experiment which occurred in the social context of the lives of the subjects, concerning events considered vital by them. The subjects were not aware that their membership and reference groups were of research interest; in fact, they did not know that the relevant information about these was available to the investigators.

Reprinted from *Journal of Abnormal and Social Psychology*, 55: 360–364, 1957, by permission of the authors and the publisher, the American Psychological Association. This study was supported by grants from the Committee for the Study of American Values at Stanford University and from the Stanford Value Theory Project. We wish to acknowledge with gratitude the assistance given by Davis W. Thompkins, Marilyn Sanchez-Corea, and Coleen Baker in the execution of this study, and the generous administrative cooperation of Elva Fay Brown, Dean of Women at Stanford University, and her staff.

1. M. Sherif and Carolyn W. Sherif, *Groups in Harmony and Tension*, New York: Harper & Brothers, 1953.

The field experiment permitted a test of the general hypothesis that both the amount and the direction of a person's attitude change over time depend on the attitude norms of his membership group (whether or not that group is chosen by him) and on the attitude norms of his reference group.

This hypothesis is tested with subjects who shared a common reference group at the time of the initial assessment of attitudes. They were then randomly assigned to alternative membership groups, some being assigned to the chosen group and others to a nonchosen group. Attitudes were reassessed after a year of experience in these alternative membership groups with divergent attitude norms. During the course of the year, some subjects came to take the imposed (initially nonpreferred) membership group as their reference group. Attitude change after the year was examined in terms of the membership group and reference group identifications of the subjects at that time.

The Field Experiment

The Ss of this study were women students at a large private coeducational university. The study was initiated shortly before the end of their freshman year, when they all lived in the same large freshman dormitory to which they had been assigned upon entering the university. At this university, all women move to new housing for their sophomore year. Several types of housing are available to them: a large dormitory, a medium-sized dormitory, several very small houses which share common dining facilities, and a number of former sorority houses which have been operated by the university since sororities were banished from the campus. These latter are located among the fraternity houses on Fraternity Row, and are therefore known as "Row houses." Although the Row houses are lower in physical comfort than most of the other residences for women, students consider them higher in social status. This observation was confirmed by a poll of students,[2] in which over 90 per cent of the respondents stated that Row houses for women were higher in social status than non-Row houses, the remaining few disclaiming any information concerning status differences among women's residences.

In the Spring of each year, a "drawing" is held for housing for the subsequent year. All freshmen must participate in this drawing, and any other student who wishes to change her residence may participate. It is conducted by the office of the Dean of Women, in cooperation with women student leaders. Any participant's ballot is understood to be secret. The woman uses the ballot to rank the houses in the order of her preference. After submitting this ballot, she draws a number from the hopper. The rank of that number determines the likelihood that her preference will be satisfied.

In research reported earlier,[3] a random sample was drawn from the popula-

2. S. Siegel, "Certain Determinants and Correlates of Authoritarianism," *Genet. Psychol. Monogr.*, 49: 187–229, 1954.

3. *Ibid.*

tion of freshman women at this university, several tests were administered to the *S*s in that sample, and (unknown to the *S*s) their housing preferences for the forthcoming sophomore year were observed by the investigator. The *S*s were characterized as "high status oriented" if they listed a Row house as their first choice, and were characterized as "low status oriented" if they listed a non-Row house as their first choice. The hypothesis under test, drawn from reference group theory and from theoretical formulations concerning authoritarianism, was that high status orientation is a correlate of authoritarianism. The hypothesis was confirmed: freshman women who listed a Row house as their first choice for residence scored significantly higher on the average in authoritarianism, as measured by the E-F scale,[4] than did women who listed a non-Row house as their first choice. The present study is a continuation of the one described, and uses as its *S*s only those members of the original sample who were "high status oriented," i.e., preferred to live in a Row house for the sophomore year. In the initial study, of the 95 *S*s whose housing choices were listed, 39 were "high status oriented," i.e., demonstrated that the Row was their reference group by giving a Row house as their first choice in the drawing. Of this group, 28 were available to serve as *S*s for the follow-up or "change" study which is the topic of the present paper. These women form a homogeneous subsample in that at the conclusion of their freshman year they shared a common membership group (the freshman dormitory) and a common reference group (the Row). These *S*s, however, had divergent experiences during their sophomore year: nine were Row residents during that year (having drawn sufficiently small numbers in the housing drawing to enable them to be assigned to the group of their choice) and the other 19 lived in non-Row houses during that year (having drawn numbers too large to enable them to be assigned to the housing group of their choice).

E-F scores were obtained from each of the 28 *S*s in the course of a large-scale testing program administered to most of the women students at the university. Anonymity was guaranteed to the *S*s, but a coding procedure permitted the investigators to identify each respondent and thereby to isolate the *S*s and compare each *S*'s second E-F score with her first.

To prevent the *S*s from knowing that they were participating in a follow-up study, several procedures were utilized: (*a*) many persons who had not served in the earlier study were included in the second sample, (*b*) the testing was introduced as being part of a nation-wide study to establish norms, (*c*) the test administrators were different persons from those who had administered the initial tests, (*d*) *S*s who informed the test administrator that they had already taken the "Public Opinion Questionnaire" (E-F scale) were casually told that this did not disqualify them from participating in the current study.

The *S*s had no hint that the research was in any way related to their housing

---

4. See T. W. Adorno et al., *The Authoritarian Personality*, New York: Harper & Brothers, 1950; and H. G. Gough, "Studies of Social Intolerance: I. Some Psychological and Sociological Correlates of Anti-Semitism," *J. Soc. Psychol.*, 33: 237–246, 1951.

arrangement. Testing was conducted in classrooms as well as in residences, and all procedures and instructions were specifically designed to avoid any arousal of the salience of the housing groups in the frame of reference of the research.

The annual housing drawing was conducted three weeks after the sophomore-year testing, and, as usual, each woman's housing ballot was understood to be secret. In this drawing, each S had the opportunity to change her membership group, although a residence move is not required at the end of the sophomore year as it is at the end of the freshman year. If an S participated in this drawing, the house which she listed as her first choice on the ballot was identified by the investigators as her reference group. If she did not, it was evident that the house in which she was currently a member was the one in which she chose to continue to live, i.e., was her reference group. With the information on each S's residence choice at the end of her freshman year, her assigned residence for her sophomore year, and her residence choice at the end of her sophomore year, it was possible to classify the subjects in three categories:

A. Women ($n = 9$) who had gained assignment to live on the Row during their sophomore year and who did not attempt to draw out of the Row at the end of that year;

B. Women ($n = 11$) who had not gained assignment to a Row house for the sophomore year and who drew for a Row house again after living in a non-Row house during the sophomore year; and

C. Women ($n = 8$) who had not gained assignment to a Row house for the sophomore year, and who chose to remain in a non-Row house after living in one during the sophomore year.

For all three groups of Ss, as we have pointed out, membership group (freshman dormitory) and reference group (Row house) were common at the end of the freshman year. For Group A, membership and reference groups were identical throughout the sophomore year. For Group B, membership and reference groups were disparate throughout the sophomore year. For Group C, membership and reference groups were initially disparate during the sophomore year but became identical because of a change in reference groups.

As will be demonstrated, the Row and the non-Row social groups differ in attitude norms, with Row residents being generally more authoritarian than non-Row residents. From social psychological theory concerning the influence of group norms on individuals' attitudes, it would be predicted that the different group identifications during the sophomore year of the three groups of Ss would result in differential attitude change. Those who gained admittance to a Row house for the sophomore year (Group A) would be expected to show the least change in authoritarianism, for they spent that year in a social context which reinforced their initial attitudes. Group C Ss would be expected to show the greatest change in authoritarianism, a change associated not only with their membership in a group (the non-Row group) which is typically low in authoritarianism, but also with their shift in reference groups, from Row to non-Row, i.e., from a group normatively higher in authoritarianism to a group normatively lower. The extent of attitude change in the Ss in Group B would be expected to be intermediate, due to the conflicting influences of the imposed membership group (non-Row) and of the unchanged reference group (Row). The research hypothesis, then, is that between the time of the freshman-year testing and the sophomore-year testing, the extent of change in authoritarianism will be least in Group A, greater in Group B, and greatest in Group C. That is, in extent of attitude change, Group A < Group B < Group C.

Results

GROUP NORMS

From the data collected in the large-scale testing program, it was possible to determine the group norms for authoritarian attitudes among the Row and the non-Row women at the university. The E-F scale was administered to all available Row residents ($n = 303$) and to a random sample of residents of non-Row houses ($n = 101$). These Ss were sophomores, juniors, and seniors. The mean E-F score of the Row women was 90, while the mean E-F score of the non-Row was 81. The E-F scores of the two groups were demonstrated to differ at the $p < .001$ level ($x^2 = 11.1$) by the median test,[5] a nonparametric test, the data for which are shown in Table 1.

Table I—Frequencies of E-F Scores Above and Below Common Median for Row and Non-Row Residents

	Residents of Non-Row Houses	Residents of Row Houses	Total
Above Median	36	166	202
Below Median	65	137	202
Total	101	303	404

ATTITUDE CHANGE

The central hypothesis of this study is that attitude change will occur differentially in Groups A, B, and C, and that it will occur in the direction which would be predicted from knowledge of the group norms among Row and non-Row residents in general. The 28 Ss of this study had a mean E-F score of 102 at the end of their freshman year. The data reported above concerning authoritarianism norms for all women residing on campus would lead to the prediction that in general the Ss would show a reduction in authoritarianism during the sophomore year but that this reduction would be differential in the three groups; from the knowledge that Row residents generally are higher in authoritarianism

5. S. Siegel, *Nonparametric Statistics: For the Behavioral Sciences*, New York: McGraw-Hill Book Company, Inc., 1956, pp. 111–116.

than non-Row residents, the prediction based on social group theory would be that Group A would show the smallest reduction in authoritarianism scores, Group B would show a larger reduction, and Group C would show the largest reduction. The data which permit a test of this hypothesis are given in Table 2.

Table 2—Freshman-Year and Sophomore-Year E-F Scores of Subjects

| | E-F SCORE | | |
Group	End of Freshman Year	End of Sophomore Year	Difference
	108	125	− 17
	70	78	− 8
	106	107	− 1
	92	92	0
A	80	78	2
	104	102	2
	143	138	5
	110	92	18
	114	80	34
	76	117	− 41
	105	107	− 2
	88	82	6
	109	97	12
	98	83	15
B	112	94	18
	101	82	19
	114	93	21
	104	81	23
	116	91	25
	101	74	27
	121	126	− 5
	87	79	8
	105	95	10
	97	81	16
C	96	78	18
	108	73	35
	114	77	37
	88	49	39

The Jonckheere test,[6] a nonparametric k-sample test which tests the null hypothesis that the three groups are from the same population against the alternative hypothesis that they are from different populations which are ordered in a specified way, was used with these data. By that test, the hypothesis is confirmed at the $p < .025$ level.

Discussion

Substantively, the present study provides experimental verification of certain assertions in social theory, demonstrating that attitude change over time is

6. A. R. Jonckheere, "A Distribution-Free K-Sample Test Against Ordered Alternatives," *Biometrika*, 41: 133–145, 1954.

related to the group identification of the person—both his membership group identification and his reference group identification. The hypothesis that extent of attitude change would be different in the three subgroups of Ss, depending on their respective membership group and reference group identifications, is confirmed at the $p < .025$ level; in extent of change in authoritarianism, Group A $<$ Group B $<$ Group C, as predicted.

Another way of looking at the data may serve to highlight the influence of membership groups and reference groups. At the end of the freshman year, the Ss in Groups A, B, and C shared the same membership group and the same reference group. During the sophomore year, the Ss in Group A shared one membership group while those in Groups B and C together shared another. From membership group theory, it would be predicted that the extent of attitude change would be greater among the latter Ss. This hypothesis is supported by the data (in Table 2): by the Mann-Whitney test,[7] the change scores of these two sets of Ss (Group A versus Groups B and C together) differ in the predicted direction at the $p < .025$ level. This finding illustrates the influence of *membership* groups on attitude change. On the other hand, at the conclusion of the sophomore year, the Ss in Groups A and B shared a common reference group while those in Group C had come to share another. From reference group theory, it would be predicted that attitude change would be more extensive among the subjects who had changed reference groups (Group C) than among those who had not. This hypothesis is also supported by the data (in Table 2): by the Mann-Whitney test, the change scores of these two sets of Ss (Groups A and B together versus Group C) differ in the predicted direction at the $p > .05$ level. This finding illustrates the influence of *reference* groups on attitude change. Any inference from this mode of analysis (as contrasted with the main analysis of the data, by the Jonckheere test) must be qualified because of the noninde-pendence of the data on which the two Mann-Whitney tests are made, but it is mentioned here to clarify the role which membership and reference groups play in influencing attitude change.

The findings may also contribute to our understanding of processes effecting attitude change. The imposition of a membership group does have some effect on an individual's attitudes, even when the imposed group is not accepted by the individual as his reference group. This relationship is shown in the case of Group B. If the person comes to accept the imposed group as his reference group, as was the case with the Ss in Group C, then the change in his attitudes toward the level of the group norm is even more pronounced.

Methodologically, the study has certain features which may deserve brief mention. First, the study demonstrates that it is possible operationally to define the concept of reference group. The act of voting by secret ballot for the group in which one would like to live constitutes clear behavioral specification of one's reference group, and it is an act whose conceptual meaning can be so directly

7. Siegel, *Nonparametric Statistics*, pp. 116–127.

inferred that there is no problem of reliability of judgment in its categorization by the investigator. Second, the study demonstrates that a field study can be conducted which contains the critical feature of an experiment that is usually lacking in naturalistic situations: randomization. The determination of whether or not a woman student would be assigned to the living group of her choice was based on a random event: the size of the number she drew from the hopper. This fact satisfied the requirement that the treatment condition be randomized, and permitted sharper inferences than can usually be drawn from field studies. Third, the test behavior on which the conclusions of this study were based occurred in a context in which the salience of membership and reference groups was *not* aroused and in which no external sanctions from the relevant groups were operative. This feature of the design permitted the interpretation that the E-F scores represented the Ss' internalized attitudes.[8] Finally, the use of a paper-and-pencil measure of attitude and thus of attitude change, rather than the use of some more behavioral measure, is a deficiency of the present study. Moreover, the measure which was used suffers from a well-known circularity, based on the occurrence of pseudo-low scores.[9]

Summary

In the social context of the lives of the subjects, and in a natural social experiment which provided randomization of the relevant condition effects, the influence of both membership and reference groups on attitude change was assessed. All subjects shared a common reference group at the start of the period of the study. When divergent membership groups with disparate attitude norms were socially imposed on the basis of a random event, attitude change in the subjects over time was a function of the normative attitudes of both imposed membership groups and the individuals' reference groups. The greatest attitude change occurred in subjects who came to take the imposed, initially nonpreferred, membership group as their reference group.

8. Sherif and Sherif, *op. cit.*, p. 218.

9. Adorno et al., p. 771; Siegel, "Certain Determinants . . . ," pp. 221–222.

Conflicting Group Membership: A Study of Parent-Peer Group Cross-Pressures

Bernard C. Rosen

MULTIPLE group membership, particularly in heterogeneous societies, often carries with it the possibility that the individual will belong to groups with mutually conflicting normative systems.[1] Since each group seeks to transmit and enforce its own particular norms and values, the individual whose membership groups conflict is likely to be caught between the cross-pressures of contradictory group expectations and role prescriptions.

This paper is a study of the influence of two membership groups on the attitude of a group of adolescents, many of whom find themselves in a cross-pressure situation. The membership groups with which we are here concerned are among the most important to which the adolescent belongs: the *family*, his first membership group and one which plays an important role in the socialization process; and the *peer* group, the group in which the adolescent in particular finds many of his gratifications. Both groups exert pressures upon the adolescent. Frequently these pressures are mutually sustaining, but in some areas they may be in conflict, demanding from the adolescent patterns of thought and behavior which are mutually incompatible. For many adolescents one of these areas is

Reprinted from *American Sociological Review*, 20: 155–161, 1955, by permission of the author and the publisher, the American Sociological Association.

1. For a systematic analysis of the possibility of multiple group membership in modern societies and its consequences for the individual see T. Newcomb, *Social Psychology*, New York: Dryden, 1950, Ch. 15; and M. Sherif, *An Outline of Social Psychology*, New York: Harper, 1948, Ch. 5.

religion.[2] In this paper we shall examine the conflicting expectations that familial and peer groups have concerning one facet of the adolescent's religious orientation. Our task is to examine the relationship between the adolescent's religious attitude and that of his membership groups, to determine what this relationship is when the groups are defined as reference groups, and to evaluate the relative influence of these groups upon the adolescent in cases where their expectations conflict.

Research Procedure

SAMPLES AND TECHNIQUES

The data for this study were collected in a small upper New York State city. The subjects are fifty adolescents—the entire universe of Jewish high school age boys and girls in the city: a fact of some importance in that it considerably facilitated charting the pressures, attractions, and structure of the adolescent's peer-clique group.

Adolescents were first questioned in unstructured interviews in order to familiarize the investigator with the formal and informal groups. Strategic adult informants, particularly youth activities leaders, and a sample of parents were also interviewed. In addition the investigator observed the adolescents at school and at play as a nonparticipant observer for about a year. At the end of the year the subjects were reinterviewed. This time a structured interview schedule was used.

INDEX OF GROUP MEMBERSHIP

Before the relative influence of the conflicting groups could be examined, it was necessary to locate the membership groups and to delineate an area in which there were conflicting norms and expectations. Information about the familial[3] group was secured from the adolescent and from a sub-sample of parents. The latter were interviewed in order to check upon the teen-agers' reports. The peer group with which we are here concerned is not the general category of the adolescent's age-mates, but only those who form his own particular sub-group or clique. In unstructured interviews adolescents were asked to describe the groupings or cliques among the Jewish adolescents of the community. A list of the names of every Jewish adolescent in town was handed to the respondent, and he was asked to tell us with whom these adolescents most

2. It is often in adolescence that the individual first questions the religious beliefs and practices accepted unquestioningly by him in his childhood and often taught to him by his parents. See A. B. Hollingshead, *Elmtown's Youth*, New York: Wiley, 1949, Ch. 10.

3. The religious norm of the familial group is here defined as expectations of the parents, since in most families in our culture the norm is set by the parents. The terms parental group and familial group will be used here interchangeably, although it is recognized that the adolescent's membership group is the familial group (i.e. parents and siblings) and not the parental dyad.

frequently associated. These data were buttressed by information gained through nonparticipant observation over a period of a year. At the end of the year each respondent was asked to list the persons among his age-mates, both Jewish and non-Jewish, with whom he most often associated. Through combining these three sources of information we were able to locate each adolescent in a particular peer group.

The issue about which there are conflicting expectations and pressures from certain familial and peer groups is one which adolescents often report as a source of conflict between themselves and their parents. It concerns a ritual practice of traditional Judaism—the use of kosher meat.[4] As a way of establishing the position of the adolescent and that of his membership groups, the respondents were asked: "When you get married are you going to use kosher meat in your home?"; and "Is kosher meat now used in your home?" Adolescents who plan to use kosher meat, and parents who use kosher meat will be called, for purposes of this study, "observant." In cases where more than half of the members of the adolescent's peer clique-group are observant, the group will be labeled observant.[5] In terms of the attitude and presumably the expectations of their membership groups, it can be seen that adolescents fall into one of four categories: those whose parent and peer groups are both observant; those whose parent and peer groups are both non-observant; those whose parents are observant and peer group is non-observant; those whose parents are non-observant and peer group is observant. Adolescents who fall into the latter two categories are those who are likely to experience conflicting expectations and pressures.

Research Findings

PARENT-PEER GROUPS AS MEMBERSHIP GROUPS

Our first task is to examine the relationship between the attitude of the adolescent toward the use of kosher meat and the attitude of his membership groups. Unless a relationship can be shown to exist, it would be meaningless to speak of a cross-pressure situation. If the data indicate that neither group is sufficiently important on this issue to influence the adolescent to the extent of having attitudes congruent with his, it is not probable that their conflicting expectations would be perceived or experienced as a cross-pressure situation.

The data in Table 1 show that a significant relationship exists between the attitude of the adolescent and the attitude of his membership groups. Children of observant parents are proportionately more likely to be observant than are children of non-observant parents: 60 per cent of the former state they are going

4. Traditional Judaism forbids the use of any but ritually clean (i.e. *kosher*) food. Only certain animals, slaughtered in a prescribed manner, may be eaten.

5. Non-Jewish members of the clique-group are considered non-observant. This is to indicate that they are not likely to exert pressures on the Jewish adolescent to be observant, although this is a possibility.

Table 1—Parent and Peer Group Attitude by Adolescent's Attitude

Adolescent Attitude	PARENT ATTITUDE		PEER GROUP ATTITUDE	
	Observant per cent	Non-Observant per cent	Observant per cent	Non-Observant per cent
Observant	60	32	80	23
Non-observant	40	68	20	77
Total per cent	100	100	100	100
Total number	25	25	20	30

Chi-square: 3.9.
P less than .05.

Chi-square: 15.5.
P less than .001.

to observe the kosher meat ritual in their homes after marriage, as compared with 32 per cent of the latter—a difference that is statistically significant at the .05 level. The picture is the same when we compare the attitude of adolescents and the attitude of their peer groups: 80 per cent of the respondents whose peer-clique group is observant are also observant, as compared with 23 per cent of those whose peer group is non-observant—a relationship that is significant at the .001 level. However, it may be asked whether the relationship between adolescent and peer group attitude is not in fact in the final analysis a function of parental influence, since parents sometimes determine their children's selection of friends. Parents may see to it that their children associate only with adolescents who share the parental point of view. This hypothesis is examined in Table 2, in which the parental attitude is controlled. It can be seen that if

Table 2—Peer Group Attitude by Adolescent's Attitude When Parental Attitude Is Controlled

Adolescent Attitude	OBSERVANT PARENTS		NON-OBSERVANT PARENTS	
	Observant per cent	Non-Observant per cent	Observant per cent	Non-Observant per cent
Observant	83	38	75	12
Non-observant	17	62	25	88
Total per cent	100	100	100	100
Total number*	12	13	8	17

Combinatorial chi-square: 8.9.
P less than .05.
* Yates correction factor used in computation.

parents seek to limit their children's associates to those who share the parental attitude (we do not know that this is the case) they are successful in only a little over half the cases. Furthermore, the relationship between the attitude of the adolescent and that of his peer group observed in Table 1 is not destroyed, although the statistical significance of this relationship is reduced to the .05 level.

There is, we note further in Table 1, a tendency for adolescents to agree more closely with their peer group than with their parents: 22 per cent of the adolescents differ from their peer group, as compared with 36 per cent who differed from their parents. Also it is apparent that membership in a particular group does not explain entirely the possession of an attitude on the part of many adolescents. In the case of this study the use of one membership group as a predictive factor would involve considerable error: in terms of the familial group this error is as high as 36 per cent.

One way of guarding against this kind of error is to relate the attitude of the adolescent to the attitude of more than one membership group. When the membership groups are found to be homogeneous in attitude on a particular issue, the probability is increased that the adolescent will possess that attitude also. Thus the relationship between the adolescent's attitude and that of his membership groups is very marked in cases where the religious orientation of the two groups is similar. The data in Table 3 show that when parent and peer

Table 3—Relationship Between Adolescents' and Membership Groups' Attitude When Membership Groups' Attitude is Homogeneous

Adolescent Attitude	Parent and Peer Group Are Observant per cent	Parent and Peer Group Are Non-Observant pe cent
Observant	83	12
Non-observant	17	88
Total per cent	100	100
Total number*	12	17

Chi-square: 12.1.
P less than .001.
* Yates correction factor used in computation.

group are both observant, 83 per cent of the adolescents are observant. When the membership groups are non-observant, 88 per cent of the adolescents are non-observant. In both cases the relationships between the adolescent's attitudes and those of his membership groups are statistically significant at the .001 level. The combined influence of the two groups, presumably both in terms of the examples they set and their expectations is very effective: in all only 14 per cent of the respondents deviate from the norms of their membership groups when the groups are homogeneous in attitude.

PARENT-PEER GROUPS AS REFERENCE GROUPS

Another, and we believe more reliable method of guarding against error, is to substitute the factor reference group for that of membership group. Not all membership groups are necessarily significant to the individual, and those which are significant for him on one issue may not be so on another. Recently, the group which consists of significant others, persons of importance to the individual and to whom he psychologically relates himself, has been termed the reference group. A major proposition of reference group theory is that the individual's attitudes stem from and are related to those of his significant others, and that this congruence of attitudes is a function of the process of interiorization and legitimation of referent's expectations.[6]

In determining the adolescent's reference group the following criteria were used: (1) perceived importance to individual, (2) perceived model for self-evaluation, and (3) perceived bond of understanding. Respondents were asked these questions:

1. Who are the people whose good opinion of you is important to you?
2. How religious would you say you are? Are you comparing yourself with someone? If so, with whom are you comparing yourself?
3. Who do you think understands you better, your parents or your friends?

In answer to the first two questions adolescents were permitted to name as many persons as they felt necessary. These criteria permit the rough classification of adolescents into three categories: (1) those who named their parents more often than their peer group; (2) those who named their peers more often than their parents; (3) those who named their parents and peers with equal frequency. The group named most frequently is considered the reference group.[7] We recognize that adolescents may have other references (e.g., teachers, or siblings) but for the purpose of this study we shall limit ourselves to only parental and peer groups as reference groups.

When the reference group rather than the membership group[8] is used as the explanatory variable, the data indicate, as in Table 4, that error (i.e. those adolescents who deviate from the norm of their designated group) is con-

6. The term "reference group" seems first to have appeared in a monograph by H. H. Hyman, "The Psychology of Status," *Archives of Psychology*, 1942, No. 269. Hyman used the term to signify some person or social category with whom the individual compares himself in evaluating his status. M. Sherif, *op. cit.*, and T. Newcomb, *op. cit.*, stress the attitude formation functions of the reference group. R. K. Merton and A. Kitt, "Contributions to the Theory of Reference Group Behavior," in *Studies in the Scope and Method of the American Soldier*, in R. K. Merton and P. F. Lazarsfeld, editors, New York: Free Press, 1950, pp. 40–105, employ the concept as a frame of reference for both self-evaluation and attitude formation.

7. A somewhat different method was employed in research reported elsewhere by the writer: Bernard C. Rosen, "The Reference Group Approach to the Parental Factor in Attitude and Behavior Formation," paper read at the annual meeting of the Eastern Sociological Society, April 3, 1954. The index employed here is not a scale and admits of neither ordinal nor cardinal properties, but is a rough categorization. However, we feel that the criteria and questions with some modifications are capable of being scaled.

8. An individual's reference group may or may not be one of his membership groups. That is, it may be a group to which he objectively belongs, believes himself to belong, or aspires to belong. In this study the reference group is also an objective membership group.

Table 4—Correspondence Between Attitude of Adolescent and Attitude of Reference Group

| | ADOLESCENT'S ATTITUDE IS | |
Adolescent's Reference Group	Like His Reference Group (cases)	Unlike His Reference Group (cases)
Parents	21	5
Parents and peers	5	1
Peers	15	1
Total number*	41	7

* Two cases designating parent and peer as reference group and corresponding to only one or the other not included.

siderably reduced, particularly as compared to situations in which only one membership group is employed as the explanatory factor. No more than 14 per cent of the entire sample deviate from their reference group. The relationship between the attitude of the adolescents and the attitude of their reference group is clearly statistically significant. In this case also it can be seen that adolescents tend to conform more closely to the norm of their peers than the norm of their parents: 7 per cent deviate from their peers as compared with 19 per cent who differ from their parents.

CONFLICTING MEMBERSHIP GROUPS

The fact that relatively few adolescents deviate from the norm of their parent-peer groups considered as reference groups, but that a sizeable number differ from these groups when defined as membership groups except in those cases where the attitude of the two groups is similar, suggests that the deviate cases may be understood in terms of the membership groups possessing different attitudes and of the adolescent interiorizing the expectations of one group rather than those of the other. When this situation obtains, the individual is likely to be placed in a cross-pressure situation in which he experiences conflicting expectations from his membership groups.

Several kinds of evidence indicate that a number of adolescents find themselves in a cross-pressure situation. Analysis of their membership groups show that 42 per cent of the adolescents belong to familial and peer groups whose attitude toward the use of kosher meat is mutually conflicting. Furthermore, these conflicting attitudes show up in the *perceived pressures* which adolescents explicitly verbalized in interviews. Usually, pressures from parents are described as contributing to the observance of rituals: many adolescents attribute their acceptance of a particular ritual to parental influence. Explanations of this acceptance were typically in terms of habituative experience in which the observance of a ritual was traced to a habit formed in the home, or in terms of constraintive experience in which case observance is more a function of parental pressure than of personal preference. The peer group on the other hand is often held responsible, both by adolescents and parents, for the adolescent's deviation from traditional norms. Respondents often ascribe their first transgression of the traditional code to the influence of their peers. This is not to say that there are not instances in which parental pressures are away from traditionalism and peer group pressures toward traditionalism; situations of this sort occur, but they are not as frequent objectively and even less frequently perceived and reported by the adolescent.

As is the case for most groups, the family and the peer groups expect conformity to their norms. Some latitude is permitted in the interpretation of these norms, but typically any radical deviation from the group pattern will be punished. In the case of the familial group the sanctions are usually verbal scoldings; in the case of the peer group deviation from the group norm may result in expulsion from the group. In one case which the writer observed a teen-age girl was isolated from her peers because of her unusually close adherence to the traditional norms of her parents, an adherence which prevented her from writing, riding, or attending sports events on the Sabbath. She is described by other adolescents as "fanatic" and "stiff necked" and is virtually without friends among her age-mates. This is an extreme situation; usually severe sanctions are rare. Ordinarily the group achieves conformity to its norms by effectively creating a climate of opinion which gently coerces the adolescent into acceptance of the group's norms.

The data in Table 5 lend tentative support to the hypothesis that when

Table 5—Correspondence of Adolescent's Attitude With Parental Attitude by Correspondence of Adolescent's Attitude With Peer Group Attitude

Adolescents' and Peers' Attitude Are	ADOLESCENT'S ATTITUDE AND PARENT'S ATTITUDE ARE	
	Like (cases)	Unlike (cases)
Like	25	14
Unlike	7	4
Total number	32	18

adolescents deviate from the norm of one group they are conforming to the norm of the other group. Thus of those adolescents who differ from their parents, 78 per cent of these agree with their peer group. Conversely, of those respondents who differ from their peer group, 63 per cent agree with their parents. Here again we note that the norm of the peer group tends to have a greater appeal than that of the parents. That is, when the adolescent differs from his parents he is proportionately more likely to agree with his peer group (78 per cent of the time) than he is to agree with his parents when he differs from his peers (63 per cent). While this difference is not statistically significant it is in the direction of our other data. We cannot be certain from these data that adolescents who deviate from the norm of one group are doing so at the instigation of the other group. For example, adolescents who reject the norm of observant parents may do so because they feel their parents to be unnecessarily restrictive, rather than because they find the norm of the peer group more acceptable or because they are reacting to the direct promptings of their peers. However, it is probable that the group with which the adolescent agrees plays at least a supporting role, if not an active role, in alienating the adolescent from the norm of the other group. Few adolescents are in rebellion against both groups. Logically, the adolescent may agree with both groups, with one of the two, or with none. Yet in only 8 per cent of the cases does he take the last alternative, indicating perhaps a need for support of at least one of these two important groups.

We can now ask the question: when parents and peer group have conflicting attitudes, with which group does the adolescent tend to agree and is this group his reference group? The data in Table 6 show that in the cases in which parent-

Table 6—Correspondence of Adolescent's Attitude With Membership Groups' Attitudes in Cases Where Groups Differ, by Adolescent's Reference Group

	ADOLESCENT'S ATTITUDE IS	
Adolescents' Reference Group	Unlike Parents and Like Peer Group per cent	Unlike Peer Group and Like Parents per cent
Parents	21	80
Peers	79	20*
Total per cent	100	100
Total number**	14	5

Chi-square: 3.6.
P less than .06 but more than .05.
* Yates correction factor used in computation.
** Two cases designating parent and peer group as reference group and corresponding to one or the other not included.

peer groups have conflicting attitudes, 74 per cent of the adolescents agree with their peers as compared with 26 per cent who agree with their parents. In each case the group with which he agrees is about four times as likely to be his reference group as is the group with which he does not agree. The probability that a difference as large as this could have occurred by chance is about 5 times out of a hundred.

Conclusions

The data indicate that a significant relationship exists between attitude of adolescents in this sample toward the use of kosher meat and the attitude of their familial-peer groups considered as membership groups. This relationship is even more marked when the membership groups are homogeneous in attitude or when the group is a reference group. In cases where the attitudes of the two membership groups are conflicting, the group with which adolescents agree tends to be their reference group as defined by independent criteria. The data, on the whole, point to the greater influence of the peer group. More often than not in cases where parent-peer groups have conflicting attitudes on the issue examined in this study adolescents agreed with their peers rather than their parents. The smallness of the sample, the ethnicity of the adolescents and the nature of the issue on which there is conflict make it imperative that any generalizations or conclusions drawn from these data be considered as highly tentative. Nonetheless, on the whole the data consistently and cumulatively indicate that for this issue and these adolescents the norm of the peer group tends to be more closely related to the attitude of the adolescent than is the norm of the parental group. Whether this relationship is a causal one and to what extent it reflects not only the pressures of the peer group but also other referents, as well as the general value system of American culture, we cannot, of course, be certain. But the data do suggest that the importance of the peer group, even in situations where parents and peer group conflict, must be taken into account in any study of adolescent attitudes.

While the necessary data to explain these findings are lacking, some tentative explanations which may lead to further research can be offered. The relationship between adolescent and parental-peer group attitudes found in this study is in keeping with a growing body of theory and empirical data which demonstrate the importance of these two groups, particularly in terms of their functions in the socialization process, in the attitude formation process. An explanation of the relative impact of these two groups on adolescents in our society may be found in the hypotheses about American character presented by Riesman.[9] His suggestion that the changing character structure of Americans is in the direction of the increasing importance of the peer group offers a potentially rewarding guide for future research. Should further research indicate that the relative number of inner-directed persons (those who internalize parental authority) is declining in our society and that the proportion of other-directed persons (those whose character is formed chiefly by the example of their peers) is growing, it would help to provide a conceptual framework in which the data in this study could be interpreted.

Whatever future research may reveal about the importance of the peer group in childhood and adulthood, it is likely to be found that at no other time is the peer group as important to the individual as it is in

9. D. Riesman et al., *The Lonely Crowd*, New Haven: Yale University Press, 1950.

adolescence. In our culture the physiological changes, the lag between physical maturation and social maturity associated with adolescence create a host of problems for the adolescent. In his effort to cope with these problems the adolescent turns to his age-mates for companionship, recognition, and support. The peer group provides the teen-ager with a sense of belongingness at a time when conflicting loyalties, identifications, and values make him unsure of himself. Within the peer group the adolescent is able to acquire the status often denied him in the adult world—a status which is more predictable and based upon values and expectations he understands and can fulfill.

Studies in Reference Group Behaviour

REFERENCE NORMS AND THE SOCIAL STRUCTURE

S. N. Eisenstadt

The Problem and the Research

THE purpose of this paper is to analyse certain problems related to reference group behaviour, a field whose importance has grown and been recognized in the recent past in both sociological and psychological works. It is hoped that the analysis presented in this paper will advance to some extent the coordination of work on reference group behaviour with systematic sociological theory. The analysis presented here is a preliminary step in a wider work, the purpose of which is to present a systematic theory of this field.

A. THE PROBLEM

Before presenting our data it would be useful to state, in a very general way, what kinds of problem related to reference group behaviour struck us as requiring a more specific and systematic investigation. We shall not present these problems and hypotheses in any great detail at this stage, as they will emerge from the presentation and analysis of the material.

In most of the available literature, the importance of reference groups as determinants of an individual's behaviour, attitudes, opinions, and beliefs has been emphasized. It has been shown that an individual may identify himself with various groups to which he may not belong, and with a variety of group norms, and that he may strive to enter into these groups.[1] Such identifications

Reprinted from *Human Relations*, 7: 191–206, 212–213, 1954, by permission of the author and the publisher.

1. See T. M. Newcomb, *Social Psychology*, New York: Dryden Press, 1950, pp. 194ff; M. Sherif, *An Outline of Social Psychology*, New York: Harper & Brothers, 1948, pp. 122ff; E. L. Hartley and R. Hartley, *Fundamentals of Social Psychology*, New York: Alfred A. Knopf, Inc., 1952, pp. 456–483; M. and C. W. Sherif, *Groups in Harmony and Tension*, New York: Harper & Brothers, 1953, pp. 157–182.

and aspirations influence his behaviour, his attitudes towards other people, and his evaluations of himself, and his own role and position as well as those of others. The analysis of the data in the *American Soldier* by Merton and Kitt, has shown the importance of such reference orientations and groups in a great variety of situations in influencing, for instance, an individual's level of aspiration and satisfaction and his standards of comparison.[2] Out of this analysis some very pertinent questions for further research have been thrown up: what are the determinants of choice of a given reference group by an individual; what are the various types of relationship between membership and reference groups, among others.

It seems to us, however, that a somewhat different approach to the whole problem of reference groups might be attempted. While this approach probably denotes only a change of emphasis in the posing of certain problems, it was felt that it might lead to their greater elucidation.

Instead of asking at the beginning what are the ways in which reference groups influence an individual's behaviour, we could ask why such an orientation is necessary at all from the point of view both of a given social system and of the individual's personality. What are the functions which such orientation fulfils in the social life-space of an individual and in his participation in the society of which he is a member?

Our main interest, then, is in finding out to what extent orientations to reference groups constitute an integral part of the social structure, and what functions they fulfil in it. The analysis presented in this paper will attempt to specify the social situations in which such orientations are evoked and the social roles through which they are maintained. It will be shown that the maintenance of such orientations to reference groups and group norms is one of the important mechanisms of social control, and that it is closely connected with the exercise of leadership and authority, and with the processes of communication in a society. It is assumed here that on the basis of such a systematic analysis of this problem it would be easier to understand the numerous concrete ways in which orientation to reference groups can influence an individual's behaviour.[3]

B. THE RESEARCH

We shall now introduce our main research data and findings. In this paper we shall present them in a rather summary way, dealing only with those aspects and problems which seem to be of greatest interest at the present stage of dis-

2. See R. K. Merton and A. Kitt, "Contributions to the Theory of Reference Group Behaviour," in R. K. Merton and P. F. Lazarsfeld, eds., *Continuities in Social Research,* New York: The Free Press, 1950, pp. 40–106.

3. Some indication of a similar approach can be found in E. L. Hartley, in "Process of Opinion Formation, A Symposium," *Public Opinion Quarterly,* 1950–51, Vol. 14, pp 668ff., and in C. Hovland, I. L. Janis, and H. H. Kelley, *Communication and Persuasion,* New Haven: Yale University Press, pp. 165–166, footnote 1.

cussion. In a second paper we hope to present more detailed case-studies and materials.

The general importance of the problems of reference groups has been recognized in the first studies on absorption of immigrants in Israel undertaken by the Research Seminar in Sociology of the Hebrew University.[4] It has been shown there that only in so far as various groups of immigrants develop orientations and references to various norms, institutions, and groups of the absorbing society—beyond the various actual roles that they have to perform in their various membership groups—can we speak of absorption and institutionalization of immigrant behaviour. These were, however, rather general orientations, and it is only through a series of later studies and researches that the problem has been systematically tackled. Some preliminary aspects of these studies have already been reported,[5] but only now have we reached the stage at which we can present a full report on those first systematic investigations.

These investigations have been undertaken on the one hand in a number of different immigrant settlements of various types (agricultural cooperatives, urban and semi-urban quarters, etc.) in which both the institutional structure and a sample of the inhabitants were studied, and on the other hand in selected samples of special "types" of immigrants—leaders of different types (communal, political, educational, etc.) and generally "mobile" persons, i.e. persons with a strong mobility orientation. The studies were made by a combination of participant observation, open-ended and "focused" interviews, and closed questionnaires, which were used interchangeably according to the specific situation. These investigations served as a first step in a more broadly based research project which is now under way.[6] At the same time it was possible to use several other research projects of the Research Seminar, such as those on youth movements, immigrant youth, and social participation,[7] for elucidation of several problems connected with this.

The research presented here is based on analysis of 400 cases, of which 250 were random samples of five different settlements and urban quarters, and 150 a sample of leaders and mobile persons from these settlements and from various special courses for community leaders and such.

4. See S. N. Eisenstadt, "The Process of Absorption of New Immigrants in Israel," *Human Relations*, Vol. V, No. 3, and "Institutionalization of Immigrant Behaviour," *ibid.*, Vol. V, No. 4.

5. See S. N. Eisenstadt, "The Place of Elites and Primary Groups in the Process of Absorption of New Immigrants," *American Journal of Sociology*, Nov. 1951; "Processes of Communication Among New Immigrants," *Public Opinion Quarterly*, Spring 1952; "Conditions of Communicative Receptivity," *Public Opinion Quarterly*, 17: 363–375, 1953; "Reference Group Behaviour and Social Integration," *American Sociological Review*, 19: 175–185, 1954.

6. On the general outline of this project, see the Memorandum submitted to the Second International Congress of Sociology, Liege, 1953, ISA/L/RD/10.

7. See "Sociology in Israel, 1948–53," submitted to this Congress, ISA/L/RD/6.

The Nature and Different Types of Reference Orientations

The first step towards ascertaining the place of reference groups in the social structure was to see what are the main types of orientation to reference groups. An answer to this could be found in the responses to such questions as "Are you satisfied or otherwise with your present job, social relations, etc., and why?" "What is good, or bad, about them?" "Why is it good or bad?" "How would you like to have it?" "Why would you like it that way?" "What do you consider to be proper standards for it?" "Is this important or unimportant for you, and why?" "When do you feel so?" etc., etc. These were included in interviews and observation schedules.[8]

The first important finding was that when talking of reference groups, as our basic analytical concept, we might be guilty of reifications. This has already been alluded to in the literature, when it was emphasized that a "reference group" is a group with whose *norms* we identify ourselves.[9] In all our interviews it became apparent that it is this norm (or, perhaps, in a broader sense, "value") that serves most as the frame of reference towards which an individual seeks to orient himself, and that only in some specific situations is such a norm tied to a concrete *group*. Thus it seems that the process of orienting oneself towards a frame of reference which transcends one's own concrete roles, is a part of the normative process in society, through which some value-orientations are maintained in concrete behaviour.

In order to be able to understand this process, it is necessary to analyse some of the more important common characteristics of such norms and frames of reference. These, on the basis of the material available, seem to be the following:

(a) All such norms contain a general evaluative element, i.e. they are *general standards* according to which various patterns of behaviour are evaluated. Thus they may be said to transcend any given concrete act of behaviour.

(b) Despite their generality, they are, at the same time, related to various clusters of roles and specifically focused on them. Hence they may be said to bring these roles into a wider context of reference.

(c) This wider context does very often, although not always (in fact in about 70 per cent of our cases) contain some elements of collectivity-orientation, i.e. some evaluation in terms of behaviour and participation

---

8. Obviously, it was mainly in the open-ended and focused interviews that clear answers to such questions could be elicited, although some general indications were also found in the closed questionnaires.

9. An interesting comment on this view can also be found in a recent paper by E. Stern and S. Keller, "Spontaneous Group References in France," *Public Opinion Quarterly*, Summer 1953, Vol. 17, No. 2, pp. 208–218, in which some of the usual assumptions of reference group theory are pertinently criticized.

in a given collectivity, not necessarily a concrete group, but more often—at least in our cases—a "total society" or some major subdivision of it. The following two excerpts from interviews can well illustrate these points:

"I think it is not proper to behave in such a way in this settlement. One should participate in its affairs and behave like a good worker. Otherwise, you are not really a member of this settlement, or even of the Yishuv at all; you are outside it. . . ."

"It is not Jewish not to help one's neighbour, even if you do not know him. We Jews always helped each other, but here it is sometimes different, and I do not know what we are becoming."

(d) These norms were usually (in about 90 per cent of the cases) perceived as prescribing the proper types of behaviour in the roles and situations to which they were referring.

(e) These norms usually served also as principles of perceptual organization of the social field for the individual; i.e. with their aid various social objects could be perceived in some organized way, for instance, as conforming with given norms or deviating from them, as exemplifying certain values, etc. (A good example of this may be found in the following excerpt from an interview: "When I know how one should behave, what is the accepted way here, I begin also to understand people, to know who is doing what . . . everything becomes clearer. But otherwise I am very confused; everything is rather blurred.")

It seems to us that these general characteristics of reference norms are not limited only to our research, or necessarily influenced by the types of questions asked. Perusal of the "raw materials" of other studies of this subject, especially of Newcomb's fully documented Bennington study and of several studies on communication,[10] indicates that most of these characteristics existed there as well, and may therefore be assumed, at least in a hypothetical way, as more or less universal attributes of reference norms.

Beyond these common characteristics, the various reference norms may be differentiated according to the kind of roles and situations to which they refer, and according to the kind of normative imperatives which they prescribe to these roles. The analysis of our material showed the following main types of such norms. Although they seem to cover the main types of institutional roles,[11] it is not claimed, however, that they are the only possible ones, and it is to be hoped that additional work will enable a wider differentiation to be made.

10. See, for instance, the material given in M. Sherif, *op. cit.*, and in T. M. Newcomb, *op. cit.* See R. K. Merton, *Mass Persuasion*, New York: Harper & Brothers, 1946; M. Janowitz, *The Community Press in an Urban Setting*, New York: The Free Press, 1952.

11. The classification found here is similar to but not identical with the one used by R. Linton in *The Study of Man*, New York: D. Appleton-Century Company, 1936, pp. 272ff.

1. General norms which seem to apply to almost any kind of roles and situations and which indicate only a very general prescription of behaviour, such as "good-bad" behaviour, "honest-dishonest," etc. They are not specifically related to any particular role and can be seen as applicable throughout a great variety of concrete forms of behaviour.

2. General norms which indicate the type of behaviour or attitudes appropriate to all members of a collectivity, and which indicate also a general type of identification with such a collectivity. A good example can be seen in the excerpt from the interview quoted earlier about the "mutual help" obligations of Jews, etc. These norms are also of a rather broad application. They do not prescribe any definite single role, but they are already clearly oriented towards a definite, even if rather wide, social setting. They may be said to prescribe the universal conditions of membership in a community.

3. Norms and values prescribing the types of behaviour appropriate to certain broad categories of social roles (i.e. age, sex, etc.) or some of the major institutional frameworks and subgroups of the society (i.e. family life, economic or religious behaviour, etc.). It is obvious that here there exist very many possibilities according to the different institutional spheres and sub-groups within a society.

4. Norms which prescribe behaviour in what may be called ambiguous, potentially undefined (at least from the point of view of a given individual) situations. These norms usually define the solution to some conflict between various demands and expectations, and also some sort of hierarchy of values and preferences.

5. Norms which prescribe the possibilities of choice between various roles in a given situation, and which prescribe the behaviour appropriate in the process of choice and in the chosen role.

These were the most important types of reference norms that were encountered in our researches. While no claim is being made that this list is exhaustive, it is already sufficient to show us that there may exist at least two different types of orientations towards such wider norms, or two types of such norms and frames of reference. First, there are those norms which emphasize or delineate the proper way of behaviour in a given concrete role or situation. They are, as it were, explicit formulations of the ultimate values which are implicit in any given social interaction. In other words, these norms give a wider, and not merely technical, meaning to the various roles, and in this way put them in the framework of wider value-orientations and some sort of collectivity identification. They do not, however, relate these roles to any other specific roles, and are firmly bound to a given concrete situation, which does not seem to be in any way problematic.

The second type of reference norms (those listed 4 and 5) seem to be of a somewhat different type, or to have at least an entirely different emphasis. They define solutions to problems, to potential conflicts (for the individual, and within the society), and delineate the points and possibilities of choice. They usually deal not with a simple, unproblematic situation (or set of situations) but with several situations or roles which have to be arranged in some relation to one another. Thus the reference to wider norms, systems of values, etc., is in this case not only a general indicator of proper behaviour and attitude but also a regulator of potentially conflicting and complex modes of behaviour. This difference between these two types of reference norms may be most clearly discerned in some of their internal characteristics. In the second type of norms there always exist, as already indicated, some sort of hierarchical arrangement of different roles, values, attitudes. There is always an emphasis on the *relative* importance of some of these spheres of relations and roles, while in the first type there is usually a more simple, unequivocal emphasis on one norm or value which is given a somewhat absolute validity. The following excerpt from an interview is a good illustration of this point: "I was told that it is usually more important to perform the various civic duties than to help friends. Helping friends is also important, but not of such great importance. Only if we shall all perform our duties to the settlement and the State, shall we and all our friends live in order and in peace."

These two different types of norms were mentioned and referred to by most of the interviewees. The first, simple type, was mentioned by about 90 per cent, while the second, the hierarchically complex one, by about 75 per cent.

Reference Orientations as Mechanisms of Social Control

This analysis, cursory as it may be, already shows us that these various frames of reference seem to fulfil an important function in society. All these reference norms are, in reality, derivations from the main values of a society. It is through the reference to these norms that the various concrete roles which an individual performs are related to the wider values of society, and to its basic identifications. As it is well known that the maintenance of common ultimate values is an important prerequisite of any society, it can be postulated that the reference to wider norms constitutes a mechanism of social control, through which proper ways of behaviour and attitudes are maintained, whether in simple, unambiguous situations, or, in the second case, in potentially conflict-ridden situations.

This does, however, only raise another problem—perhaps the most crucial one of our whole discussion—namely why, and in what cases, is such reference-norm behaviour necessary as a mechanism of social control? In order to be able to approach an answer to this question, we should first ask in what kinds of social situations are these orientations evoked and maintained? Do there exist any specific types of such situations, or are they fortuitously, randomly distributed throughout the social system?

The answer to this question is not very simple for a variety of reasons. First, it is necessary to remember that many of our data (as well as those in any social research) have been collected through some type of questioning, which usually creates a new social situation. Hence it is important to be able to discount this factor in the analysis of our data and rely sometimes more on systematic observations and open questions rather than on direct structured questioning. Secondly—and this applies mainly to our data—we have to distinguish between those situations which are the result of a specific situation of immigration, culture-change, etc., and those situations which may be assumed to exist in any stable society. We shall also see that this distinction will enable us to throw some very important light on the problem.

With these cautions in our mind, we shall attempt to give an answer to this problem. This answer is based on an analysis of altogether about 300 cases (based both on questioning and observation) in which satisfactory answers to this problem could be found. The analysis of this material shows most clearly that these references to wider norms are evoked in special social and psychological situations, which can be defined from two different points of view. First, we may ask how are they experienced and perceived by those who participate in them. Secondly, we may also ask whether there exist any specific characteristics of such situations, which define their place in the social structure. It seems best to begin with the first question, since through it we shall be able to understand the problems faced by the participants in the situation and understand the function of reference norms for them. It may then be easier to proceed to the second question. A content analysis of interviews and observations reveals that the following seem to be the most important feelings and attitudes experienced by these people:

First, there is the mere lack of knowledge of proper behaviour and of understanding of the situation. This deficiency is not usually felt simply as a technical deficiency in perception or organization, but more often as a difficulty of ordering one's aims and goals into a meaningful pattern. The different goals become discrete, and to some extent disorganized. Thus it is that the possibility of conflict is often perceived by people in such situations.

Along with this we usually find a great deal of uncertainty and anxiety about establishing relations with other people. The individual feels that he faces undefined, unknown behaviour on the part of other people and is not certain of being able to establish stable relations with them. "I do not know how to behave here . . . what is good or bad . . . I am always afraid what other people will think of me . . . whether they will think I am all right . . . whether I do what should be done . . . by them." In other words, there may exist an anxiety about denial of reciprocity on the part of those with whom one may, or may have to, participate in these new, unstructured situations.

This anxiety is closely related to the fear of not attaining, or of losing, one's place in the collectivity or wider society of which one is a member, and which makes these demands. The collectivity may be an important sub-group of a society (ethnic group, social movement, etc.), but usually there is some orientation towards the total society. "I do not feel that I am yet a member of the Yishuv, of the State, even of this town. It is so baffling; I do not know what to do; whether this is the way in which one becomes a part of the country here, or even a part of this factory I am working in."

In summarizing these various attitudes, it might be said that an individual feels in such situations some anxiety about his place and status within the community. Our material was not clinically oriented, and sometimes there is only rather indirect evidence, but there is usually some anxiety about the potential failure of the ego to integrate and guide the personality. This is, of course, closely related to the problem of perceptual and moral organization which was mentioned earlier.

These various attitudes were usually quite closely interconnected. In about 60 per cent they went always together, while in 80–85 per cent of the cases, at least three out of the four existed.

The Place of Situations in Which Reference Orientations Are Evoked in the Social Structure

The foregoing discussion has shown us the psycho-sociological meaning of certain situations for those who participate in them, and the nature of the problems they face. It has shown clearly that we deal here not with extreme individual psychological states, but with states of uncertainty and anxiety which have clear social reference points.

We shall describe the main situations which were found in our analysis. These various situations could probably be multiplied, and there exists also an overlap between them (both analytically and concretely). But even so their main characteristics can be discerned. The following are the main situations in which those reference norms which deal with potentially conflicting roles are evoked.

1. Situations in which an individual, most of whose roles are performed in a given institutional setting (especially family, home, and place of work), is called upon to perform new roles in another setting (i.e. political, ritual, educational). Some typical instances of this from our material are the following:

(a) Whenever people in a settlement or an urban neighbourhood are called upon to perform some civic duty (local or national), to join some sort of organization or association, or to participate in an election, drive, etc.

(b) When members of a settlement or of an urban area are called upon to participate in some collective ritual, parade, etc.

(c) When such people are faced with educational problems brought over by their children from the school and youth movement.

(d) Whenever such individuals become oriented to a wider setting through reading newspapers, listening to the radio and trying to understand and cope with problems presented there.

2. Whenever for an individual a real or potential conflict exists between the participation in different social settings and groups. Typical examples here are, for instance:

(a) When the demands made by the political authorities or parties seem to be in conflict with the claims of work (i.e. either in allocation of time or in the necessity to choose one's fellow workers, or in the demand to allocate work only to members of a given party);

(b) When such demands run counter to family solidarity, once more either in terms of time allocation, or of necessity to give preference to members of party or trade union and not to relatives, friends, or neighbours. Instances of this can be multiplied, and do, of course, exist in any society. However, they become more pronounced in situations of culture contact.

(c) Whenever people are faced with some new demand on their time, and more especially when such a demand is made in terms of participation in the total society (i.e. various types of national service, taxes, inauguration of a new economic or agricultural policies, etc.).

(d) The necessity to have some reference orientation becomes especially important when, in the above situations, there exists also a necessity to make an explicit choice between various roles and courses of action and/or to enter actively into a new group. Examples of this can be seen when parents have to choose for their children different types of schools (i.e. religious or secular), when there exist some possibilities of choosing between different occupational channels at the times of political elections, etc. These cases may also frequently involve the joining of a new group. The outstanding example of this is, of course, taking up military service or joining a youth movement. As we shall see later, however, in such situations some additional elements come in.

In our investigations about 87.5 per cent of all the orientations to the more complex norms were related to the types of situation outlined above. About 5 per cent did not seem to be related to any special situation while in 7.5 per cent of the cases no clear analysis could be made.

The common characteristic of all these situations is that in all of them the individual has to transfer his behaviour from one institutional sphere to another, or has to act concurrently in several institutional spheres and to relate them to one another. Analysis shows that most such situations may create some uncertainty and anxiety among individuals who participate in them. It is proposed here that this is due to the following conditions which are inherent in the institutional structure of any society and in the elementary fact of social division of labour.

(a) First, it seems that in most, or all, societies different institutional frameworks or spheres are regulated according to different principles and norms, and hence the transition from one sphere to another may involve both unfamiliarity and conflict.

(b) This possibility is especially acute because different people participate to different degrees in the various institutional spheres and hence may be more strongly involved in one than in the other.

(c) Such division of labour and different degrees of social participation exists not only in relation to different institutional spheres but also in the relation between what may be called "local" and "central" activities. Most people in any society participate actively in some sub-groups or sub-systems of a society which have only an indirect relation to the central sphere of activity and the values of a society, and yet their activity must necessarily be oriented to these values and to some extent guided by them.[12]

In other words, it may be tentatively summed up that these situations of uncertainty exist in any society because of the fact that any individual's behaviour, attitudes and identification must necessarily extend beyond the actual roles which he performs at any given time and throughout his life. This discussion should, of course, be expanded, and these institutional conditions should be analysed in greater detail. But now it seems enough to say that on the basis of the former analysis it may be proposed that the various "reference" orientations towards wider norms, groups, or values are evoked in situations of strain so as to counteract the anxieties referred to above. These orientations fulfil then the functions of mechanism of social control because they can provide the necessary perceptual and moral knowledge through which the social field can be organized, behaviour in it regulated, relations with other people stabilized, and a feeling of status-security and collective identification established.

Before proceeding with our discussion, we have still one question to answer. Our preceding analysis was mostly concerned with those types of orientations which referred to undefined situations, situations of potential conflict. What about the first (perhaps in a way more common) types of reference orientations; those which simply reaffirm the main values implicit in any concrete situation or group? In what situations are those norms evoked? The answer to these questions is both easier and more difficult than in regard to the former types of norms. It is easier because in a situation of rapid social change, such as the one we have been investigating, the evocation of these "simple" orientations and norms is frequent—perhaps even more frequent than of the more complicated norms. On the other hand, however, it is more difficult to discern and analyse exactly the situations in a stable setting in which these norms are evoked. Our data in this respect are rather impressionistic, and much more systematic research will be needed before full answers will be given.

The most general conclusion we have reached on this matter is that these norms are evoked in situations where, for one reason or another, the routine

12. These general theoretical considerations are very closely related to those outlined by Talcott Parsons in *The Social System*, New York: The Free Press, 1951, and by T. Parsons, E. Shils, and R. Bales, in *Working Papers in the Theory of Action*, New York: The Free Press, 1953.

of a given group, situation of work, or family behaviour is disturbed. The important difference between these and the former situations is that these disturbances seem to be due not to the systematic impingement of other institutional spheres on the group or situation, but mostly to some sort of internal disturbances due to individual tensions and differences, to lack of adequate motivation to perform some routine work, etc.[13]

It may thus be suggested that these "simple" unequivocal norms are evoked when the stability of a fully structured and usually accepted situation is threatened, either because those participating in it seem either apathetic in performing their roles or appear to view them in purely technical meaning, without seeing in them any full social and moral meaning. This interpretation —tentative and cursory as it is—finds support in the analysis of the data specific to the situation of social change and culture contact. In this situation it was found that the immigrants very often faced a gradual undermining of the most simple roles, in work, in family life, in neighbourhood relations. These would lose some of the meaningfulness of their relation to values and status images, and would become purely *technical* and adaptive.[14] It would not be only a conflict between relatively ordered and stable situations and norms, but a disorganization of these elementary, simple situations, of their internally meaningful organization. It is in such situations that the references to the more simple, unequivocal norms were very often evoked, looked for, and asked for. Quite often this would be intermingled with the reference to the more complex, hierarchically arranged norms. But even more often it was found that, in such a situation of change and disorganization, people could be disinterested and apathetic towards these more complex reference norms unless and until the meaningfulness and stability of the simpler situation and norms became re-established. In these situations there was usually also a very strong emphasis on some sort of collective identity and participation, and it was the lack of meaning of various roles in relation to such identity that was often especially remarked.

It may thus be proposed that the reference orientation towards the simpler, and in a way more basic, norms does also serve as a mechanism of social control, but not so much in situations of potential conflict between different sub-systems of a society as in the event of potential disorganization of a stable sub-system itself. This is evident in the relatively small emphasis on any "hierarchial" organization of norms and roles in these references. However, several situations were found in which both types of reference orientations and norms were used, and when the need for both of them was expressed by the participants. These situations were mainly of two types. First, the situations of choice already mentioned. It was quite often found that, though during the process of choice between different alternatives or possibilities the more complex norms were used

13. Further research may perhaps show that there exist some systemic conditions within a small group which do also give rise to conditions of some uncertainty. The work of R. Bales points in such a direction. But we still need much research in this field.

14. See S. N. Eisenstadt, "Conditions of Communicative Receptivity."

and referred to, once a choice had been made and the individual had entered a given group in which he had to perform some concrete role, the more simple norms were also referred to. It was found quite often that during the initial process of "socialization" within a group (army, course, new place of work, etc.), the individual would refer to both types of norms. After he became more stabilized in the new place, however, the reference to the more complex norms would be diminished. Secondly, both types of norms would sometimes be referred to also when some new demands were made by the total society—demands which would necessitate the undertaking of some very routine and discipline-demanding activities, such as civic defence, or rounds of watches.

These examples seem to substantiate our previous analysis. They show that in both these types of situation, there existed at the same time some conflict between various demands and attitudes—a conflict which had to be resolved by means of wide community participation, and also by the necessity to give wider meaning to various new concrete roles and performances.

From this analysis it is clear that there exists a multiplicity of reference norms and groups to which an individual may direct himself and that his choice between them is very largely determined by the kind of social situation he is in. These different reference norms are evoked when the impact of the institutional structure on the individual puts him in a somewhat problematic situation from the point of view of his status and collectivity aspirations. Thus it may be suggested that the kinds of reference orientations and norms that will be evoked in a given situation—whether these be simple, universal norms, or those related to specific clusters of roles (e.g. occupation, family, etc.) or the more "complex", hierarchically arranged norms—will depend on the interplay between the particular social situation in which an individual finds himself and his perception of this situation in terms of his status-image or levels of aspiration. Here there exists a very wide scope for research, some possibilities of which have already been indicated in former analyses of the problem.[15] The analysis presented here has shown, we hope, how it is possible to relate these various concrete problems to analysis of the institutional structure of society. It has shown that such orientations and references serve as mechanisms through which various concrete roles are connected with the main values of a society and regulated by them.

This raises some additional systematic problems which have to be solved before all the various ramifications of these conclusions can be fully understood.

The Communication of Reference-Orientations and Their Place in the System of Communication in a Society

The first problem is to ascertain in what ways this social control is exercised and performed. How does the orientation to reference norms and groups develop within an individual, and how is it maintained through his various

15. See R. K. Merton and A. Kitt, *op. cit.*

social activities? We have to ask who exercises this control, and by what means. It can be assumed at this stage of our discussion that some sort of general orientation is developed in any normal individual through the process of socialization.[16] Several researches now going on try to analyse systematically this process in socialization. But even if we take it for granted now, the problem still remains as to how these orientations are maintained and implemented in the main situations in adult life in which the potential need may exist.

It is through the attempt to find answers to this problem that we have come to what may be an interesting theoretical development through which another set of problems could be connected with that of reference group behaviour. In most of the situations investigated by us, it was found that:

    (a) the various reference orientations, etc., are usually communicated to people, and that these people expect to receive such communications;

    (b) that these communications are transmitted by persons in special social positions—usually of leadership—or striving to attain special positions, among whose functions is the transmission of such communications, and

    (c) that the transmission of such norms constitutes a basic part of the process of communication in the society, and

    (d) that this whole process of communication constitutes an important part of the institutional framework of the society; i.e. that special roles and situations are assigned and that these roles are connected with positions of authority.

The transmission and articulation of reference standards in situations of potential conflict (and/or rapid social change) was usually found to be the function of special people who can be broadly said to hold positions of leadership, or aspire to such positions, whether formal or informal.[17] We shall analyse in yet greater detail the various processes of selection of these leaders who were of different types—traditional, political, professional, etc.—in our situation, but here it is enough to emphasize that in most of the situations investigated there were people in positions of leadership, or authority, or aspiring to such positions, who would see it as part of their tasks to communicate these various wider norms and prescribe or propose different types of solutions to the potential conflict. Perhaps even more interesting is the fact that most of the new immigrants sought such people, and expected the communication of norms from people in these positions. The absence of such people in certain instances was very often experienced as one of the main frustrations of the new situation. About 65 per cent of those investigated here either emphasized such a frustration or a deep satisfaction at the existence of such people. As one of the interviewees put it, "I felt awful when I could not find any important people who could explain

16. See on this Talcott Parsons, *The Social System*, ch. viii.

17. See S. N. Eisenstadt, "The Process of Communication" and "The Place of Elites and Primary Groups."

to me all this and tell me how to behave . . . it was really terrible, but now it is much better, much easier when these officials explain to me this. . . . "[18]

These people, the communicators, were looked upon as interpreters of the new reality, as people who could both explain and evaluate the various situations of potential conflict. It was the absence of such people in certain situations that gave rise to a predisposition among the immigrants to go after "quack" leaders.[19] At the same time the absorbing structure and its representatives were also always looking among the immigrants for people who could act as transmitters of communications from the absorbing society to the various immigrant groups and were ready to give them positions of power and authority, in the hope that in this way their communications would be received and accepted by the various groups of immigrants. It was also found that in a great part (about 75 per cent to 80 per cent of communications analysed by us in the different settlements) of both the formal and semi-formal communications directed towards the immigrants from the absorbing society, as well as communication coming from their leaders (ethnic, religious, or professional) consisted of such reference-norms, prescriptions of behaviour and identification. Most propaganda communication covered the main characteristics of reference-norms referred to above and only purely technical communication differed in this respect.[20] Thus our analysis shows that reference-group orientations, their maintenance and transmission, are an important part of the institutional structure of a society. It seems that the same applies in a general way not only to a total society or community, but also to various small groups, organizations, etc. Thus we have found, although as yet only in a rather impressionistic way, that such informal leaders, or communicators, exist in almost every cluster of groups (family, neighbourhood, place of work). More systematic researches on these problems, undertaken elsewhere, have also shown the same general conclusions.[21]

This brief analysis of the relation between communications and reference orientations may perhaps also help to evaluate communication research in terms of systematic sociological problems and also to orient this research to such

18. See for more material on this "The Place of Elites. . . . "

19. See "Conditions of Communicative Receptivity."

20. See "The Process of Communication."

21. Evidence for this can be found in numerous studies of small groups, especially those of R. Bales at the Harvard Laboratory of Social Relations. The analysis presented here, especially that part which deals with the relation between social division of labour is, to some extent, parallel to the analysis of "phase movements" in the small groups. In additional work we hope to analyse the relation between those movements and the structure of communication within a society. Evidence on the existence of such centres of communication in everyday organization and groups can be found in E. Jacobson, "A Method for Studying the Relationship between Communication Structure and Attitudes in Complex Organizations," Survey Research Center, University of Michigan, 1952 (mimeographed), and L. Reissman, "Levels of Aspiration and Social Class," *American Sociological Review*, Vol. 18, No. 3, June 1953, pp. 233–242.

problems. Most of the more recent communication research which is not confined merely to opinion surveys is already going in such a systematic and dynamic direction. Instead of just listing the listening, reading, or movie-attending, habits of various groups of the population, this research has tended more and more to analyse the process of communication in a functional setting, in its relation to community life and to the individual's general orientation and participation in a social system. Foremost among these researches are those of Lazarsfeld and associates on the "People's Choice,"[22] Merton's analysis of the Smith broadcast[23] and of patterns of influentials in a community,[24] Herzog's and Warner's analysis of the audiences of "soap operas" and similar performances,[25] Berelson's analysis of newspaper-writings[26] and Janowitz' analysis of community press.[27] In all these researches, one way or another, it was shown that receptiveness to different kinds of communication is conditioned to a very great extent by one's status-image and aspirations, by one's aspirations to various types of community participation and quite often by seeking solutions to some dilemmas and problems of status and participation. Moreover, in these researches is also implied—mainly through the concept of "opinion leaders" and influentials on the one hand and through the analysis of the structure of mass media on the other—that the process of communication constitutes a part of the institutional structure of the society. But with the exception of Merton's analysis of types of influentials and Janowitz' analysis of the community press, there has been until now little systematic analysis in this direction. It is submitted here that such an analysis could be furthered and developed through the convergence of communication research and of reference-group research. In this way the analysis of contents of communication would receive additional significance—it could be systematically analysed as to the types of norms, orientations, etc., it transmits. The whole process of communication in a society could be analysed as an important medium of social control through which these regulative norms are maintained. . . .

Reference Norms and Reference Groups

Before summing up the main conclusions of this stage of our study we should dwell on one additional problem which is inherent in the study. We

22. P. F. Lazarsfeld et al., *The People's Choice*, New York: Columbia University Press, 1948.

23. R. K. Merton, *Mass Persuasion*.

24. R. K. Merton, "Patterns of Influence," in P. F. Lazarsfeld and F. Stanton eds., *Communications Research*, 1948–49, New York: Harper & Brothers, 1949, pp. 180ff.

25. L. C. Warner and W. Henry, "Radio Daytime Serial," *Genetic Psychology Monog.*, 1948, pp. 3–71.

26. B. Berelson, "What Missing the Newspaper 'Means'," in Lazarsfeld and Stanton, *op. cit.*, pp. 111ff.

27. Janowitz, *op. cit.*

have spoken hitherto in a very general way about reference norms, reference groups, etc., without differentiating to any extent between these terms. In particular, we have as yet not analysed the place of reference-*groups* in our whole framework. Most of the recent literature on this problem has stressed the importance of reference-*groups*, and although we have indicated already at the beginning of our discussion that such an emphasis may involve some reification, we have not analysed it systematically. It seems that the main question here is "when are *groups* the main reference points according to which a person evaluates himself and orders his behaviour?"

On the basis both of our material and of the data of other researches mentioned before, the following tentative answers to this question may be proposed:

A. Specific groups may become the main reference points of our individual in so far as they become the *symbol* of a given norm or value. This may take place, (i) if the leaders (formal or informal) seem to emphasize and symbolize some groups; and/or (ii) when the effectiveness of a given reference norm is largely dependent on the maintenance of a solidarity, best evoked through some sort of a group identification; and/or (iii) if some specific group has acquired such symbolic importance in the individual's process or socialization.

B. A group may become the main reference point for an individual if he has aspirations to become a member of it, and if it is in the direction of his mobility aspirations or role-choices. In all such cases, the group becomes the main focus of an individual's reference-norms and value orientations or one of their most important aspects. But only very rarely—and mostly only in deviant cases —does *one* group become the focus of *all* values of aspiration. Usually these are spread among several groups, thus widening the individual's potential participation in the social system.

This short analysis of the place of groups in the reference framework of an individual poses, of course, many new problems. Some of them have already been stated by Kelley,[28] whose differentiation between two different types of reference groups is very similar to that made above. But it seems to us that through the analysis proposed in this paper, the proper place of such *groups* within the institutional structure of society and within the personality structure of individuals becomes clearer and better articulated, and may help to evaluate the various concrete problems which have been proposed in the literature.

28. See H. Kelley, "Two Functions of Reference Groups," in G. E. Swanson, T. M. Newcomb, and E. L. Hartley (eds.), *Readings in Social Psychology*, New York: Henry Holt and Company, 1952, pp. 410–415.

The Communicator and the Audience

Raymond A. Bauer

I SHOULD like to present a few ideas which have grown out of the work of the Program of International Communications at Massachusetts Institute of Technology. Since these thoughts are group products, this paper could as appropriately have been presented by any one of several colleagues whose names will be mentioned in the course of this paper.

If we may judge by the glee with which physicists greeted the recent demolition of one of the theoretical underpinnings of their trade, it would seem that limited chaos is a sign of health in a science. When old models prove too simple, we expand them and add new variables. In the short run we are delighted when our work substantiates our theories. In the long run, however, it is the discarding of theories and assumptions that marks the milestones of advance. On these grounds, research in the field of social communications may be viewed with a great deal of satisfaction. A high proportion of individual pieces of research are so inconclusive that they have forced on us these ever more elaborated models of the communications process. May I cite just one major example: It is now generally conceded that the Erie County study of the 1940 elections compelled us to discard certain simple assumptions about the direct impact of the mass media upon the mass audience. The idea of the "two-step flow of communications" was introduced, and this initiated a search for opinion leaders. But opinion leaders proved not to be a single class of persons all of whom exercised their influence in the same way. We are now thrown back on looking for networks of interpersonal communication. Not only has the communications model been expanded, but the study of informal communications has now

Reprinted from *Conflict Resolution*, 2: 67–77, 1958, by permission of the author and the publisher.

blended into basic psychological research on interpersonal influence and sociological studies of the primary group.[1]

The same sort of revision is gradually taking place with respect to the classic formula of communications research: "Who says what to whom and with what effect?" Originally, communications research implicitly gave the major initiative to the communicator. The main question asked was: What sort of communications and media are most effective and under what circumstances? It would be incorrect to say that the audience was *ignored*, but it was certainly accorded very little initiative. Audiences (if I may use this term to embrace also "readers"), however, have proved intractable. They make their own decisions as to whether to listen or not to listen. Even when they listen, the communication may have no effect, or it may boomerang. More and more, researchers have had to shift their attention to the audience itself to find out what sorts of people they are dealing with under what circumstances.

I would like to go further and suggest that in the future we may come to regard the audience more and more as a system of response potentials and the communication as a signal which triggers off the response highest in the hierarchy. Or, to shift language a bit, what was once regarded as a "stimulus-bound" situation looks more and more like a "response-bound" situation. I am not proposing that this is all of what happens in *all* communications, but I *am* proposing that we are likely to find that it is profitable to look at a high proportion of communications not as *changing* behavior but as triggering the organism to do what it was very likely to do in any event. If this view of the audience is correct, it is of course not the result of, nor can it be tested by, any single crucial experiment; it is rather the reflection of the impact of a long series of research findings.

Our own attempts to understand a series of problems in the field of international communications have suggested to us the desirability of entertaining seriously the following propositions concerning the role of the audience in communications: (1) The audience influences the way in which the communicator organizes new information and thereby what he himself may remember and/or believe at a later point in time. (2) A communication once completed has an existence external to the originator. It is a sample of his behavior which he must often reconcile—as a result of social or of internal pressure—with other behavior. On this latter point we need only remember the story of Franklin Roosevelt asking Samuel Rosenman to reconcile one of his early speeches with later policy. After some deliberation, Rosenman told him that the only solution to his dilemma was flatly to deny having made the first speech. (3) Communications are seldom directed to a single manifest audience. Secondary audiences or reference groups, usually internalized and often imaginary, are important targets of communication and may at times play a decisive role in the flow of communications.

1. This trend is excellently and extensively reviewed by Elihu Katz and Paul Lazarsfeld in the first portion of *Personal Influence*, New York: The Free Press, 1955.

These propositions are not new discoveries. They may be found in the sociology of C. H. Cooley and of G. H. Mead, the psychiatry of Harry Stack Sullivan and others, and the essays of writers on communication. The rationale for presenting them in this context is twofold. First, practical problems of communications research have suggested to us their utility; second, it appears that it is presently possible to bring to bear on these propositions more systematic data than have been employed in the past. Much of what I have to say will consist of reporting of work we have done and are planning to do and of pointing to established areas of research and to individual studies which contribute with varying degrees of directness to the testing of these propositions, their implications, and their practical significance.

I. Effect of the Audience on Organization and Retention of Material

Our first proposition is that audiences influence the way in which a person organizes new information and thereby what he himself may remember and/or believe at a later point in time.

The functional approach to perception and remembering which has been so attractive to social psychologists in the past decades has led them to investigate the relationship of man's needs and interests to the way he perceives and remembers the "blooming, buzzing confusion" around him. Is it not equally plausible that one will organize new information in terms of its intended use in interpersonal relations, that a person who intends to communicate on a topic will organize and remember material on that subject as a function of his image of the audience he has in mind?

This question was posed by Harry Grace in a paper published in 1951.[2] He asked subjects to remember an array of objects which they were later to report to an experimenter. Some of the subjects were told that the person to whom they were to report was a woman; the control subjects were told nothing about the characteristics of the person to whom they were to report. It was anticipated, since some of the items might be "embarrassing" to report to a woman, that those subjects who were briefed on the sex of the experimenter would remember fewer of these items than would control subjects. Grace's data were not so conclusive as one might hope for, but he had nevertheless posed a meaningful question.

As often happens, the same question occurred to us without our having been aware of Grace's earlier work. While we were trying to organize our thoughts concerning the impact of foreign travel on American businessmen, Ithiel Pool suggested the possibility that a person might never formulate his impressions of a foreign country systematically until he was in the position of having to communicate them to someone else. In this event, the first audience to whom he addressed himself would influence the way in which he would organize

2. H. A. Grace, "Effects of Different Degrees of Knowledge about an Audience on the Content of Communication," *Journal of Social Psychology*, 34: 111–124, 1951.

his information and the terms in which he would couch his conclusions. In this way the audience would influence what he would later remember and believe. Let us consider the position of a man confronted with a new batch of information or with old unorganized knowledge, i.e., items of information which he has not previously related to each other. He is now in a position in which he views this information, whether "old" or "new," as something he may have to communicate to another person. He has a set to communicate to an audience of which he has a specified image. It is a basic assumption of both content analysis and effective public speaking, as well as the object of common-sense observation, that the communicator adapts his statements to his audience, taking into consideration its interests and expectations for purposes of more effective communication. That this set to communicate may affect what he later remembers is given plausibility by the voluminous experimental literature on the effect of set on perception and retention.[3]

One of the major problems of design in studies of the influence of set on remembering has been to prevent rehearsal of the material between periods of recall. From the standpoint of communications research, we would assume that such rehearsal is precisely what happens in the real life-situations in which we are interested. Therefore, it presents no design problem. Cooley long ago spelled out the process that we would guess to be at work. The anticipated audience would serve as—in Cooley's words—an imaginary interlocutor with whom the subject would hold internal conversations in anticipation of the eventual communication.[4] In the course of these internal conversations the material ought to be "reworked" to bring it closer to the form in which it was intended to be communicated. Cooley contended that the human personality is formed via such internal conversations with audiences real and imagined. Our goals are more modest. We should like to know what happens to the particular batch of new or newly organized information about which we have been talking. Is retention of this information indeed affected by the person's image of the audience to which he expects to communicate? The audience, in a fashion, coerces the individual into playing a role. Does this also mean, as the work of Janis and King on the influence of role-playing on attitudes[5] suggests, that the subject's attitudes are changed in this process?

We have so far undertaken only one piece of research directed at the question of the influence of the audience on what is remembered of new, incoming information. This was an experiment reported by Claire Zimmerman

3. Cf. C. E. Osgood, *Method and Theory in Experimental Psychology*, New York: Oxford University Press, 1953, pp. 562ff.

4. C. H. Cooley, *Human Nature and the Social Order*, New York: Charles Scribner's Sons, 1902, esp. pp. 61–62.

5. I. L. Janis and B. T. King, "The Influence of Role Playing on Opinion Change, *Journal of Abnormal and Social Psychology*, 49: 211–218, 1954; and King and Janis, "Comparison of the Effectiveness of Improvised versus Non-improvised Role-playing in Producing Opinion Changes," *Human Relations*, 9: 177–186, 1956.

and myself.[6] The design evolved out of a joint Harvard-M.I.T. seminar consisting of Miss Zimmerman, Ithiel Pool, Jerome Bruner, George Coelho, and myself.

The experimenter presented herself in the classrooms of a number of colleges and universities, as a representative of one of two fictitious organizations: the National Council of Teachers, identified as interested in improving the teachers' lot, or the American Taxpayers Economy League, identified as interested in saving taxpayers' money. Her organization, she said, was seeking speakers to address its members on the topic of teachers' pay, and she had arranged with the instructor to have them write sample speeches during class time one week from that day. In the meantime, she said, her organization was also interested in how well people remembered material on this topic. She then read a short passage to them—in half the instances favoring, and in the other half opposing, teachers' pay raises. There were thus four groups of 18 persons, each involving all possible combinations of materials and "audiences" both favoring and opposing raises in teachers' pay. She then asked the subjects to write from memory the passage she had just read to them, as close to verbatim as possible. On returning the next week she asked them again, before writing the sample speech, to write down the passage as literally as they could. This was an experiment in remembering, but under conditions where the subjects anticipated communicating the material to an audience of specified characteristics.

Our prediction was that, at the end of a week, subjects would remember more information in those instances in which the passage and the intended audience were on the same side of the issue (we called this a situation of "congruence") than they would if the passages to be remembered and the audience for whom they were to write a speech were in conflict (a situation we labeled "incongruent"). Thus a subject would remember more arguments in favor of raising teachers' pay if he were anticipating a favorable audience than if the intended audience were interested in saving the taxpayers' money. There were no differences among the groups in their initial recall immediately after the presentation of the material. However, there were differences in the expected direction at the end of the ensuing week. Our hypothesis was supported comfortably beyond the 0.01 level of statistical significance. Schramm and Danielson[7] have since replicated the basic experiment at Stanford University, using as subject matter a quite different issue, that of lowering the voting age to eighteen. The results once more hold up beyond the 0.01 level.

A subsidiary hypothesis was that this "audience effect" of selective remembering would be maximal for persons primarily concerned with the audience and minimal for persons primarily involved in the subject matter. The complete

6. Claire Zimmerman and R. A. Bauer, "The Influence of an Audience on what is Remembered," *Public Opinion Quarterly*, 20: 238–248, 1956.

7. W. Schramm and W. Danielson, "Anticipated Audiences as Determinants of Recall," *Journal of Abnormal and Social Psychology*, 56: 282–283, 1958.

design mentioned above was carried out on both graduate students of journalism (supposedly oriented by selection and/or training to be sensitive to the characteristics of the audience) and on students in teachers' colleges (presumably highly involved in the issue of teachers' pay). The basic hypothesis held up for both groups. But the effect, as predicted, was greater among the graduate students of journalism. The difference in effect was, again, statistically significant beyond the 0.01 level. The journalism students' rate of forgetting in a situation of "incongruence" was *double* that in a situation of "congruence." These results appear to be not only statistically but practically significant (see Table 1).

Table I—Mean Angles Corresponding to Percentage Losses for All Groups between First and Second Recall Trials*

	TAX AUDIENCE		TEACHER AUDIENCE	
STUDENTS OF	Incongruent Raise Salary Arguments	Congruent Do Not Raise Salary Arguments	Incongruent Do Not Raise Salary Arguments	Congruent Raise Salary Arguments
Journalism	55.44	26.85	54.79	27.30
Teaching	40.05	26.81	41.09	25.88

* From Zimmerman and Bauer (*op. cit.*, p. 244). The Bliss conversion formula from percentages to angles was used.

Since the completion of this experiment, several other pieces of work starting out on entirely different tacks have been done which testify to the effectiveness of a set to communicate on the organization and retention of information. Zajonc,[8] in a study directed at an understanding of cognitive processes, has found that persons who anticipate communicating a body of material organize it differently from persons who anticipate being communicated *to* on the same subject. Furthermore, by specifying that the other persons (i.e., those to whom the subjects are supposedly going to communicate or who are going to communicate to the subjects) are opposed to the subjects' own position on the issue, he was able to effect still further changes in the organization of the material. Thus in Zajonc's work, not only is the communicative set per se found relevant, but the qualitative image of the intended audience is also of importance to the way in which new information is handled.

Jones and Aneshansel[9] became interested independently in the question of the relative influence on retention of experimental subjects' own values and their intention to use controversial material for communication. They told some of their subjects that they were going to have to use the material presented to them in rebuttal to arguments with which they were to be confronted later. Their subjects remembered significantly more material counter to their own values

8. R. Zajonc, "Cognitive Structure and Cognitive Tuning," Ph.D. dissertation, University of Michigan, 1954.

9. E. E. Jones and Jane Aneshansel, "The Learning and Utilization of Contravaluant Material," *Journal of Abnormal and Social Psychology*, 53: 27–33, 1956.

when they were told they would have to use this material in an argument. Under control conditions the usual results were found. Subjects remembered more material in line with their own beliefs.

These several findings all seem to say that it is possible to affect what a person will recall of new information by telling him he will have to communicate on the subject and that his image of the audience will affect what is remembered. This indicates that the audience can, in fact, have an enduring effect on the communicator that extends beyond its influence on the form and content of individual messages.

Is it "perception" or "remembering" that is affected? All these studies suffer from the usual difficulty of distinguishing between perception, retention, and recall. In the instance of the Jones and Zajonc studies a very early effect was observed which might possibly reflect the initial organization of incoming material, i.e., perception. In the Zimmerman experiment, however, there was no observed effect on initial recall of the material. But there was a pronounced "audience effect" at the end of a week. This suggests that conscious or unconscious rehearsals of the anticipated speech resulted in accommodation of the newly acquired information to the values and expectations of the intended audience. It makes sense in light of this to look at the intended audience as an induced reference group of high salience. Presumably one's habitual reference groups regularly evoke similar internal conversations, although this process is somewhat more difficult to study.

However, we must again complicate matters. Image of the audience, information, and communicator's values appear to be in a state of active interrelationship in which any one of the elements may affect any one or combination of the others. Communicators committed strongly to the subject matter may "distort" their image of the prospective audience to bring it more in line with either their own values or the content of the incoming information and thereby reduce the "audience effect." Thus the teachers' college students were more likely than the journalists to report "objectively incongruent" audiences as "neutral" with respect to the material they were given to memorize. Furthermore, those subjects who "neutralized" an incongruent audience remembered more of the material. Because of the limited number of cases that fell in these categories, the differences in Zimmerman's data are not statistically reliable, and, in fact, some of the findings are presently ambiguous. They do, however, suggest this line of speculation.

Whereas it was previously proposed that reference groups, by acting as internal audiences, affect what one remembers (and possibly one's attitudes), it seems likely also that the individual's image of a reference group is formed and changes in the process of these internal conversations. On controversial issues, this may eventually produce a schematization of reference groups in which positive reference groups are seen as "all white" and negative reference groups are seen as "all black." This proposition, also, seems amenable to systematic study.

There are indications also that the set to communicate may have a dampening effect on the impact of the individual's own values. Most of the experiments on the influence of personal values on remembering and perception accept implicitly the position that pleasurable material will be remembered better than disagreeable material. That which is consonant with the individual's personal values is taken tacitly by most of the investigators to be pleasurable to the individual. Direct test of the proposition that agreeable material will be better remembered has produced conflicting results in quite a number of experiments.[10] The possibility that positive results of the influence of personal values on remembering and perception may be due, at least in part, to greater familiarity with consonant material may be bypassed for the moment in deference to a point more crucial to the present argument. Reinforcement of one's self-image or ego-defense is only one of the possible motives that may influence one's set toward incoming information. This is already implied in the notion of "perceptual vigilance" with the suggestion that under some circumstances the threshold for so-called "contravaluant" material will be lowered. Jones and Aneshansel make the same argument I am making now, and say: "The functionalist might suggest that we examine the total context in which perception (or learning) takes place, in an effort to determine those conditions which promote lowered thresholds for threatening material (perceptual vigilance) and those which promote higher thresholds (perceptual defense)."[11] It will be remembered that in their experiment positively valued material was better remembered in the control situation, but negatively valued material was better remembered by the experimental subjects who were told they were going to have to use the material in a later argument. Zimmerman's data also indicated that when subjects were given instructions that they would have to communicate on the topic of the material they were to memorize, this set to communicate dampened the effect of the subjects' personal values. Teachers' college students, for example, remembered material opposed to raising teachers' pay as well as they remembered material favoring raising teachers' pay. Pending more direct evidence, it is reasonable to assume that a majority of them favored high salaries for the profession they were about to enter.

To summarize the discussion of this point, I have presented evidence, argument, and speculation to the effect that one's image of the audience to which material is to be communicated affects how this material is organized and/or retained. The influence of the communicative set seems on occasion to offset the role of the individual's personal values and beliefs. However, the audience does not operate independently either of the content of the information in question or of the communicator's values. In some instances the communicator apparently accommodates his image of the audience so as to reduce the perceived incongruence between it and his values and information. Other investiga-

10. Cf. Osgood, *op. cit.*, pp. 571ff.

11. Jones and Aneshansel, *op. cit.*, p. 27.

tions, of course, have indicated that under some circumstances his values influence what he remembers.

Present evidence is at best not definitive. We have in plan further experimentation to test on larger samples some of the findings which are statistically unreliable; to ascertain to what extent Zimmerman's results reflect forgetting in any meaningful sense as opposed to a response set induced by the fact that the subjects were actually prepared to write a speech; to determine how lasting is the "audience effect" on what is remembered and whether or not attitudes are influenced. Our comparison of teachers' college students with journalism students was a lucky shot in the sociological dark but tells us less of the psychological factors which may be involved. It will be necessary to look into the psychological characteristics which differentiate persons of varying degree of "audience susceptibility" and audience resistance.

II. Communication as Personal Commitment

It is a commonplace that people on occasion say things other than precisely what they feel in their hearts. In psychological literature this circumstance has been memorialized in the distinction between "private" and "public" attitudes. Even the most honest and thoughtful person, confronted by different situations, will, quite sincerely, say different things on the same topic. What is relevant to one person in one situation is not what is relevant to another person in another situation. A disingenuous politician may well argue that he does not preach civil rights in the South because his audience is not interested in the topic. Regardless of the motives involved or the amount of disparity between private belief and public statement, the fact remains that a statement once made constitutes some degree of personal commitment.

It is easy to see how a public figure may he haunted by some utterance of his and be forced to extremes of ingenuity to reconcile it with other of his statements. We need but recall the incident mentioned previously when President Roosevelt asked Rosenman to explain away an earlier speech of Roosevelt on balancing the budget. More pertinent for us, however, is the possible effect of such commitments on the communicator's own attitudes.

Probably the most relevant body of research is that on compliance to group norms. Students of group dynamics have devoted a considerable amount of attention to the conditions under which an individual will shift his belief—at least on the overt level—to conform to the majority opinion in his group. It was Festinger who, a few years ago, called attention to the fact that overt compliance to group norms is not synonymous with covert compliance, i.e., change in private opinion.[12] It is therefore interesting to note that in a recent book Festinger devotes two chapters to the discussion of the conditions under

12. L. Festinger, "An Analysis of Compliant Behavior," in M. Sherif and M. O. Wilson, eds., *Group Relations at the Crossroads*, New York: Harper & Brothers, 1953.

which forced compliance leads to change of private opinion.[13] He cites experimental work of McBride and Burdick and Kelman's work on the effect of response restriction on opinion change.[14]

My own work on political loyalty in the Soviet Union,[15] and Bettelheim's earlier study of Nazi concentration camps[16] offer clinical evidence of opinion change when individuals are forced by external circumstances into a given line of behavior. In the light of this work on the effect of forced compliance on opinion change, it is reasonable to hypothesize that the audience, by evoking a commitment from the communicator, may have the second-order effect of causing him to accommodate his own beliefs to that commitment. This process, it would seem, is continuous with the one referred to above in which the audience affects the way in which the communicator organizes and retains information. The difference, however, is that one effect occurs in anticipation of the communication and the other follows after it. While it is easy to draw this distinction analytically, it may be difficult to draw empirically in practical situations, if an individual is involved in several successive communications.

From our contact with elite communications in this and other countries it seems to us that occurrences like the following sometimes take place. A prominent man is invited to deliver a ceremonial speech. In some instances a subordinate may draft the speech, and the speaker is rather indifferent to the content. He only wants it to be a good speech, appropriate to the occasion, that is, not blatantly divergent from his own values. On occasion the speech makes quite a hit, and the speaker is invited to make more speeches on the topic. Soon he is committed even in his own mind to this position and becomes an active advocate of it.

This sort of occurrence is probably rare among the general populace. However, among elite communicators of the sort we have been studying, this may be a problem of genuine practical significance. We have been struck with the frequency with which a public figure, bent on holding or gaining a position of influence, will deliberately seek out issues which may interest his constituency. When he hits on a successful issue and is rewarded, he becomes a vigorous proponent of that issue and in many cases converts himself even more firmly to that belief. This is exemplified in the instance of one ardent congressional spokesman for protectionism who told us that he had tried several issues on his constituency but found them uninterested until he evoked an enthusiastic response to a speech in favor of high tariffs. He has since made this his business.

13. L. Festinger, *A Theory of Cognitive Dissonence*, Evanston, Ill.: Row, Peterson & Company, 1957, chs. 4 and 5.

14. H. C. Kelman, "Attitude Change as a Function of Response Restriction," *Human Relations*, 6: 185–214, 1953.

15. R. A. Bauer, "Brainwashing: Psychology or Demonology," *Journal of Social Issues*, 13: 41–47, 1957.

16. B. Bettelheim, "Individual and Mass Behavior in Extreme Situations," *Journal of Abnormal and Social Psychology*, 38: 417–452, 1943.

We have no immediate research plans in this area. But, because of its seeming significance among elite communicators, it appears that we ought to take a closer look at the potential coercive force of the audience in evoking commitments and producing attitude change.

III. Reference Groups as Secondary Audiences

Our third and final point is that messages are seldom directed to a single manifest audience but that reference groups, acting as secondary audiences, have an influential and occasionally a crucial role in the flow of communications. The importance of secondary audiences is a matter of common experience and has often been commented on anecdotally. Anyone who wishes to refresh himself on their role in everyday life need only leaf through a few casually selected doctoral theses. It has been my experience in reading them that I could identify certain pages written for Professor A, for Professor B, and certain others for Professor C, even though none of these gentlemen obviously was going to read the thesis.

As I have said, the importance of secondary audiences has been commented on frequently in anecdotal fashion but seldom studied systematically. Systematic work on reference groups—to which I am referring in this context as potential secondary audiences—has been confined largely to their influence on the attitudes of the subjects under investigation. But, unless we consider the interview situation in which the attitudes were evoked as an instance of communication, there has been little direct research on the role of reference groups or secondary audiences in the flow of specific messages. Daniel Lerner[17] has pointed out that the reviews of *The American Soldier* were influenced by the reference groups of the reviewers. More recently, Herbert Gans[18] has presented a case study of the role of the reference groups of various movie-makers in the production of the movie *The Red Badge of Courage*. But such examples are few.

In an attempt to get at the actual role played by secondary audiences in the flow of communications, Irwin Shulman, a research assistant at M.I.T. and himself a journalist, interviewed newspapermen immediately after they had finished writing a story for their newspapers. At first he asked, "Who reads stories like this?" In response to this question he got stock answers derived from the newspaper's readership surveys. Then he shifted to asking, "While you were writing this story did you think of any person or group?" The answers to this question were quite different from those to the former question. The persons or groups of whom they actually thought while writing the story were seldom the "average middle-class man who buys this newspaper." The number of

17. In R. K. Merton and P. F. Lazarsfeld (eds.), *Studies in the Scope and Method of "The American Soldier,"* New York: The Free Press, 1950.

18. H. J. Gans, "The Creator-Audience Relationships in the Mass Media: An Analysis of Movie-Making," in B. Rosenberg and D. M. White (eds.), *Mass Culture*, New York: The Free Press and Falcon's Wing Press, 1957.

interviews was not sufficient for statistical analysis. Yet the qualitative evidence suggested that there was a patterning to these secondary audiences with respect to the type of communicator and story involved. Let me put the case more conservatively: There was in these interviews at least enough evidence that these secondary audiences are more than "noise" in the communications system to encourage us to continue the investigation.

The fact that many, possibly not all, journalists in Shulman's sample thought of secondary audiences while writing did not by any means demonstrate that secondary audiences influence the content of what is written. An experiment was conducted with journalism students who were asked to write news stories out of a set of disjointed facts.[19] The conditions of the experiment and the findings are too complicated for brief summarization. However, Pool and Shulman demonstrated that the reference groups and persons evoked were systematically and predictably a function of the material presented to the subjects of the experiment; and, much more interesting, the distortions which occurred in the handling of the material were a systematic function of idiosyncratic images which individual subjects imagined.

Both the results of Zimmerman's experiment, suggesting internal conversation in rehearsal of a speech, and Shulman's and Pool's work indicate the utility of thinking of reference groups as internalized audiences which are targets of imaginary conversations. While the existence of negative reference groups has been mentioned in the literature, almost all attention has been paid to positive reference groups. Reference groups have usually been treated as groups whose acceptance is sought or who are used as positive yardsticks for self-assessment. Our own orientation and data suggest that negative reference groups should be given more serious attention and that reference groups should be regarded as groups which one wants to influence in *any* fashion, whether it be to gain their approval or to persuade them to one's own position.

IV. Conclusion

The general import of these remarks is that there is something to be said for expanding our model of the communications process. I have proposed the utility of three propositions and presented evidence for both their plausibility and their practical import. These three propositions are, in summary, (1) images of audiences, both real and imaginary, external and internal, affect the way in which we organize and retain information and what we believe; (2) the audience often commits the speaker to a public position to which he may subsequently accommodate his private belief; and (3) finally, one seldom has in mind a single audience, and secondary, reference-group audiences may often exert the determining influence in the organization and retention of information, as well as in the flow of communication. In the simplest words, the communicator may

19. I. de S. Pool and I. Shulman, "Imaginary Audiences and the Creative Process," Cambridge, Mass., 1957, mimeo.

actually be addressing himself to someone other than the manifest audience.

It will be remembered that our interest in this expanded model of communications was generated by concern with the practical problem of the impact of foreign travel on American businessmen. It is our belief that this view of the communications process will continue to have practical implications in the field of international relations. In the recent conduct of our own foreign policy, observers have commented, the utterances of American officials, while ostensibly directed abroad, were actually directed at domestic American secondary audiences. Also, in international relations audience *images* play a crucial role. Negotiators between nations, in all probability, carry in their heads highly stereotyped images of their opposite numbers. Their absorption and retention of information will be much affected by the intervention of these images. Coelho[20] has, partially out of the stimulus of these ideas, done a doctoral dissertation on the role of audience images as reference groups in the accommodation of Indian students to the United States.

While we may talk about such practical implications abstractly, it will take a considerable amount of empirical work to establish what part audience images actually play in international affairs.

20. G. Coelho, "Acculturative Learning: A Study of Reference Groups," Ph.D. dissertation, Harvard University, 1956.

Mass Communication and the Social System

John W. Riley, Jr., and Matilda White Riley

The Recipient and His Primary Groups

A CONSIDERABLE store of theory, often summarized under the heading of reference-group theory, is at hand to describe recipients [of communications] as members of groups. As set down by such scholars as Sherif, Newcomb, Merton, and others,[1] this theory "centers on the processes through which men relate themselves to groups and refer their behavior to the values of these groups."[2] Not only do the groups provide a standard against which the individual may evaluate himself and others; more importantly, the individual's family, his community, his workmates—all of his significant "primary" groups—teach him their values and shape his values in line with theirs. During the course of his lifetime, he makes his own many of the central values of these others; the others come to constitute for him, in Mead's term, an "inner forum" before which he privately debates alternatives. Moreover, in the course of daily interaction, whenever he conforms in his acts or expressions of opinion to the values of his associates, these others are likely to approve and reward; and when he fails to conform, they may disapprove, bringing negative sanctions to bear.

Reprinted by permission of the authors and the publisher from Chapter 24, "Mass Communication and the Social System," by J. W. Riley, Jr., and Matilda White Riley, in R. K. Merton, L. Broom, and L. S. Cottrell, Jr. (eds.), *Sociology Today*. Copyright 1959 by Basic Books, Inc., Publishers, New York.

1. Muzafer Sherif, *An Outline of Social Psychology*, Harper, 1948; Theodore M. Newcomb, *Social Psychology*, Dryden, 1950; Robert K. Merton and Alice S. Kitt, "Contributions to the Theory of Reference Group Behavior," in Robert K. Merton and Paul F. Lazarsfeld (eds.), *Continuities in Social Research: Studies in the Scope and Methods of "The American Soldier,"* New York: The Free Press, 1950, pp. 40–105.

2. Merton and Kitt, *op. cit.*, pp. 41–42.

Hence, he often conforms in order to win approval or (in Veblen's telling irony) to gain "an increment of good repute."

SELECTED APPLICATIONS

Such theories are beginning to be applied to problems of mass communications. The traditional approach, as we have pointed out, has long found it fruitful to classify individuals in terms of their location in different parts of the country or different types of communities or in terms of their socioeconomic status within the larger society. In addition to this, it is now increasingly recognized that, if the recipient's values are indeed shaped in part by the primary groups to which he belongs or aspires, then his perception of a message and his response to it may be better understood in terms of his relationship to these groups and to their values. As part of the Yale program of research, Kelley and Volkart set up an experiment in which an outside adult speaker at several Boy Scout meetings criticized the Scout emphasis on the values of camping and woodcraft and advocated various urban activities instead. Attitude tests conducted among the boys before and after this speech suggest that the boys who were most strongly motivated to retain their membership in the Boy Scouts were the most resistant to a communication which ran counter to the standards of the group.[3] In another study, Festinger, Riecken, and Schachter observed the members of a religious sect at a time when they expected that the earth would be destroyed and only "believers" would be saved. Even though the prophesied event failed to occur, those who received support from others of the faithful (unlike members who faced the crisis alone) tended to regard the failure merely as a slight miscalculation and not as disconfirmation of their essential belief.[4]

Some Rutgers research illustrates an application of reference-group theory to the receipt of quite another kind of message—one which, made up of fiction or fantasy, is not explicitly designed to persuade, although it may nevertheless exert considerable influence. An exploratory study of children's mass-media preferences suggests that the individual's integration into a significant group may affect both his choice of materials to read or listen to and his interpretation of media content. In this study, children who were not disposed to talk extensively with friends—and who doubtless felt the strain of exclusion from the peer group—were found to express relatively high interest in stories which foster fantasies of aggression or escape. They were more apt than high communicators to like radio and television programs characterized by action and violence or comic books about animals, such as Bugs Bunny, which they regarded as "a rascal," "lazy," "happy-go-lucky," and likely to "get away with it." Even when the excluded child and the integrated child are exposed to the same media

3. Harold H. Kelley and Edmund H. Volkart, "The Resistance to Change of Group-Anchored Attitudes," *American Sociological Review*, 17 (1952), 453–465.

4. Leon Festinger, Henry W. Riecken, and Stanley Schachter, *When Prophecy Fails*, University of Minnesota Press, 1956.

material, the content may serve a different function for the two. In describing such a radio program as "The Lone Ranger," the low communicators typically used terms like "scary," "creepy," "hard to get out of your mind when you go to sleep"; the high communicators tended to couple exposure to this program with "playing guns" with their friends subsequently.[5]

Another piece of related research develops the hypothesis that media preferences may be associated, not only with the individual's disposition to communicate with the members of the group (parents, in this instance), but also with his agreement with their values. A sample of adolescent boys in New Jersey high schools were asked which of a list of topics they "like best to read about or listen to" in the mass media. The first step in the analysis again compared high and low communicators. The proportion of boys who named "news" as a desired topic was as follows:

	DEGREE OF COMMUNICATION WITH PARENTS	
	Low	High
Per cent who like to read or listen to news	50	65
Total respondents = 100%	(755)	(357)

This finding is consistent with the notion that the boys' media behavior tends to conform to the expectations of their middle-class parents, even when these significant others are not immediately present to exert control.

Moreover, when the boys were subdivided according to the degree to which their own aspirations (classified in terms of their responses to a series of vignettes embodying selected values of concern to adolescents) conformed to the expectations of parents or peers, the results were as follows:[6]

	DEGREE OF COMMUNICATION WITH PARENTS			
	Low		High	
Predominant agreement with	Peers	Parents	Peers	Parents
Per cent who like to read or listen to news	47	55	58	70
Total respondents = 100%	(433)	(322)	(155)	(202)

Thus it appears that a boy's selection of media materials in line with probable parental expectations is related to his predominant agreement with parental values, as well as to his disposition to interact with his parents as persons.

CONSEQUENCES FOR PRIMARY-GROUP STRUCTURE

One outcome of individual tendencies to adopt a group as a source of

5. Matilda White Riley and John W. Riley, Jr., "A Sociological Approach to Communications Research," *Public Opinion Quarterly*, 15 (1951), 445–460. See also Matilda White Riley and Samuel H. Flowerman, "Group Relations as a Variable in Communications Research," *American Sociological Review*, 16 (1951), 174–180.

6. This measure of agreement will be reported in further detail in an article now in preparation by the Rutgers Research Group.

guidance and orientation is the development of a considerable degree of homogeneity in attitudes and values among the group members. (The implementation of these values is often differentiated, of course, according to some "division of labor" among the individual roles.) Newcomb, starting from sociological theory, on the one hand, and the work of Heider, on the other, has developed a theory to account for such homogeneity, explaining how group members, as they interact and talk among themselves, feel rewarded when their attitudes coincide, and thus tend to influence one another to arrive at similar attitudes.[7] And Festinger states a set of hypotheses, developed from a wide variety of empirical experiments in the Lewinian tradition, which indicate in some detail how discrepancies in group opinion lead to pressures toward uniformity—or, failing this, toward extrusion of dissident members from the group. He suggests, for example, that the amount of change in an individual's opinion resulting from the attempts of the other members to persuade him will

—increase as the pressure toward uniformity in the group increases;
—increase as the strength of the resultant force to remain in the group increases for the recipient;
—decrease in the degree to which the opinions and attitudes involved are anchored in other group memberships or serve important need-satisfying functions for the person.[8]

CONFLICTING REFERENCE GROUPS

This mention of "other group memberships" leads to the highly important point that the individual belongs and refers, not just to one group, but to many. The expectations of such groups may reinforce one another, so that he uses them jointly as a reference. If their values conflict, however, he is in a "role conflict," or under "cross-pressure." Studies of voting behavior have shown that cross-pressured individuals, who sometimes vacillate and even withdraw from making any decisions at all, are also apt to change their vote intentions during the course of the campaign.[9]

TOWARD A SOCIOLOGICAL VIEW

These few examples suggest how this use of reference-group theory is beginning to discover the social structure which underlies and tends to integrate the great diversity of individual perceptions of and responses to the mass-communicated message. It becomes apparent that the consumer faced with a

7. Theodore M. Newcomb, "An Approach to the Study of Communicative Acts," *Psychological Review*, 60 (1953), 393–404.

8. Leon Festinger, "Informal Social Communication," *Psychological Review*, 57 (1950), 271–282.

9. See, for example, Bernard R. Berelson, Paul F. Lazarsfeld, and William N. McPhee, *Voting: A Study of Opinion Formation in a Presidential Campaign*, University of Chicago Press, 1954, p. 148, *passim*.

baffling array of brands, the voter choosing between political courses with un-known consequences, and the entertainment-seeker with untold possibilities on his television dial make choices which are not based primarily on the inherent merits of the object chosen—no matter how persuasively these merits may have been advertised to them. It further appears that these choices are widely affected, not alone by the choice object itself or by advertising and propaganda about it, but also by other people. The individual often decides to purchase or to vote or to look at television programs *with* trusted other people, rather than *for* a par-ticular brand or candidate or program. Thus his reactions are not random relative to the reactions of these others. His perceptions and his responses form part of a pattern of interactions and mutual orientations among all the members of the group.

By focusing on the recipient's place within such a pattern, reference-group theory points the way toward an extension of the traditional approach in the direction of a larger sociological view. Figure 1 begins to suggest the nature of this emerging view. The arrow from C (the communicator) to R (the recipient) indicates the traditional focus. The sociological approach makes its first contri-bution to the model by taking into account the connections between R and the many primary groups with which he interacts, which shape his values, sanction his behavior, and, accordingly, impinge upon his role as a recipient in relation to C.

Figure I

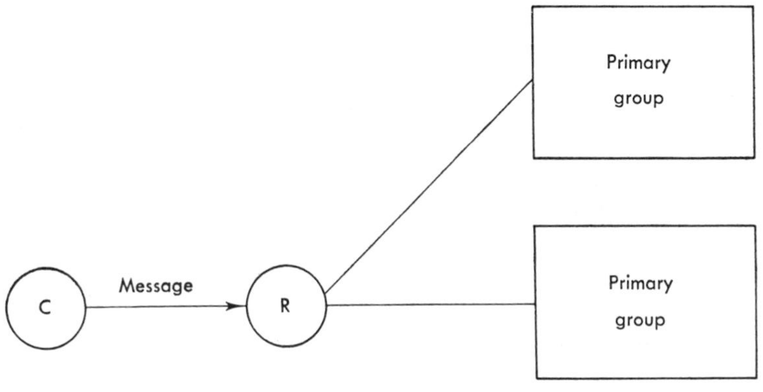

SOME FURTHER PROBLEMS

Yet, the use of this reference-group concept in research has scarcely begun. The beginnings are sufficient, however, to raise a number of fairly clear-cut questions for further study. Merton, in his detailed analysis of work on reference groups and social structure, has done a great deal to clarify the general problems at hand.[10] With specific reference to the field of mass communications, we can

10. *Social Theory and Social Structure*, Chap. 9. See also Merton and Kitt, *op. cit.*

identify some of the types of question that seem to require attention at this time, such as: How is the recipient's reaction to a mass communication related to his membership (or coveted membership) in a *single* primary group? How does this reaction vary, on the one hand, with his positive or negative feelings toward the members of this group and, on the other hand, with his agreement or disagreement with their values? How does it vary with his status in the group and the particular role he is expected to perform? How does his reference group seem to affect his reactions to different types of communication—those intended to inform, persuade, and commit him to action, and those intended merely to entertain and provide him with food for fantasy? Moreover (a far more complicated question), how does he respond when he must react to a message in multiple roles as a member of conflicting reference groups? How does his reaction vary with the relative significance of these groups to him, with the relative degree of his positive or negative feelings toward them, and so on?

Much of the methodological framework is already at hand for research on such questions. Yet, since the notion of reference group is a subtle one, often implying a mechanism which operates below the awareness of the recipient, new measurements and new experimental controls will have to be worked out.

Answers to such questions should go far toward locating the recipient in the social structure, but they will serve primarily to locate him in relation only to his diverse primary groups.[11] They cannot in themselves fully describe the structure within which mass-communicated messages are received, for, just as the audience is not composed of discrete individuals, neither is it composed of discrete primary groups. These smaller, solidary groupings must also be viewed in their interdependence with one another and as belonging to some still more inclusive system. By analogy, the economist does not (cannot) account for depressions merely by studying the personal inefficiency of given individuals or the reduced incentives for wage-earning in given families. Nor did Durkheim account for societal differences in the suicide rate as exclusively a function of personal motivation or of family integration. In both instances, the relevant theory also invokes wider structures and longer-term changes which include and also transcend the individual or the primary group as such.

The Recipient and the Larger Social Structure

Concomitant with such studies of the individual recipient and his primary groups, a quite different and less developed line of research has begun to explore the more inclusive structure of social organizations and institutions which surrounds the recipient. For, if the recipient's role is affected by the values and goals of his diverse primary groups, how do these groups themselves derive

11. The reference-group approach is not by definition limited to primary groups; it applies also to larger, more distant social groupings, as the next section indicates. As effective reference groups, however, the primary groups, with which the individual is most closely associated, seem to have the most compelling hold upon him.

such values and goals? How are the primary groups related to one another? How are they integrated within the more embracing social structure and process?

Because this larger structure transcends both the individual and his primary groups, many of the pertinent studies have their major focus, not on R (as in most reference-group research), but on the structure itself. That is, they do not start with the individual recipient and work outward through his primary groups, hoping thereby to piece together the complex network within which these groups are intertwined and interdependent. Instead, they start with the larger structure, examining first the relationships of the primary groups to the larger structure and to one another, and finally seeking the recipient's place within the whole. (Ultimately, these two complementary approaches should dovetail.)

STUDIES OF FORMAL ORGANIZATIONS

A number of studies in other fields illustrate the fruitfulness of this focus on the structure itself. The classic Western Electric investigations, for example, deal with the industrial plant as a social system made up of interrelated parts. This system is composed of a technical organization and a human organization, each of which affects the other. The human organization, in turn, is subdivided into formal and informal social organizations. Within such a system, research observations indicate the processes through which the informal groupings of friends and coworkers may function either to support or to detract from the formal organization's goal of efficient productivity.[12] In a somewhat similar fashion, studies of the combat behavior of American troops in World War II examine the formal organization which achieves its goals by ordering men to fight, and within this the informal organizations of friends which, because of the common threat, shared ideals of manliness, and the like, reinforce the goals of the formal system. As Williams and Smith conclude, "Affective ties binding the group together were important in keeping men in combat because, among other reasons, the group through its formal organization was inextricably committed to the fight: anything that tied the individual to the group therefore kept him in combat."[13]

A STUDY OF PROPAGANDA

The prototype of studies of this type in the mass-communication field is perhaps the evaluation by Shils and Janowitz of the impact of propaganda by the Western Allies on the fighting effectiveness of the German Army in World War II.[14] Contrary to earlier views of propaganda as a panacea, their findings

12. See, for example, F. J. Roethlisberger and William J. Dickson, *Management and the Worker*, Harvard University Press, 1940.

13. Robin M. Williams, Jr., and M. Brewster Smith, "General Characteristics of Ground Combat," in Samuel A. Stouffer et al. (eds.), *The American Soldier, Studies in Social Psychology in World War II*, Vol. II, Princeton University Press, 1949, p. 100.

14. Edward A. Shils and Morris Janowitz, "Cohesion and Disintegration in the Wehrmacht in World War II," *Public Opinion Quarterly*, 12 (1948), 280–315.

did not reveal that the invocation of adverse political, ideological, and cultural symbols produced any sweeping disaffection or collapse in military morale. Nor did they reveal that the extraordinary tenacity of the *Wehrmacht* was due primarily to the political convictions of the German soldier—to his direct attachment to the Nazi system itself as a reference group, as it were. They showed, rather, that his resistance to Allied propaganda and his sustained motivation to fight rested upon the persistence of the primary-group structure of the component units of the army. These analysts concluded that only when the primary groups themselves start to dissolve does propaganda (and then only certain kinds of propaganda) facilitate disintegration.

This study merits careful attention, since it seems to illustrate an important, but little exploited, approach to the study of the social structure within which mass communications are received. In order to account for the stability of the Army and its resistance to propaganda against its norms, Shils and Janowitz began with an investigation of the basic military organization and its relationship to the system of primary groups. They examined the process by which the goals of the larger bureaucratic structure were met by the functioning of smaller groups of friends, suggesting a number of linkages between the Army and these smaller groups. For example, membership in the informal social group was seen to coincide roughly with membership in the military squad. Both the larger structure and the primary group are exposed to the same external danger and share the same ideal of soldierly honor. The small but hard core of Nazis, as well as the paternally protective NCO's and junior officers, served as mediators, or linking persons, between the primary group and the Army. Moreover, the larger system was observed to exercise various controls over the smaller. Not only did the *Wehrmacht* exert authority through its officers, it also deliberately manipulated various factors affecting small-group solidarity. For example, it maintained in the same units men who had gone through a victory together and who shared the same recollections. It warned deserters of severe sanctions. It prevented family groups from weakening its own hold on the men by issuing strict injunctions against references to family deprivations in letters to the front. At the same time, it encouraged letters which would reduce the men's anxieties about their families and give the supplementary affection which the army unit could not provide.

Within this social structure and ongoing social process, Shils and Janowitz examined the ties between the individual soldier and his group of friends and finally analyzed the fundamental indifference of the troops to the millions of Allied leaflets and the continuous Allied broadcasts. Small wonder that the German soldier, bound to his fellows by spatial proximity, intimate association, and the military organization itself, paid little heed to Allied propaganda (even when he believed it) which exhorted him to desert his friends or abandon their goals! It is in this sense that R's response may be understood: first in terms of his primary groups, and secondly in terms of the larger organization in which these groups are implanted.

PRIMARY AND SECONDARY REFERENCE GROUPS

Studies with this structural focus ultimately lead back, of course, to the individual recipient of the message and his reference groups. (They deal with the same problem as reference-group studies, merely approaching it from another level.) In general, the relevant studies of the recipient tend to distinguish between his relationships to the larger, secondary system and to his primary groups. Thus the worker's productivity is viewed as the outcome of his relationships both to the formal structure of the plant and to his fellow workers. The individual soldier's willingness to fight is explainable both through his relationship to the army and through his affectional ties to his buddies and his unwillingness to let them down. (Of course, this is merely a re-emphasis of an old insight: as early as the first Christian century, Tacitus, in the *Germania*, explained the bravery of the barbarian hordes through the presence of their families with them on the battlefield.)

The findings of such studies seem to converge in emphasizing the great importance of the primary reference group within the larger reference system. A study of the reasons given by refugees for fleeing the Communist regime in North Korea reports, for example, that "the ideological repugnance to communism . . . runs a poor second to the more impelling consideration that the system has marked a member of the family for liquidation or imprisonment."[15] Accordingly, it seems that the recipient of a mass-communicated message is rarely reached directly in his role as an anonymous and isolated member of a bureaucracy or of a mass society. His receipt of this message is, rather, "mediated" through the close, informal groupings to which he also belongs. . . .

15. John W. Riley, Jr., Wilbur Schramm, and Frederick W. Williams, "Flight from Communism: A Report on Korean Refugees," *Public Opinion Quarterly*, 15 (1951), 277.

On the Possibility of Experimenting with the "Bandwagon" Effect

Donald T. Campbell

As strictly conceived, the notion of experimentation involves the controlled variation of one or more variables. For the social scientist such control is rarely possible. In the context of the present problem we have experimental control for the most part only over the application of our measuring instruments. Thus most of the experiments discussed in this symposium will for the most part be limited to problems that are intrinsically methodological, although, to be sure, the descriptive (as opposed to experimental) aspects of the studies will have much broader significance.

It is the purpose of the present paper to suggest that we can, in a limited way at least, exert experimental control over one more variable in the election prediction scene. This variable is *exposure to poll results,* and its control would enable us to study in a scientific manner the controversial "bandwagon" effect.

The general principle that *groups tend toward consensus of opinion,* and that *the communication of the opinions of members affects such consensus* is one of the most recurrent and consistent findings of social psychology. From the early work of Bridges[1] and Moore[2] on "majority prestige" or "suggestibility to group opinion," down to the present day, experimenters, using classroom situations for the most part, have repeatedly demonstrated that people will tend to modify their opinions in the direction of majority opinion when that opinion

Reprinted from *International Journal of Opinion and Attitude Research,* 5: 251–260, 1951, by permission of the author and the publisher.

1. J. W. Bridges, "An Experimental Study of Decision Types and Their Mental Correlates," *Psychological Monographs,* 1914, 17, No. 1.

2. H. T. Moore, "The Comparative Influence of Majority and Expert Opinion," *American Journal of Psychology,* 32: 16–20, 1921.

is made known. To the writer's knowledge, none have failed to find the effect to some degree at least. Usually the opinion of the face-to-face experimental group has been involved, but in two studies[3] national opinion poll results have been used. Sherif's classic experiments on judgments of the autokinetic phenomenon, although dealing with visual perception rather than social attitudes, demonstrate the principle. More recently research in group dynamics and conference behavior is rediscovering it. Festinger[4] has summarized a group of relevant experiments on "pressures toward uniformity in a group" done by the Research Center for Group Dynamics. The theoretical framework and many of the detailed principles are new, but the older general finding stands out: *the communication of opinion within the group modifies the opinions of individual members in the direction of consensus.* In the Conference Research[5] likewise, conference members are found to change opinions primarily in the direction of the central tendency of opinions expressed by other members. Studies by Newcomb[6] and by Sims and Patrick[7] give quantitative evidence of the effect of group atmosphere upon individual attitudes in non-experimental social situations. Lazarsfeld et al. in *The People's Choice*[8] have underscored that preeminently those who changed opinion in the course of a political campaign changed into conformity with their immediate social groups. Less quantitative observations of political scientists, sociologists and anthropologists contain innumerable references to this pervasive principle. Such considerations have led the social scientists to anticipate that the publication of poll results will influence the opinions of the reading public, including congressmen. The danger of the abuse of such an influence has led many to advocate the regulation and auditing of public opinion polling agencies.

The poll takers have not all accepted this expectation however. Gallup in particular has taken the lead in denying any such influence,[9] pointing to numerous instances in which the candidate originally ahead has steadily dropped in popularity as reported in the polls. Slight trends in the published Gallup reports

3. W. Allard, "A Test of Propaganda Values in Public Opinion Surveys," *Social Forces*, 20: 206–213, 1941; V. M. Sims and J. R. Patrick, "Attitude toward the Negro of Northern and Southern College Students," *Journal of Social Psychology*, 7: 192–204, 1936.

4. L. Festinger, "Informal Social Communication," *Psychological Review*, 57: 271–282, 1950.

5. H. Levin, "Personal Influences and Opinion Changes in Conferences," mimeographed interim report of The Conference Research Project, University of Michigan; D. G. Marquis, principal investigator; Harold Guetzkow, project coordinator.

6. T. M. Newcomb, *Personality and Social Change*, New York: The Dryden Press, 1943.

7. Sims and Patrick, *op. cit.*

8. P. F. Lazarsfeld, B. Berelson, and H. Gaudet, *The People's Choice*, New York: Duell, Sloan & Pearce, Inc., 1944.

9. G. Gallup and S. F. Rae, "Is There A Bandwagon Vote?" *Public Opinion Quarterly*, 4: 244–249, 1940; N. C. Meier and H. W. Saunders, *The Polls and Public Opinion*, New York: Henry Holt and Company, 1949.

for the 1943 election are against the "bandwagon" effect. Gallup regards the evidence of the 1948 elections to be crucial in this regard:

> One of the most persistent arguments raised from the very beginning against us and against all election polls was that we created a bandwagon movement. We have always argued against this theory. I honestly believe that if the political scientists of this country had set up an ideal situation to test the bandwagon theory, they could not possibly have selected a better test than the 1948 election.
>
> In 1948 not only did every single Washington correspondent and every political writer say that Mr. Dewey would win, but the polls all said Mr. Dewey would win. And the majority of the people of this country believed that Mr. Dewey would win.*
>
> So I say that probably not in the entire history of this country has there been a better test of the so-called bandwagon theory than that provided by the election of 1948. So at least we have destroyed that theory. Even the *New York Times* said in at least one of its articles that the bandwagon theory was thoroughly destroyed in this election.[10]

It is unlikely that the social scientist will accept this evidence as disproving the "bandwagon" hypothesis, and in the conflict between the data of the elections and the data of the laboratory, will be inclined to favor the laboratory, limited to classrooms though it may be. The social scientist may well argue that but for the bandwagon effect, Truman's majority would have been larger, or will point out that the forces toward conformity with the group are only part of the total complex of factors leading to the voter's final decision. He will join with Lazarsfeld[11] in emphasizing that the polls constitute a relatively unimportant source of impressions as to group opinion, and that it is probably the perceived opinion of primary, face-to-face groups rather than the expectation of national election victory *per se* that is the relevant variable. Or the social scientists, like some politicians, may argue that the bandwagon effect is obscured by the close-related effect of over-confidence and non-voting on the part of people who, had they voted, would have produced an election result closer to the results of the polls.

It is the purpose of this article to suggest that the question of a *bandwagon effect resulting from the publication of poll results* can only be settled by experi-

*It is not known what evidence Gallup had in mind on this point. However it might be noted that in an unpublished panel survey conducted in Columbus, Ohio (using student interviewers and showing a Republican bias of some 7 per cent) the proportion of respondents expecting a Republican victory increased from 68 per cent to 77 per cent between May and October, while the proportion intending to vote Republican showed, if anything, the reverse trend, ending with 57 per cent Republican. (Ohio State University, Interdepartmental Public Opinion Research Project, 1948.)

10. *Ibid.*, p. 287.

11. Lazarsfeld, Berelson, and Gaudet, *op. cit.*

mentation, and that such experimentation is, within limits, possible. Such experiments could also provide useful information on the character of identification with larger political units, and upon the kinds of topics which are most susceptible to the bandwagon effect, if any.

It is proposed that the following experimental dimensions be incorporated into the design: 1. The extensiveness of the reference group whose opinion is being reported: precinct, state, or nation. 2. The tangibility or immediacy of the poll topic: candidates, domestic issues, foreign issues. 3. The social strata: urban lower class, urban upper middle class, rural, and 4. The national region: Northeast, South, Midwest, Far West. As dependent variables, poll results and November votes are suggested: for the sampling unit, precincts. The hypotheses and considerations involved in these choices are presented more in detail below.

It is obvious that we will not have in 1952 complete control over the dissemination of poll results. However, it is anticipated that there will again be areas, both rural and urban, and in most sections of the nation, in which no major newspaper will be carrying syndicated public opinion services. In such areas, where the saturation of public opinion poll news is low, our experimental program should be able to modify significantly the degree of knowledge of poll results. This limitation will, however, make it futile to attempt a strictly representative national sample. For the purpose of this experiment such a sample is not necessary. As a rationale for dissemination it is proposed that dramatized and simplified presentations of poll results be mailed to panel respondents as a courtesy in return for their cooperation. This might be expected to result in more uniform readership than achieved from syndicated poll features in the newspapers, and would in this sense accentuate the effect under study. An alternative procedure, in which poll results would be made available through the newspapers of an experimental sample of small towns, and withheld from an equivalent sample, does not at the present time seem feasible. And while such a procedure would have great similarity to the situation about which Gallup is talking, it would have less possibility of contributing to social science in more general terms.

In the long run, the question of any bandwagon effect should be settled in terms of votes, not in terms of poll results. For this reason the smallest vote-reporting unit, the precinct, has been chosen as the essential sampling unit. Within the selected precincts, the head of every family would be interviewed, and/or provided with poll results. With this degree of saturation, any strong effects should make themselves manifest in voting behavior. Due to the processes of social diffusion, adjacent precincts should not be utilized in the experimentation, since different treatments will be involved. The use of precincts rather than individuals as the basic sampling unit results in some loss of statistical precision but seems unavoidable, in terms of other desiderata.

A series of three polls and poll-results feed-backs is proposed as the basic experimental program. This should give the bandwagon effect more opportunity to manifest itself than would a single exposure. A series of observations is also desirable for theoretical reasons. In the experimental studies reported, the effect of a single feed-back has been demonstrated. What would happen if the sequence of polling and feeding back group opinion had been continued several further steps? We should certainly expect that the subsequent feed-backs would result in less modification, and that opinion would eventually become stable at some level less than unanimity. Three observations should enable us to observe the beginnings of any such leveling process.

The first experimental dimension is *the extensiveness of the reference group whose opinion is being reported.* Identification with political units such as city, state, and nation, has certainly varied from period to period throughout history. Reading Wirth[12] suggests that true national identification came only with the media of mass communication, and that nations prior to that time tended to be congeries of cities, tribes, or principalities to which personal loyalty was given. Certainly within our own history, the importance of state citizenship has given way to national citizenship. But on the other hand, the demands of the primary group upon loyalty must in many cases be stronger than that of larger groupings, whose existence is known only second-hand. The relative degree of suggestibility to the opinion of various social groups should provide an index of relative strengths of identification. For the study of this problem, it is proposed that some precincts be fed back the precinct opinion, others state opinion, and others national opinion. As a tentative hypothesis, it is anticipated that for most regions, national opinion will be more influential than state opinion, reflecting the greater importance of the nation as an arbiter of the lives of the citizens. It is also anticipated that precinct opinion, coming close to primary group opinion, the opinion of neighbors with whom one has to live, will be most in-fluential of all. Speculations about interactions might include a greater influence for state (or regional) opinion in the South, greater influence of precinct in the high socio-economic groups, and the like. A particular statistical problem will come up in making these comparisons, and also those involving topic differences. The basic percentages involved for the state and precinct figures will differ from group to group, which will mean on the one hand that change is more easily noticed or induced in some groups (those near 50 per cent) and that the stimulus to change will be stronger in other groups (percentages showing strong majori-ties). The kind of index which will make degrees of change comparable from situation to situation will have to be explored. Possible indices would include expressing the change in terms of the standard error of the difference between the two percents, using an arc-sine transformation, or using Hovland's index[13] of the proportion change of total possible change. The laboratory experiments have avoided such problems by reporting fictitious results where it suited the experimenter's purpose, an alternative which is not judged to be available in

12. L. Wirth, "Consensus and Mass Communication," *American Sociological Review,* 13: 1–15, 1948.

13. C. I. Hovland, A. A. Lumsdaine, and F. D. Sheffield, *Experiments In Mass Com-munication,* Princeton: Princeton University Press, 1949.

the present experiment. Note that the precinct opinion will be derived from the immediate project itself, but that the project will be dependent upon the co-operation of other survey agencies for the figures on state and national opinion.

The second proposed dimension is the *tangibility of the poll topic*. In the bulk of the experimental studies, novel or remote opinion questions have been used, and when differences in suggestibility due to content have been noted, the effect has been less on the more familiar and close-to-home topics. Such an effect was noted by Steinbok[14] who found opinion shifts larger for foreign affairs topics than for domestic issues. Such an effect would be predicted from all of the work by psychologists upon the conditions under which non-objective factors influence perception and problem solving (e.g., Coffin[15]). In the present experiment we would anticipate that the bandwagon effect would be least for candidates for the presidency, greater for candidates for less conspicuous offices, and greatest for opinions on foreign policy (except in those instances where well publicized and clear-cut controversies might be involved). It should be noted that it is polls on issues which probably exert the greatest influence on congress, which, for national surveys, are never checked against any external criterion, and which are done with the smallest samples and probably the least care.

The third suggested classification criterion is *social strata*, in which we have suggested taking three points: upper-middle-class urban, lower-class urban, and rural. There are a number of considerations which would lead to anticipated differences here. The upper-middle class should show less of the effect than the lower because of greater education, implying a broader and more stable frame of reference.[16] In particular, it should show less effect for state and national opinion, due to a greater awareness of the discrepancy between its own class interests and national interests. This has no doubt been reinforced by 16 years' experience of voting for the losing candidate. Theories of rural individualism would lead to the anticipation that less bandwagon effect would be found in rural areas than among the urban masses. The doctrine of rural provincialism would lead to anticipating a greater effect for precinct opinion than for national opinion. On the other hand, the combination of physical isolation plus mass communication media lead many farm families to be in better contact with national news than with neighbors. The interaction of social strata with the reference group whose opinion is reported should help clarify our understanding of the psychological character of national citizenship. Indeed, if it should prove feasible to report upper-class and lower-class opinion to census tracts of various socio-economic levels, the character of class identification should be illuminated by any bandwagon effect observed.

14. J. Steinbok, "The Influence of Accurate and Faked National Poll Results upon the Opinions of Introductory Political Science Students," unpublished research, Department of Political Science, Ohio State University, 1948.

15. T. E. Coffin, "Some Conditions of Suggestion and Suggestibility," *Psychological Monographs*, 1941, 53, No. 4.

16. *Ibid.*

Interest in the fourth dimension, *natural region*, is similar to that of social strata. In particular it is suggested that those areas populated by persons whose parents and grandparents lived in the same area will show more influence for precinct and state opinion as opposed to national opinion than those areas populated by newcomers. On this basis we might expect the South and Midwest to differ from the Far West and the Northeast. A tradition of being at odds with national opinion should further accentuate the effect for the South. The basic data collection and experimental program can be summarized in the following table:

× 3 social strata × 4 regions

	1	2	3	4	5, 6
			Equated Precincts		
August 15	poll	poll	poll	poll	———
August 30 feed-back	———	national opinion	state opinion	precinct opinion	———
September 15	poll	poll	poll	poll	———
September 30 feed-back	———	national opinion	state opinion	precinct opinion	———
October 15	poll	poll	poll	poll	———
October 30 feed-back	———	national opinion	state opinion	precinct opinion	———
November 4	election returns	election returns	election returns	election returns	election returns
November 15	poll	poll	poll	poll	

The design calls for polling four times in 48 precincts, feeding back results of some kind in 36 precincts, and initial matching and collection of election returns for 72. If we estimate an average of 200 households per precinct, a grand total of 38,400 interviews is indicated, as well as 28,800 feed-back letters. If these grandiose figures are appalling, the following considerations might be borne in mind: (1) There is no *a priori* reason for believing that social science research is less expensive than physical science research. In fact, a good case might be made for the opposite contention. (2) The experiment would still have value even if trimmed to the extent of studying two matched precincts, one with feed-back and the other without. (3) The interviews would not need be as expensive as current polling practice might indicate. For the first three interviews, a simple one-page secret ballot is envisaged, which would be repeated in identical form each time. The use of concentrated interviewing within the precincts should also lower costs. For these interviews a field cost of 50¢ per interview might be reasonable. For the fourth interview, a long, free-response interview covering a variety of background and attitude variables would be desirable, for which a field cost of $2.00 might be necessary. Feed-back cost should run at least 10¢ per letter. Field costs at this rate would run $37,440. Allowing an approximately equal amount for analysis, a budget of $75,000 should be sufficient to undertake the project.

There still remain other variations on the experimental design which would improve our ability to generalize any effect observed. An important one of these deals with an hypothesized interaction between the polling process and susceptibility to influence. This interaction might be in either direction: as found by Hovland[17] the pretest may reduce the opportunity for influence to show, through a "consistency" effect, in that people tend to give the same answers to repetitions of a questionnaire. On the other hand there are indications that through increasing interest the pretest may sensitize respondents to possible influence. The primary reason why the polling and the feed-back processes are combined in the present experiment is that the respondent's cooperation in being polled provides a sensible context for the "courtesy" of sending him results on the poll he has participated in. Such plausible excuses for presenting persons with poll results, providing a reasonable rationale for the sender's action without casting doubt upon the authenticity or objectivity of the information are difficult to achieve. It is possible that state or national poll results might be provided in the process of requesting cooperation for a forthcoming poll, e.g., "your precinct has been selected as a sample precinct in a national survey of public opinion. Some time within the next two weeks an interviewer will call upon you and the head of every other household in your precinct. To give you some notion of the type of survey being conducted, we are enclosing a copy of the most recent national results." This would lead to the possibility of the following type design. In this, precincts of types 7 and 8 would be added to some of the designs, enabling the effect of polling to be studied independently of history, and as it might interact with opinion feed-back.

| | Equated Precincts | | | |
	1	2	7	8
August 15	poll	poll	———	———
August 30	———	national	national	———
feed-back		opinion	opinion	
September 15	poll	poll	poll	poll

Other expansions of the design will be thought of by the reader, and have been suggested in passing in the course of the present discussion. On the other hand, meaningful segments of the program could be undertaken in local communities by interested university groups. In many ways the whole design, or fragments of it, will fit in with other designs suggested in this symposium. For example, the effect of the polling process on the respondent's likelihood of voting would be shown. Likewise, in efforts to determine the root of the socio-economic bias in present polling procedures, precinct by precinct prediction should be particularly illuminating, since the precinct is the most homogeneous unit for which election returns are available. In the post-election interview, background data and personality variables would be introduced for the special study of the correlates of greater or less suggestibility to group opinion, and such

17. Hovland, Lumsdaine, and Sheffield, *op. cit.*

information could be related to such other important problems as turnout differentials, and the like.

In summary, it has been proposed that the dissemination of poll results is a variable under the partial control of the social scientist. This control makes possible experimentation both relevant to the "bandwagon effect" controversy, and of intrinsic value to social science.

Reference Groups and Interest Group Theories of Voting

Norman Kaplan

WE have previously examined the importance of relatively small, concretely defined, primary groups as points of reference for voting behavior. In apparent stark contrast stand a host of theories, speculations, and research findings which posit the importance of broadly defined population categories or "interest groups" as determinants of voting behavior. Now, some aspects of the relationship between these two types of "explanations" of voting will be explored.

When people talk of "the farmers" voting according to their interests, or when references are made to the "Negro vote," are we considering voting processes different from those we have stressed previously? Or is it the case that to the extent to which a Negro vote can be said to exist, the explanation lies, at least in part, in the intimate reference groups which have been examined? In what senses may we speak of "interest group" voting? How does such "interest group" voting come about? Why do some people appear to be voting "contrary" to their interests?

Although the Elmira Voting Study[1] was not specifically designed to answer these types of questions, an attempt to explore certain aspects of this general problem may be useful. In particular, we shall examine the extent to which "interest group" or "bloc" voting may be clarified by reference group theory. To the extent this approach seems fruitful, an attempt will be made to determine the relative effectiveness of the intimate groups already examined and population categories as points of reference for individual voting behavior. . . .

Reprinted from Chapter 9 of "Reference Group Theory and Voting Behavior," Columbia University doctoral dissertation, 1955, by permission of the author.

1. For the full report of this study, see Bernard R. Berelson, Paul F. Lazarsfeld, and William N. McPhee, *Voting*, University of Chicago Press, 1954.

The Multiple Meanings of Interest Group Voting

There are a number of ways in which interest group voting may be examined.[2] We could restrict ourselves to organized interest groups, or "pressure groups" as they are sometimes called. Examples of this type are the National Association of Manufacturers, the A.F.L. or the C.I.O., and the Farm Bureau Federation. Interest group voting could then be studied in at least two separate ways: (1) the extent to which the actual members of a given organized interest group vote a certain way in a given election—in other words, the extent to which the organization can "deliver" the votes of its members,[3] and (2) the extent to which the organization can "influence" nonmembers, either through the mass media or through the personal efforts of its members, or in some other fashion.

Although the organized interest group is undoubtedly an important type, it is not the one with which we can be primarily concerned here. Our concern is the type of "group interests" which are referred to by such phrases as "tenant farmers" or "ethnic group members." To be sure, there may be an organized interest group of tenant farmers, but not all persons who can be classified as tenant farmers are necessarily members of such an organization. Yet "tenant farmers" are sometimes spoken of as an interest group.

The use of the term "group" in this case is not justified from a sociological point of view as there is not necessarily any interaction between all persons classified as "tenant farmers." Strictly speaking, we are here dealing with a classificatory category or an aggregate of persons. We would therefore prefer to use the term "interest category," referring to an aggregate of persons assumed to have common interests but not highly organized, formally or informally.

So far, we have sought to emphasize a point which appears to be quite obvious once it is made explicit but which seems, nevertheless, to have been the object of some confusion. The point is this—we are not necessarily dealing with the same phenomenon when we talk of a farmer, who is also a member of the Farm Bureau Federation, and another farmer who belongs to no organized farm group voting for the same political party. We "understand" why the farmer who belongs to the Farm Bureau votes the way he does—he is presumably voting as a member of an interest group. What is less clear is the voting behavior of the farmer who does not belong to an organized interest group. He has been included in the same explanation, using the statistical correlation between voting in a given fashion and being classified according to one's occupation *as if* the total occupational category were the equivalent of an organized interest group. . . .

In the discussion which follows, "Catholics" will be used as an example

2. An extensive discussion of "interest groups" would obviously take us far afield. An attempt will be made, nevertheless, to touch upon some relevant aspects. For a more comprehensive discussion of the problem, the reader is referred to David Truman, *The Governmental Process*, New York: Alfred A. Knopf, 1951; V. O. Key, Jr., *Politics, Parties, and Pressure Groups*, 2nd ed., New York: Thomas Y. Crowell, 1947; and R. M. Williams, *American Society*, New York: Alfred A. Knopf, 1951, pp. 253ff.

3. This problem is discussed at length in Truman, *op. cit.*, especially pp. 315ff.

of a politically relevant membership category. Any similar category might just as well have been used as an example but Catholics were chosen because the empirical data, which will be introduced subsequently, concern Catholics specifically. The question we now turn to is this—how can the fact that Catholics tend to vote Democratic be "explained"?

One possibility which may be suggested is that Catholics, as members of the same category, tend to have similar life experiences which are relevant for voting behavior. They tend to be exposed to similar influences, read the same papers, hear the same programs, and as a result they tend to come to the same kind of voting decision, but *independently* of other Catholics. Another possibility is that Catholics are more likely to have other Catholics as close friends, that their families are likely to be Catholic, and so are most, if not all, of their intimate associates—and therefore they tend to see the world in the same way.

In both instances it is assumed that there is some factor present in the experience of being a Catholic which leads to a particular kind of voting decision as a general tendency among persons who may be classified as "Catholics." This factor may be a certain common perception of political interest, or it may be something else. The two "explanations" differ primarily with respect to the method by which a given Catholic arrives at his voting decision. In the first case, he arrives at a common interest independently of other Catholics. In the second case, it is the interaction of Catholics with each other which leads to a common perception of a "group" interest.

To test the first possibility, it would be necessary to show that: (1) Catholics do not interact with each other any more than they do with non-Catholics; (2) they do not discuss Catholic interests; and (3) each Catholic arrives at the same definition of interests and the way in which these may be served in an election. Unfortunately, the data are not available in the Elmira study. The second possibility can be tested in a limited fashion, but further discussion is postponed until certain additional alternatives can be considered.

A third possibility which may help to describe the process whereby Catholics tend to vote Democratic relies on the use of the reference group concept. Within this general framework, at least three separate possibilities may be distinguished: (1) Catholics vote with reference to the norm of the general category of Catholics, (2) the reference group norm is that of intimate associates who are likely to be other Catholics, and (3) both the category and the group of associates may be used as points of reference. Each of these possibilities will now be discussed in greater detail.

It may be argued that to the extent to which Catholics vote alike, each individual Catholic is using "Catholics" as a political reference category. He thinks of himself as a Catholic and asks himself how other Catholics (not his friends or others he knows, but Catholics in general) will vote. He satisfies himself, either directly or indirectly, that Catholics vote Democratic. Consequently, he votes Democratic.

At least two conditions seem implicit in this formulation. Firstly, the individual must identify himself with Catholics as he considers voting behavior. Put another way, Catholics must be a "salient" point of reference for his voting behavior.[4] Secondly, he must be aware of a distinctly Catholic voting norm. Whether such a norm actually exists, or how it came into being, are still other questions which cannot be considered here. It is only important that he perceive the existence of a norm.

Although it may appear strange to think of the vague membership category "Catholics" as a point of reference it does not seem very different from a number of others which were encountered in our review of previous reference group research in Chapter II. Among the examples which were encountered, we might cite "the army," "the stratum of officers," and "married civilians."

On the basis of our review of previous research as well as our own findings throughout this work, it is to be doubted that very many persons employ the vague population category as a *direct* point of reference.[5] There is probably a greater likelihood that *specific* Catholics act as a reference group. In some cases these may be the members of the neighborhood church or some specific Catholic lay organization. But of even greater interest to us is the possibility that an intimate group of associates or family members are the specific reference groups for his voting behavior. In this instance, an individual Catholic would be voting with reference to the norms of an intimate subgroup. The norm of Catholics in general would not enter at all. The statistical tendency of a "Catholic vote" emerges because Catholics tend to associate with other Catholics and use each other as points of reference for voting behavior.

The essential weakness of this argument is that it is circular. Catholics vote like other Catholics who vote Democratic.

The third possibility, mentioned above, is that *both* the intimate subgroup and the general category "Catholics" are used as points of reference for the voting behavior of many Catholics. Intimate subgroups are adopted as reference groups and these in turn determine the extent to which (as well as the way in which) the larger category may also be taken as a point of reference. The intimate reference group tends to adopt a Democratic norm because such a norm is perceived to exist generally for "Catholics."[6]

The perception of the norm which exists in the larger category will, however, be a function of the definition provided by the intimate associates. Thus, some intimate groups may provide a definition of the situation which leads to the perception of a Republican norm (or possibily the absence of a Democratic norm) for the category. In still other cases, it is conceivable that the definition

4. Cf. W. W. Charters, Jr., and Theodore M. Newcomb, "Some Attitudinal Effects of Experimentally Increased Salience of a Membership Group," in G. E. Swanson, Theodore M. Newcomb, and E. L. Hartley (eds.), *Readings in Social Psychology*, rev. ed., New York, Henry Holt and Company, 1952.

5. Cf. H. H. Hyman, *The Psychology of Status*, p. 24 on the relative infrequency with which general population categories are cited as points of reference.

6. Why such a norm exists (or persists) is still another matter which is beyond the scope of our present inquiry.

which is provided holds that there is no norm—Catholics do not and should not vote as a "bloc." But in the majority of cases, it is presumed that a Catholic in intimate association with other Catholics who share a Democratic voting norm, will perceive an identical norm for the category as a whole. . . .

Of the possibilities suggested above, the last seems to be the most promising, both theoretically and empirically. Many aspects cannot be tested with the available data and these must remain in the realm of speculation. But it would appear to be possible to test the extent to which both intimate associates and the category are taken as reference groups for voting behavior. Insofar as these data tend to confirm this hypothesis, the others will tend to become less tenable.

The general procedure for the empirical test may be described as follows. For a given population category it will be established whether a reasonable assumption can be made that a voting norm exists. The extent to which there is agreement with that norm on the part of the people in that category will then be examined. If a significant relationship is found for the members of that category, it will be assumed that the category as such could be a reference group for voting behavior. An intimate subgroup, which is likely to have some relationship to the category as a whole, will then be selected as a test case. For example, it may be assumed that a Catholic will have Catholic friends, but not necessarily Catholic co-workers—so that friends would be selected as the testing subgroup for the category of Catholic.

Once the intimate subgroup has been selected, we will examine the extent to which people in a given category are likely to have the same kind of intimate associates (politically speaking). If our expectations are fulfilled, people within a given category are likely to show a tendency to report intimates with the same kind of norm which is posited for the category as a whole.

It will now be possible to compare, systematically, the individuals in the *same* category according to the norms of their associates. If the hypothesis is tenable, we should expect to find that people will be more likely to vote with reference to the category and intimate associates when the norms are mutually sustaining. But in any situation other than perfect harmony, the norm of the intimate group should be the dominant factor. Among people in the *same category* with close associates who have different norms, the difference in the resulting behavior will be greater than the differences exhibited among people who share the same intimate group norm but are in *different categories*.

In summary, the general problem to which we devote ourselves in the rest of this chapter is the relationship between intimate subgroups of associates and population categories taken as reference groups.[7] The problem arises in the

---

7. The importance of this problem was first recognized by Merton and Kitt when they discussed the need for further research on " . . . the comparative significance of general status categories and intimate subgroups of which one is a member. . . . " Robert K. Merton and Alice S. Kitt, "Contributions to the Theory of Reference Group Behavior," in Robert K. Merton and Paul F. Lazarsfeld (eds.), *Continuities in Social Research: Studies in the Scope and Method of "The American Soldier,"* New York: The Free Press, 1950, p. 65.

study of voting behavior in trying to account for a variety of statistical correlations between membership categories and voting. The tendency to ascribe political interests to the members of a given category seems incomplete as an explanation. It has been suggested that to the extent to which interests exist among the members of a category these become given patterns of voting through reference group processes. Specific hypotheses have been advanced which may now be tested in a preliminary fashion with the Voting Study data dealing with Catholics.

An Empirical Test of the Comparative Significance of Intimate Subgroups and Population Categories as Reference "Groups" for Voting Behavior: "The Catholic Vote"

The religious vote, and more particularly the "Catholic vote," has frequently been cited as an example of "special interest" voting in the United States. For whatever reasons may have existed in the past which originally induced and sharpened this tendency, and whether or not these factors still remain the same today, the fact remains that Catholics have been strongly predisposed to vote Democratic. This is less true for Protestants as a whole, though there has been a tendency for them to be "more" Republican when compared with a Catholic counterpart. While other factors seem to modify general Protestant tendencies to vote Republican the same is not true for Catholics.[8]

It is apparently not the case that direct appeals are made to Catholics, by either the Church or the Democratic Party, to vote for the Democrats *because* they are Catholics. The official policy of both the Catholic and Protestant Churches seems to be one of neutrality in political elections, at least within the United States and particularly in national elections. And while the political parties make no overt appeals on a religious basis, and hasten to deplore and deny the aberrations which do occur from time to time, they act on a more covert level. As has already been noted, the religious affiliation of the candidates, and of prominent persons in the party hierarchy are usually open (and well publicized) secrets.

It might therefore be expected that a Catholic be predisposed to vote for a fellow Catholic—whatever the specific processes involved in such a decision. The assumption is that each individual Catholic adopts the general category of "Catholics" as a point of reference simply because he is a Catholic, and thinks that Catholics should favor other Catholics.[9]

8. See the intensive analysis by David Gold, "Influence of Religious Affiliation on Voting Behavior" (Unpublished Ph.D. dissertation, University of Chicago, 1952).

9. This is essentially the implicit assumption underlying an experiment reported by Leon Festinger, "The Role of Group Belongingness in a Voting Situation," *Human Relations*, I (1947), 154–180 in which the main experimental variable was the knowledge made available of the religious affiliation of the candidates.

But how does a Catholic choose between two Protestant candidates? Does he choose the Democratic candidate by referring directly to the norm of the general category of Catholics? Our main hypothesis would hold that he does this only to the extent that this is the norm which is provided by his intimate associates as well.

Our data show clearly the existence of a voting norm for Catholics. All respondents were asked how they thought Catholics would be voting.[10] Of the Catholics who perceived a partisan norm, 73 per cent (100) thought that Catholics would be voting Democratic. About the same proportion of Protestants thought the same. Moreover, Catholics in Elmira actually voted Democratic, as may be seen in Table 1.

Table 1—Religious Affiliation and Voting

	Catholics	Protestants
Voted Republican	36%	80%
	100% = (142)	(380)

There can be little doubt then that Catholics tend to see other Catholics voting Democratic and that they themselves also tend to vote Democratic.

The intimate subgroup which seems to be most appropriate for testing our hypothesis is the one comprised of the three closest friends. If the hypothesis is correct, then we should expect that Catholics would be more likely to have Democratic friends, while Protestants would probably have a greater proportion of close friends with a Republican preference. This is, in fact, the case as can be seen in Table 2.

Table 2—Religious Affiliation and the Political Norm among Friends

Friends:	Catholics	Protestants
RRR	34%	68%
RRD	14	16
DDR	12	4
DDD	40	12
	100% = (147)	(367)

Catholics are more than three times as likely to have close friends with a unanimous Democratic norm as compared with Protestants. They are only half as likely as Protestants to have friends with a unanimous Republican norm. It is to be noted that fully 60 per cent of the Catholics have at least *one* Republican friend, while only 32 per cent of the Protestants have at least one Democratic friend. This is still another instance of the preponderance of Republicans in Elmira noted in earlier chapters.

10. Wave I (June) Question 24: "Do you think most . . . Catholics . . . around here would be more likely to vote for the Republican, Democratic, or Wallace Third party?"

It is now possible to compare systematically the voting behavior of Catholics and Protestants according to the varying norms which exist among close associates. This is done in Table 3, which shows the proportion who voted Republican in each case.

Table 3—Religious Affiliation, the Political Norms among Close Friends, and Final Voting Behavior

		Catholics	Protestants
Voted Republican:			
Friends:	RRR	61% (39)	93% (205)
	RRD	42% (12)	84% (45)
	DDR	36% (14)	* (8)
	DDD	10% (41)	21% (34)

* Too few cases

Within each religious category, people's voting is influenced by the political norm among friends. And for each type of friendship group norm, there is a significant difference between Catholics and Protestants, with the single exception of those whose friends were unanimously Democratic. But there seems to be a stronger likelihood that the intimate subgroup of friends will be taken as the point of reference rather than the category.

This conclusion may be drawn from the fact that Catholics whose friends provide a unanimous Republican norm are more likely to vote Republican than other Catholics. The same is, of course, true for Protestants with such friends, as compared to other Protestants. Among Catholics, the differing political norms provided by close friends, result in an absolute difference of more than fifty percentage points—from 61 per cent voting Republican when friends are unanimously Republican to 10 per cent voting Republican when friends are unanimously Democratic. Among Protestants, the differences in the norms of friends produce an even greater spread—more than seventy percentage points—in the tendency to vote Republican from those with unanimous Republican friends to those with unanimous Democratic friends.

The differences between Catholics and Protestants who have friends with the *same* political norm are not nearly as great. One might say, in terms of the spread within each category, that the Catholics are more homogeneous than the Protestants as a category, and that, therefore, to the extent that the category is used as a point of reference, it is more likely to occur in the case of the Catholics. But on the whole, the evidence in favor of the hypothesis that the category is used as a direct reference point—even by Catholics—must be considered less conclusive.

Some indication that the category *may* be taken as a point of reference, especially for Catholics, is seen in the comparison of Catholics and Protestants who have the same kind of friends. Where friends are unanimously Republican or predominantly Republican (RRD), Catholics are less likely to vote Republican than Protestants. In the other remaining comparison which is possible, where friends are unanimously Democratic, there is no significant difference between the voting behavior exhibited by Catholics and Protestants. This may mean that the Protestants are not as likely to use the category of Protestants directly or even indirectly, as a point of reference for voting behavior. Whether this can be construed as positive evidence that some Catholics are using their religious category as a direct point of reference is still not certain.

But when we come to a comparison of the two religious categories when friends do not provide a unanimous norm there seems to be some tendency for people to adopt the category as a direct point of reference. When friends are predominantly Republican (RRD), the Protestant is twice as likely as the Catholic to be voting Republican. (A comparison when friends are predominantly Democratic is unfortunately not possible because of the small number of cases involved.) We find almost the same situation where friends provide no norm at all—41 per cent (32) of the Catholics compared with 74 per cent (61) of the Protestants voted Republican in this situation.

Clearly, there is a tendency to think of a "Catholic" norm—especially where close friends provide an ambiguous political norm or fail to provide a norm altogether. When an unambiguous norm is provided by close friends, it is equally clear that the intimate group exerts the greater influence. But the question of whether the category comes into play as a direct point of reference is still quite open. We are restricted to an examination of only one intimate group at a time because of the small number of cases involved. It is quite possible that Catholics with predominantly Republican (RRD) friends could turn to their families as clear-cut Democratic reference groups.[11] It is also possible that the lone Democratic friend is serving as the crucial reference individual for voting behavior. In other words, some intimate subgroup or individual, crucially related to the category, may still be serving as an intermediate link to the category.

There is still one other empirical inquiry which can be conducted in the effort to specify the extent to which there is a direct reference to the category for voting behavior. People were asked whether they considered their "religious group," among others, very important. If the category is a direct reference point, then we should expect that those Catholics who do consider their religious group important, should be more likely to vote with reference to the category norm, than those Catholics who do not—whatever the character of the political norm provided by friends. It is assumed that "religious group" could refer to the category in general, though there is no positive evidence on this point. Nevertheless, in Table 4 the voting behavior of Catholics is examined in terms of the political norm provided by friends and whether or not the "religious group" was considered important.

11. There is some tendency for Catholics, more than Protestants, to discuss politics with other family members. See *Voting, op. cit.*, p. 67.

Table 4—The Importance of the Religious Group and the Political Norm among Close Friends of Catholics as Related to Voting Behavior

Catholics Who Voted Republican	RRR	Friends: RRD/DDR*	DDD
Religious Group: Important	56% (18)	25% (12)	5% (20)
Not Important	64% (22)	50% (14)	18% (22)

* These are combined because of the small number of cases and the lack of difference between them indicated previously.

Whether or not the religious group is considered important does not result in significantly different voting behavior among Catholics. The only significant differences occur between those Catholics with unanimous Republican and those with unanimous Democratic friends, for those who considered their religious group important as well as for those who did not. There is, of course, a slight directional tendency for the Catholics who consider their religious group unimportant to vote Republican. But in the face of the really sharp differences which the different unanimous norms of close friends produce, these data must be considered as additional evidence of the relative importance of the primary group of close friends as the crucial reference group.

It may tentatively be concluded that the category of Catholics as such is not taken as a direct reference category by Catholics. Without the knowledge of the norm which exists among intimate subgroups, it is not possible to know precisely how a given Catholic will vote.[12] In the case where there seems to be direct and independent reference to the category it is not possible to determine from our data whether or not some intimate subgroup, other than friends, is mediating between the individual and the category. The mere fact that there are consistent differences in vote between Catholics and Protestants cannot be taken as an index that Catholics refer their voting behavior to the general category alone.[13]

The Catholics who are most likely to vote for the Democrats (or in accordance with the perceived norm for the category as a whole) are those who have an intimate subgroup of friends providing a unanimous Democratic norm. Without the sustaining norm of the intimate reference group, a Catholic is less likely to be voting Democratic.

Summary and Conclusions

At the outset, the fact was noted that gross correlations may be found between membership in certain categories (or political interest "groups") and a

12. It should be noted, of course, that for reasons beyond the scope of our present inquiry, the norm which such intimate subgroups tend to adopt is a Democratic one.

13. Exactly the opposite conclusion was reached by David Gold, *op. cit.*, merely on the basis of the consistent differences.

particular way of voting and a number of possible interpretations were suggested to account for these correlations. The first was that the category itself acted as the point of reference for an individual's voting behavior. We have found, however, that the people who are most likely to vote in conformity to the norm of a category are those who also have an intimate primary group which provides a norm identical with the presumed norm of the population category. The possibility that some people may, in certain circumstances, use the population category as a point of reference cannot be discounted entirely on the basis of the available data. Some of these circumstances will be discussed below, but in any event this "explanation" does not seem to account for most of the voting behavior exhibited.

The second possible interpretation, based primarily on the data in the previous chapters, is that only the intimate subgroup norm was crucial, and that the category as such did not enter into the individual decision process at all. Catholics voted like their friends; they did not use Catholics as a reference category. Enough instances were presented in this chapter to make us question this as a complete "explanation."

Finally, it was suggested that both the category and the intimate subgroup may act as points of reference. As between the two, the intimate subgroup seemed to be the more important reference group for the greater proportion of people. The data have shown that people are most likely to vote with reference to both the category and the intimate subgroup, when the norms of both are mutually sustaining. The voting behavior exhibited shows greater differences within the category, and smaller differences between categories when the norms of the intimate subgroup are taken into account. These findings and conclusions are necessarily tentative and further research is essential before they can be accepted uncritically or extended beyond the substantive confines of the present study.

Nevertheless, it seems useful to try to draw out certain implications from these findings. In the first place, there appears to be a *two-step process* involved in the adoption of these different types of groups as reference groups. The first step is the *direct* adoption of a reference group and its norms. This direct step usually will involve an intimate subgroup or primary group. Crucial in this phase is interaction and interpersonal communication and conversation. From here, it is possible to take the second step in reference group behavior—the *indirect* adoption of the norms of a reference category or even a large-scale secondary organization. This is done through the intervening "mediation" of the direct reference group. It is through the medium of this intimate group that the relevant category is selected and its norm defined.

But let us suppose that the individual is confronted with ambiguous norms among his close associates, or even with the lack of any norm among his close associates (for a given item of behavior). Then, presumably, he may narrow his associational reference to a single individual, preferably one with whom he is very close. If this is not possible then it will be a less intimate associate, but there will still be some interpersonal interaction. And this will lead in turn to the mutual adoption of a reference category. Such categories as are adopted in these circumstances need not be membership categories. In fact, the lack of satisfactory reference groups at the intimate subgroup level may be one of the major conditions which leads to the adoption of nonmembership reference categories. Under the conditions outlined above, it is possible that in extreme cases, and at a particular point in time, a category may be adopted directly as a point of reference. But as was pointed out previously, even this may be traced back to more direct reference groups by going back in time to "former" intimate associates.

Without additional research these can only be considered as preliminary speculations. As far as our data are concerned, we have seen that "interest group" voting, as such, appeared to be a gross oversimplification of a far more complicated process. Without the intimate subgroup as a reference, there was relatively little "interest group" voting; with it, "interest group" voting was maximized. Thus, even in the realm of reference category behavior, the small intimate primary group plays a crucial role.

Political Standards in Secondary Groups

Philip Converse and Angus Campbell

THE distinctive voting patterns of certain large-scale groupings in the population suggest the presence of group standards and group influence. It has generally been recognized, for example, that members of business and labor organizations, Catholics, Jews, Negroes, and other ethnic groupings tend to show a characteristic bias toward one party or another at the polls. Since the members of each of these groupings share many of the same life experiences, there has been some question as to whether this distinctiveness of political behavior reflects only parallel responses to parallel experience, or is mediated by the group in a more active sense.[1]

Current evidence concerning the more prominent of these secondary groups indicates that it is reasonable to treat them in terms of active group standards. This evidence is of two types. First, it may be shown that members of these groups remain distinctive in their partisanship when paired with nonmembers of similar background. For example, a union member is more likely to vote Democratic in the current era than the nonmember of equivalent occupation, education, income, religion, urban-rural residence, region, ethnic background, race, age, and the like. Except as some politically potent aspect of experience may escape our attention, we would conclude that life situation aside, the fact of group membership itself leads to differences in behavior.

Where the first line of evidence pits member against nonmember, the

Reprinted from Dorwin Cartwright and Alvin Zander (eds.), *Group Dynamics*, 2d ed., pp. 300–318, by permission of the authors and the publishers, Harper & Row, Publishers, Inc. Copyright 1953, 1960 by Row, Peterson & Company.

1. A. Campbell and H. C. Cooper, *Group Differences in Attitudes and Vote*, Ann Arbor, Mich.: Survey Research Center, 1956.

second depends on intragroup differences. In the 1948 study of voting conducted by Berelson, Lazarsfeld, et al., in Elmira, New York, members of ethnic and religious groups of distinctive political coloration were asked questions designed to reveal the importance or valence which the group held for the individual. Suchman and Menzel[2] have shown that members who deemed the group important were more likely to vote "with the group" than were more indifferent members.

In our national study of the 1956 presidential election we asked Catholics, Jews, Negroes, and members of labor unions to respond to the following questions in terms of their group:[3]

> Would you say you feel pretty close to (e.g., Negroes) in general or that you don't feel much closer to them than you do to other kinds of people?
> How much interest would you say you have in how (e.g., Negroes) as a whole are getting along in this country? Do you have a good deal of interest in it, some interest, or not much interest at all?

Responses to these items were combined to form a scale indicating the degree to which the member identified with the group in question. Each group had a putative Democratic voting norm. As hypothesized, highly identified members were more likely to vote Democratic than the less strongly identified.

In both the 1948 and 1956 instances, the only apparent difference between group members was the nature of the relationship with the group. Yet in each case, this difference turned out to be associated with more or less distinctive partisan choice. The conclusion once again seems to be that the partisanship which characterizes these groups as aggregates is mediated in some manner by the group *qua* group.

There are further provocative aspects to the data. It is clear, for example, that some groupings are much more solidary in their support of a particular party than are other groupings likewise thought to have partisan voting norms. If comparable nonmembers are dividing their vote 50–50 between the two major parties, then the "Democratic" group which casts 85 per cent of its votes for the Democratic party is more distinctive than the "Democratic" group which favors that party by only a 55–45 margin. We do in fact find wide differences of this sort in the degree to which groups vote distinctively.

It is apparent, too, that the partisan division of the vote among the highly identified members of certain groups departs more strongly from the vote division of the less identified members than is the case within other groups.

2. E. A. Suchman and H. Menzel, "The Interplay of Demographic and Psychological Variables in the Analysis of Voting Surveys," in P. Lazarsfeld and M. Rosenberg (eds.), *The Language of Social Research*, New York: The Free Press, 1955.

3. This study, supported by a grant from the Rockefeller Foundation, was carried out at the Survey Research Center, University of Michigan. It involved a cross-section sample of 1,772 respondents, chosen by strict probability methods from all adult citizens living in private households in the United States.

In other words, the strength of relationship between identification and vote varies substantially from group to group. Among Catholics, for example, it is relatively low; among union members it is notably higher.

Furthermore, these "within-group" and "between-group" contrasts are correlated. Where a group is more distinctive by comparison with nongroup voters, it is likely to be the case as well that its members are more differentiated one from another in their voting choice as a function of group identification. We may think of a continuum representing percentage Democratic of the two-party vote, on which we locate three or more points representing group members of varying strength of identification, along with some comparable set of non-members. If we compare continua of this sort constructed for several groups, the distances between the several points for one group will be small, while the analogous distances for another group will quite generally be larger. We may readily imagine forces emanating from the group which act to disperse these points along each continuum; and differences in distances from group to group may be taken to reflect differences in the strength of group forces operative on the membership.

It is our purpose in this paper to expand our view of the influence process to encompass these systematic differences. We may thereby cast further light on the familiar waxing and waning of partisan homogeneity within groups of this sort over time, while illuminating, at an individual level, the circumstances of deviation from group standards in this behavioral setting.

A Model for the Political Influence Situation

We are interested in the effects of a membership group upon the response of an individual toward the world of politics. Thus three elements—individual, group, and political world—are involved in the situation. Between these elements lie a triangle of relationships. Two of these involve the actor directly; we may consider the third leg, the relationship between the group and the world of politics, as having the properties which the actor perceives to exist. Logically, a proper understanding of the character of these relationships from member to member should permit us to account for the final partisan behavior of each. Let us therefore consider some of the specific properties of these relationships which we might measure and combine to form a system of explanatory variables.

THE INDIVIDUAL AND THE POLITICAL WORLD

We must recognize at the outset that group considerations aside, the individual is engaged in a set of ongoing reactions to the political process. Hence if we wished to predict the full response made by the membership of any grouping at the polls, our characterization of the relationship between the individual and politics would become elaborate indeed, involving many terms which have nothing to do with the specific group membership. The member is exposed to much political information not mediated by the group. If the party favored by the group is enveloped in scandal, this fact will make inroads on the valence it holds for the member. Similarly, a very attractive candidate proffered by the opposition cannot be written off as lightly as an unattractive one. In short, the events of politics affect the member's reaction directly in some degree, independent of group standards. The group member does not make decisions in a psychological field limited to group forces any more than a nonmember makes decisions in a vacuum.

Our purpose here is not, therefore, to account for the total response of the individual member to current politics, but rather to account for the differences introduced in this response because the group impinges on his political evaluations. It is for this reason that we have referred above not simply to group voting, but to the "distinctiveness" of group voting. The difference is readily illustrated. Several national surveys conducted in 1956 showed that the Democratic vote for President among Catholics had dipped below a 50–50 split for the first time since relevant data had been collected. In one sense, Catholic voters had suddenly "turned" Republican. It was true that the distinctiveness of the Catholic vote had been waning; but it remained Democratic relative to the vote among non-Catholics even in 1956, and this residual distinctiveness merely formed another point on a declining trend which we have had the opportunity to watch since 1948. In absolute terms the Catholic vote became sharply more Republican in 1952 and 1956, as did the vote among virtually all prominent groupings of this sort. But the degree of partisan bias *attributable to the group* did not shift violently.

It is to recognize the individual's independent access to politics as well that we wish to measure distinctiveness as a deviation from a base-line provided by a "control group" of nonmembers whose life situations are equivalent. Catholics have tended to vote Democratic in times past, but so have other individuals of lower status. Is the Democratic bias in the Catholic vote an effect of active group mediation, or would Catholics have responded to lower status with the same increase in Democratic voting independent of their religious ties? This question may best be answered by gauging their distinctiveness relative to other voters *of equivalent status*. And, since status is not the sole aspect of life situation which affects partisan response, the control groups which we have constructed to assess group distinctiveness of vote take into account a variety of other dimensions as well.[4]

4. Control groups were formed for each secondary grouping in the following fashion. Two variables whose interaction terms were known to be potent vis-a-vis partisan behavior were controlled in a "precision" matching: region (South *vs.* non-South) and urban-rural residence (3 categories). For union members, occupation status (3 categories) was controlled in the precision sense as well. Within groups so defined looser "distribution" controls were used. Thus the control groups have the same distribution as the member groups on region of navitity (2 categories), urban-rural background (3), education (3), occupation (3), income (3), generations in the United States (2), and age (3). Finally, within each group the effect of other prominent secondary membership groups was equated: the Catholic control group had the same proportion of union members and Negroes as appeared among Catholics, etc. Dis-

The use of these control groups does not mean of course that life situations have no role in the group influence process. Quite to the contrary, the distinctive needs which arise because group members find themselves relegated to peculiar positions in the social structure may contribute substantially to the motive power of the group *qua* group. What is important for our purposes, however, is the fact that shared membership appears to lend a focus and direction to behavior which is less visible for nonmembers who exist under similar conditions and can be presumed to have similar needs. This focus and direction is an integral part of what we mean by "group influence."

If we estimate the distinctiveness of our several groups in this fashion, we find the largest deviation in a Democratic direction from a base-line set by a control group to occur in the case of Jewish respondents (a difference of proportions of 45 per cent). Union members (20 per cent), non-Southern Negroes (12 per cent) and Catholics (3 per cent) follow in descending order.[5] While these are crude estimates at best, the range of variation presented is substantial. It is our assumption that this variation reflects differences in the strength of group forces in the psychological field as members evaluate the political world in reaching a vote decision. The strength of these forces is some function of (a) the relationship of the individual to the group, and (b) the relationship of the group to the world of politics.

THE INDIVIDUAL AND THE GROUP

A variety of research undertakings have lent weight to the proposition that individuals attracted to a group are more likely to conform to its standards. The findings cited above from the 1948 and 1956 voting studies may be taken as a special case of such a phenomenon. The items which we used to measure strength of member identification with the group clearly provide an assessment of the attractiveness or valence of the group for the member. While the term "identification" seems best suited for the groupings of interest here, any method of summarizing the valence which marks the individual-group relationship appears to help us in discriminating between group members who will follow or deviate from group standards.

By the same token, if "cohesiveness" refers to a summation of the attraction exerted by the group across its membership, then the relative cohesiveness of various groups can help to explain differences in their heterogeneity as voting

---

regarding redundant per cent deviations, the differences between proportions of group and nongroup controls distributed in the several categories employed was 1.2 per cent in the case of Catholics, 1.5 per cent for Jews, 1.9 per cent for union members, and for Negroes, where matching was difficult, 4.3 per cent. It might be noted that after the first precision controls had been applied and occupation was added, further variables created only trival fluctuation in the vote division of the control group.

5. The Negro and Jewish groups are considerably smaller (*N*'s of 63 and 56 respectively) than the Catholic and union contingents (*N*'s of 253 and 373, respectively). Hence estimates for these groups are subject to greater sampling error. For the same reason, much of our intra-group analyses will be restricted to the union and Catholic groups.

"blocs." We chose items to measure group identification which might be applied to a variety of groups in order to facilitate such intergroup comparisons. The resulting distribution of member identifications which characterizes each group fits our intuitive preconceptions extremely well. Negroes, in a ferment over the problem of group advancement which was approaching the proportions of a nationalist movement, responded with almost unanimous warmth to our questions concerning group identification. Similarly, Jewish respondents, members of an ethnic community commonly considered to be "tightly-knit," showed almost the same strong cohesiveness. Union members were, more often than not, positively disposed to their organizations, but there was a notable reduction in the proportion of favorable responses to the group here by comparison with Negroes or Jews. Catholics, presumed to be nearing the end of an assimilation process which has gone on in this country for many decades, registered as somewhat less cohesive still.

The ordering of these groups in terms of relative cohesiveness bears fair resemblance to their ordering in terms of partisan distinctiveness in 1956. Jews show high distinctiveness in their vote, and are highly cohesive as well. Similarly, among our four groupings, Catholics are both least cohesive and least distinctive. Thus we get a sense that trends in the partisan solidarity of groups in the national electorate may be traced in some measure to the same mechanisms which have been subjected to examination in the laboratory with face-to-face groups.

However, the match between the two orderings is not perfect, suggesting that other variables are operative which deserve recognition in any full explanatory scheme. The distinctiveness of the Negro vote, for example, is much lower than its group cohesiveness would lead us to expect, even when we restrict our focus to Negroes residing outside the South. On the basis of independent knowledge of events surrounding the 1956 election, we might well conclude that the missing term here has to do with the character of group standards which are propagated. We know, for example, that Negro leadership was badly split in its political endorsements in the 1956 campaign. Adam Clayton Powell, the foremost legislator of his race on the national scene, bolted from a Democratic affiliation to recommend the election of the Republican candidate. At the same time, the National Association for Advancement of Colored People, the major formal organization representing the group, adopted a posture of watchful waiting during the campaign, with vague intimations of a Republican endorsement from the executive secretary. Meanwhile, visible Negro political leaders in other non-Southern cities tended to hew to the traditional Democratic choice in their public pronouncements. Along similar lines, although case numbers are small, we find in our own trend data that the distinctiveness of the non-Southern Negro vote was almost cut in half between 1952 and 1956.

This case study instructs us to shift our attention from the relationship between member and group to that which the member perceives to exist between the group and the political world. Tentatively, we leave the individual-group leg of the triangle to be represented by the single estimate of member identification with the group. There are a number of directions in which the notion of a generalized group valence has been expanded,[6] and such expansions might increase the explanatory significance of this portion of the system of variables. Nonetheless, it appears that we may enhance our understanding more rapidly by proceeding directly to the third leg of the triangular relationship.

THE GROUP AND THE WORLD OF POLITICS

In a general way, we may characterize the relationship between the group and the world of politics in terms of the proximity which the individual perceives to exist between the two entities. This sense of proximity may be difficult to specify, for in many ways the world of politics is a poorly defined region. Phenomenologically, however, it does seem to have some vague boundaries. It is in this spirit, for example, that a person may decide "to go into politics"; a group should "stay out of politics"; or a public problem is "made a political issue."

The notion of proximity is closely akin to what Schachter has treated as the "relevance" of a topic for a group.[7] Yet it subsumes a manifold process which we shall wish to examine in greater detail. It is of particular importance in this setting because the secondary groupings which we are examining are not at core "political" groups. That is, the basic goals of these groups are not directly political. The labor union exists to force management to provide more liberally for the worker; the Catholic church exists for religious worship. Yet these groups are *more nearly* political than the American Bowling Congress, for example, because from time to time influential group members come to see political instruments as important for the attainment of certain group goals. How nearly political any given member perceives the group to be will affect the way in which he reacts to a particular political standard felt to emanate from the group.

Groups which take political positions frequently are likely to communicate a sense that they are more rather than less political groups. Similarly, the strength of the standard conveyed contributes to a perception of proximity between group and politics. Even where strong standards are frequently transmitted, however, there may be further barriers acting to compartmentalize the world of politics from the sphere of group activity. The member may perceive that political action is relevant for the accomplishment of group goals, yet he may have qualms about the legitimacy of group intrusion in politics. There are cultural values bound up with beliefs about democracy and the individual which inveigh against such activity. Values of this sort might prevent a sense of proximity from developing whatever other conditions obtained.

6. See K. Back, "Influence through Social Communication," *Journal of Abnormal and Social Psychology*, 46: 9–23, 1951.

7. S. Schachter, "Deviation, Rejection and Communication," *Journal of Abnormal and Social Psychology*, 46: 190–207, 1951.

Thus we would expect some of the residual differences in vote homogeneity not explained by cohesiveness to depend on such factors as the strength and clarity of the standards which have been emitted in the name of the group, their successful transmission to the membership, and the values held by members concerning the appropriateness of political standards for the group concerned.

The Strength of Emitted Standards

One of the anomalies evident as we compare the ordering of our groups on vote distinctiveness and cohesiveness has to do with the union vote. Union members do not appear greatly more cohesive than Catholics, yet they are much more distinctive in their voting. This difference is reflected in another manner as well. Within the set of union members, the degree of association between identification and vote is considerably higher than among Catholics.[8] Since this difference depends on contrasts in the behavior of more and less identified members within each group, it cannot be accounted for in terms of group identification itself, but must depend on variation elsewhere in the influence process.

There are quite obvious differences between Catholic and union groups in the clarity with which political standards are emitted. In the current era, partisan voting norms among Catholics are probably maintained by diffuse primary-group mechanisms at a mass level. Such mechanisms for influence may not be intrinsically weak, but they probably are rendered rather impotent as group cohesiveness decreases. In the union case, however, political standards are often vigorously propagated by leadership, both through public endorsements in the name of the group and through more elaborate communication to the rank and file.

The very diffuseness of norm emission among Catholics makes empirical test of these surmises difficult. Within the set of union members, however, communication channels are more readily tapped, and we know that there is a good deal of variation in the vigor with which clear political standards are disseminated.

In the degree that union political standards are propagated in published form, they tend to flow from one of three levels of a hierarchy: the local, the international, or the remains of the massive federations which were, in 1956, still visible despite the AFL-CIO merger. The federations permit a first gross comparison. We would not hesitate long in labelling the CIO as the "more political" of the two federations, in terms of differences apparent during the period of schism. While these differences were declining in later years, the CIO leadership generally had emitted many more political standards more clearly, and had challenged directly the older norms against extension of union

---

8. A Kendall tau-beta rank-order correlation between identification and vote is .10 for Catholics, .24 for union members.

activities into political areas. National surveys during the 1940's and 1950's showed quite regularly that CIO members were 5–10 per cent more Democratic in their vote than were AFL members. In 1956, at least, a contrast of the same magnitude remained even after differences in occupation status were controlled. At the level of the great federation, then, it seems to be true that the "more political" group shapes a more distinctive political response across its membership.

We know further that there are radically different approaches to the problem of politics from one international union to another. These contrasts tend to cut across the old AFL and CIO distinction in some degree, since there is a scattering of AFL unions which expend much effort in political activity, while some CIO internationals attempt relatively little.

To capture this variation in 1956 we analyzed the political content of the pre-election editions of the official journals from several dozen of the large internationals whose members fell into our sample. The differences from journal to journal were sharp, making classification quite simple. At one extreme, large portions of the journal were given over to the elections, with fervently partisan pro-Democratic materials in abundance. As the proportion of content devoted to the campaign decreased, the tone became less strident. Short factual accounts of the AFL-CIO endorsement of the Democratic ticket, with mild-mannered editorials indicating the importance of voting for "candidates favorable to labor," became typical fare. A number of other journals made no partisan comment at all, nor did they report endorsements by other related groups. Finally, the journal of one giant union, while making no endorsement, included a picture of the international president in a friendly moment with President Eisenhower.

We have no evidence that the union members involved drew their perceptions of group standards from these particular journals. But we assumed that these journals were representative of the political efforts of the internationals more generally. Whatever the actual channels of communication, it was found that members faithfully reflected differences in clarity of standard from international to international by their reports of how they thought leaders of their union would vote. Where standards were clear in the group publications, member perceptions of leader behavior were clear and unidirectional. Where no standards were communicated, a much smaller proportion felt they knew how leaders would vote, and their guesses were less unanimously in a Democratic direction.

Within internationals where standards were most clear according to the content analysis of the journals, the vote division was 67 per cent Democratic. This fell to 55 per cent where standards were weaker, and then to 51 per cent in the category where no standards were visible at all in the analysis of journals. In the final category, where there appeared to be a slight Republican standard, the vote was only 44 per cent Democratic. Since the proportion of high identifiers across each of these categories varies within a range of nearly 3 per cent, it cannot be argued that these differences result from stronger identifications held by members of more militant unions.

However, group identification does play an interesting role in the situation. Table 1 gives some suggestion of the way in which these parts of the model—identification and strength of standards—combine as factors in the influence situation. As we see, there is little systematic variation in the behavior of the weakly identified in internationals of differing standards. It is among the highly identified that the character of group standards which are disseminated affects behavior. In other words, influence only appears with clarity when both identification and unequivocal standards are present in combination. If either is missing, the evidence for influence is weak indeed.

Table 1 is informative in other directions as well. We note, for example, that there is no sign here of any substantial negative influence or "boomerang" effect. If such effect were to occur, we would expect it to attain a maximum among the least identified where standards have greatest strength. However, the division of the vote in this cell is actually higher than among low identifiers under other conditions.

Table 1—The Relationship of Union Identification and Presidential Vote for Union Members, by Strength of Group Standards

NATURE OF INTERNATIONAL UNIONS' POLITICAL STANDARD

	I Strong, Democratic	II Weak, Democratic	III None	IV Weak, Republican	Total N
High identification	81% (21)	66% (56)	59% (37)	43% (14)	128
Low identification	50% (18)	42% (50)	41% (32)	45% (11)	111
Number of cases	39	106	69	25	239
T_b, Identification x Vote	+ .33	+ .25	+ .18	− .02	

Note: The entry in each cell indicates the per cent Democratic of the two-party vote for president in the 1956 election for the designated group. Numbers of cases involved in each proportion are indicated in parentheses. Rank-order correlation coefficients (tau-beta) between union identification and vote have been calculated for each category of political standard, and are entered in the bottom row.

It is true furthermore that while there is little evidence of the effects of standards among low identifiers in terms of Table 1, these persons are more likely to vote Democratic than nonunion people of similar life situation. We must remember that in examining the strength of standards emitted by organs at the level of the international union, we are capturing only a portion of the group standards to which union members are exposed. A Democratic endorsement by the newly merged AFL-CIO could be conceived as adding a broad force in the Democratic direction for members of all unions under its jurisdiction. Further effects of this sort may occur at the level of the local even within internationals which tend to avoid partisan commitment. And finally, we must suppose that there is influence as well at the primary-group level. Pressures here would produce a visible partisan bias in the vote of union people weakly identified with the union or members of neutral internationals to the degree that such persons were influenced by companions who happened to be more strongly identified or members of more militant unions.

Festinger, Schachter and Back, in their study of college housing units,[9] were forced to assume that a relationship between the cohesiveness and behavioral homogeneity of subunits guaranteed the presence of group norms, which could not be measured directly. Although the units in Table 1 are somewhat different, the coefficients entered at the bottom of the table lend weight to this assumption. The strength of the relationship between identification and vote varies with the strength of emitted standards which we have measured. This statistic is convenient for our further use, as it reveals variation in behavior which is, on the one hand, group-based, yet which is relatively independent of variation in identification on the other. While we cannot be sure that the differences it captures are due only to the *strength* of emitted standards, we do see that variation in strength of standard produces a gradient in the identification-vote relationship.

In these terms, it seems reasonable to assume that the weaker association between identification and vote which we have noted in the Catholic case does spring from standards which are less clear and strong than they are for many union members. The same chain of reasoning accounts for the much lower distinctiveness of the Catholic vote, despite a cohesiveness not unlike that of union groupings.

OTHER SIMPLE GROUP CUES AS POLITICAL STANDARDS

We may approach the matter of the Catholic vote from another point of view. For if Catholic standards are weak in terms of partisan loyalty toward a presidential candidacy, we can find cases in which group standards for Catholics could be expected to be much clearer.

Thus far we have considered only cases in which successful transmission of standards requires some relatively elaborate communication: at least a verbal endorsement, and normally some further persuasion. When one of the candidates is cognized as a group member, however, the behavior appropriate for loyal members is apparent without further need for communication. We can examine the effects of this classic gambit of nominating conventions in the vote of Catholics for legislative seats involving contests between a Catholic and a non-Catholic.

These split-religion races do reveal a more distinctive Catholic vote than has been apparent at the presidential level, despite the fact that support of a Catholic nominee at times requires the loyal member to depart from the "normal" Democratic preference to vote for a Republican.[10] Of course no group effect would be expected save where there is actual recognition of the group affiliation of the candidate. We know that as a general rule voters are rather uninformed about the senatorial and congressional candidates for whom

9. L. Festinger, S. Schachter, and K. Back, *Social Pressures in Informal Groups*, New York: Harper & Brothers, 1950.

10. The fact that "good" Catholics appear as candidates under a Republican label in itself helps to break down the sense of a unique group tie with the Democratic party.

they vote. Of course in the case of ethnic groupings, the name of the candidate on the ballot may in itself be sufficient to indicate group membership. But if we restrict our comparisons to the set of respondents able to recall the name of the candidate for whom they have voted, we should be focussing upon individuals most likely to be aware of the group affiliation of the candidate. And indeed, the group effect, quite visible without this intensifying device, is thereby dramatized considerably (Table 2).

Table 2—The Vote of Catholics for Catholic Candidates Whose Names Can Be Recalled, in Races Involving Non-Catholics

| | CATHOLIC IDENTIFICATION | | |
	High	Low	Total Group
U.S. House of Representatives			
Catholic voters	85% (13)	69% (13)	77% (26)
Catholic control	—	—	51% (25)
U. S. Senate			
Catholic voters	86% (22)	57% (28)	70% (50)
Catholic control	—	—	49% (47)

The per cent entry refers to the proportion of the indicated group who voted for the Catholic candidates in the split-religion congressional or senatorial race. The figure in each parenthesis indicates the number of cases involved in each proportion.

If the distinctiveness of the Catholic vote *for President* is so small as to create the impression of a politically impotent group, differences in Table 2, although based on fewer cases than we would like, are large enough to challenge any sweeping conclusion of this order. Therefore it is worthwhile to reflect upon some of the generic differences between the two situations.

The most obvious distinction springs from the fact that the 1956 presidential race studied did not pit group member against nonmember, while the congressional races were chosen precisely on this basis. We would expect a much firmer equation of political object with group interest where the object is part of the group than where the group merely extends some kind of endorsement to a party or a nonmember candidate. Secondly, the pairing of member and nonmember in the competition for office in itself makes the group basis for choice more salient. This fact becomes more critical in view of the extremely limited information which appears to underlie most political decisions in the mass electorate. Lack of knowledge about legislative candidates is simply a case in point. Where ethnic background or religion is suggested by the surname of the candidate, this datum, along with the candidate's party affiliation, may exhaust the information brought to bear on partisan choice by substantial proportions of the public. In these cases, the question posed by the ballot is in effect: "Other things equal, would you prefer a member of your own group to a nonmember?" In the degree that such a situation obtains, it is likely that the group effects which we observe in these instances are virtually maximized.

It should be recognized also that Table 2 is restricted to those voters most likely to cognize the candidate's group affiliation. A parallel table including all Catholic voters shows group candidates favored by a 12 per cent increment over the proper control group, as opposed to the increment of 20–25 per cent in Table 2. We take this to mean that group effects are muted in this voting situation simply because some members lack the information necessary to recognize the relevance of group standards. As might be expected, this problem is at least equally acute where standards are less self-evident. The fact that strong standards are emitted certainly raises the probability that some standard will be perceived; but it does not ensure reception, and failures at this point further limit the operation of influence in the political setting.

The Reception of Emitted Standards

In the social groupings under consideration, the transmission of uniform political standards to a far-flung membership is a precarious process. This is bound to be true if leadership is decentralized or if propagation depends upon primary-group diffusion. But even in the union case, where channels of communication for political materials are clear-cut and much effort is devoted in some quarters to the problem of communicating political standards, there is good evidence that influence is circumscribed because portions of the membership simply fail to absorb information concerning group political standards.

Unfortunately, it is difficult to measure the cognizance of norms on the part of the member directly. In times past we have asked group members before the election whether they would predict any predominant direction in the vote of their leadership or of other members. For some uses responses to these items are illuminating. But there is internal evidence that such reports are clouded by various types of distortion. The identified member who for other reasons wishes to cast a vote against the prevailing group standard may inhibit recognition that any standard exists; the poorly identified member who is unaware of any particular standard may simply project his own intentions on the group. Since it seems clear that such distortions will occur under certain critical combinations of identification and vote intention, we are not comfortable in using these responses to cast light on variations in identification and vote.

However, we feel more confident employing these reports to validate factors which we might suppose would affect reception of standards, yet which should, by and large, cross-cut any effects due to distortion. We would hypothesize in the union case, for example, that group standards would be least evident for poorly educated members and for those whose term of membership in a union had been most brief. We know that low education means relatively slight interest and involvement in politics, and general lack of information concerning prominent political issues of the day. It also means a higher dependence upon radio and television than upon the written word as a source of political information, if indeed any mass medium is monitored at all. If the reception of an emitted standard is a probability matter, then the individual exposed to many emissions is more likely to have absorbed the message than one exposed to few emissions. The same rationale would lead to the prediction that long-term members would be more apt to cognize group standards than new arrivals.

We do in fact find sharp variation in the clarity with which standards are reported to be perceived, as a function of both education and length of membership (Table 3). Furthermore, the correlations between identification and vote,

Table 3—Recognition of Union Political Standards as a Function of Education and Length of Union Membership

	EDUCATION			T_b, UNION
Length of Union Membership	Grade School	High School	College*	IDENTIFICATION x VOTE
4 years or less	40% (20)	49% (35)	64% (22)	+ .01
5-9 years	56% (16)	69% (36)		+ .09
10 years or over	60% (48)	80% (60)		+ .34
T_b, Union identification x vote	+ .15	+ .22	+ .35	

Note: The per cent entry in each cell refers to the proportion of the indicated group which perceives the union leadership as behaving in some predominant partisan direction. The remaining respondents indicated either that they did not know how the leadership stood in partisan terms for the 1956 election, or thought that leadership would be "about evenly split" between the parties. Figures in parentheses indicate the number of cases involved in each proportion. The rank-order correlation coefficients are comparable to those employed in connection with Table 1.

* The number of college-educated people who are union members is too few for further sub-division. In a rough way, the college entry is placed appropriately on the continuum indicating length of union membership. That is, average length of membership is considerably lower here than is the case within the other education categories.

entered around both margins of the table, show precisely the type of co-variation with each of these factors which we would demand as evidence of change in influence phenomena. These gradients of relationship associated with education and length of membership closely resemble the gradient which we discovered as a function of strength of emitted standards. However, it does not appear that they are merely derivatives or artifacts of the previous gradient, as might be the case if militant unions had memberships of longer standing and higher education. Actually, differences in mean education or length of membership across internationals of differing political standards are small at best. But to the degree that differences are present, they run in the opposing direction: internationals with stronger standards have more poorly educated members who are, on the average, of more recent vintage. Thus if we had sufficient cases to examine these several gradients within the same table, we would expect each to be more rather than less steep.

In predicting that perception of standards would increase as a function of education, we relied in part upon independent knowledge that more educated citizens are more apt to draw upon written communications for political information than audiovisual media such as radio or television. Aside from direct personal confrontation which may arise in some union situations, the transmission of political standards in the union case is likely to rest much more heavily upon the written word than upon radio or television presentation.

Furthermore, people who depend primarily on newspapers and magazines for political information do tend to receive messages from radio and television as well, while persons depending on radio and television are much less likely to supplement their information from printed sources. Thus dependence upon newspapers and magazines is posited as an intervening mechanism whereby more educated people, if highly identified as well, become more apt to respond to group standards.

Data are arrayed in Table 4 to show that while education and type of media

Table 4—The Role of Mass Media and Education in the Relationship Between Identification and Vote among Union Members

Most Important Mass Media for Political News	EDUCATION		
	Grade School	High School	College
Newspapers and magazines	.16 (21)	.37 (73)	.45 (18)
Radio and television	.19 (72)	.17 (112)	.41 (18)

Note: The entry in each cell is a coefficient of correlation (T_b) between union identification and the Presidential vote of the union member. The number of cases involved in the coefficient is indicated in parentheses.

consumption are related for union members, each factor makes some independent contribution to an intensification of the identification-vote relationship. The independent role of the mass media appears trivial among grade school and college people, but quite substantial within the high-school category, where the bulk of the cases are concentrated. The evidence that both factors make an independent contribution to variation in the identification-vote relationship raises our confidence that we properly interpret these patterns as steps in a process, rather than spurious co-variation arising from the other independent variable (education or media consumption) as a "third factor."

In short, then, a number of pieces of evidence suggest that the influence process is partially undermined in the union case by failure of identified members to recognize emitted political standards. We may suppose that if political messages were more carefully attended, newer union members would become aware of standards more rapidly, and poorly educated members would show a higher recognition of such standards. In such an event, we would expect the more identified persons within these categories to respond to standards with greater clarity than is now the case.

The Legitimacy of Group Political Standards

Even where clear standards are successfully received by a membership, we have suggested that there may be resistance on value grounds against group intrusion upon political decision-making. Since the most obvious goals of these groups are not primarily political, a member may espouse these goals fervently without feeling that it is legitimate for political instrumentation to be sought.

In 1956 we asked the members of our several groups whether or not they felt it was "all right" for organizations representing the group to support relevant legislative proposals and candidates for office. The responses to these questions showed a fairly strong relationship with the group identification variable in a direction which would seem to match theoretical expectations. That is, we would expect a person who is more absorbed in a group to accord it broader jurisdiction than one who is less enthusiastic about his membership.

With identification controlled, however, there remains a substantial relationship between beliefs concerning the legitimacy of group political standards and conformity to group norms across all of the groupings analyzed (Table 5). It

Table 5—Presidential Vote Across Four Secondary Membership Groups, by Strength of Group Identification and Belief in Legitimacy of Group Political Activity

Belief in Legitimacy of Group Political Activity	GROUP IDENTIFICATION			TOTAL
	High	Medium	Low	
Strong	72% (126)	64% (95)	55% (98)	65% (319)
Medium	62% (52)	55% (55)	45% (56)	53% (163)
Weak	67% (27)	45% (60)	33% (127)	41% (214)
Total	69% (205)	56% (210)	43% (281)	—

Note: Each cell entry represents the per cent Democratic of the two-party vote for the appropriate combination of group identification and sense of legitimacy. The "Total" column shows the simple relationship between legitimacy and the vote, with no control on identification. The "Total" row shows the simple relationship between identification and the vote, without control on legitimacy.

is undoubtedly true that in some measure the beliefs of members as to the legitimacy of standards will be affected by perceived congruence of own and group political predispositions. In other words, a sense of legitimacy could be an effect, rather than a cause, of acceptance of the group position in politics.

Of course our data do not permit us to sort out these cases or estimate their contribution to the relationship portrayed in Table 5. Nevertheless, we feel that in some part at least we are tapping a set of beliefs which have independent causal status in the influence process. The pattern of correlates on the legitimacy responses are encouraging in this regard. For example, within each level of group identification, members of the two religious groups—Catholics and Jews—show much greater reluctance to accept the legitimacy statements than either of the two secular groupings. This suggests that our questions capture some appropriate underlying value structures, since taboos designed to insulate the political process from outside group pressures have been strongest where religious groupings have been concerned. Also, with identification controlled, there is somewhat less readiness to grant legitimacy among older people. This conforms with impressions that popular values opposing frank interest-group politics represent an older America.

Thus while Table 5 undoubtedly overstates the independent status of concern with legitimacy in inhibiting conformity, it seems that such concerns must be taken into account in any full assessment of the influence process in this setting.

Summary

We have attempted to explore a variety of aspects of the group influence process, as it operates in the formation and erosion of voting blocs within secondary membership groupings in the national electorate. We cannot test elements of the model which has been sketched above against the observed behavior of our several groups in any rigorous fashion. But we have some sense that it increases our understanding of the reasons which underlie differences in the distinctiveness of vote across our several groups.

On many counts, the Negro community appears most ripe in the current period for political influence in the name of the group. Its cohesiveness is extremely high. The legitimacy of group activity in politics goes almost unquestioned. Its primary deficit lies in the impoverished education of group members, a fact which may in some degree disrupt the transmission of political standards despite high levels of group motivation. However, conflicting leadership standards appear to have reduced the efficiency of the group as a national voting bloc in the 1956 election.

Similar cohesiveness among Jewish people may permit high distinctiveness of the group vote when group standards are clear. In this case, the high level of education within the group facilitates the transmission of standards, although there are greater reservations felt by group members about the role of the group in politics than is the case for Negroes.

The union grouping is more cohesive than the Catholic, but the difference is slight. Nevertheless, the transmission of standards for union members is much more persistent and obvious, despite telling variation over the total labor movement. And there is a general willingness on the part of union members to accept group activity in politics which is clearly lacking among Catholics. The result is a much more distinctive group vote in the union case, although the evidence suggests that distinctiveness could be greater if stronger standards were expressed and their transmission rendered more effective.

We can expect that a number of these group characteristics which appear critical in terms of the model will shift over time. Continuing observation of the magnitude of group effects as they vary in response to such change should give us an increasingly firm understanding of the dynamics of the influence process, with its many potentialities and limitations, as it occurs in this field setting.

Identification with Class and Political Role Behavior

Heinz Eulau

RESEARCH in political behavior is based on the assumption that the political process is characterized by the ceaseless inter-action of two major types of determinants: those "situational" factors which shape political activity irrespective of the personalities, motivations or perceptions of the participants; and those "psychological" factors which relate political activity to the motives, attitudes, or expectations of the political actors. It is the task of political behavior research to investigate the inter-penetration of specific situational and behavioral data in terms of empirically-oriented theory.[1]

It is the most general purpose of this study to report certain findings concerning the relationship between people's position in the social structure, or class, and various behavioral manifestations accompanying their role as democratic citizens in the presidential election of 1952. However, the findings are of interest not only because they may add to our knowledge of political behavior,

Reprinted from *Public Opinion Quarterly*, 20: 515–529, 1956, by permission of the author and the publisher. This analysis was made possible by the author's participation in the 1954 summer seminar on political behavior held at the Survey Research Center, University of Michigan, under a grant from the Social Science Research Council. It is based on data from a national sample survey conducted in 1952 by the Survey Research Center, under the sponsorship of the Political Behavior Committee of the SSRC. Neither the Center nor the Council are responsible for this analysis. The author wishes to express his gratitude for criticisms of an earlier draft he received from Dr. Gerald Gurin, of the Survey Research Center, and from Dr. Warren Miller, of the Department of Political Science and the Survey Research Center, University of Michigan.

1. See Avery Leiserson, "Problems of Methodology in Political Research," *Political Science Quarterly*, 1953, Vol. 68, pp. 558–584; and David Easton, *The Political System*. New York: Alfred A. Knopf, 1953, pp. 149–218.

[490]

but also because they necessitate reconceptualization of the data in terms of theoretical considerations not originally anticipated. In other words, this is in many respects a case study on the connection between empirical research and political theory.[2]

Social class has long been recognized as a significant factor in political behavior.[3] Research concerning the relationship between class and political behavior is, however, made difficult by the two obstacles implicit in the concept of class. The first is "index instability" which not only hampers quantification of political hypotheses, but also restricts theoretical generalizations to specified social situations; the second is lack of agreement as to whether "objective" or "subjective" indices are more relevant in linking class to social behavior.[4]

The first of these obstacles will not concern us here. As to the second, it can be successfully argued that meaningful explanation of the relationship between people's objective position in the social structure and their political behavior requires the introduction of an "intervening variable" in the form of their self-identification with a particular social class. For high correlations between objective class position and manifestations of political behavior may be a necessary, but need not be a sufficient condition for class-relevant political behavior. In other words, it may be held that the way in which class is *experienced* by participants in the political process makes a significant difference in their political behavior. Yet, it is not our intention to enter into this controversy. It is simply suggested that if identification with class does make a difference, it is a difference in degree rather than in kind. As Theodore M. Newcomb has pointed out, to have both objective and subjective information about a person is better than either alone.[5]

Identification with Class

Richard Centers defines classes as "psycho-social groupings, something that is essentially subjective in character, dependent upon class consciousness (i.e. a feeling of group membership), and class lines of cleavage [which] may or may not conform to what seem to social scientists to be logical lines of cleavage in the objective or stratification sense."[6] Class, Centers continues, "can well be

2. See Robert K. Merton, "The Bearing of Sociological Theory on Empirical Research," and "The Bearing of Empirical Research on Sociological Theory," in *Social Theory and Social Structure*. New York: The Free Press, 1949, pp. 83–111.

3. But see Heinz Eulau, "Perception of Class and Party in Voting Behavior: 1952," *American Political Science Review*, 1955, Vol. 49, pp. 364–384.

4. See Paul K. Hatt, "Stratification in the Mass Society," *American Sociological Review*, 1950, Vol. 15, pp. 216–222.

5. Theodore M. Newcomb, *Social Psychology*. New York: The Dryden Press, 1950, p. 559.

6. Richard Centers, *The Psychology of Social Classes*. Princeton, N.J.: Princeton University Press, 1949, p. 27.

regarded as a *psychological* phenomenon in the fullest sense of the term. That is, a man's class is a part of his ego, *a feeling on his part of belongingness to something;* an *identification* with something larger than himself."[7] Centers evidently equates class identification with class consciousness, and he uses people's self-identification as a criterion of their class consciousness.

As an index of identification with class Centers uses responses to this question: "If you were asked to use one of these four names for your social class, which would you say you belonged in: the middle class, lower class, working class or upper class?"[8] For instance, in a survey conducted in July, 1945, by the quota control method, and presumably representative of the adult white male population of the United States, Centers found that three per cent identified themselves as upper class, 43 per cent as middle class, 51 per cent as working class and one per cent as lower class, while two per cent said they didn't know to which class they belonged or didn't "believe in" classes. These answers, according to Centers, "will convincingly dispel any doubt that Americans are class conscious, and quite as quickly quell any glib assertions like *Fortune's* 'America is Middle Class.' "[9] And he asserts that "one can find textbook and dictionary definitions enough, to be sure, but these do not serve us here, for, in essence, *a class is no more nor less than what people collectively think it is.*"[10]

To support this hypothesis, Centers cites significant differences between occupational strata in regard to class identification, and he shows that class identifiers place different emphases on relevant class membership criteria. But this does not really prove that "class consciousness" is revealed by self-identification with class. Awareness of socio-economic differences may help one in identifying one's class, and people do not necessarily think or act alike because they belong to the same stratum. It is precisely for these reasons that subjective assessment of their social position may be important. But this cannot be construed to the effect that *only* subjective evaluations matter.

Centers himself does not seem to be sure of his evidence. He feels that "more evidence, something in the way of a crucial test, is demanded to support such an hypothesis." He finds a test, "although in a rather crude sense, in a comparison of the class criteria in use by people of common occupational position but of different class allegiance."[11] "If people in the same broad occupational stratum, but of different class affiliations do have interests in common with the classes with which they identify themselves they should differ in attitudes or politico-economic orientations, i.e. in conservatism-radicalism,

7. *Ibid.*, p. 27.

8. *Ibid.*, p. 76.

9. *Ibid.*, p. 76. Centers was referring to a *Fortune* survey, conducted in 1940, which showed 79 per cent of respondents identifying themselves with the middle class.

10. *Ibid.*, p. 78.

11. *Ibid.*, p. 103.

from the 'members' of their own occupational stratum and differ in the direction characteristic of the classes with which they identify themselves."[12]

Centers' data bear him out. When attitudes on socio-economic issues and voting preferences of identifiers and non-identifiers within a given objective stratum are compared, Centers finds that "the differences are substantial, statistically reliable, and in the predicted direction."[13] After having partialed out objective stratification indices, however, Centers concludes that subjective class identification is far more a function of socio-economic classification than anything else. "The several variables that are correlated with class identification to some extent or other are seen to derive most of their concomitancy of variation with those functions mainly from the strength of their association with stratification itself."[14]

Centers' theoretical formulations, sample and other methodological procedures have been severely criticized. Lipset and Bendix, for instance, have pointed out the circular nature of Centers' class concept, the likelihood of stereotypy involved in self-identification, and the abandonment of concern with social theory.[15] Walter Goldschmidt has emphasized that Centers' correlations are positive where one would expect them to be, but that they are low. In other words, people behave in the expected manner more often than not, but the population does not behave consistently with Centers' class analysis.[16]

Our own concern is less with these aspects of Centers' work than with the uses to which the concept of class identification has been put. Centers relates class identification exclusively to other *attitudinal* dimensions of political behavior—such as conservative-radical orientations, voting preferences, and other psychological differences—, but not to any behavioral manifestations of political *conduct*, such as political participation, political interest, exposure to the mass media, political effectiveness, and so on. In other words, whether class identification has an effect on conduct, in the sense that the self-identifier actually takes the *role* of the identified-with class, remains unanswered. Examining this problem is the particular purpose of this study.

Need of Reconceptualization

The present analysis is based on data from a national area probability sample survey collected both prior to and after the 1952 presidential election

12. *Ibid.*, p. 126.

13. *Ibid.*, p. 129.

14. *Ibid.*, p. 202.

15. Seymour M. Lipset, and Reinhard Bendix, "Social Status and Social Structure," *British Journal of Sociology*, 1951, Vol. 2, pp. 150–168; 220–254.

16. Walter Goldschmidt, "Social Class in America—A Critical Review," *American Anthropologist*, 1950, Vol. 52, pp. 483–498.

by the Survey Research Center, University of Michigan.[17] Of a total sample of 1,614 twice interviewed, 482 respondents had to be dropped from the study because they either failed to identify themselves as middle class or working class, or could not be located on an objective Index of Status Characteristics.[18] Table 1 shows the distribution of the final sample in terms of both objective classification and self-identification. This cross-tabulation was made in order to isolate the operation of class identification as a variable independent of the respondents' objective class position. With objective class controlled, it was then possible to divide respondents into four class groupings:

1. Those objectively classified as Working Class and self-identified as Working Class—Working Class Consistents or WW.
2. Those objectively classified as Working Class but self-identified as Middle Class—Middle Class Affiliates or WM.
3. Those objectively classified as Middle Class but self-identified as Working Class—Working Class Affiliates or MW.
4. Those objectively classified as Middle Class and self-identified as Middle Class—Middle Class Consistents or MM.

Table I—Distribution of 1,132 Respondents in Terms of Objective Classification and Self-Identification

	OBJECTIVE CLASSES		
Self-Identification	Working Class	Middle Class	Total
	N = 766	N = 366	N = 1,132
Working class	76%	36%	63%
Middle class	24	64	37
Total	100%	100%	100%

It was initially hypothesized, in line with Centers' procedure, that the affiliate groupings (WM and MW) should differ significantly from the consistent groupings (WW and MM, respectively) with regard to various manifestations of political behavior. Such differences would be indicative of the operation of

17. See Angus Campbell, Gerald Gurin, and Warren Miller, *The Voter Decides.* Evanston: Row, Peterson and Company, 1954.

18. In order to develop an Index of Status Characteristics, forty-five different combinations of occupational, income and educational status were placed in a cross-tabulation matrix which permitted each respondent to occupy different positions in the three status hierarchies, and which yielded nine summary scores for every combination of status positions possible in the matrix. The resultant status categories were combined and dichotomized into "working class" and "middle class" on the basis of the frequency distribution of all respondents located in the matrix. The terms "middle class" and "working class" were assigned to the dichotomized aggregates for convenience only, largely because on the self-identification instrument 94 per cent of objectively classified respondents accepted these terms as descriptive of their class affiliation.

class identification as an independent variable.[19] Tabulations revealed that this was in fact the case. But closer scrutiny of the relevant tables indicated that the differences between each pair of contrasted class groupings were quite dissimilar for the attitudinal dimensions of political behavior, on the one hand, and manifestations of political conduct, on the other. Identification with class seemed less effective in helping self-identifiers take the political roles of the identified-with groups than in helping them develop relevant attitudes and preferences. It became necessary, therefore, to clarify the concept of identification.

Two steps were taken. First, rather than define identification as a feeling of belongingness with its static implications, identification was conceptualized as a process, partial or limited, which involved locomotion away from and toward a region of valenced activity. It was assumed, then, that class identification might make for conflict, with the result that dependent attitudes or behaviors could be inconsistent.[20] This notion of identification as movement permitted measuring along the class identification continuum. The distance between the two consistent groupings reported on an Index of Class Identification Strength could serve as a standard for measuring the extent of identification by the affiliates in regard to dependent political behavior.[21]

Second, as inspection of the data suggested that identification conceived as locomotion away from and toward a region of valenced activity indicated more movement in regard to attitudinal than conduct patterns of political behavior, it seemed desirable to sharpen the distinction between identification in terms of attitudes, such as other identifications, demands or expectations, and identification in terms of political roles.

The literature on identification offered little guidance. Parsons and Shils, possibly because they are sociologists rather than social psychologists, seem to sense the multi-modal complexity of the concept of identification. Though they relegate their pregnant observation to a footnote, they distinguish "(1) the

19. Chi square (χ^2) was used as the statistical test to determine significant differences. The 5 per cent level of probability was accepted as the standard of significance. Degree of association between class identification and dependent political behavior variables was measured by T, which is the square root of T^2 where $T^2 = \dfrac{\chi^2}{n \sqrt{(t-1)(s-1)}}$. T would equal 1 if the association were perfect. See Lilian Cohen, *Statistical Methods for Social Scientists*. New York: Prentice-Hall, 1954, pp. 134–135.

20. For more detail, see Heinz Eulau, "Identification with Class and Political Perspective," *Journal of Politics*, 1956, Vol. 18, pp. 232-253.

21. This index is derived by subtracting one extreme position (i.e., proportion of voters within each class grouping) along each dependent variable continuum from the other extreme position. Resulting scores may be compared, and the *distance* between consistent and affiliate groupings may serve as a measure of locomotion. As it should be expected that the distance between the two consistent groupings is always greater than that between each contrasted pair, the more the distance score of the latter approximates that of the former, the less partial or limited is identification with respect to a particular aspect of an affiliate group's political behavior.

internalization of the values but not the role of the model from (2) internalization of his specific role."[22] But they do not follow up this distinction. Stuart M. Stoke, in a critical appraisal of the concept, points out that "an emotional identification cannot produce a behavioral manifestation if *capacity* for the behavior is lacking. It also seems reasonable that different degrees of capacity are bound to produce different degrees of behavioral identification, even though effort to identify is held at a constantly high level."[23] The success of behavioral identification, Stoke continues, "will be affected by the capacity of the individual to adopt the role."[24] But what is meant by "capacity to adopt the role?" In order to answer this question, an attempt was made to reconceptualize identification in terms of George Herbert Mead's theory of communication.

Identification and Communication

Once it is assumed that identification does not mean internalization of an object, as Freud and many subsequent psychologists thought, but rather movement along a continuum of valenced human relationships, one is readily led to the work of George Herbert Mead. For relationships are predicated on the presence of "Self" and "Other," their mutual interaction and expectations —in other words, the existence of reciprocally defined roles. And roles are defined through communication.

Though uninfluenced by Freud, but like Freud concerned with the development of the Self, Mead found in communication a requisite for identification. . . .

Two major types, each divisible into two sub-types, may be sorted out of Mead's discussion of communication. Only the major types need to concern us. The first type of communication is perhaps best represented by the relationship between mother and baby. The baby may react to a tense mother, without her being aware that she has communicated her feelings to the child. Communication is automatic and unconscious. Behavior as such acts as a signal setting off a response. . . .

The second major type of communication as developed by Mead is characterized by consciousness, an awareness of one's taking the part of another person. The child now consciously plays the part of his father or mother in games, or he may imagine that he is the hero of an adventure story. This, in Mead's terms, is "meaningful conduct." . . .

Now, what distinguishes this second type from the first, apart from consciousness, is the *capacity* to anticipate what the response of another person is

22. Talcott Parsons, and Edward A. Shils, *Toward a General Theory of Action*, Cambridge, Mass.: Harvard University Press, 1951, p. 310, n. 4.

23. Stuart M. Stoke, "An Inquiry into the Concept of Identification," *Journal of Genetic Psychology*, 1950, Vol. 76, p. 177.

24. *Ibid.*, p. 180.

going to be. This capacity is a function of participation in organized, goale
directed activities—at first games, but later on more functional collaborativ-
activities. The individual must not only take the attitudes of other individuals
toward himself and toward one another, but he must also take "their attitudes
toward the various phases or aspects of the common social activity or set of
social undertakings in which, as members of an organized society or social
group, they are all engaged."[25] The activity, then, has a goal, involves others,
and is participated in by way of rules or procedures to be followed. In order to
reach the goal of the activity, functions must be performed and functional roles
must be filled. Communication, then, takes place in terms of the functions to
be performed rather than in terms of feelings about particular people involved
in the activity. Regardless of one's valued orientations towards the other—
whether he is liked or not—it is possible to take his functional role. In other
words, taking the role of the other is not so much dependent on identification
with the other, but it derives from or is "built in" the unity and structure of
"the social process as a whole; and each of the elementary selves of which it
is composed reflects the unity and structure of one of the various aspects of that
process in which the individual is implicated."[26] The attitude of the whole
community or social group Mead refers to as "the generalized other."[27] And
it is through the process of "calling out a generalized other" that fully conscious
communication with others becomes possible.

Mead's discussion of communication, and particularly of his major types,
is suggestive for our analysis of identification. For identification would seem
to rest on communication. Unconscious communication, of the first type,
should also give rise to a different type of identification than conscious communication. Indeed, though not made explicit, this differentiation between
unconscious and conscious communication seems to underlie Parsons and
Shils' distinction between identification as "internalization of the values" of
the model and identification as "internalization of his specific role." As we
have seen, Mead's first type of communication, especially in its later stage, is
in many respects similar to the earliest appearance of what in Freudian terminology is called the super-ego, i.e. those norms or values which form a basic part
of the emerging personality. Here the most primitive prohibitions or values—
such as the distinction between hot and cold, or being a good child or a naughty
one—are unconsciously internalized through identification.

Internalization of role, on the other hand, would seem to be based on
Mead's second type of communication. Identification takes place not only in
terms of unconsciously communicated values, but in terms of a conscious
relationship. Since this relationship is one between Self and Other as mutually
defined, it serves as the identifying mechanism. Required for identification

25. George Herbert Mead, *Mind, Self and Society*. Chicago: University of Chicago Press,
1934, p. 155.

26. *Ibid.*, p. 144.

27. *Ibid.*, p. 154.

here is attention to the roles others perform in relation to each other, i.e. the functions they perform as interacting individuals in pursuit of a common objective. Just as communication in terms of others' roles requires capacity to anticipate the others' response, so identification in terms of role is predicated on capacity for such identification.

Capacity for both successful communication and identification in terms of role depends on the degree of actual inter-action that takes place. Such inter-action is severely limited by the particular position which a person occupies in the social structure. A union member is unlikely to be a member of the local country club, or a successful businessman is unlikely to live in a slum tenement house. Inter-action, then, is dependent on such class-relevant variables as occupation, income, or education; it is related to common characteristics rather than common interests. But as common characteristics tend to give rise to common interests, and common interests are a prerequisite for taking the role of the other—i.e. for forming an image of the activity that is required to perform different functions in terms of role—it follows that identification is also dependent on shared characteristics if role performance is to be successful. Without these characteristics the person is *incapable* of taking the role of the other. This type of identification, then, is quite different from simply the sharing of emotional feelings, attitudes or values.

Just as both types of communication continue to operate simultaneously throughout a person's life-time—though the second type becomes increasingly preponderant—so both types of identification play a continuing part in a person's career. They are certainly not mutually exclusive, and one should not expect either type of identification to preclude the other from having an effect on social behavior. *Conduct*—in the sense of actually taking the other's role—should however be more a function of capacity than of personal identification in terms of feelings, attitudes or values.

One should expect that self-identification in terms of class is more likely to be effective when it comes to other identifications or preferences which are predicated on "internalization of values," than when it comes to taking a class-related role in political conduct. Participation in politics, for instance, as a manifestation of role performance, may depend less on identification with a class than on possession of those objective characteristics which are a prerequisite for capacity to imagine and play the role of the other. This does not mean that *only* common characteristics, defined in terms of objective class position, matter in political conduct, but it may suggest why self-identification with class is less effective in political role performance than more attitudinal aspects of political behavior.

Class Identification and Political Roles

A number of expectations accompany the role which the democratic citizen should play in the course of a political campaign. He is expected to be interested in the electoral fight, participate in the campaign or, if he does not participate, at least to vote. He is expected to see that there are differences between the parties and care about the outcome of the election. To meet these expectations, he should expose himself to campaign issues and arguments by paying attention to the mass media of communication. Beyond these expectations, the democratic citizen is assumed to feel that his vote counts, and that voting is a moral obligation. He should be a regular voter who takes his role as citizen in earnest from election to election.

In spite of great social pressure to carry out these various aspects of his role as a citizen in a democracy, almost one out of every two Americans fails to register his preferences at the polls. Many studies of voting behavior have suggested that political participation and other facets of the citizen role are a function of people's socio-economic status. That people tend to inter-act with each other in terms of their objective class position, and that such inter-action is a prerequisite for capacity to perform successfully class-related political roles, raises the question of whether self-identification with social class makes a difference, *in degree* at least, as far as political role performance is concerned. If it does, one should expect that middle class affiliates will differ from working class consistents by showing better performance, while working class affiliates will differ from middle class consistents by showing worse performance. At the same time, however, the effect of such self-identification should be less than in the case of attitudinal manifestations of political behavior. In other words, the effect of self-identification on political role performance should be attenuated by capacity for such performance.

A number of questions concerning political role were asked by the Survey Research Center in its 1952 poll. For two of these, participation and exposure to the mass media, detailed tables are presented here; the others will be treated in a summary table. All of the tables show significant differences between affiliates and consistents of both classes. But Class Identification Strength scores suggest the limited and partial effect of identification and may be accepted as indicative of the importance of capacity in political role performance. A separate table summarizes these scores as well as their respective locomotion scores, and contrasts them with those obtained for the relationship between class identification and more attitudinal aspects of political behavior.

Participation in the campaign and the act of voting are probably the most tangible manifestations of political role behavior. The participation scale used in Table 2 provides for the three degrees of political participation: (a) high: those who voted and also engaged in some other political activity during the campaign; (b) medium: those who voted but did not otherwise participate; and (c) low: those who did not vote. Most evident in Table 2 is the fact that there are significant differences between the affiliate groupings and their respective consistent classes. Class Identification Strength scores indicate that the "pull" of identification, though present, is countered by a relative lack of capacity for relevant role performance.

Table 2—Class Identification and Participation

	WORKING		MIDDLE	
Participation	Working	Middle	Working	Middle
	N = 580	N = 186	N = 131	N = 235
High	22%	28%	30%	49%
Medium	47	53	53	43
Low	31	19	17	8
Total	100%	100%	100%	100%
CIS Index	− 9	+ 9	+ 13	+ 41
Tests for:	χ^2	d/f	p	T
WW—WM	10.83	2	< .01	.10
MM—MW	12.04	2	< .01	.14

Attention to the mass media of communication during an electoral campaign may be considered a form of vicarious participation. What, then, is the relative effect of class identification and capacity on this aspect of political role behavior? The "exposure to media" scale divided respondents into three groups: (a) high exposure: those who used three or four sources, of these one or more actively; (b) medium exposure: those who used one or two sources, with active use of at least one; and (c) low exposure: those who used no source at all, or made inactive use of any number of sources. Table 3 shows an exposure pattern similar to that found in connection with participation. There are significant differences between the affiliated and their respective consistent classes. But the Class Identification Strength score differences are smaller than strong identification would lead one to expect. In other words, capacity for identification to be more effective is lacking.

Table 3—Class Identification and Exposure to Mass Media

	WORKING		MIDDLE	
Exposure	Working	Middle	Working	Middle
	N = 580	N = 186	N = 131	N = 235
High	33%	48%	55%	71%
Medium	27	26	23	14
Low	40	26	22	15
Total	100%	100%	100%	100%
CIS Index	− 7	+ 22	+ 33	+ 56
Tests for:	χ^2	d/f	p	T
WW—WM	17.86	2	< .001	.13
MM—MW	10.50	2	< .01	.14

Similar tests, summarized in Table 4, were made in regard to other manifestations of political role behavior. Interest was measured by using the respondents' own assessment of their interest, the scale distinguishing between: (a) those very interested; (b) those somewhat interested; and (c) those not much interested. The "voting regularity" scale differences between: (a) those who had voted in all or most elections since reaching voting age: (b) those who had voted in some elections; and (c) those who had never voted (exclusive of those too young to have ever voted before). Concern with outcome of the election was measured by a four-point scale distinguishing between: (a) those who cared very much; (b) those who cared somewhat; (c) those who didn't care much; and (d) those who didn't care at all. "Sense of efficacy" was measured in terms of a Guttman-type scale which was based on four items which sought to elicit respondents' feelings that one's action can effectively influence the course of political events, i.e. that one's vote counts. Similarly, "sense of citizen duty" was derived from four items, also brought together in a Guttman-type scale, which sought to discover the degree of respondents' acceptance of those obligations which a democratic society expects of its members.[28]

As Table 4 indicates, there are, with one exception of working class affiliates on the citizen duty scale, significant differences between the affiliated and consistent classes, suggesting that class identification is not altogether irrelevant in connection with political role performance. But, as in the cases of participation and exposure to the media, the Class Identification Strength scores suggest that identification is countervailed by capacity for effective role behavior. The T values obtained in these tests indicate that the degree of association between class identification and political role behavior, though positive, is uniformly low.

Table 4—Class Identification and Political Role Behavior

Relationship between Identification and:	Tests for	x^2	d/f	p	T	CIS Index
Interest	WW—WM	26.81	2	< .001	.16	− 6 / + 29
	MM—MW	22.15	2	< .001	.21	+ 59/ + 26
Voting regularity*	WW—WM	11.42	2	< .01	.11	+ 68/ + 59
	MM—MW	20.36	2	< .001	.21	+ 82/ + 57
Care for outcome	WW—WM	8.04	3	< .05	.08	+ 11/ + 23
of election	MM—MW	21.28	3	< .001	.19	+ 46/ + 21
Sense of efficacy	WW—WM	18.31	2	< .001	.13	− 4 / + 18
	MM—MW	10.21	2	< .01	.14	+ 44/ + 21
Sense of citizen duty	WW—WM	22.46	2	< .001	.14	+ 23/ + 50
	MM—MW	3.06	2	< .30	.08	+ 62/ + 51

* In connection with voting regularity, the difference between the consistent class groupings is so small that there is no room for meaningful variation in role behavior as a result of class identification. The same was the case in regard to perception of differences between the two parties. In other words, neither the operation of identification nor capacity could be properly isolated and observed.

To assess the independent effect of capacity for identification on political role performance, on the one hand, and the relative irrelevance of capacity in regard to attitudinal dimensions of political behavior, one may compare the distance scores yielded by the Index of Class Identification Strength. As it should be expected that the distance between the two consistent classes (WW and MM) is always greater than the distance between an affiliate grouping and

28. For more detailed analysis of "political efficacy" and "citizen duty" as well as statistical analysis of the adequacy of these scales, see Campbell, Gurin and Miller, *op. cit.*, pp. 187–189 and 194–195.

its respective consistent class, the more the distance score of the latter (i.e. WW—WM or MM—MW) approximates the distance score of the former, the less partial or limited is the effect of class identification and the less relevant is the capacity factor for identification. In other words, the distance between the two consistent classes yielded by the CIS Index can serve as a standard for measuring the extent of identification by the affiliates as well as the force of capacity.

Table 5 reports the distance scores for the relevant pairs of class groupings as well as the differences between these actual distance scores and the "ideal" difference score of zero for a hypothetical "full" identification. For the purpose of comparison, scores obtained in two attitudinal dimension tests dealing with party identification and demands for government activity in the social welfare field have been included. As the table indicates, the differences in attitudinal manifestations of political behavior are, in general, considerably smaller than those in regard to role aspects of political behavior. This result suggests that capacity for identification is less relevant in connection with attitudes than with roles in political behavior.

Table 5—Identification Distance Scores of Class Groupings

Political Behavior	WW—MM	WW—WM	Diff	MM—MW	Diff
Party Identification	49	40	(9)	35	(14)
Govt. activity demands	30	24	(6)	23	(7)
Participation	50	18	(32)	28	(22)
Exposure to media	63	29	(34)	23	(40)
Interest	65	35	(30)	33	(32)
Care for outcome	35	13	(23)	25	(10)
Sense of efficacy	48	22	(26)	23	(25)
Citizen duty	39	27	(12)	11	(28)

DISTANCE SCORE BETWEEN

Table 5 reveals another very interesting pattern. If one compares the difference scores for manifestations of role performance, a more or less distinct rank order appears to be implicit in these manifestations. For the middle class affiliates, the difference scores are greatest for exposure, participation and interest, somewhat smaller for sense of efficacy and concern over outcome, and smallest for sense of citizen duty. In the case of working class affiliates, exposure and interest also rank among the three greatest difference scores, now joined by sense of citizen duty, while participation shows a somewhat smaller score. This outcome suggests that role manifestations of political behavior differ from attitudinal manifestations in degree rather than in kind, that there is a gradual transition from emotional or personal identification to functional or role identification. The more a given dimension of political behavior is predicated on identification in terms of role, the greater, apparently, is the need for capacity to effectuate behavior in line with identification. In other words, rather than representing a dichotomy, Parsons and Shils' types of identification —"internalization of values" and "internalization of role"—may be considered as mutually interdependent poles of the identification continuum. Our empirical findings, then, support our theoretical considerations, to the effect that both types of identification operate simultaneously, but with more or less relevance for particular aspects of political behavior.

Summary

This study has sought to examine the relationship of identification with social class and political role behavior. Identification with class, in spite of theoretical misgivings, was accepted as an "intervening variable" between objective class position and political behavior, on the assumption that both objective and subjective information about people is better than either alone. However, differences observed between attitudinal and role manifestations of political behavior suggested that class identification as an independent factor affecting political conduct is limited by capacity for identification. Capacity was made dependent, in line with theoretical considerations derived from the work of George Herbert Mead on communication, on people's actual inter-action in the social process. As inter-action is limited by objective class position, identification is more likely to be effective in connection with attitudinal than with role or functional dimensions of political behavior. The latter seem to be more dependent on capacity for identification, capacity depending on objective class position. The data reported on in this study tend to support this hypothesis. Moreover, it appears that rather than being dichotomous opposites, identification in terms of attitudes and identification in terms of role are interdependent ideal-type poles of an identification continuum—both operate simultaneously, but with more or less effect on particular aspects of political behavior.

Index of Names

Abrams, M., 73
Abrams, R. H., 269
Adams, W. A., 370
Adler, A., 247–48, 253
Adler, K. P., 281
Adorno, T. W., 249, 396, 401
Affinito, M., 7
Alexander, C. N., 354–55
Allard, W., 453
Allport, F., 5
Allport, G. W., 26, 51
Anderson, H. H., 129
Aneshansel, J., 435–36, 437
Ansbacher, H. L., 247, 254
Ansbacher, R. R., 247, 254
Asch, S. E., 131, 265

Back, K., 120, 133, 136, 138, **268–77**, 357, 479, 483
Baker, C., 394
Baker, R. W., 354
Bales, R., 423–24, 427
Bass, B. M., 245, 251, 254
Barber, B., 287
Bauer, R. A., 20–21, 323, **430–42**, 434, 439
Beal, G. M., 7, 15
Becker, H. S., 239, 281
Bendix, R., 187, 191, 198, 321, 353, 493
Bennis, W. G., 7
Benoit-Smullyan, E., 89
Berelson, B., 43–44, 47, 297, 428, 446, 453–54, 461, 474
Berkowitz, N., 7
Bernard, V., 370
Berreman, G. D., 27
Bettelheim, B., 321, 439
Blake, R., 358
Blalock, H. M., 321
Blos, P., 92–93
Bobrow, D., 281
Bott, E., 70

Boyd, G. F., 345
Brandt, H. F., 129
Brehm, J. W., 126
Brenman, M., 164
Bridges, J. W., 452
Broom, L., 443
Brown, E. F., 394
Brown, R., 258, 266
Bruner, J., 10, 434
Bullock, R. P., 185
Burlinghame, D., 224

Campbell, A., 11, 17, 19, 23, 323, **473–89**, 494, 501
Campbell, D. T., 251, 323, **452–60**
Campbell, E. Q., 354, 355
Carlson, R. O., 15
Carper, J. W., 239
Cartwright, D., 473
Centers, R., 19, 20, 186, 191, 491–94
Chapman, D. W., 76, 104, 118, 129, 166
Chapman, L. J., 251
Charters, W. W., Jr., 15, 21, 25, 88, **95–102**, 299, 300, 464
Chave, C. J., 97, 102
Chein, I., 298
Chowdhry, K., 16, 20
Clark, H. F., 215
Cochran, T. C., 291–92
Coelho, G., 434, 442
Coffin, J. E., 457
Cohen, L., 495
Converse, P. E., 11, 23, 261, 323, **474–89**
Cooley, C. H., 6–7, 52, 432, 433
Cooper, H. C., 473
Cottrell, L. S., Jr., 28, 443
Cronbach, L. J., 321
Curtis, A., 40

Dahrendorf, R., 71
Daniel, W. G., 342

NOTE: **Boldface** numerals refer to articles included in the text.

Index

DATE DUE

APR 5 '71			
GAYLORD			PRINTED IN U.S.A.